Henry Sturcke

Encountering the Rest of God

T V Z

TVZ · DISSERTATIONEN

- Matthias Mittelbach: Religion verstehen. Der theologische und religionspädagogische Weg von Hubertus Halbfas

  2002, ISBN 3-290-17237-6

- Rudolf Gebhard: Umstrittene Bekenntnisfreiheit. Der Apostolikumstreit in den Reformierten Kirchen der Deutschschweiz im 19. Jahrhundert

  2003, ISBN 3-290-17256-2

- Trix Gretler: Zeit und Stunde. Theologische Zeitkonzepte zwischen Erfahrung und Ideologie in den Büchern Kohelet und Daniel

  2004, ISBN 3-290-17312-7

- Barbara U. Meyer: Christologie im Schatten der Shoah – im Lichte Israels. Studien zu Paul van Buren und Friedrich Wilhelm Marquardt

  2004, ISBN 3-290-17220-5

- Henry Sturcke: Encountering the Rest of God. How Jesus Came to Personify the Sabbath

  2005, ISBN 3-290-17351-8

Henry Sturcke

Encountering the Rest of God

How Jesus Came to Personify the Sabbath

TVZ

Theologischer Verlag Zürich

Die deutsche Bibliothek – CIP-Einheitsaufnahme
Die Deutsche Bibliothek verzeichnet diese Publikation in der Deutschen Na-
tionalbibliographie; detaillierte bibliographische Daten sind im Internet über
<http://dnb.ddb.de> abrufbar

Umschlaggestaltung:
www.gapa.ch gataric, ackermann und partner, zürich

Druck:
ROSCH BUCH GmbH Scheßlitz

ISBN 3-290-17351-8
© 2005 Theologischer Verlag Zürich
www.tvz-verlag.ch

In memoriam C. H. S.

Inquietum est cor nostrum, donec requiescat in te.
Augustine

Contents

Preface

The reason for undertaking this work can be simply stated: I changed my mind about a tenet of faith and practice that had meant a great deal to me for nearly thirty years. After a conventional upbringing in a mainline Protestant denomination, in the course of which I memorized the Ten Commandments as a partial requirement for confirmation, I was exposed to the polemical, persuasive teaching of a fundamentalist, apocalyptic Christian group, the Worldwide Church of God. A core belief involved the command to remember the Sabbath day. This church pointed out, correctly, that the day referred to in the Decalogue command ran from Friday evening to Saturday evening. The absence of any scripture expressly transferring this command to another day (Sunday), combined with a variant of the reconstruction of church history found in many Protestant circles since the Reformation, one that traced the divergence from an idealized image of the pristine *Urgemeinde* to Emperor Constantine, made the case compelling to me at the time. So convinced was I that I studied at their college, accepted ordination and served in the ministry of the church for over twenty years. With time, however, I began to have doubts. At first I kept them to myself until I learned that several denominational leaders had similar doubts. The priceless opportunity to write a dissertation offered me the chance to slowly and painstakingly reexamine the question.

The resulting dissertation was accepted by the theology faculty of the University of Zurich in Summer Semester 2003 on the recommendation of Prof. Dr. Jean Zumstein. The list of those whose help I should acknowledge could easily run as long as the main body of this work; I must limit myself to a few. First of all, my *Doktorvater*, Professor Zumstein. The acuity of his powers of critical analysis, from which this project greatly benefitted, was balanced by his constant encouragement. The second evaluation was provided by Prof. Dr. Samuel Vollenweider; I have profited from his probing questions. The other doctoral examiners, Profs. Drs. Silke-Petra Bergjan, Pierre Bühler, and Konrad Schmid, provided a stimulating environment for my oral defense.

The loneliness of the endeavor was ameliorated by the New Testament Society at the university, that is, by fellow scholars such as Markus Anker, Pascale Rondez, Dr. Hans-Ulrich Rüegger, Dr. Esther Straub, Dr. Eva Tobler, and *Rektor* Prof. Dr. Hans Weder. The meetings of the German-Swiss NT society were also valuable, especially the feedback of Prof. Dr. Ulrich Luz and others to my presentation of the work in progress. *Privatdozentin* Dr. Daria Pezzoli-Olgiati, my officemate of many years, read most of the manuscript before I submitted it. Her constant encouragement to excel resulted in a far better project. In addition, Kathryn Davidson critically and carefully read an early version. Individual chapters were read by Dr. Konrad Haldimann, Andreas Hunzicker, Michael Johnson, Dr. Annette Schellenberg, and Wolfgang and Linda Thomsen as well. To Annette, as well as to Dr. Peter Schwagmeier, I owe the choice of topic. To Prof. Dr. Hans-Dietrich Altendorf a word of thanks for being the first to suggest that I write a dissertation. Prof. Dr. Eduard Schweizer was not only encouraging, but also loaned me his personal copy of a hard-to-find book.

The length of the bibliography is a small indication of the debt I owe to the library and librarians of the theology faculty in Zurich, especially Alice Holliger and Julia Pálffy. In addition, I spent many hours in Zurich's Zentralbibliothek, as well as libraries in Claremont, Harvard, and Princeton. At each of these institutions the staff was unfailingly helpful. The word *helpful* hardly suffices to describe the support of the unsung heroes of the theology faculty: the secretaries and computer support personnel. Again, I will limit myself to mentioning a few: Ursula Ziefle, Georgina Fischer, and Michael Hottinger.

My research was supported in part by a grant from the Swiss National Science Foundation. Portions of this work were presented in SBL congresses in Rome, Toronto and Cambridge, as well as to groups of ministers of the Worldwide Church of God and the *evangelisch-reformierte Landeskirche* of the Swiss *Kanton* of Aargau. On each occasion I gained from the necessity of preparing a presentation, as well as from the discussions that ensued. For contributions toward the cost of publication I would like to thank the Emil Brunner foundation, in connection with the *evangelisch-reformierte Landeskirche* of the *Kanton of Zurich*, and the Lang foundation, also of Zurich. Thanks are due as well to the Theologischer Verlag, Zurich, for accepting this book in their dissertation series, especially to Marianne Stauffacher for her care.

The SBL Handbook of Style: For Ancient Near Eastern, Biblical, and Early Christian Studies (Patrick H. Alexander et al., eds.; Peabody, Mass., 1999) served as primary style manual, supplemented as necessary by *The Chicago Manual of Style* (14th ed.; Chicago, 1993). I have departed from these authorities in that the honoree of a *Festschrift* is listed as part of the title both in first mention of the work in a footnote and in the Bibliography, preceded by the abbreviation *FS*.

Quotations from the Bible, unless otherwise noted, are from Bruce M. Metzger and Roland E. Murphy, eds., *The New Oxford Annotated Bible with the Apocryphal/Deuterocanonical Books: New Revised Standard Version* (New York, 1991). For the sake of consistency, I have capitalized the word *Sabbath* in quotations from the NRSV, in accordance with SBL style. I have also consistently used *ss* rather than *ß* in all German names and quotations.

Throughout the entire course of this project, my wife Edel was an unfailing source of encouragement and support. Many friends and colleagues from the Worldwide Church of God were supportive of my research, and also showed understanding for the professional change of course to which it led. *Pars pro toto* I would thank Randal Dick and John Halford. During the time I wrote, three individuals died who had been very helpful to me: Prof. Dr. Odil Hannes Steck, Prof. Dr. Fritz Stolz, and my father, Charles H. Sturcke. To the memory of the latter I dedicate this book.

Abbreviations

The abbreviations used are those of Patrick H. Alexander, et al., eds., *The SBL Handbook of Style: For Ancient Near Eastern, Biblical, and Early Christian Studies* (Peabody, Mass.: Hendrickson, 1999). Abbreviations for works not listed in the *SBL Handbook* follow Siegfried M. Schwertner, *Internationales Abkürzungsverzeichnis für Theologie und Grenzgebiete* (2d ed.; Berlin: de Gruyter, 1992). Additional abbreviations:

Barrett	C. K. Barrett, ed. *The New Testament Background: Selected Documents.* 2d ed. San Francisco: Harper, 1987 (1957).
Bauer-Aland	Walter Bauer, *Wörterbuch zum Neuen Testament.* 6th ed. Edited by Kurt and Barbara Aland. Berlin: de Gruyter, 1988.
Bill	Hermann L. Strack and Paul Billerbeck. *Kommentar zum Neuen Testament aus Talmud und Midrasch.* 6 vols. 4th ed. (vols. 1–3); 3d ed. (vol. 4); 2d ed. (vols. 5–6); München: Beck, 1961–1965 (1922–1928). [following IATG^2 instead of *SBL Handbook*'s Str-B].
BISer	Biblical Interpretation Series.
DBI	*A Dictionary of Biblical Interpretation.* Edited by R. J. Coggins and J. L. Houlden. London: SCM, 1990.
EDSS	*Encyclopedia of the Dead Sea Scrolls.* Edited by Lawrence H. Schiffman and James C. VanderKam. 2 vols. New York: Oxford University Press, 2000.
SNTW	Studies of the New Testament and its World.
Stern	Menahem Stern, *Greek and Latin Authors on the Jews and Judaism.* 3 vols. Jerusalem: Israel Academy of Sciences and Humanities, 1974-1984.
TKNT	Theologischer Kommentar zum Neuen Testament.

1

Introduction

1.1 SUBJECT OF INQUIRY

The first followers of Jesus in Jerusalem formed a subgroup of Judaism.[1] Its leader, James, the brother of the Lord, was known for his loyalty to the Torah, which certainly included observance of the seventh-day Sabbath, although none of the sources explicitly mention this.[2] Yet within a century, most Christians did not observe it; instead, we find indications of a new weekly practice, that of the Lord's Supper, on the first day of the week. At the same time, the conviction arose that a Christian did not need to, or even ought to, keep the Sabbath; Jews who confessed Christ yet continued to observe the Sabbath came under pressure to cease.[3] It is beyond dispute that this occurred, but there is no unanimity on the question of how and why. There is no passage in the sources to which we can turn to find an explicit answer. I propose to explore the reasons for this radical shift in the worship practice of early Christians.

---

[1]   An increasing number of scholars advocate the term Christian Judaism, rather than Jewish Christianity, as more appropriate to describe this original form (e.g. David C. Sim, *The Gospel of Matthew and Christian Judaism: The History and Social Setting of the Matthean Comunity* [SNTW; Edinburgh, 1998], 24–27). I will retain the traditional designation Jewish Christianity, as this study focuses on the question of the Sabbath in two forms of Christianity.

[2]   On the piety of James, as well as his martyrdom, see Hegesippus in Eusebius, *Hist. eccl.*, 2.23.4–18; see also John Painter, *Just James: The Brother of Jesus in History and Tradition* (Studies on Personalities of the New Testament; Columbia, S. C., 1997), 105–58.

[3]   Justin concedes that it is permissible for a believer in Christ to observe the Sabbath, as long as he doesn't require it of others (*Dial.* 47; PTS 47:146–8). Jerome doesn't approve of Christian Sabbath observance, but he knows of it (*Epist. ad Augustinum* 112:15, CSEL 55:384–5).

The Ten Commandments have long been considered the backbone of morality and catechetical instruction. Simultaneously, there has been a widespread consensus, dating back to the second century, that the command concerning the Sabbath (counted as the third in the Roman Catholic and Lutheran traditions, and fourth in the Reformed tradition) is not to be followed literally by Christians. Many are not aware that the biblical form of the commandment reads "Sabbath," nor that the day referred to is not Sunday, but the seventh day of the week, Saturday. Those who do understand this often assume that the change originated in the desire to memorialize the resurrection of Jesus Christ, which is commonly assumed to have occurred on a Sunday morning.

Thus, the Sabbath question represents one of the most interesting aspects of Christian reception of the Decalogue. The non-observance of the seventh-day Sabbath, or the transfer of elements of its observance to Sunday, the eighth/first day of the week, achieved a self-evidence unparalleled in the Christian view of the other nine commandments. Admittedly, there has been repeated Sabbath observance by Christians throughout history, but after the first century this was always a minority, always at the margins of the church, usually suppressed, sometimes persecuted. Such movements have been especially frequent in Eastern Europe and Russia, but two chief strands of this tradition in the West are the Seventh-Day Baptists and the various groups that have their roots in the Millerite revival in the first half of the nineteenth century, such as the Seventh-Day Adventists and the Church of God, Seventh-Day.[4]

On one level, it seems that the minority tradition is in accord with the biblical record.[5] Yet it is evident that the Sabbath has been replaced in

---

[4] Oswald Eggenberger, "Sabbatarier," *RGG*[3] 5:1260–61; idem, *Die Kirchen, Sondergruppen und religiösen Vereinigungen: Ein Handbuch* (6th ed.; Zürich, 1994), 136–7. Kurt Hutten, "Church of God," *RGG*[3] 1:1821–2. The Worldwide Church of God, a breakaway from the Church of God, Seventh-Day, moved away from literal Sabbath observance in 1995. See Markus Schmidt, *Weltweite Kirche Gottes: Von Sonderlehren zur Bibel* (Sekten, religiöse Sondergemeinschaften, Weltanschauungen 78; Wien, 1998); and Andreas Fincke, "Lehrkorrekturen," *MD* 59 (1996): 370–1. Internal views of the change are offered by Joseph Tkach, *Transformed by Truth* (Sisters, Ore., 1997) and J. Michael Feazell, *The Liberation of the Worldwide Church of God* (Grand Rapids, Mich., 2001).

[5] The Sabbath appears in the OT in connection with the creation (Gen 2:2–3), as

Christian faith and practice by Sunday, the first day of the week. Christians have been explaining the departure from the seventh-day Sabbath to themselves and to others ever since the second century, when two arguments make their appearance; they continue to appear in discussions of the question. One is the claim that some laws were not the original divine intention, but were added because of Israel's sin; they are either punitive or disciplinary.[6] The other is a differentiation between the law of God and the law of Moses.[7] Neither of these arguments is convincing when applied to the Sabbath, however, due to its presence in the Decalogue. The fact that they are nonetheless cited suggests that they are attempts to justify a step that had already been taken for other reasons. In addition, a third explanation, connection to the resurrection appearances, first documented almost as an afterthought in the *Epistle of Barnabas*, becomes more frequently cited and in time becomes one of the chief arguments for Sunday worship.

1.2 HISTORY OF RESEARCH

1.2.1 The History-of-Religions School

The History-of-Religions School devoted little attention to the departure from the Sabbath, expressing more interest in the introduction of worship on the first day of the week. Hermann Gunkel reversed the standard view of this, and derived the dating of the resurrection from a prior celebration of the first day of the week by Christians unconscious of the fact that the "lord" in whose honor the day was celebrated was

well as in the Decalogue (Exod 20:8–11; Deut 5:12–15). It was designated as a sign between God and his people (Exod 31:12–17; Ezek 20:12–20). In the NT, the Gospel of Luke tells us that it was the custom of Jesus to go to the synagogue on the Sabbath (4:16). The same author repeatedly mentions the Sabbath in connection with the missionary activity of Paul (Acts 13:14–15, 42–44; 16:12–13; 17:1–2; 18:1–11).

[6] Ezek 20:24–25 is cited to this effect by early apologists, e. g. Justin, *Dial.* 21:4 (PTS 47:103–4). See also *Ps.-Clem.* R 1.36, where the sacrifices are a concession by Moses to the idolatrous tendencies of Israel.

[7] Irenaeus, *Haer.* 4.15.2 (SC 100:154–8). This may have forerunner in Jewish thought (Philo, *Mos.* 2.188–90; *Decal.* 175; cf. Francis T. Fallon, "The Law in Philo and Ptolemy: A Note on the Letter to Flora," *VC* 30 [1976]: 45–51). This view is rejected by Rabbinic orthodoxy, *Sipre Num.* 112 (ed. D. Börner-Klein, 206).

none other than the Sun god.[8] Wilhelm Bousset agreed: "Die Entstehung
des Sonntags hat mit der Auferstehungsüberlieferung gar nichts zu tun."
There was for him a connection with the abandonment of the Sabbath,
in analogy of the displacement of the traditional Jewish days of fasting,
Monday and Thursday, to Wednesday and Friday.[9] Eduard Schwartz
also arrives at the conclusion that worship on Sunday preceded the
association of the resurrection with it, and that it was chosen for its
difference to Judaism. He comes to this by a different path, namely, by
the study of the controversies over the dating of Passover/Easter.[10]

1.2.2 Willy Rordorf

A new era in the history of the study of the Sabbath among early
Christians was initiated with the work of Willy Rordorf, which has
become a standard work on this question.[11] Rordorf rejects suggestions
that the practice of worship on the first day of the week arose in
imitation of pagan reverence for the day of the sun; the planetary week,
of which we also have record in the Roman empire of the first century,
is for him modeled on the seven-day week of Israel.[12] Both the seven-day

---

[8]   *Zum religionsgeschichtlichen Verständnis des Neuen Testaments* (2d ed.;
FRLANT 1; Göttingen, 1910), 73–76.

[9]   *Kyrios Christos: Geschichte des Christusglaubens von den Anfängen des
Christentums bis Irenaeus* (FRLANT 21; Göttingen, 1913), 31.

[10]   "Osterbetrachtungen," *ZNW* 7 (1906): 1–33; repr. in *Zum Neuen Testament und
zum Frühen Christentum* (Gesammelte Schriften, 5; Berlin, 1963), 1–41. In the course
of this article, Schwartz also takes issue with consensus positions of his time that had been
propounded by scholars such as F. C. Baur and Harnack. For instance, he maintained
that the separation of the Christian movement from Judaism was not completed in the
first century C.E., but was a slow, step-by-step process that lasted centuries. His
independently-staked positions have in the last few years become widely-held, although
he is rarely cited in conjunction with them.

[11]   *Der Sonntag: Geschichte des Ruhe- und Gottesdiensttages im ältesten
Christentum* (ATANT 43; Zürich, 1962). All further references to this work in this
chapter appear in the text, in parentheses. A companion publication, *Sabbat und Sonntag
in der Alten Kirche* (TC 2; Zürich, 1972), compiles relevant passages from the NT and
the church fathers with brief commentary.

[12]   Although the seven-day week is taken over from Judaism, the planetary week has
also exercised a certain influence. The names of most of the days of the week in most
European languages are taken from the planetary gods or their Nordic equivalents. The

week and the practice of reserving one day in seven for worship and/or rest are borrowed from the Jews.

Rordorf's most enduring contribution to the investigation of the Sabbath and Sunday is his separation of the questions *rest* and *worship*. In Judaism of the first century, the Sabbath was both a day of rest and a day of worship. In Christianity, this has not necessarily been the case. Rordorf emphasizes that the introduction of Sunday as the Christian day of rest is a Constantinian state decision, which was only subsequently reinforced theologically, so that the restrictions of the Sabbath were applied to Sunday (160–65).

Concerning the question of rest, Rordorf traces the unbinding of Sabbath rest to Jesus himself who, as he writes, "repeatedly" broke the Sabbath (67). Rordorf generally sees the Sabbath conflicts as historical reports, or, at the very least, as based on incidents in the life of Jesus (other than, for instance, Bultmann, who views them as constructions of the early church, in answer to conflicts with the Judaism of their time). The saying contained in Mark 2:27, "The Sabbath was made for humankind, and not humankind for the Sabbath" is for him a genuine word of Jesus, while he sees the following verse, 28, "so the Son of Man is lord even of the Sabbath," as a post-resurrection explication of the identity of Jesus (Son of Man, Lord), giving the reason for his freedom with regard to the Sabbath, as well as an indication of the reluctance of the early church to claim this freedom for itself (59–65).

Rordorf maintains that the Christian practice of worship on the first day of the week extends back to the earliest days of the Jerusalem congregation (213–33). To support this, he uses the reported appearances of the resurrected Christ (Luke 24:13–32; 33–43; John 20:19–23; 26–29). The language of these accounts is evocative of worship practices (gathering, meal, presence of Jesus), and John reports two successive Sunday evening gatherings. Problematic for this view is the generally

exceptions are primarily with regard to either Saturday or Sunday. The Jews named only two days, the Sabbath, and the day before, the day of preparation; the rest were numbered. The early church took over this custom of numbering the days of the week, even in contexts in which the Sabbath was not discussed (1 Cor 16:1; *Did.* 8:1; *Acts Pet.* 15–16;18). The first Christian use of the planetary names for days is found in apologetic writings of the second century that were aimed at pagan readers.

acknowledged loyalty of the Jerusalem church toward the Sabbath; Rordorf explains this as a step back following the persecution of Stephen and his followers. The Hellenists, who Rordorf assumes to have generally had a more open posture toward the law than the Hebrews, fled Jerusalem.[13] The remaining Hebrews renewed their loyalty to the law, in order to avoid persecution.

Rordorf warns, though, against placing too much weight on a Sabbath-loyalty even on the part of the Hebraists. For him, there are two conceivable reasons why even Palestinian Christians would no longer feel fully at home in the synagogues, one external, the other internal: (1) the disciples of Jesus were compromised by Jesus' arrest, trial and crucifixion. They did not dare show themselves in public. When they did preach publically, they viewed it as a special grace (Acts 4:29–31; cf. v. 13). (2) This external isolation would have been accompanied by an internal distance. Christians could not feel at home in synagogue worship because for them the decisive aspect of worship, the confession of Jesus Christ, was missing (122–3). Further, the bitter experience of the Sabbath between the crucifixion and the resurrection would have permanently colored their attitude toward the Sabbath (124–5). Lying behind Rordorf's assertion of an early alienation of the disciples in Palestine from the synagogue however is the assumption of a unified Judaism in the period before the destruction of Jerusalem in 70 C.E. While there were certainly many common features of Judaism, there was also a great deal of diversity. One only needed twelve adult males to found a synagogue (a youth who had celebrated his bar mitzvah was in this sense an adult). If the Christians indeed did not feel at home in a synagogue service lacking a confession of Jesus Christ (a plausible suggestion), what would have hindered them from founding their own synagogues?

Rordorf concludes from Gal 4:10 that Paul held that Gentile Christians were not permitted to keep the Sabbath and the Feast days (130); he believes that Romans, in which Paul recommends tolerance

---

[13] The widely-held assumption that Diaspora Jews were less observant than those in Palestine has been challenged by Philip Francis Esler, *Community and Gospel in Luke-Acts: The Social and Political Motivations of Lucan Theology* (SNTSMS 57; Cambridge, 1987), 138, 145–8.

with regard to "days," was addressed to Jewish Christians (135–6). For him it is unthinkable that Paul could have made an innovation in this question and introduced Sunday worship (215–6), without our reading of it in polemic literature such as Galatians, which for him is an indication that Sunday worship was introduced earlier, and enjoyed widespread acceptance.

Rordorf's thesis is that a regular practice of weekly gatherings of Christians is strongly established in the first century. These gatherings had the character of worship services (Lord's supper, scripture reading and exposition). Further, this practice originated in Jerusalem. It was determined not by the timing of the resurrection, but through the resurrection appearances on Sunday evening (216).

Rordorf lays great weight on reports on the gospels of Luke and John as historical reminiscences of the events in the days and weeks following the resurrection to establish the introduction of Sunday worship in Jerusalem by the risen Christ. He goes so far as to suggest that most of the resurrection appearances were on the first day of the week. This is speculative, and the fact that the day of the week is *not* given in many cases speaks against his thesis. Given the lateness of composition—Luke circa 80 C.E., John circa 90–95 C.E.—, the historicity of these accounts is open to question. It is also possible that these reports were written at a time when this had become the worship pattern, and in such a way as to evoke the practice of the community of their time.

1.2.3 Samuele Bacchiocchi

Samuele Bacchiocchi, a Seventh-Day Adventist from Rome, profited from the opening of the Roman Catholic Church after Vatican II by becoming the first non-Catholic to write a dissertation at the Pontificia Universitate Gregoriana.[14] Bacchiocchi, like Rordorf before him, discusses not only NT evidence, but also patristic literature. Although Bacchiocchi

---

[14] Samuele Bacchiocchi, *Un Esame dei testi biblici e patristiici dei primi quattro secoli allo scopo d'accertare il tempe e le cause del sorgere della domenica come giorno del Signore* (Ph. D. diss., Pontificia Universitate Gregoriana, 1974). English publication in two versions, *Anti-Judaism and the Origin of Sunday* (Rome, 1975) and *From Sabbath to Sunday: A Historical Investigation of the Rise of Sunday Observance in Early Christianity* (Rome, 1977). Page references to *Sabbath* appear in the text.

concedes that the development of Sunday worship was the result of the interaction of many factors—theological, political, social, and religious (13), he sees growing Antijudaism as the prime motivation.[15] Bacchiocchi locates the introduction of Sunday in Rome, not in Jerusalem, and dates it to the fourth decade of the second century, after the bloody suppression of the Bar Kokhba revolt in Palestine. This dating is crucial to Bacchiocchi's thesis. If he can prove that it was only *after* this time that Christians held regular worship services on the first day of the week, then he can deliver a weighty argument—he believes—in support of his reconstruction: the disfavor into which the Jews fell throughout the Roman empire, as well as the Hadrianic disabilities.

Bacchiocchi questions Rordorf's late dating of the planetary week; he marshals evidence to show that it existed in the first century B.C.E., and asserts that it included the honoring of a weekly day of the sun (242–6). This can help explain, he suggests, a possible predisposition toward the first day of the week as day of worship. He is unable, however, to adduce any evidence of honoring a regular day of the sun in the first century C.E., as he almost admits:

> Though not sufficiently explicit to establish the exact time when the day of the Sun emerged as the first and most important day of the week, these few indications do reveal however that it occurred in concomitance with the development of Sun-worship which became widespread beginning from the early part of the second century. (251)

Important for Bacchiocchi's case is his interpretation of the material in the Gospels, which for him offers a typology of the Sabbath and its messianic fulfillment; indeed, they recount the "sabbatical ministry of Jesus" (19).[16] The Sabbath healings, in particular, are understood as

[15] Bacchiocchi dissents here from the common Seventh-Day Adventist explanation for the origin of Sunday worship, which, in the train of turn-of-the-century scholars of comparative religion, saw the origin in pre-Christian Sun-worship (Robert Leo Odom, *Sunday in Roman Paganism* [Washington, D. C., 1944]. Bacchiocchi does not, however, totally discount the role of sun worship as a factor (237–69).

[16] Bacchiocchi bases this on the structure of the ministry of Christ in the Gospel of Luke: it begins on the Sabbath (Luke 4:16) and ends on "the day of preparation as the sabbath was beginning" (Luke 23:54).The overtones of the Jubilee year in his opening sermon, in which, as Bacchiocchi terms it, "the Sabbath became the liberator," provide the framework. "It is significant that Christ in His opening address announces His

enhancing the meaning of the Sabbath as redemption, joy and service (30). The reported conflicts in the Gospels "on the manner of Sabbath observance" indicate for Bacchiocchi "the serious estimate in which the Sabbath was held both in Jewish circles and in primitive Christianity." The accounts presuppose "that primitive Christians were involved in debates regarding the observance of the Sabbath"; they understood Jesus' attitude toward the Sabbath as "a new perspective of Sabbath-keeping," consisting "both in a *new meaning* and a *new manner* of observance of the Sabbath." This new manner of observance consisted in "active, loving service to needy souls." This was in keeping with deliberate actions by Jesus "to restore it to its original divine intention"; it was a "program of Sabbath reforms" (72–3).

Bacchiocchi challenges the connection Rordorf makes between resurrection appearances and Sunday worship. The resurrection is not cited in the immediate post-NT literature as the primary reason for the celebration of the Lord's Supper or for the observance of Sunday. The *Didache*, dated by Bacchiocchi between 70–150 C.E., devotes "three brief chapters" to the manner of celebrating the Lord's Supper. No allusion is made in chs. 9 and 10 to the resurrection (78–79).[17] *First Clement* 23–26 (95 C.E.) extensively discusses the resurrection, using three different symbols (the day/night cycle, the reproductive cycle of the seed, the phoenix) but omits "the most telling symbols of all," the Lord's Supper and Sunday worship, which is surprising, if, "as some hold, the Eucharist was already celebrated on Sunday and had acquired the commemorative value of the resurrection" (79).

Bacchiocchi dismisses Rordorf's interrelation of the Last Supper, the meal of the risen Lord with His disciples on Easter Sunday, the breaking of bread in the earliest community, and the Lord's Supper described in 1 Cor 11:17–34 (85). Noting the lack of mention of a meal on Easter evening in the Gospel of John, he argues "the omission of this detail can

---

Messianic mission in the language of the sabbatical year" (20). Bacchiocchi concludes that Christ identified his mission with the Sabbath in order to make the day a fitting memorial of his redemptive activities (phrased as a question on 21, answered later in the affirmative, 73).

    [17]   He relegates his discussion of *Did.* 14:1, with its mention of the Lord's Day, to a footnote (114, n. 73).

hardly be justified if the Easter-meal was regarded as the crucial starting point of Sunday-keeping." That the Gospel mentions a meal that Christ consumed with his disciples on an early week-day morning (21:13) "strongly suggests that no particular significance was attributed to Christ's Easter-Sunday evening meal." Luke, who reports a meal, makes no mention of a breaking of bread, nor wine, nor a ritual blessing (86). Although John mentions an appearance the following week, there is no mention of a meal. "No consistent pattern can be derived from Christ's appearances to justify the institution of a recurring eucharistic celebration on Sunday" (87). In fact, for Jesus to have partaken of the elements again would have contradicted his pledge not to drink wine again until in the Kingdom (Matt 26:29). Neither Matthew nor Mark make reference to any meeting of Christ with his disciples on Easter Sunday. The appearances were to be in Galilee, so would have occurred later (88). His partaking of food was not in order to institute a eucharistic Sunday worship, but to demonstrate the reality of his bodily resurrection (89).

Rordorf's reconstruction of Jerusalem as the place of origin of Sunday worship is dismissed by Bacchiocchi. Since the church there was "composed primarily of and administered by converted Jews," he judges it "impossible to assume that a new day of worship was introduced by the Jerusalem Church prior to . . . A.D. 70" (151).

Bacchiocchi deals with the key passages in the Pauline literature in an appendix added to the published version of his dissertation. He emphasizes that Paul speaks at no point of Sunday worship services (his version of the argument from silence). He accepts without discussion the reports about Paul in Acts, then uses the loyalty to the law described there to interpret the problematic passages in the epistles. In addition, he accepts the authenticity of Colossians, and uses his discussion of Col 2:14–17 to explain Gal 4:10. Both positions dissent from the mainstream consensus of NT scholars. This is, of course, his right. Problematic, though, is that he does this with no discussion.

Bacchiocchi concludes that his analysis has shown the high esteem in which the Sabbath was held both in Jewish circles and in primitive Christianity (303). Christ did not annul the Sabbath command, but enriched its meaning and function by fulfilling its Messianic typology (304). He dates the introduction of Sunday worship to the time of

Emperor Hadrian (reigned 117–138 C.E.), when "both external pressures and internal needs encouraged many Christians at that time to break radically with the Jews" (305). The connection between Easter Sunday and weekly Sunday "gives us reason to believe that both festivities originated contemporaneusly [*sic*] in Rome because of the same anti-Judaic motivations" (307). The choice of Sunday was suggested by the diffusion of Sun cults, although a rich Judeo-Christian tradition associated the Deity with the Sun and light as well. Moreover, the beginning of creation and the resurrection of Christ were both "commemorated adequately" by Sunday (308). Nevertheless, there is an internal contradiction involved in maintaining that the Sabbath was abolished, while using the Sabbath command to enjoin Sunday observance (312). The solution, Bacchiocchi proposes, is to "rediscover and restore those permanent interpretive categories which make the Sabbath, God's holy day for the Christian today" (318).

There are serious questions that can be addressed to Bacchiocchi. Increasing awareness of the variety in the early Christian movement makes it problematic to assume that the entire church was either keeping the Sabbath or keeping Sunday. Although he never directly states it, at several points he argues as if Sabbath-keeping were the universal practice of the early church, including in the communities founded by Paul and other representatives of the Antioch-based Hellenistic mission, and that this practice suddenly changed in the early decades of the second century. If, on the other hand, the question of days was treated as a matter of indifference by Paul in the churches he founded, or if he even actively opposed the introduction of the days prescribed in the OT in these churches, then we can easily picture the change coming about in a different way. Even if no Sabbath-keeping Christians ceased from keeping the Sabbath, they ceased to be the majority simply because many new people came into the church who did not observe it.

At points one must ask if Bacchiocchi has understood Rordorf's thesis, or if he has read it in good faith. Rordorf brings cogent linguistic considerations to support his interpretation of passages such as Acts 20:7–12 and Rev 1:10. Bacchiocchi rejects Rordorf's interpretations without discussing Rordorf's arguments. His use of patristic sources that would be fatal to his reconstruction appears problematic as well; he dates some of the key sources (such as *Didache*) later than is usual, and when that is not possible, as in the case of Ignatius's letter to the Magnesians, he adopts an uncommon interpretation. Bacchiocchi's dating and/or his interpretation of the patristic passages that would present difficulties for his thesis raise the question of whether his primary interest is understanding the texts, or whether apologetic interests dominate.

1.2.4 Scholarly Discussion in the Past Three Decades

The first popularization of Rordorf's research in the English-speaking world was in Paul K. Jewett's *The Lord's Day*.[18] Jewett synthesizes the work of other scholars on the history of Sunday observance and its theological grounding and displays an irenic but critical engagement with the Seventh-Day Adventist position. A notable feature is the articulation of a moderate Lord's Day position, one that is not based on an unreflective appropriation of the Decalogue command, and avoids the error of applying casuistic rules for observance. Instead, the author offers four principles—a minimal guide—on how to keep the Lord's Day (164–9).

A treatment that appeared soon after the publication of Bacchiocchi's dissertation was Roger T. Beckwith and Wilfrid Stott's *This is the Day*.[19] In the first part, Beckwith reviews the Biblical and Jewish evidence, organized according to the topics of creation, redemption, and resurrection. He identifies thirteen points of correspondence between the Lord's Day and the Sabbath, indicating for him a continuity between the two institutions, making the Lord's Day the Christian Sabbath. In the second part, far longer, Stott reviews the patristic evidence and outlines a theology of the Christian Sunday. There is also a summary of early Christian attitudes toward the Ten Commandments. The book is a useful expression of the Lord's Day variant of Sabbatarianism.

A thorough interaction of the work of Rordorf and Bacchiocchi is a volume edited by Donald A. Carson that documents a research project

---

[18] Paul K. Jewett, *The Lord's Day: A Theological Guide to the Christian Day of Worship* (Grand Rapids, Mich., 1971).

[19] Roger T. Beckwith and Wilfred Stott, *This is the Day: The Biblical Doctrine of the Christian Sunday in its Jewish and Early Church Setting* (Marshall's Theological Library, London, 1978).

by doctoral and post-doctoral students at Cambridge University.[20] The contributors engage both Rordorf and Bacchiocchi in an irenic spirit from a moderately evangelical point of view. They conclude that those who celebrate Saturday "fail to do justice to the newness of the eschatological situation brought about by God's actions in Christ, and therefore the discontinuity between the Old and New Covenants, and to the attitude of the New Testament writers . . . to the Mosaic Law." In particular, they find that "Bacchiocchi's particular treatment of the New Testament data and his reconstruction of the evidence of the post-apostolic period fail to convince at too many crucial points."[21] At the same time, the authors distance themselves from the Lord's Day version of Sabbatarianism, as well as the moderate transference view of Orthodox and Roman Catholic branches of the church. While they find much to agree with in Rordorf's work, they have "a more positive assessment of the relation of the two days, Sabbath and Lord's Day, in the progress of the history of salvation." In particular, they find that Rordorf fails to sustain his case for "the close connection he posits between Sunday observance and the Lord's Supper."[22]

A number of works have appeared recently that focus on the treatment of the Sabbath in the Gospels.[23] There will be interaction with these in the appropriate chapters. Special mention should be made however of Berndt Schaller's lecture devoted to the question of Jesus and the Sabbath.[24] Schaller engages both those who see Jesus as demonstratively breaking with the Sabbath as well as those who situate Jesus so

[20] Donald A. Carson, ed., *From Sabbath to Lord's Day: A Biblical, Historical, and Theological Investigation* (Grand Rapids, Mich., 1982).

[21] Andrew T. Lincoln, "From Sabbath to Lord's Day: A Biblical and Theological Perspective," in *From Sabbath to Lord's Day: A Biblical, Historical, and Theological Investigation* (ed. D. A. Carson, Grand Rapids, Mich., 1982), 401.

[22] Lincoln, "Sabbath," 402–3.

[23] Three that engaged my attention in particular are Sven Olav Back, *Jesus of Nazareth and the Sabbath Commandment* (Abo, 1995); Yong-Eui Yang, *Jesus and the Sabbath in Matthew's Gospel* (JSNTSup 139, Sheffield, 1997); and Martin Asiedu-Peprah, *Johannine Sabbath Conflicts as Juridical Controversy* (WUNT 2/132, Tübingen, 2001).

[24] *Jesus und der Sabbat* (Franz-Delitzsch-Vorlesung 3, Münster, 1994). See also by the same author "Sabbat III: Neues Testament," *TRE* 29 (1998): 525–7.

thoroughly in his Jewish setting that any hostile reaction on the part of his compatriots on a point of Sabbath practice is incomprehensible. He can nonetheless be considered an exponent of a revisionist position. The Sabbath infractions of Jesus were related to his proclamation of the nearness of the Kingdom of God. Schaller concludes that it is questionable whether those infractions constitute an attack on the institution of the Sabbath.[25] He views it as certain that Jesus through his Sabbath healings sought neither to separate himself from his Jewish environment nor abolish the Sabbath.[26] The Sabbath remained for him precisely in these demonstrative semiotic actions the day that God had created and set for mankind and his salvation. Schaller concludes that while not historical reports, the Sabbath healings reflect a historical core that Jesus did heal on the Sabbath, and that these healings precipitated a reaction. They were not, however, intended to be provocative.[27] He sees a broad agreement in argumentative structure between the sayings of Jesus that accompany his Sabbath healings and rabbinic sayings, namely, that saving life takes precedence over the command to rest. This points to a common *Sitz im Leben*: disputes concerning the rules of the Sabbath and its practice. The discrepancy however between them lay in the application, as the explicit mention of non-life-threatening afflictions that Jesus healed suggests. When Jesus, in one such situation, challenges his opponents with the alternative of whether, on the Sabbath, one should do good or act badly, save life or kill (Mark 3:4), this points to the meaning Jesus ascribed to the Sabbath. Schaller explicates the stress on saving life by an appeal to Jesus' overall proclamation of the Kingdom of God, tied to an eschatological meaning assigned to the Sabbath he may have shared with the Judaism of his time. The Sabbath, then, would have been for Jesus precisely the day on which the healing sovereignty of God should be expressed in deeds.[28] It is understandable, Schaller concludes,

---

[25] "Sabbat III," 29:526.

[26] *Jesus*, 20–27.

[27] *Pace* Rordorf, *Sonntag*, 65–7, 71. On the distinction between *precipitate* and *provoke*, see Donald A. Carson, "Jesus and the Sabbath," in *From Sabbath to Lord's Day: A Biblical, Historical, and Theological Investigation* (ed. D. A. Carson, Grand Rapids, Mich., 1982), 69.

[28] In addition to scholars Schaller cites, many others, including Bacchiocchi, have

that this caused opposition among those who did not share his conviction of the breaking into the present of God's sovereignty. It is open to
question whether Schaller thus has adequately explained the dissonance
between "saving life" and the non-life-threatening situations depicted.
Moreover, his case would be stronger if he could point to indications in
the text that reflect an eschatological understanding of the Sabbath,
rather than relying on an assessment of the general teaching of Jesus.[29]

The subtitle of Ernst Haag's study, *Vom Sabbat zum Sonntag*, indicates
the program: it is a biblical-theological investigation of the main texts
relevant to the question in both OT and NT.[30] This book reflects the
concerns of the established churches in Germany over diminishing
respect for Sunday as Lord's Day and increasing pressures to allow
economic activity on it. Noting that the first day, as Day of the Lord, is
never mentioned in connection with Sabbath polemic in the Gospels,
while the references to first-day worship never refer to the Sabbath and
its rest prescription, Haag concludes that the relation between these two
institutions is not clarified in the Bible. How then could the early church
claim that the Sabbath was no longer binding, he asks, and yet demand
observation of Sunday by appealing to the OT Sabbath command. "Lag
hier ein Akt kirchlicher Willkür vor, oder gab es nicht doch einen inneren
Zusammenhang zwischen Sabbat und Sonntag?" (3-4).

Haag points to the contradictory results of the work of Bacchiocchi
and Rordorf as exemplary of the dilemma. He deplores that even some
Catholic scholars have joined Rordorf's call for an abandonment of the
post-Constantinian synthesis of Sabbath and Sunday, with Sunday rest

come to this conclusion; cf. however M. M. B. Turner, who maintains that the argument
is "not that the Sabbath *is* a special day in this respect but precisely that it is *not*," ("The
Sabbath, Sunday, and the Law in Luke/Acts," in *From Sabbath to Lord's Day: A Biblical
Historical and Theological Investigation*, ed. D. A. Carson, Grand Rapids, 1982,
99–157, here 107).

[29] Cf. however Jürgen Becker, who also expresses healing on the Sabbath as an
expression of what the Sabbath itself was: a foretaste and picture of the coming Kingdom.
He would part ways with Schaller however in that these acts of Jesus did not just *seem*
violations of the Sabbath to those who didn't share Jesus' conception of his mission; they
were violations (*Jesus von Nazaret*, de Gruyter Lehrbücher. Berlin, 1996, 377).

[30] Ernst Haag, *Vom Sabbat zum Sonntag: Eine bibeltheologische Studie* (TTS 52;
Trier, 1991).

anchored in legal sanction. He cites approvingly Ratzinger's grave reservations: While it is correct that Christian Sunday does not depend on civil ordinance, to deduct from this a total opposition in the respective spiritual content of Sabbath and Sunday is to profoundly misunderstand both OT and NT. He maintains, despite the complicated historical development, that the transition from Sabbath to Sunday in church practice was "theologisch äusserst konsequent" (6). The structure of the book is sensible. It is divided into two roughly equal halves, OT and NT, each subdivided into five sections. The final NT section discusses theological aspects of Christian Sunday (ecclesiastical, eschatological). In general, Haag reports the results of exegetical investigations by other scholars, rather than contributing new insights of his own. The chief value of his work is that it serves as a handy compendium of the *status quaestionis* on the various pertinent Biblical passages.

A substantial work on the Sabbath in the NT by Andrea J. Mayer-Haas appeared after this dissertation was finished, so that I was unable to interact with it.[31] The author applies John Dominic Crossan's adequacy criterium to the Sabbath question, and asks what behavior of Jesus explains the pluriform history of the Sabbath in early Christianity (31). To answer this, she conducts an exhaustive examination of all relevant NT texts, giving priority to a synchronic reading over a diachronic. Mayer-Haas concludes that the texts reveal various stages in early Christian treatment of the Sabbath; determinative in each case was the composition and locality of each group. The course of development from Sabbath-observant community of disciples in Jerusalem to the anti-Sabbath polemic of Christian authors of the second century was by no means continuous, even if it followed a certain logic (658).

Mayer-Haas stresses that the history of Christian Sunday and its liturgical observance began independently of the Sabbath practice of early Christians (642). This is a significant advance over the work of Rordorf and Bacchiocchi, who both reason as if Christians observed either the

---

[31] Andrea J. Mayer-Haas, *«Geschenk aus Gottes Schatzkammer» (bSchab 10b): Jesus und der Sabbat im Spiegel der neutestamentlichen Schriften* (Neutestamentliche Abhandlungen, Neue Folge, 43), Münster, 2003. Page-number references will appear in the text in parentheses.

Sabbath or Sunday. The abandonment of the Sabbath by the mainstream was the result of a Christian process of self-discovery, which occurred in disassociation from synagogual Judaism and which, in light of the opening of the Christian mission to the Gentiles, was difficult to avoid. It had primarily sociological reasons, which were related to the development of an inner-Jewish group of followers of Jesus to a church composed of Jews and Gentiles and finally to a Gentile-Christian church. Theological arguments came later (644).

In the third part, the author evaluates and interprets the results of her exegetical investigation. She questions the traditional criterion of difference in the quest for the historical Jesus, which she identifies as the decisive reason for the origin of the common view of Jesus standing in critical distance toward the Sabbath, or even in enmity (647). She then introduces the criterion of historical plausibility as developed by Gerd Theissen and Dagmar Winter, which she modifies by application of Crossan's adequacy criterium: what did Jesus say and do that led, if not necessarily at least immediately, to diverse understanding? (656).

Finally, she undertakes a historical reconstruction, concluding that Jesus' Sabbath behavior did not markedly differ from that of his contemporaries, and that he taught his followers neither Sabbath criticism nor Sabbath norms (676). He did not go outside of the limits of what was possible in the Judaism of his day, although he had a liberal, practical interpretation of the command, conditioned by his life and ministry as an itinerant preacher. It was this, as well as his dealings with social and religious outsiders, that made it possible for his followers, after Easter, to pass beyond the territorial and religious borders of Israel. All in all, his relation to the Sabbath was not a prominent part of his ministry (680).

A unique contribution to the discussion is her suggestion that the conflicting chronologies concerning the events between the crucifixion and the resurrection reflect diverse Sabbath practices in the communities among which the Gospels arose. The Sabbath rest of women in Luke 23:56, for example, is seen as paradigmatic for the behavior of the Lukan Christians (367). The time indications in the Easter narrative in John, meanwhile, are a clear indication of the high estimation of Sunday in the Johannine community. Nevertheless, the question remains whether these texts have paradigmatic function. To what degree can they inform us of practices of the addressees? This question can be raised as well with regard to the repeated assertion that portrayals of Jesus teaching in synagogues are an indication that Sabbath worship services were the location of Christian scripture exposition as well (147–9, 156, 258, 400). To conclude that early Christian worship was patterned after that of the synagogue does not mean that their meetings were on the Sabbath.

Herold Weiss has authored a series of essays over the years that combine apt observations with idiosyncratic interpretations; they have now appeared in book form.[32]

Final mention in this survey of research goes to the monumental treatment of Sabbath halakah by Lutz Doering, *Schabbat: Sabbathalacha und -praxis im antiken Judentum und Urchristentum* (TSAJ 78, Tübingen 1999). This groundbreaking study was hailed upon publication as the standard treatment.[33] My treatment of the Sabbath in intertestamental Judaism is much briefer than it otherwise would have been because at many points I will refer to this.

1.3 METHOD AND STRUCTURE

In the light of the ample material that has been written on the subject, it is necessary to ask why another dissertation on the Sabbath should be written. The relevant texts in the NT after all are few and have often been discussed. There is little that can be labeled an uncontested, tangible fact. Yet there is a constant refinement of method, and each generation, indeed each individual student, brings a new perspective to any question. The intervening decades since the publication of the monographs of Rordorf and Bacchiocchi provide much of the justification for a new investigation, having brought changes to the landscape in NT and early Christian studies. Jewish-Christian dialogue, the discussion of unity and diversity in nascent Christianity, the "new perspective" on Paul, and the

---

[32] Herold Weiss, *A Day of Gladness: The Sabbath Among Jews and Christians in Antiquity* (Columbia, S.C., 2003).
[33] See, for example, the review by Friedrich Avemarie, *TLZ* 126 (2001): 622–5.

"third quest" for the historic Jesus can be cited as new approaches. The question of the Sabbath can serve as a test case for many of these and their explanatory capability.

Rordorf's landmark study sees a pattern of Sunday worship in the early Jerusalem group immediately after the resurrection appearances, using John 20 for this. Samuele Bacchiocchi's antithetical response traces the departure from the Sabbath primarily to growing anti-Jewish feeling. He implies, through his handling of texts, that the early Christian movement was principally Sabbatarian until the aftermath of the Bar Kokhba revolt (132–135 C.E.). Both Rordorf and Bacchiocchi are patristic scholars; my investigation of the NT texts yields results that differ from both. Both scholars place the question in the framework of a move from Sabbath to Sunday; this is misleading, since it gives the impression that Sunday is the Christian Sabbath, and that Christians would honor one or the other. This leaves out two other possibilities: neither, or both. To avoid this mistaken framing, I will not examine in detail the major "Sunday" texts (1 Cor 16:1–2; Acts 20:7; Rev 1:10).

What interests me instead is how to account for the rapid abandonment of Sabbath practice by many—if not most—Christians. The models of both Rordorf and Bacchiocchi are flawed. I propose a reexamination of NT texts on the basis of a historical-critical approach, supplemented by narratological and sociological considerations. The investigation will be supplemented by two texts that can also be dated to the time in which the NT texts were composed, the *Epistle of Barnabas* and the *Gospel of Thomas*. Although they did not achieve canonical status, they were widely used. It is essential, in light of current awareness of the variety in early Christianity, that these two voices be heard in this investigation.

Missing from this selection of texts is any document arguing for continued observance of seventh-day Sabbath rest. We can reasonably infer from Acts and Galatians that this position was argued at the time, but there are no primary sources for this position, imprecisely termed *Jewish-Christian*. Sadly, the two dramatic discoveries of hordes of primary documents in the middle of the twentieth century, Nag Hammadi 1945 and Qumran beginning in 1947, were not accompanied by a third: a cache of "Jewish-Christian" documents. Perhaps such a trove still awaits discovery; in the meantime, we must content ourselves with analyzing traditions contained in later works from this standpoint such as the Pseudo-Clementines, and mirror-reading the works of apologists and heresiologists. This lies outside the scope of my project, however.

I have chosen as a cut-off the Bar Kokhba revolt and the resulting Hadrianic repressions. This results in a period covering roughly the first hundred years of the Christian movement, with a reasonable number of texts to investigate.[34] Even within this period, however, choices had to be made. I have thus left out detailed examination of the Sabbath healings in the Synoptics; the topic will be touched on in my investigations of the grainfield episode (ch. 4) and of Sabbath healings in the Fourth Gospel (ch. 5). Secondly, Col 2:16, which belongs to the *Wirkungsgeschichte* of Gal 4:1–11, will be treated only in passing (ch. 3). Thirdly, with a heavy heart, I have not treated the *Didache*, whose version of the Eucharist stands in some relation to Sabbath prayers (*Kiddush*), and which also offers a clear statement of assembling on the Lord's Day.

Despite my choice of terminus a quo for this study, the question of whether Christians would worship on the Sabbath was not fully settled by then. The Hadrianic repressions were primarily aimed at Jews living in Judea and Galilee, and lapsed soon after his death. For the special case of Judea and Galilee, these events did effectively seal the fate of Torah-observant Christians: they became marginalized from both communities, lost influence, and shriveled or fled.[35] My periodization is not meant to endorse the traditional view that Judaism and Christianity parted ways at that time and that their further development was in mutual isolation. It appears that interaction continued between Jewish and Christian communities throughout the Diaspora, both within the vast extent of the Roman Empire and beyond, with Judaism continuing to represent an attractive alternative to Christianity, as the eight *adversus Judaeos*

---

[34] I did not choose this cut-off, however, on the assumption that the ancients conventionally used centuries for periodization in the way that we do. See Arndt Brendecke, *Die Jahrhundertwenden: Eine Geschichte ihrer Wahrnehmung und Wirkung*, Munich, 2000.

[35] Michael Avi-Yonah, *The Jews Under Roman and Byzantine Rule. A Political History of Palestine from the Bar Kokhba War to the Arab Conquest* (repr. New York, 1984 [1976]), 138–55.

sermons of John Chrysostom (ca. 347–407 C.E.) suggest. Nevertheless, by about 135–138 C.E. the main lines of the reasons for mainstream Christian rejection of the Sabbath were clear.

In the second chapter, I will explore the background of the question. Sabbath in OT and Judaism. A common view is that we are witnesses to a decline, that the institution decayed over time into a morass of stifling casuistic that Jesus opposed and overturned. This thesis will have to be examined and, if necessary, modified.

Chapters three through five present an exegesis of selected NT passages, representing three major streams in early Christianity: Paul, the Synoptic tradition, and John. Many overviews of the life and teaching of Jesus conclude that he opposed the Sabbath. But if Jesus did abrogate the Sabbath through word or deed, his earliest followers seem not to have known about it. This review of NT evidence will both allow an assessment of the validity and merits of the work of Rordorf and Bacchiocchi, both of whom approach the question as church historians rather than as exegetes, and serve as a basis for my own conclusions on the departure from Sabbath observance. A further chapter will examine Hebrews, *Barnabas* and *Thomas*.

Historical truth is complex and difficult to ascertain. Yet in this, as in so many cases, it arouses more than antiquarian interest. The present state of the Christian faith, and of the institutions that bear it, cause us to wonder about the Church "as it was supposed to be." For some, the solution would be a return to an earlier, pristine state. For others, it would be an adaptation of worship patterns to better reflect our digital, global age. For both, the history of the question is vital. The Sabbatarian—whether of the seventh-day or "Lord's Day" variety—has an emotional investment. If we do not observe the seventh-day Sabbath, are we violating divinely-ordained, permanent patterns?

1.4 THESIS

The Sabbatarian claim that the followers of Jesus remained universally observant of the seventh day throughout the apostolic era long received little scholarly support, but in recent years, a growing number of researchers have reassessed the relation of the emerging Christian

movement to its Jewish matrix and have suggested that the "parting of
the ways" between the two was a later development than previously
assumed.[36] Could it be that the Sabbatarian reading of NT evidence has
been correct all along? If the answer to this is no, but if there was
nonetheless no clear, early break between Christians and Jews, then a
more nuanced explanation for the abandonment of the Sabbath must be
sought. I do not propose to discover *the* reason for the change. A
convincing model must account for the diversity of formative Christianity, while bearing in mind that it was not simply a collection of doctrines,
but a lively social movement. The results of the following investigation
demonstrate that the change from Sabbath to Sunday worship was not
an event but a process. The three major catalysts in this development, I
will suggest, were the success of the Gentile mission, the cooling of the
ardor of the first generations, and the impossibility of returning to the
Sabbath when the need for a structured pattern of worship made itself
felt. This impossibility was the result of a complex interplay of factors,
the primary being the necessity of a clear separation from specifically
"Jewish" practices for the purpose of identity formation.

Finally, the project will not simply be an attempt at historical
reconstruction, but will recognize the paradigmatic value of this change
in worship practice. After all, Christianity has often accommodated itself
to new situations in which a strict orientation on the letter of the
scriptures has been viewed as a denial of the gospel to which those
scriptures witness.

---

[36] A pioneer in this perception was Eduard Schwartz (see n. 10, above). An
influential work that challenged the alternative, dominant, view was Marcel Simon, *Verus
Israel: A Study of the Relations Between Christians and Jews in the Roman Empire (AD
135–425)* (trans. H. McKeating; Oxford, 1996); trans. of *Verus Israel: Étude sur les
relations entre chrétiens et juifs dans l'empire romain (135–425)* (2d ed.; Paris, 1964).
Reflection on the metaphor *parting of the ways* and other models in Judith Lieu, "'The
Parting of the Ways': Theological Construct or Historical Reality?" (1994; repr. in
Neither Jew nor Greek? Constructing Early Christianity [SNTW; London, 2002],
11–29).

2

The Sabbath in the Old Testament
and in Intertestamental Judaism

Christianity did not arise in a vacuum. Jesus was a Jewish teacher who
spent his entire life, to judge by the sources available to us, in Galilee and
Judea, with short visits to neighboring lands. The first to proclaim the
gospel were Jews, preaching to fellow Jews. In Second Temple Judaism,
the Sabbath was not just a common practice, it was an identity marker.
Indeed, Sabbath observance is such an integral feature of Jewish identity
that it has been credited with the preservation of the beleaguered Jewish
faith.[1] This chapter, intended to serve as a background to the exegetical
investigations in the following chapters, will review research into the role
of the Sabbath in the Hebrew scriptures (2.1) and in Second Temple
Judaism (2.2). It will also examine how the Jews and their Sabbath were
viewed in the broader cultural context, one that was formed by oriental,
Hellenistic, and Roman influences (2.3). The aim will be to identity
factors that favored the retention of a Sabbath practice by the early
Christians, and those that spoke against.

2.1 THE SABBATH IN THE HEBREW SCRIPTURES

2.1.1 The Origin of the Sabbath
Viewed as a whole, in canonical order, the Hebrew Scriptures offer a dual
explanation of the origin of Sabbath observance. First, it is rooted in the
creative activity of God in the opening narrative, Gen 1:1–2:3. The
creation of heaven and earth culminates in the rest of Elohim himself on

---

[1] "The Sabbath has kept the Jews more than the Jews have kept the Sabbath,"
Ahad Ha-am, cited in Chaim I. Waxman, "The Sabbath as Dialectic: The Meaning and
Role," *Judaism* 31 (1982): 37–44, here 37.

the seventh day, after creating man as the pinnacle of his acts: "And on the seventh day God finished the work that he had done, and he ceased on the seventh day from all the work that he had done. So God blessed the seventh day and hallowed it, because on it God ceased from all the work that he had done in creation (Gen 2:2–3).[2]

The statement that God completed his work on the seventh day (2:2a) is difficult in light of v. 1, which had already declared the work of creation complete.[3] The noun *Sabbath* is not used here; instead, reference is strictly to the seventh day, mentioned three times.[4] This seventh day is nevertheless clearly the day celebrated in Israel as the Sabbath, as implicitly indicated by the two-fold use of the homophonic verb שָׁבַת.[5] Although the Sabbath is not named—thus avoiding the implication that

---

[2]   NRSV translates the verb שָׁבַת twice as *rest*; I have substituted the basic meaning of the verb, *cease*, in the sense of "come to an end," not "interrupt" (E. Haag, "שָׁבַת, *šabat*," *ThWAT* 7 [1993]: 1040–46, here 1040). In subsequent quotations from the NRSV, I have left the translation unchanged. The translation of שָׁבַת as "rest" or "celebrate" is justified in that this is the effect of completing one's work (F. Stolz, "שׁבת *šbt* aufhören, ruhen," *THAT* 2:863–69, here 864), but should be understood as a context-conditioned rendering.

[3]   This was felt in earliest times, as seen in LXX, Syr. and Sam., which read "sixth" instead of "seventh"; see also *Jub.* 2:1, 16 (O. H. Steck, *Der Schöpfungsbericht der Priesterschrift: Studien zur Literarkritischen und Überlieferungsgeschichtlichen Problematik von Genesis 1,1–2,4a* [2d ed.; FRLANT 115; Göttingen 1975], 178–9). There is no indication in the text that would suggest redactional strata (*pace* Claus Westermann, *Genesis 1–11* [3d ed.; BKAT 1/1; Neukirchen-Vluyn, 1983], 231–2). The most common explanations are to understand the sentence as declarative (Westermann, *Genesis 1–11*, 233–4) or the verb as pluperfect (Ugo Cassuto, *A Commentary on the Book of Genesis* [Jerusalem, 1961], 1: 61–62). Some suggest here a nuance that something indeed was created: the seven-day structure or the seventh-day rest (E. A. Speiser, *Genesis: A New Translation with Introduction and Commentary* [AB 1; Garden City, N. Y., 1964] 7; Jacques Briend, "Sabbat," *DBSup* 10:1132–70, here 1162); but care must be exercised: the works were finished on the sixth day (Gen 1:31–2:1). Steck concludes that what is new and special on the seventh day is that it finishes creation in another sense (*Schöpfungsbericht*, 178–87).

[4]   It is also referred to a fourth time by בֹּו in v. 3b.

[5]   The terminological similarities with Exod 20 and 31 reinforce this, showing that the seventh day of creation was understood in light of the later-instituted Sabbath (W. H. Schmidt, *Die Schöpfungsgeschichte der Priesterschrift: Zur Überlieferungsgeschichte von Genesis 1,1–2,4a und 2,4b–3,24* [2d ed.; WMANT 17; Neukirchen-Vluyn, 1967], 154–9; note however that Schmidt reverses the order of influence).

God *kept* the Sabbath—the basis for its later observance is clearly laid: "Elohim blessed the seventh day by setting it apart" (v. 3a).[6] The seventh day is set apart—*sanctified*—through the [non-]action of God in desisting from all his works.[7] The creative activity of God described in the works of the previous six days comes to a stop on the seventh for the sole reason that God himself chooses to desist. The solemnity of the occasion is reflected in the description.[8] There is no command for humans to observe the seventh day, yet the seven-day week belongs to the basic structure of creation; this has led some to consider it a "creation ordinance"[9] It was only on the seventh day that the final element through which the world

---

[6] For this translation, I have adopted Steck's suggestion that the phrase is best solved modally (*Schöpfungsbericht*, 194). In addition, I have used a literal translation of the verb קָדַשׁ, normally translated *to sanctify* or *to hallow*. This is the only time these two verbs appear together in the OT (Schmidt, *Schöpfungsgeschichte*, 157). This is the third instance of blessing in P's creation account (cf. 1:22, 28); the similarity to these works of creation that had also been blessed is that the seventh day will be propagated in an unending cycle (Steck, *Schöpfungsbericht*, 193–4).

[7] Like the term *the seventh day*, the expression מְלַאכְתּוֹ appears three times, twice qualified as אֲשֶׁר עָשָׂה, preceded by מִכָּל־ and completed by לַעֲשׂוֹת אֱלֹהִים בָּרָא אֲשֶׁר.

[8] The repetitive, rhythmic language—unmistakably that of P—, which hints at liturgical use, becomes more pronounced in 2:2–3, as if this forms a cadence at the end (Westermann, *Genesis 1–11*, 232). There are parallels in many religious traditions for the concept of divine rest at the close of creation (Raffaele Pettazzoni, "Myths of Beginnings and Creation-Myths," in *Essays on the History of Religions* [SHR 1; Leiden, 1954], 24–36; see also W. G. Lambert, "A New Look at the Babylonian Background of Genesis," *JTS* NS 16 (1965): 287–300). After the extraordinary activity involved in the creation of the world, the supreme deity enters, or returns to his natural condition, inactivity. Pettazzoni refers to this by the Latin term *otiositas*, idleness, a term that is ironically appropriate to underline the difference between God and man in light of its use in the Vulgate ("multam enim alitiam docuit otiositas," *Ecclesiastic.* 33:29) and the Benedictine Rule ("otiositas inimica est animae, et ideo certis temporibus occupari debent fratres in labore manuum, certis iterum horis in lectione divina," *Reg. Ben.* 48). Nevertheless, there is no trace of divine exhaustion in P's creation account, nor a need to withdraw after completing a creation that he has declared "very good" (1:31). If P is aware of such traditions, which is likely, the language implies dissent.

[9] E.g. Westermann, *Genesis 1–11*, 235–6. Sabbatarians, as well as those who see an application of Sabbath theology to the Lord's Day, see in this an indication that it is binding on all humanity. The concept "creation ordinance" is problematic (Martin Honecker, *Einführung in die Theologische Ethik: Grundlagen und Grundbegriffe* [de Gruyter Lehrbuch; Berlin, 1990], 291–303).

receives its constitutive order—time in a seven-day cycle, marked by a day of rest—is in place.[10] The uniqueness of the day is signaled by the lack of a closing formula such as "and it was evening, and it was morning, day seven" in analogy to the other six days.[11]

While the placement of this account certainly reflects a congruence between time as narrated and the narrative itself—the beginning comes at the beginning—the prominence this gives the seventh day in the overall flow of the canon is unmistakable, as is the tie-in to a major theme of the Hebrew scriptures taken as a canonical whole: the God of Israel is lord of creation.

The second explanation of the origin of the Sabbath observance is its prominence in the wilderness experience of Israel following the exodus (Exod 16). The lack of food in the wilderness leads to complaints about the leadership of Moses and Aaron and a desire to return to Egypt (vv. 2–3). The solution that Yahweh offers—"to rain bread from heaven"—is qualified as a way of putting the Israelites to the test, to see if "they will walk in my law" (v. 4). For six days, manna appears, with a double amount on the sixth, whereas on the seventh there is none (vv. 5, 22). Further, manna kept overnight on any other day goes bad, but on the Sabbath does not (vv. 20, 24). This continues throughout the forty years in the wilderness (v. 35; cf. Josh. 5:12).[12] The manna gathering bears

[10] Steck, *Schöpfungsbericht*, 196–7. P, with its distribution of eight creation works on six days, is often credited with imposing the seven-day scheme on what may have been an older tradition (Schmidt, *Schöpfungsgeschichte*, 67, 70; Westermann, *Genesis 1–11*, 124–5). Alternatively, it is held that the seven-day scheme itself is traditional (H.-P. Stähli, "Creatio als creatio perpetua?" *WD* NF 10 [1969]: 121–9). The uniformity of the language makes all supposition about the form of any earlier tradition hypothetical.

[11] See Gen 1:5, 8, 13, 19, 23, 31. This has been explained by the fact that the day had already been amply identified as the seventh (Hermann Gunkel, *Genesis übersetzt und erklärt* [3d ed.; HKAT 1/1; Göttingen, 1910], 116). It has however allowed for suggestions that this is a hint that the condition initiated by the completion of creation was interrupted not by the setting of the sun, but by the fall (there is no indication however that the author of P was aware of J's creation account), or is a hint of the never-ending blessedness of the world to come (both Jewish and Christian scholars. e.g., Augustine, *Conf.* 13.35–36).

[12] Polemic literature by Sabbatarian groups points to this incident to counter the objection that we cannot know when the Sabbath of creation was (e.g. Herbert W.

some traits of an etiological narrative that would account for the origin of the custom of rest every seventh day, yet lacks features typical of more straightforward etiological accounts. For instance, there is no formulation such as "for this reason . . . to this day."[13] Instead, the Sabbath is presented as something the reader is expected to know about. The question of its origin remains therefore open.

Critical study of the texts concerning the seventh day and the Sabbath has led to the consensus that neither explanation accounts for its origin.[14] There are few references to the Sabbath in the long stretch of narrative between the Pentateuch, detailing Israel's origins, and the material recounting its reconstitution after the exile.[15] An investigation of the few preexilic texts reveals that they speak either of the seventh-day or the Sabbath, but never equate the two. A prominent prexilic seventh day occurs when the Israelites first enter the promised land and encircle Jericho; the decisive march is said to occur on the seventh day. The term "Sabbath" is not used, however, nor is the increased activity of the people on that day—they marched around the city seven times, then stormed and destroyed it—explained or justified (Josh 6:1–21).[16] Meanwhile,

---

Armstrong, *Has Time Been Lost?* [5th ed.; Pasadena, 1984], an adaptation of an earlier work of the same name that had been distributed by the Church of God, Seventh Day).

[13]   E.g., Gen 26:33; 32:32.

[14]   Fritz Stolz, "Sabbat, Schöpfungswoche und Herbstfest," *WD* NF 11 (1971): 159–75, here 159.

[15]   It is not mentioned, for instance, in Joshua, Judges, or Samuel.

[16]   Other seven day periods are mentioned in the OT without explicit reference to the Sabbath. For instance, such periods are mentioned four times in the account of the Flood (Gen 7:4, 10; 8:10, 12). In addition, it is also the duration of the wedding celebration of Jacob (Gen 29:27; cf. Judg 14:12) as well as the mourning at his death (Gen 50:10). See also Job 2:13, where the friends of Job share his grief. Also: Gen 31:23; Exod 7:25; 12:15, 19; 13:6. There is no mention that any of these periods end with a Sabbath. It is unclear how far back the traditions behind these texts reach, but it corresponds to the evidence for seven-day periods in other cultures of the ancient Near East, which is not surprising given the length of lunar quarters (Willy Rordorf, *Der Sonntag: Geschichte des Ruhe- und Gottesdiensttages im ältesten Christentum* [ATANT 43; Zürich, 1962], 20–23). The view that there is an etymological connection between the word for seven and the noun Sabbath has been largely abandoned (Briend, "Sabbat," 1133; cf. however Gerhard F. Hasel, who still sees this as a possibility, "Sabbath," *ABD* 5:849–55, here 849).

2 Kgs 4:23 is one of the oldest references to the Sabbath, if not the oldest. A Shunemite woman, who had conceived a son after being promised this by Elisha, proposes to go to the prophet after her son's sudden death. Her husband replies: "'Why go to him today? It is neither new moon nor Sabbath.' She said, 'It will be all right.'" The preexilic Sabbath thus not only had meaning for the official cult but also for private religious undertakings: it was an appropriate time for visiting a man of God.[17] This indicates that a pause from normal labor was connected with the day and also that later restrictions on travel on the day were not yet known. Nothing is said about its origin, nor is there any definition of what is meant by Sabbath, or in what frequency it occurs.

2 Kings 11:4–12 narrates a putsch initiated by Jehoiada against Queen Athaliah, who is replaced by her grandson, Joash. Crucial for the plot's success is its timing, the Sabbath, when troop movements would not draw suspicion because the changing of the guard occurred then.[18] There is no concern of violating rest, nor is there any explicit reference to the seventh day.[19] This is consistent with the assumption that the change of the guard occurred monthly, as did other aspects of the administration established by Solomon (1 Kgs 4:7; 5:7; 18).[20] This illuminates preexilic observance of the Sabbath in the Jerusalem cult: it is a day on which the ruling king or queen visits the temple, and is an appropriate day for the enthronement of a king.[21] These associations with kingship correspond to what is known about the ancient Near Eastern moon cult.[22]

---

[17]   Stolz, *THAT* 2:866.

[18]   Christoph Levin dismisses the mention of the Sabbath in this account as a later insertion (*Der Sturz der Königin Atalja: Ein Kapitel zur Geschichte Judas im 9. Jahrhundert v.Chr.* [SBS 105; Stuttgart, 1982], 29–57).

[19]   Gnana Robinson, *The Origin and Development of the Old Testament Sabbath: A Comprehensive Exegetical Approach* [BBET 21; Frankfurt am Main, 1988], 79–80. He points out that the parallel account in 2 Chron 23:1–11, all the actors in the coup d'état are priests or Levites, whose prerogative to labor on the Sabbath is presumed.

[20]   Robinson, *Origin*, 79–80. In 1 Chron 9:24–32, written after the Sabbath was unmistakably identified with the seventh day, the change of guards at the temple takes place weekly, even though other administrative duties, including the changing of the palace guard, continued to rotate on a monthly basis.

[21]   Robinson, *Origin*, 74–82.

[22]   Robinson, *Origin*, 66–73.

The husband of the Shunemite woman referred to the Sabbath in parallel to the new moon (2 Kgs 4:23). In preexilic prophetic criticism of the Sabbath we find the same phenomenon (Amos 8:5; Isa 1:13; Hos 2:13).[23] The parallelism of Sabbath and new moon has led to repeated attempts to explain the Sabbath as originating as the day of the full moon.[24] Support for this is that the closest cognate to the noun Sabbath in Semitic languages is the Akkadian *šapattu(m)*, the full moon day.[25] Some have suggested that in the northwest Semitic area, the term came to be applied to the last day of each lunar quarter, not just the full moon day, but this is undocumented.[26] There is no clear indication in the OT that the Sabbath was once the celebration of the full moon, however, nor of a change to apply the name to each seventh-day.[27] Evidence based on the calculation of Shavuot, the Feast of Weeks, is not decisive. In Leviticus, it is based on seven-day periods called Sabbaths, that begin and end on the day after a Sabbath (Lev 23:15). This method of counting appears older than the context in which it is embedded, and may be an early indication of equating Sabbath and seventh-day.[28] In the festival

---

[23]   The cultic character of the observance of the new moon in preexilic Israel is indicated by the need for purification (1 Sam 20:5, 18, 24) and the offering of sacrifices (Num 28:11–15). It seems to have retained significance after the exile (Ezra 3:5; Neh 10:34; 1 Chron 23:31; 2 Chron 2:3; 8:13; 31:3). See Hans-Joachim Kraus, *Gottesdienst in Israel: Studien zur Geschichte des Laubhüttenfestes* (2d ed.; BEvT 19; München 1962), 96–108, E. Otto, "Feste und Feiertage," *TRE* 11:96–106.

[24]   Notably Johannes Meinhold in a series of publications (e.g. "Zur Sabbatfrage," *ZAW* 48, 1930, 121–38). Recent proponents include Hossfeld, *Dekalog*, 38, n. 73; 59; 251; Frank Crüsemann, *Bewahrung der Freiheit: Das Thema des Dekalogs in sozialgeschichtlicher Perspektive* (München, 1983), 55; Briend, "Sabbat," 10:1137; and Robinson, *Origin*.

[25]   Stolz, *THAT* 2:863. See however the reasons against this advanced by Hasel, "Sabbath," 5:850. The Akkadian term can also refer, by extension, to a fifteen-day period or half a month (*CAD* 17/1:449–50).

[26]   E.g. Stolz, "Sabbat," 172.

[27]   Stolz, *THAT* 2:867. The criticism directed toward "Sabbaths and new moons" in Hos 2:13 and Isa 1:13 may hint at a discrediting of these institutions, but there was certainly no memory of this, or else the term Sabbath could not have been successfully applied to the seventh day. The use of the pair "Sabbath and full moon" in later passages would suggest that the memory of another practice, if there were one, was lost (Isa 66:23; Ezek 46:1; Neh 10:32; 1QM 2:4).

[28]   Ernst Kutsch, "Der Sabbat—ursprünglich Vollmondstag?" In *Kleine Schriften*

calendar of Deuteronomy, however, the calculation is based on seven periods of seven (שִׁבְעָה שָׁבֻעֹת), suggesting that the calculation of the Feast of Weeks was not dependent on the Sabbath (Deut 16:9).

Those who hold that the Sabbath and the seventh day were always one and the same must explain the reference to only one or the other in preexilic texts.[29] Meanwhile, those who hold that the seventh day and the Sabbath were once discrete institutions bear the burden of accounting for their joining. This is commonly held to have occurred during the exile, and is normally attributed to the loss of temple.[30] The texts that bear clearest witness to the increased prominence of the Sabbath, such as Ezekiel and the Holiness Code, can support such a reconstruction. Yet the Sabbath can not be seen as a conscious replacement for the temple, since it was important for those who returned from exile to build a new temple.[31] Robinson places the joining of the two institutions after the exile.[32] A difficulty for Robinson's proposal is posed by the Elephantine papyri (ca. 475 B.C.E.), in which Doering finds evidence both for the Sabbath as referring to a weekly event and to the beginnings of halakah concerning its proper observance.[33] If he is correct, it would be hard to imagine a newly redefined Sabbath having found acceptance so far from Jerusalem mere decades after its promulgation by temple priests.

Even if the two institutions were once separate, the first steps in their later joining may have occurred earlier than the exile. Even though the

zum Alten Testament (BZAW 168, Berlin 1986), 71–77.

[29] Ernst Haag, for example, explains the non-equation of Sabbath and seventh-day in preexilic texts as reflecting stages of development. In its earlier stages, the day was simply referred to by its enumeration. Later it gained a name derived from the verb that characterized the day, שָׁבַת (Vom Sabbat zum Sonntag: Eine biblisch-theologische Studie [TThSt 52; Trier, 1991], 41–42).

[30] E.g., Julius Wellhausen, Prolegomena zur Geschichte Israels (4th ed.; Berlin 1895), 113.

[31] See also reference to the enemies of Jerusalem laughing about her Sabbaths, in a lament over the destruction of the city (Lam 1:7) as well as Lam 2:6 and its reference to the cessation of the observance of the Sabbath in conjunction with the destruction of the sanctuary.

[32] Robinson, Origin, 215–36.

[33] Lutz Doering, Schabbat: Sabbathalacha und -praxis im antiken Judentum und Urchristentum (TSAJ 78; Tübingen, 1999), 40–41.

verb שָׁבַת and the noun appear *not* to share common origin, their homophony means that it is unlikely that an association between the seventh day, on which שָׁבַת was commanded, and a *different* day, called שַׁבָּת, occurred late. The Sabbath, even if monthly, involved a degree of cessation from the normal work in order to be celebrated (2 Kgs 4:23). In addition, if the seven day cycles were recalibrated twice a year, as Robinson asserts, this took place on a "Sabbath," assuming that the term referred to a full moon before the exile (15 Abib, 15 Tishri), intimately connecting the two institutions. This may have led to association long prior to exile even though there is no textual proof of this.

2.1.2 The Sabbath after the Exile

In texts related to the exile and its aftermath, improper Sabbath observance is cited as a chief factor in the catastrophe that befell Israel; renewal is tied to its stringent solemnization. The clearest indication of an increased importance of the Sabbath are the fifteen references to it in Ezekiel. These occur in two clusters: nine of the occurrences come between 20:12 and 23:38, the remaining six in the vision of restored Jerusalem and its temple (chs. 40–48), all between 44:24 and 46:12.

Concerning the first group, the Sabbath has the character of a sign (20:12, 20; cf. Exod 31:13), both the evidence of and guarantee for the relation of Yahweh to his people.[34] It has been profaned (20:13, 16, 21, 24; 22:8, 26), implying that it is holy (cf. Exod 31:14). This profanation is viewed as a major failing, on a level with idolatry and infant sacrifice (23:38); Indeed, in 20:16, this profanation of the Sabbaths is attributed to idolatry; the logic and parallelism of 20:18–20 imply that proper Sabbath observance is the positive counterpart of idolatry. The Sabbath stands in parallel to statutes and ordinances as a third object given by God (20:11–12). Invariably, the Sabbath is referred to in plural, with a possessive suffix indicating that they belong to Yahweh (שַׁבְּתוֹתַי).[35] All of

---

[34] Walther Eichrodt, "Der Sabbat bei Hesekiel: Ein Beitrag zur Nachgeschichte des Prophetentextes," in *Lex Tua Veritas* (FS H. Junker; ed. H. Gross and F. Mussner; Trier, 1961), 65–74, here 65.

[35] This form also appears in Exod 31:12; Lev 19:3, 30; 26:2; Isa. 56:4. Robinson takes this to be a special characteristic of postexilic preaching (*Origin*, 206).

these seem to be either insertions in a text already fixed, or appear in secondary sections.[36] In one case (23:38), a reference to the Sabbath appears to be an interpolation in a redactional section.[37] The proximity to the priestly source is clear.[38] The Sabbath references in Ezekiel share a homogenous theological viewpoint, apparently influenced by the Sabbath legislation of the holiness code (Lev 17–26).[39] This finding, based on literary-critical considerations, is reinforced by the lack of the mention of the Sabbath in contexts in which it would be expected, were it a major concern of the priest-prophet, Ezekiel.[40]

Concerning the second group, in restored Jerusalem, priests will discharge their responsibility for sanctifying it (44:24), essentially reversing the conditions portrayed in ch. 22:23–31.[41] It is included in series with festivals and new moons and "all the appointed festivals of the house of Israel" (מוֹעֲדֵי, 45:17).[42] It will be marked by assemblies and sacrifices (46:1, 3–5, 12). It appears that the references to the Sabbath in this part of Ezekiel largely, if not exclusively, belong to a late stage of this book's redaction, as well.

The OT texts most clearly referring to the Sabbath in a postexilic setting are those in Nehemiah. Two appear in a section presented as the climax of the work of Ezra, dated in the text to 445 B.C.E. (Neh 8:1 [ET 7:73b]; cf. 5:14) with his public reading of the law (Neh 8), public repentance (Neh 9), and a collective undertaking of a covenant pledge (Neh 10). As part of the prayer of contrition, the people say: "You came down also upon Mount Sinai, and spoke with them from heaven, and gave them right ordinances and true laws, good statutes and command- ments, and you made known your holy Sabbath to them and gave them commandments and statutes and a law through your servant Moses

---

[36]   Briend, "Sabbat," 10:1146–7; Haag, *Sabbat,* 99–105.
[37]   Walther Zimmerli, *Ezechiel* (BKAT 13; Neukirchen-Vluyn, 1969) 1:553.
[38]   Eichrodt, "Sabbat," 68.
[39]   Zimmerli, *Ezechiel* 1:447.
[40]   Eichrodt, "Sabbat," 70–71.
[41]   Robinson, *Origin,* 210.
[42]   It is not possible to draw any conclusions about whether the Sabbath is now clearly a weekly institution, since the same four objects appear, in the same order, in the preexilic Hos 2:13 (ET 2:11).

(9:13–14)." Of all of the matters commanded in the law mediated through Moses at Sinai, only the Sabbath is mentioned specifically.[43] This has the effect of making it seem to be the essential law.[44] Then, as part of the pledge to observe the provisions of the covenant, after promising not to intermarry with the neighboring people, they promise "if the peoples of the land bring in merchandise or any grain on the sabbath day to sell, we will not buy it from them on the Sabbath or on a holy day; and we will forego the crops of the seventh year and the exaction of every debt" (10:32 [ET v. 31]).[45] In addition, the people promise financial provision for regular offerings in the rebuilt temple, mentioning in sequence of daily, Sabbath, new moon and festival, which is consistent with an understanding of the Sabbath as a weekly occasion (vv. 33–34 [ET vv. 32–33]).

Finally, in a memoir of Nehemiah's return to Jerusalem, the erstwhile governor of the city observes market activity on the Sabbath (13:15–16). Although market days were commonly not seen as work days in the ancient world, pressure to engage in trade on the Sabbath was resisted in preexilic Israel (Amos 8:5).[46] Nehemiah inveighs against the practice of his contemporaries by recalling the sins of the "ancestors" (vv. 17–18). This accords with the emphasis on Sabbath transgression in general as cause of the destruction of Jerusalem seen below in Ezekiel.[47] In addition, he undertakes measures—shutting and watching the city gates—to prevent

---

[43] The expression שַׁבַּת קָדְשֶׁךָ is unique in the OT. The closest parallel is Isa 58:13, in which the expressions "Sabbath" and "holy day" are equated through *parallelismus membrorum*.

[44] Stolz, *THAT* 2:868.

[45] The "peoples of the land" (עַמֵּי הָאָרֶץ) could include Jews who were not part of the temple community in Jerusalem.

[46] In the time before the establishment of fixed marketplaces in major cities, a development archaeologically dated to late sixth or early fifth cent. B.C.E. for a major city like Athens, it was the custom for markets to take advantage of public gatherings, including religious festivals (S. von Reden, "Markt 2: Klassische Antike," *DNP* 7: 922–5). Nehemiah's concept of Sabbath observance is stricter than the norm then, but apparently in accordance with preexilic practice (Amos 8:5). This weighs against Ernst Jenni's suggestion that the Sabbath arose as a market day (*Die theologische Begründung des Sabbatgebotes im Alten Testament* [ThSt 46, Zollikon, 1956], 12–13).

[47] Ezek 22:8; 23:38.

this (vv. 19–22). Interestingly, not only Sabbath observance, but most of the other abuses singled out by Nehemiah correspond to those the people pledged to avoid in ch. 10.[48]

The reference to carrying burdens in Neh 13:15–22—clearly transport of commercial goods for the purpose of marketing them on the Sabbath—helps illuminate the harangue presented as a prose sermon in Jer 17:19–27. In it, the prophet, using the formula "thus saith the Lord," forbids the carrying of any burden on the Sabbath (vv. 21–22); the matter is presented as one of life and death (v. 21; cf. Exod 35:2). Here, as in Neh 13:18, there is a reference to the ancestors, in this case to the command given to them, in wording reminiscent of the Decalogue ("or do any work, but keep the Sabbath day holy," v. 22). After noting the refusal of the people to obey (v. 23), there is a description of benefits promised for obedience (vv. 24–26) and of the consequence of disobedience (v. 27). The consequences recall the destruction of Jerusalem ("I will kindle a fire in its gates; it shall devour the palaces of Jerusalem and shall not be quenched"), while the benefits express the hope of restoration of the Davidic kingship (v. 25).

This is the only reference to the Sabbath in the book of Jeremiah, adding to the unlikelihood that this goes back to the prophet.[49] The similarities to the thought of Nehemiah suggest that the two texts stand in some relation. If one assumes the priority of Neh 13, this would cast light on the confused setting of this oracle: "Thus said the Lord to me: Go and stand in the People's Gate, by which the kings of Judah enter and by which they go out, and in all the gates of Jerusalem" (Jer 17:19). This could reflect a conflation of the gates by which Nehemiah observed the

<hr>

[48] Provisions for Levites, 13:10–14; cf. 10:38–40 (ET vv. 37–39); intermarriage, 13:23–30a; cf. 10:31 (ET v. 30); wood offering and first fruits, 13:31; cf. 10:35–37 (ET vv. 34–36). This correspondence suggest that the pledge of ch. 10 may have been composed as part of the redaction of the book in light of the memoir incorporated in ch. 13.

[49] Most scholars see this oracle as redactional, e.g. Jack R. Lundbom, *Jeremiah 1–20: A New Translation with Introduction and Commentary* (AB 21A; New York, 1999), 806; William McKane, *A Critical and Exegetical Commentary on Jeremiah. 1: Introduction and Commentary on Jeremiah 1–25* (ICC; Edinburgh, 1986), 416–8. A connection to Jeremiah is defended, e.g., by J. A. Thompson, *The Book of Jeremiah* (NICOT; Grand Rapids, Mich., 1980), 427–31.

commercial traffic on the Sabbath and a memory of the gate through which the king entered the preexilic temple on the Sabbath.[50] In sum, this oracle presumes the criticism of Neh 13, but expresses it in more general language, so that carrying any burden, even out of one's house (Jer 17:22), on the Sabbath was the concrete expression of the kind of work to be avoided on the day. In this way, it bears witness to an extension of Sabbath proscriptions in the time around or after 400 B.C.E.

The Sabbath plays a prominent role in Third Isaiah, figuring in three passages, two of which form the outer framework of this major section of the longest prophetic book in the OT. The passages are Isa 56:1–8; 58:13–14; 66:22–24, which I will now examine in turn before attempting to draw general conclusions.

Isaiah 56:1 opens with the *Botenformel*, "thus says YHWH" (repeated in vv. 4 and 8). The general summons to maintain justice (מִשְׁפָּט) and do what is right (צְדָקָה) is placed in an eschatological perspective: "for soon my salvation will come, and my deliverance be revealed" (v. 1). This is followed by a benediction on those who do and hold fast to two things, keeping the Sabbath and refraining from doing any evil. Both are introduced by a participial form of the verb שׁמר (cf. v. 1, where the summons is introduced with this verb in imperative).[51] Sabbath observance is thus presented parallel with, and perhaps as the equivalent of, "refraining from doing any evil." To keep the Sabbath is further qualified as to not profane it, recalling language from the Sabbath references in Ezekiel.[52] Beginning in v. 3, this blessing is specifically extended to two groups, "the foreigner joined to YHWH," and "the eunuch." The eunuchs, who could not hope to have their name perpetuated in the normal way, by producing children, are promised that they will nevertheless have an everlasting name. In this promise, to keep the Sabbath is explicated as to "choose the things that please me and hold fast the covenant." Sabbath observance is thus emblematic of covenant faithfulness (cf.

---

[50] Robinson, *Origin*, 197.

[51] See also the use of this verb in relation to Sabbath observance in Deut 5:12, Exod 31:14, 16.

[52] E.g. Ezek 20:13. Isa 56:1–6 uses the singular and plural forms of the terms Sabbath side by side. The phrase "keep my Sabbaths" (v. 4) is found in H (Lev 19:3, 30; 26:2) and Exod 31:13.

Exod 31:16–17). Likewise, the description of the foreigners who will be blessed is expanded in v. 6 compared to v. 3: those who join themselves to YHWH is expanded, "to minister to him, to love the name of YHWH, and to be his servants," while the element of keeping the Sabbath and not profaning it is expanded with "hold fast my covenant." The promise to them amounts to full integration in the temple community: "these I will bring to my holy mountain, and make them joyful in my house of prayer; their burnt offerings and their sacrifices will be accepted on my altar." The effect of this, or perhaps the reason for it (כִּי), is that "my house shall be called a house of prayer for all peoples." These measures are reformulated and summarized, again introduced by "thus says YHWH" as an extension of the regathering of Israel to include the outcasts (v. 8). We find here, then, a concentration on the Sabbath as emblem of covenant faithfulness as well as condition for inclusion in the temple community that outweighs ethnic considerations or the taint of a disability that would preclude producing more heirs of the covenant.[53]

In Isa 58:13–14, another promise is made to those who observe the Sabbath, also called "my holy day" and "the holy day of YHWH." They will "take delight in YHWH," will "ride upon the heights of the earth," and be fed "with the heritage of your ancestor Jacob." This description of the state of blessedness recalls the Song of Moses, Deut 32. There, Jacob is singled out among the nations as YHWH's portion, as "his allotted share" (v. 9). YHWH sets Jacob "atop the heights of the land" (v. 13aα).[54] This is followed by a menu of delicacies he will consume (vv. 13aβ–14). The promise in Isa 58:14 is nothing less than a restoration to the blessings associated with gift of the land, and this is conditioned on Sabbath

---

[53] In Deut 23:1, eunuchs are specifically excluded from the congregation of YHWH (cf. Lev 21:20, where this exclusion can be understood to be limited to those who suffer a disability to their reproductive organs). Isa 56:3–5 thus represents the remarkable case of a statute in the Torah being directly contradicted, and thus abolished, by a word of YHWH in the OT (Herbert Donner, "Jesaja 56: 1–7: Ein Abrogationsfall innerhalb des Kanons—Implikationen und Konsequenzen," *Congress Volume: Salamanca, 1983* [ed. J. A. Emerton; VTSup 36; Leiden, 1985] 81-95; repr. in *Aufsätze zum Alten Testament aus vier Jahrzehnten* [Berlin, 1994], 165–78).

[54] The Hebrew of Deut 32:13 resembles Isa 58:14 more closely than is reflected in the NRSV translation: אֶרֶץ (Ketib: בָּמוֹתֵי) בָּמֳתֵי עַל־בָּמֳותֵי יַרְכִּבֵהוּ, Deut 32:13; אֶרֶץ (Ketib: במותי) בָּמֳתֵי עַל־ וְהִרְכַּבְתִּיךָ, Isa 58:14.

observance. At the same time, v. 13 provides some insight into what is considered appropriate or non-appropriate behavior on it; one is to avoid "trampling" on it, or "pursuing your own interests." To honor it means "not going your own ways, serving your own interests, or pursuing your own affairs" (lit., "speaking words," וְדַבֵּר דָּבָר). Although short on specifics, this is one of the few concretizations of what might violate the work prohibition on the day.[55] Positively it means not specific actions, but calling the day a "delight" and "honorable." To delight in YHWH was part of the promised blessing (v. 14). To delight in God is an expression of a trusting relationship with him (Psa 37:4; Job 22:26; 27:10). Here, the thought is extended to the Sabbath, emblematic of the covenant that symbolizes that relationship.[56] This description of the blessings of Sabbath observance is an appendix added to a longer section describing the proper attitude to accompany fasting, which also contains promised benefits (58:1–12).

The closing words of Isaiah describe conditions after God's judgment of both Israel and the nations. A uniform cult performed by all who survive takes place "from new moon to new moon, and from Sabbath to Sabbath" (Isa 66:23).[57] Distinctions between Israel and non-Israel have disappeared; "all flesh" comes to worship. There is a correspondence between the pattern of worship defined here and the one item of observance singled out as decisive for participation in the salvation community, the Sabbath.

The attitude expressed in these passages is sometimes taken as an expression of universalism.[58] Given that the book ends with the carcasses of all those who rebelled against YHWH, however, "universalism" would not seem to be an appropriate designation. There is nothing here that

---

[55]   Others are gathering sticks (Num 15:32–36), lighting a fire (Exod 35:25), and carrying a burden (Jer 17:19), especially transporting commercial goods with the intent of selling them on the Sabbath (Neh 13:15–22).

[56]   Robinson, *Origin*, 265–72.

[57]   The pair new moon/Sabbath can be understood here as traditional, and is not decisive for the question of whether the preexilic Sabbath was celebrated weekly or monthly (Briend, "Sabbat," 10:1163). Their mention here forms an inclusion with Isa 1:13, where new moons and Sabbaths are rejected.

[58]   Paul D. Hanson, *The Dawn of Apocalyptic* (Philadelphia, 1975), 388–9.

approaches the breadth of perspective expressed in one of the Ebed-
YHWH oracles (Isa 49:1–6, see especially v. 6, but also vv. 8, 12) or of the
invitation to the nations in 55:1–5.[59] Instead, these passages, particularly
56:3, 6–7, show a concern to regulate the status of those who, as part of
the reversal of fortunes, come to serve Israel (Isa 45:14–16; 49:26;
60:9–16), as part of an overall reconfiguration of the people of God.[60] In
contrast to more exclusivist tendencies, such as those expressed in Ezra
(ch. 10) and Nehemiah (10:31; 13:15–22), there is a clear acceptance of
the possibility of non-Israelites being "joined" to YHWH and embracing
the covenant. But this welcome is restricted in its own way. Salvation is
tied to a place—Jerusalem—and observances—the Sabbaths.[61] Nevertheless, the potential of a message emanating from Jerusalem yet resonating
in the nations is seen by the use of Isa 56:7b in the accounts of Jesus
cleansing the temple (Mark 11:17 parr Matt 21:13; Luke 19:46).[62]

2.1.3 The Sabbath in the Torah

The Sabbath features prominently in the legal texts in the Torah.[63] When
Israel camps at the foot of Sinai and receives the Decalogue, the Sabbath
is included (Exod 20:8–11; cf. Deut 5:12–15). The dual explanation of
the origin of the institution of the Sabbath discussed above (2.1.1) is
reflected in a significant variation between the two versions of the Decalogue. In Exod 20:11, the climax of the creation account recorded in
Gen 2:2–3 is given as the reason for remembering and sanctifying what

---

[59] Odil Hannes Steck, however, does see the welcome to foreigners and eunuchs
as an extension of God's calling the nations in 55:1–5 (*Studien zu Tritojesaja* [BZAW
203; Berlin, 1991], 170, 244–5).

[60] Seizo Sekine, *Die Tritojesajanische Sammlung (Jes 56–66) redaktionsgeschichtlich untersucht* (BZAW 175; Berlin, 1989), 236–7; Leszek Ruszkowski, *Volk und
Gemeinde im Wandel: Eine Untersuchung zu Jesaja 56–66* (FRLANT 191; Göttingen,
2000), 124–6.

[61] A similar perspective is evident in the latter chapters of Zech, tied however to
observance of the annual fall pilgrimage, the Feast of Tabernacles (Zech 14:16–21).

[62] This despite the common omission in Matt and Luke of πᾶσιν τοῖς ἔθνεσιν.

[63] Nearly half, 47, of the 111 uses of the noun שַׁבָּת occur in the Pentateuch. Most
of the rest are in postexilic sections. The derivative שַׁבָּתוֹן appears eleven times, all in
the Pentateuch; six of these are in the expression שַׁבַּת שַׁבָּתוֹן, all of these in P (Stolz,
THAT 2:863; Hasel, 5:849).

is now termed, in contrast to Genesis, the Sabbath: "For in six days the Lord made heaven and earth, the sea, and all that is in them, but rested the seventh day; therefore the Lord blessed the Sabbath day and consecrated it."[64] In the Deuteronomy version, the exodus from Egypt is cited, not only as a reason for the observance itself, but also for the inclusion of others, even livestock, in its observance:

> Observe the Sabbath day and keep it holy, as the Lord your God commanded you. Six days you shall labor and do all your work. But the seventh day is a Sabbath to the Lord your God; you shall not do any work—you, or your son or your daughter, or your male or female slave, or your ox or your donkey, or any of your livestock, or the resident alien in your towns, so that your male and female slave may rest [נוּחַ] as well as you. Remember that you were a slave in the land of Egypt, and the Lord your God brought you out from there with a mighty hand and an outstretched arm; therefore the Lord your God commanded you to keep the Sabbath day (Deut 5:12–15).

The Sabbath enjoys prominent placement in both versions of the Decalogue (Exod 20:8–11; Deut 5:12–15).[65] Not only is the Sabbath command more extensively formulated than the other commandments, but the differences in wording are greater between the two versions of the Sabbath command than in any other commandment.[66] In addition to a difference in the reason given for the command, the command is introduced in one version by the exhortation to "remember" (זָכַר, Exod 20:8), in the other, to "observe" (שָׁמַר, Deut 5:12). Since each of these near-synonyms is typical for the circles likely responsible for each formulation of the command, however, it is difficult to determine which may have been "original" (on the assumption that the younger of two—whichever it was—represents a reworking of the other, known in

---

[64] The verb here is נוּחַ, not שָׁבַת, and is properly translated *rest*, in the sense of *repose*.

[65] Norbert Lohfink finds the prominence even greater in the Deuteronomy version, reading it as a pentalogue, with the Sabbath, at its center, as the main commandment ("Zur Dekalogfassung von Dt 5," *BZ* 9 [1965]: 17–32, repr. in *Studien zum Deuteronomium und zur deuteronomistischen Literatur 1* [SBAB 8; Stuttgart, 1990], 193–209).

[66] Extensive discussion of the differences in the two versions of the command in Frank-Lothar Hossfeld, *Der Dekalog: Seine späten Fassungen, die originale Komposition und seine Vorstufen* (OBO 45; Freiburg, Schweiz, 1982), 40–57.

its fixed, written form).[67] Both appear as infinitive absolutes, which function as strong imperatives. The positive formulation contrasts with the other items in the Decalogue, all of which, apart from the command to honor parents (Exod 20:12; Deut 5:16) are formulated negatively, as prohibitions.[68]

The Deuteronomist adds that this command is a reminder (v. 12; this phrase is added to the command concerning parents as well). This might be an indication that the version of the entire Decalogue in Deuteronomy is younger, but more likely reflects the relative newness of these two commands.[69] Hossfeld argues for reversing a scholarly trend to see the Exodus version as the older.[70] In his reconstruction, the version in Deuteronomy is shown to be a well-planned, unified composition, and the Exodus version the handwork of postexilic priestly redaction.[71]

---

[67] Christoph Levin argues for זָכֹר ("Der Dekalog am Sinai," *VT* 35, 1985, 165–91), Hossfeld for שָׁמֹר (*Dekalog*, 41). The alternative to positing the priority of one version over the other would be to attempt to reconstruct an earlier form common to both. Such an attempt is not as simple as building on the language common to both versions (roughly half of the vocabulary is shared), since a decision would still have to be made as to which opening verb, שָׁמֹר or זָכֹר, was original. In addition, such a reconstructed command would have no explanation for the day or its observance; precisely this is assumed by some, e.g. Jenni, *Begründung*, 5.

[68] Attempts to suppose an earlier negative formulation of the Sabbath command (e.g. Albrecht Alt, *Die Ursprünge des israelitischen Rechts* [Berichte über die Verhand lungen der sächsischen Akademie der Wissenschaften zu Leipzig. Philologisch-Historische Klasse. Leipzig, 1934]; repr. in *Kleine Schriften zur Geschichte des Volkes Israel 1* [München, 1959], 276–332, here 317–8) have been largely abandoned.

[69] Hossfeld, *Dekalog*, 56, against Lohfink, "Dekalogfassung," 206–07. As mentioned above, these two commands also share the characteristic of being positively formulated, while the other commands are prohibitions. They appear together in a prominent position in H (Lev 19:2). The order of the two commands is inverse in both versions of the Decalogue compared to Lev 19:2. This has the effect of aligning the Sabbath command with others governing the relationship to God, and the parents' command with those concerning fellow human beings.

[70] Hossfeld's work has won wide, but not universal acceptance. The opposite case is argued, in addition to Levin, "Dekalog," by e.g., W. H. Schmidt, H. Delkurt, A. Graupner, *Die Zehn Gebote im Rahmen Alttestamentlicher Ethik* (EdF 281; Darmstadt, 1992), 28–30.

[71] Hossfeld, *Dekalog*, 57, 247–48. Hossfeld builds on observations concerning the structure of the Sabbath command by Lohfink ("Dekalogfassung," 198–99), but reverses Lohfink's conclusion about the relative age of the two versions of the

In addition to containing a work prohibition (cf. Exod 23:12; 34:21) and a list of the beneficiaries of the command (cf. Exod 23:12), both versions contain the expression הַשַּׁבָּת יוֹם, "the Sabbath day," representing its earliest occurrences (Exod 20:8, 11; Deut 5:12, 15).[72] Those who see this command as the fusion of two previously separate institutions, the seventh day and the Sabbath, see this late appearance as a reflection of this development.[73] Another innovation compared to earlier formulations of the seventh day rest command is that this is a day "for YHWH" (Exod 20:10; Deut 5:14). Although this phrase is a novelty, and may reflect an increasing emphasis on the Sabbath as an expression of Israelite faith, it simply makes explicit what was already implicit in the practice of ceasing one day (or year) in seven: it was a recognition of the sovereignty of God.[74] From this point of view, its inclusion among the "ten words" spoken by YHWH (Deut 4:13; 10:4), the "zureichende Umschreibung des ganzen Willens Jahwehs an Israel," can be understood.[75] It is the practical application of the first commandment, "I am YHWH your God" in the rhythms of life. Thus, there is reason to challenge Ernst Jenni's thesis accounting for the presence of (diverse) explanations for the Sabbath command: "Das Sabbatgebot als solches erscheint aber dermassen willkürlich und irrational—warum soll jetzt gerade ausgerechnet jeder siebte Tag als heilig gelten?—, dass es dringend einer Erklärung und Begründung bedarf."[76] In the reconstruction adopted here, Jenni's reasoning can be reversed and taken as an indication that the practice of resting one day in seven never existed in Israel without a (theologically motivated) reason. The development of the expression of that reason,

---

command. Hossfeld's conclusions with regard to the Sabbath command have been widely accepted (e.g. Briend, "Sabbat," 10:1148–55; Haag, *Sabbat*, 45–50). The priority of Deut 5:12–15 doesn't exclude the possibility of some additions to harmonize it with the Exodus version (Haag, *Sabbat*, 45–46).

[72] Hossfeld, *Dekalog*, 38.

[73] Hossfeld, *Dekalog*, 57. The nominal formulation of the phrase is taken as an additional indication of this (Hossfeld, *Dekalog*, 248).

[74] Gerhard von Rad, *Theologie des Alten Testaments 1: Die Theologie der geschichtlichen Überlieferungen Israels* (München 1960; repr. Kaiser Taschenbücher 2; 1992), 29, n. 3.

[75] Von Rad, *Theologie*, 205.

[76] *Begründung*, 5.

from the early Exod 34:21 and (probably) 23:12, through its explicit connection to the exodus (Deut 5:15) and ultimately to creation (Exod 20:11) are an unfolding of this. The connections to the exodus and creation tell us nothing about the origin of the practice, but they do tell us that the increasing centrality of that practice followed an inner logic just as much as it may have been a response to outer pressures such as the catastrophe of the exile and the strain of forging a new national identity.[77]

At the same time, the emphasis that this is a day "for YHWH" may cohere to prophetic criticism of the Sabbath.[78] Preexilic Sabbath practice—the prophets never use the term "seventh day" in their criticism—was evidently not monotheistic. This observation may help to explain the felt need to supplant the grounding of the seventh-day Sabbath in the exodus with its explanation as something that had been hallowed by God at creation; the emphasis that Israel's god is none other than the god of creation as a consequence of growing monotheism is documented for late-exilic prophecy (e.g. Isa 40:12, 21–22, 26).

The Sabbath is repeatedly commanded in the unfolding Sinai narrative. Earlier forms of the command may be Exod 23:12; 34:21. Both refer to the seventh day, but do not call it the Sabbath. Characteristic of both is a two-part formulation. The first part is a command, formed as an antithetic pair: work six days and cease (תִּשְׁבֹּת) on the seventh.[79] The second part contains a supplementary instruction. One is found in the so-called Ritual Decalogue, Exod 34:10–26: "Six days you shall work, but on the seventh day you shall rest (תִּשְׁבֹּת); even in plowing time and in harvest time you shall rest (תִּשְׁבֹּת)" (v. 21). The mention of the two main seasons of agricultural activity has been explained in various ways.[80] The

---

[77]   The two versions of the Decalogue are generally considered no older than the exile (Briend, "Sabbat," 10:1157). Even Haag, who dates the Deuteronomic version of the Sabbath command to the time of Josiah's reform, says it was not yet part of the Decalogue, *Sabbat*, 51–55).

[78]   Hos 2:13 (ET 2:11); Isa 1:13–14; the negative correlation of Sabbath and idolatry in Ezek is also relevant here (see above 2.1.2). In Amos 8:5, however, the thrust of criticism is the impatience of merchants to resume trading.

[79]   This antithetic pair remained a common formulation in seventh-day and Sabbath legislation (Exod 20:9–10a; Deut 5:13–14a; Exod 31:15; 35:2; Lev 23:2; Briend, "Sabbat," 10:1137).

[80]   The instruction to rest appears in the midst of ordinances concerning yearly

connection with the agricultural year is clear; unclear, however, is whether this indicates that these instructions originated before the urbanization of Israelite society in the time of the kings, or whether they simply arose in an agricultural context.[81] The proximity to the command to eat unleavened bread in Abib (v. 18) suggests that the seven-day cycle originated in cultic observance and was extended throughout the year.[82]

The other is found in what is commonly referred to as the book of the covenant: "Six days you shall do your work, but on the seventh day you shall rest, so that your ox and your donkey may have relief, and your homeborn slave and the resident alien may be refreshed" (Exod 23:12). In addition to the motifs of celebration and refreshment, which are repeatedly found in Sabbath material, concern is expressed for both the socially inferior as well as domestic animals on whom the livelihood of an agricultural society depended. In place of the simple formulation "you shall work" (Exod 34:21), the Israelites are commanded "you shall do your work" (literally, "your works")[83] In contrast to Exod 34, the seventh-day is not mentioned within the liturgical calendar (23:14–17), but ahead

---

festivals. The first of these, the days of unleavened bread in the spring month of Abib, is specifically said to last for seven days (v. 18). At this time, the harvest of winter grain began; the grain harvests ended with the feast of weeks, while the time of sowing followed the feast of ingathering in the fall. Both of these festivals are mentioned in v. 22, although nothing is said of their duration. One explanation of the seventh day is that it was specifically observed at these agricultural seasons (Henri Cazelles, "Ex. 34, 21 traite-t-il du Sabbat?" *CBQ* 23 [1961]: 223–6, repr. in *Autour de l'Exode [Études]*, Paris, 1987, 295–8; see also Briend, "Sabbat," 10:1138–9). Another view, more widely held, is to see the expression as elliptic, a binomial phrase referring to the entire agricultural year (e.g. Jörn Halbe, *Das Privilegrecht Jahwes Ex 34,10–26: Gestalt und Wesen, Herkunft und Wirken in vordeuteronomistischer Zeit* [FRLANT 114; Göttingen, 1975], 189–92). Some add that the general weekly observance is emphasized for the time when the pressure to work without cease would be greatest (Martin Noth, *Das zweite Buch Mose: Exodus* [ATD 5; Göttingen, 1958], 217; Hans Walter Wolff, *Anthropologie des Alten Testaments*, [5th ed.; München, 1990], 208).

[81] For the first alternative, see Halbe, *Privilegrecht*, 191–2, 506–26, and Haag, *Sabbat*, 19–20; for the second, see Frank Crüsemann, *Die Tora: Theologie und Sozialgeschichte des alttestamentlichen Gesetzes* (München, 1992), 160–62.

[82] Haag, *Sabbat*, 22–23.

[83] In P, "you shall work" is consistently replaced by "you shall do your work" (Exod 31:15; 34:12; Lev 23:3; Briend "Sabbat," 10:1138).

of it, separated by a prohibition of mentioning the name of other gods (v. 13). In context, it appears more closely connected with the practice of allowing the land to lie fallow every seventh year (Exod 23:10–11) than with the yearly festivals.[84]

As with the Degalogue, the presence of two versions of this command has led to attempts to identify an older, "original" form of it. Rüdiger Bartelmus posits that an early form of the command can be determined from common wording shared by the two earliest texts. This yields: "Six day you shall (or may) do your work, but on the seventh day you shall (or must) cease." He further takes this to be an essential of Yahweh-religion, rather than something taken over from neighboring religious systems. Originally a taboo, it developed in two directions: cultic (Exod 34:21) and ethical (Exod 23:12).[85] Crüsemann also sees here a decisive step with the intent of differentiating the calendar used to honor Yahweh from that used to honor Baal.[86]

One of the most forceful expressions of the Sabbath command is found in Exod 31:12–17:

> The Lord said to Moses: You yourself are to speak to the Israelites: "You shall keep my Sabbaths, for this is a sign between me and you throughout your generations, given in order that you may know that I, the Lord, sanctify you. You shall keep the Sabbath, because it is holy for you; everyone who profanes it shall be put to death; whoever does any work on it shall be cut off from among the people. Six days shall work be done, but the seventh day is a Sabbath of solemn rest, holy to the Lord; whoever does any work on the Sabbath day shall be put to death. Therefore the Israelites shall keep the Sabbath, observing the Sabbath throughout their generations, as a perpetual covenant. It is a sign forever between me and the people of Israel that in six days the Lord made heaven and earth, and on the seventh day he rested, and was refreshed."

Yahweh refers here to "my" Sabbaths (plural), which constitute a sign (v. 13), connected to creation (v. 18). Sabbath observance is a perpetual

---

[84]   Briend, "Sabbat," 10:1138.

[85]   "Mk 2,27 und die ältesten Fassungen des Arbeitsruhegebotes im AT: Biblisch-theologische Beobachtungen zur Sabbatfrage," *BN* 41 (1988): 41–64, here 46–47.

[86]   *Tora*, 161. Crüsemann dates this development to the conflicts of the ninth century B.C.E.

covenant (v. 17), and transgression carries a death penalty (v. 14).[87] The cumulative effect underlines the solemn importance of the Sabbath. In context, these are the last instructions God gives to Moses during the forty days on the mountain, which had otherwise been solely concerned with instructions for the tabernacle (25:1–31:11); Exod 31:12-17 functions as an appendix in which a correspondence between holy space and holy time is suggested. Moses is then given two tablets, written by the finger of God (v. 18), but then the scene shifts dramatically as we learn what had been going on in the camp: the incident of the golden calf (ch. 32). This placement is mirrored in ch. 35: just as the Sabbath ends the instructions for the tabernacle, so it introduces the account of the tabernacle's construction (35:1–2).

This contextual emphasis corresponds to the content, which draws on earlier texts to weave its statement.[88] This results in a heavily-loaded statement in which the word *Sabbath* appears six times (once in plural), the death penalty is invoked (vv. 14, 15b; cf. Exod 35:2-3; Num 15:32–36), the Sabbath is declared both a sign (v. 13; cf. Ezek 20:12, 20) and a perpetual covenant (v. 16). When the term *sign* is repeated in v. 17—after the introduction of the term covenant—it is motivated by the creation rest of God. The conjunction of sign and covenant is tantalizing, since P knows of two earlier covenants, each accompanied by a sign (Gen 9:11-17; 17:7-14). It is not that the priestly author of this passage has accepted the Sinai covenant, otherwise unknown in P; rather, the Abraham covenant has received a second, additional sign in addition to circumcision, the Sabbath.[89]

There are many references to the Sabbath in the Holiness Code (Lev 17–26). The first occurs just after the first appearance of the formula

---

[87] The threat of death for failure to refrain from work on the Sabbath is repeated in Exod 35:1-3, which also contains one of the few details of the kind of labor prohibited: "You shall kindle no fire in all your dwellings on the Sabbath day" (v. 3).

[88] Walter Gross identifies both versions of the Decalogue, P, Gen 2 and 17, H, and Ezek 20 as *Formulierungsspender* ("'Rezeption' in Ex 31,12-17 und Lev 26,39–45: Sprachliche Form und theologisch-konzeptionelle Leistung," in *Rezeption und Auslegung im Alten Testament und seinen Umfeld* [FS O. H. Steck; ed. R. G. Kratz and T. Krüger; Freiburg, Schweiz, 1997], 45–64, here 49).

[89] Gross, "'Rezeption'," 55.

"You shall be holy, for I the LORD your God am holy" that gives the Code its name (Lev 19:2). It reads "You shall each revere your mother and father, and you shall keep my Sabbaths: I am the Lord your God (Lev 19:3)." There are several remarkable features. One is the brevity of the injunction. Another is the combination with the command to revere one's parents. The two commands appear in sequence in the Decalogue as well, where they are the only two that are positively formulated. Yet there are several differences: the order of the commands is inverse, as is the mention of the individual parents.[90] These details, as well as the second person plural form of the verbs and the different verb used with regard to parents, weigh against dependence on the Decalogue. At the same time the reference to "my Sabbaths," a feature of redactional references to the Sabbath in Ezekiel, points to postexilic provenance. The placement of these injunctions at the beginning of this chapter, immediately following the injunction to holiness, is surely intentional: these commands are emphasized by their placement.[91] Perhaps reverence of parents and observance of Yahweh's Sabbaths are seen as two steps that lead to the holy conduct and reverence of Yahweh detailed by the rest of the provisions in this chapter. The injunction to observe "my Sabbaths" appears again in v. 30, this time followed by a second, positively formulated command, introduced by the same verb as the instruction concerning parents in v. 3, "reverence my sanctuary." The repetition of the Sabbath in this chapter underlines its overall importance.[92]

The Sabbath next appears in the context of a festival calendar, Lev 23: "Six days shall work be done; but the seventh day is a Sabbath of complete rest, a holy convocation; you shall do no work: it is a Sabbath to the Lord throughout your settlements" (v. 3). This is widely seen as an

[90] This is "corrected" in the LXX; see also Sam. and Vulg.

[91] Note Ezek 22:7–8, in which lack of respect for parents and profanation of the Sabbath frame other transgressions such as oppression of sojourners, orphans and widows and profanation of "holy things" are chief evils responsible for the exile (vv. 15–16).

[92] The consideration of Lev 19 as a unit despite the diversity of topics it addresses is justified by the appearance of the formula "the LORD spoke to Moses, saying," in 19:1 and 20:1.

interpolation.[93] Not only is the seventh day unequivocally identified as the Sabbath, but this day—on which no work is to be done—is included among the feasts of YHWH (v. 2), whereby the term מוֹעֵד, *appointed time*, is used to designate them. As on all of the festivals, it is the occasion of a מִקְרָא־קֹדֶשׁ, a holy convocation. This is the first indication in scripture that the seventh day is to be used for worship services; not even the Sabbath command in either form of the Decalogue calls for this. In addition, it is described as שַׁבַּת שַׁבָּתוֹן, translated by the NRSV as "a Sabbath of complete rest."[94] The net effect is that of a clear enhancement of the Sabbath/seventh-day as an institution.

Leviticus 24:8 stipulates that the bread for the priests is set in the tabernacle each Sabbath. In Lev 25:1–8 the preexilic seventh-year land rest becomes "sabbathized" (cf. Exod 23:10–11; Deut 31:10–11), a use of the word that shows that the noun *Sabbath* does not mean *day* (of rest, of celebration). A day can be a Sabbath, but so can a year.[95] These mentions clearly run in the same direction as those already investigated.

This is true of the mention of the Sabbath in Lev 26, as well, but this passage is so significant that it warrants investigation. This chapter is a list of conditions of blessing ("if you walk in my statutes . . . , v. 3) and curses for disobedience ("but if you will not hearken," v. 14), whereby the section dealing with punishment (vv. 14–45) is longer than that dealing

---

[93] E.g. Stolz, *THAT* 2:868.

[94] This translation is influenced by the LXX, which renders the phrase σάββατα ἀνάπαυσις in all but one of its occurrences; it is left untranslated in Lev 23:32. Morphologically, שַׁבָּתוֹן is a superlative of the noun שַׁבָּת, so its translation depends on one's understanding of the simple noun. Haag, who understands *Sabbath* as day of celebration or holiday (*Feiertag*), suggests *absolute rest day, high holiday*, and *time to celebrate* (*ThWAT* 7:1049). Briend proposes translating *Sabbath observance*; but adds that it is in any case redundant ("Sabbat," 10:1159–60). Of the eleven uses of שַׁבָּתוֹן in the OT, six are in combination with שַׁבָּת, as here. All are in P (Stolz, *THAT* 2:864; Haag, *ThWAT* 7:1049). Four references are to the weekly Sabbath (Exod 16:23; 31:15; 35:2; Lev 23:3). Two are to Atonement (Lev 16:31; 23:32), three others to other holy days in seventh month (Lev 23:24, 39 [2x]), two to the land Sabbath (Lev 25:4–5). Festival days that do not fall in the seventh month (Days of Unleavened Bread, Feast of Weeks) are never designated with it.

[95] Robinson derives the seventh-day rest from the practice of seventh-year land rest, emancipation, and debt release, rather than the other way around (*Origin*, 109–41).

with blessings (vv. 3–13). The climax of an increasing series of punish-
ments is that the cities, sanctuaries, and the land itself will be given over
to desolation, with the people sent into exile (vv. 31–33). The concern
here is to give a theological explanation for the exile.[96] At the very
beginning of this, we read: "You shall make for yourselves no idols and
erect no carved images or pillars, and you shall not place figured stones
in your land, to worship at them; for I am the Lord your God. You shall
keep my Sabbaths and reverence my sanctuary: I am the Lord" (vv. 1–2).
Verse 2 repeats 19:30 verbatim. It is preceded by a prohibition of
idolatry, just as the double injunction to revere parents and keep the
Sabbath at the beginning of ch. 19 had been followed by one (19:4).
These verses may be secondary.[97] Whether original or added, their
placement makes it clear that these are understood to be the primary
ordinances on whose observance or transgression blessing or cursing
depends. Through the (secondary?) reference to an enforced enjoyment
of land-sabbaths in vv. 34–35 and 43, the desolation of the land is tied to
Sabbath theology.

The references in the Holiness Code to the Sabbath, now clearly
identified with the seventh day and the occasion for worship services,
appear to presume the exile. It is repeatedly positioned to assert that its
transgression was one of the primary factors leading to the exile.

The state of Pentateuch studies is in flux, yet there remains a broad
consensus that in its present form material from diverse strands of
tradition has been interwoven in postexilic times. The references to the
Sabbath appear in all strands of tradition.[98] For some, this is an argument
that the Sabbath was an ancient institution that was a feature of YHWH
religion from the start.[99] Alternatively, it can be argued that the presence
of several references to the Sabbath in the Pentateuch, while certainly

---

[96]   Martin Noth, *Das dritte Buch Mose: Leviticus* (ATD 6; Göttingen, 1962), 175.
[97]   Briend, "Sabbat," 10:1145.
[98]   There is no mention of the Sabbath or of the seventh day in Deut apart from
its version of the Decalogue. This is remarkable in light of efforts to read Deut,
especially chs. 12–26, as a successive exposition of the Ten Commandments (Georg
Braulik, *Die Deuteronomischen Gesetze und der Dekalog: Studien zum Aufbau von
Deuteronomium 12–26* [SBS 145; Stuttgart, 1991]).
[99]   E.g. Jenni, *Begründung*, 7.

reflecting the importance of the topic, at the same time raises the possibility that the multiplicity of commands might reflect a combination of various legal texts from various periods in Israel's history. Certain however is that the role that the Sabbath plays in the Pentateuch reflects its importance in postexilic Judaism, but leaves questions about its origin and historical development. There is no consensus among scholars on the question of the origin of the Sabbath in Israel, nor even on the etymology of the verb שָׁבַת and the noun שַׁבָּת.[100]

Relevant for later inner-Christian debates over the obligation of non-Jews to observe the Sabbath is P's view that the Sabbath was not instituted at creation, nor is mankind enjoined to keep the Sabbath. Instead, it is revealed by Israel in the wilderness (Exod 16).[101] It has been suggested that the cessation of God's work on the seventh day of creation, after the creation of humankind on the sixth day, implies universalistic tendencies in priestly Sabbath theology.[102] This seems unlikely in light of the lack of mention of the Sabbath between Gen 2 and Exod 16. It is mentioned neither in conjunction with Noah nor with Abraham. There is no evidence that the priestly motivation for a theologically-based Sabbath included a universalistic aspect. At best this was implicit in the connection to creation, and later generations drew this out.[103] Even in Exod 16, the Sabbath is not instituted as much as it is discovered.[104] When Israel is

---

[100] Although it is clear that in the OT, the noun Sabbath and the verb שָׁבַת, *to cease*, are closely related, attempts to explain the noun as originating from the verb, or the verb from the noun, have not prevailed (Stolz, *THAT* 2:863). That they were early related is seen by a wordplay in Hos 2:13 (ET 2:11): "I will put an end (וְהִשְׁבַּתִּי) to all her mirth, her festivals, her new moons, her Sabbaths, and all her appointed festivals." The wide variety of proposals of an alternate, extra-Israelite origin of the Sabbath is an important negative indicator for proponents of the position that the Sabbath was unique to Israel (e.g. Hasel, "Sabbath," 5:851.).

[101] The linguistic parallels between Gen 2:2–3 and Exod 16 (P^G) are explored by Klaus Grünwaldt, *Exil und Identität: Beschneidung, Passa und Sabbat in der Priesterschrift* (BBB 85; Frankfurt am Main, 1992), 159.

[102] Rordorf, *Sonntag*, 47.

[103] See below on Philo (2.2).

[104] If it is accepted that the Decalogue is a later insertion, and not part of the basic text of P (P^G), then the institution of the Sabbath occurs in Exod 31:12–14. See Jenni, *Begründung*, 20–22 (Exod 34:12–17); Steck, *Schöpfungsbericht*, 190–91, n. 808 (Exod 34:12–14, v. 17 is late).

commanded to cease work on the seventh day, this is nothing less than accordance with the behavior modeled by God himself at the foundation of the world (Exod 20:11; 31:17).[105]

2.2 THE SABBATH IN INTERTESTAMENTAL JUDAISM

As we have seen, the Sabbath grew in importance in the wake of the shattering experience of the destruction of the temple and the deportations to Babylon. Not only was the manner of its observance made more strict, but it gained in importance compared to other commandments, a process we observed in Ezek 20, where it becomes an object mentioned in parallel to law and commandments, and in Isa 56:3-5, in which a word of YHWH abolishes the non-admission of eunuchs in the community, as long as they were faithful in Sabbath observance. This tendency to assign increased importance to the Sabbath continued in the intertestamental period and beyond, albeit with variety of practice, as Doering has demonstrated.[106] This section has the task of sketching the broad development, to help situate Jesus, Paul, and others, among their compatriots.

A major impulse in this direction was the conflict in Jewish society in the time of Seleucid King Antiochus IV Epiphanes (reigned 175-164 B.C.E.) between those who were open to the Hellenistic cultural influences, even to the point of giving up specific Jewish practices such as Sabbath and circumcision, and those whose loyalty to the law and the covenant was so great that they were willing to forfeit their lives rather than compromise.[107] This had the result that the Sabbath increasingly

---

[105] In addition to serving as a model for Israelite Sabbath observance, there may also be a subtle connection to the construction of the tabernacle in P. The presence of a six days/on the seventh day pattern in Exod 24:15-18 has been noted (e.g., Westermann, *Genesis 1-11*, 236-7). Grünwaldt finds in the entire sanctuary account of P^G, Exod 25-40*, a correspondence to the blessing of the seventh day (*Exil*, 163-9).

[106] Doering, *Schabbat*. He summarizes his conclusions 566-79.

[107] Readiness to adopt Hellenistic practices is attested in 1 Macc 1:11-15; 2 Macc emphasizes the role of Jason, the high priest from 175-172 B.C.E. (4:7-17). Although the portrayal is less than flattering, and the legitimacy of his claim to office is questioned, this does not hide the fact that this movement was not the work of a radical fringe. For forcible repression of Jewish observances, including the Sabbath, see

became a sign of the identity of a Jew and his faithfulness to Yhwh.[108] The portrayal of Judith as a paragon of faithfulness to God and his law is illustrated, among other things, by her Sabbath observance (Jdt 10:2). Tendencies to liberalize the Sabbath, or even to give it up, were discredited, even though Hellenism continued to exert influence.[109]

The readiness of some to abandon the Sabbath reminds us that one must be cautious with generalizations.[110] Epigraphic evidence illustrates that the practice of ordinary people could vary from the teaching of the religious elite.[111] One example of the variety in pre-Tannaitic Judaism is the reported practice of fasting by Jews in Rome. Most Jews avoided fasting on the Sabbath, in keeping with its character as a day of joy, yet several Roman writers refer to fasting by Jews.[112] These references are routinely dismissed on the assumption that no Jews would fast on the Sabbath, but it is also possible that these writers did have accurate, if limited, knowledge.[113] A further example is that of marital relations,

1 Macc 1:37–50; 2 Macc 6:1–7 (Sabbath: v. 6). Resistance is narrated in 1 Macc 1:62–63, 2 Macc 6:9–11; 4 Macc 4:24–26.

[108] The Sabbath was not the sole marker of those who were loyal to the covenant, however. The two extensive martyrdom accounts that form the narrative and theological center of 2 Macc, that of Eleazar (6:18–31) and a mother with her seven sons (ch. 7), have as their flashpoint the refusal to eat pork (6:18; 7:1).

[109] A post-Maccabean hellenized Jew such as Philo cites the example of the Sabbath in denying that the discovery of the moral significance of the law by allegory, and its reinterpretation in terms of philosophy, exempted one from its concrete observance (*Migration* 89–93).

[110] While those who compromised are labeled *renegades* (παράνομοι, 1 Macc 1:11), it is well to remember that the people of Judea faced a new situation compared to that of the Persian era, when Ezra, acting as an imperial official, could promulgate a law that had widespread acceptance. The empire could then be seen as the instrument of God's sovereignty; now, in a different political situation, the concepts of divine sovereignty—exercised through immanent overlords—and law diverged (Reinhold Gregor Kratz, "Reich Gottes und Gesetz im Danielbuch und im werdenden Judentum," *The Book of Daniel in the Light of New Findings* [BETL 106; ed. A. S. van der Woude; Leuven 1993], 435–79).

[111] Doering, *Schabbat*, 387–97.

[112] Texts that document prohibition or discouragement of fasting include Jdt 8:6; *Jub.* 50:12; Josephus, *Life*, 279. References to fasting are, e.g., Suetonius, *Aug.* 76.2 (Stern, 2:110) and Martial, *Epigrams* 4.4.1–7 (Stern, 1:523).

[113] Robert Goldenberg, "The Jewish Sabbath in the Roman World up to the Time

which could be proscribed or enjoined, both in the name of honoring the Sabbath.[114] As these examples demonstrate, the specifics of Sabbath practice could vary, while the day itself was held in honor.

In spite of the importance of the Sabbath, the written Law and Prophets give few details of how it is to be observed, as we have seen. It is in this light that the body of halakah that grew up with regard to the Sabbath must be understood, not in the sense of burdensome casuistry. If the observance of the Sabbath is characterized by the cessation of work, for instance, one must know what work is.[115] This process of codification began before the suppression of the Sabbath under Antiochus, as is shown not only by passages investigated above such as Neh 13:15–22 and Jer 17:19–27, but also by the presence of lists of Sabbath regulations in *Jubilees* and the *Damascus Document* (*Jub.* 2:29; 50:6–13; CD 10:15–11:18). These lists share many similarities, and neither seems to reflect the controversies surrounding the Maccabean epoch, making it likely that both are based on traditional material incorporated in their present literary contexts.[116] The *Damascus Document* lists "his holy Sabbaths" among the secrets revealed by God to those faithful to the commandments (CD 3:12–16), indicating that matters of Sabbath observance were one of the issues separating those responsible for this document from other Jews; these sections of rules help identify what

of Constantine the Great," *ANRW* II.19.1, 414–47, here 435–6, 439–41. Margaret Williams has suggested that many of the Jews in Rome had been brought there as captives after Roman destruction of Jerusalem on a Sabbath, and that this may have been a commemoration ("Being a Jew in Rome: Sabbath Fasting as an Expression of Romano-Jewish Identity," paper presented at the international meeting of the SBL, Rome, July 10, 2001).

[114] For proscription, see *Jub.* 50:8; this may be the meaning of CD 11:4–5 as well. There is no text for the pre-Tannaitic period that clearly enjoins marital relations, but Doering finds it likely to have been a position held at that time by the Pharisees (*Schabbat*, 79–83, 516).

[115] The oft-cited 39 types of forbidden work (*m. Šabb.* 7:2) have their origin in this question (George Foot Moore's discussion remains valuable despite its age; *Judaism in the First Centuries of the Christian Era*, [2 vols.; Cambridge, Mass., 1927; repr. New York 1971], 2:27–28).

[116] Doering, *Schabbat*, 51–62, 119–51. In addition, there are other fragments discovered in Cave 4 at Qumran containing Sabbath halakah (Doering, *Schabbat*, 215–55).

some of the issues may have been. Of interest in light of the Sabbath controversies in the Synoptics is a rule concerning animals who fall into a pit on the Sabbath (CD 11:13b–14a; cf. Matt 12:11; Luke 14:5). Although there is much in common with other known legal rulings, there is a tendency toward greater strictness.[117] Balancing out this greater strictness, however, is the express denial of the death penalty for transgression (CD 12:3–6; cf. Exod 35:2; Num 15:32–36).[118] The strictness toward the Sabbath in the *Damascus Document* and other documents recovered from the caves at Qumran accord with the portrayal of the Essenes by Josephus (*B.J.* 2:147).

Above all, it is necessary to stress that the emphasis in Sabbath observance, as can be seen among Jews, both Orthodox and liberal, to this day, is not restriction for its own sake, but joy. As Moore points out: "Everything that might damp the joyous spirit of the day was shut out."[119] Nor are casuistry and strictness the same thing; in fact, the general tendency is that later halakah is less strict than earlier.[120]

Not only does *Jubilees* record one of the earliest non-canonical Sabbath codes available to us, it also witnesses to the Sabbath's importance in other ways. One remarkable feature this work—framed by the Sabbath (chs. 2; 50)—is its rereading of the creation account of Genesis. Although the description of the seventh day in Gen 2:1–3 is fulsome, it is nevertheless brief; in *Jub.* 2, the discussion of the Sabbath is more extensive than that of any of the six days that precede it, giving the impression that the world was made for the sake of the Sabbath (2:17–33).[121] Indeed, it turns out to have been celebrated by the angels in heaven prior to creation

[117] Discussion in Lawrence H. Schiffman, "Sabbath," *EDSS* 2:805–7, here 805–6.

[118] In contrast, *Jubilees*, not considered a work produced by the Qumran community because of the lack of topics prominent in other documents, but nonetheless well-represented in the Qumran finds (at least fourteen mss.), holds to the death penalty (2:17–32; 50:6–13). The denial of the death penalty in CD may apply however to violations of the rules in this code, not those in the Torah.

[119] *Judaism*, 2:37.

[120] E. Lohse, "σάββατον, σαββατισμός, παρασκευή," *TWNT* 7:1–35, here 9; as Doering points out, however, the trajectory of time is only one way of analysing differences (*Schabbat*, 10).

[121] Odil Hannes Steck, "Die Aufnahme von Gen 1 in Jubiläen 2 und 4. Esra 6," *JSJ* 8 (1977): 154–82

(2:30). By emphasizing the Sabbath, an institution unique to Israel, in this way, the Jews were, at the same time, celebrating their uniqueness as a people, and their special covenant relationship to the God who rested on the seventh day of creation. In the process, a solution is offered to the lack of mention of the Sabbath between creation and the wilderness in that the 22 creative works of God are correlated to the 22 generations between Adam and Jacob (2:23).

The conception of heavenly Sabbath worship found in *Jub.* 2:30 is expanded in the Sabbath Songs (4QShirShabb), a fragmentary liturgical composition in thirteen sections, one for each of the first thirteen Sabbaths of the year.[122] An angelic priesthood in heaven worships in conjunction with human Sabbath worship on earth. Thus, on the Sabbath, the normal boundary between the two spheres becomes permeable.

Meanwhile, continuing Jewish interaction with Hellenism, which had not ceased despite the Maccabean revolt, is evidenced in philosophical reflection on the nature of the Sabbath. Sirach notes that one day—he does not explicitly name the Sabbath—can only be said to be more important than another because they have been differentiated in the thought of their creator, who has exalted and sanctified certain of them (Sir 33:7–9). Aristobulus relates the Sabbath—which he conventionally referred to as *seventh day* [ἑβδόμην ἡμέραν]—to the cosmic order, to wisdom, and to the sevenfold structure of all things.[123] In addition, he understood the Sabbath principally as *rest* [ἀνάπαυσις].[124] In these aspects, he places himself within Greek philosophical discourse.[125] These topics reappear in Philo's writings; unlike Aristobulus, however, who applied the rest of the seventh day to mankind, Philo explicated the phrase "Sabbath of God" in light of rest as an appropriate attribute of the unchanging God

---

[122] *Angelic Liturgy: Songs of the Sabbath Sacrifice* (The Princeton Theological Seminary Dead Sea Scrolls Project 4B, ed. J. H. Charlesworth and Carol A. Newsom; Tübingen, 1999).

[123] Frg. 5 (= Eusebius, *Praep. ev.* 13.12.9–16; *OTP* 2:841–42).

[124] Frg. 5:9, 13b. With the translation of Hebrew scriptures to Greek, the interpretation of the verb שָׁבַת as rest, and the noun שַׁבָּת as rest day is fixed through the use of ἀνάπαυσις to explain σάββατον.

[125] Discussion of the Sabbath in Aristobulus in Doering, *Schabbat*, 306–15.

(*Cher.* 87–90), although he is at pains to point out that this is not inactivity (*Leg.* 1.5–6).[126]

The question of war and self-defense, acute for any nation, led to divided opinions of appropriate Sabbath behavior.[127] Foreign armies sought to gain military advantage by attacking on the seventh day.[128] During the tumults in the time of Antiochus IV Epiphanes mentioned above, Jews were attacked on the Sabbath, perishing because of their refusal to defend themselves (1 Macc 2:32–38). Mattathias, the father of Judas Maccabeus and his brothers, decides to fight on the Sabbath (2:39–41; cf. 9:34, 43).[129] Thus, the Sabbath could be subordinated in the name of defending practices such as the Sabbath. 2 Maccabees reflects no knowledge of this decision, and *Jubilees*, conventionally dated shortly after the Maccabean revolt, includes material that prohibits fighting on the Sabbath (50:12–13).[130] Nor does there appear to have been uniformity in practice during the revolt of 66–70 C.E.; Josephus reports discharging his soldiers on the day before the Sabbath because it was not permitted under Jewish law to bear arms on that day (*Life* 159–61; cf. 275).

Since the Sabbath had become a marker of identity, of helping define the question of who was a Jew, it is only natural that the question of the observance of the Sabbath by non-Jews should be considered.[131] The seventh day solemnly concludes creation week, and represents divine rest. Nothing is said about a command to humans, although the thought that

---

[126] Discussion of Philo in Doering, *Schabbat*, 315–77.

[127] Discussion in Doering, *Schabbat*, 537–65.

[128] William H. Shea suggests that the "seventh time" referred to by Sennacherib in his account of the capture of Lachish in 701 B.C.E. refers to the Sabbath, the day when its defenders rested ("Sennacherib's Description of Lachish and of Its Conquest," *AUSS* 26 [1988]: 171–80). Other examples are attacks on Jerusalem by Ptolemy I Soter (323–283/82 B.C.E.; Josephus, *Ant.* 12.4) and Pompey (Josephus, *J.W.* 1.146).

[129] See also Josephus, *Ant.* 12.276–8; cf. 13.12.

[130] 2 Macc knows of the strategy of attacking on the Sabbath (2 Macc 5:25; 15:1–5), but does not record any decision to fight back, let alone attack. Instead, Judas breaks off his pursuit of Nicanor because of the Sabbath (2 Macc 8:21–29). This accords with other features of 2 Macc that indicates that its stance is both more pious and somewhat distanced from the Hasmonean dynasty.

[131] On the subject of "who is a Jew?", see Shaye J. D. Cohen, *The Beginnings of Jewishness: Boundaries, Varieties, Uncertainties* (Hellenistic Culture and Society 31; Berkeley 1999).

those who live in knowledge of and close relation to this God would emulate the practice does not lie far. Nevertheless, as mentioned above (2.1.3), nothing is reported about a Sabbath observance of righteous Enoch and Noah, nor of the post-diluvian patriarchs Abraham, Isaac and Jacob (Israel).[132] This allowed for three basic views in Jewish tradition concerning the Sabbath and mankind. One is that all mankind originally knew it and was expected to keep it, but early fell away from it (Philo, *Mos.* 2.263). The second is that the righteous patriarchs knew it. When it is said, for instance, that Abraham had been tested and was known by God as one who would observe all statutes (Gen 26:5), subsequent Jewish exegesis discussed whether this implied that he knew of the Sabbath and practiced it.[133] The third is that, despite its prominence at the beginning, observance of the seventh day is not mentioned again until Exod 16, when Israel is introduced to it as the Sabbath.[134] The latter two observations lead to the assumption that the Sabbath was only ever intended for Israel, a view with implications for developments in the first century C.E., as we will see.[135]

Since one of the prime factors in the repeated recurrence of Christian Sabbatarianism—both in its seventh-day and Lord's Day forms—is the presence of the Sabbath command in the Decalogue, it is valuable to briefly note how the Decalogue was viewed in Judaism in the period under investigation. The idea that the Decalogue expresses the basic demands of the בְּרִית is found in Philo, *Decal.* 154. Phylacteries containing the Decalogue were among the discoveries at Qumran; the Nash Papyrus suggests that this was a practice in Egypt, as well.[136] It was recited

---

[132] This is supported by the lack of any reference to Sabbath observance among the commands given to Noah as the earth is repopulated after the flood (Gen 9).

[133] In *Jub.* 2:19–24, there is a clear statement that he did keep the Sabbath.

[134] The connection between the Sabbath and the election of Israel is made for instance by Sirach in the passage already cited (Sir 33:7–9).

[135] In *Jub.* 2:17–33 the Sabbath is depicted as an especially holy day, only to be observed by Israelites, not made for any other people (v. 30). Sabbath is exclusively for Israel: "He allowed no people or peoples to keep the Sabbath on this day, except Israel only; to it alone he granted to eat and to drink and keep the Sabbath on it" (*Jub.* 2:31).

[136] Qumran texts in *Les Petites Grottes de Qumran: Exploration da la falaise, les grottes 2Q, 3Q, 5Q, 6Q, 7Q à 10Q; le rouleau de cuivre* (DJD 3; ed. M. Baillet, J. T.

daily in the temple (*m. Tamid* 5:1), but was removed from use to disprove the contention of sectarians that only the Ten Commandments were given at Sinai (*y. Ber.* 1:3c [German trans.: Horowitz, 30]).[137]

2.3 THE JEWS IN THE ROMAN WORLD

2.3.1 Attitudes toward Jews and Judaism

Despite conflicting assessments among scholars of the prevailing attitude toward Jews and Judaism in the ancient world, it appears that Antijudaism was a feature of the pre-Christian ancient world, with roots in Hellenistic Egypt.[138] Tensions between Jews and their neighbors were not strictly political, economic and social matters, comparable to the strains between any other competing ethnic groups at the time. The underlying motif in anti-Jewish polemic in general is that it was foreign; the Jews are cast as unsocial, even misanthropic. Yet the very characteristics that made Jews and Judaism objects of scorn in some circles could make them objects of fascination and admiration in others, bringing them both converts and sympathizers.

This variety of response is true in particular of the Jewish practice most often noted, the Sabbath. Polemic concerning it centers on two major objections specifically directed toward the practice of the Sabbath.[139] First,

---

Milik, and R. de Vaux; Oxford 1962), 1:149–57 (for the text found in cave 8) and *Qumran Cave 1* (DJD 1; ed. D. Barthélemy and J. T. Milik; Oxford 1955), 72–76 (for the text from cave 1); brief discussion in Lawrence H. Schiffman, "Phylacteries and Mezuzot," *EDSS* 2:675–7. On the Nash Papyrus: Ernst Würthwein, *Der Text des Alten Testaments* (5th ed.; Stuttgart, 1988), 41–42 (description), 146–7 (photograph and transcription).

[137] Jonathan Magonet, "Dekalog 2: Judentum," *TRE* 8:413–5, here 413.

[138] John G. Gager concludes that Antijudaism in antiquity was rare (*The Origins of Antijudaism: Attitudes toward Judaism in Pagan and Christian Antiquity* [New York, 1983]). Louis H. Feldman allows that it existed, especially among the masses, but was accompanied by a general benevolent policy by the government and grudging admiration among intellectuals (*Jew and Gentile in the Ancient World: Attitudes and Interactions from Alexander to Justinian* [Princeton, 1993]). Peter Schäfer remains convinced that Antijudaism was a feature of the pre-Christian ancient world, with roots in Hellenistic Egypt (*Judeophobia: Attitudes toward the Jews in the Ancient World* [Cambridge, Mass., 1997]).

[139] Discussion, along with additional examples beside those quoted here, in

many non-Jews believed that the Jews kept the Sabbath out of indolence. Juvenal mocks the one "who has had a father who reveres the Sabbath." After listing various failings, such as flouting the Roman laws and the refusal to help the uncircumcised, he repeats: "For all which the father was to blame, who gave up every seventh day to idleness, keeping it apart from all the concerns of life."[140] Tacitus prefaces his account of the fall of Jerusalem with an account of the history and customs of the Jews. After describing their expulsion from Egypt, he reports: "They say that they first chose to rest on the seventh day because that day ended their toils; but after a time they were led by the charms of indolence to give over the seventh year as well to inactivity."[141] Secondly, refusal of self-defense viewed as stupid.[142]

The ruling classes of Rome were unhappy over the spread of Jewish practices.[143] In addition to the distaste they felt as members of the intellectual elite, this view also had a social and economic component: their comfortable style of living was sustained by the unceasing labor of slaves and other servants.[144]

Nevertheless, the Jews enjoyed a degree of legal protection. While there apparently was no official charter making Judaism a *religio licita*, there was a series of legal precedents to which Jews could refer.[145] This is both an extension of the policy of earlier Hellenistic powers—the Seleucids and the Ptolemies—and a reflection of the alliance Rome had with Judea since the time of the Maccabees.[146] This meant that the Jewish

Goldenberg, "Sabbath," *ANRW* 19.1:430–42, and Doering, *Schabbat*, 285–9.

[140] *Sat.* 14.96–106 (Barrett, 176).

[141] *Hist.* 5.4 (Barrett, 153).

[142] Goldenberg, "Sabbath," *ANRW* 19.1:430–31.

[143] Goldenberg, "Sabbath," *ANRW* 19.1:436. In the assessment of John C. Meagher, "the roster of ancient writers who expressed anti-Jewish feelings reads like a syllabus for a second-semester course in classics, ("As the Twig Was Bent: Antisemitism in Greco-Roman and Earliest Christian Times," in *Antisemitism and the Foundations of Christianity* [ed. A. T. Davies; New York, 1979], 1–26, here 6).

[144] S. Helfgott, cited in Doering, *Schabbat*, 287.

[145] See Alfredo Mordechai Rabello, *The Jews in the Roman Empire: Legal Problems from Herod to Justinian* (Varorium Collected Studies 645; Aldersgate, 2000).

[146] Goldenberg, "Sabbath," *ANRW* 19.1:418–19.

Sabbath was protected to some extent by Roman law.[147] This was sensible from considerations of *Realpolitik*.[148] There would then have been no reason for Christians prior to the destruction of the temple to distance themselves from Sabbath observance for political reasons; the situation changed thereafter.

2.3.2 Proselytes and Godfearers in the Synagogue

While (part of) the Jewish elite insisted Sabbath was not for non-Jews, Roman elite deplored Gentiles attracted to it. Apparently on the popular level this double disapproval was widely disregarded.[149] Philo reports: "While every country and nation and state show aversion to foreign institutions," this is not so with the Sabbath. "Who has not shown this high respect for the sacred seventh day by giving rest and relaxation from labor to himself and his neighbors, free-man and slave alike, and beyond these to his beasts" (*Moses* 2.20). Similarly, Josephus boasted: "The masses have long since shown a keen desire to adopt our religious observances; and there is not one city, Greek or barbarian, nor a single nation, to which our custom of abstaining from work on the seventh day has not spread" (*Ag. Ap.* 2.282).[150] Apparently, then, there were many Gentiles in the time of the Second Temple who became proselytes. By circumcision, followed by ritual immersion (baptism), they signalized their conversion and their acceptance of the Torah; they were no longer Gentiles. The exact figures are not available, but apparently this was a considerable number.

There was an even larger number of sympathizers, termed variously φοβούμενοι, σεβόμενοι, or θεοσεβεῖς, generally referred to in English as Godfearers.[151] Their adherence to the synagogue was voluntary—it might

---

[147] Evidence for this is found in several passages in Josephus, *Ant.*: 14.241–2, 245–6, 258, 263–4; 16.163, 168. These are quoted and discussed by Goldenberg, *ANRW* 19.1:415-18 (he cites according to the numeration in the Whiston translation).

[148] "It would have been foolish to embitter such a group over an issue like Sabbath-observance which could not have mattered terribly to the Romans themselves. A loyal Jewish diaspora, on the other hand, would have been a powerful unifying force, and was clearly worth the effort" (Goldenberg, "Sabbath," *ANRW* 19.1:420).

[149] See Cohen, *Beginnings*, 140–74.

[150] Josephus also mentions fasting, lighting of lamps, and food laws.

[151] State of current study on the subject: Bernd Wander, *Gottesfürchtige und*

even be limited to a financial gift—, as was their observance or non-observance of Jewish practices, including Sabbath observance. Moreover, their continued observance of ancestral practices was at their discretion.[152]

Aside from Matt 23:23, there is no evidence of an active Jewish mission to the nations. There appears to have been no concerted effort to encourage them to convert, despite the near consensus view fifty years ago that there was.[153] Nor is there any evidence of pressure exercised on the Godfearers to accept circumcision and become proselytes.[154]

Just as there was no uniform set of practices that Godfearers were expected to observe, so there was no uniform teaching in Second Temple Judaism about what these sympathizers could hope for in the world to come, the eschatological kingdom, although there seems to have been a rough consensus that they would not lose "their part," whatever that "part" might be.

2.3.3 The Nations in the World to Come

The observation that the Sabbath was given to Israel, not to the rest of mankind, led in turn to divergent views about the necessity of non-Israelite observance of the Sabbath for a part in the world to come. This view of Sabbath for Israel only was the predominant view in Judaism—concomitant with the Sabbath as an "identity marker"—related to debates over the universality of salvation. Could any Gentiles have a part in the world to come, and, if so, on what basis? As we saw, some texts in the prophets indicate the expectation that the Gentiles stream to

---

Sympathisanten: Studien zum heidnischen Umfeld von Diasporasynagogen (WUNT 104; Tübingen, 1999).

[152] Paula Fredriksen, "Judaism, the Circumcision of the Gentiles, and Apocalyptic Hope: Another Look at Galatians 1 and 2," JTS 42 (1991): 532–64, here 548.

[153] E.g., Joachim Jeremias, Jesu Verheissung für die Völker (Franz Delitzsch-Vorlesungen 1953; Stuttgart, 1956), 9–15.

[154] Martin Goodman has been prominent among those who have presented the revisionist view (see Mission and Conversion: Proselytizing in the Religious History of the Roman Empire [Oxford, 1994]). His views have been challenged in turn by James Carleton Paget, "Jewish Proselytism at the Time of Christian Origins: Chimera or Reality?" JSNT 62 (1996): 65–103. Much of the material that Carleton Paget cites as evidence of a missionary consciousness in Second Temple Judaism is more properly viewed as apologetic.

Jerusalem as a feature of the end-time (Isa 2:2–3 par. Mic 4:1–4; Zech 14:16–21).[155] Some of them tied it explicitly to various aspects of Torah observance, among them, the Sabbath (Isa 56:1–8; 66:23). Others spoke more generally of worshiping the God of Israel (e.g., Isa 25:6–8; Mal 1:11). This left open the possibility that God's will for Gentiles might be other than for Israel.[156] These OT texts are supplemented by texts from the intertestamental period that testify to the existence of an expectation that the dawning of the eschatological kingdom would be accompanied by the gathering of the nations to worship Yahweh, the God of Israel.[157]

Would they observe the Torah? Paula Fredriksen, arguing on the basis of a lack of texts anticipating their circumcision, distinguishes between *inclusion* and *conversion*. "Gentiles are saved as Gentiles; they do not, eschatologically, become Jews."[158] She interprets one passage that indicates they will join themselves to Israel, Isa 56:3–7, as referring to the future salvation of those who convert now.[159] This may place too much weight on verbal tenses. It must be granted that the number of prophetic passages that depict the worship of Yahweh by the nations is greater than those that refer to their obedience.[160] Nevertheless, while the distinction between inclusion and conversion is useful, especially in light of Paul's apparent vision of a dual salvation community consisting of Israel and the nations (Rom 11:11–12), it may obscure the fact that Israel could not

---

[155] On the other hand, when Gog and Magog march toward Jerusalem (Ezek 38–39), this is not a religious pilgrimage but a menace that is only averted by divine intervention. Cf. Joel 3:9–11; Zeph 3:8; *2 Bar.* 68:5–7; *4 Ezra* 13:5–11, 33, 49 (for additional texts that portray a Gentile invasion in which the nations are destroyed); Isa 49:23; 54:3; Mic 5:7–8; 7:16–17; *1 En.* 91:9 (texts that depict the total destruction of the Gentiles, or their subjection to Israel).

[156] Fredriksen, "Judaism," 544–8.

[157] *Ps. Sol.* 17 is interesting for its juxtaposition of two contrasting motifs: the purification of the land through the expulsion of foreigners (v. 28) and the pilgrimage of the nations to Jerusalem (vv. 30–32, 34). They come to return Jews they had taken into captivity, but they stay to worship and serve the God of Israel. In *2 Bar.* 72:2–6, God will spare those nations especially that have not exploited Israel or trampled the people underfoot.

[158] "Judaism," 546–8. Quotation from 547.

[159] "Judaism," 545.

[160] Walter Brueggemann, *Theology of the Old Testament: Testimony, Dispute, Advocacy* (Minneapolis 1997), 499–501.

imagine those saved from the nations *not* observing pilgrimage feasts such as Sukkot (Zech 14:16–21). This observance is not at their discretion, as the participation of Godfearers in the synagogue may have been. Failure to do so is met with sanctions. Although Fredriksen mentions the twice-told expectation that the nations will stream to Jerusalem and worship the God of Jacob together with Israel (Isa 2:2–4 par. Mic 4:1–2), she does not discuss the weight of the phrases "he will teach us of his ways, and we will walk in his paths," (cf. Exod 18:20), nor the implication of the fact that the Torah, the word of Yahweh, would go forth from Jerusalem/Zion.

2.4 RESULTS

The overall picture reflected in the canon is that from beginning to end the Sabbath is an important element in Israel's covenant with its God. In fact, it is so central that virtually all major themes of the Hebrew Scriptures—creation, exodus, covenant—are associated with it. This is an important finding, and directly relevant for the discussion of the fate of the Sabbath in the first hundred years of Christian experience, the topic of this investigation. The seventh day solemnly concludes creation week, and represents divine rest. Nothing is said about a command to humans, although the thought that those who live in knowledge of and close relation to this God would emulate the practice does not lie far. Still, no humans—not Noah, not Abraham—are recorded as observing it until it is discovered by Israel in the wilderness.

There are no preexilic passages that identify the Sabbath and the seventh-day; instead, they speak of one or the other. It is possible that they were originally discrete institutions, joined together no earlier than the exile. The origins of both the practice of resting every seventh-day and the application of the name "Sabbath" to the day on which this rest occurs lie in obscurity. The seven-day cycle may have originated in the length of a lunar phase, but in the Biblical texts, it runs independently of this. The etymological proximity to the Akkadian *šapattu(m)* and the presence of seven-day patterns in other ancient Near Eastern cultures suggest that there is a relation, even if the exact nature of that relationship is unclear. In particular, speculations that it may once have been a monthly obser-vance connected with the full moon, as an antipode to the beginning of each month, the new moon, find neither confirmation nor refutation. The practice of ceasing work on the seventh day appears to have been known in both the northern and southern kingdoms.[161] It appears to denote a recognition of divine ownership. The special meaning attached to it in the Hebrew scriptures cannot be derived however from ancient Near Eastern parallels. At the latest, in the time of the Babylonian exile the Sabbath and the seventh day are identified. It is an institution unique to Israel, as is the strict seven-day rhythm in which it is anchored. There was no memory of the origin of the seven-day week nor of the practice of observing the seventh day and calling it Sabbath other than that it was a divine revelation of Israel's God, understood as the creator of the universe, and that this practice was the sign of a unique relationship between Israel and their God, an identity marker.

For the time between the close of the OT and the Hadrianic repressions—the period of time in which the Jesus movement arose—it is clear that Sabbath observance was a prominent feature of Judaism, both as viewed from within and without. The Sabbath was an identity marker for Jews in the ancient world. It was the most frequently remarked feature of Jewish faith and practice by authors from the surrounding Hellenistic-Roman society, and it was characterized internally as a sign and a covenant. In addressing the Sabbath, then, we are addressing the question of religious identity and the role that normative worship practice plays in defining a group, giving it identity and cohesion at the same time that it enables differentiation from other groups.

The Sabbath became an identity marker of the people of Israel in the time of its search for regrouping after the Babylonian captivity, and only increased in importance after the failed uprisings against Roman domination deprived them, seemingly forever, of other possible sources of identity such as a homeland, a king, or a temple to serve as center of corporate worship. The nature of the identity that lies in this marker is that the people thus identified are servants of God, not slaves of other

---

[161] In addition to the evidence of the Biblical texts, a reference to "his seventh time" in Sennacherib's description of his capture of Lachish, 701 B.C.E. indicates that the Israelite practice of refraining from work on the seventh day was known to non-Israelites, who used it to their advantage (Hasel, "Sabbath," 5:853).

humans, nor of their own occupations. It is an identity marker that could be interpreted by Philo, explaining the nature of this way of life as much to himself as to other Jews confronted with the overwhelming pressure of a global culture, Hellenism, as to the Gentile readers who are his putative addressees, in such a way as to show the Jews as an entire people given to the ideals of repose and reflection, making them, in effect, an entire nation of philosophers, of friends of wisdom. Identity markers do more than make a group recognizable both to itself and to outsiders; they express the nature of that group and its members.

Yet this institution, which reveals so much about the limits of unexamined, unbounded virtues, one that expresses an existence before God characterized by freedom, social justice, celebration and praise, and reveals the people who practice it as friends of wisdom, did not become constitutive of the newly-forming Christian identity, at least not for the wide parts of it under the influence of the Pauline mission. The overview of the Sabbath in the OT and in intertestamental Judaism has shown how momentous this step would have been, somewhat surprising in light of the fierce loyalty to the Sabbath in the time of the Maccabees. Speaking for its retention by the new Christian movement were, in essence, the reasons that spoke in general for continuing to be what it began as, namely, a sect within Judaism. The Sabbath was recognized throughout the known world as an ancient and venerable institution. The right to observe it fell under the general privileges protected by Roman law. Yet believers in Christ largely abandoned Sabbath observance. It is time to turn to an examination of the NT scriptures, as well as other Christian literature of the time, to see what light can be shed on how this came to be.

3

The Scrupulous Observance of Days
(Galatians 4:8–11)

As a dominant voice in the writings that have been received by the church as canonical, Paul must be included in any investigation of early Christian observance or non-observance of the Sabbath. Instead of synthetically treating Paul's possible understanding of the question on the basis of all seven of his undisputed letters, I propose to work from the exegesis of a small section of one letter, Galatians. While Galatians cannot be considered a fully formed and balanced exposition of the gospel according to Paul—the closest we have to that is Romans—the occasion of the former letter is Paul's perception that his gospel is endangered (Gal 1:6–9). His passionate defense of that gospel is thus a good indicator of what he sees as the heart of the gospel, which bears closely on his posture toward the Sabbath.

3.1 PAUL'S REFERENCE TO DAYS

Paul's letter to the congregations in Galatia is accepted by all as genuine, and is held to be unified and in principle free of glosses. There are no text critical problems that affect the outcome of this investigation. Here is the passage:

> Formerly, when you did not know God, you were enslaved to beings that by nature are not gods. Now, however, that you have come to know God, or rather to be known by God, how can you turn back again to the weak and beggarly elements?[1] How can you want to be enslaved to them again? You are observing

---

[1]   I have altered the NRSV here, in that I have replaced "elemental spirits" with the neutral "elements." See below, 3.2.2.

special days, and months, and seasons, and years. I am afraid that my work for you may have been wasted.

The relevance of the passage for this investigation is Paul's reference to the scrupulous observance of days, months, seasons, years (v. 10).[2] This is often explicated as Paul's condemnation of Sabbath observance on the part of his audience, usually with reference to the three-part list of Col 2:16, ἑορτῆς ἢ νεομηνίας ἢ σαββάτων.[3] This despite a number of differences between the two sets of terms. In Colossians, the list runs from the greater unit of time to the lesser; in Galatians, it runs in the other direction. Further, it uses terms that are specifically associated with the Jewish calendar, while the list in Galatians uses general terms. Finally, the authorship of Colossians is disputed; it is usually viewed as a product of the Pauline school.[4] Therefore, while it may be viewed as part of the *Wirkungsgeschichte* of Galatians, one must be cautious in using it to explicate Galatians.[5]

Whereas the historic mainstream view of Galatians is that it is Paul's proclamation of Christian freedom on the basis of a law-free gospel, Sabbatarians, who, unlike some Christian Jews of the second century,

---

[2] For this translation of παρατηρέω, see BAGD, s.v., def. 3; cf. Bauer-Aland, which offers a series of terms (*beobachten, beachten, befolgen*). See also J. Louis Martyn, *Galatians: A New Translation with Introduction and Commentary* (AB 33A; New York, 1997), 412.

[3] E.g. Jürgen Becker, in Becker und Ulrich Luz, *Die Briefe an die Galater, Epheser und Kolosser* (NTD 8/1; Göttingen, 1998), 66; François Vouga, *An die Galater* (HNT 10; Tübingen, 1998), 105; Ronald Y. K. Fung, *The Epistle to the Galatians* (NICNT; Grand Rapids, Mich., 1988), 193. Cf. various proposals that sectarian or gnostic superstitions may be meant (e.g. Heinrich Schlier, *Der Brief an die Galater* (13th ed.; KEK 7; Göttingen 1965), 205–7; Walter Schmithals, "Die Häretiker in Galatien," in *Paulus und die Gnostiker* [TF 35; Hamburg-Bergstedt 1965], 9–46; Harald Riesenfeld, "τηρέω κτλ.," *TWNT* 8:139–51, here 148). Martyn on the other hand notes and comments on the generic language (*Galatians*, 414–8).

[4] Discussion in Raymond E. Brown, *An Introduction to the New Testament* (ABRL; New York, 1997), 610–15.

[5] Philipp Vielhauer, "Gesetzesdienst und Stoicheiadienst im Galaterbrief," in *Rechtfertigung* (FS E. Käsemann; ed. J. Friedrich, W. Pöhlmann, and P. Stuhlmacher; Tübingen, 1976), 543–55, here 550; and Hans-Joachim Eckstein, *Verheissung und Gesetz: Eine exegetische Untersuchung zu Galater 2,15–4,7* (WUNT 86; Tübingen, 1996), 229, n. 279.

accept the canonical authority of this letter, take a different view. They commonly argue, for instance, that the party of the circumcision (cf. 2:12) was so named because the only theological difference Paul had with them was their insistence that Gentile converts be circumcised to enjoy the full benefits of Christianity (cf. 5:2–12; Acts 15:1).[6] Paul shared with them an assumption that Christians, Gentile as well as Jewish, would continue to live according to the Ten Commandments.[7] In addition, it is sometimes maintained that the works of the law (Gal 2:16) refer to ceremonial rituals.[8]

---

[6] A view expressed by Tertullian: "Cum uero nec Titum dicit circumcisum, iam incipit ostendere solam circumcisionis quaestionem ex defensione adhuc legis concussam ab eis, quos propterea falsos et superinducticios fratres appallat" (*Marc.* 5.3,2 [CCSL 1:668]; "But when he says that not even Titus was circumcised, he now begins to make it plain that it was solely the question of circumcision which had suffered disturbance, because of their continued maintenance of the law, from those whom for that reason he calls false brethren unawares brought in" [trans. E. Evans 2:519]). Nevertheless, Tertullian believed at the same time that the Jewish Sabbath and holy days are meant by Gal 4:10, and therefore no longer in effect (5.4).

[7] The portrayal of Paul in the Acts of the Apostles is used to demonstrate a law- and Sabbath-observant apostle (see below, 4.2.2).

[8] E.g. Herbert W. Armstrong, *What Will You Be Doing in the Next Life?* Pasadena, 1967, 7. The view that the ritual, but not the moral law of the OT had been done away is documented soon after Paul (Rudolf Bultmann, *Theologie des Neuen Testaments* [9th ed.; UTB 630; Tübingen, 1984], 116–8). This distinction figures in Tertullian's exegesis of Galatians. He argues that the time of the gospel has replaced the time of the law, yet when he writes in connection with the admonition to remember the poor (Gal 2:10), "dum ostenditur quid ex lege custodiri conuenerit (*Marc.*, 5.3,7 [CCSL 1:669]; "Thus it is beyond doubt that it was a question solely of the law, until decision was reached as to how much of the law it was convenient should be retained" [trans. E. Evans 2:521–3]), it seems as if he is distinguishing between *moral* and *ceremonial* law. This view has recently gained adherents since the discovery and publication of 4QMMT, which contains the phrase מעשי התורה (C27, in *Qumran Cave 4: 5. Miqsat Ma'ase Ha-Torah* [DJD 10; ed. E. Qimron and J. Strugnell; Oxford; 1994]; cf. 1QS 6:18; see also John Kampen, "4QMMT and New Testament Studies," in *Reading 4QMMT: New Perspectives on Qumran Law and History* [SBLSymB 2, ed. J. Kampen and M. J. Bernstein, Atlanta, 1996], 129–44, esp. 138–43). Two scholars who have found 4QMMT significant for the understanding of Galatians are Martin Abegg ("Paul, 'Works of the Law' and MMT," *BAR* 20, no. 6 [November/December 1994]: 52–55, 81) and James D. G. Dunn ("4QMMT and Galatians," *NTS* 43 [1997]: 147–53). Both contend that Paul uses the phrase ἔργα νόμου because he reacts in Galatians to the kind of

Most importantly, a common argument is that the days and other
time periods that the Galatians were now observing (4:10) represented
a return (4:9, ἐπιστρέφετε πάλιν) to the pattern of worship they had
practiced as Gentiles before becoming Christians.[9] Indeed, the Sabbath
is not mentioned in Galatians, nor in any of the seven letters commonly
accepted as genuinely Pauline.[10] Further, while there is a necessary
connection between circumcision and ritual observance, there is no
necessary connection between circumcision and Sabbath observance.[11]
There were many non-circumcised visitors of the synagogue in the first
century, often referred to as Godfearers (see 2.3.2, above). Presumably,
at least some of them observed the Sabbath as a day of rest as well.

These observations and objections must be addressed in the course of
this chapter, but will not determine the flow of the argument. The
investigation will proceed in three steps: (1) explanation of the passage,
which will include discussions of his audience, the occasion for writing,
the reference to the elements of the world, and the reference to time
markers (3.2). (2) An investigation of the question of why Paul introduces
the reference to time markers and what he expects this reference to
perform in his overall argument; these questions will be addressed as part
of the more general question of how this section fits into Paul's overall
argument (3.3). (3) Finally, I will ask what light the answers to these two

---

theology contained in 4QMMT, but both refrain from considering it a technical term
that refers exclusively either to the matters discussed in 4QMMT (purity, temple,
sacrifice, priesthood) or in Galatians (circumcision, table fellowship, calendrical concerns),
with Dunn explicitly denying that this is what he meant (*The Theology of Paul the
Apostle* [Grand Rapids, Mich., 1998], 358, n. 97). The significance of the occurrence of
this phrase in connection with this investigation is that it documents the use of the phrase
by Jews to describe behavior that Jews ought to engage in. The contrary view, that
"works of law" is a Pauline coinage and designates the adoption of selected Jewish
practices by the Gentiles to ensure their salvation, must be abandoned.

[9]   Samuele Bacchiocchi, *From Sabbath to Sunday: A Historical Investigation of the
Rise of Sunday Observance in Early Christianity* (Rome, 1977), 366–7. Note however
that the *turning back* was to the elements of the world. The observance of days was
simply the evidence for this. See below, 3.2.3.

[10]   The one time the word appears, in 1 Cor 16:2, it is part of the construction κατὰ
μίαν σαββάτου and means *on the first day of the week*.

[11]   For example, a non-Israelite could partake of the Passover only after being
circumcised, Exod 12:43–44, 48.

lines of inquiry can shed on the program of the competing mission in Galatia, as well as the question of Sabbath observance or non-observance among early Christians (3.4 and 3.5).[12]

3.2 EXAMINATION OF GALATIANS 4:8–11

3.2.1 Analysis of the Unit as a Whole

The unit under examination shows a high degree of linguistic coherence. The author speaks directly to his readers, no other humans are mentioned. The subject of the first four conjugated verbs is his readership, the (unnamed) Galatians. The verbs all describe the manner of their religious behavior; the objects of these verbs (the not-gods, v. 8, the weak and beggarly elements, v. 9, the days and other time units, v. 10) describe the content of their religious behavior. If Paul describes the behavior of his readers to those readers, who after all should know what they were doing, it is to lead them to see that behavior as Paul does; his strategy is interpretive. This is reflected by his choice of verbs as well. The verb δουλέω, used twice (v. 8, 9) refers back to the discussion that immediately preceded (vv. 1–6). By doing so, however, Paul introduces a note of ambivalence in what otherwise would have been understood as a normal verb for the service of gods. In context, it receives an interpretive note. The following verb ἐπιστρέφω (v. 9) is used ironically; it would normally be understood positively, especially when used to describe a religious conversion. In effect, Paul describes a conversion in reverse.[13] Finally, the verb παρατηρέω, v. 10, could also be understood as a positive description of religious behavior. In context, though, it is not meant positively, and once again, the ambivalence of religious behavior is underlined. One is tempted indeed to read this description in light of the dichotomy beloved by dialectic theologians between religion and Christianity.

---

[12] J. Louis Martyn points out that the term *opponents* may be reductionistic, since they may have conducted their own law-observant mission to the Gentiles (*Theological Issues in the Letters of Paul* [SNTW; Edinburgh, 1997], 8–24). For this reason, he labels them neutrally, *the teachers*; this term fails to account for the polemical nature of Paul's reaction, so I will use the term *competitors* or *competing mission*.

[13] Cf. Paul's use of μετατίθεμι in 1:6.

Paul not only seeks to show the Galatians how to interpret their religious behavior; he also interprets his work among them: it was hard labor, travail, reflected by the use of the verb κοπιάω, followed by his present emotional state of fear for them, v. 11.

The unit is structured according to a then/now temporal scheme similar to that according to which the entire letter is structured (see below, 3.3.2), but with a difference. In contrast to the rest of the letter, in which the turning point is the coming of Christ, the "now" is interpreted as a return to their "then" state. These two levels of time are correlated to participial phrases concerned with the state of not knowing and being known by God. The development thus described evinces a reaction from Paul, v. 11, again structured in two levels of time, although he places the "now" first and expresses the "then" through a verb in the perfect aspect, rather than, as with the Galatians, in aorist. Both aspects make a statement about the past, but the change in aspect suggests a nuance in Paul's argument. In the case of the Galatians, their worship of not-gods presumably lasted for a long time—it was characteristic of their earlier life—and could therefore have been expressed with an imperfect. Through the use of an aorist, ἐδουλεύσατε, however, Paul emphasizes the break with the past that occurred at the point when they ceased such worship. When Paul then uses the perfect aspect to describe his hard labor in establishing the congregations in Galatia, κεκοπίακα, it conveys the idea that a foundation had been laid once and for all, from which there is no turning back.

3.2.2 Analysis of Paul's Audience

Their Past as Worshipers of Not-Gods (Verse 7): In v. 7, Paul had described the status of his readers as no longer slave (οὐκέτι εἶ δοῦλος) but that of son and heir of God. Paul now contrasts this in v. 8 antithetically (ἀλλά) with their situation before their calling: they did not know God, they were slaves of those who were "by nature" not-gods (cf. vv. 1–3). Paul does not deny the existence of the powers worshiped by the Gentiles, he denies their divinity. In a participial expression, this is described as a time of "not knowing God," followed by, in aorist, an action of service to those who by nature are no gods (compare the passive δεδουλωμένοι to the elements of the world in v. 3).

These expressions, in the writings of a first-century Jew, characterize the audience as non-Jews, since they echo a common topos of Jewish criticism of paganism.[14] The Jews in the first century C.E. lived in a world whose religious practices were dominated by polytheism. Two factors dominated their perception of the religious life around them: the multitude of beings worshiped as gods, and their plastic representation. This perception was especially sharpened by the first two commands of the Decalogue:

> I am the LORD your God, who brought you out of the land of Egypt, out of the house of slavery; you shall have no other gods before me.

> You shall not make for yourself an idol, whether in the form of anything that is in heaven above, or that is on the earth beneath, or that is in the water under the earth. You shall not bow down to them or worship them; for I the LORD your God am a jealous God, punishing children for the iniquity of parents, to the third and the fourth generation of those who reject me, but showing steadfast love to the thousandth generation of those who love me and keep my commandments (Exod 20:2–6, cf. Deut 5:6–8).

Although scholars have challenged the earlier consensus that these two prohibitions had always been features of the Yahweh cult,[15] at least the centuries immediately preceding the Christian era were marked by the worship of one God. Any other conceivable spiritual beings or forces were either subordinated as angels or demons, or were viewed as hypostases of divine qualities, such as God's spirit or wisdom.[16]

---

[14] On Jewish criticism of the polytheism of the nations around them, Wilhelm Bousset, *Die Religion des Judentums im späthellenistischen Zeitalter* (4th ed.; HNT 21; Tübingen, 1966), 304–07 (see esp. 306: paganism as service and devotion of the heavenly bodies).

[15] Fritz Stolz speaks of a paradigm shift (*Einführung in den biblischen Monotheismus* [Darmstadt, 1996], 1). Cf. Diana Edelman, ed., *The Triumph of Elohim: From Yahwisms to Judaisms* (CBET 13; Grand Rapids, Mich.,) 1995.

[16] Cf. 1 Cor 8:4–6. The origin of Jewish angelology are uncertain and contested. Older treatments: Bousset, *Religion*, 320–31, esp. 320: "Als ein Residuum fremder polytheistischer und animistischer Religion ist der Glaube an dienstbare Untergebene Gottes." and Bill 3:47–60. More recently, Klaus Koch, "Monotheismus und Angelologie," in *Ein Gott allein? JHWH Verehrung und biblischer Monotheismus im Kontext der israelitischen und altorientalischen Religionsgeschichte* (OBO 139; ed. W. Dietrich and M. A. Klopfenstein; Fribourg, 1994), 565–81.

Of the two features of polytheism, it was the practice of idolatry that was most often attacked, with emphasis on the foolishness of using elements of the creation as objects of worship (Isa 44:9–20; Jer 10:1–18). These attacks are marked by polemic naivete used as a rhetorical device, treating the images as if they were, in the eyes of the worshipers, the god itself. In a few texts, though, there appears to be a reference to the spirits thereby worshiped.[17]

The attack on polytheism is attested in intertestamental Judaism,[18] and this was carried over into Christianity. As a strict Diaspora Pharisee, Paul's pre-Christian religious experience was that of the synagogue. His calling to become a follower of Jesus Christ meant for him a radical break with his past (Phil 3:7–8).[19] Yet in this aspect, he carried over the attitude implicit in the first commandment.[20] On this point, at least, he is on common ground with his competitors.

Paul summarizes the coming to faith of his converts as a turning to God from idols, to serve the living and true God (1 Thess 1:9). Many of his comments continue the Jewish polemic against idols: they are dumb (1 Cor 12:2) and the worship of them is the root of all moral failings of the Gentile world (Rom 1:21–32). Yet Paul was a product of his world, a world from which animism had not completely disappeared;[21] although the idol is nothing (1 Cor 8:4), Paul never says that the beings they

---

[17] See the use of the loanword שֵׁדִים in Deut 32:17 and Psa 106:37.

[18] _Jos. Asen._ 2:3; 10:12; 21:13; _Jub._ 12:1–8, 12–14; 20:7–8; 22:16–18, 22; _1 En._ 99:7; _2 Bar._ 41:4; _Apoc. Ab._ 1–8.

[19] The view that Paul's experience on the road to Damascus should be described as a call rather than as a conversion achieved a broad consensus in the twentieth century, both among exponents of the mainstream view (e.g., Jürgen Becker, _Paulus der Apostel der Völker_ [3rd ed.; UTB 2014; Tübingen, 1998], 83) and those of the New Perspective (e.g., Krister Stendahl, _Paul among the Jews and Gentiles_ [Philadelphia, 1976], 7–23). John G. Gager dissents. He feels that the use of _call_ rather than _conversion_ is a false dichotomy and has no bearing on the basic issue, since Paul did repudiate certain fundamental elements of his past, a phenomenon normally associated with conversion. Gager agrees, however, that what Paul repudiated was not the legitimacy of Judaism, but the relevance of the Torah for determining the religious status of the Gentiles (_The Origins of Anti-Semitism: Attitudes toward Judaism in Pagan and Christian Antiquity_ [New York, 1983], 209–10).

[20] Becker, _Paulus_, 45–46.

[21] Werner Foerster, "Δαίμων κτλ." _TWNT_ 2:1–21, here 1.

represent are "nothing," they are simply not gods (1 Cor 8:5–6, cf. Gal 4:8). What pagans sacrifice, they offer to demons and not to God (1 Cor 10:20, 22).[22]

Their Transformation into Sons of God (Verse 9a): In v. 9, the readers are brought sharply (νῦν δὲ) out of this recollection of their past to the present. The state of these non-Jews had been transformed. They had become known by God, i.e., the God of Israel (v. 9a). The expected parallel to a time of not knowing God would be one of knowing God, and Paul indeed writes this, but then immediately corrects himself (μᾶλλον): his readers are known by God. Paul's self-correction, followed by the use of passive, νῦν δὲ γνόντες θεόν, μᾶλλον δὲ γνωσθέντες ὑπὸ θεοῦ, emphasizes the aspect of the divine initiative in this transformation.[23] He thereby underlines his insistence that they were not justified, nor did they receive the spirit, by the works of the law, but by faith (2:16; 3:2). This God had been characterized in the opening of the letter as the father when mentioned together with Jesus Christ (1:1, 3); the Galatians had become believers in Jesus Christ (3:26).

Their Return to the Elements (Verse 9b): This new relationship is called in question though by their reaction to Paul's competitors. In their state of being known by God, which is a state of maturity, in which the spirit is in the hearts of the readers (v. 6), Paul asks how it can be that his readers have turned "again" to the elements (cf. v. 3). The term "elements" is now qualified by the adjectives "weak" and "destitute." "Weak," ἀσθενής, is used by Paul at times in a paradoxically positive sense.[24] Similarly, those who are destitute, the πτωχοί, are the object of

---

[22]   Cf. Deut 32:16–17; 21. Deuteronomic criticism of Israel is transformed, as in the synagogue, to anti-pagan polemic.

[23]   Martyn sees here a polemic against the competing mission's portrayal of religion as an ascent to the true knowledge of God in a life of law-observance (*Galatians*, 413).

[24]   Paul's "unimpressive" appearance in 1 Cor 2:3; the "weakness of the flesh" in Rom 6:19 (cf. Matt 26:41); God has chosen the weak (1 Cor 1:26); Christ himself became weak (2 Cor 13:3–4; cf. Heb 5:2); weakness is a reason for joyful boasting (2 Cor 11:30); God's power is made perfect in our weakness (2 Cor 12:10); see Gustav Stählin, art. "ἀσθενής, ἀσθένεια, ἀσθενέω, ἀσθένημα, *TWNT* 1:488–92, here 489–90. Indeed, within a few verses, Paul describes his own preaching in Galatia as δι᾽ ἀσθένειαν τῆς σαρκὸς (v. 13). Josef Zmijewski credits Paul with developing a theology of weakness ("ἀσθενής κτλ.," *EWNT* 1:408–13, here 412).

one of Jesus' beatitudes (Luke 6:20; cf. Matt 5:17). Nevertheless, here the dual characterization of the elements in this way is meant to underline their impotence and poverty, making it all the more ironic that Paul's audience should desire once again to be in their thrall.[25] An additional note of irony in this characterization is that the elements, although weak and impoverished, are able to enslave, paralleling what Paul had written about the law (Gal 3:21). Less clear is the sense in which the elements are thought to be so. There is an echo of Jewish anti-idolatry polemic here.[26] The adjectives weak and destitute have been understood in connection with Paul's description of their previous objects of worship as not-gods.

There is a difficulty however with viewing the στοιχεῖα as demonic forces when one tries to apply it to the reference to the στοιχεῖα τοῦ κόσμου in v. 3. The bondage in which "we" were held in the past (Paul, who never worshiped the not-gods of the pagans, includes himself here) ends when Christ redeems us from the law (v. 5).[27] The Torah, then (cf. 3:19–23), was an expression of the στοιχεῖα, perhaps even to be numbered among them.[28] This makes Paul's employment of terms used in anti-pagan rhetoric poignant, even shocking.[29]

The return to the elements is further characterized, in a reformulation of Paul's opening charge (1:6–7), as a return to the previous state of slavery (πάλιν ἄνωθεν δουλεύειν), but with an added element. The previous service to the elements was simply a given (v. 8), which could even be expressed passively (v. 3). Now this service is active, an act of desire (θέλετε). Paul describes this change ironically as a second conversion (ἐπιστρέφετε πάλιν), or as mentioned above (3.2.1), a conversion in

---

[25] Rudolf Bultmann, *Der Stil der paulinischen Predigt und die kynisch-stoische Diatribe* (FRLANT 13; Göttingen, 1910), 103; Stählin, *TWNT* 1:491.

[26] Wis 13:18–19; cf. Martyn, *Galatians*, 411.

[27] "Paulus fasst sich selbst als Judenchristen und darum auch die Judenchristen insgesamt mit den Heidenchristen in ein Wir zusammen... auch da, wo sie aufs schärfste voneinander geschieden waren, in ihrer Vergangenheit als Juden und Heiden" (Gerhard Ebeling, *Die Wahrheit des Evangeliums: Eine Lesehilfe zum Galaterbrief* [Tübingen, 1981], 297).

[28] Hans Dieter Betz, *Galatians: A Commentary on Paul's Letter to the Churches in Galatia*, (Hermeneia; Philadelphia, 1979), 208, n. 62.

[29] Martyn, *Galatians*, 411.

reverse.[30] By saying that his audience turned again to be under the elements, they were apparently asked to understand themselves included in the "we" in v. 3 who were subject to the elements of the world. That to which they are becoming enslaved is not their previous pagan way of life, but the elements of the world to which the Jews as well had been enslaved in their minority (4:3), here described as *weak* and *beggarly*.[31] We will now turn our attention to these elements.

3.2.3 Excursus: The Elements of the World
In the passage we are examining, Paul speaks of his audience as desiring to serve, or to be in bondage to τὰ ἀσθενῆ καὶ πτωχὰ στοιχεῖα, *the weak and beggarly elements*, (Gal 4:9, KJV).[32] The note of turning back, sounded almost to surfeit (ἐπιστρέφετε πάλιν . . . πάλιν ἄνωθεν), combined with the repetition of the verb δουλεύω from v. 8, make it certain that these elements stand in close relation to the φύσει μὴ οὖσιν θεοῖς, the *not-gods*, that the Galatians served in their pre-Christian past. For this reason, many have concluded that the στοιχεῖα are some sort of elementary spirits or demonic powers.[33] They are often correlated with the Pauline expression principalities and powers (ἀρχαὶ [καὶ] ἐνεστῶται).[34] It has often been objected, though, that the texts that clearly

[30] The verb ἐπιστρέφω is used for religious conversion (BDAG s.v.).

[31] Gerhard Delling remarks: "mit beiden negativen Wendungen [ist] alle vorchristliche Religion zusammenfassend abgeurteilt" ("Στοιχέω, συστοιχέω, στοιχεῖον," *TWNT* 7:666–87, here 685).

[32] The translation offered by the RSV and NRSV, "weak and beggarly elemental spirits," reflects a decision about the meaning of this phrase; cf. the ZB: "Naturmächten der Welt," together with n. 45. "Weak and beggarly rudiments," ASV, also reflects an interpretation, albeit a different one.

[33] Betz, *Galatians*, 204–5; Clinton E. Arnold, "Returning to the Domain of the Powers: Stoicheia as Evil Spirits in Galatians 4:3,9," *NovTest* 38 (1996): 55–76. This is the definition under which Bauer lists the references to Gal 4:3, 9, as well as Col 2:8, 20, which are the only NT passages that speak of the στοιχεῖα τοῦ κόσμου; cf. BDAG s.v., which leaves the question undecided.

[34] Rom 8:38; cf. Eph 3:10, 6:12; Col 1:16, 2:15. The expression appears in Tit 3:1 as well, but possibly with another meaning, since Titus is urged to instruct those in his care to be subject to them. Ἀρχή denoted the original material from which everything evolved, but was gradually replaced in this sense by στοιχεῖον (Gerhard Delling, "ἄρχω κτλ.," *TWNT* 1:476–88, here 478).

speak of these spirits as στοιχεῖα are more recent than Galatians, but this does not exclude the possibility that they contain older traditions.[35]

As a variant of this view, some point to the heavenly bodies as a possible interpretation. The elements are connected to the heavenly bodies in that the stars are composed of the highest of the four elements, fire. In later conceptions, the stars themselves, visible gods, were called elements; combined with astrological belief, these were felt to have an influence on human life. It has been suggested that there may have been an astrological stoicheia-cult in Galatia, either prior to Paul's coming, or as propagated by the competing mission.[36] The objection of the late date of textual evidence has been raised against this as well,[37] but, again, this does not rule out older traditions.

This is the second reference to στοιχεῖα in this letter, however. In v. 3, Paul refers to the elements of the world (στοιχεῖα τοῦ κόσμου), under which "we were enslaved." These elements also have a correlate, the law (v. 5). If Paul used the term univocally in vv. 3 and 9, which is the most logical assumption, then this implies a demonic characterization of the law, which is problematic. It would seem, then, that the understanding of the στοιχεῖα as demonic powers either has to be extended to include the law, or this understanding has to be dropped.[38] Finally, this position suffers by explaining the use of the phrase in Galatians by reference to its use in Col 2:8, 20.[39]

---

[35] Arnold, "Returning," 57.

[36] Franz Mussner proposed a calendar piety similar to that attested in Jewish apocalyptic and Qumran documents (*Der Galaterbrief* [HTK 9; Freiburg im Breisgau, 1974], 298–303).

[37] Blinzler, "Lexikalisches," 432–4; Delling, *TWNT* 7:682.

[38] Arnold himself shrinks back from this logical consequence of his understanding: "It is doubtful Paul would have made the Torah coextensive with demonic powers." He seeks to deflect this by suggesting that it is "more appropriate to speak in terms of a close *association*" ("Returning," 68). Other interpreters speak of the law being in parallel to the στοιχεῖα (e.g., Dunn, *Theology*, 143), but this is inaccurate; the law and the not-gods are two examples of the στοιχεῖα. Some however see no difficulty and point to Paul's reference to the tradition according to which the Torah was mediated at Sinai by angels (3:19), understood in this sense as demons (discussion in Eckstein, *Verheissung*, 200–02). That the Torah figures among the στοιχεῖα τοῦ κόσμου is correctly seen by Delling, *TWNT* 7:684, and Eckstein, *Verheissung*, 231.

[39] Additional criticisms in Linda L. Belleville, "'Under Law': Structural Analysis and

In the search to find a common denominator for the two objects, law and not-gods, both are characterized as στοιχεῖα, some have explicated this term as referring to basic building blocks. The Greek understanding of στοιχεῖον had a basic meaning of items lined up in a row.[40] It was understood, similarly to our "element," in the sense of the basic building blocks of any subject (cf. Heb 5:12). If this meaning stands behind Paul's usage here, the term στοιχεῖα τοῦ κόσμου would mean something like the rudimentary principles of the cosmos, including of all religions.[41] At first glance, this appears attractive, since Paul uses metaphors implying childhood (3:24–25; 4:1–3). This use may mirror a claim of the competitors that they were simply filling out the rudimentary teaching of Paul.[42] The difficulty with this view is that the point of Paul's childhood analogy in 4:1–3 is to demonstrate the similarity to the situation of a slave. This state is ended not by maturation, but by liberation (cf. the time set by the father, 4:2).

On the assumption that Paul used στοιχεῖα univocally in these two references that are in close proximity to each other, the genitive construction τοῦ κόσμου in v. 3 limits the term and should help in the interpretation. The word στοιχεῖον, on the one hand, has many documented uses.[43] The phrase στοιχεῖα τοῦ κόσμου, on the other, is

the Pauline Concept of Law in Galatians 3.21–4.11," *JSNT* 26 (1986): 53–78, here 66–67.

[40] Delling, *TWNT* 7:670; cf. 666.

[41] The word στοιχεῖα is used in this sense in Heb. 5:12. Ernest D. Burton adopts this meaning for Galatians as well (*A Critical and Exegetical Commentary on the Epistle to the Galatians* [ICC; Edinburgh, 1921], 518. Recent advocates of this meaning for Galatians are Belleville, "Law," and Derek R. Moore-Crispin, "Galatians 4:1–9: The Use and Abuse of Parallels," *EvQ* 60 (1989): 203–23.

[42] Belleville, "Law," 67. Cf. Barclay, "Mirror-Reading," 82.

[43] BDAG s.v. Burton distinguishes seven meanings, but some of them (e.g., "a premise for fundamental proposition of a demonstration") do not seem to be reflected in the early Christian writings (*Galatians*, 510–14). Josef Blinzler identifies nine meanings that have been considered for explaining the usage in Gal and Col, but rejects three (alphabet, rudiments, supports) as undocumented. Three others (heavenly bodies, the spirits of the elements or heavenly bodies, spirits in general) are rejected as undocumented before Paul's time ("Lexikalisches zu dem Terminus τὰ στοιχεῖα τοῦ κόσμου bei Paulus," *Studiorum Paulinorum Congressus Internationalis Catholicus* [AnBib 17–18; Rome 1963], 2:429–43). For ancient citations, see BDAG, LSJ, and

only documented in one sense in the first century, that of the basic elements of the universe. In this usage, the elements would be the building blocks out of which heaven and earth were composed, although the Greeks did not think of our table of elements, but of the substances fire, air, earth and water (corresponding to sun, sky, land and sea).[44] These four are eternal; the material substances of our experience are various mixtures of these four (and the four are transformable into each other: think of water, ice, steam, and combustion). When matter decays (including the human body), it returns to these four basic elements. This is apparently meant in 2 Pet 3:10, 12, which speaks of the dissolution of the heavens and the earth in the day of the Lord. Speaking for this meaning in Gal 4 is the genitive τοῦ κόσμου, the significance of which would in this case be self-evident.[45] The evidence that the phrase στοιχεῖα τοῦ κόσμου was used in this way in Paul's time is overwhelming, and therefore deserves consideration. Nevertheless, there are three difficulties.[46] First, it is difficult to explain how the law could be equated with them, unless with the term νόμος Paul did not mean the Torah, but the principles of science. The context of chs. 2–5, however, argues against this (e.g. 4:4). Secondly, it is difficult to explain in what way the Galatians performed religious service to the basic elements. Thirdly, there has been no convincing explanation of how the coming of Christ could

Delling, *TWNT* 7:670–82. Vouga, *Galater*, 100, lists over fifty citations for the phrase στοιχεῖα τοῦ κόσμου in Philo alone. Recent literature, and some of the more important older scholarly works, listed in Vouga, *Galater*, 97–100. Earlier word studies listed in Blinzler, "Lexikalisches," 429. Some pertinent first century passages are quoted and commented on by Eduard Schweizer, "Slaves of the Elements and Worshipers of Angels: Gal 4:3, 9 and Col 2:8, 18, 20," *JBL* 107 (1988): 455-68, here 456–64.

[44] The teaching of these four elements seems to have originated with Empedocles, who commonly calls them ῥιζώματα (Blinzler, "Lexikalisches," 431; Delling, *TWNT* 7:672). However, at least one use of the word στοιχεῖα has survived (frg. 7, FVS 1:312). For Pythagoras, there was a fifth element, number (Dietrich Rusam, "Neue Belege zu den στοιχεῖα τοῦ κόσμου [Gal 4,3.9; Kol 2,8.20]," *ZNW* 83 [1992]: 119–25, here 121). Alternatively, beginning with Aristotle, ether appears as a fifth element (Blinzler, "Lexikalisches," 431).

[45] A recent proponent of this interpretation of Paul's term is Rusam ("Belege"). Cf. Delling *TWNT* 7:683; 685.

[46] Blinzler, "Lexikalisches," 440–41, Rusam, "Belege," 124–5.

break the power of these elements—or why it even should, for that matter. Therefore, while the only meaning of the phrase στοιχεῖα τοῦ κόσμου in the first century is as a reference to the basic, Empedoclean elements, it appears that this cannot be what Paul meant. For this reason, some have suggested that Paul uses the phrase figuratively.[47]

Blinzler, after demonstrating that this phrase was current before Paul, faces this difficulty by pointing out that Paul had transposed the term κόσμος from the realm of the physical and objective to that of ethical conditions.[48] The only support that he cites for this is Col 2:20. To identify the likely constitutive elements of the world, thus understood, he calls on systematic presentations of Paul's theology, in which σάρξ, ἁμαρτία and θάνατος are often mentioned as a triad.[49] This is undoubtedly true, and there is no question that Paul understood the cross as having broken their power. Additionally, a strength of this suggestion is that the mastery they exercise would be self-evident. Yet there are difficulties with this proposal. Aside from the use of Colossians to determine Paul's understanding of κόσμος, there are two problems: firstly, Paul does not correlate the στοιχεῖα with flesh, sin and death, but with the law and the not-gods.[50] Secondly, there are no known examples in biblical or extra-biblical literature of the flesh, sin and death explicitly identified or conceptualized as τὰ στοιχεῖα τοῦ κόσμου.[51] While Blinzler

---

[47] E.g., Delling: "Paulus gebraucht damit den Ausdruck, von dem er ausgeht..., in einer neuen Weise; aber er knüpft offenbar an einen zu seiner Zeit ganz allgemein verbreiteten Gedanken an.... Paulus benutzt sie in einem übertragenen Sinn." (*TWNT* 7: 685).

[48] "Das Rätsel seines Sprachgebrauchs löst sich, wenn man in Betracht zieht, dass bei ihm der Begriff Kosmos aus der Kategorie des Physikalisch-Gegenständlichen in die Kategorie des Ethisch-Zuständlichen transponiert ist" ("Lexicalisches," 442).

[49] Citations in Blinzler, "Lexikalisches," 442, n. 1–2; 443, n. 1.

[50] As it did for Arnold (above, n. 40), this characterization of the law presents a difficulty for Blinzler. He assures us that even though the law is an enslaving power that stands in closest connection with flesh, sin and death, it "keineswegs derselben Kategorie angehört wie diese drei Grössen (und somit nicht selbst zu den Weltelementen zu rechnen ist)" ("Lexikalisches," 443, n. 1). This reverses the textual evidence, in which the slavery to the law is expressly mentioned as an expression of slavery to the elements of the world, while flesh, sin and death are not mentioned.

[51] Belleville, "Law," 65.

does not claim that this is what the phrase means, but what Paul may have had in mind when he used it, we must conclude that this proposal is hypothetical.

Vielhauer viewed Blinzler's proposal positively, however, and argued in a similar fashion. The phrase is used in a more inclusive sense than the merely physical.[52] This is shown by the fact that he included religion (Jewish and pagan) under these στοιχεῖα, as well as the power of the στοιχεῖα, expressed by the concept of being enslaved to them (vv. 3 and 9). In one point his proposal is more nuanced than Blinzler's: flesh, sin and death are not said to be elements of the world; instead, they fit in with the Pauline series of objects that qualify this world.[53] In this way, Vielhauer implicitly takes into account the objection that these three powers are not indicated in context as the elements of the world, but this formulation moves us even farther from being able to explain how the law and the not-gods could be referred to as στοιχεῖα τοῦ κόσμου.

Another suggestion that builds on the attested meaning of the στοιχεῖα τοῦ κόσμου as the basic elements of the cosmos, while assuming that Paul offered a theological variant of it, is that of Martyn, who notes that the only other use of the word κόσμος in Galatians is 6:14–15.[54] Here Paul states that with the crucifixion of the cosmos, both circumcision and uncircumcision (i.e., the distinction of Jew from Gentile) has been removed. The cosmos had at its foundation, then, both Law and Not-Law. Drawing on 6:14–15 and 3:28, Martyn concludes that "Paul takes for granted the widespread tradition in which pairs of opposites are identified as 'the elements of the cosmos,'" and applies it to the distinctions obliterated at baptism, above all, that between the Law and Not-Law.[55] In this case, the mastery these elements exercise would be that as pairs of opposites, antinomies, they determine our existence.

Martyn's reconstruction relies on literary allusions not mentioned in the text of Galatians and, as he concedes, presupposes a certain amount

---

[52] "Gesetzesdienst," 553.

[53] "Gesetzesdienst," 553; Vielhauer expresses this however as if he is in agreement with Blinzler (553, n. 32).

[54] *Galatians*, 395–406.

[55] *Galatians*, 405. See, previously, George Howard, *Paul: Crisis in Galatia* (2d ed.; SNTSMS 35; Cambridge, 1990), 78.

of intellectual sophistication and familiarity with common philosophical theories about the nature of the cosmos.[56] It offers however a coherent explanation of the use of the term στοιχεῖα τοῦ κόσμου, both in terms of the previous religious experience of his readers and a plausible reconstruction of the message of his competitors, as well as in the context of the scrupulous observance of days and other time markers. One weakness of this proposal, however, is that the relation of the στοιχεῖα to the not-gods is "by implication."[57] Nevertheless, Martyn's thesis has the advantage of arguing from the text, as well as on the well-documented Jewish division of humanity into the circumcised and uncircumcised, those to whom the Torah had been entrusted and those to whom it had not been. Despite the caution that must be exercised because of the inevitable speculation involved, I will use this as my working hypothesis.

Regardless of what Paul may have had in mind when he used this phrase, he maintains that all mankind were subject to them.[58] The first time the στοιχεῖα are mentioned (4:3), they are correlated to an earlier time of minority and guardianship (v. 2) and with life under the law (v. 5), a life in which Paul had shared. In its second use (v. 9), it is correlated to his readers' return to a worship of not-gods (v. 8) and the scrupulous observance of time markers (v. 10). It is clear, then, that in v. 9 non-Jews are meant. The referent of "we" in v. 3 is less clear,

---

[56] *Galatians*, 396.

[57] *Galatians*, 394. Cf. Vouga, who adduces Rom 1:18–23 to suggest that Paul understood pagan worship as mistaking the elements of nature for the creator, a charge also made by Philo (*Galater*, 100; cf. Philo, *Spec.* 2.255).

[58] It could be that part of our difficulty in understanding Paul's use of this phrase is that it might have been introduced by the competing mission, as Martyn suggests (*Galatians*, 395–405). On this reading, Paul would have established common ground with the competing mission by agreeing that the Galatians had previously worshiped the elements foolishly as divinities, only to shift the ground by saying not only the Gentiles, but all humans had revered the elements (4:3). Paul adopted a phrase then in use, and known to his audience, but adapted it to fit his theology. It would then be "a typical instance of Paul's transformation of language" (*Galatians*, 405). The issue of whether it was introduced into the discussion by Paul or whether he appropriated a phrase of the competing mission can not be decided, but speaking for Martyn's reconstruction is the fact that the understanding of "fundamental principles" does not fit the thrust of Paul's argument and that the suggestions of the heavenly bodies or of spirits are too speculative.

however. As mentioned, when Paul tells his audience in v. 9 that they were turning again to the elements, it seems that they are included in the we of v. 3. Yet the common understanding of being "under" the law in the sense of obligated to fulfil its demands would weigh against this. Only Israel was subject to it in this way.[59] If however we adopt the suggestion of Howard and Martyn that all mankind were subject to the law in the sense that it was the law that divided mankind into Jews and non-Jews, then the difficulty is solved.[60] Note that in the first reference to the elements, there is a correlation to being under the law, and in v. 8 to service of not-gods. In this way, Paul is careful to avoid suggesting that the Jews, although they, too, had been subject to the στοιχεῖα, had been in servitude to not-gods. The law in v. 3, as in ch. 3, is the Torah revealed at Sinai. It is not an equivalent expression to the στοιχεῖα, but a specific form of them, just as the service of not-gods is a form of the στοιχεῖα among the non-Jews.[61]

The στοιχεῖα are weak and poor (even though, ironically, they had been mighty enough to hold mankind in servitude) because they could not do what the coming of Christ has done: bring divine adoption. In fact, on the understanding that the elements either are flesh, sin and death, or that they are the elementary distinctions that determine our existence, they themselves have been conquered through the coming of Christ, especially through the cross (not mentioned expressly here, but indicated by the motifs "born under the law" and "to redeem"). This above all demonstrates their weakness.

It appears, then, that this phrase somehow describes the pre-Christian life of both Jews and non-Jews.[62] In this way, the religious experience of Jews and Gentiles is placed on the same level; this is, as Vielhauer writes, for Jews a blasphemous statement, even coming from Paul an alienating

---

[59] For this reason, Betz concludes that v. 5a refers only to the Jews (*Galatians*, 208).

[60] Howard, *Crisis*, 18; Martyn, *Galatians*, 405.

[61] See also Becker, who credits Paul with consciously employing the full range of meaning implicit in δουλεύω. One could serve the gods through the careful observance of ritual, one could also serve the elements by considering the mixture in which they appeared in the world in one's life. In both cases, it is a matter of perceiving that they are functions that regulate life (*Galater*, 62).

[62] Delling, *TWNT* 7:684.

claim, one that has caused discomfort for interpreters.[63] Among those who find this idea unacceptable are Sabbatarian theologians, who maintain that the "turning again" in v. 9 signifies a return to paganism.[64] The new enthusiasm of the Galatians for the Torah is for Paul an indication of their return to the domain of the στοιχεῖα. That the time markers, which include but are not limited to the festival calendar of the Torah, are an expression of this, is a phenomenon that is better explained by Martyn's proposal than that of Blinzler and Vielhauer.

In order to answer the question of why Paul could use the expression στοιχεῖα to refer to both Jews and non-Jews, we must now consider the expressions he uses for periods of time.

3.2.4 Time Markers: Evidence of Apostasy (Verse 10)

In 4:10, Paul offers verification of his claim, expressed in the form of a rhetorical question in v. 9, that his readers are returning to slavery to the elements of the world. We are given a series of four terms that denote time periods; the Gentiles are said to be scrupulously observing them.[65] The periods are days, months, times and years. The "times" can be understood as "seasons," which their position in the series, from shorter to longer, confirms.[66] The question that must be addressed here is whether the practice of Paul's readers was a renewed enthusiasm for the observances of paganism (v. 9: turning back) or whether the practices of the Torah are meant.

In the priestly account of creation, on the fourth day lights are placed in the firmament (Gen 1:14). These lights have the purpose of dividing

---

[63] "[E]ine für die Juden blasphemische Aussage, eine auch im Munde des Paulus befremdliche Behauptung, die den Auslegern Unbehagen bereitet" (Vielhauer, "Gesetzesdient," 543).

[64] For the use of ἐπιστρέφω in this way, see 2 Pet 2:21–22.

[65] Παρατηρεῖσθε. The verb is used in Exod 12:42, Sym., to refer to the night of watching in conjunction with the exodus out of Egypt. On παρατηρέω, cf. BDAG s.v. and the uses in Josephus given there. More common in connection with the keeping of a Sabbath or festival would be the verb φυλάσσω or, less frequently, τηρέω. Riesenfeld suggests that the use of the compound παρατηρέω expresses the participation of the active subject (*TWNT* 8:139–51). He adds that the uses in Josephus show from the context that the decision to keep commandments or celebrate days is emphasized.

[66] See the use of καιροί for festal seasons in Exod 23:14, 17; Lev 23:4 LXX.

day from night, and serve for signs, and for seasons and days and years. Missing from this is any reference to months, but the lesser of the two lights created, the moon, not only "rules" the night (Gen 1:16), but it also defines the month's length in the Hebrew calendar. Dieter Lührmann has shown that the connection between Gen 1:14 LXX and Gal 4:10 is even closer when Philo (*Opif.* 45–61) and other Jewish literature of the time are taken into consideration.[67] Nevertheless, it remains true that in contrast to the list in Col 2:16 we are not dealing in Gal 4:10 with a list of holy days; rather, we are dealing with a system of marking time.[68]

Most commentators conclude that the turning back (v. 9) is an ironic equation of the new enthusiasm for Torah practices, evidenced by the observance of days and other time markers (v. 10), with the former way of life in paganism (v. 8). A recent proponent of the opposing view, namely, that the Galatians had returned to paganism is Troy Martin.[69] He argues, correctly, that the general terminology of the list could apply to either Gentile or Jewish time-keeping schemes, so that the meaning of the phrase can only be determined by the context. He limits this context narrowly, however, to the reference to the former pagan way of life of Paul's readers (vv. 8–9). He concedes that this creates a seeming inconsistency with the overall context of Galatians, which warns against submission to circumcision and the Jewish law, but argues that the readers had not yet submitted to circumcision, otherwise Paul's arguments against it would be pointless. On the understanding that circumcision was an entrance requirement, he concludes that they could not yet be keeping the competitors' sacred times.

---

[67] "Tage, Monate, Jahreszeiten, Jahre (Gal 4,10)," in *Werden und Wirken des Alten Testaments* (FS Claus Westermann; ed. R. Albertz et al., Göttingen, 1980), 428–45, here 432–7.

[68] This also solves the difficulty sometimes seen in that there is no documentation of Jewish Christians celebrating sabbatical years (nor of Jews in general in the time of the Second Temple); Bultmann viewed the inclusion of years as examples of argumentation through the false or laughable portrayal of the opposite view (*Stil*, 103).

[69] "Pagan and Judeo-Christian Time-Keeping Schemes in Gal 4.10 and Col 2.16," *NTS* 42 (1996): 105–19. Incidentally, Martin credits Lührmann with "correctly" noting "the pagan nature of *season* in contrast to the Jewish *festival* ('Tage', 437–8)," a reading for which I can find no basis in Lührmann's article ("Schemes," 112, n. 35).

This reasoning is flawed. First, granted that Paul assumes that his readers in general had not yet become circumcised (5:2), this does not mean that none in Galatia had. Secondly, the comparison with synagogue practice, where the Godfearers who worshiped were more numerous than the proselytes, proves that it was quite possible to observe days without becoming circumcised. Thirdly, not all exegetes are convinced that the Galatians had actually begun to observe the days, but understand Paul's statement either as a sarcastic description of religiously scrupulous behavior, or as a conative present (expressing volition or intention).[70] Martin argues that given the aversion of Gentiles to circumcision, the acceptance of the premise of the competing mission (no true Christianity without circumcision) would more likely have led to their rejection of Christianity than their acceptance of circumcision. He argues this based on the fact that most Gentiles did not become circumcised, even though the option was available to them in Judaism. This argument cuts both ways of course. It can also be considered surprising that Judaism was as attractive in the Roman empire as it was, at least before the two uprisings (see above, 2.3). This attempt to harmonize the overall thrust of Galatians with his reading of 4:10 must be regarded as more speculative than the widespread understanding that Paul believed his readers were indeed on the point of accepting circumcision.

Martin reaches the conclusion that the days and other time markers listed here represent a pagan time-keeping scheme, which in turn is for him proof that the Galatians were returning to paganism.[71] It is difficult for him to conceive of Paul objecting if the days and other time markers in question were those of the Jewish liturgical calendar.[72] Although Martin is correct to point out the dissimilarity of the time markers

---

[70] Betz, *Galatians*, 216–8; Dunn, *Galatians*, 227; Vouga, *Galater*, 105.

[71] "Schemes," 118.

[72] "Acts and 1 Corinthians as well as other Christian writings demonstrate that the Pauline communities and other early Christians adopted a Jewish time-keeping scheme in order to avoid the idolatrous systems of the pagans around them" ("Schemes," 110). "A comparison of these lists [sc. Col 2:16 and Gal 4:10] demonstrates that Gentile conversion to Paul's gospel involves rejection of idolatrous pagan temporal schemes in favour of the Jewish liturgical calendar" ("Schemes," 119).

mentioned in v. 10 to those in Col 2:16, he does not thereby prove that the time markers in Galatians represent a return to pagan time-keeping schemes. I contend that the answer to Martin's difficulty lies in the verb used, παρατηρέω. The close observance of time sequences implies the differentiation of time between holy and profane. Further, it is closely connected to Paul's decision to use general terms to describe these time markers instead of the specific terms we find in Col 2:16. As Martin correctly observes, a Gentile reader of Galatians could quite easily recognize in Paul's formulation the way in which his own earlier life had been regulated by the recurrence of astronomically (and astrologically) determined times and seasons. Important, however, is why Paul does this. This terminology helps the reader become aware of the close connection in all human culture of the measurement of time and religious belief.[73] As Martin himself noted, his interpretation leads to a tension between the immediate context of the reference to time-markers (vv. 8–10) and the overall context and purpose of the letter. On the reading adopted here, this tension is resolved. We find no indication that Paul was arguing for one calendar (and set of religious observances) in place of another, but for a freedom from such (and the old patterns of belief inextricably tied to them). In a world where the quality of time had changed with the coming of Christ, there had to be a discontinuity. This explains the fact—difficult for us to grasp—of why Paul mentions time markers, of all things, in 4:10 as evidence of his readers' apostasy.

The mention of scrupulous observance of time-markers then is Paul's exemplification of this return to bondage. The reason he uses general terms is to stress the commonality of Jewish calendars and pagan worship. The believers were new creatures in Christ. They were non-Jews and non-Greeks (3:28), just as the gods his readers formerly worshiped were now revealed as not-gods. Faith in Christ transcended the old, including old religious observances, both Jewish and non-Jewish.

The slavery warned of in v. 9 is demonstrated by a scrupulous observance of days and other markers of time (v. 10). Since Paul is striving to show his readers the common denominator in their previous

---

[73] See Mircea Eliade, *The Myth of the Eternal Return, or, Cosmos and History* (trans. Willard R. Trask; Princeton, 1954).

religious experience and the law-observant form of the Christian faith that his competitors are propagating, he uses general terms, although the echo of Gen 1:14 makes it clear that these terms include the Jewish calendar, even if they do not exclusively refer to them.[74]

The transformation of the Galatians from slaves of the not-gods to sons of God had taken place through the labors of Paul. Their apostasy, evidenced by their scrupulous observance of time markers, evokes from him an exclamation of pathos: were those labors in vain (v. 11)?[75]

3.3 THE FUNCTION OF GALATIANS 4:8–11 IN PAUL'S ARGUMENT

3.3.1 Overview of the Epistle to the Galatians

The coherence we observed in the unit under examination is characteristic of Galatians as a whole. It is a closely-argued polemical letter, the occasion of which is announced immediately after the epistolary greeting in 1:6–9: his readers are turning to a different gospel, which is nevertheless not another gospel (1:6–7). This change of allegiance is expressed another way in the passage under examination: they are turning back to bondage (4:9). Insight into this other gospel, as well as the nature of the bondage, is provided by a formal restatement of the letter's theme in 2:15–21: we are justified through faith in Christ, not through works of the law (2:16).

The urgent tone suggested by the occasion is reflected in the opening. Galatians begins conventionally for a letter of the antiquity with the prescript, containing the name of the sender, the addressees, and a

---

[74] Martyn is an exception among commentators in that he addresses the question of Paul's use of general terminology (*Galatians*, 414–8). He concludes, first, that "Paul is drawing an astonishing connection between creation and the realm ruled over by the enslaving elements" and second, that "[i]f the distinction of holy times from profane ones is an element of the old creation, then it is basic to all peoples" (*Galatians*, 417). Becker offers a simpler explanation for Paul's use of general terms: both he and his readers would have understood what he was referring to (*Galater*, 66). We can certainly assume that they did, but this does not explain what we, as readers, are to make of the phrase, especially in light of the literary parallels (which Becker himself adduces) and the use of these days as evidence of falling back into service to the elements of the world.

[75] Cf. 3:4: were their sufferings in vain?

greeting formula. Paul uses an atypical expansion of his name that hearkens back to the manner of his calling as well as being closely tied to his self-defense (1:11–12).[76] The greeting formula is typical for Paul: χάρις ὑμῖν καὶ εἰρήνη ἀπὸ θεοῦ πατρὸς ἡμῶν καὶ κυρίου Ἰησοῦ Χριστοῦ κτλ. (cf. Rom 1:7; 1 Cor 1:3; 2 Cor 1:2; Phil 1:2; 1 Thess 1:1; Phlm 3). Paul breaks form in Galatians, though, in that the prescript is not followed by the usual prayer of thanksgiving (formula: εὐχαριστῶ; cf. Rom 1:8; 1 Cor 1:4–9; Phil 1:3; 1 Thess 1:2–9; Phlm 4–6). Paul has nothing to be thankful for in this situation. This terseness reflects the theological tenor of the letter: the Galatians are turning away to a different gospel. In place of the prayer of thanksgiving, an element not only typical of Paul, but of Hellenistic correspondence in general, there is a sharp rebuke of his addressees, including a twice-expressed curse on those who preach a different message (1:6–10), indicating the severity of Paul's view of his difference with the competing mission.

The danger thus so brusquely announced is met in the body of the letter in three steps. Immediately after this first indication of his purpose in writing, Paul cites his authority: it is divine, not human (1:10–12).[77] This leads to a first expository section, a narrative apology, in which Paul rehearses his life in Judaism (1:13–14), his calling (1:15–17), his dealings with the pillar apostles, confirming his calling (1:18–2:10), and the incident at Antioch (2:11–14). The importance of this incident is

---

[76] See the commentaries on this, e.g., James D. G. Dunn, *The Epistle to the Galatians* (BNTC; Peabody, Mass., 1993), 23–27, who suggests that the epexegetical use of the term ἀπόστολος was occasioned by the challenge in Galatia to his status. It is not used in the opening to the Thessalonian letters, but is used invariably in all later letters (26, cf. 18).

[77] Vouga, following Pitta, sees in this the main thesis: the gospel that Paul preaches is not dependant on man, but is a revelation from God (*Galater*, 6). In this understanding, 2:16 is part of the first of four demonstrations of 1:10–12, in which the meaning of God's revelation in Christ is illustrated. The significance of this shift in accent, however, would be to assert that the argument of justification by faith is simply an illustration of Paul's main concern, the demonstration of his direct reception of divine revelation. The traditional understanding of this letter, adopted here, is that Paul's assertion of direct revelation, and the apostolic authority that this implies, is at the service of the truth of the message at stake, justification by faith, not by works of the law.

indicated by its location at the culmination of this narrative, immediately before Paul states his proposition.

The next section is clearly marked by the direct address to the readers: "O foolish Galatians" (3:1). In this section, Paul argues his case; he reaffirms the truth once clearly seen by the Galatians (3:1–4:11). Finally, in an emotional appeal, Paul urges his readers to return to the freedom of the gospel (4:12– 5:12).[78] According to this scheme, the section under consideration, 4:8–11, occupies a critical place: it forms the climax of Paul's argumentation and lays the groundwork for his appeal.

Following this appeal, Paul brings a section of paraenesis, typical for him in a letter to a congregation, but closely related to the argumentation of the letter in that the paraenesis is discussed under the aspect of the (positive and negative) use of Christian liberty (5:13–6:11). Paul then closes this letter in a personally written conclusion (6:11–18). This, too, is atypical; it lacks the usual benediction and greetings (cf. Rom 16). It does, however, contain a recapitulation of the letter's important themes (cross, circumcision). Although these final two parts of the letter, paraenesis and conclusion, are not, rhetorically speaking, part of the argumentation, this thematic connection is an indication of Paul's awareness of how much was at stake in this letter.

As this brief overview shows, this letter is a focused response to a challenge that Paul variously describes as another gospel and a return to bondage. In his eyes, the crux of the difference between his message and that of the competing mission is whether justification comes through

---

[78] For the terminology narrative apology, argument, and emotional appeal see R. Dean Anderson, Jr., *Ancient Rhetorical Theory and Paul* (CBET 18; Kampen, 1996), 125. Hans Dieter Betz, who launched the use of rhetorical criticism in NT studies with his Galatians commentary, offers a slightly different structure (*Galatians*, 16–23). For him, the *narratio* begins in 1:12 and runs to 2:14. The remaining verses to 2:21 are for Betz the *propositio*. The next section, termed *probatio* by Betz, runs from 3:1 to 4:31. He then terms 5:1–6:10 the *exhortatio*. Hans Hübner, as Anderson, would see the argument as running to 5:12, with the paraenesis beginning at 5:13 ("Der Galaterbrief und das Verhältnis von antiker Rhetorik und Epistolographie," *ThLZ* 109 [1984]: 241–50). Becker (*Galater*, 11) groups the two sections 3:1–4:7 and 4:8–5:12 as a "doppelt angelegte probatio oder argumentatio." As Vouga reminds us, in the absence of a paratext (paragraphing, subtitles, foreword) any structuring of the text is a construction of the reader (*Galater*, 5).

works of the law or faith in (or of) Jesus Christ.[79] This finding will be relevant in 3.4, when I ask whether Paul's focus on circumcision makes sense as a refutation of the position of the competing mission. First we will consider how Gal 4:8–11 is integrated in its context.

3.3.2 Galatians 4:8–11 in Context

The unit under investigation is well-integrated in its context through the vocabulary used and through the temporal scheme. The verb δουλεύω, used in vv. 8 and 9, picks up on a key term in the argument in 4:1–7, the noun δοῦλος (vv. 1 and 7, cf. 3:28). The noun στοιχεῖα repeats another key term from the argument (v. 3), and the theme of not knowing/being known by God reflects the new relationship as a son that replaces the status of δοῦλος, slave, established through the sending forth of the son and of the spirit (vv. 4–7). An important connection both to the preceding and subsequent material is established through the phrase δουλεύειν θέλετε (v. 9). In v. 21, Paul addresses his readers, or at least part of them, as οἱ ὑπὸ νόμον θέλοντες. The state of believers before their redemption was also described as ὑπὸ νόμον (v. 5), and indeed the son was born under the law (v. 4).[80]

Galatians displays a consistent two-step temporal structure, then/now. In 3:23–29, Paul had divided time into two parts, defined by the coming of faith (3:23). The earlier time is described as "under the law" (ὑπὸ νόμον). In this way, "law" and "faith" are set in polarity. Faith is men-

---

[79] For an introduction to the debate over the meaning of διὰ πίστεως Ἰησοῦ Χριστοῦ, see Martyn, Galatians, 270–71. That Paul intends these to be mutually exclusive alternatives in spite of the normally exceptive ἐὰν μή (2:16) is clear when he concludes ἵνα δικαιωθῶμεν ἐκ πίστεως Χριστοῦ καὶ οὐκ ἐχ ἔργων νόμου, ὅτι ἐξ ἔργων νόμου οὐ δικαιωθήσεται πᾶσα σάρξ (cf. Eckstein, Verheissung, 20–21; Martyn, Galatians, 251, 264, n. 158; A. Andrew Das, "Another Look at ἐὰν μή in Galatians 2:16," JBL 119 [2000]: 529–39). On the expression ἔργα νόμου, see Martyn, Galatians, 260–63.

[80] To be under (ὑπο) something is to be under the power of it. Martyn identifies ten occurrences of this construction in chs. 3–5, with seven of these uses concentrated in 3:22–4:5 (Galatians, 370–73). In five of the ten occurrences, it is law that one is under. Other things one is said to be under: a curse (3:10); sin (3:22); a confining custodian (identified as the law, 3:24–25); guardians and overseers (4:2) and the elements of the world (4:3).

tioned five times in seven verses (3:23–29), and an explicit connection is made to Jesus Christ in v. 26 (διὰ τῆς πίστεως ἐν Χριστῷ Ἰησοῦ). It is through this faith that Paul's readers have become children of God. Christ Jesus, or Christ, is mentioned six times. Taken together, faith and Jesus Christ are the characterizing features of the new time in which the readers, children of God, find themselves.[81] Contrasted with this the law is viewed as a restraint (3:23) and as a guardian servant (παιδαγωγός) of youths (3:23–24). Through the latter term, the earlier time takes on the quality of minority. The time of the law is a time in which the subjects of the law were not yet adult.

The new time, which can also be termed as having begun in baptism (3:27), is a time, in keeping with the symbolism of baptism, of new life, expressed here in terms of having "put on Christ." This new identity has the effect of surmounting dichotomies that characterized the old time, Jew/Greek, slave/free, male/female (3:28). It is further characterized as that of the offspring of Abraham, and therefore heirs according to the promise. The nature of the new identity as surmounting the old dichotomies corroborates Martyn's explanation of the στοιχεῖα τοῦ κόσμου (3.2.3, above).

This picture is expanded in the next section, 4:1–7. The then/now scheme is repeated, this time with the metaphorical change in relationship from slave to the elements of the world to son of God. The new identity, in which his readers are revealed as the offspring of Abraham (by virtue of their immersion into Christ), will now be explained by a picture in which Paul again uses the metaphor of the situation of a child. The child, although an heir, is in a situation no different than that of a servant until he reaches maturity. In v. 4, Paul refers to the fulness of time (τὸ πλήρωμα τοῦ χρόνου). This is comparable to the appointed time set by the father in v. 2, but perhaps more is meant. At any rate, the coming of Christ marks a clear break, marking an end to the previous time, described in v. 1 (ὅσον χρόνον) and v. 8 (τότε). This is consistent with the understanding of time evident in 3:23–29.

---

[81] Stendahl notes that "faith" here could be substituted by "Christ"; faith for Paul is totally defined by its content (*Paul*, 21).

3.4 Verification

We have seen that the most likely explanation for Paul's reference to time markers in v. 10 is that it is due to the fact that his readers had begun to observe the Sabbath (as a part of the festival calendar of the OT), although it is not explicitly named. We have seen as well why Paul uses general terminology, however, to describe these time markers: the generality of the terms corresponds to the point he is making to his (formerly idol-worshiping) readers, namely, that of the structural similarity of their former observances to the new enthusiasm for an identifiably Jewish way of life, as shown by Paul's characterization of both as στοιχεῖα τοῦ κόσμου. It remains for us to verify this finding in two directions: (1) does this make sense as a refutation of the position of Paul's competitors (3.4.1)?[82] (2) does this make sense in Paul's overall theological approach (3.4.2 and 3.4.3)?

3.4.1 Refutation of the Competing Mission

Paul never names his opponents;[83] his refusal to do so, combined with characterizations such as "the circumcision," may reflect his contempt for them and their position.[84] Based on the information available to us in the

---

[82]   Franz Mussner summarizes discussion from the third quarter of the last century (*Galaterbrief*, 14–24). His own solution is that they are "judaisierende Judenchristen" who lay special emphasis on calendar piety, and who cannot definitely be identified with any known groupings in the Judaism or Christianity of the time (25). For a brief survey of the wider question of whether a global, unitary opposition to Paul can be imagined, see E. Earle Ellis, "Paul and his Opponents: Trends in the Research," in *Christianity, Judaism and Other Greco-Roman Cults* (FS Morton Smith; ed. J. Neusner), 1:264–98. This overview remains useful even if one remains unconvinced by the author's stance, which harmonizes the opponents in all thirteen Pauline and Deuteropauline letters into a common front. For additional overview discussions, see Becker, *Galater*, 12–13 and Fung, *Galatians*, 3–9. Recent contributions are Thomas Söding, "Die Gegner des Apostels Paulus in Galatien. Beobachtungen zu ihrer Evangeliumsverkündigung und ihrem Konflikt mit Paulus," in *Das Wort vom Kreuz: Studien zur paulinischen Theologie* (WUNT 93; Tübingen, 1997), 123–52; and Jerry L. Sumney, '*Servants of Satan,*' '*False Brothers*' *and Other Opponents of Paul* (JSNTSup 188; Sheffield, 1999).

[83]   This is all the more remarkable when one considers that, as Fung points out, the agitators feature in every chapter of the letter (2:4–5; 3:1; 4:17; 5:10–12; 6:12–13; *Galatians*, 3).

[84]   In addition, the omission of an explicit refutation of the opponents' position is

text of the letter of Galatians, the point of contention between Paul and the competitors is their endeavor to encourage the Galatian believers to become circumcised (6:12).[85] Paul reminds his readers however that the circumcised are obligated to keep the whole law (5:2–3).[86] We learn from this that circumcision does not stand alone, in its function as the key identity marker between Jews and non-Jews.[87] Circumcision is at issue here because it is the entrance gate to Judaism, and initiates a life of Torah-observance, as Paul's repeated contrast of justification through faith in (or of) Christ, διὰ πίστεως Ἰησοῦ Χριστοῦ, and the works of the

a break with Betz's proposed model of forensic rhetoric. See Becker, *Galater*, 11.

[85] The word group περιτέμνω (verb) and περιτομή (noun) features prominently in Galatians. In the context of presenting his gospel together with Barnabas to those "of reputation" in Jerusalem, Paul reports that Titus, their Gentile companion, was not compelled to be circumcised (2:3). The result of this meeting was the recognition that Peter had received a commission to the circumcision, and Paul to the uncircumcision (2:7–9). Peter's subsequent withdrawal from common table fellowship in Antioch is ascribed by Paul to a fear of the circumcision (2:12). Paul then asserts that the offense of the cross would cease and he could avoid persecution were he to preach circumcision (5:11, lit., "still preach," εἰ περιτομὴν ἔτι κηρύσσω). This may be a reference to his pre-Christian days, although there is little evidence that Paul or any other Jews were engaged in an active mission to convert Gentiles to Judaism. Mussner however concludes that Paul presents an unreal case as if it were real, in order to point out the consequences it would have (*Galater*, 359, n. 112). Whatever Paul meant, it remains clear that if at sometime in his career as a Christian missionary to the nations he had urged circumcision on his converts, the competitors would have seized on it as evidence of inconsistency.

[86] If Paul thinks he is telling his audience something they do not know about circumcision and the obligation to live according to the Torah, perhaps he believes that the competing mission had followed a policy of gradualism: of telling converts only a little at a time. Given the fact that circumcision was the biggest obstacle to conversion, however, this seems unlikely.

[87] Although circumcision as a practice was not limited to the Jews in the first century C.E., it was enough of an identity marker that from a Jewish point of view the world could be divided into "the circumcised" and "the uncircumcised." This is reflected in the way this word pair is used in 2:7–9, 5:6 and 6:15, and could mean that in 2:12 those whom Peter fears are simply Jews, although the term there could refer instead to those within the church who urge circumcision on non-Jews. On the occurrence of circumcision in the first century C.E., see Meyer, *TWNT* 6:74–75. For an extensive examination of the OT, intertestamental, pagan and NT texts bearing on the subject, see Andreas Blaschke, *Beschneidung: Zeugnisse der Bibel und verwandte Texte* (TANZ 28; Tübingen, 1998).

law, ἐξ ἔργων νόμου, makes plain (2:16; 3:2). The law in question is that given at Sinai (3:17; cf. 4:24).

This is a soteriological matter for Paul, and apparently for his competitors as well. Underlying Paul's exegetical arguments in ch. 3 is the assumption that only children of Abraham are full covenant participants, and therefore the salvation community. This consideration may well have been introduced into the discussion by the competitors, and by this they meant those who were circumcised, as all descendants of Abraham were to be.[88] Paul grants the point of the importance of descent from Abraham, but reinterprets true descent christologically and pneumatologically. His Gentile audience has received the spirit (3:2); through Christ they have become not only children of Abraham but children of God (3:26–29). Connected with the idea of salvation is that of justification, of being righteous. The proximity of this to salvation is shown in that Paul interprets this christologically (2:16) as well.[89] His radical alternative, faith or works of law, shows that he categorically rejects a synergistic model.

Our attempts to understand the exact nature of the competing mission are frustrated by the nature of a letter as half of a conversation.[90] Paul is writing in response to a teaching that is so radically different from his own that he terms it "a different gospel, which is not another"

---

[88] This custom is recorded as being the sign of the covenant God made with Abraham (Gen 17:9–14). Not only are all male descendants of Abraham to be circumcised, but also all male children of any household servants, as well as any newly acquired slaves. Discussion of the suggestion that the competitors introduced this topic in Galatia in G. Walter Hansen, *Abraham in Galatians: Epistolary and Rhetorical Contexts* (JSNTSup 29; Sheffield, 1989), 167–74.

[89] Paul's use of δικαιόω and the related word group thus differs from that of Second Temple Judaism. For him, it is an absolute term that signifies being set in (covenantal) relationship with God. In Judaism, it is both a qualitative and quantitative term. Of those saved, some are said to have certain deeds counted for righteousness (cf. 3:6, in which Paul quotes Gen 15:6 LXX, ἐλογίσθη αὐτῷ εἰς δικαιοσύνην, but uses it in his characteristic understanding). Failure to observe this difference in usage has contributed to the view that Paul characterizes Judaism as a religion of self-salvation through performance of meritorious deeds. See Martyn, *Galatians*, 249–51, 263–75.

[90] Anderson, *Theory*, 102. Martyn, *Galatians*, 13, uses the metaphor of a drama; when we read the opening lines, it is as if we are coming in as the curtain is rising of the third or fourth act.

(Gal 1:6–7). We do not possess any writings of these opponents, nor do we have an answer from the Galatians to this letter of Paul. The most we can hope to do is to reconstruct the other position from Paul's refutation, taking into account the likelihood that our view of these competitors may be filtered by the fact that Paul's intention was not to write a calm disposition of the history of the theological positions involved.

On the basis of a study of indications in Galatians itself, John M. G. Barclay concludes that the following is certain or virtually certain about the competing mission: they were Christian; they wanted the Galatians to be circumcised and to observe at least some of the rest of the law, including its calendrical requirements; they brought into question the adequacy of Paul's gospel and his credentials as an apostle; and their arguments were attractive and persuasive for many Galatians Christians.[91]

Although Barclay had striven to approach the data with caution, not even this minimum of description has won complete approval. For instance, Witherington sees "no evidence that the agitators openly questioned Paul's apostolic status or his commission to preach to the Gentiles, nor . . . that the Galatians doubted Paul's apostolic office or commission."[92] As we have seen, Sabbatarians would question whether the competing mission urged calendrical requirements. Nevertheless, I will adopt Barclay's conclusions, with the exception of one point as noted below, as a working hypothesis. In particular, Paul's astonishment that his readers are hastily turning (ταχέως μετατίθεσθε) to a different gospel, qualified as a perversion of the gospel of Christ, is a certain indicator. The ambivalent characterization ("a different gospel, which is not another") leads us to conclude that these teachers, at least in their self-understanding, are Christian teachers.[93] As Becker observes, they do not call Christian baptism into question, otherwise the argumentation in 3:26–27 would make no sense. In addition, they combat Paul's Christol-

[91] "Mirror-Reading a Polemical Letter: Galatians as a Test Case," *JSNT* 31 (1987): 73–93, here 88.

[92] *Grace*, 25.

[93] Marcion, who placed an abbreviated and altered version of Galatians at the head of his Ἀποστολικόν, his collection of Paul's letters plus an edited gospel of Luke, believed that Galatians was an attack on Judaism, a view in which Tertullian concurs (*Marc.* 5.2).

ogy with one that brings law and Christ in unison (3:1–5:12).[94] Their program is not offered in place of belief in Jesus Christ, but as an extension of it.[95]

The reverse side of Barclay's affirmations about the competing mission is a number of proposals about it that he feels are incredible: that the competitors were Gnostics or gnosticizing to an appreciable degree; that they were libertines or played on the Galatians' "Hellenistic libertine aspirations"; that they were syncretists with cosmic or mystical notions about circumcision, the law or keeping festivals; that they were directly commissioned by the Jerusalem apostles; or that Paul was fighting against two distinct groups.[96]

Equally interesting is a list Barclay draws up of the points on which Paul and his competitors would have agreed: scripture, God's word, is now reaching its fulfilment through Christ; salvation is now available to Gentiles, in fulfilment of the promises to Abraham; the Spirit has been given to the people of God who believe in the Messiah; and God's people should abstain from idolatry and the passions of the flesh.[97]

There is much that we would like to know about the theology of the competing mission but cannot. Perhaps they shared Paul's conviction

[94] Galater, 81.

[95] Martyn, Galatians, 121.

[96] In contrast to Barclay, I see no reason why a circumcision-based, Torah-observant Christian mission could not also reflect notions on the cosmic significance of the law that we might consider syncretistic, as if the two were mutually exclusive. In particular, the introduction of a divinely ordained calendar, anchored in the movements of the heavenly bodies, lends itself to such as combination. "Da das Gesetz, mit der Weisheit identifiziert (Sir 24), als Schöpfungsmittlerin und Durchwalterin des Kosmos galt, muss man solche Sonderlehre nicht gleich für eine ausserjüdische Überfremdung halten" (Becker, Galater, 82). Note as well the widespread identification of Abraham as an astronomer/astrologer in intertestamental Judaism. His origin in the land of the Chaldees (Gen 11:31) served as the bridge, since the Chaldeans were noted for their study of the heavenly bodies. Some sources treat Abraham's departure from Ur of the Chaldees as his rejection of astronomy or as his going beyond it to the knowledge of God (Jub. 12:16–21; Josephus, Ant. 1.155–7; Philo, Abr. 69–71; cf. Migr. 177–87; QG 3:1). Others however treat the topic positively, and credit him with introducing it to other nations (Ps.-Eupolemus and Artapanus, in Eusebius, Praep. ev. 9.17–18). The Sibylline Oracles however reject the view that Abraham knew Chaldean astrology or astronomy (Sib. Or. 3.218–31).

[97] "Mirror-Reading," 89.

that the hour had arrived for the nations to be gathered, and were therefore engaged in their own mission to the nations, with the difference, of course, that these converts should become proselytes (become circumcised and live according to the Torah). Perhaps they did not, and were simply trying to repair the damage done by the fact that Paul was engaged in such a mission but failed to circumcise his converts. At any rate, they maintained that full participation in the salvation community is only available to Gentiles if they become proselytes (circumcised, Torah-observant; cf. Acts 15:1, 8).

The program of the competing mission was Christian—faith in Jesus Christ. This faith allowed for the remission of past sins, part of the baptism theology in common with all Christians of that time. This new state of purity permitted one to enter into a covenant relation with God, provided one took the steps prescribed in the Torah: circumcision, followed by faithful observance of the law. We view this position today through the filter of Paul—especially since his writings have entered the canon. It is helpful, though, to consider that the position of this other mission was carefully considered, and consistent with OT teaching.[98] The struggle lying behind Galatians was between varieties of Christianity, not between Christianity and Judaism as such. Paul's contribution to the discussion entered the canon. The view of the competing mission can only be reconstructed; it is otherwise a lost voice of the Christian dialogue.[99]

Further evidence for the plausibility of this reconstruction lies in second century sources. Ignatius of Antioch, writing ca. 110 to congregations in Asia Minor, is aware of Gentile believers attracted to Jewish practices, including Sabbath and circumcision. In his letter to the Magnesians, after exhorting to unity by upholding the authority of their bishop, he confronts the error of living according to Judaism, which he equates with a confession of not having received grace (*Magn.* 8.1).[100] For

---

[98] Martyn, *Issues*, 12–20.

[99] Hans Dieter Betz suggests that 2 Cor 6:14–7:1, widely recognized as a non-Pauline interpolation, is in fact an anti-Pauline fragment that would fit the opposing viewpoint in the incident of Antioch ("2 Cor 6:14–7:1: An Anti-Pauline Fragment?" *JBL* 92 [1973]: 88–108).

[100] κατὰ Ἰουδαϊσμὸν ζῶμεν, ὁμολογοῦμεν χάριν μὴ εἰληφέναι (ed. Fischer, 166).

Ignatius, questions of practice can reflect having received grace, which he also expresses as living according to Jesus Christ, which, he maintains, the prophets did (*Magn.* 8.2).[101] He points to those who had lived according to old practices, but had now come to new hope. This is demonstrated by the fact that they no longer observed the Sabbath, but lived according to the Lord's Day, on which our life rose through him and his death (*Magn.* 9.1–2).[102] From this we see not only the position that Sabbath observance is incompatible with "Christianity," as well as the information that some Christian Jews had abandoned Sabbath observance, but also that Gentile believers continued to "judaize," to adopt Jewish practices as part of their Christian faith (*Magn.* 10.3).[103] The "Judaism" against which Ignatius contrasts his "Christianity" includes however efforts to demonstrate Christian claims from the Scriptures of Israel (*Phld.* 8.2).[104] In response, Ignatius claims that it is

---

[101] οἱ γὰρ θεώτατοι προφῆται κατὰ Χριστὸν Ἰησοῦς ἔζησαν (ed. Fischer, 166).

[102] Εἰ οὖν οἱ ἐν παλαιοῖς πράγμασιν ἀναστραφέντες εἰς καινότητα ἐλπίδος ἦλθον, μηκέτι σαββατίζοντες, ἀλλὰ κατὰ κυριακὴν ζῶντες, ἐν ᾗ καὶ ἡ ζωὴ ἡμῶν ἀνέτειλεν δι᾽ αὐτοῦ καὶ τοῦ θανάτου αὐτοῦ (ed. Fischer, 166). The phrasing is elliptical and obscure. Those who once lived in ancient practices could be the prophets mentioned in *Magn.* 8, but are more likely Christian Jews who had abandoned Jewish practices, *pace* Richard B. Lewis, "Ignatius and the Lord's Day," *AUSS* 6 (1968):46–59. The word "day" in English is supplied from the sense of the passage. The only known Greek MS with the shorter recension adds ζωήν between κυριακὴν and ζῶντες to read "living according to the Lord's life." The critical editions correct this according to the Latin translation, which is based on a superior Greek MS (Fischer, *Die apostolischen Väter*, Darmstadt 1993, 139). The addition of ζωήν would not change the sense; the Lord's Day is emblematic of the Lord's life in the resurrection. This is not a reference to a different manner of Sabbath observance, *pace* the longer recension, which does contrast Sabbath observance in the Jewish manner (idleness) with a spiritual manner (meditation on the law). This reflects the later practice in the East of Sabbath commemoration *and* Sunday worship. The most likely referent for αὐτοῦ is κύριος, even though this appears in genitive.

[103] For Ignatius an absurdity: ἄτοπόν ἐστιν, Ἰησοῦν Χριστὸν λαλεῖν καὶ ἰουδαΐζειν (ed. Fischer, 168). Ignatius is the first to use the term χριστιανισμός, *Magn.* 10.1,3; *Rom.* 3.3; *Phld.* 6.1; William R. Schoedel, *Ignatius of Antioch* (Hermeneia; Philadelphia, 1985), 126.

[104] ἐπεὶ ἤκουσά τινων λεγόντων, ὅτι, ἐὰν μὴ ἐν τοῖς ἀρχείοις εὕρω, ἐν τῷ εὐαγγελίῳ οὐ πιστεύω (ed. Fischer, 200). "Gospel" for Ignatius is the oral tradition concerning Jesus, primarily his death and resurrection (Charles Thomas Brown, *The Gospel and Ignatius of Antioch* [Studies in Biblical Literature 12; New York, 2000]). On the ἀρχεῖα

better to hear Christianity from a man who is circumcised than Judaism from one who is uncircumcised.[105] Yet the connection Ignatius makes between using the scriptures and attraction to Jewish practices is an indirect confirmation of the point made above: the Torah-observant mission to the nations could make a strong scriptural case for their position. For all of Ignatius's appeals to unity, there was still a lively discussion within the Christian communities of Asia Minor more than a half century after Paul's letter to the Galatians, with one position held by uncircumcised Gentiles attracted to practices including Sabbath observance.[106]

In addition, the source underlying *Ps.-Clem.* Recognitions 1.27–71 reflects a Jewish Christian community that is faithful to the law and has a mission to Gentiles, yet is anti-Pauline (ch. 70).[107] The mission to the nations is necessary because some Jews failed to believe:

> But since it was necessary for the nations to be called in the place of those who remained unbelievers so that the number that was shown to Abraham might be filled, the saving proclamation of the kingdom of God was sent out into the whole world (1.42.1, Lat. [Jones, *Source*, 72]).

> Then the gospel will be proclaimed to the nations as a testimony to you, so that your unbelief might be judged on the basis of their belief (1.64.2, Lat. [Jones, *Source*, 99]).

Paul is not named, but is readily identified:

> that hostile person had received a commission from Caiaphas the high priest to persecute all who believed in Jesus, and to go to Damascus with his letters so that

as the OT, see Schoedel, *Ignatius*, 208.

[105] ἄμεινον γάρ ἐστιν παρὰ ἀνδρὸς περιτομὴν ἔχοντος Χριστιανισμὸν ἀκούειν, ἢ παρὰ ἀκροβύστου Ἰουδαϊσμόν (ed. Fischer, 198).

[106] Schoedel is correct to point out that Ignatius directs his comments in *Phld.* against scriptural interpretation, and those in *Magn.* to questions of practice, but he puts too fine a point on it when he suggests that the Philadelphian Judaizers, in contrast to the Magnesian, were more interested in the idea of Judaism than the practice (*Ignatius*, 200–3).

[107] From the growing literature on the Clementine corpus, see esp. F. Stanley Jones, *An Ancient Jewish Christian Source on the History of Christianity: Pseudo-Clementine Recognitions 1.27–71* (SBLTT 37/SBL Christian Apocrypha Series 2; Atlanta, 1995). Other examples of second-century Christian anti-Paulinism: *Ps.-Clem.* H 17:13–20; *Acts Pet. Paul*; *Ep. Pet.*

even there, when he had gained the help of the nonbelievers, he might bring destruction on the believers; but he was hastening particularly to Damascus because he believed that Peter had fled there (1.71.3–4, Lat. [Jones, *Source*,108]).

He is made responsible for the failure of the mission to the Jews:

> When the matter had reached the point that they should come and be baptized, a certain hostile person entered the temple with only a few others and began to shout and say, "What are you doing O Israelite men? Why should you be so easily duped? Why are you led headlong by the most miserable persons who have been deceived by a magician?" (1.70.1–2, Lat. [Jones, *Source*, 106]).

Further, it is he who pushed James to his death: "When in the meantime that hostile person had made his way to James, he pushed him from the highest flight of stairs" (1.70.8, Lat. [Jones, *Source*, 107]).

The source in question does not interact with Paul's letters and its criticism of the law, however, so it may reflect an abiding suspicion of Paul from his pre-calling activities prior to anything he wrote to the Galatians.[108] Nevertheless, it remains significant that this attitude is retained by Christian Jews a century later.

3.4.2 Paul's Position: Why Was It Controversial?

Not only the polemic of Galatians but also the narrative of Acts reflect tensions within the Christian community over the admission of non-circumcised, and therefore, non-Torah-observant Gentiles. Luke portrays proselytes—non-Jews who had adopted a Jewish life-style (see above, 2.3.2)—as constitutive of the church from its founding in Jerusalem (2:10) and crucial to its spread; this apparently occasioned no controversy. The account of Cornelius in Acts 10, however, reports the crossing of a boundary; although Paul is normally associated with the mission to the nations, it is Peter who facilitates Cornelius's entry into the Christian community in Luke's narrative. Cornelius is a Godfearer, not a proselyte, a sympathizer with Judaism but not a convert (10:2, 22). He and his household are baptized without being circumcised (10:48). This step is justified by his prior reception of the Spirit (10:47; 11:15–17). The prominence given in the narrative to the motifs of Peter's reluctance

---

[108] Gerd Lüdemann, *Paulus der Heidenapostel. 2: Antipaulinismus im frühen Christentum*, Göttingen, 1983, 246–7.

(10:14–15) and the opposition of other believers (11:1–2) underlines the controversial nature of this step. While the acceptance of a Godfearer and his household is not the same as initiating a mission to the nations, its role in the overall narrative of Acts as well as its placement between the calling of Paul (9:1–30) and his missionary activity (from 11:19 on) shows that Luke presents it as a step in the direction that the church will take in the future.

In one way, the practice of the synagogue is being repeated: Gentiles are not actively recruited, but are welcome to convert.[109] At the same time, the synagogue categories are transcended. This leaves Cornelius in an ambiguous situation: he has not been circumcised, but he (and his household) have been immersed, which normally followed circumcision. Is his status in the community analogous to his Godfearer-status in the synagogue, that of a welcome guest, or is he considered a full member? His receipt of the Spirit, associated by the believers with divine adoption and therefore participation in the salvation community, indicates the latter. Yet there is no discussion of his status vis-à-vis the Torah. One may assume that as a Godfearer he would have been sympathetic to its demands and practices, yet, not having been circumcised, he had undertaken no commitment to observe them. No mention is made in the narrative that his relation to the Torah had changed by becoming baptized.

At mid-point in the overall structure of Acts, ch. 15, the basis on which Gentiles could be included as joint heirs of salvation is defined; even those who had not previously become proselytes to Judaism were fully welcomed in Christian fellowship. James, the brother of the Lord, known for his loyalty to the Temple, and implicitly to all things Jewish, endorses the mission to the nations as the fulfillment of what the prophets saw in connection with the rebuilding of the Davidic tabernacle (15:17, cf. Amos 9:11–12). The gathering of the nations, a key feature of eschatological expectation (e.g., Isa 2:2; see above 2.32), could not fail to accompany the time that will culminate in "the restoration of all

---

[109] The prominent element of divine initiative must not be overlooked, but is never absent from conversion narratives, so there is no difference to the synagogue experience in this.

things" (Acts 3:21). To be determined was the basis on which common
fellowship would be possible. Four rules are given: "to abstain only from
things polluted by idols and from fornication and from whatever has
been strangled and from blood" (15:20). The principle by which these
four, and only these four, are selected is not mentioned. Apparently, they
relate to perceived ritual impurity of Gentiles, and possible Jewish
scruples about associating with them because of this. They are certainly
not the most important features either of Jewish or of Christian moral
teaching. Sabbath observance is not made an entrance requirement for
Gentiles, nor a condition for fellowship with Jewish members. Unclear
is the relation of the next verse, connected with γάρ, to the foregoing.
That Moses "in every city, for generations past, . . . has had those who
proclaim him, for he has been read aloud every Sabbath in the synagogues" (v. 21) is somehow the basis for the decision, or of the access of
the Gentiles to God's promises.[110]

The central character in the narrative by this point is Paul, firmly
embarked on his mission to the nations. Luke's portrayal of this mission
shows the pattern, to Israel first, then to the nations, recurring in every
new area that the apostle to the Gentiles enters.[111] "As was his custom"
(17:1), he first enters the local synagogue (as does Jesus at Nazareth,
Luke 4:16); his hearers divide sharply. After a period of time—Paul is
portrayed in Thessalonica, for instance, as teaching in this manner on
three consecutive Sabbaths (Acts 17:2)—he withdraws, or is cast out,
taking with him the nucleus of a new Jesus-believing synagogue.[112] Many
of those who go with him are "devout Greeks" (Acts 17:4), i.e.,

---

[110] This is the second use of this reasoning in Acts. In the course of his sermon in
Pisidian Antioch, Paul says: "Because the residents of Jerusalem and their leaders did not
recognize him or understand the words of the prophets that are read every Sabbath, they
fulfilled those words by condemning him" (13:27). The Sabbath is a day for public
reading of the law (v. 15) and the prophets.

[111] Express mention of the Sabbath or of teaching in a synagogue, or both, introduces
crucial phases of Paul's ministry: after his Damascus experience (9:20); upon his arrival
at Antioch Pisidia to initiate his missionary activity (13:14); and as his first action after
arriving in Europe (16:13). Additional mentions of entering the synagogue, without
express mention of the Sabbath, in 13:5, 14:1, and 17:10.

[112] Note the thrice-repeated saying "we are now turning to the Gentiles" (Acts 13:46;
see also 18:6, 28:28).

proselytes and Godfearers. In at least one case, they ask to meet with him "the next Sabbath" (13:42–44).[113]

This is hard to reconcile with Paul's self-presentation in his letters.[114] We have noted the two-stage schematization according to which Paul classifies the experience of his readers: they did not know God, then, in Christ, they became known by God (Gal 4:8–9; see 3.2.2, above). There is no intermediate stage that would correspond to visits to a synagogue. This can be explained as indicating that the congregations to which he wrote were located in a part of Galatia inhabited by few Jews, hence containing no synagogues, and that they represented an exception to the habitual strategy portrayed by Luke, a strategy that on the face of it appears to be eminently sensible.[115] But there is no indication that Paul

---

[113] While not expressly stated, this is suggested for Paul's lengthy stay in Corinth as well (18:4–18).

[114] The relation of Paul as depicted in Acts to Paul as known from his letters has been long noted and widely discussed. Scholarly opinion is divided on whether the differences are irreconcilable, thereby casting the believability of one author, usually taken to be Luke, in doubt, or significant yet understandable if Luke was a minor figure in the Pauline circle who traveled with him occasionally and was unfamiliar with his letters. The classic statements of the difference between the Paul of Acts and of the letters are Philipp Vielhauer, "Zum 'Paulinismus' der Apostelgeschichte," *EvT* 10 (1950–51): 1–15 and Ernst Haenchen, *Die Apostelgeschichte* (KEK 3; Göttingen, 1956), 109–14; 120–24. A recent critique and defense of close relation between the two is Stanley E. Porter, "The Paul of Acts and the Paul of the Letters: Some Common Conceptions and Misconceptions," in *The Paul of Acts: Essays in Literary Criticism, Rhetoric, and Theology* (WUNT 115; Tübingen, 1999), 187–206; cf. 172–86, in which he discusses the issue of Paul and the law in Acts. David C. Sim radically questions both accounts (*The Gospel of Matthew and Christian Judaism: The History and Social Setting of the Matthean Community* [SNTW; Edinburgh, 1998], 79–107).

[115] For the purpose of this investigation, it is not necessary to decide between the southern (*Provinzhypothese*) and northern Galatian (*Landschaftshypothese*) hypotheses (see Werner Georg Kümmel, *Einleitung in das Neue Testament*, 21st ed.; Heidelberg, 1983, 258–60, to which can be added Ben Witherington III, *Grace in Galatia: A Commentary on St. Paul's Letter to the Galatians* [Edinburgh, 1998], 2–8 [southern], and Martyn, *Galatians*, 15–17 [northern]). The northern view is stronger, in my judgment, but neither of the two insights one might hope to gain from this are conclusive. First, Paul divides the experience of his audience into two epochs, their pagan past and their present status as Christian believers (see below, 3.3.1). There is no evidence of Jewish inhabitants in northern Galatia, the highlands around Ancyra, in the first century. Therefore, knowledge of Jewish laws and customs would have come primarily

views the path of his Galatian readers as exceptional. Whether or not he operated according to the strategy Luke ascribes to him, in his own view, God was turning the nations to faith through him; before that, they had not known God. It is not denied that they may have come to know God in some way as respectful listeners in the synagogue; it is simply not addressed.

Not only does Luke show Paul entering the synagogue (on the Sabbath) as his first step in evangelizing a new city, his Paul is at pains to demonstrate his loyalty to Jewish observance. He shows his respect for the temple, on the advice of James and the elders of Jerusalem, by demonstrating that he was Torah-observant (21:24–26). He hurries to Jerusalem, even though it means foregoing a stop in the important missionary center of Ephesus, so as to arrive in time for the Day of Pentecost (20:16).[116] His defense before Festus is that he has offended in no point against the law of the Jews, the temple, nor Caesar (25:8).[117] Far from it, since the message he preaches is based on the law and the prophets, so that he continues to worship the God of his fathers (24:14). This is not implausible. From the letters, we know of the importance he places on a collection for the poor of Jerusalem (cf. e.g. Rom 15:25–28). Nevertheless, the last words attributed to him, spoken to leaders of the Jewish community at Rome, assert that Israel's rejection of the Gospel is a work of the Holy Spirit, foretold by the prophets, and that salvation now is sent to the nations, and they will hear it.

---

from Paul or from the competing mission. But this two-fold division of time could have been chosen by Paul to serve a polemic purpose. Second, if his audience were proposed primarily of ethnic Galatians, which would be more likely in the north than in the south, then his reference to their pre-Christian past might reflect a distinctively Celtic religion. This could have implications for various explanations of the "elements" they are said to have served. Yet the nature of Paul's description seems to owe more to stock Jewish views of paganism in general, and are not differentiated on the basis of special experience (Betz, *Galatians*, 213–5).

[116] Compare 18:21 in the Western text and in the Byzantine text tradition.

[117] The putative offense against the law of Caesar would be the propagation of a *religio illicita*. Luke characterizes the Christian church as a Jewish sect. It is a matter of debate whether this was solely apologetic, to fend off the charge of illegal activity, or whether Luke intend it to reflect on the self-understanding of Christians in his days.

We have, then, a complex picture of Paul's relation to Judaism. He does not reject it, it rejects him. This corresponds to the experience of Jesus in the first part of Luke's two-part work. Luke emphasizes that Jesus is the hope of Israel; the birth narrative he composes to open his gospel is redolent with echoes of the Jewish scriptures in their Greek translation. It appears as if Luke makes a careful distinction: Jews and their leaders are guilty of putting to death the Messiah, the Son of God; Judaism has not however become thereby invalid. In fact, had the leaders understood their own scriptures, "read every Sabbath day," they would not have made this grievous error (Acts 13:27).

There seem to have been a number of interrelated concerns. One was soteriological: could a person even be a member of the salvation community without accepting the sign of the covenant, circumcision, thus taking on the obligation to live according to the Torah? Both Acts and Galatians, despite the difficulties of reconciling the two accounts, attest that this was answered in the affirmative, but not without controversy (Acts 15:1–29; Gal 2:1–10). There is no need to assume that those who would have answered negatively were categorically opposed to the presence of such Gentiles in the congregation. Their synagogue experience would have made this seem normal, but would have also led them to consider these non-circumcised Gentiles sympathetic guests, not members. Although not stated in these terms, the agreement reached by Paul and the pillar apostles was in effect a decision not to perpetuate the synagogue distinction proselyte/Godfearer in the congregation.

Paul reports that the agreement resulted from the recognition by the pillar apostles that Paul had been entrusted with "the gospel of uncircumcision," as Peter had been with "the gospel of circumcision," ὁ εὐαγγέλιον τῆς ἀκροβυστίας καθὼς Πέτρος τῆς περιτομῆς (2:7). This genitive construction does not refer to the content of the gospel, as if Peter preached circumcision, whereas Paul preached uncircumcision. Instead, as v. 9 makes clear, each had his own target group. Unclear, though, is whether Luke envisions this distinction geographically or ethnically. The former alternative makes little sense, since the Jews lived throughout the Roman empire, as well as beyond its boundaries. Therefore we can assume that the distinction was meant ethnically. This raises a further question, however: how discrete were the two missions to be? If Peter arrived at a synagogue to preach to the circumcision, did he ask the Godfearers to leave? Similarly, the most sensible starting point for Paul, in his attempt to reach uncircumcised Gentiles with the gospel, would be those who already had some knowledge of the God of Israel, in other words, those with some contact with the synagogue. What happened to those who responded to the message? Were they then segregated into circumcision and uncircumcision congregations? It may be from the perspective of Jerusalem, this was not important enough to worry about. But in a large Hellenistic city with a sizable Jewish diaspora community, such as Antioch, this was bound to come up.

This consideration leads to the second issue, that of common table fellowship (see 2.3.2, above). It was on this issue that Jewish and Christian concerns collided in an irreconcilable way, since their opposing positions were constitutive for the identity of each community. For Jews, the observance of food laws and other matters of purity was emblematic of their unique status among the nations. Jews, especially in the Diaspora, did not shun contact with Gentiles in matters such as table fellowship, but they displayed scruples, as shown by the later existence of Talmudic instructions to regulate such situations.[118] At the same time, the practice of common table fellowship among believers was an issue that was vitally important for the Christian community.[119] The common meal had become an identity marker for Christians, a practice through which their shared identity was expressed and reinforced. It had what we would call, perhaps with a slight anachronism, eucharistic significance.[120] For this reason, the question of whether circumcised, Torah-obedient, and non-circumcised, non-Torah-obedient Christians could share a common table

---

[118] Cf. Acts 10:28; 11:3; Gal 2:12. It is undeniable that separation was urged and practiced by significant numbers of Jews. Older treatments portray this however as the dominant tendency (e.g., Bousset, *Religion*, 86–96; cf., more recently, J. N. Sevenster, *The Roots of Anti-Semitism in the Ancient World* [Leiden 1975], 89–144). If one never eats with a Gentile, though, one needs no guidelines to regulate it.

[119] This does not mean that one community was more *inclusive* than the other. For both, it was a matter of who was *in* and who was *out* (cf. *Did.* 9:5, which prescribes that only the baptized are to share in the eucharistic cup).

[120] The use of εὐχαριστία to refer to the celebration of the Lord's Supper was however an early development (*Did.* 9:1, 5; Ign. *Eph.* 13:1; Ign. *Phld.* 4; Ign. *Smyrn.* 8:1; cf. τὸ ποτήριον τῆς εὐχαριστιας at 1 Cor 10:16 in F, G, 365).

could not be a matter of indifference. But on what basis would the
fellowship take place? As we have seen, Luke narrates a four-point
consensus promulgated by James (Acts 15:19–20; cf. 29). These are
commonly understood as a minimum requirement on the part of Gentile
believers to enable Jewish believers to engage in full fellowship with them
without compromising their consciences; doubts that this decree was
promulgated by James seem justified.[121] It is especially difficult to picture
Paul agreeing to it; based on his reaction in Gal 2, we gather that he
would have viewed this as tantamount to compelling the Gentiles to
judaize (2:14). His speech to Peter revolves around the question: will this
full fellowship be on the basis of Gentiles living as Jews, or Jews taking
a step—compromising their concept of ritual purity—that, in effect,
meant they were living as Gentiles?[122]

A third issue was that, if Gentiles were not obligated to obey the
Torah and still be heirs of salvation, what implication did this have for
Jewish believers? Acts 20:20–21 reports an accusation that Paul taught
diaspora Jews not to circumcise their infant boys or observe the Torah.
While it is unlikely that Paul did teach this, his clear assertion that
salvation could not be achieved by observance of the Torah does raise
the question of the role the Torah should play in the life of Jewish
believers in Christ. At the very least, as we have seen, Paul expected
Jewish believers in mixed congregations to lay aside their scruples over
purity issues in the interest of full table fellowship. The accusation Luke
reports appears then to be not totally ungrounded and reflects uncertainty over this question.

---

[121] Philip Francis Esler, *Community and Gospel in Luke-Acts: The Social and
Political Motivations of Lucan Theology* (SNTSMS 57; Cambridge, 1987), 97–99; Sim,
Gospel, 90–91.

[122] Howard points out that there is no explicit mention that either Peter or Paul had
given up Jewish food laws in the account of the incident at Antioch. The issue is that
Jews ate with Gentiles, not *what* they ate (*Crisis*, xix). While this observation is correct
as far as it goes, it leaves us with the question what Paul meant when he said that Peter
conducted himself as a Gentile, ὑπάρχων ἐθνικῶς (2:14). Jews ate with Gentiles in the
diaspora (Howard, *Crisis*, xix–xx; Fredriksen, "Judaism, the Circumcision of Gentiles,
and Apocalyptic Hope: Another Look at Galatians 1 and 2," *JTS* 42 [1991]: 532–64,
here 554). There is no suggestion that this constituted living as a Gentile.

A fourth possible source of tension is expressed in Fredriksen's suggestion that the opposition to Paul then caused by the question of whether it was appropriate to engage in a mass mission (see 2.3.3, above). Fredriksen sees a greater degree of continuity between Paul and Second Temple Judaism in the matter of how the nations would serve the God of Israel in the age to come, but fails to demonstrate this, for Paul not only resisted circumcision—those saved of the nations are saved as Gentiles—but also the imposition of Torah-observance.

Is it possible to identify which of this these four questions was foremost in the minds of the competing mission?[123] The apocalyptic component in Paul's thinking is widely recognized.[124] He was convinced that the turning point in human affairs had arrived with the coming of Jesus Christ. He seems to have rearranged chronology however: the gathering of the full number of the Gentiles (through his ministry) would occur in the brief interval between the coming of the son of God and his parousia, his return.[125] This gathering would precede, and provoke, the salvation of Israel (Rom 11:11–14). The insistence that the Gentiles not become circumcised, not become Jews, meant that for Paul that the salvation community, both the age to come and in the church in this age, would contain both Jews and Gentiles. As Blaschke has noted, Paul was an innovator in this. Paul categorically rejects circumcision, and thereby its commitment to the (rest of) the law, for "his" Gentile Christians, yet places them nonetheless soteriologically and ecclesiologically on an equal footing with "Israel." Paul's position can not be explained on the basis of the Godfearer model. Nor is it a necessary conclusion from his Damascus experience, from the Jesus tradition, from Hellenist Jewish

---

[123] Howard believes that the competing mission saw Paul as an ally, being unaware that he preached non-circumcision since he had only recently revealed this fact to the pillars in Jerusalem, and news of this had not become generally known (*Crisis* 8–9, 34–45). There are two difficulties with this view: (1) Paul had been an active Christian missionary for roughly fifteen years by this time. Did no one know he had not circumcised Gentile converts? (2) If the crisis in Galatia was simply the result of a misunderstanding on the part of the competitors, we are at a loss to explain the vehemence of Paul's response.

[124] E.g. Martyn, *Galatians*, 97–105.

[125] Sanders, *Paul*, 172.

Christianity, nor from the literature of the OT or intertestamental Judaism. His dual insistence that the Gentile believers not be circumcised yet at the same time be accepted in full membership was without precedent.[126] Therefore, this is the most likely reason for the opposition of the competing mission. His opposition to Peter at Antioch shows however that this did not, in his mind, take the form of two churches, one circumcised, one not. There would be only one salvation community, and therefore only one church. Its unity would not be achieved by the Gentiles becoming Jews, however, and therefore ceasing to be Gentiles. Rather, the unity was that of a new creation.

The elements of Paul's mission can be thus summarized:

- The eschatological ingathering of the nations was taking place in his ministry.
- It was enough for the nations to worship the God of Israel, especially as revealed as the father by the coming of the son, Jesus Christ.
- This worship must be exclusive. It meant a rejection of polytheism and the sexual immorality associated with it as Jews perceived it.[127]
- These Gentile believers were not to become Jews (circumcised, Torah-obedient).
- At the same time, they were full participants in the salvation community.

Paul's view, rooted in the experience of the synagogue throughout the diaspora, in effect weighed some prophecies over others, such as those that speak of the nations taking part in Sabbath and pilgrim festivals, or accepting restrictions in the matter of foods.

It could well be that Paul's position is adequately explained by the common Jewish opinion of the time that Gentiles were not expected to fulfil the demands of the Torah and that this explains the origin of his mission as well as its acceptance by the "pillars" at Jerusalem. As long as they acknowledged the supremacy of Israel's God, the Gentiles would

---

[126] *Beschneidung*, 487–90.

[127] To this extent, Paul was in accord with the apostolic decree, even though he differed on the consumption of meat offered to idols, holding that one only need refuse it to avoid offending the conscience of another, 1 Cor 8:4–13; 10:25–32.

not lose "their part" in the world to come—however indeterminate that part remained. In this case, Paul's self-understanding as an instrument in the eschatological project of the universal acknowledgment of God's sovereignty sums up his mission. Yet we may question whether this is indeed all there is, given the sharpness of the polemic he carried on with the maximalists—those who insisted on full observance. Just as approaches from the social sciences have arisen to supplement NT scholarship because traditional historical criticism had seemed to consider Paul and other early Christians only as thinkers, so we are now confronted with an opposite danger: that his theological achievement is undervalued. Not only his, but that of his competitors. In a sense, the maximalists were early systematizers. They shared the conviction that the coming of the Messiah had a meaning for the nations, not exclusively for Israel; they were not content with the vagueness of the "part" Gentiles could attain in the world to come. The negative connotation the inaccurate, but commonly-used term *judaizers* awakens may obscure the possibility that they wished to extend the full benefits of salvation to all.[128] They simply sought to define the basis on which this could occur. Galatians therefore not only bears record to Paul's uncompromising position, it also gives us tantalizing hints of another Christian position, one that represented a different attempt to rethink the questions of law,

---

[128] The verb *judaize* (used in the NT only in Gal 2:14) refers to the adoption of a Jewish way of life. It was used in two ways at the time: either the actual conversion to Judaism, above all in accepting circumcision, or a sympathy with Judaism leading to the takeover—partial or total—of Jewish customs (W. Gutbrod, "Ἰσραήλ κτλ.," *TWNT* 3:356–94, here 385). To judaize then would reflect a sliding scale of sympathy with or adoption of Jewish customs, with circumcision as the culmination (Dunn, "Incident," 149, and Cohen, *Beginnings*, 175–97). The term did not refer to those who might encourage such a step. The common designation of Paul's competitors in Galatia as judaizers is incorrect and misleading. This usage goes back to Marcion (Adamantius, *Dial.* 2, PG 11:1784). Ferdinand Christian Baur's characterization as "judaisirende Gegner" or "judaisirende Irrlehrer" exercises influence to the present ("Die Christuspartei in der korinthischen Gemeinde, der Gegensatz des petrinischen und paulinischen Christenthms in der ältesten Kirche, der Apostel Petrus in Rom," 1831, repr. in *Historisch-kritische Untersuchungen zum Neuen Testament*, vol. 1 of *Ausgewählte Werke in Einzelausgaben* [ed. Klaus Scholder; Stuttgart-Bad Cannstatt, 1963], 1–146, here 47–48). A recent example of the depiction of the competitors as "Judaisten" is Becker, *Galater*, 12–14, 81–83.

covenant and the nations in the light of the coming of the Messiah. That Paul, followed by mainstream Christianity, rejected this should not blind us to the theological achievement that such an attempt would have represented.

3.4.3 Days in the Overall Context of Paul's Theology

The fate of Sabbath practice in the first century church can best be examined in its relation to the various forms of Christian proclamation. Since Paul's was a major voice in that proclamation, we need to see how Paul understood the gospel he preached. His self-understanding as apostle, called to preach Jesus, the Son of God, to the nations (Gal 1:16), means that we may consider his views on any other topic as subordinate to that gospel, and that we may examine them in their relation to that gospel. Our sources for understanding Paul's proclamation are primarily the seven generally accepted Pauline letters and secondarily the reception of Paul in earliest Christianity as demonstrated by the Deuteropauline letters and the book of Acts.

The examination of the letter to the Galatians has shown that Paul understood the question of whether or not to be circumcised as one of whether or not to come under the obligation of observing the whole law, the Torah. At key points in his argumentation, he brings in two concrete points of Torah-observance, purity laws (probably including food laws) and days. Although Paul does not present these topics systematically, *de facto* he has included the three main markers of Jewish identity in the Roman-Hellenistic world, if we can judge by those aspects of Jewish faith and practice that were singled out for pagan criticism.[129] For this reason, it is appropriate to view Paul's question to Peter, Why do you compel the

[129] Menachem Stern, "The Jews in Greek and Latin Literature," in *The Jewish People in the First Century: Historical Geography, Political History, Social, Cultural and Religious Life and Institutions* (ed. S. Safrai and M. Stern; Assen 1974), 1/2:1101–59, here 1150–59. Cf. the items singled out and grouped together in the earliest preserved Christian apology: Sabbaths, new moons, Passover, the great fast (probably the day of Atonement), fast, circumcision, and foods (Aristides, *Apol.* 14). Viewed from within Judaism, the identity-forming elements could be expressed more generally (Torah and temple); in a situation of cultural conflict, circumcision, food laws, Sabbath and yearly festivals would be expressly mentioned (2 Macc 6:6, 10–11, 18).

Gentiles to judaize? (2:14) as the *leitmotiv* of the letter, and of Paul's answer to the competing mission in Galatia.

Having seen that Paul included the matter of days, implicitly including the Sabbath, in the process of engaging the position of his competitors, it is now important to ask whether this opposition to Sabbath observance is consistent with Paul's theology. After all, did he not urge the Romans to exercise tolerance in the matter of days (Rom 14:5–6)?

In order to adequately answer this question, it is necessary to ask in what context Paul decries the scrupulous observance of days. When we have answered this, we will see what, in his view, was at stake. Shortly before the passage we have investigated is a sentence that Martyn calls the theological center of the letter, containing nearly all of the letter's major motifs, relating them to one another in such a way as to state the good news of Paul's letter to the Galatians: "So with us; while we were minors, we were enslaved to the elemental spirits of the world. But when the fullness of time had come, God sent his Son, born of a woman, born under the law, in order to redeem those who were under the law, so that we might receive adoption as children" (4:3–5).[130]

The observance of the Sabbath, then, was among those things that were characteristic for Paul of a time of minority. In preparing this assertion, he has described the time of the law as one of being under the care or authority of a παιδαγόγος. This assertion, of itself, would not have been surprising for a Torah-observant person. The surprise comes in the conclusion that he draws from this metaphor: that this state is only valid for a time of minority, and that in the normal course of events it will end. Not even the OT expectation of a new covenant foresaw this. Jeremiah 31:31–33, which spoke of the covenant being irrevocably broken, thereby making a "new" covenant necessary, described the "new" as a change in location of the law—from tablets of stone to the mind and heart.[131] The law was the constant, the point of continuity; there was no

---

[130] *Galatians*, 388.

[131] On the brokenness of the first covenant, see Walter Gross, "Erneuerter oder Neuer Bund? Wortlaut und Aussageintention in Jer 31,31-34," in: *Bund und Tora: Zur theologische Begriffsgeschichte in alttestamentlicher, frühjüdischer und urchristlicher Tradition* (WUNT 29; ed. F. Avemarie and H. Lichtenberger; Tübingen, 1996), 41–66, here 52–56.

expectation of the Torah being thereby superceded. Yet we have seen in our discussion so far that this is exactly what Paul sees as having happened.[132] To what degree was this view prepared by indications in the OT, and to what extent was this a new view?

There are two ways in which Paul's position in Galatians is understood within his overall theology.[133] One, which is a continuation of mainstream interpretation, at least since Luther, is that Paul came to a radically new understanding of human existence, and therefore the law, at the time of his calling.[134] It can be exemplified by the writings of Rudolf Bultmann.[135]

Bultmann's approach is anthropological, with human experience divided into two parts by the revelation of πίστις.[136] Part one of his treatment is devoted to humanity before this revelation. After a discussion of key anthropological terms as understood by Paul, Bultmann treats the topics flesh, sin and the world. He then turns to humanity under πίστις, arranged according to a four-fold structure: δικαιοσύνη θεοῦ, the righteousness, or justice of God, χάρις, grace, πίστις, faith, and ἐλευθερία, freedom. This approach has the effect of viewing salvation from the perspective of the dilemma of human existence. Speaking for this structure is the fact that it corresponds roughly to the flow of Paul's argumentation in his letters, especially Romans.[137]

[132] In a less polemic situation, however, Paul would deny that his teaching was in contradiction to Jer 31:33; it was precisely κατὰ τὸν ἔσω ἄνθροπον that he was in joyful agreement with the law of God (Rom 7:22). This does not change the fact that in Galatians he wrote as if the time of the law had ended (Gal 3:23–25) and highlights the difficulty of formulating a coherent "Pauline" teaching on the law.

[133] An exhaustive survey of the discussion of the question of Paul and the law is not possible within the space limits of the present investigation. Overview of recent publications in Calvin Roetzel, "Paul and the Law: Whence and Whither?" *CurBS* 3 (1995):249-75.

[134] An important element of this interpretation is a perceived congruence in the respective situations of Paul and Luther (Ebeling, *Wahrheit*, viii).

[135] Bultmann, *Theologie*, 187–353.

[136] This observation must be relativized by Bultmann's famous equation of Pauline theology and anthropology (*Theologie*, 192; cf. Ebeling: "Dass es ihm [Paulus] um das Evangelium geht und dass es ihm um Menschen geht, ist ein und dasselbe" (*Wahrheit*, 307).

[137] Interestingly, Dunn, though he can be reckoned among the proponents of the

In Bultmann's treatment, the law is subordinated as the final topic in the discussion of human existence pre-faith. Yet he notes the ambivalence in Paul's statements. Though expressed in the Torah of the OT, it is the concrete demand of God on all humanity (Rom 2:14–15). While "radikal abgetan," radically abolished, for the believer, it was given for the purpose of being fulfilled and leading to life (Rom 7:10).[138] Indeed, Paul speaks of it as holy, righteous, and good (Rom 7:12), and spiritual (Rom 7:14). For Bultmann, Paul goes beyond saying that no one *can* attain salvation by fulfilling the law to saying that no one *should* (264). Paul presents works of the law and faith in Christ as mutually exclusive alternatives (Gal 2:16). His decisive thesis is: τέλος γὰρ νόμου Χριστὸς εἰς δικαιοσύνεν παντὶ τῷ πιστεύοντι (Rom 10:4). This is so not simply because striving to gain salvation by fulfilling the law not just leads to sin, it *is* sin (265). The meaning of the law in the history of salvation is to lead humanity to sin; not only in that it provokes us to disobey, but in that it offers us the ultimate possibility: the perversion of the law as a means for establishing our own righteousness.

> Sein Vorwurf gegen Juden und Judaisten ist nicht der: der Gesetzesweg ist deshalb falsch, weil er infolge der Übertretungen nicht zum Ziele führt, sondern weil seine Richtung eine verkehrte ist, weil es der Weg ist, der zur ἰδία δικαιοσύνη führen soll (Rm 10,3; vgl. Phl 3,9). Nicht allein und nicht erst die bösen Taten machen den Menschen verwerflich vor Gott; sondern schon die Absicht, durch Gesetzeserfüllung vor Gott gerecht zu werden, sein καύχημα zu haben, ist Sünde (268).

While this perversion of the law applies in principle to all of humanity, Bultmann sees it as the special problem of those to whom the law had been given, calling the effort to establish one's own righteousness through works the "Jewish madness" [den jüdischen Wahn].[139] The kerygma proclaimed by the Hellenistic community with which Paul first

New Perspective, organizes his *Theology* along a similar, Romans-based outline.

[138] *Theologie*, 262. Subsequent page references will be given in parentheses in the main text, unless there is a comment to be made in a footnote.

[139] *Theologie*, 427. Bultmann was by no means the first to describe Second Temple Judaism in these terms; cf. the volume his replaced in the earlier Grundriss der theologischen Wissenschaften series, Heinrich Weinel, *Biblische Theologie des Neuen Testaments: Die Religion Jesu und des Urchristentums* (3d ed.; Tübingen, 1921), 270.

came in contact was not only that Jesus had been resurrected and was the promised Messiah, but also called the law into question. Therefore, to accept this message meant recognition "im Kreuz Christi das Urteil Gottes über sein bisheriges Selbstverständnis," which Bultmann explicates as the condemnation of the Jewish effort to achieve righteousness through the fulfilment of the law (189).

For the purpose of this investigation it is important to recall that Bultmann's comments are directed toward the entire law. Paul, he notes, does not differentiate between the ritual and moral law (260). Nevertheless, apart from Galatians, where he had occasion to speak of the ritual law, it appears that Paul generally has the law's moral demands in mind. This is the case both when he speaks of God's enduring demand on humanity, as well as the perversion of the law in a boastful effort to earn salvation by meritorious works. The difference is not in the content of the law. What has changed is that faith in Christ frees us to see that the law has led to death and to accept salvation as grace, as a gift. For those who have had this change of mind, the law appears as what it was always intended to be: God's gracious gift (269).

We are left with a paradox: Paul's teaching against the "works of law," the fulfilment of the Torah, was occasioned by Galatian adoption of the Torah, as evidenced by willingness to accept circumcision and observe the Hebrew calendar with its holy days. Before the letter ends, he writes that the law of Christ (Gal 6:2) will be fulfilled out of love by those who have faith in Christ. It is *ritual* matters that have elicited from Paul a fundamental teaching about the entire law: he does not say that only these ritual matters have been superceded by the coming of Christ. Nevertheless, there is no rehabilitation of these ritual matters in the letter. Even his other letters, where he does not write polemically about the law, they are matters of indifference (1 Cor 7:19; Rom 14:1–5).

In keeping with Bultmann's anthropological approach, justification by faith is understood as the solution to the problem of individual sin, including the sin of boasting in one's righteous achievement, and placed firmly in the middle of Paul's theology. In this Bultmann has been widely followed, notably by Ernst Käsemann.[140] Noting however that justifica

---

[140] Note however that Käsemann, though generally critical of one of the first

tion by faith only plays a central role in Galatians and Romans, Becker modifies this and sees Paul's central insight as God's gracious acceptance of sinners apart from their performance. This underlies three stages that Becker then detects in Paul that are characterized by three concrete expressions of this theme: election (1 Thessalonians), the theology of the cross (1 Corinthians) and justification through faith (Romans).[141] Others would say that justification through faith is the constant, but that it required the polemical situation of Galatians to bring Paul to write clearly about it.

Set against this is a second, revisionist position, that of the New Perspective, which can be exemplified by E. P. Sanders.[142] Adherents of this position would see Paul's self-understanding defined more by his calling than his theology or his anthropology. He had been called to gather the nations as a fulfilment of many prophecies.[143] Sanders dissents from one of the fundamental assumptions underlying the conventional view, the portrayal of Paul in opposition to a Judaism that is understood as a system of earning salvation by meritorious works.[144] This leads to a key difference in his understanding of Paul's teaching when compared with that of Bultmann. Sanders understands Rom 10:2–3 and Phil 3:9 as referring to pride in corporate possession of the Torah in contrast to the nations, rather than boasting in individual meritorious achievement (140). Finally, Sanders contends that the use of a Romans-based structure to present Paul's theology obscures the process by which Paul arrived at

expressions of the New Perspective (Krister Stendahl, "The Apostle Paul and the Introspective Conscience of the West," 1963, repr. in *Paul among the Jews and the Gentiles*, 78–96), concedes that Stendahl and his friends are correct to protest against "die individualistische Verkürzung der christlichen Botschaft" ("Rechtfertigung und Heilsgeschichte im Römerbrief," in *Paulinische Perspektiven* [2d ed.; Tübingen, 1972], 108–39, here 132).

[141] *Paulus*, 294–304.

[142] *Paul, the Law, and the Jewish People* (Philadelphia, 1983). Page references will be given in the text in parentheses.

[143] Stendahl understands this as the content of the revelation to Paul (*Paul*, 7–9, cf. Gal 1:16).

[144] His refutation of this picture is documented at length in *Paul and Palestinian Judaism: A Comparison of Patterns of Religion* (Philadelphia, 1977). In this work, he presented the concept of *covenantal nomism* (summary: 422–3).

his theological insights. To begin with the existential dilemma of humanity can make it seem as if Paul himself had been struggling with this problem prior to his call on the road to Damascus.[145] The dramatic turnaround in Paul's life was occasioned by the revelation of Jesus, the crucified one, as resurrected (125). This led him to the conviction of humanity's universal sinfulness and the inability of the law to save. As Sanders puts it, the answer led to the question (35). Therefore, although the acceptance of the kerygma as he had heard it preached by the Hellenistic congregation meant the simultaneous acceptance of their mission to the nations (cf. Gal 1:15–16), the implications this had for the law were the result of his theological homework afterward (152).[146]

Sanders deals with the ambivalence that Bultmann noted in Paul's statements about the law and seeks to explain it. He concludes that "there is no single unity which adequately accounts for every statement about the law." This is not inconsistency, though: "Paul held a limited number of basic convictions which, when applied to different problems, led him to say different things about the law" (147). The different problems, to use Sanders's terminology, are those of *getting in* and *staying in*.[147] Although he uses different terminology, we find in Sanders a correspondence to the paradox we noted in Bultmann. He credits Paul with two teachings on the law and the Gentiles. On the one hand, it must not be required of them (or of Jews for that matter) as an entrance requirement. The law does not justify, or in Sanders's term, *righteous*,

---

[145] This understanding of Paul's state of mind before his Damascus experience is also refuted by Bultmann (*Theologie*, 189).

[146] Without reference to Sanders, Eckstein reaches a similar conclusion: "So entscheidet sich für Paulus an der Person des Gekreuzigten und Auferstandenen, wie die Bedeutung der Sinai-Tora zu bestimmen ist—und nicht umgekehrt. . . . Die Frage: 'was ist und soll demnach das Gesetz?' (Gal 3,19) ergibt sich also für den Pharisäer Paulus infolge seiner Christuserkenntnis unmittelbar—und nicht erst im Laufe der Auseinandersetzung mit den judaistischen Gegner" (*Verheissung*, 254).

[147] This terminology has been targeted for much of the criticism directed against Sanders. When he repeatedly asserts that justification by faith applies to entry, and that other topics, such as judgment by works, are connected with behavior after entry, it has the negative effect of obscuring the fact that justification is a soteriological term, even though Paul prefers to speak of salvation as a future event. Sanders himself qualifies his slogan-like pair of alternatives, though this is often overlooked (159).

only Christ's death does. On the other, all those in the salvation community must live according to the will of God. Paul seems to have thought of that will in terms of the Torah, but in the case of the Gentiles, he opposed, in addition to circumcision (an entrance requirement), the Sabbath and the food laws. What these three things have in common is that they were identity markers of Judaism. Gentiles were to be saved as Gentiles; this overrode any systematic concerns.

Sanders's correction of the conventional view of Judaism is valuable. His understanding of boasting in the works of the law as pride in the fact that the Torah had been given to Israel and not to the nations is convincing. It makes sense of how Paul could speak of all humanity as having been under the law; it has been made especially fruitful, as we have seen, by Martyn in his proposed solution to the difficult assertion that the law is a form of the στοιχεῖα τοῦ κόσμου (above, 3.2.2).[148] This does not however automatically disqualify Bultmann's insights of how possession of the Torah can lead to confidence in one's achievement. When another exponent of the New Perspective, Heikki Räisänen, writes that in reading Bultmann, "one gets the impression that zeal for the law is more damaging than the transgression," this overlooks a sense in which Bultmann has recognized something fundamental about human nature, as well as the critical hermeneutical potential of the cross (1 Cor 1:18–31).[149] Therefore, while Sanders has provided a sounder exegesis of Paul's reference to the works of law in Galatians, as well as Paul's references to boasting in the law in Phil 3:9 and Rom 10:2–3, the Luther-Bultmann tradition is an appropriate relecture of Paul, as long as it is not set against "Jewish madness" but against a recurring problem of *homo religiosus*.

The New Perspective is correct to point out that it is not proven, but simply assumed, that the pre-Pauline Hellenistic congregations had forsaken the law. Therefore, it is not necessary that the end of the law for

---

[148] Rom 2:14–15 cannot be used here to show that the Gentiles were under an *obligation* to keep the law, the other possible meaning of being *under* the law. The ἔργον τοῦ νόμου written in their hearts certainly did not include the very practices—circumcision, ritual purity, calendrics—that Paul rejects for them in Galatians.

[149] Heikki Räisänen, *Paul and the Law* (Tübingen 1983; repr. Philadelphia 1986), 169.

salvation came to Paul as part of the revelation on the road to Damascus, but as a result of his reflection on that experience. Nevertheless, when Paul reports on his life immediately prior to his calling, he places statements about his zeal for the law and his persecution of the church side by side (Gal 1:13–14). There must have been some connection in his mind. This corresponds to a failure on the part of the New Perspective to adequately take into account Paul's view of the law in Galatians. Something has clearly happened to the law in it. The time of its guardianship over the Jews has ended with the coming of Christ. Its power is a power to curse (3:13); it could not give life (3:21). It is arrayed with negative powers such as sin and the elements of the cosmos.[150] The Gospel as Paul understands it means justification through faith in Jesus Christ rather than through works of the law. Not only for the nations, but for all, there is one avenue. He characterizes the message of his competitors as a non-Gospel (1:6). It is something other than Paul's gospel, and irreconcilable with it. This accounts for the vehemence of his writing and the urgency of his argumentation.

Adherents of the New Perspective generally agree that justification is important in Paul's thought, but deny that it was central.[151] In this view, justification by faith is understood as Paul's answer to the specific question of the relationship of Jews and Gentiles. This would explain its concentration in the two letters that dealt with this problem. On this reading, chs. 9–11 are seen as the heart of Romans, rather than chs. 3 or 7.[152]

Whichever of these two positions more adequately expresses Paul's thinking, the result for the question of the Sabbath is the same. We have found that Paul's attack is not only on the demand of "circumcision," but of circumcision as the entrance gate to a whole way of life in conformity to the Torah. The Sabbath is included in this way of life, and is clearly included in the days of 4:10. Therefore, as far as Paul is concerned, the

---

[150] Martyn, *Galatians*, 373.
[151] While some (e.g., Sanders) would without hesitation subscribe to Albert Schweitzer's conclusion that justification is merely a subsidiary crater in the landscape of Paul's thought, others (e.g., Dunn) strive to harmonize the results of the New Perspective with a view that retains the importance of justification.
[152] Stendahl, *Paul*, 4.

issue of whether Gentile converts needed to keep the Sabbath was already settled, prior to the visit of Peter to Antioch.

Although Paul in other contexts could speak very positively of the law (Rom 7:12, 14) and even urge tolerance in questions of days (Rom 14:5–6),[153] we see here where Paul drew the line: whenever the message of faith in Christ was combined with a teaching that Gentiles must take on observance of the Torah, whether as a condition of salvation or to be fully accepted into Christian fellowship, then he did not tolerate it. As a result, we find the proclamation of the gospel flourishing in a Gentile context within roughly twenty years after the death and resurrection of Christ. And despite the non-mention of the term *Sabbath*, we have a clear statement from Paul, despite the general terminology he used: there is no obligation to keep the Sabbath in the congregations he founded.

3.5 RESULTS

In this letter, written to Gentile Christian congregations in Galatia, the apostle struggles to retain the commitment of his readers to the gospel as he had preached it. These congregations, founded by Paul, had come under the influence of a competing mission to Gentiles characterized by loyalty to the Torah, expressed by their urging of circumcision on their hearers. Galatians can be read as documentation of two theological positions within the early Christian movement, both of which strive to understand how the inclusion of the nations in the salvation community can be understood in light of God's promises to Abraham and his revelation of his law to Israel. The answer that Paul gave has been preserved in the canon of the NT; the answer of the competing mission was rejected and can only be inferred.

To describe the life of his readers as believers in Christ, Paul had used the language of relationships, portraying their experience of coming to

---

[153] Martyn feels that in Rome, Paul took measures to correct a hostile interpretation of God with regard to his portrayal of the law and Israel (*Galatians*, 29–34). "When he writes to the Romans, Paul does not reverse himself as regards there being a connection between the Sinaitic Law and tyranny; but his concern that he is accurately understood by Law-observant Jewish Christians (both in Rome and in Jerusalem) does lead him to a carefully nuanced formulation of that connection" (32).

faith as a change from slavery to the most intimate of relationships, family. This change corresponds to the terms one of the basic antinomies of the letter, slavery/freedom (4:1–7).

Now, in contrast to the language of personal relationships, Paul describes his readers's pre-Christian life (and that to which they are in danger of returning) as a relationship to impersonal forces, the στοιχεῖα and time markers. This corresponds to Paul's conviction that the God who has called them, the father of Christ and, through adoption, of all believers, is the only personal being properly denoted as "god." Any competing objects of thought in the spiritual realm are "not-gods" (v. 8), an element of his continuity in thought with his Jewish background, in contrast to his stress of the discontinuity of the Christian faith with regard to the Torah. We note as well that the religious experience of time—a division of time into sacred and profane—is aligned with an inferior level of experience when compared with the experience of being known by God.

There is no insurmountable difficulty in Paul's use of the term στοιχεῖα τοῦ κόσμου to express the commonality of the new Torah enthusiasm of his audience, nor in his use of the scrupulous observance of time to exemplify this. At any rate, the missionaries would have seen in it a legitimate expression of their Torah-piety. That the reality of the world conforms to the Torah, that cultic observance and times must be in accord with this, and that all of reality breathes of the same divine will as the Torah—that is, that a life in harmony to creation and cult is simply the other side of conformity to the Torah, is all in accord with early Jewish theology. The law possesses therefore soteriological quality, which Paul contests on the basis of his Christology.

Despite the characterization of his competitors as "the circumcision," the issue at stake between the two positions, that of Paul and that of his competitors, is not limited to that. When Paul speaks of days and other time markers in 4:10, it is not because the Galatians are returning to their previous pagan observances, but because they have begun to observe the days mandated in the Torah. Paul is showing the parallel with that out of which the Galatians had come. For this reason, he uses general terms for time markers. He wants to show the similarity of the underlying phenomena. When Paul speaks of days and other time markers in

Gal 4:10, he is speaking of the Sabbath and other days prescribed in the Torah. The general terminology refers back to the creation, when there were no Jews or Gentiles. The new scrupulous observance of Torah-mandated time markers is phenomenologically no different from their earlier involvement with polytheistic worship, in which careful observance of planetary motion, and the time markers that resulted from that, played an important role.

Paul is ambivalent about the law as such. It is precisely that of which Israel boasted—that they alone had received the law—that required that the coming of Christ should bring the end of the law (Rom 10:4). Paul's belief of this is related to his conviction that the coming of Christ inaugurated the promised time of the gathering of the nations. The law can not at the same time be the exclusive possession of Israel and have a role in the gathering of the nations. Yet while at an end as a way of salvation, the law remains as an expression of the will of God. Nevertheless, there are some aspects of the law that are neither a way of salvation nor do they express the will of God for Gentile believers. Explicitly, they are the so-called identity markers (circumcision, ritual purity, and the observances of the Hebrew calendar). Paul does not systematize this. He does not differentiate between moral and ceremonial law, nor between the ten commandments and the rest. Still, his message is clear: faith in Jesus Christ is the way of salvation for all, Jew and Gentile. Jews do not need to stop being Jews to be saved, but believe in Jesus as their promised Messiah. Belief in Jesus as the seed of Abraham in whom all nations would be blessed meant at the same time that Gentiles did not need to become Jews, specifically as expressed by adoption of markers of Jewish identity such as circumcision, nor the observance of days such as the Sabbath. As Ebeling wrote, "hier definitiv beseitigt ist, was Juden und Heiden vor Gott trennt."[154]

Implicitly, his criticism of the scrupulous observance of time markers, couched as it is in general terms, would also mean that he did not foresee the rise of a Christian church year, marked by occasions such as Christmas and Easter. He lived in the last days, when the coming of the Christ had changed the very quality of time, overcoming its division into sacred

---

[154] *Wahrheit*, 294.

and profane just as surely as it had overcome the division of Jew and Gentile. All that mattered was the gathering of the elect and their preparation for the culmination of the day of the Lord. As it is, time has continued, and a "Christian" calendar developed parallel to the growing awareness that the end was not imminent. This is not surprising, nor is the fact that this "new" calendar merged features of the calendars it replaced.

Understanding the context in which Paul wrote can act as a safeguard against a neo-Puritanism that would view the common Christian celebrations with as much suspicion as those of Israel. At the same time, the words of Paul, preserved in the Christian canon, have a critical potential that can constantly remind us of the power of calendrics not only to unify through the observance of days, but also to divide.

4

Gleaning Grain on the Sabbath
in the Synoptics

The last twenty-five years have not only seen a reevaluation of Paul; the so-called "third quest for the historical Jesus" has brought a reassessment of Jesus, as well.[1] The criteria of the second quest—difference and consistency— have been supplemented by a readiness to accept as probably historical any words or deeds of Jesus that fit with what we know of first-century Judaism, or can account for the rise of early Christianity.[2] Whereas traditionally the discussion centered on the canonical gospels, there is a growing readiness to use non-canonical writings as sources (one of these will be discussed in ch. 6). In addition, newer methodological tools such as narrative and social criticism have enriched our perspective; the former has given us renewed respect for and insight into the text as we have it, the latter has rounded out our

---

[1]   The phrase *third quest* was coined by N. Thomas Wright in his supplementary chapter to Stephen Neill, *The Interpretation of the New Testament 1961-1986* (2d ed.; Oxford, 1988), 379. For an overview of research on the historical Jesus since the Enlightenment, see Gerd Theissen and Annette Merz, *Der historische Jesus: Ein Lehrbuch* (Göttingen, 1996), 21–33. For reports on and assessment of research in the last two decades, see Anne Dawson and Michael Lattke, "Nachtrag: Bemerkungen zum Stand der Jesusforschung," in Hubert Leroy, *Jesus: Überlieferung und Deutung* (3d ed.; EdF 95; Darmstadt, 1999), 129–58; and Bernard Brandon Scott, "From Reimarus to Crossan: Stages in a Quest." *CurBS* 2 (1994): 253–80.

[2]   "Was im jüdischen Kontext plausibel ist und die Entstehung des Urchristentums verständlich macht, dürfte historisch sein," Theissen and Merz, *Jesus*, 29. On the criteria of the second quest, see John P. Meier, *The Roots of the Problem and the Person* (vol. 1 of *A Marginal Jew: Rethinking the Historical Jesus*; ABRL; New York, 1991), 167–95 and Gerd Theissen and Dagmar Winter, *Die Kriterienfrage in der Jesusforschung: Vom Differenzkriterium zum Plausibilitätskriterium* (NTOA 34; Fribourg, 1997).

picture of life in Palestine (Judea and Galilee) in the first century C.E., the time of Jesus.[3] This has led to a reinterpretation of the incidents recorded in the gospels concerning the Sabbath.[4] Berndt Schaller, for example, concludes that it is questionable whether Jesus' Sabbath infractions constitute an attack on the institution of the Sabbath.[5] In this he follows a succession of scholars who have approached the gospel accounts from a Jewish perspective and have failed to see anything in Jesus' Sabbath behavior that would have provoked persecution and death.[6] The very small basis of texts on which to verify these views expanded dramatically in the twentieth century. The Dead Sea Scrolls, for instance, included a number of other, previously unknown documents that testify to the diversity of Judaism in the time before the destruction of the Herodian Temple in 70 C.E. In addition, the presence in Qumran of manuscripts of previously known texts has allowed them to be placed for the first time with certainty in first-century Palestinian Judaism. All of this has permitted greater insight into the world of Jesus, and has given scholars confidence that statements can be made about the earthly Jesus with a higher degree of certainty than had been thought possible.[7]

[3]   For an introduction to the application of narrative criticism to the NT, see Mark A. Powell, *What is Narrative Criticism?* (GBS; Minneapolis, 1990) and Daniel Marguerat and Yvan Bourquin, *La Bible se raconte. Initiation à l'analyse narrative* (Paris, 1998). For an introduction to the application of the social sciences to NT studies, see Bengt Holmberg, *Sociology and the New Testament: An Appraisal* (Minneapolis, 1990).

[4]   The implications of this "third quest" for the interpretation of Jesus' actions on the Sabbath are clear when Theissen and Merz write: "Jesus ist der Gründer einer 'innerjüdischen Erneuerungsbewegung', deren Intensivierung von Thora und Eschatologie formal anderen 'radikaltheokratischen' Bewegungen entspricht" (*Jesus*, 29).

[5]   It remains "fraglich, ob die Sabbatverstösse Jesu durch Krankenheilungen einen Angriff gegen die Einrichtung des Sabbats selbst beinhalten, auch wenn mit ihnen die Grenzen gängiger Sabbathalacha überschritten sind" ("Sabbat III. Neues Testament," *TRE* 29:526). As Theissen and Merz (cf. n. 4), Schaller relates the actions of Jesus to his proclamation of the nearness of the Kingdom of God.

[6]   An extreme assessment is that of Pinchas Lapide: Jesus recognized "grundsätzlich die genaue Einhaltung des Sabbats als Bibelgebot" (*Er predigte in ihren Synagogen: Jüdische Evangelienauslegung* [GTBS 1400; Gütersloh, 1980], 66).

[7]   On the significance of the Dead Sea Scrolls for Jesus research, see James H. Charlesworth, *Jesus Within Judaism* (ABRL; New York, 1988), 54–75, and that of the

As impressive as these developments are, they must be verified against the writings that have formed the Christian canon. I propose to examine one of the key passages in the Synoptic Gospels with regard to the Sabbath question, the controversy arising out of gleaning in a grainfield (Mark 2:23–28 par.).

The fifty-one references to the seventh-day Sabbath in the four canonical gospels can be grouped into twelve or thirteen incidents.[8] This has led some to rate the likelihood that Jesus came in conflict with his contemporaries over the Sabbath as one of the most certain traits of the tradition.[9] Yet tradition and source criticism reduced the number of episodes likely to date back to the historical Jesus; the rest are considered formations of the Christian community or creations of the evangelists.[10] This does not mean that Jesus did not experience opposition over his behavior with regard to the Sabbath; it simply means that the likelihood of this cannot be determined quantitatively.[11] For this reason, a passage

---

Pseudepigrapha, ibid., 30–53.

[8]   Five of these occur in Mark and parallels: Mark 1:21 par. Luke 4:31 (Jesus enters the synagogue to teach; Matthew has the incident, but strikes the reference to the Sabbath); Mark 2:23–28 par. Matt 12:1–8/Luke 6:1–5 (the grainfield incident); Mark 3:1–6 par. Matt 12:9–14/Luke 6:6–11 (the healing of the man with the withered hand); Mark 6:1–6a par. Luke 4:16(?) (rejection at Nazareth; Matthew has the incident, but strikes the reference to the Sabbath); Mark 16:1 par. Matt 28:1/Luke 23:54,56/John 19:31 (the Sabbath in conjunction with the crucifixion). Matthew has one additional reference to the Sabbath (Matt 24:20, flight in a time of tribulation, see below, 4.2.4). Luke has two additional healing incidents (Luke 13:10–17; 14:1–6), and John has two incidents unique to his Gospel (John 5:1–18; 9:14–16). The word σάββατον occurs an additional five times with the meaning of "week"; four of these refer to the first day of the week in conjunction with the resurrection.

[9]   Joachim Jeremias, *Neutestamentliche Theologie, 1: Die Verkündigung Jesu* (Gütersloh, 1971), 265. More recently, Ben Witherington III, *Jesus the Sage: The Pilgrimage of Wisdom* (Minneapolis, 1994), 168.

[10]   Eduard Lohse, "Jesu Worte über den Sabbat," in *Judentum, Christentum, Kirche* (FS J. Jeremias; ed. W. Eltester; BZNW 26; Berlin, 1960), 79–89, here 79.

[11]   Schaller, *TRE* 29:526. Lohse, after reducing the number of Sabbath sayings that may go back to Jesus, still concludes that the report of his conflict with his environment over that Sabbath is one of the surest traits of the tradition ("Jesu Worte," 84; "σάββατον, σαββατισμος, παρασκευή," *TWNT* 7:1–35, here 22, n. 172). Even Bultmann, noted for his scepticism regarding the possibility of reconstructing a life of Jesus from the Gospels, lists transgression of the Sabbath as one of the few characteristics that can be attributed

that contains material generally assigned to the earliest stages of Jesus traditions is the most suitable for our purposes.[12] In addition, the incident of gleaning grain on the Sabbath appears in all three of the Synoptics, allowing for a fruitful synoptic comparison. This will enable us to ask whether trajectories can be traced in the transformation of the material presented, and whether these shed light on questions of practice.

This is the only narrated Sabbath dispute in the life of Jesus that does not involve a healing. The canonical gospels mention seven incidents of healing on the Sabbath; there is no other day of the week identified in conjunction with a healing.[13] In general, the lines along which the discussion of these run are similar to those we will discover in our investigation of the grainfield pericope. Whereas in the Synoptics and John, the Sabbath healings are consistently the occasion of conflict, there is doubt whether this is historically accurate. Again, Schaller, who views it as certain that Jesus through his Sabbath healings sought neither to separate himself from his Jewish environment nor abolish the Sabbath, can serve to illustrate the revisionist position.[14] The Sabbath was for Jesus precisely the day on which the healing sovereignty of God should be expressed in deeds.[15] It is understandable, Schaller concludes, that this

to the historic Jesus ("Das Verhältnis der urchristlichen Christusbotschaft zum historischen Jesus" [1960], in *Exegetica: Aufsätze zur Erforschung des Neuen Testaments* [ed. E. Dinkler; Tübingen, 1967], 445–69, here 451–4). See also Martin Dibelius, *Jesus* (3d ed.; Berlin, 1960), 95, cf. 103; Günther Bornkamm, *Jesus von Nazareth* (14th ed.; Stuttgart, 1988), 88–89, Herbert Braun, *Spätjüdisch häretischer und frühchristlicher Radikalismus: Jesus von Nazareth und die essenische Qumransekte* (2d ed.; 2 vols.; Tübingen, 1969), 2:69–73.

[12] Lohse considers the saying contained in Mark 2:27 one of three that originate with the historical Jesus. The others are Mark 3:4 par. and Matt 12:11–12 par. Luke 14:5 ("Jesu Worte," 84–89). Cf. Jürgen Becker, who agrees with regard to Mark 2:27 and 3:4, but finds that the difficulty involved in reconstructing the original form of the saying contained in Matt 12:11–12 and Luke 14:5, as well as its parallels in Jewish discussion of the time make the ascription of authenticity less certain (*Jesus von Nazaret* [Berlin, 1996], 4). On the possible historicity of the episode, see below 4.4.3.

[13] Mark 1:21–28 par. Luke 4:31–37; Mark 1:29–31 par.; Mark 3:1–6 par.; Luke 13:10–17; 14:1–6; John 5:1–18; 9:1–41.

[14] *Jesus und der Sabbat* (Franz-Delitzsch-Vorlesung 3. Münster, 1994), 20–27. See discussion above, 1.3.

[15] Among others who have come to this conclusion, see Werner Kahl, "Ist es erlaubt,

caused opposition among those who did not share his conviction of the breaking into the present of God's sovereignty. Similar considerations led Bacchiocchi to speak of a "Sabbath ministry" of Jesus through which his messianic mission was primarily revealed.[16] Yet he goes considerably beyond Schaller and others when he claims that by fulfilling the redemption typology of the Sabbath, Jesus made the day a permanent fitting memorial of his redemptive mission.[17] The opposite conclusion is expressed by M. M. B. Turner, who maintains that the argument is "not that the Sabbath *is* a special day in this respect but precisely that it is *not*."[18] This fails to fully account for the mention of Sabbath healing conflicts. Because the Sabbath was what it was and meant what it did, there was no question of Jesus interrupting on that day his work, which was equally appropriate for every other day as well.[19]

I have opted, however, for the grainfield pericope precisely because it does not involve anything so dramatic as a healing, but what seems to be a petty and avoidable infraction of Sabbath norms. The words attributed to Jesus here, widely accepted as authentic, have been understood as expressing most clearly his rejection of legalistic restrictions, indeed, of the Torah itself, in the name of human needs or of human freedom.

I propose to carry out the investigation of this account in four steps. In the first, I will examine the incident as reported in the Gospel of Mark. Before asking what this text can tell us about the Sabbath practice and understanding of Jesus and his earliest followers, we must determine what it reveals about Mark and his intended readers (4.1).[20] This analysis

---

am Sabbat Leben zu retten oder zu töten? (Marc 3:4): Lebensbewahrung am Sabbat im Kontext der Schriften vom Toten Meer und der Mischna," *NovT* 40 (1998): 313–35.

[16] Samuele Bacchiocchi, *From Sabbath to Sunday: A Historical Investigation of the Rise of Sunday Observance in Early Christianity* (Rome, 1977), 25–26.

[17] *Sabbath*, 37–38.

[18] "The Sabbath, Sunday, and the Law in Luke/Acts," in *From Sabbath to Lord's Day: A Biblical Historical and Theological Investigation* (ed. D. A. Carson; Grand Rapids, 1982), 99–157, here 107.

[19] The conclusion drawn in the Gospel according to John concerning Sabbath healings must be examined separately (below, ch. 5). We will see, however, that it is precisely here that we have a point of contact between John and the Synoptics.

[20] Any reference to Jesus in this step, as well as in the following step, in which

will provide a benchmark for the subsequent steps. In a second step, I will examine the use made of the account in Mark by Luke and Matthew (4.2–4.3). Each made use of Mark's account, but made changes. If a theological tendency can be discovered behind these changes, then we have further evidence of the way in which the Sabbath may have been viewed in various Christian communities.[21] The third step will investigate the tradition preserved in the grainfield pericope prior to its incorporation in the Gospel of Mark (4.4). Finally, in a fourth step, I will ask whether the results enable us to test the various assertions that have been made about Jesus and the Sabbath (4.4.3).

This topic has implications for the broader, and much discussed question of the attitude of Jesus, the evangelists, and their communities toward the law, although a detailed examination of this lies outside the scope of the present project.[22]

4.1 THE GRAINFIELD EPISODE IN THE GOSPEL OF MARK

4.1.1 Analysis of Mark 2:23–28

The incident we will examine forms a pericope that is self-contained yet well embedded in its context.[23] A narrative introduction indicates that the

Matthew and Luke will be examined, should be understood as a reference to the narrative figure in each Gospel by that name.

[21] This sequence presupposes the use of the two-source hypothesis as my working model. This episode offers acute challenges to the two-source hypothesis, particularly because of the number—fifteen—and quality—especially the striking of the Jesus logion Mark 2:27—of minor agreements. Yet the synoptic comparison conducted below (4.2 and 4.3) will reach the conclusion that even with regard to this pericope that this hypothesis offers the most satisfying explanation of the relation between the three synoptic gospels (so also Lutz Doering, *Schabbat: Sabbathalacha und -praxis im antiken Judentum und Urchristentum* [TSAJ 78; Tübingen, 1999], 408). On the various attempts to solve the problem of the relationship of the three synoptic gospels in Kümmel, *Einleitung*, 13–53; Brown, *Introduction*, 111–22; and Joel Marcus, *Mark 1–8: A New Translation with Introduction and Commentary* [AB 27A; New York, 1999], 40–47.

[22] Brief discussion in Becker, *Jesus*, 337–87. To his thorough bibliography, 337–8, can be added William R. G. Loader, *Jesus' Attitude Toward the Law* (WUNT 2/97; Tübingen, 1997).

[23] The previous pericope, concerning fasting (Mark 2:18–22), had ended with a

incident in question occurred on the Sabbath;[24] beyond this, we are given no precise indication of the time.[25] "He" (Jesus, cf. 2:19) is underway in a grainfield; the precise location is not narrated. He is accompanied by his disciples; as they go, they glean heads of grain.[26] The Pharisees, who had already been introduced in the Gospel narrative among those hostile to Jesus (2:16, 18), address an accusatory question to "him"; The nature

saying of the Lord. The narrative framework of v. 23 is typical for Mark for the beginning of the new pericope (Καὶ + ἐγένετο, as here, 1:9; more common is καὶ + a verb of movement or change of place). The unit ends with a saying of the Lord, and the following verse (3:1) brings a narrative framework, including the identification of a new location, for the next incident, a healing on the Sabbath. Though clearly demarcated, the unit is firmly embedded in its context, preceded by a question of pious practice, fasting, in which the practice of the disciples provides the occasion for a question to Jesus (v. 18), and is followed by an incident to which it is connected by the common topic of Sabbath.

[24] ἐν τοῖς σάββασιν, plural. The use of σάββατα when a single Sabbath is meant has been variously explained as a purely vocal addition to reproduce the Hebrew -t in Greek (Lohse, *TWNT* 7:7, n. 39), or, more probably, a misunderstanding of the Aramaic emphatic singular שַׁבְּתָא (Jeremias, *Theologie* 1:17, n. 42).

[25] Since the grain was edible, the time may have been between Passover and Pentecost, but this is not mentioned, making it unlikely that the evangelist envisioned that they were reaping the omer, the first of the spring barley harvest, cf. Lev 23:9–14 (*pace* Etain Levine, "The Sabbath Controversy according to Matthew," *NTS* 22 [1976]: 480–83, and Matty Cohen, "La Controverse de Jésus et des Pharisiens à propos de la cueillette des épis, selon l'Évangile de Saint Matthieu," *MScRel* 34 [1977]: 3–12).

[26] The Greek is awkward, which speaks for Markan priority (Doering, *Schabbat*, 408). Jeremias suggests a reversal of the primary and secondary actions in the Greek construction due to an unskilled translation of a Semitic paratactical construction (*Theologie* 1:161, with n. 20). Maurice Casey proposes in addition a further mistranslation that arose from mistaking an R for a D, and thus rendering עבר, *to pass*, as עבד, *to make*, ("Culture and Historicity: The Plucking of the Grain [Mark 2.23–28]," *NTS* 34 [1988]: 1–23, here 2). This presupposes that the Aramaic original of this incident existed in written form, which is conjectural. J. D. M. Derrett accepts the Greek as it is and claims that the problem was not the gleaning but the clearing of a path, thereby creating a road for the Messiah ("Judaica in St Mark," in his *Studies in the New Testament 1: Glimpses of the Legal and Social Presuppositions of the Authors* [Leiden, 1977], 85–100, here 90–94). Marcus accepts that there may be indeed be an allusion to Isa 40:3 (*Mark 1–8*, 239–40, cf. Mark 1:3), but denies that this is the point of the objection, as the example of David shows (cf. Frans Neirynck, "Jesus and the Sabbath: Some Observations on Mark II.27," 1974, repr. in *Evangelica* 1 [BETL 60; Louvain, 1982], 637–80, here 666–8).

of their objection is not specified.[27] He responds with a two-part answer
(vv. 25–28):

> And he said to them, "Have you never read what David did when he and his
> companions were hungry and in need of food? He entered the house of God,
> when Abiathar was high priest, and ate the bread of the Presence, which it is not
> lawful for any but the priests to eat, and he gave some to his companions." Then
> he said to them, "The Sabbath was made for humankind, and not humankind for
> the Sabbath; so the Son of Man is lord even of the Sabbath."

The first part is in the form of a counter-question, citing an example from
the life of David (with altered details compared to the account in
1 Sam 21:1–7 to make the example correspond more closely to the
situation of Jesus and his disciples).[28] The second part, loosely connected
to the first (καὶ ἔλεγεν αὐτοῖς), is in itself two-parted. A saying defining
the relationship of the Sabbath and humankind (ὁ ἄνθρωπος), for whose
sake the Sabbath is said to exist, is followed by a conclusion on the basis
of this (ὥστε) concerning the relationship of an individual (ὁ υἱὸς τοῦ
ἀνθρώπου) and the Sabbath, expressed in terms of lordship. The topic
Sabbath clearly frames the episode.

On the primary narrative level, no persons are named. Indeed, the
only individual who appears is Jesus, although he, as well, remains
unnamed. All other persons appear not as individuals, but in one of two
groups. These groups appear in relationship to Jesus. This relation is

[27] This has given rise to a variety of explanations, such as those discussed in the
previous two footnotes. A third suggestion is that in the first century gleaning was only
permitted for day-laborers working in the fields, and that the transgression was petty
theft, made the more serious because it occurred on the Sabbath (Jarmo Kiilunen, *Die
Vollmacht in Widerstreit: Untersuchungen zum Werdegang von Mk 2,1–3,6* [AASF:
Dissertationes Humanarum Litterarum 40; Helsinki, 1985], 209). On balance, the
evidence of the passage indicates that gathering food on the Sabbath is the action to
which the Pharisees objected (cf. Neirynck, "Jesus and the Sabbath," 664–71; Doering,
Schabbat, 427–8). On the Pharisees in Mark's Gospel, see Marcus, *Mark 1–8*, 519–24.
The objection of E. P. Sanders to the historical likelihood of Pharisees lurking in the
grainfield ("Jesus and the Constraint of Law," *JSNT* 17 [1983], 19–24, here 20; *Jesus
and Judaism* [Philadelphia, 1985], 265) has been answered by Casey ("Historicity," 4–5).
Important for the investigation at this stage however is the function they fulfil in the
narrative.
[28] Discussion in Rudolf Pesch, *Das Markusevangelium, 1. Einleitung und
Kommentar zu Kap. 1,1–8,26* [HTKNT 2/1; Freiburg, 1976], 181–2.

established for the first group by their designation (μαθηταί, followers) and for the second by their function: they pose an accusatory question. In this way, the term Pharisee is implicitly defined as a negative counterpart to follower, an opponent. By presenting the two groups in their relation to Jesus, the narrative makes him the central figure, even though it is not his action that is called into question, as it would have been in the case of a healing episode, but that of his followers.

When Jesus cites an example from scripture, he introduces a secondary narrative level. On this level, in contrast to the first, two individuals are named. The second of these, however, Abiathar the high priest, appears in a prepositional phrase introduced by ἐπί; the phrase is usually taken as an indication of the time of the incident.[29] It thereby corresponds to the phrase ἐν τοῖς σάββασιν on the primary narrative level. There is a Jewish tradition that the incident narrated here occurred on the Sabbath, but this is neither stated in 1 Sam 21 nor here.[30] The

---

[29] Vincent Taylor, *The Gospel According to St. Mark: The Greek Text, with Introduction, Notes, and Indexes* (London, 1952), 217. The mention of Abiathar is difficult, since he was not the high priest at the time, but not unparalled (Josephus, *Ant.* 6.12.1). Derrett suggests "in the presence of" ("Judaica," 92; also Kiilunen, *Vollmacht*, 200). Alternatively, and more likely, the mention of the more famous son instead of Ahimelech, the father, is, for David Daube, "manifestly the kind of error likely if you do not look up your text" ("Responsibilities of Master and Disciples in the Gospels," *NTS* 19 [1972/73]: 1–15, here, 6). Codices D, W and a few other manuscripts omit the phrase, thus harmonizing the text with that of Matt 12:4 and Luke 6:4. Many others seek to solve the difficulty by adding τοῖς, "in order to permit the interpretation that the event happened in the time of (but not necessarily during the high priesthood of) Abiathar" (Bruce Manning Metzger, *A Textual Commentary on the Greek New Testament: A Companion Volume to the United Bible Societies Greek New Testament* [3d ed.; London, 1975], 79). A decision on this question is not necessary for the purpose of this investigation.

[30] Doering, *Schabbat*, 430-1. The references to the traditions can be found in Bill 1:618–9. It can reasonably be inferred that Jesus and the Pharisees of his day, who lived in a high context society, i.e., one that shared a broad range of common experience, shared knowledge of this tradition (a consideration that would apply to the early Aramaic-speaking community as well). Additionally, "when the Sabbath is mentioned five times in six verses, it does not have to be mentioned again at vss. 25–26" (Casey, "Historicity," 21). Nonetheless, Mark seems aware of having better knowledge of Jewish customs that did his readers (cf. 7:2–4), therefore it remains significant that he explicitly mentions hunger, and not the Sabbath, when citing this example. On high- and low-

correspondence of the phrases ἐν τοῖς σάββασιν on the primary narrative level and ἐπὶ Ἀβιαθὰρ ἀρχιερέως on the secondary demonstrates that the point of comparison between the two incidents is not their timing, but the innocent eating of something normally forbidden (οὐκ ἔξεστιν, vv. 24 and 26). Unlike the consumption of meats such as pork, which was forbidden per se in that society, we see in both cases a substance normally allowed (grain) that was forbidden only circumstantially. In the case of David and his followers, this was because the bread had been dedicated in the house of God; in the case of the followers of Jesus, because the grain had been gleaned on the Sabbath.[31]

With the naming of Abiathar thus accounted for, this leaves David, the other named individual, who is also accompanied by a group of followers, οἱ μετ᾿ αὐτοῦ, as the central figure on this level, thereby corresponding to Jesus.[32] There is no group corresponding to the Pharisees on the secondary narrative level. No accusation is brought against David. By implication, no accusation should be brought on the primary level either.

The correspondence between David and Jesus is, however, asymmetrical. David is the active agent, entering the house of God (not mentioned in 1 Samuel), taking the bread (in 1 Samuel it is given to him by the priest) and giving it to his followers (again, not mentioned in 1 Samuel,

context societies, see Bruce J. Malina and Richard L. Rohrbaugh, *Social-Science Commentary on the Synoptic Gospels* (Minneapolis, 1992), 11–13.

[31] While gleaning was expressly permitted in the Torah (Lev 19:9–10; 23:22; Deut 23:25 [23:26 MT]), the law in question involves the definition of work prohibited on the Sabbath, a matter of oral Torah exposition (halakah). The written Torah expressly forbids harvesting on the Sabbath (Exod 34:21; cf. *Jub.* 50:12); the objection of the Pharisees is apparently based on the view that gleaning was a form of harvesting, a view that is attested in the Mishna (*m. Šabb.* 7:2, cf. y. *Šabb.* 7:2 [9b–c]; Doering, *Schabbat*, 428–9). These codified definitions of work appear in sources later than the time of Jesus, but Philo expresses a strict first-century view (*Mos.* 2.22; *Spec.* 2.66–70). On the other hand, there is no unanimity in the rabbinic sources that gleaning should be prohibited on the Sabbath (*b. Šabb.* 128a). There is even less likelihood that this view formed part of a universally accepted halakah before the ascendancy of the Pharisees after the destruction of the temple (Casey, "Historicity," 5–6).

[32] This is the first mention of David in Mark's Gospel; we, as readers of Mark, do not yet know of a Davidic ancestry of Jesus (cf. 10:47–48).

although this did cause some rabbinic discussion on how David could consume five loaves) to satisfy not only his own hunger, but theirs.[33] The effect of this shift in accent is that Jesus accepts the responsibility for the disciples' action implicit in the fact that the question was addressed to him, rather than to his disciples (cf. 2:18).[34] At the same time, without being expressly stated, a comparison of David and Jesus is established, in which, according to the argumentative practice of the time, Jesus is seen as the greater of the two (*a minori ad maius*).

Jesus describes David, in need and hungry, taking the bread of presence from the house of God and sharing it with his followers (vv. 25–26).[35] Jesus specifically mentions David's companions as being co-beneficiaries of David's action. By formulating their question as a matter that is "not allowed" (cf. 10:2; 12:14; John 5:10), the Pharisees had identified the matter as a question of law.[36] By repeating the phrase οὐκ ἔξεστιν, the relevance to the question of the Pharisees is established.

The repetition by Jesus of the phrase οὐκ ἔξεστιν helps resolve the further question of how this answer is meant to respond to the accusa-

---

[33]   In 4Q52 (4QSam^b), now recognized as offering a reading superior to that of the MT(Frank Moore Cross and Donald W. Parry, "A Preliminary Edition of a Fragment of 4QSam^b [4Q52]," *BASOR* 306 [May 1997]: 63–74, here 69), the priest says "you (plural) may eat of it" (frg. 7, line 17).

[34]   Rudolf Bultmann concludes from this that the story is an invention created to defend the post-resurrection practice of the disciples (*Die Geschichte der synoptischen Tradition*, [10th ed.; FRLANT 29; Göttingen, 1995], 14). On the responsibility of a master for his disciples, however, see Jeremias, *Theologie* 1:265–6; Daube, "Responsibilities," 3–7 and Jürgen Roloff, *Das Kerygma und der irdische Jesus. Historische Motive in den Jesus-Erzählungen der Evangelien* (Göttingen, 1970), 55.

[35]   On the regulations for bread of presence, literally the *loaves of setting forth*, (ἄρτοι τῆς προθέσεως, used in the LXX to render various Hebrew phrases, see Lev 24:5–9). Twelve fresh loaves (David asks for five, 1 Sam 21:3) were placed on a table in the sanctuary, the outer part of the tent of meeting, each Sabbath. The descendants of Aaron could eat the old bread in the sanctuary after it had been replaced. The loaves were large; Lev 24:5 specifies that one-fifth of an ephah of flour should go into each loaf, which could have been as much as 2.4 liters (M. A. Powell, "Weights and Measures," *ABD* 6:897–908, here 904). Josephus says they were unleavened (*Ant.* 3.142); they were shared by the two courses of priests, the outgoing and the incoming (*b. Sukkah* 56a).

[36]   On use of οὐκ ἔξεστιν as a technical legal term in Jewish casuistic, see Lohse, "Jesu Worte," 86.

tion. It is often pointed out, correctly, that the accusation against the disciples in v. 24 was based on transgression of the orally-transmitted, halakic interpretation of what constituted forbidden activities on the Sabbath.[37] In the *Streitgespräch* (controversy dialogue) on ritual purity, this distinction figures both in the narrative framework and the answer of Jesus, which portrays Jesus distinguishing between the commandment of God, which he implicitly accepts, and the tradition of men, which he implicitly rejects (Mark 7:3, 8–9).[38] No such distinction between written and oral law is made here. Indeed, by taking up the phrase οὐκ ἔξεστιν, Jesus appears to concede that something illegal has happened.[39] The conduct is justified because of scriptural precedent, not because of invalidity of the accusation. There are two possible reasons why the precedent applies. One is that the pleonastic mention of need and hunger is meant to mitigate David's action and, by implication, that of the disciples.[40] The other is that Jesus implicitly assumes an authority similar to that of David that overrides the commandment. There is no hint in Jesus' answer however that the law concerning the Sabbath is in some way no longer binding on (Jesus and) his disciples.

Since the example of David and his followers would seem to establish the innocence of the followers of Jesus, the presence of a second answer, the appeal to the relation of humankind and the Sabbath (2:27–28), seems redundant.

The accusation of the Pharisees had been answered by a return question and a scriptural appeal, characteristic of Jewish wisdom teachers but also reported as a practice of Jesus.[41] Since the objection carried in

[37] On the relation between written Torah and oral halakah in the time of Jesus, see Becker, *Jesus*, 343–5. He cites parallels to the disqualification of the halakah of an *opposing* group as human tradition; the halakah of one's own group, as well as halakah that had found consensus acceptance that transcended the boundaries of a group, possessed authority similar to that of the Torah.

[38] Pesch, *Markusevangelium*, 181.

[39] Sven-Olav Back, *Jesus of Nazareth and the Sabbath Commandment* (Åbo, 1995), 82.

[40] Discussion in Back, *Jesus*, 82–84.

[41] Bultmann, *Geschichte*, 42; Schaller, *Jesus*, 22–23. For rabbinic examples, see Bill 1:861–2. Other examples of the use of this technique by Jesus are Mark 3:4; 11:29; 12:10, 26. Malina and Rohrbaugh term these exchanges *challenge-riposte* and identify

itself the implicit alternative that Jesus was either ignorant of the law or careless of its demands, the return question of whether they had never read concerning an incident from scripture is apposite.[42] However, the answer had not come from the Torah, but from the Prophets (1 Samuel forming part of the *Nebi'im* in the Hebrew canon).

The second answer, however, is based on the Torah, although not on the legal code therein contained. Rather, it is an argument from the order of creation (cf. Matt 19:4). In this second answer, Jesus appeals to the relationship of humanity and Sabbath in the creation order,[43] asserting that the Sabbath was made for humanity, not the other way around (v. 27).[44] He then draws a conclusion from this (ὥστε), asserting that the

them as examples of a competition for honor, played out in public (*Commentary*, 188). D. M. Cohn-Sherbok, after showing that the analogy to David is poor from a rabbinic hermeneutical perspective, says that Jesus was "teaching on his own authority . . . far removed from the technical casuistry of the Scribes, Sadducees and Pharisees" ("An Analysis of Jesus' Arguments Concerning the Plucking of Grain on the Sabbath," *JSNT* 2 [1979]: 31–41, here 34). It may well be that "Jesus was not an adept in rabbinic debate" (William D. Davies and Dale C. Allison, *A Critical and Exegetical Commentary on the Gospel according to Saint Matthew* [ICC; Edinburgh, 1988], 2:308), but the point is moot; more pertinent is that those who formulated the gospel tradition did not become masters of it. To conclude with Cohn-Sherbok and Davies and Allison that Jesus was arguing here on his own authority is to read too much into the account (perhaps from the Sermon on the Mount). The Gospels record statements that have the form, if not the quality, of rabbinic debate, in which Jesus is assumed to be a master. None of the Gospels has an opponent reply that Jesus argued poorly. In the grainfield incident, they are silent. This silence, followed by their plot to kill (surely not the standard practice when a teacher has argued poorly), portrays their inability to answer.

[42] David Rhoads and Donald Michie, *Mark as Story: An Introduction to the Narrative of a Gospel* (Philadelphia, 1982), 86.

[43] ἐγένετο; on γίνεσθαι as a circumlocution for the action of God, see Jeremias, *Theologie* 1:201. Compare ἐκτίσθη in W and λ, also reflected in sy^{s.p}. See however Carson, "Jesus and the Sabbath," who argues against this conclusion (65, with 89, n. 57). His objection is based in part on concerns that the Sabbath, if a creation ordinance, would then be thought of as binding on all (68). Alternatively, γίνεσθαι could refer to the giving of the law at Sinai (discussion in Back, *Jesus*, 97–98).

[44] In both Sabbatarian and Lord's Day circles, the argument that the Sabbath was made for humankind is taken to mean that it was meant to be *kept* by humans (Herbert W. Armstrong, *Which Day is the Christian Sabbath?* [Pasadena, 1962], 22–23; Francis Nigel Lee, *The Covenantal Sabbath* [London, 1966], 195). Bacchiocchi, a Sabbatarian, rejects this suggestion, on the grounds that this reading violates the context (*Sabbath*,

"Son of Man" is lord even of the Sabbath. The principle expressed in v. 27 is attested in rabbinic thought, and based on this it was widely accepted that Sabbath rest could be violated to save life (see below, 4.4.3). Jesus goes significantly beyond this here; there is no suggestion that the disciples are on the brink of starvation and will die if they do not eat. Instead, there is a categorical principle that the divine institution, the Sabbath, is subservient to the needs of those for whom it was created. Taken alone, v. 27 would seem to suggest that the innocence of the disciples is not because of the mitigating circumstance of their hunger (as v. 26 suggested), but because they have grasped the meaning of the day.[45] This conclusion must, however, be verified by v. 28.

The consequence drawn in v. 28 from the principle expressed in v. 27 is that the Son of Man is lord also of the Sabbath. In the context of the Gospel of Mark, both *Son of Man* and *Lord* are christological titles; this is the second use of both terms.[46] In the first use of the Son of Man, the power (ἐξουσία) to forgive sins is claimed. Now, this figure is said to be lord *also* of the Sabbath.[47] It is Jesus, then, who is lord of the Sabbath.

56–57; so also Carson, "Jesus," 64–65). By *humankind*, *Israel* is understood (cf. *Jub.* 2); this is not an extension of the Sabbath to the Gentiles (*pace* Roger T. Beckwith, in R. T. Beckwith and W. Stott, *This is the Day: The Biblical Doctrine of the Christian Sunday* [London, 1978], 11–12). In the rabbinic saying that comes closest to this (*Mek. Šabbata* 1[on Ex 31:12–17]; Bill 1:623), it is the people of Israel who are meant. On the other hand, Jesus is not expressing the idea that it was given only to Israel (Neirynck, "Jesus and the Sabbath," 660–62; Doering, *Schabbat*, 418–9).

[45] *Pace* Wilhelm Bousset, *Kyrios Christos: Geschichte des Christusglaubens von den Anfängen des Christentums bis Irenaeus* (FRLANT 21; Göttingen, 1913), 41; Francis W. Beare, "The Sabbath Was Made for Man?," *JBL* 79 (1960): 133–4. Compare Gerhard Barth, "Das Gesetzesverständnis des Evangelisten Matthäus," in G. Bornkamm, G. Barth, H. J. Held, *Überlieferung und Auslegung im Matthäus-Evangelium* (WMANT 1; Neukirchen-Vluyn, 1960), 76.

[46] In 2:10, in a clear self-reference, the Son of Man had been revealed in his power on earth to forgive sins; for Mark, this is a christological term. The previous use of κύριος, *lord*, was in the Deutero-Isaiah quotation referring to the work of John the Baptist in preparing the way for the coming of Christ (1:3). On the question of whether Jesus himself used the term, and whom he may have meant by this, see below, 4.4.2.

[47] There is a tension between these first two uses of the phrase, with their claim of authority, and the three predictions that "the Son of Man" would suffer (8:31; cf. 9:31, 10:33–34).

Unclear, however, is how his lordship over the Sabbath would be based in a creation relationship of humanity and Sabbath, as the conjunction ὥστε would indicate. In addition, this argument, if understood christologically, as Mark does, would only carry weight within the community of those who saw Jesus in these terms.

4.1.2 The Sabbath in the Context of Mark's Gospel

The ministry of Jesus is beset with conflict from the outset. The beginning of his public proclamation is subsequent to John's arrest—a premonition of Jesus' own fate (1:14). But there is no notice of where he begins to preach, in what circumstances, to whom, or how they react. Instead, there is an account of the call of the first four disciples (1:15–20). Only then do we read of a description of his preaching (1:21–22). This report is relevant for our topic for two reasons. First, it occurs in a synagogue on the Sabbath. Second, the astonished listeners bring Jesus in relation to the scribes, the legal experts who presumably represent the customary synagogue teachers. The relationship is one of dissonance: Jesus is *not* like the customary teachers, and the difference is identified as his possession of authority (ἐξουσία, v. 22). This term is emphasized by its repetition as they express their summary reaction to both the teaching and the exorcism Jesus then performs; the reaction is amazement (καὶ ἐθαμβήθησαν ἅπαντες), with the observation that Jesus brings a new teaching with authority (κατ' ἐξουσίαν, v. 27; cf. 2:10).[48] The primary referent of this new, authoritative teaching is the summary description in v. 14: the time is fulfilled, the kingdom of God has come near; repent and believe the gospel.[49] We, as readers of the Gospel, are

[48]   On the uncertainty of whether κατ' ἐξουσίαν in v. 27 refers to the teaching, the exorcism, or both, see the variants in the apparatus in NA[27], and the discussion in Taylor, *Mark*, 176, n. 2, Metzger, *Commentary*, 75, and G. D. Kilpatrick, "Some Problems in New Testament Text and Language," in *Neotestamentica et semitica* (FS Matthew Black; ed. E. E. Ellis and M. Wilcox; Edinburgh, 1969), 198–208, here 198–201.

[49]   The reaction of the listeners is strictly related to his teaching and the subsequent exorcism; there is no conflict concerning the Sabbath in this pericope. Mark's mention of the day is sufficiently explained by its relation to Jesus' presence in the synagogue. It is not necessary to infer that Mark hints at eschatological expectations tied to the day (Carson, "Jesus," 59).

nevertheless invited to apply this dual assessment to all of the subsequent teaching of Jesus as well—that it is new, and that it is authoritative—including his teaching not only *on* the Sabbath, as here, but *about* the Sabbath, as well.

There was no controversy associated with the healing of Simon's mother-in-law on the Sabbath (1:29–31), presumably because of its relatively private occurrence. Other healings and exorcisms in Capernaum took place after sunset, thus not on the Sabbath (v. 32).

The scribes, who have been introduced indirectly by reference (1:22), first appear as figures in the narrative in 2:6. By this time, the fame of Jesus was such that he was no longer able to preach publicly. Now he has returned to Capernaum and was in a house.[50] Nevertheless, a crowd had gathered in this private setting, including some scribes. They find it blasphemous that Jesus would pardon sins; they keep the thought to themselves, but Jesus knows it. In this way, both conflict and the superiority of Jesus to the conventional teachers of the law is expressed. Mark then skillfully weaves a pattern of a widening circle of opposition.[51] When the scribes are next mentioned, as the opponents in the next pericope (2:13–17), they are the scribes "of the Pharisees" (2:16). By being first mentioned in this way, the Pharisees, too, are presented as exponents of the conventional legal and religious establishment. The next pericope, concerning fasting (2:18–22), deals with a practice the Pharisees share with the disciples of John. In the grainfield episode, it is the Pharisees who accuse. When Jesus answers their question by citing the example of David, he shows himself to be both their equal—he is able to use their style of argumentation—and their superior—they are not able to answer him. In the next pericope, in which a man's withered hand is restored in the synagogue on the Sabbath (3:1–6), it is the

---

[50]   For the purpose of this study, it is unnecessary to decide between alternative textual readings in v. 1, ἐν οἴκῳ (NA[27], based on 𝔓[88], ℵ, B, D, L, etc.) and εἰς οἶκον (A C 090, 0130 *f*[1.13] 𝔐) nor the implications of each, including the possibility that the house in question in Capernaum was Jesus' own. See Metzger, *Commentary*, 77. Important is that Jesus is in a private setting, normally reserved by Mark for private teaching to the disciples (cf. Rhoads and Michie, *Mark*, 67) but here turned into a semi-public setting both by the crowd seeking his help and the authorities seeking to accuse.

[51]   Rhoads and Michie, *Mark*, 86.

Pharisees who, together with another group, the Herodians, plot the destruction of Jesus.

Therefore, while the scribes had already concluded that Jesus was guilty of a capital offence with their (unspoken) accusation of blasphemy (2:7), the active plot to destroy him arises from his practice regarding the Sabbath.[52] A Sabbath visit by Jesus to the synagogue in Nazareth results in rejection (6:1–6). This is the last time Jesus enters a synagogue in Mark's Gospel. There is one further reference to the Sabbath: the women rest on it after the crucifixion before purchasing spices and going to the tomb (16:1).

Despite the role the Sabbath plays in the plot to kill Jesus in 3:6, it is not mentioned when Mark reports Jesus' examination by the Sanhedrin (14:53–65). Instead, it is mentioned that no testimony could be found that would merit the death penalty (vv. 55–56). In the end, it is through a veiled self-admission (the ambiguous "I am") coupled with a reference to the eschatological Son of Man (v. 62) that leads to his condemnation. Christological considerations predominate: in the end, it is who he is, not what he has done, that leads to his crucifixion.[53] There are two parallels between the teaching and conflict narrative at the beginning of Mark's Gospel and the passion account that ends it: the hostility of the leaders of the Jews and the acclamation of the crowd. These provide consistency in Mark's portrayal of the relation between Jesus' actions and his death. The absence of the Sabbath in the passion account as a charge against Jesus shows that this was not as important to the narrator as the

---

[52]   It is none other than the experts in and defenders of the law who see in Jesus' interpretation of the law as a divine creation meant to serve humankind as an occasion to accuse him is. This is for Mark, a sign of their guilt, not his (Rhoads and Michie, *Mark*, 117).

[53]   This discussion is concerned with the literary presentation of Mark. Historical considerations, such as the observation that the Sanhedrin, predominantly though not exclusively Sadducean at that time, was a different group than the Pharisees with whom Jesus is portrayed as coming in conflict in Galilee (cf. Kurt Schubert, *Jesus im Lichte der Religionsgeschichte des Judentums* [Wien, 1973], 41), are relevant only in the sense that the account of Jesus' passion is a more firmly fixed tradition. For a proposed historical reconstruction—as opposed to the consideration of the literary level presented here—see Paula Fredriksen, *Jesus of Nazareth, King of the Jews: A Jewish Life and the Emergence of Christianity* (New York, 1999), 245–59.

conflict it engendered. The remainder of the narrative stands under the shadow cast by this plot to kill him.[54]

4.1.3 The Practice of Mark's Community

Mark does not directly report on the practice of his community.[55] Any conclusions we draw in this matter are inferences, drawn from his depiction of the experience of Jesus with his disciples. Caution is necessary; the likelihood that Mark has incorporated traditional material (see below, 4.4.1) means that any light shed on questions of practice may reflect those of an earlier time. Nevertheless, since Mark has incorporated the material, our working assumption should be that he did not disagree with what he used. At the very least, he understood it in such a way that did not contradict his own views.

Mark does not explain the Sabbath to his readers, this does not prove that his readers kept the Sabbath. Rather, it attests how well known it was throughout the empire as a custom of the Jews. The statement that the Son of Man, understood as Jesus, is the lord of the Sabbath (2:28) presumes the continued existence of the institution, not its abrogation. Scriptural example, as authoritatively interpreted by Jesus, absolves the disciples, even though they had done what was not permitted (vv. 25–26). The recovery of the intended place of the Sabbath in the creation order qualifies it as a divine gift to humans, subservient to their

---

[54]   Jeremias suggests that the dispute in the grainfield constitutes a formal admonition before witnesses and that the following incident, in which his opponents were laying in wait to see what he would do, made him liable for the death penalty, something that the religious authorities in Galilee would have had the power to carry out since, at the time, it was not directly administered by Rome (*Theologie* 1:265–6).

[55]   Although, as Richard Bauckham maintains, the gospels intend to address Christians generally, each would have been affected by the circumstances of its origin, as Bauckham concedes ("For Whom Were the Gospels Written?" in *The Gospels for All Christians: Rethinking the Gospel Audiences* [Grand Rapids, Mich., 1998], 9–48). There is therefore no difficulty in referring to "Mark's community." Despite the concerns of Dwight N. Peterson, with careful use of tools such as redaction criticism, we can hazard conclusions about the communities in which the evangelists lived and wrote. Nevertheless, the attention he draws to the circularity of arguments based on a postulated community is valuable (*The Origins of Mark: The Markan Community in Current Debate* [BISer 48; Leiden, 2000]).

needs. This would suggest that the Sabbath was neither abolished in the Markan community nor strictly observed (the hunger of the disciples was not life threatening).

This corresponds to the thrust of the healing narrative that immediately follows this unit (3:1–6). Criticism of the healing of a man with a withered hand in the public setting of a synagogue is countered by Jesus with a rhetorical question that equates doing good on the Sabbath with saving life (3:4).[56] There would have been wide acceptance of violating the Sabbath to save life, but this man's disability, though chronic, was not life threatening. The effect appears to be the extension of the principle of saving life in the direction of doing good, as exemplified in the healing activity of Jesus, as an overriding principle. The contrast of doing good and saving life with doing evil and killing, with no middle ground, shows that human need, here expressed in the concrete form of one who is chronically disabled, not only *permits* suppression of the Sabbath, it *requires* it.[57]

As mentioned above (4.1.2) Jesus never enters a synagogue after his rejection in Nazareth (6:1–6). Although not direct evidence for the practice of the Markan community, it would be consistent with an assumption that it kept at a distance from (non-Christian) synagogues. This corresponds to the rejection of the scriptural understanding of the Pharisees expressed in 2:25. On the other hand, in 13:9 Jesus warns his followers that they will be beaten in the synagogues (where the scribes take the best seats, 12:39), implying that his disciples will visit the synagogue after his death. This does not, however, prove that Mark and his intended readers still visited the synagogue, it could, instead, simply show that they were aware that disciples of Jesus continued to do so after his death.

Finally, as noted, the women purchase spices and go to the tomb *after* the Sabbath (16:1). It is self-evident that they had rested. Nevertheless,

---

[56]   The asymmetry in Greek of ἀγαθὸν ποιῆσαι and κακοποιῆσαι is rarely reflected in translation. Jesus was not placed before the alternative of performing a good act or performing a bad act; not to act would have been to act badly (Hans-Ulrich Rüegger, *Verstehen, was Markus erzählt: Philologisch-hermeneutische Reflexionen zum Übersetzen von Markus 3,1–6* [WUNT 2/155; Tübingen, 2002], 101–5).

[57]   Doering, *Schabbat*, 451–3.

their Sabbath observance correlates with their preparations for care of a corpse; it is done in ignorance of what they would experience at the tomb, early on the first day of the week.[58] This would imply that any further Sabbath-observance was subordinate to commemoration of the resurrection on the following day.

Taken together, these references to the Sabbath in Mark's Gospel contain no dominical saying abrogating the Sabbath, nor is there any hint that its observance is prohibited. Its continued validity is presumed in both 2:27–28 and 3:4, but relativized by the primacy of human needs. It is not an occasion for gathering in synagogues where scriptural interpretation is in the hands of those who reject the claims of Jesus. It has diminished in importance, perhaps even been eclipsed, by celebration of the resurrection of Jesus.

The inferences made about the Sabbath so far can be supplemented by consideration of Mark's handling of other recognizably Jewish practices. The unit immediately preceding the grainfield episode (2:18–22) indicates that the disciples of Jesus did not fast in accord with the practice of the Pharisees, nor of the disciples of John. Mark's assumption that his readers know of the Sabbath, with its strict requirement to rest, even to the point of definition of the kinds of work that were not "permitted" (2:24), stands in contrast to his explanation of the custom of ritual washing (7:2–4), which demonstrates that he is aware that the social world of his readers is not identical with that of Jesus.[59] This pericope on ritual purity (7:1–23) also includes the comment καθαρίζων πάντα τὰ βρώματα (v. 19b). Although the NA[26] punctuates this as if it were part of the question posed by Jesus that begins in v. 18, it is

---

[58] A. T. Lincoln suggests that they rested because they had not yet worked out the implications of Christ's ministry ("From Sabbath to Lord's Day: A Biblical and Theological Perspective," in *From Sabbath to Lord's Day: A Biblical Historical and Theological Investigation* [ed. D. A. Carson; Grand Rapids, Mich., 1982], 344–412, here 364).

[59] Philip G. Davis concludes that the Gospel of Mark reflects a distinctively Christian self-understanding and self-definition by the second generation of the church. It was aware of, and perhaps little concerned about, its differences from Judaism ("Christology, Discipleship, and Self-Understanding in the Gospel of Mark," in *Self-Definition and Self-Discovery in Early Christianity: A Study in Changing Horizons* [FS B. F. Meyer; ed. D. J. Hawkin and T. Robinson; Lewiston, Maine, 1990], 1–30).

more likely a redactional comment.[60] It shows two things that are relevant for this study: first, that Mark viewed the distinction between clean and unclean meats (cf. Lev 11; Deut 14:3–20) as a matter that belonged to the past. Secondly, that he was ready to correct the tradition he received to accord with the convictions of a church that accepted Gentiles (just as Matthew in turn "corrects" Mark on this point by striking this comment, 15:17, as well as by specifying at the end of the pericope that the matter under discussion was ritual handwashing; see below, 4.2.3). But he seems not to have created pericopes out of whole cloth simply to support such doctrinal developments. For instance, there is no controversy dialogue to reflect the question of whether Gentiles should be circumcised and adhere to the Torah.[61] From this we can suppose that Mark did not invent Sabbath controversies; they were a part of the traditional material out of which he shaped his Gospel. The point for Mark is not the question of whether the disciples would keep the Sabbath, and certainly not the halakic one of how far exceptions could go.[62] Rather, it is an occasion of strife, building on questions of forgiveness of sin, table fellowship, and fasting, that results in plans to destroy Jesus. More important for Mark than the question of Jesus' stance toward the law in general or the Sabbath in particular however is how that stance determined his fate.

4.1.4 Summary

The text portrays Jesus operating in a society that placed a high value on the Sabbath and had high expectations for its fulfillment.[63] Mark

---

[60]   Compare NA²⁷, which retains this decision, but notes in the apparatus that Origen and John Chrysostom understood this as a parenthetical comment. See Marcus, *Mark 1–8*, 452–8.

[61]   R. Meyer, "περιτέμνω, περιτομή, ἀπερίτεμνος," *TWNT* 6:72–83, here 81.

[62]   Neither the gleaning of grain nor the healing recounted in the next narrative unit were "necessary"; for this reason they are not "exceptions" to Sabbath rest (Andreas Lindemann, "Jesus und der Sabbat: Zum literarischen Charakter der Erzahlung Mk 3,1–6," in *Text und Geschichte: Facetten theologischen Arbeitens aus dem Freundes- und Schülerkreis* [FS D. Lührmann; ed. S. Maser and E. Schlarb; Marburg, 1999], 122–35). On the question of whether Jesus created halakah, see below, 4.4.3.

[63]   While Israel was not unique in distinguishing between holy and profane time (see Barbara C. Sproul, "Sacred Time," *ER*, 12:535–44, esp. 542–3), the veneration of the

describes Jesus as coming into conflict with these expectations. At times it is the behavior of the disciples of Jesus that is attacked, as in the passage under consideration (cf. 2:18, which concerns the fasting practice of the disciples, and 7:5, which concerns their lack of regard for purity regulations). But more often, it is a healing, an act of mercy, that is the occasion of the conflict. The "new, authoritative teaching" (1:27) with regard to the Sabbath is that this divine institution has to serve those for whom it was created. This is consistent with the overall teaching of Jesus concerning the law (12:31–34).

On the one hand, the freedom exercised by the disciples with regard to Sabbath practice is presented as a matter for which their master, Jesus, is held responsible and which becomes a factor in the decision of his opponents to destroy him. On the other, this freedom is not based on an abrogation of the Sabbath (in 16:1, the women, followers of Jesus, wait until after the Sabbath to anoint the body of Jesus). Instead it is based on the lordship of "the Son of Man," Jesus, lord over the Sabbath as the new and greater David, who has acted to restore the original intent of the Sabbath (2:27–28).[64] In addition, in keeping with the emphasis on Jesus as authoritative teacher, it is defended by his exposition of the scriptures of Israel (vv. 25–26).[65] Jesus, as portrayed in the Gospel of Mark, reinterprets the Sabbath but does not abrogate it. The statement that the Sabbath was made for humanity, indeed, that it is a divine institution, presumes the continuance of the Sabbath, and its continued observance, yet with an increased freedom and responsibility of the individual for determining how to use it.[66] It may be used more freely than the prevailing restrictions of its time (see above, 2.2). But there is no

---

seventh-day was frequently noted by non-Jews (see above, 2.3).

[64] Marcus suggests a link with the example of David and his companions: "the implication is that his disciples may share in his sovereignty over the Sabbath" (*Mark 1–8*, 245).

[65] The presence of these two answers, unique among the controversy dialogues in Mark, demonstrates the need for diachronic analysis; see below, 4.4.

[66] It is worth reflecting, however, how this freedom was meant. Carson comments: "Jesus is not suggesting that every individual is free to use or abuse the Sabbath as he sees fit, but that Sabbath observance in the Old Testament was a beneficial privilege, not a mere legal point—an end in itself" ("Jesus and the Sabbath," 65).

basis for saying, with Bacchiocchi, that it has messianic significance (see above, 1.2.2).

The Sabbath is something then with which both Mark and his intended readers are acquainted, yet it is an institution that has been reinterpreted by Jesus, the anointed one, and subordinated to his authority. This has implications for one of the two elements in Sabbath practice, the question of rest; a command to rest that can be set aside is a command that has lost its force.[67] We cannot be as certain concerning the other element, that of worship. While, for Mark, the food taboos of the Torah clearly belong to the past (7:19), this does not automatically mean that the Sabbath has met the same fate. Immediately preceding the grainfield episode, we read the logion of new wine and new wineskins (2:22). While this saying belongs to the preceding pericope, concerning fasting (2:18–22), it is with these words fresh in our minds that we come to the Sabbath controversies. Mark shows us Jesus rejecting the letter of the Torah in the question of divorce, as well, but in favor of restoring the creation intent of marriage (10:6). It is thinkable that he and his readers could have understood 2:27–28 in a similar way, but this is not certain.[68]

The argument thus far has been based strictly on inferences from the text of Mark's Gospel. This can be supplemented with a brief attempt at historical reconstruction. Based on the discussion in ch. 3, we can assert that this congregation, which was located outside of Palestine, and included a significant proportion of non-Jews, was founded either by an Antiochene-type mission such as that of Paul, or it was founded by a law-observant Gentile mission. The ignorance that Mark presumes his readers to have in the matter of ritual washing as well as his understanding that Jesus' words about ritual impurity had rendered all meat ritually clean weigh against the latter alternative. Nor are there any contrary indications in the Gospel of Mark that his community was Torah-

---

[67] For Doering, this points already to the later position that the Gentile church would take: "Wenn aber, wie die Exemplarität des Ährenraufens zeigt, beliebige Sabbatbrüche gerechtfertigt werden können, scheint hier bereits die Position der heidenchristlichen Kirche auf, der der Sabbat ein Tag ohne verpflichtenden Charakter ist" (*Schabbat*, 430).

[68] There is no correspondence to the phrase "from the beginning" here (Carson, "Jesus," 90, n. 60).

observant. It is then doubtful that the members of that community (certainly those who were non-Jews) ever felt compelled to observe the Sabbath. This historical consideration coincides with a conclusion that the text does permit us to make, namely, that the grainfield episode was included not primarily to defend the freedom of Mark and his community with regard to the Sabbath but rather to explain the death of Jesus.

4.2 LUKE'S USE OF THE GRAINFIELD EPISODE

4.2.1 Analysis of Luke 6:1–5

A comparison of the account in Luke 6:1–5 to that in Mark reveals roughly thirty variants; many are in the introductory narrative, and tend to be stylistic.[69] Some of his changes seem dictated by the logic of storytelling, such as adding the details that the disciples rubbed the corns in their hands and ate them. "Some of the Pharisees" make the accusation, and Luke makes their tone less aggressive by striking ἴδε.[70] Luke identifies Jesus by name as the one who answers. None of these changes affect my enquiry, however. There are a few other changes, however, that do. Luke changes the narrative time reference from plural to singular, although this is probably without theological significance.[71] He changes the verb ποιέω to second person plural, which means either that the accusers address

---

[69] Brief description of Luke's treatment of Mark's material in Joseph A. Fitzmyer, *The Gospel According to Luke I–IX. A New Translation with Introduction and Commentary* [AB 28; New York, 1981], 107–8. With regard to context, Luke has retained, unlike Matthew, the order of the accounts in Mark. This pericope is preceded by the dispute over fasting (5:33–39), and is succeeded by the dispute occasioned by the healing of a man with a withered hand on the Sabbath (6:6–11).

[70] François Bovon however suggests that the addition of τινές may make this more polemic (*Das Evangelium nach Lukas. 1. Lk 1,1–9,10* [EKK 3/1; Zürich, 1989], 270, n. 22).

[71] As we saw above (4.1.1), Mark's plural may have been the result of misunderstood Aramaic. A widely attested textual variant identifies the time as the δευτεροπρώτον, "second-first" Sabbath. J. M. Baumgarten proposes that this phrase is a Hebraism meaning that it was the second Sabbath of the first month. This would heighten the antinomist thrust of the passage, as new grain could not be eaten until the wave sheaf had been offered, which would have occurred during the subsequent week ("The Counting of the Sabbath in Ancient Sources," *VT* 16 [1966]: 277–86). Discussion of other proposals in Fitzmyer, *Gospel*, 607–8, and Bovon, *Lukas*, 266–7.

their question to the disciples, and then Jesus answers on their behalf, or that they include Jesus in the accusation.[72] If the latter were the case, Luke would have eliminated any possible interpretation that would exclude Jesus from the action in question. A similar tendency is even more evident in Luke's treatment of the story within the story, the narrative of David and the bread of presence. Here he makes far fewer stylistic modifications than in the introductory narrative. Aside from the striking of the reference to Abiathar in the interest of historical accuracy, he makes other changes that are theological in import. He strikes the circumstantial χρείαν ἔσχεν in the narrative of the David episode, which could have had the effect of mitigating David's action. He adds the adjective μόνους to the explanation that the bread of presence was forbidden (οὐκ ἔξεστιν) to any but the priests. Finally, he switches the order of the clauses, so that the mention of the bread's forbidden nature comes last, for emphasis.

The most glaring difference in Luke's account compared to Mark's comes however in the second answer from Jesus, in which Luke strikes the first half of the answer, the two-part argument from the creation order (v. 5; cf. Mark 2:27–28). He retains Mark's introductory formula, including the imperfect aspect of the verb ἔλεγεν, but then goes directly to the second half. The absence of the first half make both the conjunction ὥστε and the adversative καὶ superfluous, and he strikes both. The same change is made by Matthew (below, 4.3.1). The effect of this absence in context is to emphasize the christological understanding of Jesus' word. In fact, given that in Luke this saying follows directly on the example of David, without the intervening material that appears in Matthew, the effect is heightened. As in the Gospel according to Mark, any freedom exercised by the disciples toward the Sabbath is derived from the lordship of Jesus as the Son of Man over the Sabbath.

4.2.2 The Sabbath in the Context of Luke–Acts

As in Mark, Luke depicts Jesus inaugurating his public ministry with teaching in the synagogue (cf. Mark 1:21–28). In Luke 4:16, Jesus goes

---

[72] Bovon adopts the first of these alternatives (*Lukas*, 268), Fitzmyer, the second (*Gospel*, 608).

into the synagogue on the Sabbath, "as his custom was", and stood up to read. Unlike in Mark, this is not in Capernaum, but in his hometown of Nazareth. The has elements of Mark's Nazareth rejection story (Mark 6:1–6). In Mark, however, there is no indication of what Jesus preached. The content of Jesus' sermon is unique to Luke, who has evidently moved the Nazareth episode forward to provide the narrative framework for the first teaching. Both in form—Jesus goes according to his custom—and in content—the fulfilment of scripture—he stresses that the ministry of Jesus, thus inaugurated, stands in continuity with the faith and practice of Israel. At the same time, the reaction of the listeners, who seek to put Jesus to death, foreshadows Jesus' violent end. Yet in contrast to Mark, where the purported Sabbath transgressions of Jesus lead to opposition and a plot to kill, Jesus narrowly escapes a violent end *despite* his pious observance of the command. After he escapes from Nazareth, he come to Capernaum, and teaches there on the Sabbath (Luke 4:31). This introduces Luke's version of Mark 1:21–28 (Luke 4:31–37).

In 6:6–11, Luke brings his version of the healing of a man with a withered hand in a synagogue. As in Mark and Matthew, this follows the grainfield episode. In the introduction, v. 6, he makes it clear that this occurs on another Sabbath, thus resolving the ambiguity of Mark 3:1 in the opposite direction to Matthew. There are other added details, one that is significant is that he expressly mentions that Jesus taught.

There are two Sabbath healing controversies that are unique to Luke (13:10–17; 14:1–6). In both, Jesus defends his action with an appeal to humane practices for the benefit of animals (13:15; 14:5). The second of these closely parallels the sheep-in-the-pit saying that Matthew, but not Luke, had added to the withered hand episode (Matt 12:11). By virtue of arguments *a minori ad majori*, Jesus asserts the suitability of the healing. Thus, although Luke had stricken Mark 2:27 in the grainfield episode, it was not because he disagreed with its assertion that the Sabbath was made for humankind. It must have been because, like Matthew, he did not see the logic of tracing the lordship of the Son of Man over the Sabbath from the creation order.[73]

---

[73] Kiilunen, *Vollmacht*, 200–201.

Finally, when Luke reports the behavior of the women between crucifixion and visit to the tomb, he mentions that the women prepared spices as the Sabbath was drawing on (thus reversing the order of Mark 16:1), then rested on the Sabbath "according to the commandment" (Luke 23:56). This express mention of the obedience to the commandment is unique to Luke.

The Codex Bezae Cantibrigiensis (D) offers an additional saying in place of the declaration of the Son of Man's lordship over the Sabbath, which is displaced in this manuscript to the close of the next pericope, between our 6:10 and 6:11, where it "functions as the climax and justification for the whole set of [three] stories."[74] Instead we read at 6:5: "On the same day, seeing someone working on the Sabbath, he [Jesus] said to him, Man, if you know what you are doing, you are blessed. But if you do not know, you are cursed and a transgressor of the law."[75] Formally this is an apophthegm; it is a unified composition: the saying was always transmitted with its narrative frame.[76] The saying is constructed in antithetic parallelism; being blessed or cursed is related to a condition of knowing or not knowing. The parallelism is uneven, however. The consequence of not knowing is not only being cursed, it also means being a transgressor of the law. Some take this as an indication that the second half, the negative aspect, is emphasized.[77] Yet the pronouncement of a curse on a Sabbath-breaker is nothing new; the novelty is that one can violate the Sabbath not only without guilt, as did the priests in the temple (Matt 12:5), but even be praised for it.[78]

The difference between being blessed and cursed (as a transgressor of the law) is solely determined by knowledge. There have been various

---

[74] Ernst Bammel, "The Cambridge Pericope: The Addition to Luke 6:4 in Codex Bezae," *NTS* 32 (1986): 404–26, here 406.

[75] Based on the literal translation in Joel Delobel, "Luke 6,5 in Codex Bezae: The Man Who Worked on the Sabbath," in *À Cause de l'Évangile: Études sur les Synoptiques et les Actes* (FS Jacques Dupont; LeDiv 123; Paris, 1985), 453–77, here 453.

[76] Bultmann, *Geschichte*, 24.

[77] Jeremias, *Jesusworte*, 62; Doering, *Schabbat*, 438–9. Bammel counsels against making too much of this in light of the echoes of legal terminology from the Holiness Code (Lev 17–26) and Num 5 and 7 ("Pericope," 410–13).

[78] Delobel, "Luke 6,5," 466; see also Bammel, "Pericope," 413.

conjectures about what this knowledge might be. In its present context as the middle episode in a series of three that conclude with the statement that the Son of Man is lord of the Sabbath, it would be appropriate to take the required knowledge to refer to this.[79] Certainly the scribe who inserted the saying here understood it in this way. This is consistent with Luke's understanding of the grainfield episode; the lordship of the Son of Man had decisive weight, so that Mark 2:27 was left out. In this case, the saying would have arisen to counter libertine tendencies: Only the Sabbath transgression that is consciously placed under the authority of the Son of Man is approved.[80] Speaking against this explanation is that, while it fits the present context in D, the saying itself does not illustrate the idea that Jesus is Lord of the Sabbath.[81] A second common proposal is to see this saying addressed to those who separate themselves from the law without knowing what they are thereby doing.[82] Proponents of this solution point to the Pauline beatitude in Rom 14:22b–23a: "Blessed are those who have no reason to condemn themselves because of what they approve. But those who have doubts are condemned if they eat, because they do not act from faith."

The position concerning the Sabbath for the author of the apophthegm would be, in this case, comparable to Pauline freedom.[83] There are no indications in the text however that would permit us to conclude this with certainty.[84]

---

[79] Doering, *Schabbat*, 439. In this case, the worker would act in conscious imitation of Jesus (Walter Käser, "Exegetische Erwägungen zur Seligpreisung des Sabbatarbeiters Lk 6,5D," *ZTK* 65 [1968]: 414–30, here 429–30). Similar are Delobel's suggestion that Jesus is now the fulfilment of divine rest, thus obviating literal Sabbath observance, but only for those who know this ("Luke 6,5," 464) and Bammel's that the knowledge in question concerns the nature of God (cf. John 5:17, see below, ch. 5; "Pericope," 421–2).

[80] Charlesworth, *Jesus within Judaism*, 65.

[81] Derrett, "Luke 6:5D," 243.

[82] Adolf von Harnack, "Über einige Worte Jesu, die nicht in den kanonischen Evangelien stehen, nebst einem Anhang über die übersprüngliche Gestalt des Vater-Unsers" (Sitzungsberichte der königlich preussischen Akademie der Wissenschaften. V. Sitzung der philosophisch-historischen Classe von 21. Januar, Berlin, 1904), 15.

[83] Doering, *Schabbat*, 439.

[84] Doering, *Schabbat*, 440.

The pleonastic introduction ("that day . . . on the Sabbath") indicates that the anecdote is not part of the original Lukan text. Its appearance here could be due to attraction; Luke contains more Sabbath pericopes than the other Gospels. In addition, acquaintance with Matthew's Gospel on the part of the redactor of D (shown by the harmonizing additions to the text of Luke) would mean that he was aware of additional saying at this point in the text of Matthew, concerning the priests and their guiltless profanation of the Sabbath (12:5). This saying, although completely different in content and vocabulary, makes a similar point.[85] At the same time, the saying corresponds formally to the concern of the one responsible for the insertion of the example of David: a *criterion* for Sabbath-breaking is given.[86]

It seems unlikely that this saying goes back to Jesus himself.[87] It is unlike the other stories in its context. There are no opponents, Jesus takes the initiative.[88] While beatitudes are a well-attested feature of his teaching, the conditional form of this is unusual. Further, he upbraids the man, on the condition that he does not know what he is doing, as a transgressor of the law; this is singular among dominical sayings.[89] Finally, despite "near-parallels" in the canonical Gospels, the emphasis on knowing or not knowing as the determining factor in being blessed or cursed sets it apart from the canonical Gospel tradition.[90]

---

[85]   Delobel, "Luke 6,5," 473. Less convincing are two suggestions of Käser: (1) that the presence of the sayings introduced by μακάριοι/οὐαί in the context (Luke 6:20–26) attracted this saying, based on the pair μακάριος/ἐπικατάρατος; (2) the redactor noticed Luke's propensity for three-fold structures and therefore created an additional example ("Erwägungen," 417).

[86]   Doering, *Schabbat*, 440.

[87]   Delobel, "Luke 6,5," 465–8; Doering, *Schabbat*, 440. Joachim Jeremias argued for authenticity (*Unbekannte Jesusworte* [3d ed., ATANT 16, Zürich. 1961], 61–64), as did Bammel, "Pericope," 22.

[88]   It is not however unique in the wider context of the gospels, e.g. Mark 12:44 (cf. Bammel, "Pericope," 418).

[89]   Jeremias makes this observation, but limits it to the Sabbath sayings (*Theologie*, 150).

[90]   Doering, *Schabbat*, 440. The parallels John 7:49, 9:41; Luke 11:52/Matt 23:13Q and Matt 23:3 are offered by J. Duncan M. Derrett, "Luke 6:5D Reexamined," *NovT* 37 (1995):232–48, here 246–7.

To sum up: the understanding of the Sabbath reflected in Luke 6:5D is that if one knows what one is doing, one may work on the Sabbath, but thoughtless transgression of the Sabbath is not justified. In common with canonical Sabbath sayings, there are conditions under which an act normally forbidden on the Sabbath can be guiltless. This saying goes beyond the others, though, in saying that it could even be grounds for blessing. The saying and its setting seem "to belong to a period and an environment where the Jewish Sabbath law could provoke real questions or controversies."[91] As such, it bears witness to a Christian conviction that the Sabbath is neither abrogated nor absolutely binding.

In addition to Luke's Gospel, we have a second work from his pen, the Book of Acts. These are separate books, and thus do not necessarily present a single theologicial position.[92] Nevertheless, the fact that they are the work of one author allows us to consult both to determine how Luke may have viewed the Sabbath. Based on the discussion above (3.4.2), it appears that the evidence of Acts is that the Sabbath is neither abolished nor binding on believers from the nations.

4.2.3 The Practice of Luke's Community

When picturing the community in which the Third Gospel may have been formulated, we have an advantage that we do not have in thinking about the communities of Matthew, Mark or John. Rather than be limited to drawing inferences from the portrayal of the followers of the earthly Jesus, we can draw on the description of the post-Resurrection community in Acts. The community is depicted as a mix of Jews and Gentiles. These Gentiles had been associated with synagogues before becoming Christians, gaining acquaintance with the scriptures of Israel (Acts 15:21). Even after becoming followers of Jesus, they accepted minimal Torah-based restrictions to enable table fellowship; beyond this, they were not "troubled" with Torah observance (v. 19). Luke's own community may have recognized itself in this portrait.[93]

---

[91] Delobel, "Luke 6,5," 473.

[92] Jacob Jervell, *Die Apostelgeschichte* (KEK 3; Göttingen, 1998), 91.

[93] Philip Francis Esler, *Community and Gospel in Luke-Acts: The Social and Political Motivations of Lucan Theology* (SNTSMS 57; Cambridge, 1987), esp. 24–45.

In Luke's portrayal of the church, a high proportion of its members can be assumed to have familiarity with Jewish customs and be well disposed toward them. The Jerusalem believers continue to frequent the Temple (Luke 24:53; Acts 2:46, 3:1). When the synagogue congregation in Pisidian Antioch divides over Paul's proclamation, those who responded favorably to his message ask him to speak to them again the following Sabbath, effectively forming a new synagogue of Jews and proselytes (13:42–44).[94] At the same time, Acts contains what may be the oldest literary evidence for Christian worship on the first day of the week (20:7–12).[95] Crucial for this understanding is the phrase συνηγμένων ἡμῶν κλάσαι ἄρτον in v. 7. The participial verb form shows that the author is presenting the accompanying circumstances of the story to be told, namely Paul's sermon and the waking of Eutychus. We may infer beyond this that this implies it was their regular practice to meet to break bread on the first of the week at evening.[96] A synthesis of these indications would suggest that the Sabbath continued to be an occasion for worship and scriptural instruction, while evening meals with eucharistic character after the Sabbath were attended by all, even Gentile believers who did not observe the Sabbath.[97] The question of whether this would have been Saturday or Sunday evening cannot be decided with certainty,

---

[94] A similar development, without express mention of the Sabbath, is reported in Corinth, where the newly constituted group meets next door to the synagogue, with the leader of the synagogue among them (18:7–8).

[95] 1 Cor 16:1–2, in which Paul urges his readers to set something aside for the collection for the saints on the first day of the week, is even older, but it is not clear whether they were each to set it aside in their own homes or at a meeting hall (which in Corinth would have been a house church centered on an extended family) as part of worship. It has therefore no probative value, other than to show that the Jewish reckoning of a seven-day week was presumed by Paul even when writing to a Gentile congregation.

[96] The question of the exact meaning of breaking bread is not relevant for my question. It is often debated as if meeting for a communal meal and celebrating the Lord's Supper were distinct practices, though this distinction may be anachronistic (although see Paul's instructions in 1 Cor 11:17–34, which would predate Acts, and which appears to plead for the separation of communal meal and Lord's Supper).

[97] Jervell, *Apostelgeschichte*, 502; Bovon, *Lukas*, 271. Haenchen points out that this cannot be taken as evidence of a Sunday worship practice on the part of Paul, but reflects the time of Luke (*Apostelgeschichte*, 562).

but it is more likely to have been Saturday evening.[98] Either way, we are dealing with a regular occurrence that was referred to as occurring on the first of the week, regardless of the evening in question.

The observation that Sabbath for Luke is neither abolished nor binding on Gentile believers is, however, not so much a resolution of the tensions involved in the creation of one community out of observant Jews and non-observant Gentiles as it is a truce. The pericope concerning ritual purity (Mark 7:1–23; Matt 15:1–20) is instructive. For Mark, this meant the abolition of distinction between clean and unclean foods. Matthew rejected this interpretation and limits the topic to ritual handwashing. Luke's solution is telling: delete the pericope. This is symptomatic of the tendencies in Luke-Acts. These are sometimes ascribed to an apologetic interest: Luke wishes to make the church appear inoffensive to (non-Christian) Jews and non-threatening to Romans. This may have numbered among Luke's concerns, but more pressing was the need to safeguard a fragile unity within the community.

4.2.4 Summary

When compared with Mark's account of the grainfield incident, we see that Luke has stricken details that would tend to mitigate the offense. As does Matthew, he deletes the reference to the divine origin of the Sabbath in creation; the freedom of the followers of Jesus is based solely in the lordship of the Son of Man. Luke assumes the continuing validity of Judaism, as evidenced by the visits to the temple and Paul's professions of loyalty.[99] Charges that Paul has departed from Torah-observance, or taught other Jews to do so, are refuted (Acts 21:17–26; 24:13–14). Implicit in this is that Jewish believers in Christ will continue to observe the Sabbath, although subordinated to humanitarian concerns. Gentile believers, on the other hand, are not to be placed under this

---

[98] Peter Wick, *Die urchristliche Gottesdienste: Entstehung und Entwicklung im Rahmen der frühjüdischen Tempel-, Synagogen- und Hausfrömmigkeit* (BWANT 150; Stuttgart, 2002), 286–7). Cf. the discussion by Turner, "Sabbath," 128–33, who argues for Sunday evening. He bases his conclusion on the assumption that both Luke and his readers were Gentiles; if they were proselytes or Godfearers, however, his arguments lose their force.

[99] See Acts 21:20: the Judean believers in Christ are "all zealous of the law."

yoke.[100] As long as they refrain from idolatry and the sins commonly associated with this practice in the Jewish mind, they are accepted in full fellowship as co-heirs of salvation (Acts 15:20, 29; cf. 21:25). The absence of the Sabbath from the four points in James's decree that were essential for Gentile believers (15:28–29) indicates that they were not required to keep the Sabbath. The mixed community formed of observant Jews and believing, non-observant Gentiles is a continuation of the best of Israel.

4.3 MATTHEW'S USE OF THE GRAINFIELD EPISODE

4.3.1 Analysis of Matthew 12:1–8

In addition to making stylistic changes and corrections of detail similar to those made by Luke, although not always identical, the synoptic comparison of Matthew with Mark reveals three areas to address.[101] The first are the modifications to Markan material that might indicate nuances with regard to Matthew's understanding of the significance of this episode for the question of the Sabbath. The second is that Matthew has two additional sayings of Jesus in answer to the accusation of the Pharisees (vv. 5–7). The third is that Matthew, in common with Luke, does not have the first half of what in Mark is a two-part saying concerning the Sabbath, creation, and the Son of Man.

With regard to modifications of Markan material, in the narrative introduction (v. 1) there are two significant added verbs, in addition to numerous stylistic changes. Matthew specifies that the disciples were hungry (ἐπείνασαν) and that they ate (καὶ ἐσθίειν) the grains. Both make explicit details that were implicit in the Markan account. Yet the express mention of hunger ties the action of the disciples more closely to that of

---

[100] Note however how this term, used in a positive sense for the Torah, is qualified as unbearable, albeit by Peter, not Paul. See Robin Scroggs, "The Earliest Christian Communities as Sectarian Movements," in *Christianity, Judaism and Other Greco-Roman Cults* (FS Morton Smith; ed. Jacob Neusner; SJLA 12/2; Leiden, 1975), 1–23, esp. 10–11 and 16–17.

[101] For a detailed discussion of the difference between Matthew's version and those of Mark and Luke, see Robert H. Gundry, *Matthew: A Commentary on his Literary and Theological Art* [Grand Rapids, Mich., 1982], 220–30.

David and his followers (ἐπείνασεν καὶ οἱ μετ᾿ αὐτοῦ, v. 3). In addition, specifying their need suggests an extenuating factor in their action.[102] This may be significant in light of the call for mercy in v. 7. It has been suggested that the second addition, the specific mention that they ate the grains they gleaned, also comes from an intent to minimize the gravity of their action.[103] The reader of Mark's account would however hardly imagine that they did not, given that the example cited in their defense involved David and his followers eating bread. This second addition, therefore, cannot be understood as reflecting a nuance in Matthew's view of the Sabbath compared to Mark's. We are left however with the possibility that the first added detail might well do so.

In reporting the challenge of the Pharisees, Matthew specifies that the action of gleaning grain was not allowed ἐν σαββάτῳ (v. 2). This clears up an ambiguity in Mark's narrative. In addition, Matthew may have found it important to specify that the problem was that the gleaning was on the Sabbath. It was, as noted above (4.1.1), the oral traditions that identified gleaning, an activity expressly permitted in the Torah, as a form of harvesting, and therefore an activity expressly forbidden in the Torah on the Sabbath. In this case, this added detail may reflect a greater concern for the nuances of legal discussion.[104]

Matthew's account of the narrative within the narrative, the example of David and the bread of presentation (vv. 3–4), ends with the double emphasis that it was not allowed for *him*, David—nor those with him—to eat it, but *only* the priest. This degree of explicitness makes it clear to the point of redundance that the bread was taboo.[105]

---

[102] Günther Bornkamm, "Enderwartung und Kirche im Matthäusevangelium," in G. Bornkamm, G. Barth, H. J. Held, *Überlieferung und Auslegung im Matthäus-Evangelium* [WMANT 1; Neukirchen-Vluyn, 1960], 29, n. 1. Barth suggests that this insertion is evidence that Matthew's community kept the Sabbath. "Es soll der Konsequenz wehren, als sei am Sabbat *alles* erlaubt" ("Gesetzesverständnis," 76).

[103] W. F. Albright and C. S. Mann: "Mark, less concerned with legal interpretation, almost makes the incident an act of idle destruction" (*Matthew: A New Translation with Introduction and Commentary* [AB 26; Garden City, N. Y., 1971], 150).

[104] Martin Dibelius, *Die Formgeschichte des Evangeliums* (3d ed.; Tübingen, 1959), 142.

[105] Daube suggests that this may reflect a desire to counter a possible argument that the bread, which a non-priest normally was not permitted to eat, was no longer holy

Thus while most of the Matthean alterations can be classified as stylistic, there are a few that suggest a greater concern for what was and was not allowed. Yet there may be a tension between providing the disciples with an extenuating factor that would excuse their behavior yet stress the illicit nature of that of David and his companions.

The second way in which Matthew's account differs from that of Mark is the presence of an additional argument in three steps (vv. 5–7). Jesus cites the example of the priests, who desecrate the Sabbath weekly through their scripturally-mandated service, yet remain guiltless (v. 5), followed by the declaration that something greater than the temple is here (v. 6), and rounded off by the assertion that if the Pharisees had properly understood the will of God as expressed by the prophet (Hos 6:6), they would not have accused the guiltless, by which his disciples are meant.[106] These verses may incorporate traditional material, but on the level of the Matthean text, they are well integrated with the preceding material and unified, so that they may be considered as elements of one argument.[107] The first of these statements, the innocence of the priests in desecrating the Sabbath to fulfil Num 28:9–10, was generally accepted in Second Temple Judaism.[108] The condemnation of

when removed from the sanctuary ("Responsibilities," 7).

[106] This is Matthew's second use of this quotation; the first is in 9:13, in the context of table fellowship with tax collectors and sinners, material that occurs in Mark in proximity to the grainfield episode (Mark 2:13–17). The repetition implies that the Pharisees had not learned the lesson (Gundry, *Matthew*, 224). Note the progression "go and learn" (9:13) and "if you had known" (12:7; Lena Lybaek, "Matthew's Use of Hosea 6,6 in the Context of the Sabbath Controversies," in *The Scriptures in the Gospels* [ed. C. M. Tuckett; BETL 131; Leuven, 1997], 491–9, here 496). *Pace* Back (*Jesus*, 104), the Pharisees are not accused of ignorance (the question οὐκ ἀνέγνωτε, v. 5, would have the expected answer that they had indeed read), but of not understanding what they could be expected to know.

[107] Reinhart Hummel, *Die Auseinandersetzung zwischen Kirche und Judentum im Matthäusevangelium* (BEvT 33; München, 1963), 44. The catchwords that integrate vv. 5–7 with vv. 1–4 are shown by Back, *Jesus*, 102.

[108] This is even the case with the Essenes, who were as far as we know the strictest in their interpretation of the Sabbath (CD 11:18; 11Q19 [*Temple Scroll*] 13:17; cf. *Jub.* 50:10–11). On the six exceptions to the Sabbath in Tannaitic literature, see Yong-Eui Yang, *Jesus and the Sabbath* (JSNTSup 139; Sheffield, 1997), 91–92 and material in Bill 1:620–22. With the exception of intervention to save life, they were cases in which the

the innocent stems not so much from a false understanding of the Sabbath as it does from a failure to "recognize in Jesus the mercy of God."[109] Matthew inserted this chain of reasoning because he found the example of David insufficient.[110] While the example he shares with Mark draws from the *Nebi'im*, the prophets, the new example is drawn from the Torah; in fact, attention is drawn to this (ἐν τῷ νόμῳ, v. 5). Additionally, since these three verses in effect replace Mark 2:27, Matthew may have felt this provided a better preparation for the concluding statement that the Son of Man is lord of the Sabbath.[111] The "something greater" would then be the mercy evident in the work and message of Jesus.[112] This mercy, at the same time, fulfils the Sabbath commandment.[113] It does not follow, however, that the disciples of Jesus are counterparts of the priests in that they serve God accompanying Jesus.[114] They glean to satisfy their own hunger, not his.[115]

The argumentation would be tighter if the narrative showed the disciples exercising mercy. Instead, they glean to satisfy their own hunger. Mercy here apparently refers to an attitude displayed by others that would permit this. Alternatively, since the hunger of the disciples is emphasized, one might conclude that Matthew here expands the halakah of his day. It was agreed that hunger overrides the Sabbath if there is the suspicion that it is life-threatening. Yet Matthew intimates nothing of the kind. Instead, that behavior is acceptable which reflects the divine will as

---

law decreed a certain time for the fulfilment of a commandment (Ulrich Luz, *Das Evangelium nach Matthäus [Mt 8-17]* [2d ed.; EKK I/2; Zürich, 1996], 231).

[109] Lybaek, "Use," 497.

[110] E.g., Davies and Allison, *Matthew* 2:313; D. Hill, "On the Use and Meaning of Hosea vi.6 in Matthew's Gospel," *NTS* 24, 1978, 114–5; Hummel, *Auseinandersetzung*, 41–42; Neirynck, "Jesus and the Sabbath," 640. Compare the recent discussion of Doering, *Schabbat*, 432–6, whose position is largely followed here.

[111] This argument assumes that Mark 2:27 was known to Matthew.

[112] Luz, *Evangelium*, 2:280–81; Doering, *Schabbat*, 434.

[113] Lybaek, "Use," 494.

[114] So Back, *Jesus*, 103.

[115] Joachim Gnilka, *Das Matthäusevangelium: 1. Kommentar zu Kap. 1,1-13,58* (HTKNT 1; Freiburg im Breisgau, 1986), 445; Anthony J. Saldarini, *Matthew's Christian-Jewish Community* (Chicago Studies in the History of Judaism; Chicago, 1994), 130.

proclaimed by Matthew's Jesus. In the perspective of mercy, Sabbath violations that are committed by those who have need can be justified.[116] The third way in which Matthew's account differs from that of Mark is that he, in common with Luke, strikes the first half of the closing saying (Mark 2:27), as well as the connecting participle ὥστε from v. 28.[117] There is much discussion of this, one of the most striking of the fifteen "minor agreements" in this pericope.[118] These common omissions have given rise to a variety of proposed solutions. Aside from latter-day proponents of a modified Griesbach hypothesis, which holds to a Matthean priority, a proposal that creates more problems than it solves, the proposals fall into three groups. The first is that one evangelist, usually held to be Luke, had access to the work of the other in addition to Mark's Gospel.[119] A variation of this proposal is that both had access to common traditions other than Mark.[120] Secondly, it is proposed that Matthew and Luke had access to a copy of Mark's gospel that did not contain these verses, either because it was defective, or because it was the first edition of a work that later was reissued in a second, the form that entered our canon.[121] The third possibility is that each independently

[116] Luz, *Evangelium*, 2:232; Saldarini, *Community*, 131

[117] There is a similar case in the previous pericope, concerning the question of fasting, where the second part of Mark 2:19 has no parallel in Matthew or Luke.

[118] These are listed in *The Minor Agreements of Matthew and Luke against Mark with a Cumulative List* (ed. F. Neirynck, T. Hansen, and F. van Segbroek; BETL 37; Louvain, 1974), 74–76.

[119] E.g., Gundry, *Matthew*, 222. There are, however, a number of changes made by Matthew that Luke does not adopt; for instance, Luke retains καὶ ἔλεγεν αὐτοῖς (6:5).

[120] Albright and Mann, *Matthew*, 150. Hans Hübner proposes, for instance, that Q contained a version of Mark 2:23–28 (*Das Gesetz in der synoptischen Tradition* [Witten, 1973], 113–28, esp. 117–21). Yang, who is reticent about the existence of Q, refers instead to "common tradition" (*Jesus* 163; similarly Back, who calls it "parallel tradition," *Jesus*, 71–73). Yet the assumption of such a tradition fails to explain why both Matthew and Luke followed it, rather than their Markan *Vorlage* (Kiilunen, *Vollmacht*, 202–3).

[121] E.g., Hermann Aichinger, "Quellenkritische Untersuchung der Perikope vom Ährenraufen am Sabbat. Mk 2,23–28 par Mt 12,1–8 par Lk 6,1–5," in *Jesus in der Verkündigung der Kirche* (ed. A. Fuchs; SNTSU 1; Freistadt, 1976), 110–53, here 141–53, esp. 148–9; Helmut Koester, *Ancient Christian Gospels: Their History and Development* (Harrisburg, 1990), 276; Luz, *Evangelium*, 2:229. The phrase is missing from Mark 2 in D, but this is generally understood as a having occurred to harmonize

decided to strike it.[122] Without entering into the debate of the general relationship of these three gospels, I will note simply that the third possibility is sufficient both to explain this common omission, as well as a number of other minor agreements in this pericope.

Those who see in this an editorial decision offer a variety of explanations. The most widely held is that the community stepped back from the freedom expressed in these words.[123] It is possible that, by the time Matthew and Luke wrote, this saying was interpreted in this way and that both acted to preserve a modified observance of the law.[124] Alternatively, it is suggested that the deletion occurred because in Mark 2:27 observance of the Sabbath, while relativized, is still presumed.[125] These two explanations are mutually exclusive. It is not necessary to make recourse to either if we consider the effect of the change: both change the word order so that ὁ υἱὸς τοῦ ἀνθρώπου comes last. By striking the reference to the original purpose of the Sabbath, each brings out more clearly the christologically understood point of the remaining saying about the Son of Man and the Sabbath.[126] For Matthew, the fact that the Son of Man is lord of the Sabbath is the reason (γάρ) why the Pharisees should not have accused the innocent.[127]

4.3.2 The Sabbath in the Context of Matthew's Gospel

In contrast to Luke, who follows Mark's narrative order (see above, 4.2.1), Matthew separates the two pericopes dealing with the Sabbath

it with Matthew and Luke.

[122] So Bultmann *Geschichte*,14 ("überwiegend wahrscheinlich"), followed, among many others, by Lohse, "Jesu Worte," 84–85, cf. *TWNT* 7:22, n. 175.

[123] E.g., Barth, "Gesetzesverständnis," 85, n. 1; cf. Becker, *Jesus*, 375. This view is usually held by those who, with Käsemann, hear in Mark 2:27 the cry of freedom ("Das Problem des historischen Jesus," 1954, repr. in *Exegetische Versuche und Besinnungen* 1:187–214, here 206–7). This is not convincing in the case of Matthew, however; fear that the saying would have encouraged laxity would also have forestalled the insertion of a comparison to the temple service of the priests (vv. 5–6; Gundry, *Matthew*, 225).

[124] So Lindemann, "Jesus," 104.

[125] Georg Strecker, *Der Weg der Gerechtigkeit: Untersuchung zur Theologie des Matthäus* (3d ed.; Göttingen, 1971, 33, n. 1).

[126] Doering, *Schabbat*, 430.

[127] Gundry, *Matthew*, 225.

from the three that had preceded it in Mark's Gospel. In fact, they have
been moved to the next narrative block, where they follow the second of
the five speeches (ch. 10, with prelude in 9:35–38), according to which
Matthew appears to have structured his gospel.[128]

Not only does Matthew divide the five pericopes by the insertion of
additional material, he also separates them thematically by striking any
express mention of the Sabbath before the grainfield episode (12:1).[129]
The Sabbath is now mentioned eight times in twelve verses, then again
only in 24:20 and 28:1. In addition, Matthew binds the grainfield
pericope to the healing episode that follows more closely than does
Mark by the phrase μεταβὰς ἐκεῖθεν in 12:9.[130] The effect is a concentration of Matthew's presentation of Jesus' practice and teaching concerning
the Sabbath.

Moreover, this teaching on the Sabbath is skillfully prepared.
Immediately preceding is Jesus' invitation to the weary and burdened
who come to him, in which he offers rest (κἀγὼ ἀναπαύσω ὑμᾶς,
11:28–30).[131] Jesus speaks of his easy yoke and light burden, and this is

[128] On the structure of Matthew, see Brown, *Introduction*, 173.

[129] There is no correspondence in Matthew's Gospel to the Sabbath teaching and
exorcism in the synagogue of Capernaum (Mark 1:21–28); its place is taken, in effect,
by the Sermon on the Mount (Matt 5–7; Luz, *Evangelium* 1:197). Thus, the healing of
Simon's mother-in-law is not connected to the Sabbath (8:14–15). This may have been
motivated by a desire to downplay the degree of conflict Jesus provoked through healing
on the Sabbath (so Bornkamm, "Enderwartung,", 29, n. 1), although neither the
exorcism nor the healing provoked any in Mark's narrative. Matthew retains the notice
that many others were brought "when evening had come" (8:16), but strikes the second
part of Mark's determination of the time, "when the sun had set," which is more strongly
indicative of the Sabbath.

[130] Lohse, *TWNT* 7:24 with n. 194. Luke interpreted Mark's ambiguous time
indication in the opposite direction (Luke 6:6). Since there is no new temporal indication
in Mark 3:1, it has been argued that Mark intends the reader to understand that this
incident occurred on the same Sabbath (Fitzmyer, *Gospel*, 604–5). The narrative
framework is enough, however, to identify 3:1–6 as a separate pericope. To mention that
Jesus went into the synagogue "on the Sabbath" would have been superfluous. The lack
of explicit detail means that Mark's account can be read both ways, as evidenced by a
comparison of the other two synoptics.

[131] On the possible relation of this to expectations of a great, eschatological Sabbath,
see Davies and Allison, *Matthew*, 2:287–9. See also below, ch. 6, on Heb 4.

immediately followed (ἐν ἐκείνῳ τῷ καιρῷ) by the grainfield episode. This juxtaposition has the effect of characterizing the approach of the accusing Pharisees to the Sabbath, which was supposed to give rest, as burdensome.[132] Taken together with the grainfield and Sabbath-healing episodes—a triptych—the effect is that of reinterpreting the Sabbath in christological terms. Noteworthy as well is the thematic correspondence to the following pericope, 12:15–21, which includes a brief summary notice describing Jesus' ministry as well as the longest of Matthew's scriptural quotations, from the first of the songs of the suffering servant, Isa 42:1–4, with its twofold mention of the nations.[133] The two Sabbath pericopes serve a crucial role in Matthew's narrative as a whole. As in Mark's Gospel, they provide the first clear indication that in the end, Jesus' messianic words and deeds would lead his opponents to kill him.

There are only two further references to the Sabbath after this cluster. In 24:20, Matthew expands a saying of Jesus found in Mark 13:18 about the timing of (eschatological?) tribulation with the phrase "and not on the Sabbath." There is no widely-accepted explanation for this phrase.[134] A common proposal is that the avoidance of flight on the Sabbath would be to avoid antagonizing Jewish authorities.[135] Speaking against this is that fact that a Sabbath flight would have been acceptable to these authorities, the saving of life being a legitimate violation of the Sabbath. Banks suggests that the reason was the practical difficulty that would be involved in a predominantly Jewish setting.[136] Both suggestions would

---

[132] Davies and Allison maintain that it is not "necessary to be so exclusively specific" (*Matthew*, 2:288). For the view that the burdens are those of Pharisaism, see Barth, "Gesetzesverständnis," 148, and Robert Banks, *Jesus and the Law in the Synoptic Tradition* (SNTSMS 28; Cambridge, 1975), 113. B. Charette understands the reference to the weary and heavily laden to refer solely back to 11:5 and 9:36 and that Jesus has come to proclaim rest for those who have suffered under the withdrawal of divine favor occasioned by Israel's sin ("To Proclaim Liberty to the Captives: Matthew 11.28–30 in the Light of OT Prophetic Expectation," *NTS* 38 [1992]: 290-99).

[133] Yang, *Jesus*, 148.

[134] Survey of views in Graham M. Stanton ("'Pray that your Flight may not be in Winter or on a Sabbath': Matthew 24.20," in *A Gospel for a New People. Studies in Matthew* [Edinburgh, 1992], 192-206).

[135] Barth, "Gesetzesverständnis," 86.

[136] Banks, *Jesus*, 102.

make sense only if the flight envisaged were one that Christians undertook at a time when their Jewish, non-Christian neighbors did not. The disciples are to pray that their flight would not be in the winter or on the Sabbath, most assume that does not mean that they would not flee if it were. Eduard Schweizer disputes this and contends that there is no inherent contradiction in the position of a congregation that would extend help to *others* even when life was not threatened, yet be so strict in its own Sabbath observance that it would refuse to flee to save its *own* life.[137] The Maccabean decision to engage in battle on the Sabbath to defend their lives was not universally accepted in first-century Judaism (see above, 2.2). While the exact meaning of the phrase may elude us, it remains a further example of modifications in the gospel tradition that reflect a Jewish-Christian setting for Matthew. It is often taken as proof that the Matthean community observed the Sabbath.[138] Taken on its own, the reference is too obscure to carry the burden of proof. Yet considered in the overall context of Matthew's Gospel, it is consistent with an assumption of continued Sabbath observance.

Finally, in 28:1 the women go to the tomb after the Sabbath (cf. Mark 16:1, which mentions that the women buy [embalming] spices after the Sabbath). Although Matthew does not explicitly state that the women rested on the Sabbath, this is assumed. As in Mark and Luke, this is consistent with the picture of the followers of the earthly Jesus as Torah-observant.

With this, the mentions of the Sabbath in Matthew are exhausted. Strikingly, both of the Sabbath controversies are taken over from Mark. There are none shared with Luke, leading to the likelihood that there were no Sabbath-critical sayings of Jesus in Q, nor are there any controversies unique to Matthew, unlike Luke. Of the four canonical Gospels (on John, see below, ch. 5), Matthew's is the least negative with regard to the Sabbath. If we had no knowledge of subsequent developments, and had only the Gospel of Matthew, we would not conclude

---

[137] "Mattäus 12,1–8: Der Sabbat—Gebot und Geschenk," in *Glaube und Gerechtigkeit* (FS R. Gyllenberg; ed. J. Kiilunen, V. Riekkinen and H. Räisänen; Helsinki, 1983), 169–79, here 172.

[138] E.g., Bornkamm, "Enderwartung," 29.

that Christians had broken with Sabbath observance, but that it had been subordinated to the practice of mercy and identified with Christ.[139] The subordination (but not abrogation) of the Sabbath command to the practice of mercy corresponds to the overall stance of Matthew toward the law.[140] A number of details, such as the reference to the kingdom of heaven rather than the kingdom of God (e.g. Matt 4:17; cf. Mark 1:14) indicate that Matthew's community identifies strongly with its Jewish (-Christian) heritage, yet is poised to begin a mission to the nations (placement of Matt 28:18–20).[141] In the Sermon on the Mount, the first of the five major speeches into which Matthew has gathered sayings material, Jesus avers that the Torah retains its validity, expanding on a saying in Q (5:17–20; cp. Luke 16:16–17). The last of these five speeches, ch. 23, is a scathing denunciation of the scribes and Pharisees who interpreted that law, but whose behavior is characterized as hypocrisy. A clear reflection of this is the way that Matthew recasts the purity controversy to remove any suggestion that a rejection of ritual handwashing—a "tradition of the elders" (v. 2), and therefore a matter

[139] This can be seen in the second Sabbath controversy (Matt 12:9–14). Barth compares Matthew's account of the Sabbath healing of the man with the withered hand to that of Mark and notes that the change in v. 12b removes the point of Mark 3:4 and takes away some of the radicality of Jesus' answer, thus turning it into a positive rule for behavior of the congregation. This in turn presumes that the congregation would be keeping the Sabbath; nonetheless, the Sabbath is clearly subordinated to the love command (καλῶς ποιεῖν; "Gesetzesverständnis," 73–74).

[140] Luz, *Evangelium* 2:233–4.

[141] Sim argues that Matt 28:19 merely records the acceptance of the legitimacy of a mission to the nations, not involvement in it (*Gospel*, 236–47). This proposal has the merit of taking seriously the anti-Gentile tone of the pearls before swine saying (7:6), but does not resolve the tension this saying creates with 28:19 any better than the mainstream view. The main difficulty, according to Sim, is that the mainstream view sets the beginning of the mission to the nations after the destruction of Jerusalem, yet Matthew places the command to do so in the mouth of Jesus at his first appearance to the disciples after his resurrection. This difficulty rests however on an excessively historicist reading of the text. Viewed in reader-response terms, the Gospel as a whole performs the function of moving a (Christian-Jewish) reader from the anti-Gentile posture formulated (also in the mouth of Jesus) in 7:6 and exclusive mission focus on Israel (9:37–10:42; 22:1–10; 23:29–36) to the recognition that the time has come for a mission to the nations.

of oral tradition (i.e., "human precepts," v. 9), not of the written Torah—had any effect on the distinction between clean and unclean foods (v. 20; cf. Mark 7:19). The Gospel seems engaged in a double front: against Pharisaic-led Judaism on the one hand, and on the other a form of Hellenistic Christianity that, through accentuation of the Christ of glory, had lost sight of the validity and salvific meaning of the Law.[142]

For all of Matthew's concern to combat lawlessness and to correct the teaching that Jesus had abrogated the Torah, the summons to obedience is to that which Jesus commanded (28:20), namely, the righteousness that exceeds that of the (Torah-expounding) scribes and Pharisees (5:20), one that finds its supreme expression in the dual love command (22:37–40), which is, at the same time, nothing other than discipleship to Jesus Christ.[143] The sayings attributed to Jesus in the Sabbath pericopes, 12:1–14, appear to share this concern.

4.3.3 The Practice of Matthew's Community

The lack of explicit mention of the post-resurrection practice of the Matthean community has permitted both the interpretation that Matthew was a participant in the inner-Jewish debate over Sabbath observance and that he viewed the Sabbath as obsolete.[144] As in the case of Mark's community, we must work from inference. The extension of the prayer concerning flight to cover the Sabbath (24:20) indicates a greater concern about the Sabbath, but does not carry the burden of proof that the community observed it. More telling is the appeal to mercy in the grainfield episode. This does not abrogate the Sabbath, but relativizes it. The appeal to mercy as an overriding principle provides a key for decisions concerning behavior, and suggests that the Sabbath was observed as a day of rest, and probably worship, but that its observance

---

[142] Günther Bornkamm, "Der Auferstandene und der Irdische: Matt 28,16–20," in Zeit und Geschichte (FS Bultmann; ed. Erich Dinkler; Tübingen, 1964), 171–91, here 180. This has been developed and expanded in recent works on the Matthean community. In addition to Saldarini, Community, see David C. Sim, The Gospel of Matthew and Christian Judaism: The History and Social Setting of the Matthean Community (SNTW; Edinburgh, 1998).

[143] "Enderwartung," 21 (cf. 26); "Der Auferstandene," 187.

[144] Serious participant: Saldarini, Community, 126–34; obsolete: Yang, Jesus, 306.

was not strictly regulated through fixed halakah.[145] Beyond this, a significant indicator is Matthew's overall teaching on the law and against teachers of ἀνομία, supplemented by his reworking of the controversy over ritual purity (15:1–20, cf. Mark 7:1–23, especially the striking of 7:19b).[146] The weight of evidence indicates that Matthew assumes that the Sabbath would be observed, but that, as with tithing (23:23), such observance must be subordinated to the "weightier matters" of the law, κρίσις, ἔλεος, πίστις.

With its decided christological orientation in combination with insistence on the continued validity of the entire Torah, the Gospel of Matthew is the earliest witness to Jewish Christianity.[147] Its presence in the canon of the NT, together with writings such as James and Revelation, gives reason to doubt the widely-held view that Jewish Christianity lost its foundation with the murder of James in 62 C.E. and the destruction of the Temple in 70, and quickly became marginalized. There is no inherent reason why this must be so. Non-Christian Judaism was able to cope with this loss and reconstitute itself. With the confession of Jesus as the hoped for Messiah, Christian Jews possessed a powerful resource for such coping. In addition, his death, interpreted as "for us," provided a hermeneutical key for explaining the impossibility of a continued sacrificial cult. Writings such as Matthew's Gospel, James, and Revelation

---

[145] Doering, *Schabbat*, 435–6.

[146] Note his use of πᾶς in law-contexts, e.g., 23:3; 3:15; 5:18; 28:20 (so Barth, "Gesetzesverständnis," 66).

[147] The term *Jewish Christianity* is notoriously difficult to define. For the purpose of this study, I will adopt a simple definition: it is Christian, in that it recognizes Jesus as the promised Messiah; it is Jewish, in that Torah-observance is taught. This should not obscure the fact that there was a variety of ways in which the recognition "Jesus is the Messiah" was understood; Jewish Christianity was not *ipso facto* adoptionist, nor were all early Christians who held an adoptionist Christology Jewish Christians (Justin, *Dial.* 47; Jean-Daniel Kaestli, "Où en est le débat sur le Judéo-Christianisme," in *Le déchirement juifs et chrétiens au premier siècle* [ed. D. Marguerat; MdB 32; Geneva, 1996], 243–72, here 256–8). In the matter of Torah-observance a spectrum of views was possible as well: not all Jewish Christians would insist that the *entire* Torah be observed; some held to a two-law interpretation of the Torah, with the commandments that related to the sacrificial system viewed as secondary, the result of Israel's sin, and not part of the eternally valid law (*Ps.-Clem. R* 1.36.1–2). This tenet could be held in conjunction with the view that the sacrificial system was fulfilled in Christ, and therefore obsolete.

demonstrate not only a lively intellectual endeavor to simultaneously assert discipleship to Jesus and the continuity of the faith of Israel, but also the fact that this endeavor occurred in the context of the wider Christian movement, which took notice of these writings and canonized them.[148] This fits with the evidence of the Ignatian correspondence and the Clementine literature (see above, 3.4.1).

4.3.4 Summary

Matthew has retained the grainfield incident from Mark's Gospel. As in Mark, it is followed by the healing of the man with a withered hand on the Sabbath, which culminates in the plot of the Pharisees (he deletes Mark's reference to the Herodians) to destroy Jesus (12:14). By separating these two pericopes from the conflicts that preceded them in Mark, and placing before them the thematically related invitation of Jesus to enter into his rest (11:28–30), Matthew underlines the nature of this section as providing Jesus' teaching on the Sabbath. There are stylistic differences between the two accounts, with Matthew tending toward explicitness, as well as exactness concerning the OT. Two additional sayings have been variously interpreted as augmenting the argument from a Jewish standpoint or as emphasizing the christological claim made. Finally, there is the omission of Mark 2:27, best understood as an editorial decision that heightens the christological emphasis.

None of Matthew's references to the Sabbath prove that he or the community for which he wrote was Sabbatarian, although we can be reasonably certain that a community concerned with ritual purity would also retain some form of Sabbath observance. The conclusions that can be stated with the greatest certainty are three points that Matthew shares

---

[148] This was also true in reverse. Jewish-Christian writings know and interact with other Christian literature. In contrast to the assumptions of heresiologists, the Jewish Christian *Preaching of Peter*, as reconstructed from the basic *Grundschrift* underlying *Ps.-Clem.* R and H) does not seem to know of a Jewish Christian gospel (Georg Strecker, "Zum Problem des Judenchristentums," appendix to *Rechtgläubigkeit und Ketzerei im ältesten Christentum*, by Walter Bauer [2d ed.; BHT 10; Tübingen, 1964], 243–314, here 261). Instead, it knows and quotes the four canonical gospels, evidence that Jewish Christianity had not closed itself off from the "great church," but can accept in fundamental openness the development of the NT canon (Strecker, "Problem," 262).

with Mark: Jesus is portrayed in conflict with religious figures in his society; in part this is over the Sabbath; this conflict was severe enough to foreshadow his death; a question of the behavior of the disciples on the Sabbath is resolved by a christological appeal. At the same time, the likelihood that the Matthean community retained some kind of Sabbath observance demonstrates that the Jesus tradition *alone* did not suffice to lead Christians to conclude that the Sabbath had been abolished.

4.4 THE GRAINFIELD EPISODE BEFORE MARK

4.4.1 Evidence for a Pre-Markan Tradition

The trend to see Mark as an author, rather than merely a collector or redactor of tradition, has meant an emphasis on synchronic over diachronic analysis. Nevertheless, Mark is heavily rooted in tradition, however much he has shaped this tradition through organization and linguistic formulation to form a work that bears his own stamp.[149] So for the purpose of this study, it is appropriate to investigate whatever can be recovered about the traditions behind the Gospel. This in term will enable us to make inferences about how the Sabbath was viewed by the carriers of these traditions.

The grainfield episode itself offers ample grounds for diachronic consideration. Unlike the two controversy dialogues immediately preceding it, the grainfield pericope has two answers to the accusation of the Pharisees. That this pericope, too, had only one answer in a pre-Markan stage is widely accepted, but which one? Most scholars determine that it was the appeal to the example of David (vv. 25–26).[150] Arguments raised in favor of this view include:

---

[149] Jens Schröter, *Erinnerung an Jesu Worte: Studien zur Rezeption der Logienüberlieferung in Markus, Q und Thomas* (WUNT 76; Neukirchen-Vluyn, 1997), 78–83.

[150] Bultmann, *Geschichte*, 14–15; list of additional scholars prior to 1975 holding this position (by far the majority), in Neirynck, "Jesus," 641, n. 8. Subsequently, Pesch, who summarizes arguments in favor of this view, such as keywords shared by the narrative setting and the example of David, the relevance of the hunger of David and his followers, and the possibility of independent transmission of vv. 27–28 (*Markusevangelium*, 179), and Kiilunen, *Vollmacht*, 203–17.

- The correspondence of the accusation of the Pharisees and the defense of Jesus, as seen in the catchwords οὐκ ἔξεστιν (vv. 24, 26), ποιεῖν (vv. 24, 25).[151] This argument is reversible, however. The language of the David example could have been formulated with a view toward its insertion here.[152] In addition, the correspondence in formulation does not solve, as Kiilunen asserts that it does, the singularity of this pericope compared to other controversy dialogues in which the behavior of Jesus or his disciples give rise to criticism. In the other examples he lists (2:6–7; 2:16; 2:18; 7:5; 3:2), the correspondence is between the narrative exposition and the accusation.[153] Here, it is between the accusation and the reply. The grainfield episode remains singular in this aspect, regardless of the position taken concerning the original reply.

- The connecting phrase καὶ ἔλεγεν αὐτοῖς (v. 27) is typical for introduction of an added saying.[154] It is undisputed that this phrase is more natural for the second in a series of arguments, but this is not proof that the argument that follows it was the added argument. The insertion could have been placed after the original introduction, καὶ λέγει αὐτοῖς, v. 25, with the new introduction placed before the reply that had now been pushed back to v. 27.[155]

- It is easier to see how vv. 25–26 drew v. 27 to them than the other way around. Through v. 27, vv. 25–26 were clarified and generalized with regard to the Sabbath theme.[156] This is not as much a proof as a reading based on an exegetical decision. Were one to take the opposite position, then it would seem that the justifying

---

[151] Pesch, *Markusevangelium*, 1:179; Kiilunen, *Vollmacht*, 205.

[152] Lindemann, "Jesus," 85–86; Wolfgang Weiss, *"Eine neue Lehre in Vollmacht"*: *Die Streit- und Schulgespräche des Markus-Evangeliums* (BZNW 52; Berlin, 1989), 41; Klaus Scholtissek, *Die Vollmacht Jesu: Traditions- und Redaktionsgeschichtliche Analysen zu einem Leitmotiv markinischer Christologie* (NTAbh NF 25; Münster, 1992), 175; Doering, *Schabbat*, 410.

[153] Kiilunen, *Vollmacht*, 205.

[154] Kiilunen, *Vollmacht*, 206–7.

[155] Weiss, *Lehre*, 42–42; Doering, *Schabbat*, 410–11.

[156] Kiilunen, *Vollmacht*, 215.

factors χρείαν ἔσχεν and ἐπείνασεν (v. 25) explicate the διὰ τὸν ἄνθρωπον of v. 27.[157]

Speaking further against the originality of vv. 25–26 is the fact that they do not deal with a Sabbath transgression, nor do they have any immediate connection to gleaning.[158] At the same time, the emphasized details χρείαν ἔσχεν, ἐπείνασεν (v. 25) and ἔφαγεν, καὶ ἔδωκεν καὶ τοῖς σὺν αὐτῷ οὖσιν (v. 26) can be read into the narrative exposition (v. 23) but do not come from it.[159] Finally, it would be unusual to find an argument from scripture at this early stage of tradition.[160]

Some arguments advanced in favor of v. 27 (perhaps with v. 28), however, can also be effectively countered. For instance, it is claimed that the usage of the Son of Man title in v. 28 runs counter to the narrative strategy of Mark, and therefore represents an unassimilated tradition.[161] Yet not only did Mark include it, but taken together with v. 10 seems to have used it to frame this section. Other arguments, however, retain their force. One is that v. 27 (perhaps with v. 28) represents a more appropriate answer to the charge in v. 24.[162] The Pharisees had asked why the disciples did what was not permitted on the Sabbath, and Jesus answers that the Sabbath was made for humanity, not the other way around. The second argument is based on the purported genesis of controversy dialogues in the oral tradition, which postulates that the narrative framework is secondary, formulated to carry an aphorism. The aphorism is can be transmitted in isolation; it makes its point independently of the controversy dialogue.[163] This cannot be claimed for vv. 25–26.

Arguments against accepting the originality of v. 27 include:

- The change from τοῖς σάββασιν (vv. 23–24) to τὸ σάββατοῖντοῦ σαββάτου (vv. 27–28).[164] This cannot be taken as proof of a break,

---

[157] Weiss, *Lehre*, 45.

[158] Weiss, *Lehre*, 43–44.

[159] Doering, *Schabbat*, 411.

[160] Heinz-Wolfgang Kuhn, *Ältere Sammlungen im Markusevangelium* (SUNT 8; Göttingen, 1971), 74.

[161] Kuhn, *Sammlungen*, 75, with n. 133.

[162] Doering, *Schabbat*, 411.

[163] Weiss, *Lehre*, 273.

[164] Pesch, *Markusevangelium*, 1:179.

since such switches between singular and plural in the same context are documented.[165]

- If v. 27 is original, then v. 24 is no longer in its original form, but in one that has been linguistically adapted to correspond to v. 26.[166] This argument, based on the assumption of a fixed wording in tradition, proves nothing beyond the fact that the document we have is carefully constructed.

- That a formal and thematically closed apophthegm such as vv. 23–24, 27 would represent would be expanded, and thereby destroyed, by such different material is, on the face of it, unlikely.[167] This is admittedly the biggest challenge to any attempt to establish v. 27 (especially if already combined with v. 28) as original to the grainfield episode. Why would an argument understood by then as christological be supplemented with an argument from scripture? While a complete answer would require an examination of the use of arguments from scripture in the early Jesus movement, which lies outside the scope of this study, two suggestions can be offered: 1) the mention of need and hunger in v. 25 offers a criterion for the Sabbath-breaking of the disciples, countering a possible impression that anything is allowed on the Sabbath. As mentioned above, they explicate what it means that the Sabbath was made for humanity.[168] 2) The use of this example may have been suggested by the Davidic ancestry of Jesus.[169]

Clearly this question can be argued convincingly in either direction. On balance, however, the minority view can make the stronger claim; in the word about humanity and the Sabbath in the creation order we have the answer.[170] It must now be determined whether v. 27 alone formed

---

[165] Doering, *Schabbat*, 410, with references in Josephus, n. 73.

[166] Kiilunen, *Vollmacht*, 205.

[167] Kiilunen, *Vollmacht*, 215.

[168] Doering, *Schabbat*, 431–2.

[169] Doering, *Schabbat*, 431.

[170] In addition to Doering (*Schabbat*, 411-2) and Weiss (*Lehre*, 44–45), this is also the decision reached by the Jesus Seminar; see Robert W. Funk, *The Acts of Jesus: The Search for the Authentic Deeds of Jesus* (San Francisco, 1998), 67–68. Older proponents of this view are discussed in Neirynck, "Jesus," 645–47.

this answer, or whether v. 28 did not form part of the answer from the outset.[171]

Many scholars maintain that the saying about humanity and the Sabbath is older than that about the authority of the Son of Man over the Sabbath.[172] Some argue this on the basis of the of the Tannaitic parallels, while others see in v. 27 a greater radicality that is said to be limited and weakened by v. 28 (these two arguments are mutually exclusive).[173] Yet those who take this position understand the terms *Son of Man* and *Lord* in their christological significance.[174] On the level of the

---

[171] Other possibilities in addition to the two I will consider. One is that the Son of Man saying existed first and gave rise to the more general statement about the relation of humanity and the Sabbath (Koester, *Gospels*, 276). Eduard Schweizer once held this position ("Der Menschensohn [Zur eschatologischen Erwartung Jesu]," 1959, repr. in *Neotestamentica* [Zürich, 1963], 56–84, here 72, n. 48), but later adopted the view that the two parts originally formed a unit (*Das Evangelium nach Markus* [NTD 1; Göttingen, 1967], 39). The other possibility is that the two sayings circulated independently and were joined because of thematic similarity (Weiss, *Lehre*, 50–52). Yang, *Jesus*, 191, attributes this view to Morna D. Hooker, *The Son of Man in Mark: A Study of the Background of the Term "Son of Man" and its Use in St Mark's Gospel* (London, 1967), 95–102, mistakenly, I believe, especially in light of her *The Gospel according to Saint Mark* (BNTC 2; London 1991), 105, in which it is clearer that she considers the two sayings to have formed a unit. She does in her earlier work raise independent circulation as a possibility, but does not seem to adopt it herself. Since, with Bultmann, *Geschichte*, 87–88, it is inconceivable that the principle expressed in Mark 2:28 could have originated as a free saying, and since it flows logically from the previous verse, it is difficult to imagine v. 28 circulating separately, which makes these two possibilities much less likely than the two considered in the main text.

[172] E.g., Lohse, "Worte," 82–83. References to the history of discussion in Neirynck, "Jesus," 652. Bultmann considers both possibilities and leaves the question undecided (*Geschichte*, 14–15, 87).

[173] Tannaitic parallels: *Mek. Šabbata* 1 (on Ex 31:12–14) par. *b. Yoma* 85b (Bill 2:5); discussion in Neirynck, "Jesus," 656–63. The second variant is most famously the position of Käsemann; it is for him an example of the criterion of dissimilarity despite similar rabbinic formulations because the contexts in which these sayings have been preserved limit the principle expressed to life-threatening situations ("Problem," 207). Previously Dibelius, *Formgeschichte*, 61–62, and taken over by many since.

[174] This term, which appears roughly 80 times in the four Gospels, almost always in a saying attributed to Jesus, yet only three times in other NT writings (aside from a quotation from Ps 8 in Heb 2:6), has been the object of a great deal of scholarly interest, since on the one hand we seem here to be tantalizingly close to the historical Jesus, yet on the other we are confronted with a rich and complex array of statements that do not

Gospel, this is certainly correct. However, since, as Scholtissek observed, "die älteste erreichbare Gestalt der vormarkinischen Tradition *2,23f.27 hat noch keine christological Interpretation," then the question arises whether this sentence, stripped of christological interpretation these terms acquired, makes sense. I will argue not only that this is the case, but that it is the preferable interpretation, since it makes better sense of the logical connection ὥστε.[175]

The saying in Mark is a two-part logion, a wisdom *mashal*.[176] Part one is in turn two-parted and chiastically constructed: humanity was not made for the Sabbath, but the Sabbath was made for humanity. While not the universal view in the time of Jesus (see *Jubilees*), the thought makes sense given the order of events in the first creation account in Genesis and has, as mentioned, parallels in Tannaitic literature.

Part two has an organic connection to the first part; the pair humanity/individual human is familiar in Hebrew parallel expressions.[177] Yet this saying lacks any reference to suffering or to eschatological glory; it is unlikely that v. 28 is a creation of the Christian community. The phrase ὁ υἱὸς τοῦ ἀνθρώπου is here neither a self-designation, nor is it a reference to the eschatological figure in Daniel and other apocalyptic literature (cf. 13:26, 14:62; Dan 7:13).[178] It is a case of an individual example of a generic category.[179] Of the fourteen OT occurrences of this

yield a simple picture (Theissen and Merz, *Jesus*, 471). For a recent overview of the vast literature on this question, see Delbert Burkett, *The Son of Man Debate: A History and Evaluation* (SNTSMS 107; Cambridge, 1999).

[175] The quotation is from *Vollmacht*, 177. Scholtissek understands v. 28 as carrying christological significance (177–80), although he is one of many who recognizes the logical difficulty caused by ὥστε if v. 28 is taken as having been *formulated* with this christological significance in mind (174).

[176] Bultmann, *Geschichte*, 84.

[177] This was pointed out by Hugo Grotius in the seventeenth century (details in Neirynck, "Jesus," 647–8, n. 36; further details of the history of discussion 648, nn. 37–38).

[178] For the argument that it is a veiled self-reference, see esp. Geza Vermès, *Jesus the Jew* (2d ed.; London, 1983), 163–8; Casey, "Historicity," 17. The parallels that have been adduced are from Tg. texts (Gen 4:14 in Tg. *Neof.* 1 and in the Cairo Tg. B text) and have been rejected as not relevant for the NT usage because of their late date (Fitzmyer, *Gospel*, 209).

[179] Hans Bietenhard, "'Der Menschensohn'—ὁ υἱὸς τοῦ ἀνθρώπου. Sprachliche und

pair, an apposite example is Ps 8:4 (MT 8:5), since—as here—it deals
with the sovereignty of humankind over the works of God's creation
(cf. v. 6): "what are human beings (אֱנוֹשׁ) that you are mindful of them,
mortals (בֶן־אָדָם, sg.) that you care for them?" For this reason, it is
reasonable to conclude that, in the original formulation of this saying, it
may have meant *a human*, and was not a title.[180]

Unlike Ps 8:4 (MT 8:5), Mark 2:27–28 is not constructed in parallel.
Rather, a conclusion is drawn (however weakly ὥστε is to be understood
here and elsewhere in the NT in contrast to classical Greek).[181] Yet the
use of ὥστε to connect the two statements is easier to explain if these
were a unit before the christological understanding of Son of Man
prevailed.[182] A second difficulty is the presence of καί in Mark's
formulation. In context this makes the Sabbath one more thing, such as
the power to forgive sins, over which the ἐξουσία of the christologically-
understood Son of Man extends (see 2:10).[183] But what could it mean if
it were present in the saying when it existed on its own? At that level, the
sovereignty of the individual—the child of Adam and Eve—would be
that spoken of in Genesis when the Lord gave Adam and Eve dominion
over the works of creation. In that case καί—*and, even*—would mean
that the Sabbath was not exempted from the works of creation but was
also placed under the feet of Adam and Eve.[184]

The sayings, in so far as they were transmitted in Christian circles,
were quite possibly a unit from the beginning. The phrase yields good
sense in context, especially in light of the parallelism implicit in the
pairing of humankind (v. 27) and the son of man (v. 28). Verse 28
assigns to the individual an authority that the church assigned to Jesus.

---

religionsgeschichtliche Untersuchungen zu einem Begriff der synoptischen Evangelien.
1. Sprachlicher und religionsgeschichtlicher Teil," *ANRW* 25.1:265–350, here 274.

[180] Delbert Burkett's survey of the history of the suggestion that the son of man
should be understood in a nontitular way concludes that this has failed to convince, yet
allows that Mark 2:28 parr. is one of three exceptions (with Mark 2:10 and Matt 12:32
par.) for which a generic interpretation is plausible ("The Nontitular Son of Man: A
History and Critique," *NTS* 40 [1994]: 504-21).

[181] BDR § 391.2, n. 3.
[182] Doering, *Schabbat*, 420.
[183] Kuhn, *Sammlungen*, 73, 83; Gnilka, *Evangelium*, 1:120–21.
[184] Pesch, *Markusevangelium*, 1:185; Schaller, *Jesus*, 18, n. 58.

This authority goes a step beyond anything known in contemporary Judaism (howbeit a small step) and is therefore not likely to be taken over by Jesus or the community from Judaism.

This contradicts the way that the authors of the synoptics understood *Son of Man*, namely, as a reference to Christ. A developing Christology attached special significance both to the term *lord* and the phrase *Son of Man*. While the first shift may well have occurred in an Aramaic milieu (מרא or שׁ'לם),[185] the second likely coincided with the translation of the proclamation into Greek.[186] At any rate, the christological understanding of both phrases was firmly in place by the time the Gospel of Mark was written. As a result, the freedom expressed vis-à-vis the Sabbath shifted from a direct freedom (that of an individual who had received the Sabbath as a gift to humankind and understood it in accord with this original intent) to an indirect freedom, mediated through the lordship of Jesus. This is verified by the scriptural precedent cited in the discussion: the significance of David (type of Jesus, the son of David) is that he was the active agent who exercised the freedom to take the bread of presence to give his hungry companions the bread (grain) that they needed.

If, by the time the gospels of Matthew and Luke were composed, the use of Son of Man to refer to Jesus in all three aspects of his earthly ministry, his suffering, and his eschatological role was so strongly fixed that the Semitic parallelism of the original saying was overlooked, then the connection between the two parts of the saying as preserved by Mark may well have no longer been evident.

But do we have an authentic saying of Jesus? As we saw above (4.1), Lohse considers the first half of the saying (Mark 2:27) one of three authentic words of Jesus concerning the Sabbath in the Gospels. Verse 28, on the other hand, is for him an extension created by the community.[187] The fellows of the Jesus Seminar decided that both vv. 27–28 probably go back to Jesus. A radically different position is expressed by Beare, who denies that it can be authentic because no Jewish teacher

---

[185] Casey, "Historicity," 17.
[186] C. Colpe, ὁ υἱὸς τοῦ ἀνθρώπου, *TWNT* 8:403–81, here 408.
[187] "Worte," 82–83.

would have said it.[188] In both cases, it is the supposed difference to Jewish teaching of the time that forms the basis for the conclusion. Yet, as we have seen, there are parallels in Jewish literature that have long been recognized. These have usually been discounted, however, because the context in which they have been transmitted deals with life-threatening situations. There is a methodological inconsistency of treating the saying of Jesus as an isolated saying and refusing to do the same with rabbinical sayings; the sayings themselves show a marked similarity.[189] In addition to those that directly express the priority of humankind over the Sabbath, *2 Bar.* 14:18 indicates the same relationship of humanity and the world. It is also important for our investigation since it expresses the thought of humankind's guardianship over the works of creation: "And you said that you would make a man for this world as a guardian over your works that it should be known that he was not created for the world, but the world for him."[190] The concept of lordship or dominion over the creation is well attested in the OT (Gen 1:26–28; Ps 8:4–8 [MT 8:5–9]). *Second Baruch* 14:18 combines the thought that the work of creation was for humankind, rather than the other way around, with that of man in a function of responsibility over the work of creation: the same conjunction found in Mark 2:27–28.[191] In addition, in 2 Macc 5:19 the relation between humans and holy space is defined in a way similar to that between humans and holy time in Mark 2:27: "But the Lord did not choose the nation for the sake of the holy place, but the place for the sake of the nation."

Clearly, the criterion of dissonance, which led scholars such as Lohse and Käsemann to conclude that Mark 2:27 (but not v. 28) was an authentic word of Jesus, cannot safely be applied to this saying. Nor is Beare correct to assert that no Jewish teacher would say such a thing. His

---

[188] "Sabbath," 32.

[189] Lindemann, "Jesus," 88–89; Schaller, *Jesus*, 18.

[190] OTP 1:626; cp. 15:7, in light of the debate whether the Sabbath applies to all humanity on the basis of Mark 2:27: "And with regard to the righteous ones, those whom you said the world has come on their account, yes, also that which is coming is on their account."

[191] Colpe rejects the solution adopted here because he understands the dominion in question as the authority to validate or cancel the Sabbath (*TWNT* 8:455).

comment not only assumes the radicality of v. 27, but also rests on a preconceived notion of Jewish teachers as invariably demanding strict adherence to the law in disregard of humane considerations. On the other hand, the criteria used by the third quest—plausibility in a Jewish context and understandability in the founding of the early Church—would lead to the conclusion that this saying, both vv. 27 and 28, may well be historical. In other words, the criteria of the second quest fail to prove that Jesus *did* say it, but those of the third quest would counter that he might well have.

When we examine the core sayings preserved in the Sabbath controversy dialogues as a whole, certain patterns emerge, both in form and content. The construction of Mark 2:27—two-part, chiastic—is found in other sayings of Jesus; it is also documented for other Jewish teachers (cf. 4.3.2, above). The pericope subsequent to the grainfield incident incorporates in Mark the saying: "Is it lawful on the Sabbath to do good or to do evil, to save life or to kill?" (3:4). This double question is shortened in Matthew's Gospel to a general rule to guide a Sabbath-keeping community in their Sabbath practice.[192] In its longer form, however, it was accepted by Lohse as an authentic saying, although his reason for doing so is open to question.[193]

Luke 13:15–16 contains an argument from the lesser to the greater: "Does not each one of you on the Sabbath loose his ox or his donkey from the stall, and lead it away to water it? So ought not his woman, being a daughter of Abraham, whom Satan has bound—think of it—for eighteen years, be loosed from this bond on the Sabbath?" Once again, Jesus defends his behavior in the form of a question. The thought expressed here appears again in two other Sabbath controversy dialogues (Matthew 12:11–12; Luke 14:5), an indication that this saying belongs

---

[192] Lohse, "Jesu Worte," 86.

[193] "Denn Heilungen am Sabbat hat es nirgendwo in der Urgemeinde, die sich noch in Ehrfurcht an das Gesetz der Väter gebunden wusste, gegeben" ("Jesu Worte," 85). Aside from the obvious objection that Lohse has no way of knowing this, his argumentation is not consistent here. This would be the same community that, according to him, had made the rule of doing good the guiding principle in determining Sabbath practice. Why would they have shied away from healing on the Sabbath?

to an early stage in the transmission of the words of Jesus.[194] There are no known parallels to the opening "who among you"; this saying fulfils the criterion of dissimilarity and can with confidence be accepted as an authentic saying.[195]

Although it is generally assumed that in the Gospel of John the words attributed to Christ are at a further remove from anything that may have been spoken by the earthly Jesus, it is striking to notice the Sabbath saying preserved in John 7:22–23: "Moses therefore gave you circumcision (not that it was from Moses, but from the fathers), and you circumcise a man on the Sabbath. If a man receives circumcision on the Sabbath, so that the law of Moses should not be broken, are you angry with me because I made a man completely well on the Sabbath?" Again we find a rabbinic type of argumentation, from the lesser to the greater (see above, 4.3.1), which is also attested as an argument in favor of intervening in a life threatening situation on the Sabbath.[196] John has made use of traditional material here.[197] Once again, however, the criterion of dissimilarity precludes us from deciding for certain authenticity, although we must leave the possibility open that Jesus may well have made use of this argument.[198]

Based on this examination of the three related questions of the possible unity of the two-part saying, the meaning of "child of Adam and Eve," and whether Jesus could have said it, the thought expressed in v. 27 is quite conceivable in Second Temple Judaism, and could easily exist by itself, whereas v. 28 is an extension of the first thought, drawn out of it as a conclusion—and not a necessary conclusion. While this second thought would have been more controversial among Judeans than the first, nevertheless we do not have to go outside of the framework of Second Temple Judaism to imagine someone saying it. And that someone *could* have been Jesus. The consonance with Jewish teaching

---

[194] Lohse, "Jesu Worte," 81. He concludes that the form of this saying found in Matthew is the more original.

[195] Lohse, "Jesu Worte," 86.

[196] Rudolf Bultmann, *Das Evangelium des Johannes* (21st ed. KEK 2. Göttingen, 1986), 208.

[197] Lohse, "Jesu Worte," 80, n. 2.

[198] Meyer, *TWNT* 6:81–82.

of Jesus' time means, when we apply the criterion of dissimilarity, that we cannot definitely say that the earthly Jesus said it. Yet if both sayings formed a unit from the beginning, as may well be the case, then the dissonance between this unit in its original meaning (as I postulate it) and the way it was understood in the post-resurrection community (as witnessed by Matthew and Luke's striking of Mark 2:27) makes it more likely that Jesus said it than that the community formulated it.[199]

4.4.2 Inferences about the Carriers of Tradition

At the outset, it should be stated that the question of the life-setting of the community that transmitted this episode does not depend on the position taken in the much-discussed question of whether it was part of a pre-Markan collection. The formal and thematic similarities shared by the grainfield episode with the pericopes in its immediate context led throughout the twentieth century to proposals that this pericope belonged to such a collection. There is no consensus, however, on the extent of such a proposed collection.[200] For Albertz, the collection included the five episodes that comprise 2:1–3:6. Subsequent scholars have argued for a three- or four-part collection.[201] Other scholars deny

---

[199] The other saying attributed to Jesus in this pericope must be judged differently. For example, the use of a scriptural example (David and the bread of presence, Mark 2:25–26, cf. 1 Sam 21:1–7) means that it is not necessary to trace the saying back to Jesus, although it is not impossible that he could also have cited it (So Bultmann, *Geschichte*, 50–51, cf. 109; against: Funk, *Acts*, 68). This does not mean that Jesus could not conceivably have made the statements ascribed to him, simply that it cannot be proven.

[200] See Karl Ludwig Schmidt, *Der Rahmen der Geschichte Jesu: Literarkritische Untersuchungen zur ältesten Jesusüberlieferung* (Berlin, 1919), 104; Dibelius, *Formgeschichte*, 39; Martin Albertz, *Die synoptischen Streitgespräche: Ein Beitrag zur Formgeschichte des Urchristentums* (Berlin, 1921), 5–16. Later scholars, such as Joachim Jeremias, expanded the notion of pre-Markan collections, reducing Mark's editorial activity to no more than arranging collections (*Die Abendmahlsworte Jesu*. [4th ed. Göttingen, 1967], 85–86). For a recent discussion of the question of Mark as collector of material and as redactor who shaped this material according to a theological point-of-view, see Marcus, *Mark 1–8*, 57–62.

[201] Kuhn: four-part, minus 3:1–6 (*Sammlungen*, 214; cf. 84, where he lists his reasons for excluding 3:1–6 from the collection). Pesch: four-part, minus 2:1–12 (*Markusevangelium*, 149–51). A three-part collection, minus both 2:1–12 and 3:1–6,

the existence of such a collection; Kiilunen's detailed study, for instance, led him to conclude on linguistic and structural grounds that it was Mark who placed these pericopes in the sequence in which they are found in his Gospel.[202] Whether or not a formal collection existed prior to Mark, it is evident that the grainfield episode was one of a number of similarly structured narratives, such as those concerning table fellowship and fasting (Mark 2:15–22*).[203] All three deal with conflicts arising on the basis of pious Jewish practices. In each case, these are reinterpreted by Jesus, the authoritative teacher. It can easily be imagined that such controversy dialogues served in inner-Christian discussions in a context in which questions of practice that Jewish believers in Christ might raise is addressed.[204] In none of them is the practice in question abrogated.

How might the community in which such controversy dialogues were formed have viewed the Sabbath? While Mark includes these incidents to show how the teaching and healing activity of Jesus resulted in plans to destroy him, in none of the disputes once situated in an inner-community discussion of Jewish practices is there a total break with Judaism.[205] With regard to the Sabbath, this would mean that without

is proposed by, e.g., Robert A. Guelich (*Mark 1–8:26* [WBC 34; Dallas, 1989], 82–83) and Scholtissek, *Vollmacht*, 137–47.

[202] Kiilunen, *Vollmacht*, 249. Others who reject the notion of a pre-Markan collection include Weiss, *Lehre*, 22–40 and Schröter, *Erinnerung*, 78–79, n. 82

[203] James D. G. Dunn, Note added to "Mark 2.1–3.6: A Bridge between Jesus and Paul on the Question of the Law." (1984) for repr. in *Jesus, Paul and the Law: Studies in Mark and Galatians* (Louisville, Ky., 1990), 35.

[204] *Sammlungen*, 229–34; this represents a sharpening of Bultmann's proposed *Sitz im Leben* of community discussions over the law (*Geschichte*, 42).

[205] Having identified the grainfield incident as belonging to a pre-Markan collection used to discuss questions that might be raised by traditionally-minded Jewish Christians, and the subsequent healing episode, with the concluding verse, 3:6, as the product of Markan redaction, Kuhn concludes that Mark takes a more severe view of the practices at issue. He feels that by juxtaposing the criticisms raised against the behavior of Jesus and his disciples and the decision of Jewish leaders to seek his death, Mark views the claims of these members as false: "[d]er Textzusammenhang stellt jetzt heraus, dass es von den hier aufgeworfene Fragen nur zur Kreuzigung Jesu kommen kann.... Offenbar verurteilt damit Mk bewusst noch schärfer als die Sammlung selbst von ihm für falsch gehaltene Ansprüche des Judenchristentums in seiner Gemeinde" (*Sammlungen*, 223).

being totally rejected, it is nonetheless viewed within the community as not absolutely binding.[206]

The question has been raised of whether the choice of gleaning may have been conditioned by the experience of early followers of Jesus. Jesus is called to account in the grainfield pericope not for his own behavior but for that of his disciples. For this reason, many have concluded that this pericope is the creation of the post-resurrection community in an effort to justify its own Sabbath practice.[207] Others have maintained that there is no insurmountable difficulty in the account that would prevent us from placing it in the ministry of Christ.[208] But they have not thereby proven that the account *is* historic, since their arguments could apply equally well to an origin in the post-resurrection Palestinian community. It must be kept in mind that the account does not purport to be historical; the location of the grainfield is not given, there is no date, the accusers are not named. It is stylized according to a form of which we have numerous examples in the synoptic gospels.[209] One doubts that it was the regular practice of a community to glean on the Sabbath.[210] This specific application of Sabbath freedom could reflect instead the situation of rural itinerant preachers, a lifestyle that was an extension of that which the disciples had shared with Jesus during his ministry in Galilee. Both the need to glean in a grainfield on the Sabbath as well as the urgency not to postpone a healing to the next day are explicable from this.[211] The point of the anecdote would have been to justify the relative freedom the followers of Jesus, who continued the life style of their master, that of

---

[206] Kuhn, *Sammlungen*, 90. One wonders whether Kuhn is here making too fine a point; at any rate, it is difficult to do justice to it in translation. The verbs he uses are *beseitigen*, "to set aside," to describe what is not done to the Sabbath, and *aufheben* to describe what *prinzipiell* counts for the community. *Aufheben* means literally to lift up, but has a range of meaning that includes both "preserve" and "abolish."

[207] E.g., Bultmann, *Geschichte*, 14–15.

[208] Ernst Haenchen, *Der Weg Jesu: Eine Erklärung des Markus-Evangeliums und der synoptischen Parallelen* (2d ed.; Sammlung Töpelmann 2/6; Berlin, 1968), 121–22; Derrett, "Judaica," 85–100; Casey, "Historicity"; Daube, "Responsibilities." See also Pesch, *Markusevangelium*, 183.

[209] Bultmann, *Geschichte*, 39–56.

[210] Haenchen, *Weg*, 122.

[211] Theissen and Merz, *Jesus*, 329–30; cf. 161.

itinerant radical charismatics, exercised with regard to Sabbath restrictions that were workable for the more stable segments of society. The difficulty with this proposal as that wandering charismatics did not claim the right to self-support, but to support by the communty.[212] In this case, gleaning is meant paradigmatically.[213]

In the earliest formulations, this freedom could be one that still lies within the bounds of inner-Jewish discussion of proper Sabbath observance.[214]

4.4.3 Inferences about the Historical Jesus

The following words express the scholarly consensus about the historical Jesus twenty years ago:

> In seiner Verkündigung der Herrschaft Gottes und in seinem Verhalten und Umgang lag ein Ärgernis, das die Grenzen der damaligen Judentums zu sprengen drohte. Jesu Polemik gegen Gesetzeskasuistik, Sabbatgebot und Reinigungsvorschriften offenbarte eine Freiheit, die die Tora, die existentielle Lebensgrundlage der Schriftgelehrten und Pharisäer, der Sadduzäer und Ratsältesten radikal in Frage stellte.[215]

The general tenor of the many works that have appeared since these words were written, whether they portray Jesus as an apocalyptic teacher, a Cynic sage, or Galilean hasid, share the common assumption that Jesus is understandable within the Judaism of his time.[216] In that society, as we saw in ch. 2, there was a general agreement that the Sabbath was a divine command, but a broad spectrum of opinions on how it should be kept.[217]

---

[212] 1 Cor 9:13, Did. 13:3; Kiilunen, Vollmacht, 218–9.

[213] Doering, Schabbat, 412.

[214] Well expressed by Kiilunen: "Proklamiert wird nicht Freiheit vom Sabbat, sondern am Sabbat" (Vollmacht, 219–20).

[215] From the summary to Michael Lattke's survey of research on the historical Jesus, originally published as "Neue Aspekte der Frage nach dem historischen Jesus," 1979, republished in Leroy, Jesus, 129–33. Quotation from 132.

[216] On Jesus the apocalyptic teacher, Helmut Merklein, Jesu Botschaft von der Gottesherrschaft: Eine Skizze (SBS 111; Stuttgart, 3d ed., 1989); E. P. Sanders, The Historical Figure of Jesus (London, 1993); Dale C. Allison, Jesus of Nazareth: Millenarian Prophet (Minneapolis, 1998); and Fredriksen, Jesus. On Jesus the cynic, John Dominic Crossan, The Historical Jesus: The Life of a Mediterranean Jewish Peasant (New York, 1991). On Jesus the hasid, Vermès, Jesus.

[217] If objections to Sabbath behavior are raised before 70 C.E., it is important to

The grainfield episode, along with the other Sabbath conflict material in the synoptics, has been read as showing Jesus participating in this discussion.[218] This has led some scholars to conclude that Jesus was establishing halakah.[219] For them, the essence of the conflicts between Jesus and his critics was not whether the Sabbath was to be held, but how. More precisely, whether there could be additional exceptions to the general prohibition of work on that day beyond the two generally recognized: to save one's own life or that of another human or an animal.[220] On the basis of the pericope at question here, we see Jesus operating much as other sages. A question of practice is raised, a minor issue indeed. Yet this petty matter—it takes neither a great deal of thought nor physical effort to pluck a ripe ear of grain, rub it in one's hands, and chew the wheat berries that remain after blowing away the chaff—becomes the occasion for reflecting on the will of God in creating both humanity and the Sabbath. And this is precisely the dynamic process by which halakah was created.[221] As long as this is kept in mind, then I would concur with those

remember that these do not represent anything that can be considered normative. No other ancient society was so torn by religious strife (Shaye J. D. Cohen, "The Political and Social History of the Jews in Greco-Roman Antiquity: The State of the Question," in *Early Judaism and Its Modern Interpreters* [ed. R. A. Kraft and G. W. E. Nickelsburg; Atlanta, 1986], 48).

[218] Saldarini, *Community*, 124–33; 160–64.

[219] E.g., Theissen and Merz, *Jesus*, 328–29; Phillip Sigal, *The Halakah of Jesus of Nazareth According to the Gospel of Matthew* (Lanham, Md., 1986), 125–8; Herold Weiss, "The Sabbath in the Synoptic Gospels," *JSNT* 38 (1990): 13–27, here 22.

[220] Theissen and Merz, *Jesus*, 328. In their reconstruction, the difference lay in the fact that the general relativizing of the Sabbath commandment for the sake of life was viewed as fulfillment of the Sabbath command, whereas Jesus portrays this as a breaking of the Sabbath. In their opinion, however, this represents however just a small step beyond those tendencies already present in his time. Therefore, Jesus does not go outside of the framework of the Judaism of his time. "In der Sabbatfrage vertritt er eine generelle indikativische Maxime (Mark 2,27), die mit der Thora übereinstimmt, um mit ihr eindeutige Übertretungen des Thorabuchstabens zu rechtfertigen" (330).

[221] Whenever the subject of the halakah of Jewish teachers is mentioned, we have to guard against *a priori* assumptions about the nature of Judaism as a dry system of legalistic observance, in which rabbinic discussions revolved around sophistic distinctions far removed from daily life. In such a view, Jesus is imagined as representing a revolutionary break with such hair-splitting.

who maintain that the roots of this anecdote can be found in a discussion over the law, whether in the early community or in the life of Jesus.

Yet in another sense, what is recounted here is not simply an exception to Sabbath rest, but a fundamentally different way of approaching the question.[222] The point of the grainfield episode coincides with that of the healing episodes, including the words ascribed to Jesus in them: the Sabbath must be understood according to its original intent, and subordinated to the overall will of God. The eschatological urgency of Jesus' mission doubtless played a role, but the principle is presented as a general axiom, not one conditioned by the urgency of the moment. Subordination of the Sabbath to the overall will of God meant that the ministry of Jesus could not be interrupted for the Sabbath.

This general result, that Jesus fits in the context of his time and stands out against it, is exemplified in the son of man saying, in which a sovereignty over the Sabbath was ascribed to any child of Adam and Eve. It was both understandable in a Jewish context and bold enough that it stood out and was remembered by his disciples.

In the life and teaching of Jesus, insofar as it can be reconstructed, it appears that we have neither a yes nor a no to the Sabbath as such, but a subordination of Sabbath observance (as well as the rest of the law) to radical obedience to the love command in the light of the breaking in of the Kingdom of God.

4.5 Results

In this chapter, I have examined the question of Jesus and the Sabbath on the basis of the pericope of gleaning grain on the Sabbath (Mark 2:23–28 and par.). This was undertaken in three steps: an analysis of the pericope in Mark, a synoptic comparison with Matthew und Luke, and the grainfield narrative and the sayings it contains prior to their inclusion in Mark's Gospel. In all three synoptic Gospels, Jesus is quoted as saying that the Son of Man is lord of the Sabbath. The presence of

---

[222] Doering, whose purpose in studying NT references to the Sabbath was to analyze what they can tell us about Jewish practice and halakah, concludes that Jesus was not interested in a halakic protection of the Sabbath (*Schabbat*, 424).

these words, and the incident in which they are embedded—a controversy dialogue—allows for a fruitful synoptic comparison.

The Synoptics portray Jesus operating in a society that placed a high value on the Sabbath and had high expectations for its fulfilment. They describe him coming into conflict with these expectations. Usually, it is an act of healing, an act of mercy, that is the occasion of the conflict. In this case, however, it is the behavior of the followers of Jesus that is attacked. In defending the disciples, Jesus cites the example of David, the ideal king, a messianic figure, who also did something "not allowed" in a situation of need and hunger. In a second answer, he refers to the original intent of the Sabbath as having been instituted for the benefit of humanity, but then extends the priority of the individual human over Sabbath in terms of lordship. The phrase for individual human, the Son of man, is understood in the context of the Synoptics as Jesus. Unclear, however, is how this dominical authority is deduced from the creation order.

Jesus has the last word in the pericope. His opponents have been silenced, but this does not mean that they have been convinced. In the very next pericope, Jesus heals in the synagogue on a Sabbath after asserting the right to do good on that day. This results in a resolve to do away with Jesus. The Sabbath is an occasion of strife, building on questions of forgiveness of sin, table fellowship, and fasting, that results in plans to destroy Jesus. More important for the evangelists than the question of Jesus' stance toward the law in general or the Sabbath in particular is how that stance determined his fate.

The pericope is well defined in all three gospels and was transmitted in the pre-gospel tradition. The Synoptics understood this pericope in connection with a decision to kill Jesus, which exists in a certain tension with the reports of his appearance before the Sanhedrin in Jerusalem prior to his crucifixion. The pericope was taken over by both Matthew and Luke. The character of conflict remains, but each author sets his own accents. This is especially the case with Matthew, who not only inserts additional material, but also recontextualizes the pericope, which has the effect of concentrating his material on the Sabbath. In addition to stylistic changes, some of which they have in common, they both strike the first half of the second answer, τὸ σάββατον διὰ τὸν ἄνθρωπον ἐγένετο καὶ οὐχ ὁ ἄνθρωπος διὰ τὸ σάββατον (Mark 2:27). Although we cannot discount the possibility that the text of Mark that each possessed did not include this statement, it is also plausible that this was a conscious editorial decision independently taken by each. The effect is to highlight the christological emphasis of the final statement, a conclusion supported by the observation that both change the word order so that ὁ υἱὸς τοῦ ἀνθρώπου comes last. By striking the reference to the original purpose of the Sabbath, each brings out more clearly the christologically understood point of the remaining saying about the Son of Man and the Sabbath.

This understanding was the result of post-resurrection reflection. Originally, this two-part logion was about humankind (collective/individual) in relation to the Sabbath, seen in the perspective of the will of God expressed in creation. As such, it fits in a Jewish setting and gives us some indication of the possible conduct and teaching of Jesus concerning the Sabbath. Conflict with his environment on this question was not based on a categorical rejection of the Sabbath on his part, but on the way that he subordinated it to his proclamation, through word and deed, of the imminent Kingdom of God.

The Jesus who emerges from this investigation fits well in a Jewish context. In that context, there was a broad agreement that the Sabbath was to be kept, but a wide spectrum of opinions on practice. Even the saying recorded in Mark 2:27–28 is understandable within this spectrum; its categorical subordination of the Sabbath to the lordship of humankind (understood of course as those humans fulfilling the creation will of God, therefore Jews) stood out enough that it was remembered by his disciples, but was not unthinkable in the discussions of the time. This finding means however that it does not fulfill the criterion of double dissimilarity, and so cannot be accepted with certainty as a word of Jesus. The point on which it fails to fulfill this criterion, however, is not, as often supposed, the teaching of the early church, but with contemporary Judaism.

The incident in which this saying is embedded is not impossible for the life of Jesus, but it is not a historical report. It is more likely originated among early post-resurrection community as a framework to contain the sayings.

There is nothing in the words or deeds of Jesus that led his earliest followers to believe he had abrogated the Sabbath. The eschatological ethic of his proclamation elevated human needs (the double commandment of love) over "ritual" observance. The common denominator of the Sabbath-related words and deeds of Jesus recorded in the Synoptics is that the Sabbath must be understood according to its original intent, and subordinated to the overall will of God.

By the time of the composition of the written Gospels, the eschatological hour announced in the proclamation of Jesus has become a generalized way of life; the days of the wandering charismatic are passing over into those of settled congregations. Freedom with regard to the Sabbath, originally rooted in the urgency of proclamation, has become a principle. Human needs (the law of love) are elevated above ritual observance as matter of principle. Yet even at this stage, however much this incident and others recounted in the gospels relativize the Sabbath and its observance, there is no express abrogation of it in the Synoptics. Given the non-Palestinian location of their redaction, and the changed historical circumstance (e.g., the Pharisees are no long a competing movement, but have become the elite of post-temple Israel), this is a significant negative finding. Nevertheless, there are clear indications of later developments. On the one hand, they saw in the Sabbath conflicts a part of the explanation for the hostility of the Jewish elite toward Jesus. On the other, there was a reinterpretation of rest as a theological category that found its fulfillment in Jesus, rather than in a period of time.

Can these results explain why the movement that gathered around Jesus in his lifetime eventually broke with Judaism after his death? At an earlier stage, the motif of the Sabbath had already been an element in conflict dialogues. While they are, in the form that we have them, products of community discussions, it is inherently probable that Jesus debated with other Jews about proper Sabbath observance.

The communities in which the canonical gospels were formulated may well have differed in their own Sabbath practice. We found no reason to believe that Mark's community observed the Sabbath (of course, this does not mean that Jewish members of that community would have been expected to stop observing the Sabbath). The Matthean community may have had a different practice. While there is no direct evidence of Sabbath observance (some would see it in Matt 24:20, but this will not carry the burden of proof), the general tenor of the Gospel, the concern for the law, and specific indications such as Matthew's reworking of the pericope on ritual purity, give us reason to believe that the community was observant—perhaps even to the point of expecting Gentile converts to live according to a Christ-interpreted Torah. Perhaps not, but at least Matthew resists the notion that a law-free, pneumatological Christianity should be normative. We can speculate, given the Matthean emphasis on Jesus as a teacher and the Christian life as discipleship, that community worship centered on a synagogue with regular teaching on the Sabbath, but this must remain speculation. The fact that all three found the grainfield pericope useable is an indication that the traditions passed down about Jesus and the Sabbath were capable of sustaining a variety of practices.

Whether or not Jesus thought of himself as the Messiah, the conviction that the imminent Kingdom of God was breaking into the present in his ministry seems central to his self-understanding (Luke 11:20). Those of his words and deeds on the Sabbath that led to conflict (and the tradition retained no other kind) seem to be rooted in this. This provides at one and the same time both the evidence that Jesus is well placed within a first-century Jewish context as well as the seeds of the impetus that led to Christianity becoming a movement that had a separate existence outside of the Judaism that did not share this understanding of Jesus and his mission.

5
The Sabbath in the Fourth Gospel

The independent and reflective manner in which the Gospel of John shapes traditional material to form its own theological statement is evident in its treatment of the Sabbath. While the Fourth Gospel contains two incidents reminiscent of Sabbath controversies in the Synoptics, the question of the Sabbath is subordinated to the central purpose of this Gospel: to strengthen and deepen the faith of believers in Jesus as the Son of God. This can be said, of course, of every gospel, but it is expressly true of the Gospel of John (20:30–31).[1] Thus, while the Sabbath is subordinated to christological concerns in the Synoptics, as seen in the previous chapter, this is more clearly so in John. Indeed, it is precisely controversies concerning the Sabbath that serve to introduce teaching about the identity of Jesus and his soteriological significance. At the same time, the Sabbath is an occasion for misapprehension of the nature of the one sent.

The Sabbath is mentioned in John ten times, in four passages.[2] In addition to three conflict scenes in the life of Jesus, the word is used in the passion account to explain the removal of his body from the cross: it was the preparation day before a Sabbath (19:31). The first four occurrences of the word are clustered in a complex, John 5:9b–18, that will be the primary focus of the investigation. In this passage, "the Jews" charge him with doing something destructive to the Sabbath (ἔλυεν, v. 18), often translated as *broke*.[3] The next passage to touch on the

---

[1] See Jean Zumstein, "Das Johannesevangelium: Eine Strategie des Glaubens," in *Kreative Erinnerung: Relecture und Auslegung im Johannesevangelium* (Zürich, 1999), 31–45.

[2] The word also appears twice in accounts in the resurrection appearances as part of an expression that means *first [day] of the week*, τῇ [δὲ] μιᾷ [τῶν] σαββάτων (20:1, 19).

[3] E.g., in addition to the NRSV cited here, all other English translations consulted

Sabbath refers to making a man whole on the Sabbath; presumably the man in the incident in ch. 5, since no Sabbath healing is recounted (7:21–23). A second Sabbath healing, that of a man born blind, is subsequently narrated (ch. 9), an episode that shows compositional similarities to the account in ch. 5. In order to round out the picture of worship days in John, it will also be necessary to consider whether, in light of the resurrection appearances on successive Sunday evenings (20:19, 26), the Johannine community had a pattern of Sunday worship.

The relevant passages will be presented and assigned to stages in the development of the text of the Gospel (5.1–5.2). Then the charges leveled against Jesus will be examined (5.3), as well as the defenses raised against these charges (5.4). Some explanatory models for the fate of the Sabbath will be reviewed (5.5), then the question treated of whether the results can be correlated to the history of the community in which this text was formulated and transmitted (5.6). The results will be summarized in 5.7.

5.1 A SABBATH HEALING CONTROVERSY (JOHN 5:1–18)

5.1.1 Text and Structure

Here is the text of the first passage under consideration:

> After this there was a festival of the Jews, and Jesus went up to Jerusalem.
>
> Now in Jerusalem by the Sheep Gate there is a pool, called in Hebrew Beth-zatha, which has five porticoes. In these lay many invalids—blind, lame, and paralyzed.[4]
>
> ... One man was there who had been ill for thirty-eight years. When Jesus saw

(18 in all), dating back to William Tyndale's, with one exception, plus the French Segonde ("il violait"), and most German translations (11 consulted), with four exceptions. The exceptions: Lamsa (translated from Aramaic): "weakening;" Wilckens and Revidierte Elberfelder in German (forms of "aufheben"); as well as the Konkordant in German ("auflöste").

[4] Verses 3b–4 are a later addition; they are missing from older mss. such as $\mathfrak{P}^{66}$, $\mathfrak{P}^{75}$ and B (Bruce Manning Metzger, *A Textual Commentary on the New Testament: A Companion Volume to the United Bible Societies Greek New Testament [third edition]*[corrected ed.; London, 1975], 209). It may, however, have restored traditional material associated with this location that John chose not to use (Raymond E. Brown, *The Gospel According to John: A New Translation with Introduction and Commentary* [AB 29, 29A; Garden City, N. Y., 1966, 1970], 1:207).

him lying there and knew that he had been there a long time, he said to him, "Do you want to be made well?" The sick man answered him, "Sir, I have no one to put me into the pool when the water is stirred up; and while I am making my way, someone else steps down ahead of me." Jesus said to him, "Stand up, take your mat and walk." At once the man was made well, and he took up his mat and began to walk.

Now that day was a Sabbath. So the Jews said to the man who had been cured, "It is the Sabbath; it is not lawful for you to carry your mat." But he answered them, "The man who made me well said to me, 'Take up your mat and walk.'" They asked him, "Who is the man who said to you, 'Take it up and walk'? Now the man who had been healed did not know who it was, for Jesus had disappeared in the crowd that was there. Later Jesus found him in the temple and said to him, "See, you have been made well! Do not sin any more, so that nothing worse happens to you." The man went away and told the Jews that it was Jesus who had made him well. Therefore the Jews started persecuting Jesus, because he was doing such things on the Sabbath. But Jesus answered them, "My Father is still working, and I also am working." For this reason the Jews were seeking all the more to kill him, because he was not only breaking the Sabbath, but was also calling God his own Father, thereby making himself equal to God.

Chapter 5 occupies a prominent position; it is generally considered to open a main section of the first half of the Gospel of John (5:1–10:42, within the larger section 1:19–12:50). There are two remarkable features of this section: it is structured into episodes related to the feasts of the "Jews," and these episodes are the occasion for mounting hostility to the one sent, Jesus.[5] The chapter can be divided into three sections: the healing miracle (vv. 1–9a), the exchanges that arise out of the miracle (vv. 9b–18), and a discourse of Jesus (vv. 19–47), a sequence that fits well in the general nature of the first half of John, with its account of the public ministry of Jesus. The beginning of a new episode, the healing miracle, is clearly

---

[5] See Brown, *Gospel* 1:CXXXVIII–CXLIV; Rudolf Schnackenburg, *Das Johannesevangelium, 2: Kommentar zu Kap. 5-12* (5th ed.; HTKNT 4/2; Freiburg im Breisgau, 1990), 1–5; R. Alan Culpepper, "Un exemple de commentaire fondé sur la critique narrative: Jean 5,1–18," in *La communauté johannique et son histoire: La trajectoire de l'evangile de Jean aux deux premiers siècles* (ed. J.-D. Kaestli, J.-M- Poffet, and J. Zumstein; *MdB* 20; Geneva, 1990), 135–51, here 138–40; Martin Asiedu-Peprah, *Johannine Sabbath Conflicts as Juridical Controversy* (WUNT 2/132; Tübingen, 2001), 4–5.

marked by a geographical and temporal transition (v. 1).[6] The previous pericope (4:46–54), in which Jesus heals the son of a "royal" (official? member of the royal family?) is identified as the second sign Jesus did, having come from Judea into Galilee (4:54), thus forming an inclusion with the wine miracle at a wedding in Cana (2:1–12).[7] The next change of place and time occurs in 6:1, so that all of ch. 5 forms one unit. The double formulation, Ἀπεκρίνατο οὖν ὁ Ἰησοῦς καὶ ἔλεγεν αὐτοῖς, combined with the solemn ἀμὴν ἀμὴν λέγω ὑμῖν (v. 19), can be taken, though, to mark a transition from narrative and dialogue to discourse.[8] What follows is an uninterrupted discourse of Jesus, which is nonetheless connected with the passage under examination in that it is an explication of the relation to God spoken of in vv. 17–18 and a defense of it. The Sabbath plays no direct role in the discourse, however, so that its relation to the theme of the discourse can only be suggested.[9] Formal grounds—the transition from narrative and dialogue to discourse—combined with the disappearance of the Sabbath as an explicit topic thus permit breaking off the examination at v. 18.[10] I will therefore

[6] Culpepper, "Exemple," 138–9. This essay was subsequently published in English, the language in which it had originally been written ("John 5:1–18: A Sample of Narrative Critical Commentary," in *The Gospel of John as Literature: An Anthology of Twentieth-Century Perspectives* [ed. M. W. G. Stibbe; NTTS 17; Leiden, 1993], 193–207. I will cite the page numbers of the French version.

[7]   On the pairing of miracles in the Gospel of John, see René Kieffer, "Different Levels in Johannine Imagery," in *Aspects on the Johannine Literature* (ed. L. Hartmann and B. Olsson; ConBNT 18; Uppsala, 1987), 74–84, here 80.

[8]   Ernst Haenchen, *Das Johannesevangelium: Ein Kommentar* (Tübingen, 1980), 274–5. Cf. vv. 24–25, which are introduced by the double affirmative formula alone.

[9]   See however Asiedu-Peprah's reading of the discourse as a response to the dual accusation of Sabbath-breaking and blasphemy (*Conflicts*, 26–29).

[10]   So most scholars, e.g., Rudolf Bultmann, *Das Evangelium nach Johannes* (21st ed.; KEK 2; Göttinger, 1986), 177, 183; C. K. Barrett, *The Gospel According to St John: An Introduction with Commentary and Notes on the Greek Text* (2d ed.; London 1978), 257; Udo Schnelle, *Antidoketische Christologie im Johannesevangelium: Eine Untersuchung zur Stelle des vierten Evangeliums in der johanneischen Schule* (FRLANT 144; Göttingen, 1987), 112. Dissenting: Brown, *Gospel*, 1:201; Schnackenburg, *Johannesevangelium*, 2:116, 126 (both of whom end the unit at v. 15); Jacques Bernard, "La Guérison de Bethesda: Harmoniques judéo-hellénistiques d'un récit de miracle un jour de sabbat," *MScRel* 33 (1976): 3-34, here 7–8; Rainer Metzner, "Der Geheilte von Johannes 5—Repräsentant des Unglaubens," *ZNW* 90 (1999): 177-93, here

limit my examination to the healing incident and the controversy dialogues that arise out of it.

Verses 1–18 show some similarities to a miracle story and some to a Sabbath controversy. Until the mention of the Sabbath in v. 9b there is no indication that we have anything other than an account of a miraculous healing, culminating in its demonstration (v. 9a) and possibly a closing admonition by Jesus, which may still be reflected in v. 14.[11] Yet in the form in which we have the episode, a Sabbath controversy is narrated as well (vv. 9b–18). The resulting unit, vv. 1–18, displays a different structure from that of Sabbath healing controversies in the Synoptics.[12] With few exceptions, there is a general consensus on two

---

178; Klaus Wengst, *Das Johannesevangelium. Teil 1* (TKNT 4/1; Stuttgart, 2000), 181 (all of whom end it at v. 16).

[11] Scholars who see in v. 14 the vestige of an earlier version of the account include Ernst Haenchen, "Johanneische Probleme," in *Gott und Mensch: Gesammelte Aufsätze* (Tübingen, 1965), 78–113, here 107–8; followed by Robert T. Fortna, *The Gospel of Signs: A Reconstruction of the Narrative Source Underlying the Fourth Gospel* (SNTSMS 11; Cambridge, 1970), 53, but not in his subsequent *The Fourth Gospel and its Predecessor: From Narrative Source to Present Gospel* (Philadelphia, 1988); Michael Labahn, "Eine Spurensuche anhand von Joh 5.1–18," *NTS* 44 (1998): 159–79, here 167; Severino Pancaro, *The Law in the Fourth Gospel: The Torah and the Gospel, Moses and Jesus, Judaism and Christianity According to John* (NovTSup 42; Leiden, 1975), 10–12; L. T. Witkamp, "The Use of Traditions in John 5.1–18," *JSNT* 25 (1985): 19–47, here 21. Rainer Metzner finds it unlikely ("Geheilte," 178, n. 3; see also Johannes Frühwald-König, who calls it unproven and unprovable, especially since it relies in part on the analogy to the non-Johannine account of the adulteress, 8:11 (*Tempel und Kult: Ein Beitrag zur Christologie des Johannesevangeliums* [BU 27; Regensburg, 1998], 146, n. 702. This reconstruction has become more likely however through the combination of P. Egerton 2 and P. Köln 255 (Dieter Lührmann, "Das neue Fragment des P Egerton 2 [P Köln 255]," in *The Four Gospels 1992* [FS F. Neirynck; ed. F. van Segbroeck; BETL 100; Leuven, 1992], 3:2239–55).

[12] Synoptic Sabbath healing accounts share a common structure: (1) the Sabbath is mentioned to introduce the story; three of the four Synoptic accounts place the events in a synagogue; (2) a sick person is present; Jesus' critics watch to see if he will heal the person, thus breaking the Sabbath; (3) Jesus proposes to heal the sick person in spite of the Sabbath law against work; he directs sharp remarks to his critics; (4) his remarks silence the critics, or at least meet no opposition; in one of the stories (Luke 14:1–6) this element is given twice (vv. 3–4a and vv. 5–6); (5) Jesus heals the sick person. The story in Luke 13:10–17 diverges from this pattern. The critical remarks of Jesus, the third element in the common pattern, have undergone two changes: (a) they have been

points: first, that the evangelist has incorporated traditional material here,[13] and second, that an original miracle story describing the healing was subsequently transformed into a Sabbath controversy.[14] Opinions differ, however, as to whether the evangelist is responsible for this transformation. The result is that both a two-stage and a three-stage model of development are proposed.[15] In the discussion that follows, I

expanded into a dialogue between Jesus and the synagogue ruler, so that the opposition is no longer silent, and (b) this dialogue now comes after rather than before the miracle. The creation of a dialogue may, as has been supposed for John 5 and 9, reflect later church-synagogue conversations.

[13] This includes both scholars who posit a written source of miracle stories (SQ; e.g. Bultmann, *Evangelium* 177; Fortna, *Gospel of Signs*, 48–54; J. Louis Martyn, *History and Theology in the Fourth Gospel* [2d ed.; Nashville, 1979], 68; Jürgen Becker, *Das Evangelium nach Johannes* [3d ed.; ÖTK 4/1; Gütersloh, 1991], 279–80), and those who do not (e.g. C. H. Dodd, *Historical Tradition in the Fourth Gospel* [Cambridge, 1963], 178–9; Haenchen, "Probleme," 107–8; Pancaro, *Law*, 10–12). Recent discussion critical of the SQ hypothesis briefly in Udo Schnelle, *Einleitung in das Neue Testament* (3d ed.; UTB 1830; Göttingen, 199), 502–5, more extensively in his *Christologie*, 168–82. A recent trend sees oral tradition as a source of the Fourth Gospel (Michael Labahn, *Jesus als Lebensspender: Untersuchungen zu einer Geschichte der johanneischen Tradition anhand ihrer Wundergeschichten* [BZNW 98; Berlin, 1998], 78–112; Matthias Rein, *Die Heilung des Blindgeborenen [Joh 9]: Tradition und Redaktion* [WUNT 2/73; Tübingen, 1995], 166–293.

[14] A variant of the reconstruction presented here is that we have the result of the fusing of two traditional stories: a miracle story in Jerusalem and a Sabbath controversy set in Galilee (Dodd, *Tradition*, 174–80; Peder Borgen, "John and the Synoptics," in *The Interrelations of the Gospels* [ed. D. Dungan; BETL 95; Leuven, 1990], 408–37, here 423, 430; Barnabas Lindars, *The Gospel of John* [NCB; London, 1972], 52–53, 209–10; Witkamp, "Use,", 21–31). In this way, the presence of motifs also found in Mark 2:1–3:6 (carrying the pallet and walking, the connection of healing and forgiveness of sins, holding Jesus responsible for the Sabbath-transgressing activities of others, a Sabbath controversy as the occasion for the first mention of the intent to kill Jesus), a section of several pericopes set in Galilee, in an episode set in Jerusalem in John. Not all of these elements are of equal weight, and none necessarily tied to Galilee (these motifs are also cited by those who claim John's literary dependence on Mark, see below, 5.2.2).

[15] For a presentation of the two-stage model, one that assigns the transformation to the evangelist, see Fortna (*Gospel of Signs*, 53; *Fourth Gospel*, 115–7; cf. Haenchen, *Johannesevangelium*, 270–3; Schnackenburg, *Johannesevangelium*, 2:117–8; Schnelle, *Christologie*, 108–14). The three-stage model, which holds that the expansion of healing episode to Sabbath controversy had already taken place before the material came down to the evangelist, is proposed by Bultmann (*Evangelium*, 177–8, 208) and refined by

will presume the three-stage model as the one that best accounts for the introduction, then subordination, of the Sabbath topic.[16] At the same time, such diachronic concerns must not overshadow a reading of the text as we have it; the evangelist has taken over traditional material, yet had made it part of his own proclamation.

5.1.2 The Healing Miracle (John 5:1–9a)

The healing miracle consists of five elements, the order of which is in accord with the pattern for miracle stories, as a comparison with the Synoptics shows.[17]

First there is an introductory verse, supplied by the evangelist, which marks the transition from previous material (v. 1).[18] Jesus "ascends" (ἀνέβη) to Jerusalem.[19] The temporal transition is signaled both by the

Harold W. Attridge, "Thematic Development and Source Elaboration in John 7:1–36," *CBQ* 42 (1980): 160–70; see also the recent presentations in Rainer Metzner, *Das Verständnis der Sünde im Johannesevangelium* (WUNT 122; Tübingen, 2000), 40–61, and Labahn, *Jesus*, 213–64.

[16] Lacking a written document representing an earlier stage of transmission, all reconstructions are hypothetical. The reconstruction of Johannine sources is more complicated than that of the Synoptics. Not only do we have one of the written sources of Matthew and Luke, Mark, but the independent use each makes of the sayings source, Q, is a valuable control. Neither of these is the case for John (unless the discourses were composed in conscious distancing from the dialogues that were one of the sources of *Dial. Sav.* [NHC III,5]; cf. Helmut Koester, *Introduction to the New Testament*[2d ed.; Berlin, 2000], 2:182–6). Additionally, the recensions through which the Gospel passed appear to have been the work of a school, sharing a characteristic vocabulary (sociolect), making differentiation more difficult (on the Johannine school, see Schnelle, *Einleitung*, 447–9).

[17] Labahn, "Spurensuche," 166; cf. Bultmann, *Evangelium*, 177; Dodd, *Tradition*,174–80; Martyn, *History*, 24–25, 68. As noted above (5.1.1), the episode as a whole (vv. 1–18) has a structure unlike that of synoptic healing miracles.

[18] Cf. 2:12, 6:4, and 7:2; Bultmann, *Evangelium*, 179; Labahn, "Spurensuche," 164.

[19] That one "goes up" to a feast in Jerusalem is suggested by the fact that Jerusalem lies higher, and the temple in Jerusalem higher yet. However in Johannine usage, it is likely that there is a suggestion of the ἀνάβασις of the Son of Man (3:13, 6:62, 20:17; cf. C. H. Dodd, *The Interpretation of the Fourth Gospel* [Cambridge, 1953], 385; Frühwald-König, *Tempel*, 171–2).

phrase μετὰ ταῦτα and the reference to a feast "of the Jews."[20] Second, the description of the setting (vv. 2–3a, expanded subsequent to the circulation of the Gospel by v. 3b and 4). The scenic description is, however, fairly detailed for a miracle story.[21] The mention of the pool reflects both knowledge of Palestine and the assumption that the reader may not share this knowledge (cf. the explanation that the name of the pool as Εβραϊστὶ, i.e. Aramaic).[22] The third element is the focus of attention on one of the sufferers gathered there and his disability, thus preparing for the miracle(v. 5). The man is not named, nor is his illness mentioned.[23] From the man's answer to Jesus in v. 7 we learn that he can move, but slowly; the cause is not named.[24] The length of his illness is given, though, 38 years.[25] The situation of the man is hopeless, therefore

[20]　This is the second of a minimum of four trips to Jerusalem that Jesus makes in the Gospel of John. In the Synoptics, his only visit there as an adult is the trip he makes that ends with his crucifixion. The occasion is always a feast (2:13; 7:2, 10; 12:1, 12) The feast mentioned in 5:1 is unique however in that it is not identified (assuming with NA[27] that the anarthrous reading is original; cf. Metzger, *Commentary*, 207), leading both ancient scribes and modern scholars to try to remedy this. The feast plays no further role in the narrative; it is best to accept the *lectio difficilior* and conclude that it is simply mentioned in order to move Jesus to Jerusalem for the conflict to be played out there (Haenchen, *Johannesevangelium*, 266).
[21]　Dodd, *Tradition*, 179. For discussions of the textual difficulties in v. 2, see Metzger, *Commentary*, 207–8; Bultmann, *Evangelium*, 179; Haenchen, "Probleme," 105, n. 5; W. D. Davies, *The Gospel and the Land: Early Christianity and Jewish Territorial Doctrine* (Berkeley, 1974), 307–8; Frühwald-König, *Tempel*, 140–43. On the discussion of the identification of the pool, see Joachim Jeremias, *Die Wiederentdeckung von Bethesda*, (FRLANT NF 41; Göttingen, 1949); rev. and expanded for the ET: *The Rediscovery of Bethesda, John 5:2* (Louisville, Ken., 1966).
[22]　R. Alan Culpepper, *Anatomy of the Fourth Gospel: A Study in Literary Design* (FF; Philadelphia, 1983), 217; D. L. Mealand, "John 5 and the Limits of Rhetorical Criticism," in *Understanding Poets and Prophets* (FS G. W. Anderson; ed. A. G. Auld; JSOTSup 152; Sheffield, 1993), 258–72, here 259–60. Accurate geographical knowledge does not of itself guarantee the authenticity of the tradition, *pace* Witkamp, "Use," 22.
[23]　In the similarly worded P. Egerton 2 (with P. Köln 255), Jesus heals a leper, but there is no indication here that this is the nature of the illness.
[24]　Wengst, *Johannesevangelium*, 184–5.
[25]　This is the only NT use of this number. Most see in this no more than a description of a very long time (e.g. Bultmann, *Evangelium*, 180, n. 7; Schackenburg, *Johannesevangelium*, 2:120–21; Haenchen, "Probleme," 108, n. 2), cf. Wengst, who

the miracle will be great.[26] Fourth, the exchange between Jesus and the man, culminating in the command of Jesus, executing the miracle (vv. 6–8).[27] There is a switch from aorist and imperfect verb tenses to durative (historical present) to report the words of Jesus to the man (λέγει), this has the effect of moving the reader into the scene.[28] Jesus takes the initiative; the action starts because he knows and sees (v. 6).[29] For Jesus to take the initiative is rare, but not singular.[30] At the same time, it runs counter to the pattern established in the first two signs in the Gospel of John, in which a request is made of Jesus that he expresses a reluctance to fulfil.[31] The question of Jesus, θέλεις ὑγιὴς γενέσθαι, seems superfluous, since the assumption would be that it was for this purpose that the man was at the pool.[32] The question has therefore been taken to imply that Jesus was questioning the man's desire.[33] It is possible, however, that this is nothing more than a narrative means of initiating

attempts to correlate this to the wilderness experience of Israel (Deut 2:14; *Johannesevangelium*, 183–4). Mention of the duration of the malady is a topic of healing stories (Mk 5:25; Lk 13:16; cf. Bultmann, *Evangelium*, 177, n. 3).

[26] Witkamp, "Use,", 30. The characterization of need is a typical feature of miracle stories (Bultmann, *Geschichte*, 236; Gerd Theissen, *Urchristliche Wundergeschichten: Ein Beitrag zur formgeschichtlichen Erforschung der synoptischen Evangelien* [6th ed.; SNT 8; Gütersloh, 1990], 61–62).

[27] There is no change of setting, nor are the many others present shut out, as in many healing miracle stories (Theissen, *Wundergeschichten*, 70–71).

[28] Culpepper, *Anatomy*, 30–31.

[29] This is usually understood as supernatural knowledge, a characteristic of Jesus in the Fourth Gospel (1:42; 2:24–25; 4:17–18; Culpepper, *Anatomy*, 108–9; Labahn, *Jesus*, 230–31). Wengst limits instances of the motif of the special knowledge of Jesus to the word family connected to οἶδα; he understands γινώσκω here in its basic sense of to arrive at the knowledge of something, *Johannesevangelium*, 184.

[30] Examples of this are Mark 1:30–31; 3:1–6; Luke 7:11–17; 13:10–17, 21–22; John 9:1, 6.

[31] Culpepper lists seven ways in which this episode differs from the previous signs ("Exemple," 142–3).

[32] The adjective ὑγιής (v. 6) is used by John only in reference to this episode (vv. 11, 14, 15; 7:23), an indication that he is using traditional material here.

[33] Dodd, *Interpretation*, 319–20; *Tradition*, 178–9; Brown, *Gospel*, 1:209; Culpepper, *Anatomy*, 137–8, "Exemple," 147–8.

the healing.[34] It permits the man to describe his plight.[35] Just as the question of Jesus is often interpreted as a negative feature, though, so is the man's answer.[36] Rather than answering Jesus' question directly, the man, described here as ὁ ἀσθενῶν, describes the circumstance that has prevented his healing. In light of the general failure of the world to comprehend the one sent into the world (1:10), this response could reflect misunderstanding of the nature of the help offered (cf. 3:4, 9; 4:11–12, 15, 33).[37] Jesus nonetheless performs the healing by commanding him to rise, to take up his pallet and walk (v. 8; cf. Mark 2:9, 11).[38]

The fifth element is a demonstration of the effect of the miracle (v. 9a).[39] The words take effect, and the man responds immediately to Jesus' instruction.[40] The miracle story does not, however, conclude with a reaction of the man or of bystanders.[41] Possibly there was, as a sixth

---

[34] Bultmann, *Evangelium*, 180–81.

[35] Becker, *Evangelium*, 278–9.

[36] E.g. Dodd, *Interpretation*, 320; Haenchen, "Probleme," 107; Donald A. Carson, "Jesus and the Sabbath in the Four Gospels," in *From Sabbath to Lord's Day* (Grand Rapids, Mich., 1982), 57–97, here 80.

[37] Haenchen, *Johannesevangelium*, 269; Culpepper, *Anatomy*, 152–65; Witkamp, "Use," 25. Theissen notes the connection of this motif to the taking of the initiative by the miracle-worker (*Wundergeschichten*, 65). On misunderstanding as an aspect of Johannine style, see Hubert Leroy, *Rätsel und Missverständnis: Ein Beitrag zur Formgeschichte des Johannesevangeliums* (BBB 30; Bonn, 1986) and François Vouga, *Le cadre historique et l'intention théologique de Jean* (BeRe 3; Paris, 1981), 15–36.

[38] The question of whether John knew and used Mark's Gospel has been reopened by Frans Neirynck ("John and the Synoptics," in *L'Evangile de Jean* [ed. M. de Jonge; BETL 44; Leuven, 1977], 73–106; "John 5,1–18 and the Gospel of Mark," in *Evangelica 2* [ed. F. Neirynck; BETL 99; Leuven, 1991], 703–8).

[39] On demonstration as a motif of miracle stories, see Theissen, *Wundergeschichten*, 75–76; cf. Labahn, who notes parallels from the ancient world (*Jesus*, 235–6). It is not necessary to consider the pallet superfluous to the story, even though no illness is described that would require lying on one. The man's lengthy presence at the pool supplies adequate justification for this detail (*pace* Lindars, *Gospel*, 210).

[40] Theissen, *Wundergeschichten*, 75–76. Witkamp, "Use," 26, sees here a further indication that John tried to clamp his two streams of tradition closer together by substituting ἐγένετο ὑγιής, which comes from v. 6, for ἠγέρθη, which we would expect after ἔγειρε (v. 8) and because of the Markan parallel (2:12).

[41] Cf. the reactions recorded in 2:10; 4:53; 6:14; 9:8; 11:45; see also Brown, *Gospel*, 1:210; Culpepper, "Exemple," 141–4; Witkamp, "Use," 26–27.

element, a dismissal saying, the essence of which may still be discernible in v. 14.[42] Jesus draws the man's attention to the fact that he has been made well and warns him against unspecified consequences of continued sin.

To sum up: in vv. 2–9a we have a clearly organized healing episode with no necessary connection to the Sabbath. The narrative interest in the episode prior to its reworking is to demonstrate the miracle-working power of Jesus. The local knowledge points to a Palestinian, Jewish-Christian context. This does not rule out the possibility that John has shaped the tradition to suit his purpose.[43]

5.1.3 The Controversy Dialogue (John 5:9b–18)

The narrator uses the demonstration of the healing, an element of the traditional healing story, to provide a means by which the story may be given a dramatic expansion.[44] The healing, that is, the command of Jesus to the man to take up his pallet and walk, leads to a reaction of a group not mentioned in the miracle story, characterized as "the Jews."[45] The

[42] On dismissal sayings, see Theissen, *Wundergeschichten*, 77.

[43] Elements that can be assigned to the evangelist are the introductory v. 1 with its mention of a feast, the time indication in v. 5, the supernatural knowledge of Jesus in v. 6; see Bultmann, *Evangelium*, 177; Witkamp, "Use," 22; Metzner, *Verständnis*, 40–41. The addition of 38 years as the duration of the illness, which emphasizes the grandeur of the miracle, demonstrates that although reworkings change the emphasis of an account, they do not necessarily reject the original point (Schnelle, *Christologie*, 113).

[44] Haenchen, *Johannesevangelium*, 92. This passage and the miracle story share stylistic features: the reuse of ὑγιής (vv. 9, 11, 14, 15; cf. 7:23; only Johannine uses); the return of the formulation of Jesus' command (v. 8, reused three times in vv. 10–12). The correspondence is close in vv. 8–10, with a chiastic pattern formed around the suture where the Sabbath motif was introduced (Bernard, "Guérison," 6–11).

[45] The term οἱ Ἰουδαῖοι, which reflects the alienation and distance felt by a community expelled from the synagogue, becomes in the Gospel of John, in contrast to the Synoptics, the primary—though not exclusive—term for the opponents of Jesus (cf. "Pharisees" and "chief priests," used together in 7:32, also used separately in other passages). As used in the Gospel, the term denotes a collective literary figure, representatives of the world hostile to Jesus (Bultmann, *Evangelium*, 59–60; Culpepper, *Anatomy*, 126). At the same time, not all Judeans are opposed to Jesus (8:52; 10:19–21; 11:45; 12:11). Although the term applies to a cluster of referents (Urban C. van Wahlde, "The Johannine 'Jews'—A Critical Survey," NTS 28 [1982]: 33–60), the use of one term is significant (Culpepper, *Anatomy*, 126). I have decided to retain the traditional translation

reason is the introduction of a new detail, "and it was Sabbath" (v. 9b).[46] This is skillfully placed; it sets the stage for the conflict that follows, for to carry a pallet was a violation of the Sabbath (see below, 5.2.5).[47] It is presented as an afterthought and draws the reader's attention to this detail, causing him to reconsider what has been narrated so far in a new light (cf. 6:4; 9:14).[48] The reference to the Sabbath acts as a hinge, marking the transition from narrated miracle (it defines the timing of the miracle) to the controversial exchanges (it is the reason for the controversy).[49]

This passage, the first conflict dialogue in John, describes exchanges that can be divided into four scenes on the basis of the varying pairs of dialogue partners.[50]

of οἱ Ἰουδαῖοι as "Jews," placed in quotation marks, to stress the fact that the term refers to the collective figure in the Johannine narrative. In chs. 5 and 9 Jesus and those whom he healed are interrogated by figures who hold positions of authority in the community (see the interchangeability of the terms *Jews* and *Pharisees* in ch. 9).

[46]   The placement of this remark is often taken as an indication that an earlier healing episode was subsequently transformed into a Sabbath conflict; e.g. Bultmann: "nachklappt" (*Evangelium*, 177, n. 3). This alone does not determine whether the motif was original or secondary, since the delayed mention of time could be a stylistic feature (cf., in addition to the similar introduction of the Sabbath motif in 9:14, the reference to the Passover in 6:4, and to the night in 13:30). These references were added in such a way that they draw attention to themselves. Brown dissents from the consensus and maintains that the Sabbath was an element of the story from the beginning, yet nevertheless concedes that 9b–13 may be a secondary expansion (*Gospel*, 1:210). The importance of the Sabbath motif for introducing christological concerns leads Asiedu-Peprah to reject the view that the Sabbath motif is secondary to the healing narrative (*Conflicts*, 6–7, n. 17; repeated 43; 66–67, with n. 66). There is however no reason why an added motif can not be important to the unfolding of the narrative as it now stands in the text. Asiedu-Peprah fails to grasp the difference between the addition of a trait to a traditional account and the intention of the text in the form that we now have it.

[47]   Culpepper, "Exemple," 149.

[48]   On the omission of essential information until the point where it is required as a feature of Hebrew narrative (e.g. 1 Sam 21:7), see Robert Alter, *The Art of Biblical Narrative* (New York, 1981), 66, and Jeffrey L. Staley, "Stumbling in the Dark, Reaching for the Light: Reading Character in John 5 and 9," *Semeia* 53 (1991): 55-80, here 60.

[49]   With ἦν δὲ σάββατον, the verbal tenses return to imperfect.

[50]   Culpepper, "Exemple," 143; cf. Martyn, *History*, 69. Culpepper also points out the technique of the pairing of characters. V. 14 has the same pair as v. 5–9a (ibid.).

In the first scene, vv. 10–13, the partners are the "Jews" and the man. In contrast to the Synoptic Sabbath healing controversies, it is not Jesus who is first accused, but the anonymous person who had benefitted from the work of Jesus. That which Jesus commanded him to do demonstratively infringed on the Sabbath, at least in the eyes of the accusers, for whom this represented the carrying of a burden, thus a violation of the Sabbath (v. 10).[51] The questioners show no interest in how he gained his mobility; their interest is focused on why he is carrying his pallet on the Sabbath.[52] This reaction implies that scrupulous observance of Sabbath regulations has led to a skewed perspective, in which the act of carrying a pallet on the Sabbath arouses more interest than the occurrence of a work of God in their midst.

The man, now referred to with a different participle, ὁ τεθεραπευμένος, the one who had been healed (cf. Mark 3:2), has to answer for his offence, but he does not formulate an argument to defend his action.[53] Instead, he passes the responsibility to the one who healed him (v. 11). Since, as we will subsequently learn, the man does not know who Jesus is, the latter is referred to as well by a participial expression, ὁ ποιήσας με ὑγιῆ. The phrase could have been used of a medical practitioner who had exercised his profession, which would have been a clear violation of the Sabbath. But, as we saw, no action of Jesus is recorded, only a word that effectuates the result. The words of the command are quoted, but the first command, ἔγειρε, is omitted. The "Jews" do not follow up on this description of Jesus as the one who made well, but simply ask about "the man" who told him to carry his pallet (v. 12). Nor do they take note of the power to heal implicit in such a command. The man, who is now referred to with yet another participle, ὁ ἰαθείς, does not know who

---

[51]   Haenchen, "Probleme," 108.

[52]   Brown, *Gospel*, 1:207. Carson suggests that the pallet-carrying was potentially more serious and less debatable that the charge of breaking the Sabbath by healing ("Jesus," 81). This is surprising in light of the Sabbath healing controversies in the Synoptics, and runs counter to Carson's assertion that the command contravenes no clear ordinance and that Jesus did not intend to precipitate a crisis over the Sabbath.

[53]   His identity is not important for the story (he is not named), but the change in his condition, expressed by the change in participles, is.

commanded him (v. 13).[54] Nor can he point Jesus out; he had disappeared into the crowd.

The second scene contains a note of irony. The one sought, Jesus, finds the man, in the Temple (v. 14).[55] It is not surprising that Jesus finds the man there.[56] When he finds him, he points to the healed condition of the man, then warns him not to go on sinning lest something worse happen.[57] The sharp words not to go on sinning create a tension in the context of the Gospel of John because of the explicit rejection of a connection between sickness and sin in 9:2–3; there is no explicit connection between sin and the infirmity of the man, however, in 5:14, so that this tension should not be overly stressed. They hearken back to an earlier stage of tradition, when the common consensus of Second Temple Judaism on this matter was shared by the Christian community, as the disciples are portrayed as doing in ch. 9.[58] In other words, it would fit well the likely setting of the healing episode (see 5.2.2, above).[59] Its similarity to other sharp warnings at the close of episodes in which the forgiveness of sin was the topic (e.g., the non-Johannine 8:11) suggest that an earlier form of this verse may have been the original conclusion of the healing episode, even though the forgiveness of sin had not been an explicit topic in it.[60] On the level of tradition, the meaning of

[54] In ch. 9, the blind man knows that it is Jesus who opened his eyes, but he cannot say, when asked, where Jesus is (9:12).

[55] This is the second Temple appearance of Jesus. The first was provocative (cf. the early placement of the temple cleansing by John, 2:13–25; the Synoptics bring it during the passion week, Mark 11:15–19, par. Matt 21:12–17; Luke 19:45–48).

[56] Another instance of the supernatural knowledge of the Johannine Jesus, already demonstrated in v. 6 (see above). After receiving a divine blessing such as a healing, it was appropriate to go to the temple to present a thank offering, but nothing about this is said, and it is unnecessary to resort to such explanations to account for what Jesus knows.

[57] The imperative μηκέτι ἁμάρτανε, present tense, is a general command or summons to continuation.

[58] Bill 1:495–6; 2:193–7, 527–9; also Luke 13:1–5. But cf. Wengst, who objects to the view that Second Temple Judaism unanimously believed that all sickness is the result of sin (*Johannesevangelium*, 189). On Wengst's view, see also 5.2, below.

[59] Haenchen, "Probleme," 107.

[60] Cf. Mark 2:1–12, where a healing episode demonstrates the authority of Jesus to forgive sins. Examples of healings in the Synoptics in which a command follows the recovery: Mark 1:44 par.; Mark 5:19 (=Luke 8:39); Mark 8:26; see also the non-

something worse is that of a relapse to a more serious illness.[61] John retained it, not only out of respect for his tradition, but because it was susceptible of new meaning in context of the Gospel.[62] The meaning in context reflects a typical Johannine topic, proper perception of the identity of the one sent.[63] The man did not know the identity of the one who had healed him (v. 13); once Jesus encounters him with this warning about continued sin, he does know, as v. 15 shows.[64]

This reference to sin implicitly underlines what the sin is *not*. Despite the accusations of the authorities, the man had not sinned by carrying his pallet on the Sabbath; it is negative only in the eyes of those who fail to understand the sign. By warning against sin, Jesus' moral credentials are established beyond doubt *before* he is accused by the "Jews" of being a sinner.

In the third scene, vv. 15–16, the partners, as in scene one (vv. 10–13), are the "Jews" and the man. We are not told that Jesus had identified himself, but the man is now able to identify him to the "Jews" (v. 15).[65] This scene is presented as a narrative rather than as a

Johannine John 8:11 (cf. Pancaro, *Law*, 11).

[61]   Metzner points to the use of χείρων in the saying about the return of an unclean spirit in Matt 12:45 par. Luke 11:26 (*Verständnis*, 49).

[62]   Witkamp posits reverence for tradition ("Use," 25). Fortna, in a similar vein, suggests a reluctance to change a text known and loved in the community (*Fourth Gospel*, 8–9).

[63]   Dorothy Ann Lee, *The Symbolic Narratives of the Fourth Gospel: The Interplay of Form and Meaning* (JSNTS 95; Sheffield 1994), 117; Metzner, *Verständnis*, 48–57.

[64]   Labahn remarks: "Das traditionelle Fragment der älteren Heilungsgeschichte, v. 14, wird so sekundär zu einer Kritik des Geheilten, der die im Wunder durchscheinende Doxa Gottes und seiner Gesandte weder erkennt noch anerkennt" (*Jesus*, 234).

[65]   It is not necessary to view the action of the healed man as betrayal (*pace* e.g. Bultmann, *Evangelium*, 182; Martyn, *History*, 71; Culpepper, *Anatomy*, 137–8, 194; Metzner, *Verständnis*, 53–55). The basic meaning of the verb ἀναγγέλλω is to *report* or to *inform* (BDAG, s.v., Broer, *EWNT* 1:129–32, esp. 130–31, L&N 33.197). It is used in John in the positive sense of proclamation (4:25; 16:13–15; 16:25 v.l.; cf. Ignace de la Potterie, *La Vérité dans Saint Jean. 1: Le Christ et la vérité, l'Esprit et la vérité*, AnBib 73, Rome 1977, 445–53), and it is possible, given Johannine ambivalence, that this should be heard here as an overtone. This does not mean that the man's intention was to proclaim (*pace* Thomas, "Stop sinning," 18–19; Sjen van Tilborg, *Imaginative Love in John* [BISer 2; Leiden, 1993], 218–9). Brown mediates between positive and negative assessments of the man's motivation in reporting the identity of Jesus to the "Jews,"

discourse.[66] The man does not speak again, and indeed disappears from the account after this.[67] No change of location is mentioned; evidently we are to picture this, too, as taking place in the temple.[68]

The denouement of this story underlines its importance for the overall plot of the Fourth Gospel. Verse 16 is a conclusion from the perspective of the narrator. Now Jesus is accused, or, more accurately, persecuted (διώκω). This, although the "Jews" have not yet confronted Jesus. This is proleptic, and looks toward the only other use of this verb in John, in the farewell discourses, as a prediction there of the post-resurrection experience of the disciples (15:20).[69] The imperfect tenses in v. 16, ἐδίωκον, ἐποίει, indicate ongoing persecution, based on continual, or repeated, actions (ταῦτα) of Jesus.[70] These may be the two actions of healing and commanding to carry the pallet. In light of the imperfect verbs, it is likelier that a series of Sabbath infractions (healings?) is meant (cf. however the emphatic ἕν in 7:21).[71] At any rate, the charge is not specified.[72]

The fourth scene, vv. 17–18, representing the "Jews" and Jesus, differs because no dialogue is narrated.[73] These verses present the defense of Jesus and the reaction of the "Jews." He defends himself in terms that

attributing it to "persistent naïveté" (*Gospel*, 1:209). The man has unwittingly become an agent of betrayal, and yet, ironically, of proclaiming that it is Jesus who heals. Nevertheless, that he reveals the identity of Jesus to the opponents, following directly on the warning not to go on sinning—in Johannine terms, persist in unbelief—, is an indication that the man has not become a follower of Jesus; the contrast to the healed man in ch. 9 (see below) is clear (Metzner, "Geheilte," 177–93); cf. Labahn: the negative characterization of the man does not depend on the evaluation of his report to the authorities, his deficient reaction to God's emissary suffices (*Jesus*, 248).

[66] Martyn, *History*, 69.

[67] Staley suggests that the evangelist shifts to narrative here to protect the man ("Stumbling," 61). More likely, his purpose in the story is fulfilled.

[68] Bultmann, *Evangelium*, 182; Haenchen, *Johannesevangelium*, 273.

[69] On the use of prolepses in John, see Culpepper, *Anatomy*, 61–70.

[70] This is a sharpening of the question posed by the "Jews" after the cleansing of the temple (2:18). In their eyes, the messianic claim implicit in doing *these things* (ταῦτα) required further authentication.

[71] Becker, *Evangelium*, 1:280.

[72] Frühwald-König, *Tempel*, 167.

[73] Lee however finds elements of a dialogue in the discourse (*Narratives*, 107).

intensify the conflict, however, since he invokes his imitation of the continuing work (ἐργάζεται) of "my" Father. The subsequent dialogue shows which "works" are meant: the divine activities of giving life and judging.[74] Yet he refers to the continuing work of the Father with a prepositional phrase that implies its termination (ἕως ἄρτι), which has given rise to discussion over possible implications for the Sabbath question (see below, 5.5.1). Before Jesus defends himself, the "Jews" had laid one charge against him. Now they have two: (1) he has "loosed" (imperfect) the Sabbath; (2) he has made himself equal to the Father (v. 18). "Therefore they sought all the more to kill him." This is the first use of ἀποκτείνω in John's Gospel. As in v. 16, the verb is imperfect; the quest to kill Jesus is not a one-time event, but recurrent or continual (cf. 8:59; 10:31; 11:8; 19:7).

This first mention of murderous intent, in the context of a Sabbath controversy, invites comparison to the Synoptic tradition. The combination of sovereign behavior vis-à-vis the Sabbath, combined with the participation in divine authority implicit in such an action, elicits from his compatriots a lethal hostility similar to that recorded in Mark 3:6. In Mark, hostility to Jesus is first aroused by his claim to exercise a prerogative that is God's alone, the forgiveness of sins (2:7; cf. John 5:17), and the first mention of a plot against Jesus springs from a Sabbath healing (3:6). In John these two steps of escalating strife are retained but conflated into one confrontation. Yet by relating the first stage, described as persecution, to alleged Sabbath violations and the second stage, dually signaled by the comparative μᾶλλον and the stronger verb, *destroy*, to the perceived claim of equality with the Father, we have again a subordination of the Sabbath issue to the Christological. Thus even in the reaction of the opponents, the evangelist achieves his aim of emphasizing the nature of the Son and his relation to the Father.

Verses 17–18 were composed by the evangelist to prepare for his use of the healing and resultant Sabbath controversy as a springboard for the subsequent discourse. While they duplicate v. 16, they pick up the theme

---

[74] The lexeme ἔργον in the LXX is used consistently of the works of God both in creation (cf. Gen 2:2–3; Ψ 8:4 [ET 8:3]; 103:24 [MT, ET 104:24]) and salvation (cf. Exod 34:10; Ψ 43:2 [MT 44:2, ET 44:1]; 65:5 [MT, ET 66:5]).

of the Sabbath and subordinate it to the christological issue of the participation of the Son in the unceasing activity of the Father. This provides a fitting conclusion for this subsection, since the accusers do not speak again in this chapter, the rest of which is devoted to a long discourse by Jesus.

To sum up: there is a change in protagonists compared to the healing story. There, the infirm man had been passive. Here, he is the constant figure in the first three scenes, which gives him central importance in the unfolding of the narrative. More crucially for the narrative strategy of the overall Gospel, a previously unmentioned group, the "Jews," enters.[75]

The "Jews" contend first with the man who had been healed, then with Jesus.[76] The two-stage dialogue between the "Jews" and the man, interrupted by an intermezzo in which Jesus encounters the man anew and instructs him (v. 14), enabling the man to identify Jesus to the accusers (v. 15), culminates in a dual charge: breaking (literally *untying*) the Sabbath and a claimed equality with God, accompanied by the intent to destroy Jesus (v. 18), a step beyond the first mention of persecution (5:16). The narrated conflict ends here; the rest of the chapter is devoted to a discourse by Jesus in which he defends his authority by explicating this relationship of the Son and the Father (vv. 19–30) and cites the necessary witnesses (vv. 31–47).

This material is a reworking of a miracle story into a Sabbath controversy.[77] Details in the original story lent themselves to this transformation, being susceptible to a deeper meaning in the new context. Carrying the pallet, originally a demonstration of the healing, becomes a transgression of the Sabbath and provokes the controversy.[78]

---

[75] Ch. 5 introduces the theme of conflict with the "Jews," a theme that extends throughout the first half of the Gospel, which describes the public ministry of Jesus, and reaches its culmination in the role of the "Jews" in the trial of Jesus. This episode thus occupies a privileged position in the Gospel as a whole (Culpepper, "Exemple," 138).

[76] The ultimate identity of the "Jews" as representatives of the world hostile to the Revealer is revealed in their role in the judgment scene, 18:28–19:16 (Jean Zumstein, "Der Prozess Jesu vor Pilatus (ein Beispiel johanneischer Eschatologie)," in *Kreative Erinnerung* [Zürich, 1999], 145–55, here 150).

[77] The result could be described in Theissen's terminology as a "Normenwunder" (*Wundergeschichten*, 66).

[78] Haenchen, *Johannesevangelium*, 286. Similarly, the command of Jesus, ἔγειρε,

Because of the lack of explicit reference to the Sabbath in the following discourse, this transformation can be assigned to an intermediate stage between the formulation of the traditional healing episode (5:2–9a) and the composition of the Fourth Gospel.[79] Johannine features are redactional, indications that the evangelist has intervened in the conflict scene, just as he had in the miracle story, to mold it to his own perspective.[80] In particular, through the composition of vv. 17–18, he has prepared the way for the following discourse, in which the meaning both of the original healing and the characterization of it as a Sabbath work are subsumed to the overriding Johannine theme of the work of the one sent and his relation to the Father.[81] Just as the original ending of the healing episode may have been retained despite its transformation into a Sabbath controversy, so the original ending of the Sabbath controversy, replaced by vv. 17–18, may still be present in the Gospel (7:19–24; see below, 5.1.4).

Though the Sabbath is extraneous to the miracle itself, and subordinated in the resulting controversy dialogues and discourses to the issue of Jesus' identity, i.e., to Christology, it is not irrelevant, as if just any issue could have provoked the more important revelation. The Sabbath plays a role in the unfolding purpose of the narrative, which does not proceed directly from a non-Sabbath healing story to the discourse on sharing in the Father's work. For the evangelist, it is a *Sabbath* healing that signifies that Jesus shares in the divine prerogative of giving life.[82] In the final argument of the discourse, Jesus claims the Torah as a vehicle through which the revelation of the Son could have occurred. Yet it had not. His opponents persist in an understanding of the law of Moses that

---

with its echo of Jesus' own resurrection, portrays Jesus as life-giver and is a bridge to the discourse (5:21); Haenchen, *Johannesevangelium*, 92, 270. See the use of ἐγείρω in John 2:19, 22; 21:14.

[79] Metzner, "Geheilte," 178–9; Labahn, *Jesus*, 244–7.

[80] Metzner, "Geheilte," 179; Labahn, "Spurensuche," 169–70.

[81] Labahn, *Jesus*, 248–9. On union with God as the leading idea of John, see Dodd, *Interpretation*, 187–200; John Painter focuses on the aspect of unity of activity (*The Quest for the Messiah: The History, Literature and Theology of the Johannine Community* [Edinburgh, 1991], 187–91).

[82] Pancaro, *Law*, 16; Asiedu-Peprah, *Conflicts*, 75–76.

prevents their recognition of the true identity of Jesus. It is not accidental that the conflict that will govern the further unfolding of the narrative of the Gospel ignites over a critical issue of Torah-loyalty, the Sabbath.

5.1.4 A Second Reference to this Healing (John 7:14–24)

The next Sabbath reference in the Fourth Gospel is in 7:22–23, where Jesus refers to a Sabbath healing he has performed, although none is narrated in context. Evidently, this refers back to the healing in 5:1–9. After an extensive narrative and discourse back in Galilee shortly before a Passover (ch. 6), a new literary unit begins.[83] Jesus rejects the urging of his brothers, said to be based on unbelief (v. 5), to go to Jerusalem for Succoth, Tabernacles, the third of the annual pilgrimage feasts, to demonstrate his identity. When he does go, it is in secret (v. 10). The feast is half over before he appears, teaching in the temple (v. 14). This provokes a new controversy with the "Jews" about his qualification to teach (v. 15).[84] In the course of this, he again defends his Sabbath healing:

> About the middle of the festival Jesus went up into the temple and began to teach. The Jews were astonished at it, saying, "How does this man have such learning, when he has never been taught?" Then Jesus answered them, "My teaching is not mine but his who sent me. Anyone who resolves to do the will of God will know

---

[83] Indications of the beginning of a new unit are a marker of time change, μετὰ ταῦτα, and mention of location, Galilee, 7:1, mention of an upcoming feast, v. 2, and new characters, his brothers, v. 3, cf. 2:12. Many reckon with a confusion of the original order (e.g. J. H. Bernard, *A Critical and Exegetical Commentary on the Gospel According to St. John* [ICC; Edinburgh, 1928], xvi–xx; Bultmann, *Evangelium*, 177–8; Becker, *Evangelium*, 1:34–36; 191; Schnackenburg, *Johannesevangelium*, 2:6–11, 115; already proposed by Tatian, *Diatesseron* §§ 19–20; 22 [*ANF* 10:72–75, 77–78]). Though this solves some difficulties, it raises others (cf. Haenchen, *Johannesevangelium*, 53–57; Attridge, "Development," 165–70; Wengst, *Johannesevangelium*, 1:180). The present order of the Gospel, though admittedly problematic, is increasingly accepted as intentional (D. Moody Smith, "Johannine Studies," in *The New Testament and Its Modern Interpreters* [ed. E. J. Epp and G. W. McRae; Atlanta, 1989], 271–96, here 275; cf. Schnelle, *Einleitung*, 495–501).

[84] The interplay of "crowd" and "Jews" here is confused. P. Egerton 2, 1 verso, 7 has heightened the probability that "Jews" in John has replaced a term for the leaders in the traditional material taken over by the evangelist (Helmut Koester, *Ancient Christian Gospels: Their History and Development* [Harrisburg, Penn. 1990], 209).

whether the teaching is from God or whether I am speaking on my own. Those who speak on their own seek their own glory; but the one who seeks the glory of him who sent him is true, and there is nothing false in him.

"Did not Moses give you the law? Yet none of you keeps the law. Why are you looking for an opportunity to kill me?" The crowd answered, "You have a demon! Who is trying to kill you?"

Jesus answered them, "I performed one work, and all of you are astonished. Moses gave you circumcision (it is, of course, not from Moses, but from the patriarchs), and you circumcise a man on the Sabbath. If a man receives circumcision on the Sabbath in order that the law of Moses may not be broken, are you angry with me because I healed a man's whole body on the Sabbath? Do not judge by appearances, but judge with right judgment."[85]

The passage as I have delimited it consists of a discourse of Jesus (vv. 16–24), introduced with a description of the situation: time, place, activity of Jesus, and the reaction of the crowd to that activity (vv. 14–15). The crowd is astonished that Jesus would teach without the customary training.[86] To dare do this meant that Jesus was either self-taught, thus unreliable and prone to heresy, or that he was the Messiah.[87] Jesus disallows the first alternative by denying that the teaching is his own. The claim that his doctrine is that of the one who sent him is dual, pointedly not uttering the name that was conventionally not spoken in Second Temple Judaism and at the same time underlining his own identity as the one sent (v. 16). The reference to doing the will of God would have been understood by the "Jews" as the divine will as codified in the Torah. "Hier wird also die sachliche Übereinstimmung dieses Gotteswillens der Tora mit dem vorausgesetzt, was Jesus lehrt."[88]

---

[85] I have chosen to limit the passage under consideration with this gnomic saying of Jesus. The next scene is introduced by a time indicator, v. 37. The intervening verses report the divided opinion of the crowd (vv. 25–27; 30–31), interspersed by an utterance of Jesus concerning his identity, origin, and knowledge of the one who sent him (vv. 28–29), the reaction of the Pharisees and their joint attempt with the chief priests to arrest Jesus (v. 32), a further saying of Jesus concerning his return to the one who sent him (vv. 33–34), and the misunderstanding of the crowd (vv. 35–36).

[86] The verb *astonished*, ἐθαύμαζον, should be understood here with the meaning that they were disturbed (BDAG s.v. θαυμάζω, cf. Bertram, θαῦμα κτλ, *TWNT* 3:28).

[87] Wengst, *Johannesevangelium*, 277.

[88] Wengst, *Johannesevangelium*, 278.

Jesus charges his opponents with not doing the Torah (v. 19). This should be understood in light of v. 21. Jesus refers to "one work," contrasting it to the repeated failure of his interlocutors to "do" the law; the reference is evidently to the one Sabbath healing so far narrated in the Gospel, that of ch. 5 (cf. the expression ὑγιῆ ἐποίησα in 7:23, which points back to 5:11, 14, 15).[89] The defense revolves around that fact that the "Jews" themselves suppress the Sabbath by performing circumcision (see below, 5.4.1).

The defense of Jesus closes with an appeal for right judgment, as opposed to judgment according to appearances. This can be understood as common sense wisdom, and continues to live as such. But in Johannine context those in danger of a judgment according to appearances, and therefore a wrong judgment, are not only those who reject Jesus because they fail to see in Jesus' works that they are works of God, and therefore reject him, but also those who accept Jesus because they see in the works merely σημεῖα, and therefore remain with, to Johannine eyes, an inadequate Christology. Jesus is not only the man of God who works while it is day; he is the light of the world.

The introduction of the Sabbath topic is unexpected in context. On the narrative level, several months—perhaps a year—have elapsed since the healing that is referred to.[90] The course of the argument takes a sudden turn. Jesus had defended himself against the charge of being unlearned with the aid of emissary Christology (vv. 16–18); he then goes

---

[89] Markku Kotila, *Umstrittene Zeuge: Studien zur Stellung des Gesetzes in der johanneischen Theologiegeschichte* (AASF Dissertationes Humanarum Litterarum 48; Helsinki, 1988), 39. Wengst understands it in light of v. 17: those who resolve to do the will of God will recognize his teaching as divinely authenticated. Therefore those who reject Jesus do not do the law (*Johannesevangelium*, 280). This recalls the concluding argument in ch. 5: properly read, Moses points to Jesus (5:47).

[90] The incidents narrated in ch. 7 occur during the Feast of Tabernacles, in the fall. The previous chapter, ch. 6, had been set shortly before the Passover, which falls in the spring. The feast mentioned in ch. 5 is unspecified. No biblically mandated feasts fall between Tabernacles in the fall and Passover in the spring, although the Feast of Dedication (Hanukkah), which commemorates the rededication of the temple by the Maccabees falls in the winter (10:22). Purim, which falls one month before Passover (Esth 9:17–19), was not mandated in the OT, nor is it mentioned in the NT. On the mandated feasts, see Lev 23 and Deut 16:1–17.

over to the attack, charging his interlocutors, identified in v. 15 as "the Jews," with failing to observe the law of Moses and intending to kill him (v. 19). The reaction of "the crowd" is surprise; they appear not to know of an intent to kill (v. 20), although some Jerusalemites do know about this (v. 25). These tensions in the narrative have led many to conclude the presence of foreign material in this section. The most common solution is to propose that 7:15–24 have been moved subsequent to the work of the evangelist from their location after 5:47, either by accidental displacement or by intent.[91] A redaction critical solution, such as that of Markku Kotila, is simpler, and therefore to be preferred.[92] On this reconstruction, the evangelist, who constructed the controversy in its present context and who is responsible for the emissary Christology, made use of traditional material in 7:19–24 as an illustration of the teaching of Jesus that he had received from his Father.[93] Seen in light of 5:17, added by the evangelist, this example serves as an additional demonstration of the deep unity between Father and Son.[94]

More pertinent to the present study is that the appeal to the precedent of circumcision on the Sabbath stems from the stratum of tradition in which the original healing narrative was transformed into a Sabbath controversy.[95] The experience reflected in this stratum is one of conflict

---

[91]   Bultmann, *Evangelium*, 177–8; Becker, *Evangelium*, 1:309 (both displacement); Schnackenburg, *Johannesevangelium*, 2:183–4 (intent). For a critical analysis of this proposal, see Labahn, *Jesus*, 213–4.

[92]   Kotila, *Zeuge*, 34–46. See also Attridge, "Development," 165–6; Labahn, *Jesus*, 249–51.

[93]   This determination of the function of vv. 19–24 in its present context was already made by Bultmann, *Evangelium*, 178, n. 3. Kotila finds it paradoxical that this example, rabbinical in form, with its argument from the example of circumcision, is set against the teaching expected by the "Jews" (*Zeuge*, 43). But there is no indication in the text that this teaching is being set against that of the "rabbis;" the point of the objection is that it is unseemly for a man who had not undergone the approved course of study to presume to teach. It is possible that it is precisely the "rabbinic" form of argumentation that commended itself to the evangelist to demonstrate that Jesus was qualified by virtue of having received his teaching from the Father.

[94]   Labahn, *Jesus*, 252. There is also secondary in 7:21–24: the pronoun ὑμῖν in v. 22 (evangelist); the parenthetical phrase, not Moses, etc, in v. 22 (scribal gloss); see Labahn, *Jesus*, 251.

[95]   Kotila, *Zeuge*, 42. Once again, Bultmann was here first, in that he suggested that

over the Sabbath, and the concern is to defend the practice of Jesus in terms of the law. This material is taken up and used as an illustration by the evangelist, whose interest is christological. The emissary Christology of 7:16–18 corresponds to the discourse of 5:19–47, which elucidates the claim of Jesus to share in the work of the Father in 5:17. For the evangelist, Sabbath conflict is an occasion for unfolding the identity of Christ, and not a subject of direct interest. Yet though his concern is other than that of the tradition he uses, it is not contrary to it. Just as he quotes Jesus closing the discourse in ch. 5 with the assertion that belief in Moses should lead to belief in the Son, so he has Jesus claim that a genuine desire to live a life in accordance with the will of God—i.e., in conformity to the Torah—would recognize his teaching as that of the one sent.

5.2 A SECOND SABBATH HEALING (JOHN 9)

The next reference to the Sabbath in the Gospel of John is in ch. 9. In the Gospel as we have it, the section 9:1–10:21 forms an artfully constructed unit similar to that encountered in ch. 5, consisting of a narrated healing, a controversy, and a discourse in which the identity of Jesus is further unfolded. The decision on delimitation of the unit is not clear-cut.[96] The dialogue with "the Jews" concerning competing claims to Abraham's heritage ends with the attempt to stone Jesus, who departs from the temple (8:59).[97] Chapter 9 opens with Jesus *along the way* (καὶ

7:19–24 stood as the conclusion to 5:1–18 in his proposed SQ (*Evangelium*, 208) although, as Kotila points out, he overlooked that the consequence of his observation was that it was unnecessary to assign the present placement of the text to a redactor subsequent to the evangelist.

[96] The phrase ἀμὴν ἀμὴν λέγω ὑμῖν in 10:1 is an important structural marker, indicating the transition from narrative to discourse; note however that it is repeated in 10:7. The lack any mention of a change of time, place, or addressees weigh against separating the discourse from the preceding narrative unit. Discussions in Rein, *Heilung*, 159–65; Labahn, *Jesus*, 307.

[97] The next controversy dialogue also ends with this motif (10:31), reflecting an inability to answer the arguments of Jesus, as well as murderous intent, an element introduced into the narrative in 5:18.

παράγων).[98] Subsequent material is introduced by the mention of another festival, ἐγκαίνια, the commemoration of the rededication of the temple at the time of the Maccabees, Hanukkah (10:22). Yet lack of sharp breaks at either end indicate that this section is also part of a larger unit. The location remains Jerusalem, the time is during the same pilgrimage to the Feast of Tabernacles reported in 7:1, 10. Nor is there any report of Jesus leaving the city between the two festivals, so that the conflict between Jesus and "the Jews," introduced in ch. 5, becomes the main feature of a long narrative span that continues until Jesus leaves Jerusalem (10:40). When he returns, it is to be, in the vocabulary of the Fourth Gospel, *lifted up*.[99]

The narrative 9:1–38 can be structured into seven scenes according to the dramatic persons.[100] The first scene introduces the narrative (vv. 1–5). Along the way Jesus sees a man born blind (9:1). Before Jesus acts, however, there is an exchange between the disciples and Jesus whether the sin-related cause for the blindness lay with the man himself or with his parents (v. 2), a causality denied by Jesus (v. 3): this case of natal blindness is for the demonstration of God's work.[101] Thus the miracle

---

[98] The only appearance of this phrase in the Fourth Gospel.

[99] On the compositional unity of ch. 7–10, despite use of traditional material, see Ludger Schenke, "Joh 7–10: Eine dramatische Szene," *ZNW* 80 (1989): 172–92.

[100] Francis J. Moloney, *The Gospel of John* (SP 4; Collegeville, Minn., 1998), 291–6. Labahn's structure differs slightly, since he does not use the dramatic persons as organizing principle (*Jesus* 309–10). He combines the first two of Moloney's subunits into the depiction of the miracle (vv. 1–7), interrupted by an apophtegmatic discussion of the sin that may have caused the blindness (vv. 2–5), followed by a controversy in four scenes with various dialogue partners (vv. 8–34), climaxing with the confession of the healed man of Jesus as the Son, initiated by Jesus (vv. 35–38). He understands 9:39–41 as the provisional conclusion of a controversy dialogue between the Jews and Jesus, rather than as the introduction to the discourse, as Moloney does.

[101] On blindness as a punishment by God, see Wolfgang Schrage, τυφλός, τυφλόω, *TWNT* 8:270–94, here 283. The remarks of Jesus refer to the present case; the tension between this and 5:14 should not be exaggerated. See however Metzner, who resolves the tension by understanding the remark of Jesus in v. 3 as a rejection of posing the question of guilt, not as a rejection of the connection between sin and illness (*Verständnis*, 82). Wengst suggests that the sin in question is idolatry, the only sin sanctioned with punishment on a succeeding generation. By reporting that Jesus makes the man see—an act with messianic connotations—the evangelist assures his readers that their confession

that will be narrated is proleptically interpreted as a work of God, as well as a demonstration of the identity of Jesus (the light of the world, v. 5). The exchange also foreshadows plot developments: both the parents (vv. 18–23) and the allegation of being born in sin (v. 34) will recur in the juridical scene that follows.

The second scene, vv. 6–7 describes the healing miracle itself, including a terse report of the actions of Jesus, his command to the blind man to wash in Siloam, the report of this being carried out and the verification of the healing.[102]

The third scene, vv. 8–12, narrates the reaction of others, which, though it had been lacking in the healing account in ch. 5, is a common feature of healing miracles.[103] Remarkable, in light of the further course of the controversy, is the element of doubt in the reaction; people who had known him seem reluctant to believe that it could be he. The man gives a detailed answer, repeating the actions Jesus and he took. The reaction to the miracle takes up more narrative space than the account of its performance.

The Sabbath is introduced in the fourth scene. The healed person is brought to the Pharisees for a new round of questioning:

> They brought to the Pharisees the man who had formerly been blind. Now it was a Sabbath day when Jesus made the mud and opened his eyes. Then the Pharisees also began to ask him how he had received his sight. He said to them, "He put mud on my eyes. Then I washed, and now I see." Some of the Pharisees said, "This man is not from God, for he does not observe the Sabbath." But others said, "How can a man who is a sinner perform such signs?" And they were

of Jesus is not idolatry, but an expression of the confession of the God of Israel (*Johannesevangelium*, 352–4). Despite the evidence he marshals to support his contention, there is no reference to idolatry in the text. It is possible that author and original readers would have recognized the allusion, making explicit reference unnecessary, but there is no way we can know this. Even if Wengst is correct, however, this would not invalidate the general connection made between sin and illness at the time, since this would be a specific instance of it.

[102] The application of a saliva-earth paste and the washing in a pool may seem to compete as means of healing, but there are parallels in other ancient accounts of folk medicine, so that no conclusions about the history of transmission of the account can be drawn from this (Labahn, *Jesus*, 327–35).

[103] Theissen, *Wundergeschichten*, 78–80.

divided. So they said again to the blind man, "What do you say about him? It was your eyes he opened." He said, "He is a prophet."

As in ch. 5, the mention of the Sabbath is delayed. In light of this new fact, the plastic details of Jesus' activity—mixing his spittle with earth, kneading the mud, applying it to the eyes, which could well have been part of a traditional healing story that once had no connection to the Sabbath—take on an added significance.[104] Now they seem to purposefully violate several precepts connected with proper Sabbath observance.[105] Nevertheless, there is a report of schism among the Pharisees, with some arguing that the sign precludes the judgment that Jesus is a sinner.[106] The issue is thus cast in terms of an alternative: Jesus is either from God, or he is a sinner (see below, 5.4.3). The formerly blind person is pressed for his opinion; for him, Jesus is a prophet.

The opponents, now termed "Jews," turn to the person's parents in the fifth scene, vv. 18–23. The element of doubt recurs as motivation for this. The parents confirm that the person is their son and that he had been born blind, but evade offering an opinion on how he came to see. The reason given is their fear of expulsion from the synagogue as disciplinary measure against anyone confessing Jesus as the Messiah, an anachronistic feature.

In the sixth scene, vv. 24–34, the formerly blind person is again interrogated. In defending himself, he develops into a protagonist, boldly deriding his tormentors for their lack of insight. The "Jews" reject him as one who had been born in sins (cf. 9:2), and "drove him out" (v. 34), which in light of v. 22 can be understood as expulsion from synagogue fellowship.

---

[104] The story reported in vv. 1–7 is widely viewed as traditional (e.g. Bultmann, *Evangelium*, 249–50; Dodd, *Tradition*, 181–8; Fortna, *Gospel of Signs*, 70–74). As in the case of the story in ch. 5, however, this story too shows evidence of Johannine reworking (esp. v. 4, τὰ ἔργα τοῦ πέμψαντός με). Kneading is one of the 39 works forbidden on the Sabbath (*m. Šabb.* 7:2). An additional violation is that Jesus used matter that was not normally used during the week to anoint eyes (ibid.).

[105] Cf. the stress on πηλὸν ἐποίησεν, 9:6, 11, 14, πηλὸν ἐπέθηκέν, v. 15.

[106] Blindness was considered incurable apart from divine power (Schrage, *TWNT* 8:273–5). Previous mentions of schism: the neighbors of the blind man (9:9), the crowd (7:43); followers of Jesus (6:60, 66).

Jesus, who had been absent from all four controversy dialogues, encounters the formerly blind person and leads him to a fuller confession in the seventh scene, vv. 35–38.[107] This culminates in a controversy dialogue with opponents, Pharisees, in which Jesus declares who the truly blind in this story are (vv. 39–41). This reference to blindness acts as a summary to the narrative and as an introduction to the discourse in which Jesus reveals himself as the good shepherd, 10:1–18, which leads to another mention of division, this time among "the Jews," with some asserting that Jesus is demon-possessed and mad, which others, citing the works, deny (vv. 19–21).

The account bears many similarities to the healing in ch. 5. In addition to the parallel structure of healing, controversy, and discourse, as well as the delayed mention of the Sabbath, there are details such as the lengthy infirmity of the person healed, and the prominence of a pool of water.[108] Significantly for the purpose of this inquiry, as in the discourse 5:19–47, the Sabbath is not explicitly discussed.[109] Yet there are contrasts as well, such as the portrayal of Jesus physically acting to work a cure (v. 6; cf. the effectuation of the healing by a command in 5:8), as well as the injunction to the man to participate in his own cure.[110] Jesus is never called to

---

[107] Whereas in v. 17, the man had referred to Jesus as a prophet, now he is asked by Jesus if he has faith in the Son, identified as the one whom he has seen and who is now speaking to him (cf. the words of Jesus to the woman at the well, 4:26). The man expresses his belief both in word and his action (by bowing before Jesus). As in NA[27], the variant *Son of Man*, attested in 𝔓[66] and [75], ℵ, B, D, and W, is to be preferred over *Son of God* (Metzger, *Commentary*, 228–29). Earlier uses of Son of Man: 1:51; 3:13–14; 5:27; 6:27, 53, 62.

[108] See Bultmann, *Evangelium*, 178; Attridge, "Development," 166, n. 12; Culpepper, *Anatomy*, 139–40 and Lee, *Narratives*, 105–6, for discussions of the similarities. Schnackenburg suggests that the parallel episodes in chs. 5 and 9 may have been adjacent in a collection of miracle stories prior to being transformed into Sabbath controversies (*Johannesevangelium*, 1:117). In Mark 8:22–26, a blind man is healed in Bethesda, which shows an interesting mingling of what represents two traditions in John (cf. the variant reading Βηθεσδά in many mss. of John 5:2).

[109] For this reason, the shepherd discourse is seen by some as part of the secondary redaction of the Gospel (e.g., Becker, *Evangelium*, 1:265–7). Metzner finds no convincing reason for this (*Verständnis*, 67–68).

[110] On the motif of using physical means in a miraculous healing, see Theissen, *Wundergeschichten*, 72. On the ancient belief in the efficacity of spittle for working

account, unlike in ch. 5, although the primary aim of the proceedings is to pass judgment on him (vv. 16, 24), and only secondarily on the man, should he be convicted of confessing that Jesus is the Christ, not of breaking the Sabbath (v. 22). When Jesus reappears, it is not to warn the healed person, as in 5:14, but to lead the man to a more appropriate (i.e., Johannine) faith (vv. 35–38).

A final point of comparison is that in contrast with Sabbath controversies in the Synoptics, but in consonance with ch. 5, it is the person healed, rather than Jesus, who is first examined by the authorities.[111] In fact, other than in ch. 5, the examination takes on the features of formal juridical proceedings.[112] Taken together with the anachronistic mention of expulsion from the synagogue, this has raised the question of the extent to which the experience of the Johannine community is reflected in these narratives, or even more, whether these narratives can help reconstruct the history of that community (see below, 5.6).

There are tensions in the account, the most obvious being the alternative naming of the opponents as "Pharisees" and "Jews." In addition, the length of the reaction compared to the account of the miracle is an indication that the miracle is not recounted for its own sake (vv. 8–12). This is immediately confirmed by the delayed mention of the Sabbath (v. 14). Doubts are expressed about the reality of the miracle or at least the identity of the person who sees in two scenes (vv. 8–9, 18). In the intervening scene, however, the Pharisees divide over the interpretation of the miracle, not its reality (v. 16). In the discussion of John 5, three phases were distinguished: a traditional healing story, its transformation into a Sabbath conflict, and its use by the evangelist for Christological purposes. It would appear that at a minimum the same

cures, see citations in Wengst, *Johannesevangelium*, 356–7.

[111] This in spite of the fact that the man had not violated the Sabbath. Unlike the carrying of a pallet, there were no restrictions against washing one's face, which is all that Jesus had commanded him to do (v. 7).

[112] Indications of this include the threat of sanction—exclusion from the synagogue, v. 22—and the formula, δὸς δόξαν τῷ θεῷ, v. 24, used to elicit a confession from an unwilling witness, Josh 7:19; see Josef Blank, *Das Evangelium nach Johannes* (GSL.NT 4/1b; Düsseldorf, 1981), 198.

stages are represented here.[113] Not even in the phase in which the healing narrative is transformed into a Sabbath conflict does the conflict revolve around proper Sabbath observance, but on the religious evaluation of the miracle worker.[114]

Within the overall narration of conflict between Jesus and "the Jews," the special function of the section 9:1–10:21 is to inform about the threat to those who confess and follow Christ, and encourage these followers to continue in public profession of their faith.[115] In the account of healing and conflict, as in that recorded in ch. 5, the Sabbath is a transparently supplemental feature, but one that serves a narrative purpose. It is not mentioned to plead either for or against its observance directly, but serves as the issue over which the claim of the believing community concerning Jesus are challenged. Yet a negative connotation is clear in the way it functions to make the blindness of the opponents of Jesus evident.

5.3 THE CHARGES AGAINST JESUS

5.3.1 Jesus Tells the Man to Carry His Pallet

Carrying the pallet, commanded by Jesus in 5:8, is referred to three times in the controversy exchanges (vv. 10, 11, 12). It is this, rather than the healing itself, that provokes critical comment, first toward the man who had carried the pallet, then toward the one who had commanded it. If the man has violated the Sabbath in doing this, then Jesus, by his command, shares in the responsibility for the violation, as the "Jews" know (v. 16). The prohibition of carrying of any burden on the Sabbath (Jer 17:21–22), though it refers to merchandise or agricultural produce (see above, 2.1.2), is worded generally, and may have been understood generally in the first century. Therefore, this injunction, though found in the Prophets, not in the Torah, could have been understood as forbid-

---

[113] Labahn distinguishes four, finding no necessary connection between the experience of expulsion with the phase in which the healing was transformed into a Sabbath conflict (*Jesus*, 358).

[114] Labahn, *Jesus*, 356, against Kotila, *Zeuge*, 68–69.

[115] Labahn, *Jesus*, 305–6.

ding the carrying of a pallet on the Sabbath, and may be the basis of the criticism voiced by the "Jews."[116]

Does the narrator accept this viewpoint? It is conceivable that the evangelist has knowledge of distinctions between written law and oral interpretation, or between the law and the prophets and that he makes no mention of it because he expects his readers to share this knowledge. Lacking any indication of this in the text, however, it must be considered unlikely.[117] There is thus no basis for denying that, in terms of this text, the Sabbath had been violated.[118] The healed man does not attempt to defend himself by pointing to any such distinction. Further, the choice of the term "the Jews" to describe the opposition underlines the fact that it is not only authoritative but also representative; this, too, weighs against any suggestion that the Johannine Christ was simply opposing a sectarian oral interpretation. Finally, there is the repeated characterization by Jesus of "your" or "their" law (e.g. 8:17; 10:34; 15:25). This would seem to imply that if the law is conceded to the opponents (although, if they read it correctly, it would point to Jesus, 5:46–47), then their interpretation goes along with it.

The dramatic strategy in this section revolves around a provocative transgression of Sabbath norms. At the behest of Jesus, the man has done what would have been considered a transgression of the Sabbath. As in Mark 2:9, but other than in Mark 2:11, Jesus uses the verb περιπατέω (*walk around*), which in context of the chapter as we have it should be understood here in its full sense, which would be demonstrative, even provocative.[119] Yet from the perspective of the Gospel, it is not this that

---

[116] Doering, *Schabbat*, 468–9; he also cites material from Qumran (4Q265) and Philo (*Migr.* 91) as possible evidence for such a halakic understanding.

[117] Cf. 15:25, in which Jesus, citing "their law," quotes from a Psalm (35:19). The Greek νόμος appears to carry here the same range of meaning as the Hebrew תּוֹרָה. For an example of explicit attention drawn to oral precepts, see Mark 7:9, together with vv. 3–4.

[118] Pancaro, *Law*, 14–15.

[119] So Emanuel Hirsch, *Das vierte Evangelium in seiner ursprünglichen Gestalt verdeutscht und erklärt* (Tübingen, 1936), 157; Haenchen "Probleme" 107; Schnackenburg, *Johannesevangelium*, 2:122. Against this, Bultmann, *Evangelium*, 181, n. 2, finds that περιπατέω is used generally, as it is in many places in the NT (cf. BDAG *s.v.*, 1c). This is the case in Mark 2:9 (not spoken on the Sabbath), as the comparison with v. 11

is his sin, but his failure to grasp the identity of his benefactor—another indication that the issue of Sabbath observance has been subordinated to Christology.

5.3.2 Jesus Abolishes the Sabbath and Makes Himself Equal to God (5:18)

As we will see (5.4, below), Jesus defends himself from the charge of Sabbath-breaking in terms that, for the Johannine community, clear him of any suspicion of having broken it. The reaction of the opponents is however radically different. It leads to a heightened intent to destroy him (v. 18). Whereas in v. 16 they persecute him for *doing* unspecified things, presumably Sabbath violations—now reformulated as having *loosed* (ἔλυεν) the Sabbath—they now accuse him of something more serious: making himself equal to God. We will look at these accusations in turn.

As mentioned above (5.1), ἔλυεν is commonly translated *broke*, but there are two considerations that speak against the suggestion that John writes here that Jesus broke the Sabbath: (1) the verb is not in aorist, but imperfect. Whatever Jesus had done to the Sabbath, it is either recurring or lasting; (2) the verb λύω does not mean *to break*, in the sense of transgress. The basic meaning is *to loose*, as, for instance, the laces of a sandal (1:27). It means to unbind, but the word can also be used in the sense of *to destroy* (2:19).[120] The opponents, then, claim not that Jesus had broken the Sabbath, but that he had unbound or destroyed it.[121]

Jesus' defense ὁ πατήρ μου ἕως ἄρτι ἐργάζεται κἀγὼ ἐργάζομαι (5:17) may contain two elements offensive to his listeners in the view of the evangelist. The adversaries hear in the reference of Jesus to "my" Father

---

shows. Carson finds no compelling reason to suppose that Jesus is precipitating a crisis over the Sabbath ("Jesus," 81).

[120] BDAG, s.v.; Karl Kertelge, *EWNT* 2:909–12, esp. 910. In Mark 2:23–28, where the disciples had broken the Sabbath, it is expressed with the phrase "to do what is not allowed." Cf. Wengst: "In der vorangehenden Erzählung hat Jesus allerdings nicht 'den Sabbat aufgelöst,' sondern ihn in einem bestimmten Fall übertreten. Dass hier dennoch so grundsätzlich formuliert wird, dürfte Wiederspiegelung dessen sein, dass die johanneische Gemeinde unter Berufung auf Jesus eine freiere Sabbatpraxis übte" (*Johannesevangelium*, 194–5). *Pace* Bultmann, *Evangelium*, 182, n. 8.

[121] Cf. Lohse: "Den Juden gilt Jesus als sabbati destructor," (*TWNT* 7:29, n. 224; cf. Tertullian, *Spect.* 30).

a claim to an exclusive relation (πατέρα ἴδιον, v. 18).[122] Secondly, to presume to exercise the unique prerogatives of one's father is offensive in a culture that normally assumed the subordination of sons to fathers.[123]

The two charges levied against Jesus therefore are that he has loosened, or destroyed, the Sabbath, and—worse yet—that in claiming equality with God he has shown himself to be a rebellious claimant to divine prerogatives.[124] These are the accusation of the opponents, however. They mistake his origin (7:52; 6:42). In the parallel charge in 5:18, as elsewhere (6:42; 10:33; 19:7), they misunderstand the nature of his relationship to the Father. From beginning to end of this Gospel, we read of Jesus, the Logos incarnate, the Son of God.[125] Yet this is not something that Jesus *made*; it was given to him by virtue of his being sent.[126] The discourse, especially in its first half (vv. 19–30), shows that what is claimed is an equality of function, and that this is not rebellion but obedience.[127] Nevertheless, there is complexity. "It is possible to read the text as qualifying, but still endorsing the view initially stated by the opponents."[128]

---

[122] When Mary meets the resurrected Jesus at the tomb, he commissions her to tell "his brothers" that he is ascending to his Father and theirs (20:17), showing that the reference of Jesus to "my" Father does not exclude one to "our" father, at least after he is "raised up." It is the response of the adversaries that makes it so, although this is seemingly confirmed by Jesus when he refers pointedly to "your father" (8:41).

[123] Schnackenburg, *Johannesevangelium*, 2:128–9; James F. McGrath, "A Rebellious Son? Hugo Odeberg and the Interpretation of John 5.18," *NTS* 44 (1998) 470–73.

[124] The escalation is indicated in the text by the formulation οὐ μόνον . . . ἀλλὰ καὶ.

[125] In addition to the prologue, see the witness of John the Baptist (1:15–34) and the confession of Thomas, 20:28, which frame the narrative.

[126] See Wayne Meeks, "Equal,", 309–21, here 317.

[127] Wengst, *Johannesevangelium*, 1:194.

[128] Mealand, "Limits," 263; similarly Culpepper: false charges against Jesus are ironically true in John's world (*Anatomy*, 171, 177). Cf. however Dodd: "It seems that if the evangelist had been asked whether or not he intended to affirm that Christ was ἴσος τῷ θεῷ, he would have been obliged to reply that ἴσος, whether affirmed or denied, is not the proper term to use in this context. He does not here offer any alternative term, but sets forth with great precision the actual facts, and leaves the reader to reflect upon them," (*Interpretation*, 327–8). Or, as Barrett puts it, "[t]his complaint (like others in this gospel) is at once both valid and invalid" (*The Gospel of John and Judaism*, London 1975, 16).

Thus, from the narrator's perspective, the charge contained one element of truth, the perceived equality with the Father, combined with a misunderstanding of how it came to be. Based on this, we would expect a parallelism with the first part of the accusation. Perhaps John shares the belief that Jesus has done *something* to the Sabbath. Perhaps in the "ironic truth" of the Johannine world (to borrow Culpepper's phrase), Jesus did not break the Sabbath, but did unbind it. Ambivalence remains. Matthew, perhaps aware of the same charge being levied against Jesus, quotes Jesus as explicitly denying that he has come to destroy (καταλῦσαι) the law or the prophets (Matt 5:17). John lets the opponents levy the accusation, and does not directly counter it. No violation of the Sabbath is conceded by the Johannine Christ, including in his command to the man to walk about with his pallet (not just to go home, as in Mark). And even had there been a violation, this does not fully account for the verb λύω in the accusation.

A possible aid in resolving the question can be found in 7:19–24, material that has been identified as once forming the conclusion of the Sabbath healing controversy. This material was displaced by the evangelist when he added 5:17–18, but not deleted. In its present location, the comparison circumcision/Sabbath healing offers an anaphoric comment on the question of abolishing the Sabbath. If the Jews (properly) performed circumcision on the Sabbath in order *not to* abolish the law, then it is hard to see how the evangelist could share the charge of abolishing the law through a Sabbath healing.[129] At the same time, the two charges in 5:18 share a common denominator. The accusation of abolishing the Sabbath is, just like the parallel charge of making himself equal to God, a charge that Jesus had assumed divine prerogative. In both charges we have an indirect, involuntary recognition on the part of the adversaries of the import of Christ's activity. And it is a charge that, although false, contains in an ironic way, an element of truth. Therefore, it appears likely that the narrator would agree that something—what exactly is not clear—has happened to the Sabbath.

---

[129] With Labahn, *Jesus*, 253, n. 202.

5.3.3 Jesus Is a Sinner (9:16, 24), Demon-Possessed and Mad (10:20)
Attempts to deny the reality of the healing of the man born blind fail
(9:8–9). To resist accepting the implications of a work that cannot be
denied, those who oppose Jesus formulate a series of charges. Not only
has Jesus healed on the Sabbath, but he did so in ways that contradicted
specific Sabbath halakah. Jesus is directly accused of not keeping the
Sabbath (τὸ σάββατον οὐ τηρεῖ, v. 16). For some of the "Jews," Jesus is
a *sinner*, ἁμαρτωλός (vv. 16, 24); a charge that is never levied in the
Synoptics, where he is accused of associating with sinners.[130] In the OT
and Judaism, to designate a man an ἁμαρτωλός (רָשָׁע) is more serious
than to say that he has committed sin; it suggests that in a state of sin and
implies a deliberate refusal to seek the will of God.[131] The gravity of this
charge is heightened by the prior claims of Jesus that those who
genuinely believed in Moses would believe in him (5:46) and that those
who genuinely intended to fulfill the will of God would recognize the
divine origin of his teaching (7:16–18). Additionally, the opponents seek
to convict him of being a false teacher who leads the people astray
(9:24–34; cf. Deut 13:2–5). At the close of this unit, after the discourse
in which Jesus proclaims himself to be the good shepherd, some of the
"Jews" assert that he is demon-possessed and mad (10:20; cf. 7:20;
8:48, 52).[132] This is the reaction to his words, not, as in the Synoptics, an
alternate explanation of the works of Jesus (Mark 3:21–30 par.
Matt 12:24–29, Luke 11:15–22).

In this complex of charges, three motifs are intertwined: the performance of works that require superhuman power, whether divine or
demonic; the disregard of Sabbath halakah; and the claims made by Jesus

[130] See Mark 2:15–16 par. Matt 9:10–11, Luke 5:29–30; Luke 15:2; cf. Pancaro,
Law, 46. The term ἁμαρτωλός is used nowhere in the Fourth Gospel other than ch. 9
(vv. 16, 24, 25, 31), and was likely present in the tradition used by the evangelist
(Labahn, *Jesus*, 352).
[131] On the implications, see Pancaro, *Law*, 30–52. The chiastic construction of v. 16
shows that the alternative to being an ἁμαρτωλός is being παρὰ θεοῦ; cf. Pancaro, *Law*,
20.
[132] The charge is perhaps tautological. Mania was seen by the Greeks not only as a
pathological expression but also as a religious phenomenon (H. Preisker, μαίνομαι,
TWNT 4:363-4).

to be the fulfilment of messianic expectations. Significant, since it is an indication of the purpose of the evangelist, is that the charge of demoniacal mania follows his discourse rather than, as in the Synoptics, his works. The works, prodigious as they are and possessing sign character as they do, are subordinated to the revelation in discourse of the identity of the one sent. This raises the possibility that the Sabbath motif—with its transparently supplemental character—accomplishes the same aim in the Gospel as we have it. Namely, that attention is deflected from the prodigious nature of the miracle to its Sabbath-breaking character, and that this is done not in the interest of developing a Johannine position on the Sabbath, but for the affirmation of christological revelation.

5.3.4 Summary

The three sets of charges raised against Jesus as a result of his Sabbath healings are all based on the perception of his opponents that the Sabbath had indeed been violated.[133] There are nevertheless differences. In ch. 5, Jesus himself has done nothing illegal; the cure is effected by a word, not by any healing activity. The guilt of Jesus is limited to his instigation of the only objective Sabbath violation in the incident, that of the man carrying his pallet. It is unclear whether the evangelist shares the perception that the Sabbath has been violated by this. The charge that follows in v. 18, that Jesus has loosened, or abolished, the Sabbath, is all the more surprising for this. Its only possible motivation is found in the formulation employed in 5:16, which suggests repeated or continual Sabbath violations. This although only one Sabbath incident has been narrated, which accords to the emphatic "one deed" of 7:21, which apparently points back to this incident. The evangelist sees no need to elucidate or harmonize, which probably should be explained by its subordinate position within 5:18. However surprising the charge appears in light of what has been narrated so far, and however far-reaching its possible consequences for Sabbath observance, it is less important—both

---

[133] The three sets of charges appear in two settings, ch. 5 and ch. 9 (with discourse 10:1–18). There are no charges verbalized in ch. 7, an observation in line with other literary critical tensions that suggest that material has been used here that was once in a different setting.

for the opponents and for the evangelist, to judge by the contents of the following discourse—than the relation to the Father implicit in Jesus' defense in 5:17.

In ch. 9, in many ways parallel to ch. 5, there are several reversals. The man healed has done nothing wrong, but it is he, not Jesus, who must face the brunt of the interrogation. Jesus, who unlike in ch. 5, has acted to perform the cure, and acted in a way that involves several halakic violations, is charged *in absentia* with being a sinner—showing willful indifference to the will of God. He is also directly accused of not keeping the Sabbath (9:16). As in ch. 5, a second charge—in this case, that of demon-possession—is raised with no direct relation to his Sabbath activity (10:20).

5.4 Jesus Defends His Sabbath Activity

5.4.1 The Comparison to Circumcision (7:23)

Jesus points out that the "Jews" were confronted with two demands of the law: to rest from physical activity on the seventh day, and to circumcise every male child on the eighth day (i.e., one week after its birth). Faced with the dilemma of the case of a boy born on the Sabbath, they were convinced that the need to perform circumcision when commanded overrode the command to rest.[134] For that reason, they broke the law so as not to destroy the law, taking up the verb used by the accusers in ch. 5 to describe what Jesus had done to the Sabbath, λύω (5:18).[135] The use of two different verbs here suggests that the issue is not that of choosing between two demands of the law and deciding which to observe ; instead, the principle appears to be that sometimes transgression of the law is required to preserve the law. The conclusion for Jesus and his followers was clear: if the Sabbath law can be overridden to take something (the foreskin) away from one part of a human body, then there can be no objection to his making a whole person well. A similar thought is documented in the Talmud, arguing that if circumcision is

---

[134] Documented in *m. Šabb.* 18:3; 19:6.

[135] ἵνα μὴ λυθῇ ὁ νόμος Μωϋσέως, 7:23; cf. the discussion of the use of λύω in 5:18 above, 5.3.2.

necessary on the Sabbath, then it is even more so to save a whole person; the conclusion made, however, is that one can heal or save one who is in danger of death.[136] The argument of Jesus goes decisively further than this; there is no indication that the man's life is in danger.[137] It would not be hard to think of a suitable answer to this argument, for instance, the fact that in the one case the Sabbath was overridden to fulfill an express command of the Torah, whereas in the other case Jesus had intervened to do something that could legally have been done on six other days of the week.[138] In addition, the Sabbath was suppressed in one case on the basis of a common decision, whereas Jesus acted independently, on his own initiative.[139] John feels no need to continue the debate on the point, however, once Jesus had spoken.[140]

This argument *a minori ad maius* is similar to rabbinic argumentation *qal-wahomer*. As such, it appears to be more traditional than the argumentation used in 5:16–47.[141] It is reminiscent of arguments brought in the Synoptics.[142] Further, such an argument, while establishing Jesus' activity as weightier, nonetheless presumes the continued validity of the less weighty, circumcision, as well.[143]

The positive valuation of circumcision (7:22–23) points to a Jewish-Christian setting. The apologetic direction of the argument confirms this, and reflects a conflict situation in a synagogue setting.[144] This accords with the fact that, although there is an implicit concession that the Sabbath had been violated, this is presented as being nonetheless in

---

[136] *T. Šabb.* 15:16, attr. to R. Elieser, ca. 90 C.E.; *b. Yoma* 85b, attr. to R. Eliesar ben Azariah, ca. 100 C.E. (Bill 2:488).

[137] Kotila, *Zeuge*, 41.

[138] Pancaro, *Law*, 163. This point is expressed by opponents in Luke's Gospel (13:14).

[139] Wengst, *Johannesevangelium*, 281.

[140] Cf. Pancaro, for whom this proposed speciousness is an indication that this argument was *not* presented in the manner of the humanitarian arguments of the Synoptics (*Law*, 167).

[141] Attridge, "Development," 166.

[142] Mark 2:25–26 par.; Matt 12:11–12; Luke 13:16.

[143] Labahn, "Spurensuche," 173.

[144] Labahn, "Spurensuche," 176.

keeping with the will of God, and therefore of the true intent of the Sabbath.[145]

In v. 19, the issue is introduced of who is obedient to the law. Complete alignment with the will of God, and therefore obedience to the Torah, is claimed for Jesus and, implicitly, his followers, the Johannine community. Anyone who properly understood Moses would recognize this (5:47). These are not the words of a community that had consciously broken with the Sabbath.[146] Their opponents did not recognize them as keeping it, but as acting as if it had been abolished (see below, 5.4.2). Just what they were doing, aside from continuing the healing activities that Jesus apparently engaged in, is not known. It is possible that the same activities were in the time of Jesus part of a spectrum of Sabbath behavior within Judaism, but in the consolidating orthodoxy after 70 C.E. were no longer so.

In one detail the argument may go beyond other, humanitarian, arguments: Jesus has made a whole man well (ὅλον ἄνθρωπον ὑγιῆ ἐποίησα). One could speak of healing both as making a person whole and of making him well. Here the two expressions are combined (note the reversal of the words ὅλον and ἄνθρωπον in 𝔓[75]; perhaps because of the strangeness of the phrase). If we assume that this exchange is the original conclusion of the healing story in ch. 5 after it had been transformed into a Sabbath controversy but before the composition of

---

[145] Cf. Pancaro, who has difficulty with this implied concession of a Sabbath violation (*Law*, 163–4).

[146] This is based on the words in their presumed original setting. In the context of the Gospel as we have it, the remarks 5:47 and 7:19–24 are separated by the insistence that it was God, not Moses, who gave manna in the wilderness (6:30–35). This devaluation of Moses stands in tension, then, with what precedes it and what follows. It is not possible here to go into the possible presence of redactional material in ch. 6; the tension is one more indication that the Fourth Gospel reflects a diachronic development. For a first orientation, see Hans Weder, "Die Menschwerdung Gottes: Überlegungen zur Auslegungsproblematik des Johannesevangeliums am Beispiel von Joh 6," in *Einblicke ins Evangelium: Exegetische Beiträge zur neutestamentlichen Hermeneutik* (Göttingen, 1992), 363–400. Note that the testimony of the Baptist also contrasts Moses and Jesus, allocating grace and truth, in contrast to the law, to Jesus Christ (1:17). This provides the reader with the framework through which all subsequent references to Moses in the Fourth Gospel in its present form are to be read.

the Gospel of John, we can see in this expression a clue to why John did not simply replace it with the defense of 5:17, leading to the discourse of 5:19–30.[147] Precisely in light of the interpretation of healing as life-giving that the discourse presumes we understand the salvific overtones of making the *whole* man well.

This defense differs from those mentioned in ch. 5 and 9. It is only here that the legitimacy of Jesus' Sabbath violation is argued on the basis of the law, which is presumed to be still valid. It reflects a stage in the tradition of material about Jesus when there was still concern to validate a lenient Sabbath practice to fellow Jews. This is also reflected in the form of argumentation, which fellow Jews would have recognized.[148]

In the Gospel as we have it, however, this argument has been separated from the incident to which it refers and is brought simply as an example of the teaching of Jesus. The concern in context is to legitimate Jesus as the one sent. This transformation corresponds to the discourse that the evangelist added to the Sabbath controversy (5:19–47).[149]

5.4.2 Participation in the Unceasing Work of the Father (5:17)

In compelling the man to carry his pallet as he walked about, Jesus caused a demonstrative transgression of the Sabbath. This observation exists in tension with the answer Jesus gives to his persecutors. He does not defend his actions by an argument based on humanitarian (cf. Luke 13:15–16; 14:5) or scriptural grounds (cf. the precedent of circumcision, John 7:22–23, referring back to this incident). Instead, he cites the continuing activity of the Father (durative verbal aspect) as the model for his own activity (5:17).[150] As the Son, he can only do what he

---

[147] It is often proposed that this material was the original end of the healing story of ch. 5, at least in the form in which it had been cast when it was transformed into a Sabbath controversy (Bultmann, *Evangelium*, 208; Haenchen, "Probleme," 107; Attridge, "Development"; Labahn, "Spurensuche," 160, 172–4). Bultmann also believed that in the first edition of the Gospel, before it had become disordered, that 7:15–24 had followed 5:47 (*Evangelium*, 205).

[148] Kotila, *Zeuge*, 41–42.

[149] Kotila, *Zeuge*, 43–44.

[150] Paratactical construction (κἀγώ) with the meaning of *just as . . . so also* (cf. Bultmann, *Evangelium* 182, n. 11).

sees the Father do (v. 19). This implies that there was no violation of the Sabbath on his part, any more than the Father's unceasing activity implies any violation on the part of the Father. The closest analogy in the Synoptic tradition is Mark 2:28 par. (cf. 4.1.2, above). There is a difference, however. In the Mark 2:28, the Sabbath controversy ends with a statement, introduced by ὥστε, expressing the sovereignty of the Son of Man over the Sabbath. It is a conclusion drawn from the purpose of the Sabbath as a divine institution. The implication is that this figure, understood in the Synoptics as Jesus against the background of the eschatological judge, has authority to do as he chooses on the Sabbath. Here, no absolute sovereignty is claimed, but the participation of the Son in the work of the Father.[151]

The position Jesus takes can be understood against the background of the discussion of the Sabbath in creation week, Gen 2:2–3. Underlying it is the widespread, but not universal (cf. Jub 2:18), assumption in Second Temple Judaism that God does not interrupt his work on the weekly Sabbath.[152] This is not presented as controversial: it is not contested by Jesus' hearers. They object to his claim to share in this work. The topic of the shared work of the Father and the Son recurs in the discourse (vv. 20, 36). The work that the Father continually performs is therefore specific work, life-giving and judgment, and it is his prerogative to do it. For "Jews" in the first century, this in no way diminished or contradicted the Sabbath; their negative reaction is to the claim of a mere mortal, in their eyes, to participate in this work. For those who share the conviction of the Johannine community about the identity of the Son, there is no question of his right to participate in this work, even on the

---

[151] Schnackenburg, *Johanesevangelium*, 2:126–7.

[152] On Philo, see above, 2.2. Two lines of reasoning are known from rabbinic writings. One was based on the lack of a prohibition of being active in one's own dwelling, and pointed out that the cosmos was God's dwelling. The other posits that there are some activities that God neither delegates to his angels nor interrupts on the Sabbath. These include the giving of life and the exercise of judgment, topics prominent in the discourse in John 5. Discussions in Bultmann, *Evangelium*, 184; Dodd, *Interpretation*, 20–21, 320–23; Bacchiocchi, "John 5:17: Negation or Clarification of the Sabbath? *AUSS* 19 (1981): 3–19, here 4–10; Labahn, *Jesus*, 258–9.

Sabbath. There is no word about how this would exonerate the healed man, however, who had disappeared from the narrative.

5.4.3 The Identity of Jesus as One Sent from God

Jesus is not a participant in the controversy that arises out of his healing of a blind person, 9:13–34. The evangelist devises a different strategy to respond to the charges raised; Jesus does not defend himself, others speak for him. When the Pharisees first learn of this miraculous Sabbath healing, they divide into two camps. In answer to the charge of one that such Sabbath activity disproves the claim that Jesus is a divine emissary, the other answers that the miracle speaks for itself, and makes it clear that Jesus is not a sinner, i.e., one who had acted in blatant disregard for the will of God (v. 16). The man who had received his sight, for whom Jesus is a prophet, (v. 17), argues in a similar way: the work speaks for itself (v. 27). When pressured, the man becomes bolder; he taunts his interrogators (v. 27), then makes light of their confessed ignorance about the origin of Jesus(v. 30), before reaffirming the main thrust of the counter argument: the deed speaks for itself (vv. 31–33).

The strategy employed here, with its apparent trust in the power of the miracles to authenticate the identity of Jesus, and therefore reflect a stage in the tradition prior to the evangelist, is subtle. The argument is not decided; it is ended by the expulsion of the man healed, now a follower of Jesus. This is in keeping with the Johannine understanding of the ambivalence of works or signs.

Meanwhile, Jesus is not present to defend himself, but does not need to be; others are emboldened to speak for him. It is also in keeping with the evangelist's strategy that the charge of demon-possession that follows the good shepherd discourse is not answered by Jesus, but is countered by others with a question (10:19–21). Again, Jesus provokes division; some speak for him. Yet by formulating the defense in the form of counter questions, the evangelist challenges the reader by placing him before the same dilemma faced by the investigating Pharisees: Jesus has worked miracles, therefore he is a man of God; he has done them on the Sabbath, therefore he is not a man of God, because he is a sinner. The strategy employed in 9:13–10:21 has implications for the Sabbath question. The contention that Jesus' power over the Sabbath shows him to be the Son of God, which was the essence of the defense in ch. 5, and can thus be assumed to be a factor in shaping the reader's response here, has meaning only within the context of this otherwise insoluble dilemma posed in ch. 9.[153] It is crucial for the narrative strategy employed by the evangelist that the Sabbath retains validity, at least within the narrative world in which the conflict is played out. For Pancaro, this is an indication that the Sabbath was still seen as binding by the Johannine community, a conclusion that we will leave aside until the question of the relation between narrative and history has been discussed (5.6, below).[154]

5.4.4 Summary

Sabbath violation is conceded in traditional material taken over by the evangelist, but defended as legitimate through an argument that uses the Torah. It is not conceded, however, in the material supplied by the evangelist. In neither case is it admitted that Jesus has sinned by healing on the Sabbath. Jesus commands the man healed to pick up his pallet and walk about (5:8). Yet the action of Jesus is justified by two lines of reasoning—the comparison with circumcision (7:23, see 5.4.1, above) and the participation in the unceasing work of the Father (5:17, see 5.4.2, above)—neither of which concedes that the Sabbath was illegitimately violated. Jesus had acted, depending on the reasoning in question, according to the true intent of the law, or on the basis of divine prerogatives in which he shared on the basis of his unique identity. The Sabbath violation in question was in either case legitimate, at least in the eyes of those who shared the assumptions of the evangelist. If the action was legitimate, then its demonstration is also legitimate, even necessary for the purpose of proclaiming the mission of the revealer. We must be cautious about assuming that a more general freedom was seen in this action. There is a conceivable connection between the two arguments brought in defense of the Sabbath healing of the infirm man: the only male babies who would be circumcised on the Sabbath are those who had been born one week earlier, on the Sabbath. It was precisely the repeated empirical observation that birth and death did not cease each week on

---

[153] Pancaro, *Law*, 29, with n. 64.
[154] Pancaro, *Law*, 530.

the Sabbath that led to the conclusion that God did not rest from his activities as giver of life and as judge, the works in which Jesus is said to participate in ch. 5. As there is no explicit link between these two arguments in the Gospel of John, however, it would be unwise to make too much of this.

5.5 THE SIGNIFICANCE OF THE SABBATH IN THE FOURTH GOSPEL

5.5.1 Does ἕωσ ἄρτι (5:17) Imply an End to the Sabbath?

As mentioned above (5.2.4), the defense Jesus mounts could imply an end to the Father's continuing activity (5:17). The phrase ἕως ἄρτι looks back on and summarizes a condition in the past from the standpoint of the present.[155] Normally this would be done because the past situation is coming to an end.[156] If the phrase is used thus here, then Jesus is not only describing the continuing past activity of the Father, but also announcing its conclusion. Bultmann suggests that this end might be the time expressed in 9:4, the *night* in which no one can work.[157] Cullmann extends this: the close of the work of revelation is the time when the earthly work of atonement is completed in the death and resurrection of the Son, thus inaugurating the eschatological Sabbath of God.[158] This expectation is documented in Second Temple Judaism, is also found in early Christian literature.[159] In this conception, the weekly Sabbath rest is a type of the new age in which God's work of salvation had been achieved. Once fulfillment comes, its type has been superceded. Jesus'

---

[155] H.-J. Ritz, ἄρτι, *EWNT* 1:382–3.

[156] E.g. John 2:10: the good wine has been held back until now, it is no longer being held back; cf. 16:24: the disciples have hitherto asked nothing in Jesus' name, now they are to do so.

[157] Bultmann, *Evangelium*, 184.

[158] Oscar Cullmann, "Sabbat und Sonntag nach dem Johannesevangelium. ἙΟΣ ᾿ΑΡΤΙ (Joh. 5,17)," 1951, repr. *Vorträge und Aufsätze, 1925–1962*, Zürich 1966, 187–91.

[159] On the eschatological interpretation of the Sabbath in Second Temple Judaism, see Gerhard von Rad, "Es ist noch eine Ruhe vorhanden dem Volke Gottes: Eine biblische Begriffsuntersuchung," 1933, repr. in *Gesammelte Studien zum Alten Testament* (3d ed.; TB 8; München, 1965). Christian texts that reflect this concept include Heb 4:10; *Barn.* 15; Irenaeus, *Haer.* 5.28. Cf. ch. 6, below.

revelatory work puts an end to the Sabbath by fulfilling it. On this basis, Cullmann concludes that the text bears indirect witness to a theological reflection that connects the OT day of rest with the resurrection day.

Before discussing the merits of the theses of Cullmann's argument, I will examine the linguistic claim underlying them, namely, that the adverbial phrase ἕως ἄρτι announces the conclusion of the activity of the Father. This phrase is not documented before its nine uses in the NT.[160] In most of these, no end is in view. In some cases, an end could be hoped for or expected, though this is subordinate to the point of the statement (1 Cor 8:7; 15:6; 1 John 2:9). These could be considered implicit termini ad quem. In one case, 1 Cor 4:13, the stress is on the unceasing or continual nature of the condition, the sufferings of the apostle, who does not describe them as coming to an end; the condition obtains up to the present hour (ἄχρι ἄρτι ὥρας, 4:11) and will continue to characterize apostolic existence.[161] This spectrum of use, expressing both continuity and culmination, corresponds to the Hebrew עוֹד. The NT uses are restricted to the writings of those who write semitically-flavored Greek; it is the kind of mistake one would make who speaks Greek but thinks Hebrew or Aramaic.[162] This is all the more understandable since the conjunction ἕως alone can express not only the end of a period of time but also continuation as such (*as long as, while*).[163]

In the passage under consideration, John 5, this statement is an answer to persecution over Sabbath-breaking activities of Jesus; the meaning *continually, without interruption*, is more appropriate. Bacchiocchi, by the way, understands the syntax as placing the emphasis on the adverb, suggesting that the constancy implied by ἐργάζεται must be subordinated to the culmination implied by the adverb ἕως ἄρτι. Since

[160] Christian Maurer, "Steckt hinter Joh. 5:17 ein Übersetzungsfehler?" *WD* 5 (1957): 130–140, here 135.

[161] In Matt 11:12 and 2 Thess 2:7 (ἄρτι ἕως), the meaning is open to interpretation and can not help us determine how the phrase should be understood.

[162] Maurer, "Übersetzungsfehler?", 136, following a conjecture in Bultmann *Evangelium*, 183, n. 6, that ἕως ἄρτι represents an unskillful translation of a semitic original. There is no indication that John 5:17 is a translation, though, so the title of Maurer's essay is misleading.

[163] BDAG, s.v.

however the verb is placed last in the clause pertaining to the Father, and then repeated—again in the final position—when referring to the Son, the opposite would appear to be the case.[164] The phrase ἕως ἄρτι does not announce an end to the activity of the Father.

Although the linguistic observation on which Cullmann based his arguments must be rejected, it is worthwhile to consider his theses. There are four: First, God's revelatory activity comes to an end in the death and resurrection of the Son. The revelation of God indeed reaches its culmination in the coming of Christ, and this, in turn, in the *raising up* of the Son (cf. the final word of the Johannine Jesus, τετέλεσται, 19:30).[165] Doubts have been raised as to the suitability of applying the metaphor *night* from 9:4 to express the time inaugurated by this event, especially if, with Cullmann, the resurrection is understood as a prolepse of the *day* of the Lord.[166] Yet the Gospel cites Jesus as applying the term *night*, with its negative connotations in the Gospel, to the end of his earthly activity, so we are confronted with an ambivalence within the Gospel itself. A resolution of this does not belong to in this study; we must simply note that this objection cannot be sustained.[167] A more serious question is that of the appropriateness of the concept of a forced end (οὐδεὶς δύναται ἐργάζεσθαι, 9:4) to the work of God. Is the *night*, whatever it means, more powerful than God, that it can force an end to his activity? The rest enjoined in the Sabbath command is an expression of the freedom not to labor, not the inability to do so (Exod 20:10; Deut 5:15). Divine rest expresses divine sovereignty, not the prevention of further work by the coming of night.

Second, the death and resurrection of the Son inaugurate the eschatological Sabbath. Although one can, with Bultmann, understand

---

[164] John 5:17," 10–12.

[165] See Jean Zumstein, "Die johanneische Interpretation des Todes Jesu," in *Erinnerung*, 125–44.

[166] Herold Weiss, "The Sabbath in the Fourth Gospel," *JBL* 110 (1991): 311–21, here 318.

[167] Another objection that can not be sustained is that there is a shift in emphasis from the work of the Father (5:17) to that of the Son (9:4) (Maurer, "Joh. 5,17," 130–31; Barrett, *Gospel*, 256). This objection carries little weight because of the Johannine unity of the work of the Father and the Son, which is the point of 5:17.

many of the references to ἡ ὥρα in John as speaking of the eschatological moment, there is no express mention in the Gospel of John of an eschatological Sabbath.[168] It is possible that the ambiguous, previously undocumented, phrase μεγάλη ἡ ἡμέρα ἐκείνου τοῦ σαββάτου in 19:31 suggests this.[169] In this case, it would refer to the condition that had now obtained with the death of Jesus, the eschatological Sabbath. This must be regarded as speculative, however.

Third, when the fulfilment comes, its type is superceded and passes away. Although there is no necessary reason why this conviction would mean that one no longer observed the weekly Sabbath, since a type can continue to live on as a memorial of its fulfilment, the parallel with 4:21–24 shows that in the Johannine conception fulfilment does imply transcendence and abolition. Yet the parallel with the fate of the concept of holy places that can be drawn from Jesus' encounter with the Samaritan woman reminds us at the same time that this fulfilment was Jesus himself. We would expect the same to be true with regard to holy time; in Johannine terms, it is fulfilled and transcended by Jesus himself, not an eschatological Sabbath.[170]

Fourth, this is an indirect witness to a reflection that connects the OT day of rest to the day of resurrection. There is indeed ample evidence that Jews of that time connected the weekly Sabbath with the rest of the

---

[168] On ἡ ὥρα as *die eschatologische Zeit*, see e.g. *Evangelium*, 139–40.

[169] On the level of the canonical gospel, this remark in light of John 18:28 and 19:14 is a reference to the Passover, the first day of the Feast of Unleavened Bread, although the designation *great Sabbath* in combination with holy days is otherwise unknown in Jewish literature until later; when it does appear, it is used to refer to a weekly Sabbath *before* a holy day (I. Abrahams, *Studies in Pharisaism and the Gospels* [Cambridge, 1924], 2:67–69). Bultmann suggests that this detail is from a tradition, in which, as in the Synoptics, Jesus is crucified on the Passover, rather than the day before (*Evangelium*, 524, n. 8). In that case, the Sabbath in question would be the weekly Sabbath during Unleavened Bread in which the wave sheaf was presented (Lev 23:10–11). The reference to a *great Sabbath* (ὄντος σαββάτου μεγάλου) in conjunction with the death of Polycarp (*Mart. Pol.* 8:1)—in February—is dependent on this passage.

[170] *Pace* Bacchiocchi, who maintains that there is a lack of any suggestion that Jesus by his participation in the work of the father has brought the Sabbath to an end by fulfilling the ultimate purpose of the day ("John 5:17," 9–10). It must be granted that this is not made explicit in the Gospel.

world to come. To the degree that this possibility can be entertained, it should be connected to the unusual reference to the Sabbath between crucifixion and resurrection being a *great day* (19:31), and not to the phrase ἕως ἄρτι. The discussion of Cullmann's second point applies here as well.

Despite these difficulties, Cullmann's thesis remains valid on the level on which he presented it: a theological reflection. Because the secondary meaning of ἕως ἄρτι, *culmination*, is not definite in 5:17, but only possible, and because of the conceptual difficulties mentioned, Cullmann's proposal is not conclusive. Finally, such an end to activity, though implied, is not in view in 5:17; rather, the emphasis is on the unceasing activity of both Father and Son. There is therefore no indication in the text that the Johannine community had given up a Sabbath practice in the belief that the eschatological Sabbath had come.[171]

Even if one were to maintain that it were the (unstated) conviction of the Johannine community that the phrase ἕως ἄρτι implies an end to the activity of the Father (and therefore the Son), and that this end arrived with the end of the earthly activity of the Son, inaugurating an epoch known from other sources as the eschatological Sabbath, there is no necessary reason why this conviction would mean that one no longer observed the weekly Sabbath. To maintain that the phrase ἕως ἄρτι is intended by the evangelist as having consequences for the weekly Sabbath goes beyond the evidence of the text, and must be dismissed as speculative. The same can be said of Paul K. Jewett's contention that the connection of the Sabbath to the day of the resurrection would include the transfer of the divinely mandated day of rest.[172] For the counter-

---

[171] *Pace* Weiss, who generalizes from the Sabbath controversies that the Christian communities remained observant of the Sabbath law, even if engaged in the continuous process of defining the how of its observance ("Sabbath," 313–4). He recognizes the intertwining of the Sabbath issue with issues that were more important to the Johannine community, especially Christology, yet expresses the relationship as one of a Christological understanding of the Sabbath. Nevertheless, he concludes that by the time of the final redaction of the Gospel of John the community was no longer concerned with the how of Sabbath observance. Every day is a Sabbath in which they are to perform the works of the Son (ibid., 319–20).

[172] *The Lord's Day: A Theological Guide to the Christian Day of Worship*, Grand Rapids 1971, 84–87.

suggestion of Bacchiocchi there is even less basis. He suggests that John reports the sabbatical saying about God's working in 5:17 (and 9:4) to justify the understanding and practice of the Sabbath-rest of the community as a day to experience God's redemptive working by ministering to the needs of others. He thereby misses the point of Jesus' defense and his participation in the continual work of his Father: he ministered not *because* it was the Sabbath, but *despite* the Sabbath.[173]

5.5.2 Is the Sabbath a Symbol of Divine Reality?

Dorothy Ann Lee suggests that in John 5 the Sabbath becomes a symbol of the ministry and mission of Jesus, and therefore of the divine reality to which the coming of Jesus points (108, 121).[174] The Sabbath however is a middle term between the healing of an infirm man—an expression of the giving of life—and the claim of equality with the father that this participation in the life-giving work of the Father implies. The Sabbath, as we have seen, is not explicitly discussed in the discourse that follows the brief controversy, but Lee finds it implied in three ways. One is that Jesus participates in the unceasing work of the Father. Yet the accent here shifts if we, with Lee, describe these activities as "the Sabbath work of God" (110, 119). As mentioned above (5.5.1), the Father—and Jesus—do these not because it is the Sabbath, but in spite of the day. The second is the theme of judgment (vv. 39–47), which recalls the controversy provoked by the healing (100). The third is the appeal by Jesus to the law of Moses—this law being of course that which the action of Jesus had putatively broken. The law acts as a symbol, too: for those who see the divine reality to which the law points, it is clear who Jesus is (119, 124). The opponents see only the law, thus showing that they are tied to this world. For those who perceive the symbolic reality of the law, it is clear that Jesus had not broken it (112). The work of enabling an infirm man to rise and walk about points to the life-giving work of the father. But this sparks opposition through the middle element, the Sabbath. It is unclear whether Lee's typology would make the crucial term the infirm

---

[173] Bacchiocchi, "John 5:17," 19.

[174] *Narratives*, 108, 121. Subsequent references to page numbers within this section will be set in the text.

person or the Sabbath. She expressly states, though, that the Sabbath becomes a symbol. It is not however the Sabbath in ch. 5 that points to divine reality (which we would expect), but the non-keeping of the Sabbath that points to it. To conclude with Lee that the Sabbath is a symbol of divine rest is to read the account in terms of the well documented expectation of a divine Sabbath, eschatological rest, but *not* in terms of the Gospel itself.

Even were we to say that the Sabbath points to a divine reality beyond itself, we still could make no conclusion about the Sabbath practice, or lack of it, of the Johannine community. Recognition of its symbolic value could just as easily imply a continuance of observance as a cessation of observance. It is however the *refusal* to rest, to cease activity, that points to divine reality in 5:17. This implies that the identity of the community was forged in conflict with a synagogue-based Judaism and that this conflict was based in part on the Sabbath activity of the community, activity that opponents viewed as arising from a conviction on the part of the Johannine community that the Sabbath had been loosed. It would be more accurate to turn Lee's thesis around: the Sabbath had *previously* served to symbolize divine reality. Both the work of God, achieved at the end of creation week and solemnly brought to conclusion by his rest, and his presence among his people, symbolized by their participation in that rest, are now superceded. It is in Christ that the work, indeed the presence of God is experienced (5:19–30).[175]

5.5.3 The Great Sabbath of John 19

Although the suggestions of Cullmann and Lee have been found to face difficulties, both were correct to sense that Sabbath was more than an indication of time for the Fourth Evangelist. The Key to its significance is suggested by the final mention of the Sabbath in the Gospel. As mentioned above, there is, in addition to the Sabbaths mentioned in conjunction with healing controversies, a Sabbath mentioned in the account of Jesus' passion. It forms an inclusion with the first Sabbath in the Gospel. On that occasion, Jesus had said, "My Father is still working, and I also am working" (5:17). This theme is picked up on the occasion

---

[175] The possibility of this reversal was suggested to me by Konrad Haldimann.

of the second Sabbath healing: "We must work the works of him who
sent me while it is day; night is coming when no one can work" (9:4).
Night does come, and it is noted in conjunction with the departure of
Judas to betray Jesus (13:30). As soon as Judas leaves, Jesus announces:
"Now the Son of Man has been glorified, and God has been glorified in
him" (v. 31). The aorist, following the adverb νῦν, *now*, could serve to
mark the moment that the glorification takes place; the NRSV reflects
such an understanding. More likely, it should be taken in an ingressive
sense: the moment marks the beginning of the events that will rapidly,
within the next few hours, culminate in the lifting up of the Son of Man
(BDAG, s. v. νῦν, 1.a.α.ἰ). When this glorification reaches its culmination
in the departure out of the world of the one sent , it is Jesus himself who
announces it with his final words, "it is finished" (19:30). The work the
Son came into the world to do has now been accomplished. In the next
verse, "the Jews" make another appearance. Oblivious to the poignancy
of the moment, their concern is for the solemnity of the Sabbath. The
bodies must be removed from the cross (v. 31).[176] Thus, at the end of the
narrative, they remain as they were at the beginning; their concern is for
proper observance of their sacred day, blind to the significance of Jesus
both in life and in death, subject to the judgment of God (cf. 9:39–41).
Thus the Sabbath serves to introduce teaching about the identity of Jesus
and his soteriological significance. At the same time, it is an occasion for
misapprehension of the one sent by those who hold to the strict
observance of the day.

5.5.4 The Sunday Evening Appearances of the Risen Jesus

After the "great Sabbath," but—significantly for John—while it was still
dark (cf. Mark 16:2), Mary Magdalene goes to the tomb and finds the
stone rolled away (John 20:1). She tells Simon Peter and the beloved

---

[176] It would have been necessary on any day to remove the body so that it did not
remain overnight (Deut 21:22–23). The imminence of the holy day increased the normal
desire to have bodies removed before nightfall (Brown, *Gospel*, 2:939). The motif of the
approaching Sabbath as occasion for taking down the body was traditional (Mark 15:42),
but is transformed in the Fourth Gospel by the fact that the request is made by "the
Jews," rather than Joseph of Arithmathea, motivated by concern for the purity of the
Sabbath, not with affording an appropriate burial.

disciple, but only the latter "believes" (v. 8). Mary then encounters the risen Jesus, which she reports to the disciples (vv. 11–18). That evening, Jesus appears to a gathering of the disciples (vv. 19–23). One, Thomas, is absent and doubts their report, leading to his dramatic confrontation with Jesus and his confession, which serves as the climax of the Gospel (v. 28). This occurs one week later (μεθ' ἡμέρας ὀκτώ), which implies that the disciples had once again gathered on a Sunday evening.[177]

As we saw in ch. 1, Rordorf sees in these two resurrection appearances to the gathered disciples in a closed room in Jerusalem on successive Sunday evenings an indication that the Jerusalem congregation began weekly celebrations of the resurrection on the first day of the week immediately after Easter. Given the length of time between the events surrounding the resurrection appearances and the composition of the Fourth Gospel, the likelihood of this must be determined by considerations of the relation between tradition and redaction in these accounts.

The appearance to disciples at the close of the day on which the empty grave was discovered is traditional (cf. Luke 24:28–49).[178] The report that Thomas doubted takes up the traditional motif that some disciples did (Matt 28:17; Luke 24:37–38). Thomas is identified by the non–Johannine εἷς ἐκ τῶν δώδεκα (John 20:34), indicating that the story of a second appearance for his benefit may have existed in a written passion narrative used as a source by John, even though there is no such second appearance in the Synoptics.[179]

For what purpose? The first appearance has been edited to symbolize the fulfillment of Jesus' promise in 14:18.[180] The second to dramatize and personify the traditional theme of apostolic doubt.[181] Unlike in Luke 24, there are no eucharistic elements in either.[182] The express mention of the second meeting as coming one week later may neverthe-

---

[177] Brown: "The impression is given that there were no gatherings and hence no appearances during the elapsed week" (*Gospel*, 2:1025).
[178] Bultmann, *Evangelium*, 534–5.
[179] Bultmann, *Evangelium*, 537.
[180] Bultmann, *Evangelium*, 535.
[181] Brown, *Gospel*, 2:1031–2.
[182] Cf. Barrett, who finds liturgical traces and concludes that the presence of Christ may suggest the Eucharist and the spoken word (*Gospel*, 477).

less indicate that by the time of the composition of ch. 20 such a pattern was likely well-established.[183]

It has been objected that the gathering was not for worship but for fear of the "Jews." But the "fear of the Jews" is mentioned not to motivate the gathering, but the locking of the door, and this detail is mentioned to heighten the miraculous nature of Jesus' appearance.[184]

Hard to determine is the chronological sequence. Was there a time when both practices overlapped and the Johannine community observed, in their own way, the Sabbath while commemorating the resurrection on Sunday evening? Or had their commitment to any form of Sabbath observance waned before they had established a regular pattern of Sunday evening worship. Without knowing this, and I see no way in which this can be determined, we can not speak of the one practice replacing the other.

5.6 FROM NARRATIVE TO HISTORY

In none of the passages investigated has there been any direct statement about the Sabbath practice—or lack of it—of the community in which the Gospel was introduced, nor any direct instruction from the author to the reader. Yet the question of the experience of a community in which healing narratives were transformed into Sabbath controversies, and the view of an author who subordinates these controversies to christological concerns, poses itself. There has been a variety of answers to the question, from the assumption of a community loyal to the Torah and retaining some form of Sabbath practice, albeit more liberal than that of fellow Jews, to a setting in which the Sabbath is trampled underfoot.[185]

---

[183] Cf. Ign., *Magn.* 9:1. On the proximity of Ignatius to John, see Haenchen, *Johannesevangelium*, 5–7.

[184] Bultmann, *Evangelium*, 535.

[185] Roloff, for instance, concludes two of the three healing miracles in John involve a Sabbath controversy, there is no doubt that the Sabbath was an important issue for the Johannine community (*Das Kerygma und der irdische Jesus. Historische Motive in den Jesus-Erzählungen der Evangelien* [Göttingen, 1970], 81). Wengst maintains that it is not the Sabbath as such under discussion in the Johannine community, but Sabbath halakah (*Johannesevangelium*, 360). Pancaro sees a community loyal to the Torah (*Law*, 530). Lohse, in contrast, understands the command to carry the pallet in 5:9 as an indication

The step from narrative world to historical reconstruction, difficult with any text, appears especially challenging in the case of the Gospel of John. Jesus is absent during the controversy that results from his healing of a blind person in ch. 9. It is the healed man, not Jesus, who is subjected to forensic examination. This absence of Jesus from the conflict about his work led Bultmann to suggest that the Johannine tradition was shaped in the controversy between the community and the synagogue.[186] Other anachronistic features include the reference to persecution, 5:16, the fear of expulsion from the synagogue, 9:22, and the fact that juridical authority is in the hands of the Pharisees, 9:13. These text signals indicate that for the Johannine community, the earthly ministry of Jesus was transparent for their own situation. Bultmann's suggestion has been taken up and expanded by J. Louis Martyn.[187] Martyn's thesis builds on a major premise of form criticism: the materials used in the gospel pericopes often rest on tradition, and their formulation reflects the life-setting of the transmitting community. Martyn takes this a step further when he maintains that the Johannine community, reading its own experience back into the earthly ministry of Jesus, has created a two-level drama. Indeed, Martyn postulates a literal correspondence, in which Jewish Christian teachers reenact the words of Jesus in the lives of believing Jews. For instance, Martyn sees in 5:16 a reference to the level of the earthly ministry of Jesus and v. 18 a reference to the experience of the Johannine community.[188]

Martyn's proposal has been influential in Johannine studies, but the difficulties of reading this Gospel as if it were transparent to the history of the community in which it was produced are increasingly apparent.[189]

---

that the Sabbath had been abandoned by the Johannine community (*TWNT* 7:28); an opinion expressed with a violent figure of speech by Hirsch: "Das Sabbatgesetz wird öffentlich mit Füssen getreten als eine Nichtigkeit" (*Evangelium* 157); cf. Bultmann: those who benefit must share in the freedom (*Evangelium*, 185).

[186] *Evangelium*, 178–9.

[187] *History*. Prior to Martyn, this suggestion of Bultmann's was developed by E. L. Allen, "The Jewish Christian Church in the Fourth Gospel," *JBL* 74 (1955): 88–92.

[188] *History*, 70–72.

[189] Robert Kysar, "Expulsion from the Synagogue: A Tale of a Theory," (paper presented at the annual meeting of the SBL, Toronto, 25 November 2002).

There are four areas of difficulty. The first of these is the correlation by Martyn of a general ban of Christians from the Synagogue to the *Birkat ha-Minim*, the *Benediction against the Heretics* the twelfth petition of the *Shemoneh Esreh*, the *Eighteen Benedictions*, which he dates ca. 85–90 C.E.[190] This has been widely challenged both on the specificity of the dating and the question of whether this petition was aimed at followers of Christ.[191] This is not fatal to Martyn's theory, however, since the limited experience of the Johannine community and their local synagogue would suffice.

More serious are the other difficulties. The retrojection of all the details of the text into the life of the community disregards the nature of narrative. The narrative world is not the same as the real world that author and community share.[192] In addition, we must reckon with the aspect of fiction in narrative texts.[193] The needs of story-telling, not reportage, govern the selection of details.

Third, given the evidence of a history of transmission, the question must be posed of the stage in which the expulsion from the synagogue was a current concern.[194] Martyn reads the entire Gospel in light of this conflict, but it appears to have been settled by the time of the composition of the Gospel.[195] This is not only seen by the absence of "the Jews" in the farewell discourses, but also the manner in which the Sabbath topic is subordinated to christological concerns in the two episodes that have been investigated here. For this reason, the experience of expulsion is best related to the stage of pre-Gospel tradition.[196]

[190] *History*, 34–62.

[191] Recent critical discussion, with further literature, see Labahn, *Jesus*, 34–41.

[192] Zumstein, "Zur Geschichte des johanneischen Christentums," in *Erinnerung*, 1–14, here 2.

[193] Labahn, *Jesus*, 43.

[194] Kotila faults not only Martyn, but also Brown and Wengst with failing to consider the strata (*Zeuge*, 44–45).

[195] Wengst disagrees with Martyn on the direct relevance of the בִּרְכַּת הַמִּינִים, yet shares the view that the expulsion from the synagogue was a contemporary problem of the Johannine community (*Gemeinde*, 75–104).

[196] Labahn, *Jesus*, 359–60, n. 288. Labahn also see terminological grounds for assigning the conflict with the synagogue as prior to the composition of the Gospel ("Spurensuche," 174–5).

Finally, the high degree of theological reflection in the Fourth Gospel alerts us to the possibility that the step from text to community may be larger than it is in Mark, for example.

This does not mean that it is impossible to reconstruct the historical situation from the text. A text originates in a particular historical, cultural and social location. Though we lack the information that would be needed to identify this more than generally, the text does contain information that permits a relative dating of reconstructed tradition.[197] Two phenomena, in particular, can be observed. First, at some stage in the transmission of Jesus tradition, healing accounts were turned into Sabbath controversies. As discussed above (5.3.2), it is the opponents who claim Jesus has loosened or abolished the Sabbath (5:18). At the very least, this charge reflects the perception that they had formed of the behavior of their Jesus-confessing compatriots on the Sabbath. Secondly, the present Gospel uses Sabbath controversies as prominent plot elements, though no longer primarily interested in defending Jesus from the charge of Sabbath-breaking. While there is no necessary connection between the view of the text and the practice of the community in which the text was formulated, we would be safe in concluding that it is not the intention of the text to defend a strict Sabbath observance. Whether the Johannine Christians themselves believed that the Sabbath had been abolished, or whether they simply had a freer practice based on their memory of the example of Jesus cannot be decided.[198]

5.7 RESULTS

As do the Synoptics, John incorporates traditional miracles of healing and words of conflict. Yet he handles them in ways that diverge sharply from those followed in the Synoptics. The charges made against Jesus concerning his Sabbath activities are stronger and more direct than in the Synoptics. In John, Jesus is said to abolish the Sabbath (5:18), and to not keep it (9:16), and that he is a sinner (9:16, 31).

[197] Labahn, *Jesus*, 41–43.
[198] Cf. Wengst, *Gemeinde*, 117, n. 46, and idem, *Johannesevangelium*, 194–5.

Five texts have been examined to determine what the Gospel of John has to say about the Sabbath. The first, John 5:1–18, is important for the narrative strategy of the Gospel as a whole, especially the first half, for it is in this passage that the hostility of the "Jews" is first recounted. This provides the context in which the rest of the public ministry of Jesus is narrated, a tale of rejection, division, and repeated attempts to kill him. The last words in this section are spoken by Jesus, who solemnly avers that he has faithfully fulfilled the mission of the One who sent him (12:49–50). For this reason, to reject him is to reject the Father (12:44–48).

The introduction of this central topic, the hostility of the "Jews," is achieved through a healing miracle that has been recast as a Sabbath controversy. Jesus commands the man healed to carry his pallet, a violation of the Sabbath. The ensuing controversy leads to a discourse in which the sign value of the healing miracle is brought out (life-giving/judgment). The discourse closes with the assertion that a proper reading of Moses points to him (5:46–47).

Not only life-giving words, but also a warning of judgment, are spoken to the man healed, an elusive figure whose character has been assessed in diametrically opposing ways. The warning against continued sin indicates that he had *not* sinned in obeying Jesus and carrying his pallet. Jesus never concedes that he had sinned by healing on the Sabbath. The accusation of having violated the Sabbath is first addressed to the healed man. Only he can be charged with a verifiable offense, carrying his pallet. But this accusation disappears, and only the putative violation of Jesus plays a role, although the charge is not specified (ταῦτα ἐποίει, v. 16). The indeterminate nature of Jesus' Sabbath offenses (plural, cf. ἕν, 7:21) is an additional indication that the interest of the evangelist does not lay primarily here but with their role in leading to the revelation of the participation in the work of the Father. It is this topic that is explored and expanded in the subsequent discourse, 5:19–47, not the meaning and purpose of the Sabbath. Jesus' defense involves his participation in the unceasing activity (life-giving and judging) of the Father, his prerogative by virtue of being the Son. For any mere human to have claimed this right would have been presumptuous rebellion. This argument, unlike that from circumcision in ch. 7, can carry no weight with outsiders: one has to recognize the identity of Jesus in order to accept the validity of his claim. Although reflecting its origin in the setting of conflict with the synagogue, it is not suitable for dialogue with the synagogue.

The phrase ἕως ἄρτι in 5:17 implies an end to the activity of the Father, and therefore the Son. This end is not in view in 5:17, however. Rather, the emphasis is the unceasing activity of both—an observation that also weighs against the suggestion that the Sabbath is a symbol of the ministry and mission of Jesus, and therefore of the divine reality to which Jesus points, for it is his refusal to rest that reveals his identity. There is no indication in the text that the Johannine community believed that it had entered the eschatological Sabbath.

When Jesus defends his action by an appeal to his participation in the unceasing activity of "his" Father, the "Jews"—a term that here and in many other references in this Gospel probably refers to the authority figures in the synagogue—formulate a dual charge against him: he had unbound the Sabbath and has made himself equal to the Father. The second of these charges was a central issue in the conflict between the Johannine community and its fellow "Jews" (cf. 10:33). While containing an element of truth—the divine origin and mission of the Son—it reflects a misapprehension: this is not something Jesus made. If the same thought is applied to the first charge, it would mean that it, as well, reflects synagogue debate with the Johannine community, yet the charge as formulated would be rejected as being based on a misapprehension. Nevertheless, the charge does allow insight into how the behavior of the Johannine Christians appeared to their fellow Jews, for whom these followers of Jesus seemed to act as if they believed the Sabbath had been abolished. At the same time, the course of the argument makes it clear that the Sabbath question has been subordinated to christological concerns.

The second passage examined, 7:14–24, refers back to this episode. Jesus not only affirms that his teaching (and by implication, his actions, including healing on the Sabbath) is in accord with the will of God, hitherto understood as expressed in the Torah, but also that anyone with the desire to do that divine will would recognize the genuine nature of his mission (7:17). Jesus appeals to the practice of circumcision, which was carried out on the Sabbath as on any other day. The argument from the lesser to the greater presumes the validity of circumcision and points to a Jewish-Christian setting. Complete alignment with the will of God, which in such a setting would mean obedience to the Torah, is claimed for Jesus and those who recognize his divine mission, i.e., the Johannine community. Tensions in the text suggest that traditional material is preserved here, and that the argument employed reflects a time when the community was still concerned to justify a Sabbath violation as nevertheless in keeping with the law. For the evangelist, this is no longer a concern; the material is used simply to demonstrate the teaching of the one sent.

The third passage is a healing miracle that displays many parallels to that in ch. 5, including the supplemental way in which the Sabbath is mentioned (9:14). In contrast to ch. 5, where the miracle was effectuated by a commanding word, Jesus works a cure for blindness that in several details conflicts with Sabbath halakah. Two facts—that Jesus has healed and that he has done so on the Sabbath—are paradoxical, and lead to division among the Pharisees. Yet it is not Jesus who is summoned for interrogation, but the formerly blind man. He is not charged with breaking the Sabbath—Jesus is—but is expelled from the synagogue for confessing Jesus. This opens a window into the history of the Johannine community, who apparently continued to work as Jesus had done, causing their fellow Jews to conclude that they were acting as if the Sabbath had been abolished. Although they are not equal with the Father, they share in the unceasing activity of the Son (cf. 20:21). This could explain the evidence in the Gospel of the Sabbath as a point of contention between the Johannine community and the synagogue. To their fellow Jews, the Johannine Christians acted as if the Sabbath had been abolished, all the while convinced that it was they, not their compatriots, who truly fulfilled the will of God. Their self-understanding was that they were not disobeying the law. Yet their behavior was not recognized by their contemporaries as Sabbath-observant.

The second Sabbath healing leads to the charge that Jesus breaks the Sabbath and is a sinner (9:16). The discourse that follows the controversy results in the formulation of the charge that Jesus is demon-possessed and mad. Although in context the reaction to his words, this charge appears in the Synoptics as an alternate explanation of his works, whereas here it follows the messianic claims in the discourse. The revelation in works has been subordinated to the revelation in discourse. This raises the possibility that the mention of the Sabbath—with its transparently supplemental character—is meant in the same way.

The final mention of the Sabbath follows immediately on Jesus' final words, announcing the completion of his mission (19:30–31). The Jews take no cognizance of the soteriological significance of his having been raised up in this way; their concern, as before, is with the purity of Sabbath observance. This forms an inclusion with the first mention of the Sabbath in 5:9. The few mentions of the Sabbath in the Fourth Gospel thus form a consistent picture: it is an occasion both for the revelation of the work of the divine emissary as well as the failure to understand of the paramount representatives of the world, "the Jews."

The two appearances of the resurrected Jesus to the disciples on consecutive Sunday evenings that John narrates (20:19–29) show that the evangelist has reworked tradition, which does not allow us to make any conclusion about historic events that transpired in Jerusalem in the first Easter week. Nevertheless, they could indicate that in his community a practice of weekly gatherings for the Lord's Supper on Sunday evening had become established. Whether it had replaced a Sabbath practice or existed alongside of it can no longer be determined.

John builds on traditions that Jesus' healing activities took precedence over respect for the conventions of Sabbath observance among his co-religionists. These traditions are still evident in 7:21–24. But a number of text signals are anachronistic and point beyond the historical situation of Jesus (see 5.6, above). In additions, there are tensions that indicate a literary development of the material (the tension between ἕν, 7:21 and ταῦτα, 5:16; the supplemental addition of the Sabbath, 5:9b and 9:14; as well as, possibly, between the understanding of the relation between sin and illness in 5:14 and 9:4). These have shown that analysis of the question of the Sabbath in John should proceed along diachronic lines as well as synchronic. A possible reconstruction of the development reflected in these texts would begin with a loosened commitment to the Sabbath that had its origins in the behavior of Jesus, based on a reordering of priorities, not its abolishment. This led to behavior that was judged by fellow Jews as improper (cf. "abolished," 5:18). We must keep in mind the development in Judaism during the first century, with the narrowing of diversity in the time of consolidation after the destruction of the temple. Behavior that in the early part of the century that may have been controversial but within the spectrum of Jewish practice may later have been judged as sinful. As a final development, we can imagine that in a situation of enforced expulsion from the synagogue, primarily over the high Christology of the Johannine community, their Sabbath freedom became a negative identity marker, leading eventually to abandonment of the practice. Statements that are hard to reconcile with a community that had consciously broken with the Sabbath (7:19–24) exist side by side with statements that suggest that Jesus had indeed loosened, or abolished, the Sabbath (5:18). We have seen however that the Sabbath is introduced for the purpose of emphasizing Christology, and of emphasizing that the crucial location of that Christology is not the works (signs) but the self-revelation in discourse. The discourses are nothing other than an explication of the works of Jesus, which in turn consist of effective words and eloquent signs.

As in the Synoptics, there is no explicit answer to the question of whether Christians are to observe the weekly Sabbath. The Johannine community may have continued to observe the Sabbath, but there is no proof that it did. Two things however are clear: to fellow Jews, they appeared to have abandoned it. Secondly, the topic is introduced neither for urging followers of Jesus to continue Sabbath observance nor establishing Sabbath halakah. The Sabbath healing in ch. 5, for instance, is not recounted to show Jesus' superiority over the law, but to prepare for the portrayal of his relation to the Father.[199] The community understood itself as sharing in this relationship with the Father by virtue of the ascension of Jesus (20:17), so that it could well as felt free to share in the life-giving and judging activity that justified the Sabbath activity of Jesus in their eyes, without necessarily feeling that the Sabbath had thereby been abolished.

The Gospel of John was composed at a time after the conclusion of dialogue with the synagogue (9:22; 16:1–4). The broad characterization of the opponents as "Jews" is an indication of distance, implying that the

---

[199] Haenchen, *Johannesevangelium*, 284.

Johannine community now perceived its identity in negative terms, that is, as *non*-Jews. This did not prevent them from claiming to be the legitimate heirs to Moses and the Torah (5:46–47; 7:17–19; cf. 4:22), an honor the evangelist in no way concedes to the rulers of the synagogue. It is they who view discipleship of Jesus and discipleship of Moses as antithetical, not John. Yet the Johannine claim was not merely that Jesus was the appropriate successor of Moses, but that he was the one toward him the scriptures of Israel had pointed (cf. 1:17), which implies a different concept of succession. If this had not led already to the abandonment of such signs of Jewish identity as the Sabbath, it was only a matter of time until it would. Henceforth, the positive identity of the group would be oriented toward the mainstream church.[200]

---

[200] On this function of the epilogue (ch. 21), see Jean Zumstein, "Die Endredaktion des Johannesevangeliums," in *Kreative Erinnerung*, 192–216, esp. 206–11.

6
Additional Writings
from the First Christian Century

After the extensive examination of texts from three major strands of NT theology—Paul, the Synoptic tradition, and the Johannine school—this chapter will round out the picture of what can be recovered from the first century of Christian belief and practice. In the first section, an additional NT text will be considered. In the second section, we will look at evidence from *Barnabas*, one of the writings collectively known as the Apostolic Fathers. The third section will be devoted to a reference to the Sabbath in the most famous of the noncanonical writings, *The Gospel of Thomas*. The latter two texts may be especially helpful in determining the variety of faith and practice in the first Christian century, since they may reveal a perspective that was not represented in the writings included in the canon.

6.1 THE SABBATH CELEBRATION THAT REMAINS (HEBREWS 4:9)

In the investigation so far, we found no statement of a clear abrogation of the Sabbath. In the passage to which we now turn, we find the only NT statement that a celebration of the Sabbath remains for the people of God (Heb 4:9). This merits our attention in light of what we have seen. In all four canonical gospels, the Sabbath activity of Jesus and his followers is uniformly an occasion for strife. Paul, writing to the Galatians, resisted the notion that congregations he had gathered from the nations should observe days. Knowing this, we should avoid a hasty conclusion that this text indicates a practice of weekly Sabbath observance on the part of

either the author of Hebrews or his intended readers.[1] The determination
of what is meant by the Sabbath celebration that remains for the people
of God can only be made by its use in context.

6.1.1 Analysis of the Context

The mention of the Sabbath appears near the conclusion of an illustration
that is, in itself, a miniature "word of exhortation."[2] In 3:1–6, the
faithfulness of Christ is compared to that of Moses and found superior,
though the latter's faithfulness is not called into question.[3] The material
that follows immediately, 3:7–4:13, does not however continue the
discussion, so central to the Book of Hebrews as a whole, of the superiority of Christ, but elucidates the quality by which he is here compared to
Moses, faithfulness. It investigates and illustrates this quality by drawing
on an example of its opposite, unfaithfulness. The example is apt in that

---

[1]   Adolf von Harnack's suggestion that the anonymity of this letter may be due
to the involvement in its authorship of a woman, someone like Prisca, is attractive
("Probabilia über die Adresse und den Verfasser des Hebräerbriefes," ZNW 1 [1900]:
16–41). It is however speculative, and the use of a masculine participle in 11:32
weighs against it. I will use the masculine pronoun when referring to the unknown
author.

[2]   In 13:22 the author refers to his text as a "word of exhortation." Lawrence
Wills has identified several smaller units in this form in the book ("The Form of the
Sermon in Hellenistic Judaism and Early Christianity," HTR 77 [1984]: 277–99).
Cf. Harold W. Attridge's characterization of this section as an "excellent little example
of the homiletic form" (The Epistle to the Hebrews [Hermeneia; Philadelphia, 1989],
17; in n. 139 he references an early identification of the sermon form of this passage
(by C. Clemen in 1896).

[3]   See Craig Koester on the general stance toward Judaism in Heb. As with the
reference to Moses, the author freely refers to other heroes of Israel as examples of
faith in ch. 11. In addition, he cites institutions of Israel such as Jerusalem, the
tabernacle, its sacrifices, and the levitical priesthood. He does not speak of an old and
a new Israel or contrast Israel and the church, "but perceives the continuity in the
people of God under the old and new covenants (Hebrews: A New Translation with
Introduction and Commentary [AB 36; New York, 2001], 76–77, 272). He always
assumes that the reader is familiar with these, and points to the superiority of Christ
in each case without adopting or condemning these forerunners. Their value is that of
a type (Heb 8:5, drawing on Exod 25:40) or model (9:23). See also the designation
"shadow," σκιά (10:1). The passage under examination here is unique in Heb in using
an example (ὑπόδειγμα, 4:11) that is clearly negative.

it concerns those who followed Moses out of Egypt yet were refused entry into the land of promise because they withheld trust in God. The import for those who follow Christ is clear.

To make this point, and in keeping with the form of a word of exhortation, this passage consists of (1) an exemplum, ascriptural quotation (3:7–11), (2) application, drawing out the significance of the exemplum for those addressed (3:12–4:10), and (3) an exhortation (4:11, perhaps vv. 12–13 as well).[4] We will now briefly examine each of these.

(1) Exemplum (3:7–11). In 3:7, a quotation from Ψ 94:7d–11 (= Ps 95:7d–11) is introduced with a formula that attributes the words to the Holy Spirit:[5]

7 Therefore, as the Holy Spirit says,
"Today, if you hear his voice,
8 do not harden your hearts as in the rebellion,
as on the day of testing in the wilderness,
9 where your ancestors put me to the test,
though they had seen my works 10 for forty years.
Therefore I was angry with that generation,
and I said, 'They always go astray in their hearts,
and they have not known my ways.'
11 As in my anger I swore,
'They will not enter my rest.' "[6]

---

[4]   Albert Vanhoye, whose work on the structure of Heb has been widely followed, ends the section at v. 11 and treats vv. 12–13 as a discrete unit (*La structure litteraire de l'Épître aux Hébreux* [2d ed.; StudNeot 1; Paris, 1976], 92–104). Otfried Hofius however sees in vv. 12–13 not only the conclusion to the entire section but also the support for the exhortation in v. 11 (*Katapausis: Die Vorstellung vom endzeitlichen Ruheort im Hebräerbrief* [WUNT 11; Tübingen, 1970], 138; see also Craig Koester, *Hebrews*, 276–7, n. 133).

[5]   Διό, καθὼς λέγει τὸ πνεῦμα τὸ ἅγιον. Cf. however the reference to David in 4:7. This psalm is ascribed to David in the LXX, although it is not in the MT. Behind this reference lies apparently the concept of David as author of the Psalter. This is in keeping with the general early Christian use of the Psalter, as seen in other NT writings (Luke 20:42–43; Acts 2:25, 34–35; Rom 4:6; 11:9–10). The Holy Spirit is also said to have spoken through him in 2 Sam 23:2; Matt 22:43; Mark 12:36; Acts 1:16; 4:25; this makes David's role akin to that of the prophets (cf. Acts 2:29, where David is called a prophet).

[6]   On the differences between this text and the LXX, see in addition to the commentaries, Judith Hoch Wray, *Rest as a Theological Metaphor in the Epistle to the*

The verb "speaks," λέγει, is in durative; this sets the stage so that when the listener hears the first word of the quotation, σήμερον, "today," he feels directly addressed and does not immediately think of a day many years earlier when the psalm may first have been uttered.[7] The day in which we are to "hear his voice" is our ever-new today. This is confirmed in the argument and exposition, which begins by encouraging the readers to exhort one another ("every day, as long as it is called today," 3:13).[8]

The quotation culminates in an oath by which God declares "they" (the wilderness generation) will not enter into his rest (εἰς τὴν κατάπαυσίν μου).[9] Rest is a key term for this passage, the only extended discussion of this theme in the NT.[10] The concept is one of the most common associations with the Sabbath in the OT and Judaism, but rest was not exclusively tied to the Sabbath. As the quotation from Ps 95 shows, the land of promise was also associated with rest.[11]

(2) Application (3:12–4:10). In keeping with the homiletical nature of this passage, the psalm—the "sermon text"—is used to structure this section. Parts of the psalm quotation are repeated at strategic points in the argument.[12] These have been identified as the center of three segments,

---

Hebrews and the Gospel of Truth: Early Christian Homiletics of Rest (SBLDS 166; Atlanta, 1998), 64–66.

[7] Σήμερον is repeated at key locations in this passage (3:13, 15; 4:7 [2x]).

[8] καθ᾽ ἑκάστην ἡμέραν, ἄχρις οὗ τὸ σήμερον καλεῖται. This "today" will not continue indefinitely however. The coming of the Son is evidence of the "last days" (1:2; 9:26). The generation now living is the last one (11:40). There remains just a little while (10:37); the day of completion is near (10:25). Cf. the use of ἄχρι, ἄχρις οὗ, μέχρι (Otto Michel, *Der Brief an die Hebräer* [13th ed.; KEK 13; Göttingen 1966], 188). The strongly emphasized "today" in relation to hearing God's voice is the existential moment of decision. It is not tied to any specific day of the week.

[9] The LXX of Ψ 94 woodenly took over the literal form of a Hebrew curse. The author of Hebrews left it as he found it. See BDR § 454,5.

[10] This is underlined by vocabulary statistics. The noun κατάπαυσις is used eight times in this section (3:11, 18; 4:1, 3 [2x], 5, 10, 11); the only other NT use is in Acts 7:49. The cognate verb, καταπεύω, is used three times (4:4, 8, 10). Again, there is only one other NT use (Acts 14:18).

[11] Note esp. Deut 12:9; 25:19, where both "rest" and "inheritance" are used in reference to the land (cf. Heb 9:15, where inheritance is used as a metaphor for salvation). See also Josh 1:15; 21:43–44; 22:4; 23:1.

[12] 3:15 (= 3:7–8a), 4:3b (= 3:11), and 4:7b (= 3:7–8aα).

each delimited by an inclusion.[13] In addition, words from the quotation appear in 3:17–18, as part of a series of rhetorical questions about the identity of those who did not enter, and 4:5, in which words of the curse quoted in 3:11 are repeated.

The first of these segments (3:12–19) presents an exposition of the argument drawn from the exemplum and can be subdivided in turn into three units. In the first, the addressees are urged to see to it that they do not have an "evil, unbelieving heart," with *heart* serving as a catchword (3:12–14).[14] An *unbelieving* heart contrasts negatively with the faithfulness displayed by Moses and Christ (3:2, 5). In the second unit, the relevant passage is repeated from the scriptural quotation (3:15), while in the third, a series of rhetorical questions affirms the identification of those who failed to enter God's rest, concluding that the reason for this was their unbelief (3:16–19). The section ends with δι᾽ ἀπιστίαν, forming an inclusion with 3:12. The function of this segment in the overall argument is to warn.

The second segment (4:1–5) applies the argument to the addressees. The same words out of which the author drew a warning of failure and curse serve also to reveal a promise (4:1–2). In 4:1, the author points out that a summons or promise to enter remains (καταλειπομένης) and adds, in v. 2, that we have been "evangelized" just as they. In addition, an important word for the book of Hebrews as a whole, πίστις, *faith*, makes the first of its 32 appearances in 4:2 in a significant way.[15] Those for

---

[13]   3:12–19; 4:1–5; 4:6–11 (Attridge, *Hebrews*, 114). Note that this third inclusion takes in v. 11, which is taken by many to be the beginning of an exhortation, vv. 11–13. As Attridge writes, "[s]ome of the difficulty in analyzing the structure of Hebrews is due not to the lack of structural indices, but to their overabundance" (ibid., 16).

[14]   The quoted scripture mentioned "heart" twice (the exhortation not to "harden" the heart, 3:8, and God's assessment that the wilderness generation always erred in its heart, 3:9). "Heart" is understood here as the organ of thought, will and decision, as in Hebrew thought (Hans Walter Wolff, *Anthropologie des Alten Testaments* [5th ed.; München, 1990], 68–90).

[15]   Two-thirds of these uses (24 of 32) are in ch. 11, which is a mirror to this section. Here the wilderness generation serves as a negative example of those who did not receive the promises because of disobedience (ἀπείθεια, 4:6, cf. 3:18), which is related to unbelief (ἀπιστία, 3:12, 19). There, the heroes of faith, although a positive

whom the word was of no benefit have previously been described as having a faithless heart. Here they are said not to have been joined in faith with those who heard. While faithlessness is referred to as a quality of heart, a characteristic one can have, its opposite, faith, is qualified relationally, as the basis of a community in which one can be joined with others. Those with whom they could have been, but failed to be joined are those who *heard*.[16] The text is not explicit about the identity of those who heard. Moses, Joshua and Caleb may have been meant, but since the logic of the argument is that no one has yet entered God's rest, then apparently those who have heard are those who are being addressed.[17] Strikingly, in v. 3, "we" who believe enter the rest. This assurance, expressed in the durative tense, indicative mood (εἰσερχόμεθα), was apparently made possible by the wooden Greek translation of a Hebrew oath repeated here, which literally says "if they enter into my rest."

A connection is made between the oath and the completed works of creation, although the concessive logic of the connection made—καίτοι, "though,"—is not fully clear.[18] The bridge between the experience of the wilderness generation and creation is achieved through the common element of "works," although in the quotation from Ψ 94, the works that are in view are the divine interventions on behalf of the Israelites recounted in the narratives of Exodus and Numbers.

The connection to creation having been made, a further quotation is introduced, with the help of which the concept of God's rest will be

counterpart, also have not yet received the promises and will not without "us" (11:40).

[16] This presupposes a connection between hearing and believing that is also important for Paul (Rom 10:14).

[17] The difficulty of the thought may be the reason for the textual variants in this verse, as well as the variety of connectives in the next verse. See the apparatus of NA[27] and Metzger, *Commentary*, 665–6. Cf. however Michel, who argues for the poorly attested μὴ συγκεκερασμένος τῇ πίστει τοῖς ἀκούσασιν ("the word did not combine itself through faith with the hearers," i.e., the exodus generation) on the grounds that it is theologically unique and found in diverse locales (*Brief*, 193; so also Erich Grässer, *An die Hebräer: 1. Hebr 1–6* [EKK 17/1; Zürich, 1990], 206).

[18] Attridge discusses possibilities and suggests that the meaning is that rest was the sequel of works (*Hebrews*, 130). Grässer understands God's rest as one of the works of creation; that its primeval existence underscores its value, as well as the promissory character of God's word (*Hebräer*, 1:208–9).

redefined (4:4–5): "For in one place it speaks about the seventh day as follows, 'And God rested on the seventh day from all his works.'"(4:4).[19] The off-handed way in which this is done, however, contrasts with the introduction of the Psalm quotation in 3:7.[20] Intuitively, we would expect that words from the Torah, the five books of Moses, would carry great authority, but this expectation is rooted in the inner-Jewish (and Jewish-Samaritan) debates over the extent of scripture and canon. Our author, rooted in Greek–speaking Judaism, has no problem accepting all of the Greek Bible as "scripture" and if he makes a differentiation at all, it is in viewing the Psalm as a prophetic utterance (3:7) through David (4:7) and therefore having a direct immediacy as a divine utterance that a narrative text such as the Genesis creation account does not have.[21]

This impression is reinforced when the subject of the Genesis quotation is identified: περὶ τῆς ἑβδόμης, [concerning the seventh (day)] (4:4). This is a legitimate way of referring to the Sabbath and corresponds to the reference to the day within the quotation (ἐν τῇ ἡμέρα τῇ ἑβδόμῃ).[22] It is interesting however in light of the fact that the related word for "week," ἡ ἑβδομάς, is avoided in the NT in favor of τὸ σάββατον (Luke 18:12) to the point that even in the resurrection accounts, the first day of the week is referred to as ἡ μία σαββάτου or ἡ μία [τῶν] σαββάτων.[23]

---

[19] Καὶ κατέπαυσεν ὁ θεὸς ... ἀπὸ πάντων τῶν ἔργων αὐτοῦ. As Barrett points out, the middle would have been more appropriate. Philo notes this and takes the active literally: "God caused to rest" (*Leg.* 1.6). In Heb 4:8, the active is given its proper meaning, and it may be that Heb understands Gen 2:2 as did Philo: "God prepared a rest for his people" ("The Eschatology of the Epistle to the Hebrews," in *The Background of the New Testament and its Eschatology* [FS C. H. Dodd; ed. W. D. Davies and D. Daube; Cambridge, 1956] 363-93, here 367).

[20] Cf. however 2:6, in which a psalm quotation (Ps 8:5–7) is introduced with the words διεμαρτύρετο δέ πού τις λέγων. Michel points to a combination of scriptural citation from Torah and Ketubim in Heb 7:1–25; such a combination was felt to be especially weighty (*Brief*, 194).

[21] This fits with, and could have helped pave the way for, a view of scripture that did not give primacy to the law but to prophetic utterance as more clearly pointing to the fulfillment of the plan of salvation in Christ.

[22] Cf. ἡ ἑβδομος, Acts 21:27 D; this was Philo's preference for referring to the Sabbath (*Abr.* 28; *Mos.* 2.209, 215, 263).

[23] ἡ μία σαββάτου: 1 Cor 16:2; Mark 16:2 D; ἡ μία [τῶν] σαββάτων: Matt 28:1; Mark 16:2; Luke 24:1; John 20:1, 19; Acts 20:7; 1 Cor 16:2 v.l. Another variant is

Within the quotation, mention is made that God rested from his works, thus connecting two of the terms, ἔργα and κατάπαυσιν, that had been important to the author in the quotation from Ψ 94. The rest in Ψ 94 is that of the land of Canaan, a place of rest. Through a form of argument commonly used in Jewish exegesis, *gezera shawa*, in which a word in one text is explained by its meaning in another, this rest is interpreted as that which God entered after completing the works of creation.[24] The introduction of the notion of God's rest after creation week however redefines the concept.[25] The rest of God is not simply to be equated with possession of the land.[26] Key words from the curse, εἰ εἰσελεύσονται εἰς τὴν κατάπαυσίν μου, form an inclusion with εἰσελθεῖν εἰς τὴν κατάπαυσιν αὐτοῦ in v. 1.

In the third segment (4:6–11, with v. 11 serving both as the conclusion of this segment and the beginning of the exhortation), a conclusion is drawn from the fact that the wilderness generation was refused entry into God's rest (3:11, 4:5), combined with the prophetic call to hear God's

---

πρώτη σαββάτου, Mark 16:9.

[24] The argument works however only in Greek, in which κατάπαυσις is used in both contexts. On *gezera shawa*, one of the seven hermeneutical rules of Hillel, see Günter Stemberger, *Einleitung in Talmud und Midrasch* (München, 1992), 28–29.

[25] Ernst Käsemann saw Philo's discussion of God's rest as the background of its use here (*Das wandernde Gottesvolk: Eine Untersuchung zum Hebräerbrief* [2d ed.; FRLANT 55; Göttingen, 1957], 40–45). The differences between Philo and Heb are outlined by Barrett, "Eschatology," 368–9, 373, 377–8, 387–8. Overview of the discussion in Helmut Feld, *Der Hebräerbrief* (EdF 228; Darmstadt, 1985), 38–42.

[26] George Wesley Buchanan is frequently cited as one who claimed that it was. Yet he too recognized that possession of the land alone was not enough. He interpreted the rest of Heb 3–4 in terms of the promise of rest in the land of Canaan, and posits a meaning for this that is the same as that of Jewish writers of the time (*To the Hebrews: Translation, Comment and Conclusions* [AB 36; Garden City, N. Y., 1972], 64–65. Yet this inheritance is also "heavenly" (ibid., 256, 258) in that it will be an everlasting kingdom of peace, such as Israel had never experienced in their periods of sovereignty (ibid., 73–74, 246–7). As such, his understanding is a corrective of the general tendency of interpreters to understand *rest* spatially (cf. the fact that even Hofius, who rejects so much of Käsemann's position, translates κατάπαυσις as *Ruhestätte*) yet identify it with the heaven that now is. Yet heaven, too, will be shaken (12:26) and rolled up like a cloak (1:10–12). Nevertheless, Buchanan's reading does not fully grasp the effect of the introduction into the argument of the "rest of God" from Gen 2 in Heb 4:2, nor the substitution of *rest* with *Sabbath celebration* in 4:9.

voice today (3:7): it remains for some to enter it (4:6). This is followed
again by an appropriate statement from the quotation of Ψ 94 (4:7). An
inclusion is formed by a reference to entering into it/that rest, εἰσελθεῖν
εἰς αὐτήν/ἐκείνην τὴν κατάπαυσιν as well as by a reference to faithlessness,
δι' ἀπείθεισαν/τῆς ἀπειθείας, thereby echoing and combining both of the
previous inclusions. The inclusions thus created unify the three segments
of the application and underline its main themes. In 4:8, the author takes
the words of David as proof that not even the next generation, which *did*
enter into the land, had entered into God's rest, for "Jesus" (i.e. Joshua,
but this might not have been immediately clear to the listeners) did not
give them rest. The catchword ἀπολείπεται from 4:6 is taken up in the
climatic statement (ἄρα) in 4:9: "So then, a Sabbath celebration still
remains for the people of God."[27] This draws our attention to the use of
σαββατισμός in place of what we have come to expect through its frequent
repetition in this section, God's κατάπαυσις.

Hebrews 4:9 is the only NT occurrence of the word σαββατισμός.[28]
The word is rare, but not obscure. It is a normal construction, making a
noun out of a verb to refer to the activity described by that verb.[29] The
verb σαββατίζω means to *observe* or *celebrate the Sabbath*, so the noun
refers to the observance or celebration of the Sabbath.[30] But the nature of
the Sabbath referred to here is determined by the author's argument
leading up to this statement. It is a figurative expression for entry into
God's rest, itself a metaphor of salvation. At the same time, it redefines
the notion of rest, since it is not simply a synonym. The celebration of the
weekly Sabbath included worship and praise as well as rest.[31]

---

[27] NRSV reads "Sabbath rest." This reflects only one aspect however of what it
meant to observe the Sabbath.

[28] Undue weight should not be placed on this, however, since this is but one of at
least 150 hapax legomenae in Heb (Ceslas Spicq, *L'Épître aux Hébreux* [Paris, 1952],
1:157). More than 90 other words, including κατάπαυσις and καταπεύω, appear in
only one other NT text, usually Luke–Acts.

[29] BDR § 109, 1.

[30] It is used in this sense by Plutarch, *Mor.* 166a, a text in which dependence in
either direction is unlikely, as well as by Justin (*Dial.* 23.3), whose knowledge of Heb
is not demonstrated. Other citations in early Christian literature are probably
influenced by Heb (these are examined by Hofius, *Katapausis*, 104–5).

[31] E.g., *m. Tamid* 7:4, in explaining why Ps 92, a song of praise, is a Sabbath

In v. 10, the catchword *works*, which has been used both to describe God's saving intervention in the wilderness and his creative activity at the dawn of the world, reappears. We are told that those who have entered into God's rest have rested from their own works, as God rested from his own.[32] To enter the rest of God means to no longer depend on one's own achievements. This statement stands in a certain tension to the next, though, which serves both as the conclusion of the third segment of the exposition (catchword ἀπείθεια) and the entire mini-sermon.

(3) Exhortation (4:11–13). The concluding exhortation, "let us strive to enter the rest" seems self-contradictory (v. 11). To strive is normally the opposite of being at rest. Yet the mastery of rhetoric displayed throughout Hebrews leads one to suspect that this paradox was consciously and ironically meant.

The logic of the argument is that God promised that the Israelites would enter his rest. They failed, out of unbelief. It is a consequence of the argument that other people would enter in place of the people who failed.[33] But when we are told that he sets another *day* (4:8), this is surprising, since the failure had nothing to do with a unit of time.[34] On the other hand, the argument is not introduced to justify the practice of worship at a different time than the weekly Sabbath (see below on *Barn.* 15). This other day is *today*, the present experience of the believer.

6.1.2 The Meaning of God's Rest and the Σαββατισμός
The Sabbath celebration for the people of God that remains is presented in parallel to entry into the rest of God, and is both a circumlocution for it and a redefinition of it. This is natural because of the close connection

psalm; see Hofius, *Katapausis*, 108–13.

[32] The comparison to God's own works militates against interpretations of *rest from works* as cessation of evil deeds. An alternative view, that of Bacchiocchi, suffers from reading a Pauline conception of grace and works into the text that is otherwise not indicated (*Sabbath*, 67–68; this is also pointed out by Attridge, *Hebrews*, 131, n. 110).

[33] Cf. the emphatic *we* in 4:2.

[34] Among the acts of disobedient unbelief in the wilderness were violations of the weekly Sabbath (Exod 16; Num 15:32–36), but the author does not single these out. They were part of a general pattern of disobedience.

of the concepts of Sabbath and rest in the OT and in Second Temple Judaism. The rest of God, introduced through scriptural quotation first in connection with the land of Canaan and then with the seventh day of creation week, is said to be open to believers, although no one had previously entered into it. This creates a dissonance with the background of these concepts in Second Temple Judaism, both on the literal and figurative levels. On the literal level, while the exodus generation was refused entry into the land of promise, the next generation did enter, under the leadership of Joshua.[35] Further, weekly Sabbath rest is explicitly tied to divine rest on the seventh day of creation week in the Exodus version of the Ten Commandments (Exod 20:8–11). On the figurative level, Jewish apocalyptic literature knows of the hope "that we may rest with the fathers" (2 Bar. 85:9). Yet repeated loss of sovereignty in the land, tied to failure to properly observe the Sabbath (Jer 17:21–22, 27; Ezek 20:18–24), meant that the assertion made by Hebrews was not totally new.

As the quotation from 2 Baruch indicates, rest is documented as a term for salvation in Second Temple Judaism. This could be expressed either as eschatological rest in a new land or city, or as a place of rest in the heavens.[36]

---

[35]   After the Jerusalem temple had been built and the ark of the covenant installed in it—that is, when the divine presence in Israel had also found its resting place—Solomon pronounced a blessing on Yahweh, "who has given rest to his people Israel according to all that he promised" (1 Kgs 8:56).

[36]   An example of the former is T. Dan 5:12: "the saints shall refresh themselves (ἀναπαύσονται) in Eden; the righteous shall rejoice in the New Jerusalem, which shall be eternally for the glorification of God." The latter idea is expressed in Jos. Asen. 15:7: repentance "prepared a place of rest in the heavens." Hofius examines these and many other texts (Katapausis, 59–74). There are also excurses on the concept of rest in many commentaries on Hebrews. One that combines concise, balanced treatment with ample reference to source materials is Attridge, Hebrews, 126–8. Käsemann saw the references to κατάπαυσις and σαββατισμός in Heb 4 as evidence that its author was aware of speculation an already-traditional Sabbath-hebdomas speculation, particularly as found in Philo, which he characterized as Alexandrian Gnosticism (Gottesvolk, 40–45). In light of this, he saw a heavenly journey of the soul as the central theme of Hebrews. A short summary of the discussion of Käsemann's thesis can be found in Feld, Hebräerbrief, 42–48. An influence in the opposite direction with regard to the κατάπαυσις concept, namely of Heb on later literature such as the gnostic-Christian

It has been suggested, however, that the meaning of *rest* in Hebrews refers to a tranquility that the believer experiences now in his relationship to God.[37] In this case, the promise inherent in *today* would imply a present participation, even though this might not yet be the fulfilment. While *today* is emphasized in this passage, however, it is presented as the time of striving, of taking heed, not yet the time of rest.[38] While the verb *enter* is indeed in the durative tense, this can mean that the addressees are in the process of entering God's rest, and does not mean they have already done so.[39]

There is a parallel thought, via the catchword *enter* (εἰσέρχομαι), with the sanctuary. Jesus has entered the heavenly tabernacle (9:12, 24–25), and in 6:19–20 *hope* follows him into it.[40] Believers now approach God through prayer (4:8–10). This is not insignificant, yet is not the fulfillment. As Craig Koester expressed it, the present time is like the forecourt where people are still at some remove from God (9:8–10).[41] In a similar way, a believing response to a promise of entry into rest affords a certain participation in that rest in this life, without being the fulfilment of it. Another expression for the goal of the believer in Hebrews is a heavenly city, the new Jerusalem (11:8–9). Although a future goal, the addressees are also told "you *have come* . . ." (12:22). This can be seen as paradoxical, in the way that salvation is often expressed in the NT as an interplay of present and future. Hofius, however, who understands the refusal to enter the land against the backdrop of Num 14 rather than the entire wilderness experience, sees in Heb 12:22 an expression of the same

homily *Gos. Truth* is suggested by Wray, *Rest*, 16, 141–2.

[37] Wray, *Rest*, 80. Cf. Barrett: "Christians, though living in this world, have already begun to experience the world to come" ("Eschatology," 365).

[38] This is conceded by Wray, *Rest*, 86.

[39] BDR § 319. Another possibility, suggested by Michel, *Brief*, 194, and C. Koester, *Hebrews*, 270, is that it is used in a future sense (cf. BDR § 323,3). Given the end-time perspective of the text, there is not much to be gained by drawing a clear distinction between present and future.

[40] In addition, the verb is used in 10:5 to express Christ's coming into the world. See also 4:16, where the related verb προσέρχομαι is used in urging the addressees to come to the throne of grace, an alternate expression for the inner sanctuary in the heavenly tabernacle where Jesus now is.

[41] *Hebrews*, 103.

situation: that the people of God "schon an den Toren des himmlischen Jerusalems angelangt ist und nur noch auf das Offenbarwerden der βασιλεία ἀσάλευτος wartet, die zu empfangen sie im Begriff steht."[42] Thus we see the same structure in three metaphors of salvation in Hebrews. The addressees are spoken to as those living in anticipation. To the degree that such an expectation itself represents participation in the awaited goods, one can speak of a present participation in rest for believers. This should be carefully distinguished from the use of rest in the *Gospel of Thomas*, as well as more fully developed gnostic Christian writings such as the *Gospel of Truth*.[43]

To enter into divine rest then is an expression of salvation. Sabbath celebration, used in parallel to the notion of divine rest, is best understood as a metaphor of salvation as well. This concept is paralled in Jewish apocalyptic literature, according to which Sabbath rest is a symbol of the resurrection of the age to come; for this reason, it is improper to mourn for more than six days.[44] Given the use of rest as a soteriological metaphor, it should not surprise us that the world to come was also thought of as a Sabbath in rabbinic Judaism.[45]

In Jewish thought, celebration of the eternal Sabbath is a result of having kept the weekly Sabbath faithfully.[46] This is not mentioned in Hebrews, but could have been a mental association made by the readers.

---

[42] *Katapausis*, 148.

[43] On the concept of rest in gnostic writings, particularly in *Gos. Truth*, see Jan Helderman, *Die Anapausis im Evangelium Veritatis: Eine vergleichende Untersuchung des valentinianisch-gnostischen Heilsgutes der Ruhe im Evangelium Veritatis und in anderen Schriften der Nag-Hammadi-Bibliothek* (NHS 18; Leiden, 1984), supplemented by Wray, *Rest*, 34–49.

[44] "Quia septimo die signum resurrectionis est futuri seculi requies, et in die septimo requievit dominus ab omnibus operibus suis" (*L. A. E.* 51:2–3; ed. Anderson and Stone, 75).

[45] In addition to *Tamid* 7:4, already cited, see *Pirqe R. El.* 18 (9d), according to which God made seven worlds (aeons), six of which are for the coming and going of man, the seventh however is all Sabbath and rest in eternal life; *'Abot R. Nat.* 1: when the righteous sit with their crowns on their heads; *Gen. Rab.* 17:5 (the teaching of R. Hanina about various types: the type of the world to come is the Sabbath).

[46] In the prophets, Sabbath observance is linked to future blessings (Isa 58:13–14; Jer 17:19–27).

Yet there is no similar statement about weekly Sabbath observance in Hebrews. The term "rest" is not used after 4:11, nor is it explicitly connected with other expressions of the goal of the believer. Yet the attentive listener might be expected to retain the metaphor of rest and connect it to the other goals the believer is to enter, the inner chamber of the tabernacle sanctuary and the heavenly Jerusalem. Hebrews explicitly expresses the conviction that the altar service is no longer to be practiced, not because of the destruction of the temple—this is not mentioned—but because in Jesus the ultimate sacrifice had been offered. The reference to *foods* in contrast to *conscience* (9:9) and *grace* (13:9), disparaging references to the purity regulations associated with the sacrificial system, may indicate that the distinctions between meats—an identity marker of Jews in the Roman world—had been relegated to the past for the author. Nor did the designation of the goal of believers as a new city, the heavenly Jerusalem, correspond to an orientation toward the earthly Jerusalem. Based on the understanding that the consecrating suffering of Jesus had occurred "outside the gate," the readers are urged to go "outside the camp"—to turn their backs, as it were—on the earthly Jerusalem, as an expression of their quest of the city that is to come (13:11–13). Based on these parallels, there is no reason to suppose that the author expected his readers to observe the weekly Sabbath as an expression of their hope of entering into the rest of God.

Supporting this conclusion are additional considerations. The *first* Testament/Covenant (the author is aware of the dual reference of διαθήκε) is viewed throughout as superceded and passing away, replaced by one that is new, better, and eternal.[47] The fact that no appeal is made to the Decalogue, in which the Sabbath holds a central place, even when paraenetic exhortation touches on topics that are covered in it, such as adultery and coveting, is significant as well (13:4–5). Note also the previously mentioned use of ἡ ἑβδόμη rather than τὸ σάββατων.

---

[47] See 7:22; 8:6–13; 9:15–20; 12:24; 13:20. This is not only a theological but also an historical judgment. From the perspective of the author, there was no way of knowing that the efforts to consolidate and redefine Judaism after the loss of the temple would be successful (assuming he knew of them, which is not certain).

Beyond this, the overall thrust of the Book of Hebrews should also be considered. The occasion of the letter is the spiritual exhaustion of the addressees (6:12; cf. 5:11). Members are irregular in their attendance when the congregation gathers for worship (10:25). Delay of the expected Parousia led to doubts of the validity of God's promises (10:23, 35–36). The author perceives a danger that they could abandon their faith through neglect (10:35–39). In this wavering condition, the addressees appear to exhibit "nostalgia for the Jewish roots of the Christian proclamation."[48] This does not prove however that they were native Jews; their knowledge of Israelite customs could have arisen from the use of what Christians now refer to as the Old Testament as their scriptures.[49] Additionally, Jews and Judaism were well known in the ancient world and they were met not only with antipathy and rejection, but also with sympathy and curious interest (see above, ch. 2). Therefore, in a situation in which the Greek scriptures were utilized as scriptures, it is not surprising that the customs described therein exercised attraction on Christian readers. This makes it understandable that the Sabbath, an identity marker of Jews and Judaism, is reinterpreted.[50]

Finally, when the listeners are urged to be more faithful in participation in gatherings of the community (10:25), there is no reference when these gatherings took place, neither to the Sabbath nor to the first day of the week.[51] The *today* of which our text speaks is the time between the first and second comings of Christ, not a specific day of the week.

In short, there is no indication that the observance of a weekly Sabbath formed an exception to the general pattern of Hebrews. Whereas in Jewish thought celebration of the eternal Sabbath is the result of having

---

[48] Brown, *Introduction*, 697.

[49] They, like the author, seem to have known them in a Greek version very similar to that known to us as the LXX; see Kenneth J. Thomas, "Old Testament Citations in Hebrews," *NTS* 11 (1964/65): 303–25.

[50] Cf. however Michel: "Der Brief fürchtet nicht einen Rückfall in die Vergangenheit, sondern einen Abfall vom Glauben überhaupt" (*Brief*, 188). If the addressees had not previously been Jews, then it would not be a case of returning to (their) past. For the Exodus generation, one expression of falling away was their desire to return to Egypt (Num 14:4; Acts 7:39).

[51] Michel suggests that they were daily (*Brief*, 188).

kept the weekly Sabbath faithfully, in Hebrews, participation in the world to come is tied to holding fast to the confession of faith (in Christ).

6.1.3 Summary

The reference to σαββατισμός fits in well with the rest of the work. Themes from the OT, especially from the cultic field, are taken up and through a comparison with Jesus Christ newly interpreted and subordinated to him. The Sabbath, and the related concept of rest, though not expressly related to Christ, is no exception.[52] In this writing, adopted into the Christian canon, we have the appropriation of Sabbath celebration as one of a number of metaphors for salvation. This concept was already present in Second Temple Judaism, and could well have been taken over from it by the author. There, however, the idea of participation in the eternal Sabbath, the world to come, is strongly linked to the observance now of the weekly Sabbath. This link may have been present in the minds of the addressees, but no reference to the weekly Sabbath is made. Hebrews subtly claims the language of the Sabbath as a continued way of speaking of salvation while uncoupling it from the notion commonly associated with it, weekly observance of a day.

To elucidate the meaning of the "rest of God," the passage here examined draws on two OT texts, each of which describes one of the two references of the Sabbath in the OT, creation and exodus (see above, ch. 2). The wilderness example is cited as a cautionary example: the word of promise was of no use to them, because it was not combined with faith (3:19).

By repeatedly stressing "my rest" and then, in the climax of the argumentation, substituting for it "a celebration of a Sabbath," the text

---

[52] That the Sabbath and rest are not christologically interpreted is pointed out by Wray, *Rest*, 54. Cf. Matt 11:28–29, where the concept of rest is expressly related to Christ. Jon Laansma claims that Christology is the key to a cluster of ideas summed up in the "today" of 4:7 (*'I Will Give You Rest': The Rest Motif in the New Testament with Special Reference to Mt 11 and Heb 3–4* [WUNT 2/98; Tübingen 1997], 291). The relation he posits between these terms, taken from throughout Hebrews, is however fragile. Although there is no explicit link between rest/Sabbath and Christology, this should not be overemphasized, since in the context of the book as a whole, participation in the world to come is linked to confession of the Son.

attempts nothing less than a redefinition of the Sabbath—an extension of its conventional sense through emphasis on an experience that had long been associated with the concept of weekly Sabbath rest, fellowship with God.

To be fully understood, this has to be seen in the context of the whole of Hebrews, especially in light of the topic of entry into the divine presence, now and future. The causal link between weekly Sabbath observance and entry into the divine Sabbath in the future is broken, confession of Christ taking the place of weekly Sabbath rest.

6.2 THE SABBATH IN THE *EPISTLE OF BARNABAS*

Another early Christian document that seeks to reinterpret the institutions of the religion of Israel for Christianity is that known as *Barnabas*.[53] But whereas the view of Hebrews towards elements of the covenant with Israel never denies the validity of the historical experience of Israel and God's soteriological dealings with them, that of *Barnabas* is ahistorical, viewing the practices of Israel as mistaken or even as result of the influence of an evil angel (9:4). The value of their experience is that it contains τύποι—the word appears at least thirteen times in

---

[53] In addition to this strategy of reinterpretation, *Barn.* shares with Heb a formal similarity: the framework of each is epistolary, while the body shows features of another genre—in the case of *Barn.*, that of treatise. The characterization of Hans Windisch, "eigentlich kein Brief, sondern ein leicht in Briefform gekleideter erbaulicher Traktat," has achieved near-consensus status (*Die Apostolischen Väter 3: Der Barnabasbrief* [HNT-Ergänzungsband; Tübingen, 1920], 411). Although epistolary features are limited to chs. 1 and 21, and lack any indication of author, his location, addressees and their location, or an occasion for writing, these do not prove that the writing was not actually sent (discussion in Reidar Hvalvik, *The Struggle for Scripture and Covenant: The Purpose of the Epistle of Barnabas and Jewish-Christian Competition in the Second Century* [WUNT 2/82; Tübingen, 1996], 72–75). Hvalvik follows the current fashion that applies rhetorical categories to written works and describes *Barn.* as a protreptic letter (*Struggle*, 159). He does not however reflect on the differences between speech and letter, nor the caution with which modern analyses of the characteristics of a given genre should be applied to an ancient text. In addition, given the author's eagerness to dissuade his readers from adopting certain practices, it is a question whether—to remain within the terminology chosen by Hvalvik—it would not be more accurate to label *Barn.* an apotreptic letter.

Barnabas—pointing usually to Christ, but in one case to the future people of God (13:5).[54] In the course of the book, various OT practices are reinterpreted; one of these is the Sabbath. It forms the subject of ch. 15, which we will now examine.[55] After this, we will consider how the teaching of *Barnabas* on the Sabbath fits with the general thrust of this document. The results will then be evaluated to see what they tell us about how some Christians viewed the Sabbath one hundred years after the resurrection.

6.2.1 Examination of Barnabas 15

This chapter can be easily structured into four sections on the basis of textual markers. Verses 1–3 introduce the subject and cite three quotations. These quotations are then interpreted in a second section, vv. 4–5. A further quotation is introduced and interpreted in vv. 6–7, while in a last section, vv. 8–9, the related topic of the eighth day is introduced. Here is the first section, vv. 1–3:

> Furthermore it was written concerning the Sabbath in the ten words which he spake on Mount Sinai face to face to Moses, "Sanctify also the Sabbath of the Lord with pure hands and a pure heart." And in another place he says, "If my sons keep the Sabbath, then I will bestow my mercy upon them." He speaks of the Sabbath at the beginning of the Creation, "And God made in six days the works of his hands and on the seventh day he made an end, and rested in it and sanctified it."[56]

---

[54] Klaus Wengst characterizes this as allegory, rather than typology (*Didache [Apostellehre], Barnabasbrief, Zweiter Klemensbrief, Schrift an Diognet* [Schriften des Urchristentums 2; Darmstadt, 1984], 134; for a more nuanced view, see Hvalvik, *Struggle*, 114–34). The self-evidence with which *Barn.* employs the term τύπος indicates that definitions were still fluid (L. Goppelt, τύπος κτλ, *TWNT* 8:246–60, esp. 253–7). See also the discussion of the use of τύπος in *Barn.* in Ferdinand Rupert Prostmeier, *Der Barnabasbrief* (KAV 8; Göttingen, 1999), 271, n. 41.

[55] Apart from *Barn.*, the lexeme σαββάτων appears only once in the corpus known conventionally as the Apostolic Fathers, in *Did.* 8:1, where it is part of an expression referring to Monday (δευτέρα σαββάτων); the sole relevance of this to the Sabbath question is that this yields additional evidence for the use of the Jewish seven-day week among Christians. The passage under consideration here can therefore be considered as the chief contribution to the Sabbath question in the Apostolic Fathers.

[56] Ἔτι οὖν καὶ περὶ τοῦ σαββάτου γέγραπται ἐν τοῖς δέκα λόγοις, ἐν οἷς ἐλάησεν

In v. 1, the subject of the chapter, the Sabbath, is introduced by the formula ἔτι οὖν καὶ περὶ + genitive. A similar construction occurs in 16:1 to introduce the next subject, the temple, so that ch. 15 forms a unit that is clearly delimited. The chapter opens with a series of three quotations, introduced in turn by γέγραπται, καὶ ἐν ἑτέρῳ λέγει, and λέγει ἐν ἀρχῇ τῆς κτίσεως. The first of these serves to identify scripture as the authoritative basis of the discussion.[57] It is identified as coming from the Decalogue, but it contains wording from Jer 17:22 and Ψ 23:4a (MT Ps 24:4a) as well as from Exod 20:8 or Deut 5:12. Significantly, in light of the further course of the argument, the phrase τὴν ἡμέραν τῶν σαββάτων, found in both versions of the Decalogue as well as in Jer 17:22, is modified to τὸ σάββατον. "Sabbath" here functions as a name for the day, rather than as a characteristic of its content. This is understandable considering the development traced in ch. 2, above, yet given the program of reinterpretation in *Barnabas*, it is worth considering whether this change has to do with the author's intention: the Sabbath must be sanctified, but not necessarily the Sabbath *day*; there is no question of a devaluation of the Sabbath here, though, as the author's addition of the qualification κυρίου, *of the Lord*, shows. Another departure from Decalogue forms of the Sabbath command is the addition of the reference to pure hands and heart from Ψ 23. This may also be occasioned by the author's purpose; in light of what follows, it suggests that the commanded consecration of the Sabbath stands under a condition that God alone can fulfill.[58] The words are identified as having been spoken personally (κατὰ

ἐν τῷ ὄρει Σινᾶ πρὸς Μωϋσῆν κατὰ πρόσωπον· καὶ ἁγιάσατε τὸ σάββατον κυρίου χερσὶν καθαραῖς καὶ καρδίᾳ καθαρᾷ. καὶ ἐν ἑτέρῳ λέγει· ἐὰν φυλάξωσιν οἱ υἱοί μου τὸ σάββατον, τότε ἐπιθήσω τὸ ἔλεός μου ἐπ᾽ αὐτούς. τὸ σάββατον λέγει ἐν ἀρχῇ τῆς κτίσεως· καὶ ἐποίησεν ὁ θεὸς ἐν ἓξ ἡμέραις τὰ ἔργα τῶν χειρῶν αὐτοῦ καὶ συνετέλεσεν ἐν τῇ ἡμέρᾳ τῇ ἑβδόμῃ καὶ κατέπαυσεν ἐν αὐτῇ καὶ ἡγίασεν αὐτήν. English translations are from Lake, LCL. Verses 14:8 and 9 are transposed in ℵ, so that the last half of 14:8, οὕτως λέγει κύριος ὁ λυτρωσάμενός σε, "thus saith the Lord the God who did redeem thee," functions as the opening of the topic "Sabbath"; Prostmeier, *Barnabasbrief*, 474–5.

[57] "Diesem allgemeinen Rekurs zufolge ist die Schrift nicht nur für Juden, sondern nach wie vor auch für Christen unstrittig die autoritative Argumentationsbasis," Prostmeier, *Barnabasbrief*, 478.

[58] Prostmeier, *Barnabasbrief*, 481. There is a modification of the Psalm wording;

πρόσωπον) to Moses on Mount Sinai, but the verb ἁγιάσατε, consecrate, is in second person plural, in keeping with the form in Exodus.[59] The intended audience was then originally all of Israel, but in the context of *Barnabas* should be understood as all Christians (cf. 1:7).

A second quotation follows in v. 2. The idea of keeping the Sabbath comes from Exod 31:16, although there the verb φυλάσσω is in future tense and in *Barnabas* subjunctive, in keeping with the conditional formulation of the sentence. In Exod 31:16, the subject of the verb is the sons of Israel, in *Barn.* 15:2, it is "my sons," a difference that will facilitate the application of the (reinterpreted) Sabbath command to the readers.[60] As in v. 1, the Sabbath is referred to in singular; in Exod 31:16, it is in plural. It is not certain where the promise to place his mercy on them comes from; perhaps Isa 44:3b is in view (ἐπιθήσω το πνεῦμά μου ἐπὶ τὸ σπέρμα σου καὶ τὰς εὐλγίας μου ἐπὶ τὰ τέκνα σου) as well as Isa 56:1–2, where φυλάσσω and τὸ ἔλεός μου occur together.[61] The conditional offer of mercy is not unparalleled in early Christian literature, one need only to remember the Sermon on the Mount (Matt 5:7; cf. 6:12).

The third quotation, v. 3, is from the creation account in Genesis.[62] It contains the first use of the noun *God* in the chapter; he had been the

---

ψ 23:4 qualified the reference to hands with the adjective ἀθῷος, a translation of Heb יָקִנ, "free of guilt."

[59] The expression κατὰ πρόσωπον is especially appropriate with regard to Moses in light of Deut 34:10; Prostmeier, *Barnabasbrief*, 479, n. 12.

[60] א was corrected to "Israel," perhaps to harmonize with Exod 31:16.

[61] Prostmeier, *Barnabasbrief*, 482. Windisch suggests that this is a general summary of Jer 17:25–26 (*Barnabasbrief*, 381); it is hard to see what that might be other than the conditional formulation of the relation between Sabbath observance and salvation. There are a number of statements in *Barn.* identified as quotations by the use of introductory formulae but are not identifiable in any canonical or known non-canonical works (6:13; 7:4, 8; 10:7; 16:6). Windisch proposed the use of a testimony collection (*Barnabasbrief*, 410); a suggestion taken up and extended by Pierre Prigent, *Les Testimonia dans le Christianisme primitif: L'Épître de Barnabé 1–16 et ses sources* [EBib; Paris, 1961]. The use of testimony collection may be the best way to account for some of the anomalous quotations, such as here in 15:2. In other cases, the wording may have been altered for editorial purposes.

[62] The quotation formula may be intended to identify the location; cf. λέγει ἐν ἀρχῇ τῆς κτίσεως and the opening words of Gen. 1:1 LXX: ἐν ἀρχῇ.

implied subject of ἐλάλησεν, v. 1, and ἐπιθῆσω, v. 2. God's activity in creation is expressed through four verbs, all in aorist: ἐποίησεν, *made*, συνετέλεσεν, *completed*, κατέπαυσεν, *rested*, ἡγίασιν, *consecrated*. These all appear in Gen 2:2–3, although in a slightly different order. For the first time, there is specific mention of the seventh *day* (ἡ ἡμέρα ἡ ἑβδόμη); it is perhaps significant that the text does not mention that God blessed the day (cf. Gen 2:3a LXX: καὶ ηὐλόγησεν ὁ θεὸς τὴν ἡμέραν τὴν ἑβδόμην καὶ ἡγίασεν αὐτήν), nevertheless, in the order in which the author arranges the four verbs he does take over, ἡγίασιν comes last, and is therefore emphasized. Against the LXX, but in agreement with the MT, *Barnabas* ascribes the completion to the seventh day.[63] It refers to the entire work of creation, rather than the time of its completion, and appears to be related to the author's decision to take the verb ποιέω from the relative clause in which it appears in Gen 2:2 and place it at the beginning of his series of four verbs.

The second section of the chapter, vv. 4–5, begins in v. 4 with the interpretation of the third of the quotations, introduced by the question τί λέγει τό:

> Notice, children, what is the meaning of "He made an end in six days"? He means this: that the Lord will make an end of everything in six thousand years, for a day with him means a thousand years. And he himself is my witness when he says, "Lo, the day of the Lord shall be as a thousand years." So then, children, in six days, that is, in six thousand years, everything will be completed. "And he rested on the seventh day." This means, when his Son comes he will destroy the time of the wicked one, and will judge the godless, and will change the sun and the moon and the stars, then he will truly rest on the seventh day.[64]

---

[63] The use of the cardinal number ἕξ in place of the ordinal τῇ ἕκτῃ is paralleled in Philo (Prostmeier, *Barnabasbrief*, 485).

[64] προσέχετε, τέκνα, τί λέγει τὸ συνετέλεσεν ἐν ἕξ ἡμέραις· τοῦτο λέγει, ὅτι ἐν ἑξακισχιλίοις ἔτεσιν συντελέσει κύριος τὰ σύμπαντα· ἡ γὰρ ἡμέρα παρ᾽ αὐτῷ σημαίνει χίλια ἔτη. αὐτὸς δέ μοι μαρτυρεῖ λέγων· Ἰδού, ἡμέρα κυρίου ἔσται ὡς χίλια ἔτη. οὐκοῦν, τέκνα, ἐν ἕξ ἡμέραις, ἐν τοῖς ἑξακισχιλίοις ἔτεσιν συντελεσθήσεται τὰ σύμπαντα. Καὶ κατέπαυσεν τῇ ἡμέρᾳ τῇ ἑβδόμη, τοῦτο λέγει· ὅταν ἐλθὼν ὁ υἱὸς αὐτοῦ καταργήσει τὸν καιρὸν τοῦ ἀνόμου καὶ κρινεῖ τοὺς ἀσεβεῖς καὶ ἀλλάξει τὸν ἥλιον καὶ τὴν σελήνην καὶ τοὺς ἀστέρας, τότε καλῶς καταπαύσεται ἐν τῇ ἡμέρᾳ τῇ ἑβδόμη.

The readers are directly addressed for the first time, an additional signal of the transition from citation to interpretation. The term used, τέκνα, *children* (repeated later in the verse), reflects the relationship the author assumes with them (see also 7:1; 9:7: 21:9). He was reluctant to describe himself as a teacher (1:8; 4:9), but functions as one who is able to authoritatively interpret scripture. Finally, the turn to the readers for the purpose of interpretation is introduced with a verb from the domain of teacher/pupil relations, προσέχω, *to pay close attention*, in imperative (see also 7:4, 6, 7, 9; 16:8).

Focus of the interpretation is two of the four verbs from the quotation, συντελέσει and κατέπαυσεται. Both are changed to future tense in the interpretation, although nothing is said about this change. The completion of all things takes on an eschatological dimension not present in Genesis. What follows is a chiliastic reinterpretation of the creation week, using the technique of *gezera shawa* (see above, 6.1.1). For this purpose, a fourth quotation is introduced, from ψ 89:4 (MT Ps 90:4), in which a day by human standards of reckoning is equated with a thousand years in God's sight. A reversal of the terms gives the application an import not present in the original statement; a reflection on the transience of life becomes an equation for converting God-time to human counting methods.[65] *Barnabas* makes the eschatological use of this quotation explicit by the insertion of two terms not present in the LXX, ἔσται, *will be*, and κυρίου, *of the Lord*. The second of these is used to modify ἡμέρα, *day*, creating the phrase used in the OT to denote the day of God's wrathful intervention.[66] This quotation is unlike the first three in function; it serves as proof of his interpretation rather than as the object of his interpretation. The unusual formula by which he introduces it, αὐτὸς δέ μοι μαρτυρεῖ, may be an indication that, whereas he had drawn on traditional collections of quotations concerning the Sabbath for the material in vv. 1–3, this is his own interpretation.[67]

---

[65] Windisch, *Barnabasbrief*, 382. The equation of a day and a thousand years is also documented in Jewish tradition (*Jub.* 4:30), the NT (2 Pet 3:8), and other early Christian writers (Justin, *Dial.* 81.3; Irenaeus, *Haer.* 5.23.2; 28.3).

[66] E.g. Isa 2:12. The replacement of the term θεός with κύριος in the quotation from Genesis (L retained *deus*) is probably in keeping with this.

[67] Klaus Wengst, *Tradition und Theologie des Barnabasbriefes* (AKG 42; Berlin,

Although in the quotation of Gen 2:2 in v. 2 the completion is correlated to the seventh day, in the interpretation, the author reverts to the wording of the LXX; it is mentioned in conjunction with the six days in which God actually worked.[68] Rest is reinterpreted to point to the return of Christ, who is not named here. He is spoken of as "his [God's] son." His coming is correlated to a triad of verbs in future tense pointing to the completion of God's work: καταργέω, "put an end to," κρίνω, "judge," ἀλλάσσω, "change."[69] These verbs correlate to three domains affected by this divine intervention: that of spiritual powers (the time of the lawless one), the human realm (the impious), and the cosmic sphere (the change in sun, moon and stars). It is not said to what they are changed, but variations of this expectation appear frequently in apocalyptic literature.[70] It is not clear whether the Lord (i.e., God) or his Son (Jesus) is the subject of these verbs. Grammatically it would normally be the former. This plus the lack of any verbs that express the positive aspect of the role of the returning Son in the fulfillment of salvation suggest a subordinate role for the Son. When the work of defeating, judging and changing is accomplished, then God can well, or properly (καλῶς) rest on the seventh day, the thousand-year Sabbath (also known from Rev 20:4).

The next step in the argument, vv. 6–7, is formally signalized by the phrase πέρας γέ τοι ("and furthermore"):[71]

> Furthermore he says, "Thou shalt sanctify it with clean hands and a pure heart." If, then, anyone has at present the power to keep holy the day which God made holy, by being pure in heart, we are altogether deceived. See that we

1971), 49.

[68]   Discussion of the difference between MT and LXX above, 2.1.1.

[69]   Subject of the verbs however is God (cf. v. 3) also referred to as the Lord (v. 4). In v. 3, Barn's change of Gen 2:2–3 resulted in the correlation of three verbs to the seventh day; in v. 7, three verbs describe the soteriological activity. This may be intentional (Prostmeier, *Barnabasbrief*, 484). The three verbs are in subj. in H; discussion Prostmeier, *Barnabasbrief*, 475.

[70]   E.g. Joel 2:10; cf. *4 Ezra* 7:39: "for thus shall the Day of Judgment be whereon is neither sun, nor moon, nor stars"; *Jub.* 1:29: at the end of the Jubilees, "all the luminaries (shall) be renewed"; *1 En.* 91:15–17 after the great eternal judgment, "the powers of heaven shall be given seven-fold light." See also *2 Bar.* 59:5; *As. Mos.* 10:5; Mark 13:24–25 par; 2 Pet 3:10–13; Rev 6:12–13; 21:1.

[71]   BDAG s.v. τοι.

shall indeed keep it holy at that time, when we enjoy true rest, when we shall be able to do so because we have been made righteous ourselves and have received the promise, when there is no more sin, but all things have been made new by the Lord: then we shall be able to keep it holy because we ourselves have first been made holy.[72]

In this section, the text takes up again the phrase concerning clean hands and heart with which the first quotation, from the Decalogue, had been expanded. The verb form, however, has been changed from aorist imperative second person plural to future second person singular. While there is a certain interchangeability between imperative and future in both Hebrew and semitically influenced Greek, with the future expressing a stronger command, this change is significant in light of the reinterpretation of the Sabbath as a future, eschatological event. The strategy now is not reinterpretive, but that of showing the impossibility of a literal fulfillment of this by humans. Presuming the human inability of meeting this condition "now"—i.e., in the present age—especially with regard to inner purity, a "pure heart," he claims that the alternative, if it were nonetheless possible, would be that we are completely deceived (ἐν πᾶσιν πεπλανήμεθα). The verb πλανάω, together with the noun πλάνη, is one of the main terms by which the text refers to the failure of the Jews. It is connected especially with their religious observance.[73] The statement that forms the second part of v. 6, εἰ οὖν, ἦν ὁ θεὸς ἡμέραν ἡγίασες, νῦν τις δύναται ἁγιάσαι καθαρὸς ὢν τῇ καρδίᾳ, ἐν πᾶσιν πεπλανήμεθα [If, then,

---

[72] πέρας γέ τοι λέγει· ἁγιάσεις αὐτὴν χερσὶν καθαραῖς καὶ καρδίᾳ καθαρᾷ. εἰ οὖν ἦν ὁ θεὸς ἡμέραν ἡγίασεν, νῦν τις δύναται ἁγιάσαι καθαρὸς ὢν τῇ καρδίᾳ, ἐν πᾶσιν πεπλανήμεθα. ἴδε ὅτι ἄρα τότε καλῶς καταπαυόμενοι ἁγιάσομεν αὐτήν, ὅτε δυνησόμεθα αὐτοὶ δικαιωθέντες καὶ ἀπολαβόντες τὴν ἐπαγγελίαν, μηκέτι οὔσης τῆς ἀνομίας, καινῶν δὲ γεγονότων πάντων ὑπὸ κυρίου· τότε δυνησόμεθα αὐτὴν ἁγιάσαι αὐτοὶ ἁγιασθέντες πρῶτον. Verse 7 is syntactically difficult, with no unity among the manuscripts. Lake's opening of v. 7 is based on a conjectured Gk. text ἴδε ὅτι, reconstructed from *videns ergo* in L. Kraft begins the sentence with a conjectured εἰ δὲ οὐ νῦν (*Épître de Barnabé*, [introd. and comm. by P. Prigent; SC 172; Paris, 1971]). Discussion in Prostmeier, *Barnabasbrief*, 476.

[73] Cf. 16:1: ἔτι δὲ καὶ περὶ τοῦ ναοῦ ἐρῶ ὑμῖν, ὡς πλανώμενοι οἱ ταλαίπωροι εἰς τὴν οἰκοδομὴν ἤλπισαν καὶ οὐκ ἐπὶ τὸν θεὸν αὐτῶν τὸν ποιήσαντα αὐτούς, ὡς ὄντα οἶκον θεοῦ; [I will also speak with you concerning the Temple, and show how the wretched men erred by putting their hope on the building, and not on the God who made them, and is the true house of God]; Hvalvik, *Struggle*, 87.

anyone can now, by being pure in heart, treat as holy the day God declared holy, we are entirely deceived], is reminiscent of 1 John 1:8: ἐὰν εἴπωμεν ὅτι ἁμαρτίαν οὐκ ἔχομεν, ἑαυτοὺς πλανῶμεν καὶ ἡ ἀλέθεια οὐκ ἔστιν ἐν ἡμῖν [If we say that we have no sin, we deceive ourselves, and the truth is not in us]. Yet the differences are telling. In 1 John 1:8, for instance, the conjunctive particle introduces a subordinate clause that is a verbal claim, in aorist subjunctive, εἴπωμεν, whereas in *Barn.* 15:6, it introduces a statement of a possible action, in indicative, δύναται ἁγιάσαι: it can often happen that someone could make the verbal claim to be without sin. The mode in *Barn.* 15:6 is indefinite; it is left open whether anyone can indeed keep the Sabbath now with a clean heart.[74] A second difference is the congruence in person between the subordinate and main clause in 1 John 1:8. In both cases, it is second person plural: whenever *we* say this, *we* err. In *Barn.* 15:6, however, only the verb in the main clause is first person plural; the condition of the subordinate clause applies to an indefinite third person, τις: if *anyone* could keep the Sabbath with a clean heart, *we* err. A final noteworthy difference is that the verb πλάνομαι in *Barn.* 15:6 is in the perfect tense; as if this were not strong enough, it is modified by ἐν πᾶσιν. A more devastating result of the possibility of someone keeping the Sabbath today in a pure heart can hardly be imagined: if it were possible, then the entire basis of Christian preaching would be in error. Either people prior to the coming of Christ had fulfilled the will of God, making the suffering of Christ (to cite the aspect emphasized by *Barnabas*) unnecessary, or they had failed to do what was in their power to do, making redemption impossible.[75] The adverb νῦν does not emphasize the present in contrast to the past, but in contrast to the future, which has been in view since the mention of the return of Christ in v. 5. It refers to the entire present condition of mankind since creation, including the entire experience of Israel in spite of the Ten Words having been personally (κατὰ πρόσωπον) spoken to Moses (v. 1).

[74] Prostmeier identifies ἁγιάσαι as an optative (*Barnabasbrief*, 492), then it would be a potentialis.
[75] See the references to the suffering of Christ in 5:1, 5; 7:2–3, 5.

The motif of human inability to properly keep the Sabbath is not unknown in Jewish thought, but it is never suggested that this is a reason for not keeping it at all.

Following as it does what appears to be the climactic statement in the chapter, v. 7 attempts to tie together the interpretation of all three quotations cited in the first section of the chapter. The condition of clean hands and clean heart, finally being capable of fulfillment, since the time of the lawless one will have come to an end, means that the command to consecrate the Sabbath can be observed by believers in the same way as by God (v. 5 τότε καλῶς καταπαύσεται; v. 7 τότε καλῶς καταπαυόμενοι).[76] Pictured however is not the periodic weekly observance of a Sabbath day in the messianic age (foreseen in Isa 66:22–23, for instance), the Sabbath itself having been reinterpreted in vv. 4–5 to mean that age itself. It is that age that the justified will consecrate. The middle quotation of the three (v. 2) was not touched on in the explanation of vv. 4–7, but is implicitly included. Believers having been made holy, having become capable of fulfilling the first half of the quotation, of observing the Sabbath, will then be the sons on whom the mercy of God can remain.[77]

The phrase πέρας γέ τοι returns in v. 8, signaling another argumentative step (vv. 8–9), although it would seem that all issues raised by the three quotations in vv. 1–3 have been settled:

> Furthermore he says to them, "Your new moons and Sabbaths I cannot away with." Do you see what he means? The present Sabbaths are not acceptable to me, but that which I have made, in which I will give rest to all things and make the beginning of an eighth day, that is, the beginning of another world. Wherefore we also celebrate with gladness the eighth day in which Jesus also arose from the dead, and was made manifest, and ascended into Heaven.[78]

---

[76] There is parallelism with v. 5; in addition to the reference to proper rest on the Sabbath, there are parallels in the end of lawlessness and the change in the universe. But the parallelism is incomplete: there is now no reference to the judgment of the impious. In view now are solely the saved, those who have been made righteous and have received the promises.

[77] There is an unresolved tension between this thought and references to believers already being a new creation (6:11–16; 16:8).

[78] πέρας γέ τοι λέγει αὐτοῖς· Τὰς νεομηνίας ὑμῶν καὶ τὰ σάββατα οὐκ ἀνέχομαι. ὁρᾶτε, πῶς λέγει; οὐ τὰ νῦν σάββατα ἐμοὶ δεκτά, ἀλλὰ ὃ πεποίηκα, ἐν ᾧ καταπαύσας τὰ πάντα ἀρχὴν ἡμέρας ὀγδόης ποιήσω, ὅ ἐστιν ἄλλου κόσμου ἀρχήν. διὸ καὶ ἄγομεν

Encountering the Rest of God

Instead of additional explanation, *Barnabas* offers one more quotation, the most negative statement in the entire OT about the Sabbath, Isa 1:13b.[79] The use of a negative statement about the Sabbath shows that the author is not imposing an interpretation that is unprecedented.[80] The exegesis that follows, introduced by a phrase reflecting again the teacher/pupil relationship between the author and his readers (ὁρᾶτε, πῶς λέγει), is dual. First, it seems to repeat and confirm what has already been said: the Sabbaths (and new moons, not otherwise treated in this chapter, there being no discernable connection between the reference to the change of sun, moon and stars and the rejection of Sabbath and new moons) of the present (i.e. of the Jews, as λέγει αὐτοῖς makes clear) are not acceptable to God. Following the logic of *Barnabas*, they could not have been, since it was impossible to meet the condition of clean hands and heart. Instead, another day will be set that can be pleasing to God. But instead of the coming seventh thousand-year messianic age, we hear of an eighth day, the beginning of another world. Jewish eschatology featured both seven-day and eight-day outlines of the plan of God; *Barnabas* appears to adhere to an eight-day scheme.[81] The Sabbath age in which God, at the coming of his son, puts down sin and lawlessness, and even effects astronomical change, normally associated with the new world, is not yet the new world, but apparently the preparation for it.[82]

τὴν ἡμέραν τὴν ὀγδόην εἰς εὐφροσύνην, ἐν ᾗ καὶ ὁ Ἰησοῦς ἀνέστη ἐκ νεκρῶν καὶ φανερωθεὶς ἀνέβη εἰς οὐρανούς.

[79] This had already been cited in *Barn.* 2:5 as part of the scriptural proof for rejection of the sacrifices.

[80] A similar strategy is used in the interpretation of fasting (ch. 3).

[81] Details in Hofius, *Katapausis*, 114.

[82] Cf. Rev 21:1, 23 for astronomical change correlated to the time after the messianic age. The tension created by correlating astronomical change with the seventh day, but then speaking of the eighth as signifying the new world, has led some to suggest that these are the same in *Barn.*'s scheme (e.g. Prostmeier, *Barnabasbrief*, 496–9). Speaking for these proposals is the lack of clear differentiation in the purpose of the eighth, as opposed to the seventh day. Both are times of salvation, of the fulfillment of God's promises. In light of a 400-year messianic age in *4 Ezra* 7 it is interesting that *Barn.* does not specifically say that the messianic age will last one thousand years and the new world, the eighth day, will begin after that time, but in light of his application of Ps 90:4 (Ψ 89:4), this is a logical assumption. Admittedly, the equation of a day for a thousand years breaks down when one speaks of the final

The distinction seems to be indicated by the two forms of ποιέω in v. 8. The eschatological Sabbath has already been created by God (πεποίηκα). In that time, having brought the universe to rest, he will prepare (ποιήσω) the eighth day, the new world.

The tension between the seventh and eighth day is one of the difficulties that led to suggestions that there have been interpolations in the chapter.[83] The author does not seek to outline an eschatological chronology but to encourage knowledge and obedience in his readers in the present. Barrett's conclusion is apt: "The only point that is really clear is the only point that *Barnabas* wanted to make: the Jews with their sabbaths are in the wrong, the Christians with their sabbaths are in the right."[84]

In v. 9, we come to the last point: for this reason (διό), the author and his readers observe the eighth day, i.e., the day after the seventh day of the week, our Sunday. This is done out of allegiance to the new, post-messianic age. This is the first recorded use in Christian literature of the verb ἄγω in combination with the eighth, or first, day.[85] It is also a day for

day, whether the seventh or eighth day, since it is pictured as the world without end. Nevertheless, to combine the seventh and eighth days in *Barn.*'s eschatological scheme would undermine his own justification for observing the eighth, rather than the seventh, day; cf. Windisch: "Dennoch bleibt bestehen, dass der Anfang der neuen Welt 1000 Jahre später angesetzt ist als der in 5" (*Barnabasbrief*, 383). At any rate, there are difficulties with both readings, as Prostmeier admits (*Barnabasbrief*, 498–9).

[83]   Windisch judged that vv. 8–9 were either subsequently interpolated or taken from another document (*Barnabasbrief*, 383). Survey and critique of interpolation theories in James Carleton Paget, *The Epistle of Barnabas: Outlook and Background* (WUNT 2/64; Tübingen, 1994), 72–78. A somewhat different solution is proposed by Wengst, who posits successive stages in the development of the material in ch. 15, although he attributes all of it to the author of *Barn.* (*Tradition*, 51). This theory does not resolve the tension between the seventh and eighth days.

[84]   "Eschatology," 320. Barrett's conclusion can be supplemented by the formal observation that temporal aspects are treated in all three "paratexts": in ch. 1, he writes that the lord (δεσπότης) has, through prophets, given us knowledge of the past and present, as well as a foretaste of future things (1:7). In the transitional material, however, he seems to indicate that he has limited his exposition to things past, since present and future things are hidden in riddles, and so cannot be understood by his readers (17:2).

[85]   See Prostmeier on the use of ἄγω to denote the ritual observance of the Sabbath and other occasions, *Barnabasbrief*, 500, n. 114.

rejoicing, as the Sabbath was for Jews. Not only the mention of the eighth day in a context that rejects literal Sabbath observance, but also the use of terminology traditionally associated with the Sabbath documents that within the time period chosen for this investigation, the hundred or so years between the resurrection and the Bar Kokhba uprising, we have record of some Christians, at least, adapting the language of Sabbath observance and applying it to the eighth day. They can be seen not only as observing that day but doing so consciously in place of the Sabbath.

On the other hand, the author does not use the verb ἁγιάζω, "consecrate." If humans are unable in this age to consecrate the seventh day, why should they be able to consecrate the eighth? Therefore, we do not yet have a full transfer of Sabbath teaching to Sunday. It is not yet a Christian Sabbath.

The reference to the eighth day is expanded (ἐν ᾗ) through reference—again a triad—to the resurrection, appearance and ascension of Jesus, who is mentioned for the first time in this chapter.[86] The writer apparently conceives of all three events occurring on the same day of the week.[87] The significance of this is dual. On the one hand, this is the first mention of the resurrection events in conjunction with the practice of the observance of the day. The resurrection accounts in the Synoptics make no reference to the disciples observing the day, with the possible exception of the consecutive Sunday evening appearances in John; yet even the latter falls short of making an explicit connection (see above, 5.5.3). On the other, this is not stated as the primary reason for Sunday observance.[88] Nor is it mentioned to explain the change from Sabbath to Sunday.

6.2.2 The Sabbath in the Context of the Epistle of Barnabas

Our understanding of the teaching of *Barnabas* on the Sabbath and the eighth day can be deepened by considering both its formal placement

---

[86] There are 21 uses overall in *Barn.*, all of them in the first major section, chs. 2–16.

[87] Luke 24:51; Mark 16:9; *Gos. Pet.* 13:56. See Prostmeier for references to this tradition in early Christian literature, *Barnabasbrief*, 500–01, n. 118.

[88] William H. Shea characterizes it as an afterthought ("The Sabbath in the Epistle of Barnabas," *AUSS* 4 [1966]: 149–75, here 172).

within the overall structure of the book and its relation to its purpose. The main body is a treatise in two sections of unequal length, separated by a transition (17:1–18:1).[89] The first section is devoted to the reinterpretation of OT practices, while the second contains a version of the two ways teaching. The Sabbath is the next to last subject treated, with the mention of the temple being the last (ch. 16). It shares the introductory phrase καὶ περὶ + genitive with ch. 16. This has the dual effect of tying both of these chapters to the previous material, chs. 2–14, yet also setting them apart.[90] The reason for the placement of the material concerning the temple appears related to its relevance at the time of composition. It is apparently the only reference to a contemporary event outside of the world of the text.[91]

---

[89]   For centuries, the only version known was that of L, which only contains the first 17 chapters. Not long after the discovery of the first complete copy of *Barn.*, in א, 1859, the first copy of Didache, which also contained the two ways teaching, was discovered, in H, 1873. The first assumption was that *Barn.* 19–20 was appended as an epilogue to *Barn.* The unity of the work is now generally accepted (dissent: Leslie William Barnard, "The 'Epistle of Barnabas' and its Contemporary Setting," *ANRW* 27.1:159–207). The author clearly divides his work into two parts, with the two ways teaching representing a different kind of knowledge and teaching (ἑτέραν γνῶσιν καὶ διδαχήν).

[90]   Prostmeier, *Barnabasbrief*, 476.

[91]   There is no agreement, however, on the meaning of this reference. Suggestions that it refers to Roman permission to rebuild the Jewish Temple (e.g., Barnard, "Epistle" *ANRW* 27.1:174–5) suffer from the legendary nature of such reports. Many scholars prefer to see here a reference to the construction of a Jupiter temple on the site, commanded by Hadrian in 130 C.E. (e.g. Wengst, *Didache*, 115). Speaking against this is the verb "rebuild" (ἀνοικοδομέω, 16:4); this is not insurmountable, given the near-equation the text makes of pagan and Jewish rites (16:2). If this is the reference, then the letter can be dated to a period of two years between Hadrian's command and the outbreak of the Bar Kokhba revolt. Since this cannot be proven, it is perhaps preferable not to be more precise than Harnack: "dass unser Brief an den Schluss des Zeitraumes 80–130 zu rücken ist" (*Geschichte der altchristlichen Litteratur bis Eusebius. 2/1: Die Chronologie der Litteratur bis Irenäus nebst einleitenden Untersuchungen* [Leipzig, 1897], 418). The reference to the ten kings of Daniel (4:3–5) is sometimes used in dating *Barn.* (e.g. J. B. Lightfoot, *The Apostolic Fathers: A Revised Text with Introduction, Notes, Dissertation and Translations* [London, 1890], 240–01, followed by Simon Tugwell, *The Apostolic Fathers* [Outstanding Christian Thinkers; London, 1989], 29–30). This disregards the nature of apocalyptic thought, which readily adapts after each new disconfirmation by finding new ways in which a

There are three passages to which special attention must be paid in posing the question of the purpose of this writing: the opening and closing chapters (1, 21) and the transition between the two main sections (17:1–18:1). The present state of the readers is that they are spirit-filled believers (1:3b: ὅτι ἀληθῶς βλέπω ἐν ὑμῖν ἐκκεχυμένον ἀπὸ τοῦ πλουσίου τῆς πηγῆς κυρίου πνεῦμα ἐφ᾽ ὑμᾶς).[92] The author writes to perfect their knowledge (1:5d: ἵνα μετὰ τῆς πίστεως ὑμῶν τελείαν ἔχητε τὴν γνῶσιν).[93] But his purpose is not exhausted in better knowledge, nor is the work an expression of Gnosticism. It is good to walk according to all of the ordinances of the Lord; on this the outcome of life depends, either glorification in the Kingdom of God or destruction (21:1). What they need, and why the author writes, is the faithful fulfillment, as long as one is in the flesh, of every commandment.[94] This movement from knowledge to performance is reflected in the two halves of the letter, both characterized as knowledge and teaching (18:1: γνῶσιν καὶ διδαχήν).

Windisch, writing at a time when the opinion of Harnack that church and synagogue had parted ways so completely that there was no contemporary contact was widely accepted, saw no concrete occasion.[95] Early

---

prophecy can be fulfilled. Such explanations only work in reverse: when we know the date of writing, then we can attempt to understand how the author saw the ten kings and little horn. Discussion in Hvalvik, *Struggle*, 25–32.

[92] "Because I truly see in you that the Spirit has been poured out upon you from the Lord, who is rich in his bounty."

[93] "That your knowledge may be perfected along with your faith."

[94] 21:8–9a: ἕως ἔτι τὸ καλὸν σκεῦός ἐστιν μεθ᾽ ὑμῶν, μὴ ἐλλείπητε μηδενὶ ἑαυτῶν, ἀλλὰ συνεχῶς ἐκζητεῖτε ταῦτα καὶ ἀναπληροῦτε πᾶσαν ἐντολήν· ἔστιν γὰρ ἄξια. διὸ μᾶλλον ἐσπούδασα γράψαι, ἀφ᾽ ὧν ἠδυνήθην [While the fair vessel is with you (i.e., while you are in the body) fail not in any of them, but seek these things diligently, and fulfill every commandment; for these things are worthy. Wherefore, I was the more zealous to write to you of my ability, to give you gladness]. This is sometimes characterised as a legalistic teaching of works righteousness (e.g. Wengst, *Didache*, 136), but caution must be exercised. While obedience to τὰ δικαιώματα κυρίου is constitutive for salvation, there are no "degrees" of salvation pictured, but a strict alternative, glorification or destruction. The passion of Jesus opened the way to forgiveness of sins and the possibility for believers to inherit the covenant/testament.

[95] "Ein aktueller Anlass konnte nicht entdeckt werden" (*Barnabasbrief*, 411). Harnack's view can be consulted, for instance, in *Geschichte*, 415–6. A significant exception to the consensus opinion was Eduard Schwartz, "Osterbetrachtungen,"

Christian *Adversus Judaeos* literature in general was not seen as written because of contemporary threat from Judaism; anti-Jewishness was academic, theoretical, at the service of inner-Christian doctrinal debate. A newer generation of scholars, working under the influence of the paradigm shift effected by Marcel Simon, has sought to read *Barnabas* as a document reflecting rivalry between Synagogue and Church for converts among Gentile sympathizers.[96]

There is little in the letter that can help decide between these alternatives. Appeal is made to the emphasis on the ritual practices, all admittedly found in Scripture, but the "selection of topics seems to indicate that the author takes into consideration Judaism as a living religion: they all belong to the hallmarks of Judaism, the rites and institutions most typical of the Jews."[97] To formulate the terms of the debate so categorically—either Scripture or contemporary, lived Judaism—is needlessly dualistic. These hallmarks had already been traditional for centuries, and could well have been part of inherited discourse on Jews.

The text refers to the Jews as *them*, ἐκεῖνος, in contrast to *us*.[98] They are introduced in 2:9 without further explanation; the author expects the readers will know who is being referred to. For Hvalvik, this is an indication that the author and readers were well-acquainted with Jews.[99] They may well have been, but perhaps only as figures of rhetoric. Alternatively, the motif *them* could have been well-known whenever OT and those who followed its practices (ancient Israel) were referred to. What the text allows us to say is that it portrays Judaizing and or Judaism as a real threat. Whether this was because of inherited discourse of past battles or an actual danger facing its readers is difficult to determine. There is no evidence the addressees had begun to observe the Sabbath; the

---

(1906); repr. *Gesammelte Schriften* 5:1–41, here 12–13.

[96] Marcel Simon, *Verus Israel: A Study of the Relations between Christians and Jews in the Roman Empire (AD 135–425)* (trans. H. McKeating; Oxford, 1986; repr. London, 1996); two works written from this point of view are Carleton Paget, *Epistle*; Hvalvik, *Struggle*.

[97] Hvalvik, *Struggle*, 94.

[98] See 2:9–10; 3:6; 4:6–7; 8:7; 10:12; 13:1, 3; 14:5.

[99] *Struggle*, 87.

tone adopted by the author suggests that he may have expected his readers to be ambivalent toward his message.[100]

A related question is that of whether the author perceives the danger as being a Torah-observant Christianity, or conversion to Judaism per se. Two statements in particular are relevant. *Barnabas* 3:6 is sometimes read as a warning to its readers against becoming proselytes to Judaism.[101] Yet the warning is only against conversion to "their law" (. . . ἵνα μὴ προσρησσώμεθα ὡς ἐπήλυτοι τῷ ἐκείνων νόμῳ).[102] In 4:6 there is invective against those who claim that *their* covenant is *ours* as well (προσέχειν νῦν ἑαυτοῖς καὶ μὴ ὁμοιοῦσθαί τισιν ἐπισωρεύοντας ταῖς ἁμαρτίαις ὑμῶν λέγοντας, ὅτι ἡ διαθήκη ἐκείνων καὶ ἡμῶν).[103] This seems to envision a situation—untenable for *Barnabas*—in which two groups share the heritage of the same covenant. These observations point in the direction of an inner-Christian debate over the extent of usage of OT practices, rather than conversion to Judaism. It has been noted that the position of *Barnabas* is more extreme than that of the eventual mainstream, and that its polemic could be directed against any Christian teachers who saw validity in Israel's history, and assumed that the Christian faith had a certain continuity with it.[104] Yet aside from the insistence that there is one covenant rather than two, there seems no evidence for this. The practices that *Barnabas* reinterprets (food laws, sacrifices including the ritual for the Day of Atonement, Sabbath) are practices that were commonly seen in the early church as evidence of what they called judaizing.

The discussion of the Sabbath was introduced with a quotation identified as belonging to the Ten Commandments. These are for

---

[100] Although the author clearly is a teacher, he denies acting as one: "I will show you a few things, not as a teacher, but as one of yourselves" (1:8; see also 4:9). Meanwhile, he flatters his audience (1:2–3). The combination is reminiscent of rhetorical rules prescribed for a situation in which the audience is ambivalent toward the speaker (Hvalvik, *Struggle*, 52–53).

[101] On the basis of *we* in 14:5 and 16:7, it can be assumed that both author and readers were Gentile Christians (discussion in Hvalvik, *Struggle*, 45–46).

[102] ". . . that we should not be shipwrecked by conversion to their law."

[103] ". . . take heed to yourselves now, and be not made like some, heaping up your sins and saying that the covenant is both theirs and ours." The ending of 4:6 is badly corrupted. Most scholars use L to reconstruct what the Gk. text could have been.

[104] Wengst, *Didache*, 113.

Barnabas the key demands of the covenant. The covenant, in turn, is a central concept for *Barnabas*, as the root of all of the other distinctive teachings. There is only one covenant, spoken by God to Moses, lost by Israel forever through idolatry before it was even practiced, which led to the smashing of the tablets (4:7–8). Their observance was not that intended by God, but was a mistaken, physical practice. *Barnabas* reinterprets these physical practices, as the extreme Jewish allegorists known to Philo had done, showing that their true intent was moral; this moral intent is then binding on those to whom *Barnabas* is addressed, the people of the inheritance, those who have received the one and only covenant through the one who inherited it, Christ (14:4–5).

Finally, there is a certain symmetry in the subordinationist Christology reflected in ch. 15 and the subordination of the Christological explanation *Barnabas* offers for Sunday observance, the connection to the resurrection appearances.

6.2.3 The Significance of the Results for This Investigation

The question of the relation of Israel and the church, as well as the appropriate validity of the scriptures claimed by both, occupied the minds of many, with a variety of models proposed, ranging from that of the Torah-faithful mission opposed by Paul in Galatia to Marcion's dismissal of the OT as the work of a lesser god, not the Father of Jesus. *Barnabas* stands out as offering a radical, consistent solution, especially to the question of the applicability of the law. While many post-NT writers sought to differentiate between a moral and a ritual code, with the former retaining its validity for believers in Christ, *Barnabas* focuses primarily on the ritual aspects of the law and reinterprets them through the use of allegory so that even they are revealed as placing moral demands on the believer. In this, it had forerunners within Judaism and in Christianity.[105] Yet by rejecting the practical application of these laws as mistaken and/or demon-inspired, he denies the validity of Israel's historical experience and seeks to end the awkward situation whereby the same set of scriptures was

---

[105] Judaism: Aristeas and Philo on food laws, cf. *Barn.* 10:9. In both cases, however, continued literal observance is presumed (Hvalvik, *Struggle*, 120–22). Christianity: Paul on circumcision, cf. *Barn.* 9:5.

shared by two groups emerging as arch-rivals, even as mutual enemies. This thrust makes *Barnabas* an uncomfortable book for Christians to read in light of the Holocaust, so that while suggestions abound that the *Gospel of Thomas* or other writings should be added to the Christian canon, there are no serious suggestions that *Barnabas* should join them. Yet this should not blind us to the fact that *Barnabas*'s program offered an ingenious solution to a specific issue that dogged all efforts to distinguish between a ritual and moral law within the Torah, namely that of the Sabbath. For when Christians sought to define which specific aspects of the law retained validity, they commonly looked to the Decalogue, either first or, more commonly, after the love commands invoked by Jesus. Yet the Sabbath poses an obstacle to all attempts to ground moral law in the Decalogue, since this supposedly ceremonial matter occupies a central position in it. *Barnabas* meets this issue head on, by citing the Decalogue at the beginning of its discussion (v. 1).[106] It then adopts two strategies to fit the Sabbath into his overall conception of an enduring moral law behind the ritual demands given to Israel. First, it reinterprets the Sabbath as the messianic age at the close of six thousand years of human history. Until that time, neither God nor humankind could truly rest. Secondly, though, and in some tension to his first solution, the author shows that he and his readers kept the eighth day as a conscious counterpart of the Sabbath. Thus the teaching that Sunday is in some way a Christian Sabbath has roots that extend back to the early second century.

The thoroughgoing emphasis *Barnabas* places on observance of a morally reinterpreted law has led at times to a characterization of this writing as legalistic, or teaching works righteousness. The treatment of the Sabbath question must relativize this judgment. The Sabbath must indeed be observed, in its reinterpreted sense of the consecration of the entire Messianic age, but this is only possible for those whom God has justified and consecrated. The initiative remains God's. In the meantime, God and

---

[106] Prostmeier notes that the author of *Barn.* is the only Christian writer of the second century who mentions this (*Barnabasbrief*, 479). Others apparently chose to avoid an obvious but inconvenient fact.

humans share in an unusual fellowship: neither are able to properly rest until the return of the Son.

Barnabas is a remarkable achievement in its inner consistency, but exposed to serious weaknesses in dialogue with other positions. For example, in its assumption that the meaning or import of ἁγιάζω, *to consecrate*, remains unchanged whether the subject is God or man. Or in the insertion of "clean hands and clean heart" into the wording of the commandment and then using that as the criterion of whether the Sabbath can be kept at all in a way pleasing to God.[107] The force of the argument is blunt—it can only serve to dissuade non-Jews from Sabbath observance. It would be useless in dialogue with Jews themselves. Another example is the logical inconsistency of assuming that problems he diagnoses in Sabbath observance are solved by observance of a different day. One might also point to its use of the free admission in Jewish thought that Sabbaths kept in this age are not kept perfectly, but are merely an image of the world to come. Yet this is not seen by those who admit this as a reason not to keep it at all. Aside from the assumption that if God commanded it, it was possible to obey in a way pleasing to him, there is the attractive thought that present-day Sabbath observance—to the degree that it is realized—brings a proleptic participation in the rest of the world to come.

To the specific issues regarding ch. 15 can be added the overall untenability of the attempt to take over the entirety of the scriptures, and the covenant (or testament) as exclusive property of Christians. This might help to explain why, despite its widespread popularity in the second and third centuries and its apostolic ascription, it did not become part of the canon.

At the same time, it reveals something about Christian claims: faith in Christ makes possible a complete moral regeneration not available through the religious practices of Israel. This is reflected in the moral earnestness of the entire letter—but precisely with regard to the Sabbath, it reveals itself as something that cannot be achieved in this life.

---

[107] A "clean heart" in Judaism was not the result of perfect behavior, but of confession, restitution, and forgiveness.

An analogue in Paul is the road to Damascus. His visionary confrontation with the ascended Jesus brought with it the recognition that if God
identified with the one crucified, then the system God had given did not
work. Others may have concluded that Jesus was the fulfilment to which
the whole dispensation had pointed, but Paul questioned the system. After
all, the connivance of Jewish leaders in the death of Jesus meant that those
who were putatively responsible for "correct" observance had helped
bring about the death of the Son of God. If that were so, then the system
Paul had zealously lived by and defended was flawed.

6.2.4 Summary

The treatment of the Sabbath in *Barnabas* is consistent with its handling
of the OT law and Jewish customs in general: it is only in light of the
coming of Christ that it can be correctly understood. Yet it differs in that
it offers no moral interpretation for the present-day life of believers,
which it consistently does with regard to all other topics. This difference
is all the more remarkable, since a possible alternative—the eighth
day—was available, and even mentioned in context. The refusal of the
text to make this association is nevertheless consistent with its overall
approach, since the celebration of the eighth day was also a practice, not
a moral issue. Nevertheless, although it is late in the period I am
examining, and based on an understanding of the covenants not accepted
by the mainstream, *Barnabas* does provide evidence of emerging Sunday
observance. Important for the development of Sunday worship is that it
does *not* transfer the notion of consecration from the seventh to the
eighth day.

6.3 THE SABBATH IN THE *GOSPEL OF THOMAS*

The *Gospel of Thomas*, which has been the object of more interest, both
scholarly and popular, than all the rest of the writings found near Nag
Hammadi in Upper Egypt, refers to the Sabbath in one logion, the twenty-
seventh of the 114 logia into which *Thomas* is conventionally divided:[108]

---

[108] Numbering system introduced in the editio princeps, *Evangelium nach Thomas:
Koptischer Text herausgegeben und übersetzt*, (ed. A. Guillaumont, et al.; Leiden,

"If you do not fast as regards to the world, you will not find the kingdom. If you do not observe the Sabbath as a Sabbath, you will not see the father."[109]

The public fascination with this collection of sayings in which Jesus speaks in a voice simultaneously strange and familiar corresponds to the scholarly controversies over the nature of these sayings and their relation to the NT.[110] Since there is no consensus on the question of whether *Thomas* represents an independent line of tradition or whether it was from its earliest formulation a secondary work derived from the Synoptics, nor in the question of the location of its general theological position, it is important to begin with an examination of the text itself. Then the individual saying can be read in light of *Thomas* as a whole, which in turn must be read as a theological document in its own right before seeing it in relation to either the Synoptic tradition or Gnosticism. The dictum that its independent or secondary nature can only be decided on the basis of

1959); simultaneous editions in Dutch, English and French, a Spanish edition followed in 1981. The codex ms. does not have a numbering system. The work takes its name from its colophon, ΠΕΥΑΓΓΕΛΙΟΝΠΚΑΤΑΘΩΜΑϹ, the *Gospel of Thomas*. Note however that the incipit designates the work as a collection of sayings: ΝΑΕΙ ΝΕ Ν̄ϢΑΧΕ ΕΘΗΠ, "These are the secret sayings . . ."; cf. James M. Robinson, "LOGOI SOPHON: On the Gattung of Q," in idem and H. Koester, *Trajectories through Early Christianity* (Philadelphia, 1971), 71–113, esp. 76–80. The story of the discovery in December 1945 of thirteen leather-bound codices, containing more than fifty works in whole or in part, has been assiduously pieced together by Robinson and reported by him in a number of publications, e.g. "The Discovery of the Nag Hammadi Codices," *BA* 42, 1979, 206–24, which is generously illustrated with maps, diagrams and photos.

[109] Translation by Thomas O. Lambdin in *Nag Hammadi Codex II,2–7 together with XIII.2*, Brit. Lib. Or. 4926 (1), and P. Oxy. 1, 654, 655*, (B. Layton, ed.; NHS 20; Leiden, 1989), 65. Coptic text (with conjectured reconstructions in pointed brackets): <ΠΕΧΕ Ι̅Ϲ̅ ΧΕ>ΕΤΕ<ΤΝ>ΤΜ̄ΡΝΗϹΤΕΥΕ ΕΠΚΟϹΜΟϹ ΤΕΤΝΑϨΕ ΑΝ ϹΤΜΝ̄ΤΕΡΟ ΕΤΕΤΝ̄ ΤΜ̄ΕΙ ΡΕ Μ̄ΠϹΑΜΒΑΤΟΝΝ̄ϹΑΒΒΑΤΟΝΝ̄ΤΕΤΝΑΝΑΥ ΑΝ ΕΠΕΙ ΩΤ (ibid., 64). All Coptic texts and translations in this section are taken from this critical edition, although, apart from brackets, critical sigla will be omitted.

[110] For an expression of a non-theologian's reading of *Gos. Thom.*, see Harold Bloom, "A Reading," in Marvin W. Meyer, *The Gospel of Thomas: The Hidden Sayings of Jesus* (San Francisco, 1992), 111–21. For the main lines of scholarly debate, see Francis T. Fallon and Ron Cameron, "The Gospel of Thomas: A Forschungsbericht and Analysis," *ANRW* 25.6:4195–251, supplemented by Gregory J. Riley, "The *Gospel of Thomas* in Recent Scholarship," *CurBS* 2 (1994): 227–52.

careful examination of the individual sayings in context of the collection as a whole is axiomatic for NT exegesis, but must be explicitly stated with regard to *Thomas*.[111] This is because of the invitation to the reader to find the hidden meaning of the sayings: "And he said, 'Whoever finds the interpretation of these sayings will not experience death'" (log. 1).[112] Yet support for the application of the usual methods of biblical study can be found as well: "Jesus said, 'Recognize what is in your sight, and that which is hidden from you will become plain to you. For there is nothing hidden which will not become manifest'" (log. 5).[113]

Happily, this saying also is known to us in Greek from the Oxyrhynchus papyri.[114] This examination will proceed primarily on the basis of the Greek text as the earliest recovered form of the saying.[115]

---

[111] The order of steps outlined reverses that proposed by Ernst Haenchen, *Die Botschaft des Thomas-Evangeliums* (TBT 6; Berlin, 1961), 37–38. Haenchen's goal however was to determine the degree to which *Gos. Thom.* is a gnostic document, whereas the present investigation seeks to determine what the saying examined here reveals about how the Sabbath was viewed in this early Christian text.

[112] ⲀⲨⲰ ⲠⲈⲬⲀϤ ⲬⲈ ⲠⲈⲦⲀ2Ⲉ ⲈⲐⲈⲢⲘⲎⲚⲈⲒⲀ ⲚⲚⲈⲈⲒϢⲀ ⲬⲈ ϤⲚⲀⲬⲒ †ⲠⲈ ⲀⲚ ⲘⲠⲘⲞⲨ; cf. P. Oxy. 654, 3–5: καὶ εἶπεν· [ὃς ἂν τὴν ἑρμηνεί]αν τῶν λόγων τούτ[ων εὕρη, θανάτου] οὐ μὴ γεύσηται. The thought has its roots in the wisdom tradition; cf. Prov. 3:1–2: "My child, do not forget my teaching, but let your heart keep my commandments; for length of days and years of life and abundant welfare they will give you." It has a parallel in the Johannine tradition (e.g., John 8:52: ". . . Whoever keeps my word will never taste death"). *To keep* and *to understand* are variants in the wisdom tradition, so that it is not possible to say which formulation is more traditional.

[113] ⲠⲈⲬⲈ ⲒⲤ ⲤⲞⲨⲰⲚ ⲠⲈⲦⲘⲠⲘⲦⲞ ⲘⲠⲈⲔ2Ⲟ ⲈⲂⲞⲖ ⲀⲨⲰ ⲠⲈⲐⲎⲠ ⲈⲢⲞⲔ ϤⲚⲀϬⲰⲖⲠ ⲈⲂⲞⲖ ⲚⲀⲔ ⲘⲚ ⲖⲀⲀⲨ ⲄⲀⲢ ⲈϤ2ⲎⲠ ⲈϤⲚⲀⲞⲨⲰⲚ2 ⲈⲂⲞⲖ ⲀⲚ; cf. P. Oxy. 654, 27–31: λέγει Ἰη(σοῦ)ς· γ[νῶθι τὸ ὂν ἔμπροσ]θεν τῆς ὄψεώς σου, καὶ [τὸ κεκαλυμμένον] ἀπό σου ἀποκαλυπφ<θ>ήσετ[αί σοι· οὐ γάρ ἐσ]τιν κρυπτὸν ὃ οὐ φανε[ρὸν γενέσεται], καὶ τεθαμμένον ὃ ο[ὐκ ἐγερθέσεται].

[114] λέγει Ἰ(ησοῦ)ς· ἐὰν μὴ νηστεύσηται τὸν κόσμον, οὐ μὴ εὕρηται τὴν βασιλείαν τοῦ θ(εο)ῦ· καὶ ἐὰν μὴ σαββατίσητε τὸ σάββατον, οὐκ ὄψεσθε τὸ(ν) π(ατέ)ρα (P. Oxy. 1, verso, lines 4–11; Harold W. Attridge, "The Greek Fragments," in *Nag Hammadi Codex II,2–7*, 118). The papyrus uses contracted forms of Ἰεσοῦς, θεός, and πατήρ in a way known from biblical manuscripts. The *nu* at the end of line 10 is suppressed, represented by a supralinear letter, as is usually the case in P. Oxy. 1 (Attridge, "Fragments," 97). On the relationship of the P. Oxy. fragments to the Coptic translation, see Attridge, "Fragments," 99–101.

[115] There is no guarantee that the Greek versions are closest to the original.

6.3.1 Examination of Logion 27 in Greek and Coptic

The elements of this logion may once have been separate sayings, but this is not documented.[116] In the form in which we have them, they are arranged in *parallelismus membrorum*, reminiscent of Hebrew poetry, and can therefore be treated as a unit. It will have to be determined whether the parallelism involved is synonymous or synthetic in the course of the investigation.[117] "To find the kingdom of God" is set in parallel with "to see the father."[118] Before consulting the rest of *Thomas* it appears that these are both expressions of the goal of human existence, metaphors for salvation. Fasting from the world and "sabbatizing the Sabbath" appear then as conditions for achieving the goal of salvation.

Fasting, an ascetic practice of going without food, is known in many cultures, including Israel. But here it is used metaphorically; instead of food, one is to fast from the world.[119] Ascetic behavior of some sort with regard to the world is presented as a condition for reaching the goal of salvation, here expressed as finding the Kingdom of God. The juxtaposition of κόσμος and βασιλεία suggests that they are two contrasting realms.

It is clear that the act of Sabbath observance is meant as a parallel practice to that of fasting, but there has been no consensus on the concrete meaning of the expression. Since it is introduced in parallel to fasting, it is likely that the negative aspect of Sabbath observance, refraining from work, is in view here, rather than the more positive aspects such as celebration. Some see in these words "a strong admonition

[116] For the suggestion that these were once separate, see Jacques-É. Ménard, who points to the καί introducing the second statement (*L'Évangile selon Thomas* [NHS 5; Leiden, 1975], 120).

[117] Since each phrase introduced with the negative of the conditional (ἐὰν μή . . . οὐ μή / καὶ ἐὰν μή . . . οὐκ), it is unlikely that an antithetic parallelism is meant.

[118] The Coptic translation omits "of God" from the reference to the Kingdom.

[119] Τὸν κόσμον: accusative of respect, instead of the more usual genitive. This unusual construction is retained in the Coptic: ⲉⲧⲉ<ⲧⲛ̄>ⲧⲙ̄ⲣ̄ⲛⲏⲥⲧⲉⲩⲉ ⲉⲡⲕⲟⲥⲙⲟⲥ. The construction is not unusual in Coptic, however, since the preposition ⲉ can also introduce the object after a verb of separation (Antoine Guillaumont, "ΝΗΣΤΕΥΕΙΝ ΤΟΝ ΚΟΣΜΟΝ [*P. Oxy. 1*, verso, 1.5–6]," BIFAO 61 [1962]: 15–23, here 17). Guillaumont suggests the Greek is a translator's mistake from Aramaic, while Ménard sees in it the influence of Syriac (*L'Évangile*, 120).

to keep the Jewish Sabbath law."[120] Others observe that it unlikely that a reference to a literal practice would follow in parallel to a figurative usage.[121] Among the possibilities suggested have been to correlate the reference to Sabbath to the sayings referring to rest in *Thomas*, to view *Sabbath* as alternative term for world, or to see in this reference an appeal for the sanctification of the whole week or of one's entire life. These will be discussed below.

In the Coptic version, rather than the combination of verb and noun, the noun CABBATON, Sabbath, in repeated and combined with the verb *to make*. In one case, it is spelled CAMBATON, in the other CABBATON, but this may be because the second instance occurs at a line break.[122]

6.3.2 Exploration of the Old Testament Background

The combination of fasting and Sabbath observance may have its background in two OT contexts. The phrase σαββατίσητε τὸ σάββατον,

---

[120] April D. De Conick, *Seek to See Him: Ascent and Vision Mysticism in the Gospel of Thomas* (SVigChr 33; Leiden, 1996), 129. De Conick's reading, according to which the Thomasine Christians observed the Sabbath as "a weekly celebration for them of their return to Paradise and the sinless condition of the First Man" is based on an understanding that the Sabbath occurred before the fall (*Seek*, 135). This is certainly the view in Genesis. In the absence of reflection in *Gos. Thom.* about the origin of sin and the timing of the fall, it is impossible to determine, however, whether *Gos. Thom.* shares this view, or the alternate ("gnostic") view that the physical creation *was* the fall. If the latter, then the connection of Sabbath and creation takes on another, negative view. Gilles Quispel assigns this logion to his conjectured Jewish-Christian source behind *Gos. Thom.* ("The *Gospel of Thomas* Revisited," *Colloque International sur les Textes de Nag Hammadi, Québec, 22–25 août 1978* [B. Barc, ed.; BCHN 1; Québec, 1981], 218–66, here 243). This logion illustrates the difficulty of Quispel's theory, since he also posits a (separate) encratite source, to which a reference to fasting, such as that contained in logion 27, could also belong.

[121] E.g., Adolf Harnack, *Über die jüngst entdeckten Sprüche Jesu [B. P. Grenfell and A. S. Hunt, ΛΟΓΙΑ ΙΗΣΟΥ, Sayings of Our Lord from an Early Greek Papyrus, London 1897]*, Freiburg, 1897, 8–9.

[122] CABBATON is not found frequently in the NHC, nor does it figure prominently in descriptions of gnostic systems in early heresiologies. Other instances in NHC are *Gos. Phil.* 8, (NHC II,3); *Gos. Truth* 32:18, 24 (NHC I,3); *Interp. Know.* 11:18, 31, 33 (NHC XI,1); and *Ap. John* 11:34–35 par. (NHC II,1). See Tjitze Baarda, "The Sabbath in the Parable of the Shepherd, *Evangelium Veritatis 32:18–34*," in *Essays on the Diatessaron*, 133–45, here 133.

literally, to "sabbatize" the Sabbath, is similar to two phrases in the LXX, although σάββατον appears in singular, whereas it appears in plural in the two LXX occurrences.[123] Leviticus 23:32 concerns Yom Kippur, the Day of Atonement, the one day in the year when fasting was commanded by the Torah: σάββατα σαββάτων ἔσται ὑμῖν, καὶ ταπεινώσετε τὰς ψυχὰς ὑμῶν· ἀπὸ ἐνάτης τοῦ μηνὸς ἀπὸ ἑσπέρας ἕως ἑσπέρας σαββατιεῖτε τὰ σάββατα ὑμῶν [It shall be to you a Sabbath of Sabbaths, and you shall deny yourselves; on the ninth day of the month, from evening to evening you shall keep your Sabbath].[124] The phrase σαββατιεῖτε τὰ σάββατα ὑμῶν is, apart from the plural form of the noun, a literal translation of the Hebrew תִּשְׁבְּתוּ שַׁבַּתְּכֶם. This is one of the limited number of places in which the translators of the LXX understood the Hebrew verb שָׁבַת in its secondary meaning of *celebrate (a Sabbath)* rather than in its basic meaning of *to stop, to come to an end.*[125] The phrase is not used in connection with any other of the festivals of Israel, but only for this day, a day of fasting.

The second context that combines fasting and Sabbath observance is Isa 58. In a disquisition on fasting, a prophetic indictment is made against a practice described by its outward manifestations ("to bow down the head like a bulrush, and to lie in sackcloth and ashes," v. 5), yet it is accompanied by a contentious attitude (v. 4): "Look, you fast only to

---

[123] On the use of σάββατα when a single Sabbath is meant see n. 24 in ch. 4, above. In addition, the verb in Lev 23:32 LXX is in future indicative, which is typical in place of imperative for OT-influenced Greek (BDR § 362), whereas in P. Oxy. 1, it is in conjunctive, which is normal in Koine Greek for a negatively formulated expectation introduced by ἐὰν μή (BDR § 376).

[124] The other occurrence of the phrase, 2 Chron 36:21, is not concerned with an observance of the weekly Sabbath by humans. It appears after the account of the fall of Jerusalem and refers to the fallow state of the abandoned land as a forced land Sabbath: τὰ σάββατα σαββατίσαι. On the institution of land Sabbath, see Exod 23:10–13; Lev 25:1–7; cf. Deut 15:1, in which the sabbatical year is understood as a year of release from debt and indentured service. Not to be overlooked however is the role assigned to improper Sabbath observance, or lack of it, in leading to the fall of Jerusalem and the deportation of its inhabitants (e.g. Ezek 20:18–24; Neh 13:15–18). The failure to practice agricultural sabbatical years would be seen then as a parallel phenomenon, and the fallow state of the land an ironic means of compensation.

[125] E. Haag, שָׁבַת, *šābat*, *ThWAT* 7:1040–46, here 1046.

quarrel and to fight and to strike with a wicked fist." This is contrasted with works of social justice, the practice of which is accompanied with a promise of divine favor (vv. 8–12). A briefer but similarly structured saying about the Sabbath follows, connected by the catchword חֵפֶץ (vv. 3, 13), which denotes *that in which one takes pleasure* or, as in this case, *an interest*.[126] It refers to the personal cares and concerns that prevented the addressees from sincere fasting and Sabbath observance (vv. 13–14):

> If you refrain from trampling the Sabbath,
> from pursuing your own interests on my holy day;
> if you call the Sabbath a delight
> and the holy day of the LORD honorable;
> if you honor it, not going your own ways,
> serving your own interests, or pursuing your own affairs;
> then you shall take delight in the LORD,
> and I will make you ride upon the heights of the earth;
> I will feed you with the heritage of your ancestor Jacob,
> for the mouth of the LORD has spoken.

As we have seen, Yom Kippur was an annual Sabbath on which fasting was commanded and might be in the background of the combination of these two themes in Isa 58, but there is no express reference to this.[127]

While there is no promise of a *visio dei* in Isa 58, as in *Gos. Thom.* 27—the phrase "seeing the father" is not found in the OT, nor is "finding the kingdom"—we do find "true" fasting and Sabbath observance, as opposed to that which is merely outward, correlated in one context as conditions for divine guidance, favor and presence (vv. 8–10, 14).[128]

6.3.3 The Sabbath in the Context of the Gospel of Thomas
Until now, the primary object of investigation has been the Greek form of the saying, with the Coptic version consulted for comparison. The next

---

[126] In v. 3, it is related to seeking the will of God (G. J. Botterweck, חָפֵץ, *ḥāpeṣ*, חֵפֶץ, *ḥepaeṣ*, *ThWAT* 3:100–16, here106–7), whereas in v. 13 the things in which the addressees take their pleasure are their normal pursuits, i.e., their business.

[127] This text is postexilic, by which time Judeans observed additional communal fasts to commemorate national disasters.

[128] The connection between proper (i.e. heartfelt) Sabbath observance and divine favor or salvation is also made in Jer 17:21–27, Ezek 20:18–24. On the Jewish linkage of Sabbath observance and participation in the world to come, see above, 6.1.2.

step—situating the logion in context of the entire document—requires that we draw on the fourth century Coptic manuscript. Paleographic analysis indicates that roughly 150 years lie between the two. While the two versions of the saying concerning the Sabbath differ little (the primary difference being that the noun Sabbath is repeated, rather than the noun and verb combination in Greek), other parallels between the papyri and the NHC show that we can not be sure whether in the subsequent two centuries sayings have been added or deleted, or whether the language has been modified either in the direction of harmonization with the canonical gospels (which demonstrably happened among the canonical gospels themselves) or in the direction of a more pronounced gnostic interpretation.[129]

Logion 27 contains several key terms for the *Gospel of Thomas* as a whole. The nouns ⲕⲟⲥⲙⲟⲥ (world), ⲙⲛ̄ⲧⲉⲣⲟ (kingdom), and ⲉⲓⲱⲧ (father) are each used more than a dozen times, as are the verbs ⲍⲉ (fall, find) and ⲛⲁⲩ (see). The verb ⲛⲏⲥⲧⲉⲩⲉ (fast) appears less frequently, but its other

---

[129] Wolfgang Schrage's comparison of *Gos. Thom.* with the various Coptic translations of the NT, widely criticized for methodological weakness that did not support the conclusions that he had hoped to draw, did at least demonstrate linguistic affinities that could indicate assimilation (*Das Verhältnis des Thomas-Evangeliums zur synoptischen Tradition und zu den koptischen Evangelienübersetzungen. Zugleich ein Beitrag zur gnostischen Synoptikerdeutung* [BZNW 29; Berlin, 1964]). One indication of modification that may have been motivated by gnostic concerns appears in the saying under examination here, which has *kingdom* instead of *kingdom of God*, as in P. Oxy. 1. The Coptic version generally avoids *God* as designation of the supreme being, preferring terms like *father* (e.g. log. 27) or *the living one* (log. 59). God (ⲛⲟⲩⲧⲉ) appears in only two sayings. Both have synoptic parallels, but show distinctive differences. In log. 30 (// Matt 18:20), the promise of Jesus's presence reads in part "[w]hen there are three gods, they are gods" (ⲡⲙⲁ ⲉⲩⲛ̄ ϣⲟⲙⲧ ⲛ̄ⲛⲟⲩⲧⲉ ⲙ̄ⲙⲁⲩ ⲍⲛ̄ⲛⲟⲩⲧⲉ ⲛⲉ). It is uncertain whether this reading is the result of a deliberate change or a verbal error. The Greek P. Oxy. 1 is badly damaged at this point, and the conjectured reconstructions vary (Attridge in *Nag Hammadi Codex II, 2–7*, 67). In log. 100, the response of Jesus to a question about taxation (// Mark 12:13–17 par.) concludes "and give me what is mine" (ⲁⲩⲱ ⲡⲉⲧⲉ ⲡⲱⲉⲓ ⲧⲉ ⲙⲁⲧⲛ̄ⲛⲁⲉⲓϥ), making God, in effect, the middle term between Caesar and Jesus, which could imply that Jesus is greater. The combination of limited usage of the term, combined with the ambivalent usage in its two appearances, suggests that for the Copic translator, ⲛⲟⲩⲧⲉ refers to a divine being, but not to the supreme being.

uses contrast significantly with this. The exception is the term ⲤⲀⲂⲂⲀⲦⲞⲚ (Sabbath), which appears only in this saying. While the other terms are reappear in various combinations and with a complex and subtle range of meaning, reflecting their importance in the overall message, the topic of Sabbath is conspicuous by its single usage.

Beyond statistics of word usage, a look at how these terms are used may cast light on the interpretation of this saying. We have already noted the apposite contrast of cosmos and kingdom in this saying. In *Thomas* as a whole, the cosmos, or world, is that from which the disciple should maintain distance. In log. 21, a saying about guarding one's house against the expected coming of a thief, known to us from the Synoptics, becomes a specific warning to be on guard against the world as that which can enter to steal one's goods.[130] The nature of those goods becomes clear when we reconsider log. 27: the discovery of the kingdom was not possible without an abstention from the world; if the world is nevertheless able to break in "the house of his domain" (ⲘⲚ̄ⲦⲈⲢⲞ, translated *kingdom* in log. 27), those goods, the knowledge of the kingdom, can be lost.

A contrast to the discovery of the kingdom in log. 27 is offered in log. 110, which calls on those who have found the world and become rich to turn around and renounce it.[131] It has been questioned whether this saying presents the world as something evil. An alternative reading is

---

[130] Log. 21 is a cluster with at least three elements. It is not possible here to analyze all of them and their possible interrelation. The part to which reference is made here appears as the middle element, between a saying about children in a field that is not theirs and one about that refers to the quick harvesting of ripe grain: ⲀⲓⲀ ⲦⲞⲨⲦⲞ †ⲭⲱ Ⲙ̄ⲘⲞⲤ ⲬⲈ ⲈϤϢⲀⲈⲓⲘⲈ Ⲛ̄Ⳡⲓ ⲠⲬⲈⲤⲂ̄ⲚⲎⲈⲓ ⲬⲈ ϤⲚⲎⲨ Ⲛ̄Ⳡⲓ ⲠⲢⲈϤⲬⲓⲞⲨⲈ ϤⲚⲀⲢⲞⲈⲓⲤ ⲈⲘⲠⲀⲦⲈϤ Ⲉⲓ Ⲛ̄ϤⲦⲘ̄ⲔⲀⲀϤ ⲈϢⲞⲬⲦ Ⲉ2ⲞⲨⲚ ⲈⲠⲈϤⲎⲈⲓ Ⲛ̄ⲦⲈ ⲦⲈϤ ⲘⲚ̄ⲦⲈⲢⲞ ⲈⲦⲢⲈϤϤⲓ Ⲛ̄ⲚⲈϤ ⲤⲔⲈⲨⲞⲤ Ⲛ̄ⲦⲰⲦⲚ̄ ⲆⲈ ⲢⲞⲈⲓⲤ 2Ⲁ ⲦⲈ2Ⲏ Ⲙ̄ⲠⲔⲞⲤⲘⲞⲤ ⲘⲞⲨⲢ Ⲙ̄ⲘⲰⲦⲚ̄ ⲈⲬⲚ̄ⲚⲈⲦⲚ̄†ⲠⲈ 2Ⲛ̄ⲚⲞⲨⲚⲞϬ Ⲛ̄ⲀⲨⲚⲀⲘⲓ ϢⲓⲚⲀ ⲬⲈ ⲚⲈ ⲚⲀ2ⲤⲦⲎⲤ 2Ⲉ Ⲉ2ⲓⲎ ⲈⲈⲓ ϢⲀⲢⲰⲦⲚ̄ ⲈⲠⲈⲓ ⲦⲈⲭⲢⲈⲓⲀ ⲈⲦⲈⲦⲚ̄ϬⲰϢⲦ ⲈⲂⲞⲖ 2ⲎⲦⳠ̄ ⲤⲈⲚⲀ2Ⲉ ⲈⲢⲞⲤ [Therefore I say, if the owner of a house knows that the thief is coming, he will begin his vigil before he comes and will not let him dig through into his house of his domain to carry away his goods. You (pl.), then, be on your guard against the world. Arm yourselves with great strength lest the robbers find a way to come to you, for the difficulty which you expect will (surely) materialize].

[131] Log. 110: ⲠⲈⲬⲈ Ⲓ̄Ⲥ̄ ⲬⲈ ⲠⲈⲚⲦⲀ2ϬⲓⲚⲈⳡ Ⲙ̄Ⲡ̄ⲠⲔⲞⲤⲘⲞⲤ Ⲛ̄ϤⲢ̄ Ⲡ̄ⲘⲘⲀⲞ ⲘⲀⲢⲈϤⲀⲠⲚⲀ Ⲙ̄ⲠⲔⲞⲤⲘⲞⲤ [Jesus said, "Whoever finds the world and becomes rich, let him renounce the world"].

offered, according to which the point is the necessity of grasping its limited value at the right moment.[132] Yet even on this reading, according to which the discovery of the world and the discovery of the self are seen as successive, complementary processes of knowledge, the world is not assigned a positive quality in *Thomas*. Instead, recognition of the true nature of the world leads to the insight that it is dead and destined to decay.[133]

At the same time, though set in set in opposition to the world, *Thomas* denies that the kingdom is confined to the hereafter: "His disciples said to him, 'When will the kingdom come?' <Jesus said,> 'It will not come by waiting for it. It will not be a matter of saying "Here it is" or "There it is." Rather, the kingdom of the father is spread out upon the earth, and men do not see it.'"[134]

---

[132] So Thomas Zöckler: "Man mag an der Welt teilnehmen, durch sie hindurch-gehen, am Ende jedoch, wenn das an Erfolg und Gewinn in ihr Mögliche ausgeschöpft ist, gilt es über sie hinauszugehen" (*Jesu Lehren im Thomasevangelium* [NHS 47; Leiden, 1999], 114). See also Antti Marjanen, who classifies the relevant sayings in a three-fold scheme, finding there are some that refer to the world with a positive connotation, others that make the world a stage for soteriological events and actions, and finally some that consider the world worthless and threatening. The closest correlate for this conception is in his estimation that of the Johannine writings. Both speak relatively little of the creation of the world. In neither of these writings is the relation of God as creator and the evil character of the world reflected. The question of whether their views of the world are gnostic depends on the definition of *gnostic*. There is no distinction between a good, eternal God and a perishable, malevolent creator, as in two other texts used for comparison, *Gos. Phil.* and *Apoc. John*. If however the fact that a writing regards the world as evil and as being in opposition to the divine realm makes its conception of the world gnostic, then both *Gos. Thom.* and John are. Marjanen situates the view shared by them as having moved from the view of Jewish wisdom tradition toward a gnostic conception ("Is *Thomas* a Gnostic Gospel?" in *Thomas at the Crossroads: Essays on the Gospel of Thomas* [ed. R. Uro; SNTW; Edinburgh, 1998], 107–39).

[133] Cf. log. 56: ΠΕΧΕ Ι͞C ΧΕ ΠΕΤΑ2ϹΟΥⲰΝΠΚΟϹΜΟϹ ΑϤ2Ε ΕΥΠΤⲰΜΑ ΑΥⲰ ΠΕΝΤΑ22ΕΕ ΑΠΤⲰΜΑ ΠΚΟϹΜΟϹ Μ͞ΠⲰϢΑ Μ͞ΜΟϤ ΑΝ [Jesus said, "Whoever has come to understand the world has found (only) a corpse, and whoever has found a corpse is superior to the world"].

[134] Log. 113: ΠΕΧΑΥ ΝΑΥ Ν͞GΙ ΝΕϤΜΑΘΗΤΗϹ ΧΕ ΤΜΝ͞ΤΕΡΟ ΕϹΝ͞ΝΗΥ Ϯ Ν̄ΑϢ Ν̄2ΟΟΥ <ΠΕΧΕ Ι͞C ΧΕ> ΕϹΝ͞ΝΗΥ ΑΝ 2Ν̄ ΟΥ2ⲰϢΤ ΕΒΟΛ ΕΥΝΑΧΟΟϹ ΑΝ ΧΕ ΕΙ Ϲ2ΗΗΤΕ Μ͞ΠΙ ϹΑ Η ΕΙ Ϲ2ΗΗΤΕ ΤΗ ΑΛΛΑ ΤΜΝ͞ΤΕΡΟ Μ͞ΠΕΙⲰΤ ΕϹΠΟΡⲰ ΕΒΟΛ 2Ι Χ͞Μ ΠΚΑ2 ΑΥⲰ Ρ͞ΡⲰΜΕ ΝΑΥ ΑΝ ΕΡΟϹ.

The presence of the kingdom is emphasized in *Thomas* from the outset: "Jesus said, 'If those who lead you say to you, "See, the kingdom is in the sky," then the birds of the sky will precede you. If they say to you, "It is in the sea," then the fish will precede you. Rather, the kingdom is inside of you, and it is outside of you.'"[135] In contrast to the negative correlation of cosmos and kingdom in log. 27, the parallelism according to which this saying is constructed relates the discovery of the kingdom positively to the *visio dei*. Just as with regard to the kingdom, this vision of the father is accomplished, if at all, in this lifetime: "Jesus said, 'Take heed of the living one while you are alive, lest you die and seek to see him and be unable to do so.'"[136]

In log. 3, cited above, when the kingdom is found, it is in and around the seeker. Connected to that is mutual recognition: "When you come to know yourselves, then you will become known, and you will realize that it is you who are the sons of the living father."[137]

Therefore, the ideas of finding the kingdom and seeing the father, although joined in Jewish and Christian eschatology as well, are more tightly interrelated in *Thomas*. They are in turn connected to the self-

---

[135] Log. 3:1–3: ΠΕΧΕ ΙC ΧΕ ΕΥϢΑΧΟΟC ΝΗΤΝ ΝϬ ΝΕΤ CⲰK 2ΗΤ ΤΗΥΤΝ ΧΕ ΕΙ C2ΗΗΤΕ ΕΤ ΜΝΤΕΡΟ 2Ν ΤΠΕ ΕΕΙ Ε Ν2ΑΛΗΤ ΝΑΡ ϢΟΡΠ ΕΡⲰΤΗ ΝΤΕ ΤΠΕ ΕΥϢΑΝΧΟΟC ΝΗΤΝ ΧΕ C2Ν ΘΑΛΑCCΑ ΕΕΙ Ε ΝΤΒΤ ΝΑΡ ϢΟΡΠ ΕΡⲰΤΝ ΑΛΛΑ ΤΜΝΤΕΡΟ CΜΠΕΤΝ2ΟΥΝ ΑΥⲰ CΜΠΕΤΝΒΑΛ. Cf. P. Oxy. 654,9–16: λέγει Ἰ[η(σοῦ)ς· ἐὰν] οἱ ἕλκοντες ἡμᾶς [εἴπωσιν ὑμῖν· ἰδοὺ] ἡ βασιλεία ἐς οὐραν[ῷ, ὑμᾶς φθήσεται] τὰ πετεινὰ τοῦ οὐρ[ανοῦ· ἐὰν δεἴπωσιν ὅ]τι ὑπὸ τὴν γῆν ἐστ[ιν, εἰσελεύσονται] οἱ ἰχθύες τῆς θαλά[σσης προφθάσαν]τες ὑμᾶς· καὶ ἡ βασ[ιλεία τοῦ θεοῦ ἐντὸς ὑμῶν [ἐσ]τι [κἀκτὸς]. See also log. 77, in which the ubiquity of Jesus is expressed (wood/stone). On the eschatology of *Gos. Thom.*, Zöckler detects a tension comparable to that evident in the NT. Yet instead of the "now" / "not yet" tension seen there, that found in *Gos. Thom.* is best described as "always has been" / "now" (*Lehre*, 178–80).

[136] Log. 59: ΠΕΧΕ ΙC ΧΕ ϬⲰϢΤ ΝCΑ ΠΕΤΟΝ2 2ⲰC ΕΤΕΤΝΟΝ2 2Ι ΝΑ ΧΕ ΝΕΤΜΜΟΥ ΑΥⲰ ΝΤΕΤΝϢΙΝΕ ΕΝΑΥ ΕΡΟϤ ΑΥⲰ ΤΕΤΝΑϢϬΜ 2ΟΜ ΑΝ ΕΝΑΥ.

[137] Log. 3:4–5: 2ΟΤΑΝ ΕΤΕΤΝϢΑΝCΟΥⲰΝ ΤΗΥΤΝ ΤΟΤΕ CΕΝΑCΟΥⲰ(Ν) ΤΗΝΕ ΑΥⲰ ΤΕΤΝΑΕΙΜΕ ϪΕ ΝΤⲰΤΝ ΠΕ ΝϢΗΡΕ ΜΠΕΙⲰΤ ΕΤΟΝ2 ΕϢⲰΠΕ ΔΕ ΤΕΤΝΑCΟΥⲰΝ ΤΗΥΤΝ ΑΝ ΕΕΙΕ ΤΕΤΝϢΟΟΠ 2Ν ΟΥΜΝΤ2ΗΚΕ ΑΥⲰ ΝΤⲰΤΝ ΠΕ ΤΜΝΤ2ΗΚΕ. Cf. P. Oxy. 654, 16–21: [ὃς ἂν ἑαυτὸν] γνῷ, ταύτην εὑρή[σει, καὶ ὅτε ὑμεῖς] ἑαυτοὺς γνώσεσθαι[ι, εἴσεσθε ὅτι υἱοί] ἐστε ὑμεῖς τοῦ πατρὸς τοῦ ζ[ῶντος· εἰ δὲ μὴ] γνώσ(εσ)θε ἑαυτοὺς, ἐν [τῇ πτωχείᾳ ἐστὲ] καὶ ὑμεῖς ἐστε ἡ πτω[χεία]. On the mutuality of being known in *Gos. Thom.*, see Zöckler, *Lehre*, 175–8.

recognition that is another, important aspect of the soteriology of this gospel.

In log. 6 fasting appears first in a list of four pious practices (the others are prayer, alms-giving, observing purity in matters of food) about which the disciples ask Jesus.[138] Jesus does not give a direct answer, telling them not to lie or do what they hate, followed with a thought familiar from the Synoptics that there is nothing hidden that will not be revealed, which repeats a thought from log. 5. The implication is that these injunctions are to be followed instead of the observances about which they asked. A direct answer to the question posed here comes in log. 14; Jesus expressly mentions these four practices and rejects them. Taken alone, log. 6 could be read as a reminder of the inner sincerity that must accompany pious practices if they are to be pleasing to God (cf. Matt 6:2–18). In light of log. 14, however, which rejects these practices as spiritually harmful, log. 6 should be understood to mean that these acts are lies and hateful deeds. Finally, in log. 104, Jesus resists an exhortation to fast and pray.[139]

There is not, as sometimes has been supposed, a contradiction between these negative sayings, since they concern fasting as traditionally understood, refraining from food, and log. 27, in which the practice is reinterpreted as a restraint from the world.[140] Nevertheless, the negative

---

[138] The correlation of fasting, prayer and almsgiving Jewish ethical tradition is documented in Tob 12:8: ἀγαθὸν προσευχὴ μετὰ καὶ ἐλεημοσύνης καὶ δικαιοσύνης, ἀγαθὸν τὸ ὀλίγον μετὰ δικαιοσύνης ἢ πολὺ μετὰ ἀδικίας, καλὸν ποιῆσαι ἐλεημοσύνην ἢ θησαυρίσαι χρυσίον [Prayer is good with fasting and alms and righteousness. A little with righteousness is better than much with unrighteousness. It is better to give alms than to lay up gold]. This is the text of B and A; ℵ reads ἀληθείας instead of νηστείας.

[139] ΠΕΧΑΥ ⲚΙⲤ ϪⲈ ⲀⲘⲞⲨ ⲚⲦⲚⲰⲖⲎⲖ ⲘⲠⲞⲞⲨ ⲀⲨⲰ ⲚⲦⲚⲢⲚⲎⲤⲦⲈⲨⲈ ΠⲈⲬⲈ ⲒⲤ ϪⲈ ⲞⲨ ⲄⲀⲢ ΠⲈ ΠⲚⲞⲂⲈ ⲚⲦⲀⲈⲒ ⲀⲀⲨ Ⲏ ⲚⲦⲀⲨⲬⲢⲞ ⲈⲢⲞⲈⲒ ⲌⲚⲞⲨ ⲀⲖⲖⲀ ϨⲞⲦⲀⲚ ⲈⲢⲰⲀⲚ ΠⲚⲨⲘⲪⲒⲞⲤ ⲈⲒ ⲈⲂⲞⲖ ⲌⲘ ΠⲚⲨⲘⲪⲰⲚ ⲦⲞⲦⲈ ⲘⲀⲢⲞⲨⲚⲎⲤⲦⲈⲨⲈ ⲀⲨⲰ ⲘⲀⲢⲞⲨⲰⲖⲎⲖ [They said to Jesus, "Come, let us pray today and let us fast." Jesus said, "What is the sin that I have committed, or wherein have I been defeated? But when the bridegroom leaves the bridal chamber, then let them fast and pray"]. The reference to the departure of the groom is related to Mark 2:19–20 par. See Marjanen on the symbolism of the bridal chamber as a metaphor for salvation in early Christian literature ("Thomas and Jewish Religious Practices,"in *Thomas at the Crossroads: Essays on the Gospel of Thomas* [ed. R. Uro; SNTW; Edinburgh, 1998], 163–82, here 171–2).

[140] Bertil Gärtner, for example, see in this a double attitude toward fasting indicative of different traditions from which *Gos. Thom.* gathered material (*The*

attitude toward the physical practice of fasting indicates that the theology of *Thomas* is not that of monastic ascetics.

Thomas presents a generally negative reaction to conventional practices of Jewish piety, yet at the same time, takes over the language. Some of the sayings may have originally been formulated as criticism of mere outwardness in religious practice. The most striking example is that of sabbatizing the Sabbath in log. 27, but there is also the reinterpretation of circumcision in log. 53.[141] At the same time, log. 12 affirms the leadership of James, the brother of Jesus who led the Torah-observant Jerusalem community, and it does so in terminology documented in Jewish sources to describe the righteous of Israel.[142] Yet the subsequent log. 13 relativizes this.[143] It is significant that the leaderless imitation of Thomas immediately follows the affirmation of the leadership of James. The effect on the reader is that a certain structure for the congregation is established but immediately superseded, though not suppressed. This may be a case in which a text phenomenon allows us to draw a conclusion about historical development.[144] If so, the picture painted is of a community that has its

Theology of the Gospel According to Thomas [ET; New York, 1961], 58).

[141] ΠΕΧΑΥΝΑΥ N̄CI NЕЧMΑΘΗΤΗC ΔЄ ΔΟΥΤЧΤЄ M̄ΠΡΟΘΗΤΗC ΔΥΩΔ ΔЄ 2M̄ΠI CΡΔΗΔ ΔΥΩ ΔΥΩΔΔЄ ΤΗΡΟΥ 2ΡΔΪ N̄2ΗΤΚ ΠΕ ΔΔЧ ΝΔΥ ΔЄ ΔΤЄΤN̄ΚΩ M̄ΠЄΤΟN2 M̄ΠЄΤN̄M̄ΤΟ ЄΒΟΔ ΔΥΩ ΔΤЄΤN̄ΩΔ ΔЄ 2Δ ΝЄΤΜΟΟΥΤ ["His disciples said to him, 'Is circumcision beneficial or not?' He said to them, 'If it were beneficial, their father would beget them already circumcised from their mother. Rather, the true circumcision in spirit has become completely profitable"].

[142] "The disciples said to Jesus, 'We know that you will depart from us. Who is to be our leader?' Jesus said to them, 'Wherever you are, you are to go to James the righteous, because of whom heaven and earth came into being." The world was also said to be created for Abraham (*Gen. Rab.* 14:6; cf. *Gen. Rab.* 43:7), Moses (*Gen. Rab.* 1:4), Israel (*Sipre Deut.* 47; *4 Ezra* 6:55–59), and righteous men in general (*2 Bar.* 15:7–8).

[143] In a saying reminiscent of Mark 8:27 par., Jesus invites his disciples to compare him. Simon Peter and Matthew suggest respectively an angel and a philosopher, but Thomas states that it is inutterable: "Master, my mouth is wholly incapable of saying whom you are like." As a result, Jesus tells him alone three sayings, which Thomas in turn refuses to divulge.

[144] This has been suggested by many, e.g. H. Koester, in *Nag Hammadi Codex II,2–7*, 40–41. This argument is not probative, however, given the prominence of James in gnostic literature, as witnessed by the presence of two apocalypses ascribed to him (V,3–4) and an Apocryphon (I,2) in the NHC, as well as the claim of the

roots among Jewish, Torah-observant followers of Jesus oriented toward James, yet has developed into an independent, principally leaderless circle, without obliterating all traces of its origin. This accords with what we observe in the discussion of Jewish religious practices: engagement, yet criticism and at times outright rejection, coupled with a willingness to adopt the terminology and use it in non-literal ways.

6.3.4 Comparison of Logion 27 to the New Testament

The question of the relation between *The Gospel of Thomas* and the writings of the NT canon, particularly the synoptic Gospels, is one of the most vigorously debated in all of *Thomas* research. As has been pointed out, there is a risk of positions taken and defended, rather than discussed.[145] This can only be overcome by careful examination that starts with individual sayings. Therefore, the aim of this section is modest. It will consist of three steps. In the first, common language and phrasing will be identified. Secondly, the general outlines of the cult-critical remarks attributed to Jesus in the canonical Gospels will be summarized. Thirdly, we will consider whether log. 27 is possibly a saying of Jesus.

Naasseners to have received their teaching from him (Ταῦτά ἐστιν ἀπὸ πολλῶν πάνυ λόγων τὰ κεφάλ[αια], ἅ φασι παραδεδωκέναι Μαριάμμῃ τὸν Ἰάκωβον, τοῦ κυρίου τὸν ἀδελφὸν [Hippolytus, *Haer*, 5.7.1; PTS 25:142]).

    [145] Christopher Tuckett, "Thomas and the Synoptics." *NovT* 30 (1988): 132–57, here 132. The vehemence with which the interrelated questions of possible dependence on the Synoptics, the presence or absence of gnostic material, and the date of composition have been discussed betrays the fact that there is much at stake in the outcome of the question (Cf. Risto Uro, "Introduction," in *Thomas at the Crossroads: Essays on the Gospel of Thomas* [ed. R. Uro; SNTW; Edinburgh, 1998], 1–3). Fueling the debate have been the contradictory results of studies of individual sayings or groups of sayings. There is, for instance, a remarkably high number of parallels with Q, which had been imagined to be a sayings gospel long before *Gos. Thom.* was discovered. H. Koester and others have focused on these, identifying instances where the wording of *Gos. Thom.* seems to be original (see also Koester's references to the work of Wendling and Bultmann in "GNOMAI DIAPHOROI: The Origin and Nature of Diversification in the History of Early Christianity," in *Trajectories*, 114–57, here 129). Tuckett meanwhile has gathered evidence of sayings that share traits with elements of synoptic sayings often regarded as redactional. But this does not mean that all sayings in *Gos. Thom.* with no parallel are automatically late and composed with a gnostic slant.

First, with regard to phrasing, there are a number of parallels. Sentences beginning with ἐάν and ἐάν μή that express conditions for attaining salvation are not rare in the Gospels.[146] Seeking and finding the kingdom, and seeing the father, are also well-represented.[147] Lacking, however, are the two expressions that give this saying its distinctive statement, to "fast with regard to the world" and to "sabbatize the Sabbath."

This does not make this saying automatically alien to the thought-world of the Synoptics, and so we turn now to the references found there to fasting and the Sabbath, which can be considered part of the general cultic criticism attributed to Jesus in the canonical gospels. A number of Jesus's words and actions, such as cleansing the temple (Mark 11:15 par.; John 2:13–16), may be understood in the tradition of cult criticism such as we saw in Isa 58. That is, they may reflect a concern with the restoration of honest intent, not abolition of the practice. This is especially pronounced in Matthew, who reports criticism of prayer, fasting and almsgiving that is directed against empty outwardness; not necessarily against the customs themselves (Matt 6:2–18).[148] The view toward fasting expressed in log. 6 is not so distant from this that one cannot detect a common source in tradition. At the same time, abstention from the world has some affinity with the Johannine tradition.[149] Concerning the Sabbath, it is enough to recall the results of chs. 4 and 5 of this study in the examination of sayings that the Sabbath made for man (Mark 2:27), that it is lawful to do good on the Sabbath (Mark 3:4 par.), and the appeal to the continuing activity of the father (John 5:17). Although these statements can support a reading that understands them as signalizing a break with the Sabbath, it is possible, as we have seen, that in early tradition they were expressions of concern for proper intent in its

---

[146] Harnack points to Matt 18:3; Mark 10:15; Luke 18:17; Matt 16:26; Mark 8:36; Luke 17:33 (*Sprüche*, 8).

[147] On seeking the kingdom: Matt 6:33 par. Seeing the father: John 6:46; 14:7–9; cf. "see God" in Matt 5:8; John 1:18; 1 John 4:20; 3 John 11.

[148] Matthew's concern is evident as well in the modifications he makes to Mark's account of the controversy over ritual purity (Matt 15:1–20; cf. Mark 7:1–23).

[149] E.g. 1 John 2:15. On the Johannine attitude to the world, see Bultmann, *Theologie*, 367–73.

observance. This reading has also been applied to the phrase "sabbatize the Sabbath" in log. 27 (see below, 6.3.6).

This leads to the third step, that of whether this saying could be viewed as "authentic," that is, valuable for the reconstruction of the history of Jesus. Here the nearly universal opinion of scholars has been negative since the discovery of P. Oxy. 1, including among those who are prepared to accept the presence of primary material in *Thomas*.[150] Harnack's argument remains cogent: the picture we have otherwise of Jesus is of a figure firmly rooted in the beliefs and practices of his people. Whenever he speaks of fasting, praying, almsgiving and Sabbath observance, it is invariably with reference to the literal practices. A metaphorical reference loosened from the concrete is otherwise unknown. Logion 27 stands alone in this regard. Harnack wrote before the formulation of the criteria used in the second and third quests, but can be seen to have applied them. The criterion of dissimilarity is met, yet the saying is inconsistent with the picture we are otherwise able to construct of Jesus.

The question of the age of the saying remains open. Its presence in P. Oxy. 1 proves that it was in the collection by that time (ca. 200 C.E.). How much earlier than that it may have been composed is unknown, as

---

[150] Harnack, *Sprüche*, 10–11; Resch, *Agrapha*, 68; Joachim Jeremias, *Unbekannte Jesusworte* (3d ed.; ATANT 16; Zürich, 1961), 17–18. H. Koester considers the sayings that reject the ritual and theological claims of the OT (log. 6, 14, 27, 52, 104) as well as those that consider the Pharisees as guardians of that tradition (log. 39, 102) as traditional. They have been retained because they fit the author's theology (*Nag Hammadi Codex II, 2–7*, 40). But he groups log. 27 with others in such a way that it is not possible to determine whether he would be prepared to argue that authenticity of its comments on fasting and the Sabbath in the form in which they appear in this saying. Baarda dissents; he believes that log. 27, or at least the sayings contained in it, belonged to "a very archaic Jewish-Christian tradition" that "may have preserved items of preaching of Jesus, in which both the practice of fasting and the observation of the sabbath were said to be conditions for the life of the believer" ("'If You Do Not Sabbatize the Sabbath . . . ': The Sabbath as God or World in Gnostic Understanding [*Ev. Thom.*, Logion 27]" [1988] repr. in *Essays on the Diatessaron* [CBET 11; Kampos, 1994], 147–71, here 149). It is uncontested that Jesus spoke both of fasting and the Sabbath, and that "very archaic Jewish-Christian tradition" considers these part of the will of God for the life of the believer. At stake in the decision regarding the possible age and origin of this logion however is the distinctive metaphorical usage of these terms.

is the question of whether this saying figured among traditional material worked into *Thomas* or whether it was composed for this collection. In the latter case, we would have a terminus ad quem of 140 C.E., with the question of how much earlier it may have been composed left open.[151] Here the dissonance of a positive reference to metaphorical fasting and the negative reference to the physical practice in log. 6, 14, and 104 may be significant. The other sayings dealing with fasting, prayer, and almsgiving seem to draw on the same tradition of cult criticism that Matthew especially is aware of, yet interpreted more radically. The polyphony may have begun with Jesus's earliest followers.[152] It is characteristic of charismatic leaders to evoke response among a variety of people, each of whom reacts in a different way. This could be in part because of different facets of the message, or simply because of the different reception. Further, the effect is such that various individuals may each feel that they understand especially well. Yet the figurative use of fasting and Sabbath observance in log. 27 reveals a degree of reflection that coincides with the overall tendency of the collection as a whole, so that the best guess—it is no more than that—is that it was composed for the collection, and should be dated together with it to an unknown time prior to 140 C.E.[153]

6.3.5 Analogous Statements in Early Church Fathers

While there are no parallels in the NT for the two key phrases in log. 27, to "fast to the world" and to "sabbatize the Sabbath," there are some parallels in other early Christian literature.[154] The similar phrase "fasting

---

[151] See the arguments for this dating by Grenfell and Hunt, *The Oxyrhynchus Papyri, Part 1* (Egypt Exploration Fund 1; London, 1898), 2.

[152] Cf. Jacobus Liebenberg, *The Language of the Kingdom and Jesus: Parable, Aphorism, and Metaphor in the Sayings Material Common to the Synoptic Tradition and the Gospel of Thomas* (BZNW 102; Berlin, 2001), 523. James A. Robinson attributes the variety evident in early Christianity to a bifurcation of tendencies inherent from the earliest stages (*Trajectories*, 10).

[153] For a contrary opinion, see again Baarda: "It is very improbable that the collector himself should have faked his readers by making up some saying that suited his own goals," ("Sabbatize," 149).

[154] In addition, the juxtaposition of world and kingdom found in log. 27 is paralleled. Examples are cited by Harnack, *Sprüche*, 9–10.

from the world" could be said to have become a technical term, as exemplified by Clement of Alexandria: "Those who have castrated themselves from all sin for the sake of heaven's kingdom are fortunate: They are the ones who fast from the world."[155] While the usage may not have the same meaning, it does show that we are not obligated to assume a gnostic interpretation for the saying under investigation.[156]

The phrase to "truly sabbatize the Sabbath" is also documented. It appears in a homily attributed to Macarius of Egypt.[157] As in the *Gospel of Thomas*, sabbatizing is not a liturgical act of the Christian community, but the asceticism of the individual soul. It is possible, given the phrase's existence in the LXX, that both *Thomas* and Pseudo-Macarius draw on a common tradition, and that they each independently chose to use this as a metaphor for spiritual life. Aelrud Baker argues, however, for the dependence of Pseudo-Macarius on *Thomas*.[158] In that case, this homily could be considered part of the *Wirkungsgeschichte* of *Thomas*, but does not elucidate the background of *Thomas*'s use. The use of the verb σαββατίζειν to designate spiritual observance of the new law, in contrast to Jewish practices, is documented in Justin.[159] Similarly, Tertullian

---

[155] ἀλλ᾽ οἱ μὲν εὐνουχίσαντες ἑαυτοὺς ἀπὸ πάσης ἁμαρτίας διὰ τὴν βασιλείαν τῶν οὐρανῶν, μακάριοι οὗτοι εἰσιν, οἱ τοῦ κόσμου νηστεύοντες (*Strom.* 3.15.99.4 [PG 8:1200B]). The phrase has been likened to the beatitude μακάριοι οἱ ἀποταξάμενοι τῷ κόσμῳ τούτῳ in *Acts of Paul and Thecla* 5 (ed. Lipsius, 238); cf. ἀποτάσσετε κόσμῳ in *Pistis Sophia* (Resch, *Agrapha*, 68).

[156] Gärtner points out however that such an attitude applied only to "special Christians" who adopted ascetic practices, while in gnostic circles this could be exalted into a general requirement for salvation (*Theology* 239–40). But it must be independently determined whether *Gos. Thom.* is addressed to all believers or a spiritual elite.

[157] καὶ ἀληθινὸν σάββατου σαββατίζει (ed. Dörries, et al., 263). The phrase is paralleled by καὶ ἀληθινὴν ἀνάπαυσιν ἀναπαύεται, "to truly rest [the] rest."

[158] "Pseudo-Macarius and the Gospel of Thomas," VC 18 (1964) 215–25.

[159] σαββατίζειν ὑμᾶς ὁ καινὸς νόμος διὰ παντὸς ἐθέλει [the new law requires you to keep perpetual sabbath], *Dial.* 12 [ed. Marcovich, 90]). See also the concept of celebrating the Sabbath according to the spirit in Ps.-Ignatius, *Magn.* 9: ἕκαστος ὑμῶν σαββατιζέτω πνευματικῶς (PG 5:768). A similar thought can also be expressed in Jewish-Christian circles; Ps.-Jerome refers to an obscure Judaeo-Christian Baptist sect: 'Masbothei dicunt ipsum Christum esse qui docuit illos in omni re sabbatizare' (*Indiculus de haeresibus* [PL 81:636]; [the Mosbothites says that it was Christ himself who taught them to sabbatize in all things]).

understood Sabbath celebration as the obligation to refrain from all "servile" works, not just on one day, but perpetually.[160]

6.3.6 Possible Interpretations of the Sabbath in Logion 27

Some possible interpretations of what it might mean to "sabbatize the Sabbath" in log. 27 have been mentioned above (6.3.1). A few have seeen in this expression a reference to the observance of a literal Sabbath[161] The parallelism with the figurative use of fasting would seem to exclude this, however, and so a number of non-literal suggestions have been made. One suggestion is to read it in light of the topos of rest, thereby correlating it to a major metaphor for salvation in *Thomas*.[162] There is however no

---

[160] [S]abbatizare nos ab omni opere seruili semper debere, et non tantum septimo quoque die, sed per omne tempus (*Adv. Jud.* 4.2, CCSL 21347–8; [we . . . ought to observe a Sabbath from all servile work always, and not only every seventh day, but through all time]. The term *servile work* comes from the instructions for the annual festivals (Lev 23:7–8, 21, 25, 35–36). In context, it probably is meant to allow for the work necessary for staging a festival (cf. Exod 12:16: "no manner of work . . . save that which every man must eat"). This may explain why the term does not appear in conjunction with the Day of Atonement; since it was a day of fasting, no food preparation was required. Instead, the command was to perform no manner of work (Lev 23: 31), which is the same instruction given for the weekly Sabbath (v. 3). Tertullian is able to interpret this because of the common topos of "slavery to sin" (e.g. John 8:34; Rom 7:25). Servile works, then, are sinful acts; these are to be laid aside "per omne tempus."

[161] In addition to De Conick, cited above (n. 119), see Stephen J. Patterson's note on log. 27 in *The Complete Gospels: Annotated Scholars Version* (ed. R. J. Miller; 3d ed.; San Francisco, 1994), 310.

[162] Ménard, *L'Évangile*, 47–48; Michael Fieger, *Das Thomasevangelium: Einleitung, Kommentar und Systematik* (NTAbh NF 22; Münster, 1991), 110; Richard Valantasis, *The Gospel of Thomas* (New Testament Readings; London, 1997), 101; and cautiously, Zöckler, *Lehren*, 114. Here too there is a reinterpretation of a traditional conception, as the reference to the "rest of the dead" in combination with "the new world" in log. 51 shows. Phillip Vielhauer examines *Gos. Thom.*'s references to rest in light of the more fully developed concept in gnostic writings. He concludes that while the Thomasine concept lacks many of their characteristic features, its teaching on rest fits in with their speculations ("Ἀνάπαυσις, zum gnostischen Hintergrund des Thomasevangeliums," in *Apophoreta* [FS E. Haenchen; ed. W. Eltester and F. H. Kettler; BZNW 30; Berlin, 1964], 281–99). This demonstrates that it is possible to read *Gos. Thom.* through gnostic eyes, which is not the same as showing that it is a gnostic document.

explicit connection between Sabbath and rest in this saying, nor even an implicit relation through contextualization. Another suggestion, based on the parallelism of the saying, has been to equate Sabbath and cosmos.[163] This draws on later gnostic usage.[164] A third reading sees in this reference a call to sanctify one's entire life.[165] This draws on parallels in patristic literature, such as the passage in Justin's *Dialogue* mentioned above. A variant of this view is based on the use of the term *Sabbath* to refer to the week.[166] The difficulty with this view is the assumption that the same term is used in one sentence with two meanings. Finally, a fifth suggestion, which has the merit of remaining internal to the saying being interpreted, sees Sabbath as an epexegesis of *fast*.[167]

The variety of these suggestions reflects a certain opacity in the saying itself. It could be that one of these interpretations, or even another that no longer suggests itself to us, was the subject of oral interpretation.[168]

[163] Baarda, "Sabbatize."

[164] Baarda points to *Interp. Know.* 11:18–19, where the Sabbath is identified with the world: "From [being counted] with the female, sleep [brought labor] and the [sabbath] which [is the] world." In this difficult and imperfectly preserved writing, the female is Sophia/Eve. The fall was the division of originally androgynous, spiritual humanity into male/female. The equation of Sabbath and world is apparently based on the Sabbath as the completion of creation of this world. This does not mean that the two terms are interchangeable, or that we may conclude with Marjanen that it symbolizes abstinence from the world and its values, to the exclusion of a relevance in the question of literal Sabbath observance. It does raise the possibility however that it is precisely its connotation as a memorial of creation that may have made the practice suspect in circles that did not assign positive value to the physical creation.

[165] Harnack, *Sprüche*, 11. Cf. Johannes Leipoldt: the Christian's entire life should be a festival (*Das Evangelium nach Thomas: Koptisch und Deutsch* [TU 101; Berlin, 1967], 62).

[166] Most recently by Paterson Brown, who appeals to the use of *Sabbath* in both Greek and Coptic to refer to the week as well as to the seventh day ("The Sabbath and the Week in Thomas 27," *NovT* 34 [1992]: 193).

[167] Haenchen, who paraphrases log. 27: "If you don't fast (i.e. withdraw) from the world the way a Jew does once a week . . ." (*Botschaft*, 50). This may well have been the oral interpretation of a Thomasine teacher, but it fails to respect the parallelism of the saying. The addressees are to sabbatize as well as to fast.

[168] Bruce Lincoln shows how *Gos. Thom.* may have been read within a community consisting of novices, initiates, masters, and "perfects" ("Thomas-Gospel and Thomas-Community: A New Approach to a Familiar Text," *NovT* 19 [1977]: 65–76).

In contrast to these suggestions, I propose interpreting the saying on a text-internal basis. Taken on its own, the exhortation to celebrate the Sabbath as a Sabbath could be seen as a summons to heartfelt observance in accord to its true intent, similar to the concern expressed in Isa 58. The appearance of fasting in parallel to this is not surprising, again given the prophetic precedent, directed against empty compliance with the letter. A similar criticism of surface piety is attributed by Matthew to Jesus. Nor is the admonition to fast with respect to the world necessarily gnostic, as parallels in Clement show. A heritage that combined Isaiah's pointed reminder that abstention from food alone was not a sufficient indicator that a heart had turned to God with an attitude toward the cosmos as shorthand for everything from which the true follower of Jesus should turn (John) could easily account for the origin of the expression "fast with respect to the world" to describe an ascetic practice that did not *only* refrain from eating but *also* signified a heart turned toward God.

Yet in the context of the *Gospel of Thomas* the statement takes on another meaning. Here the literal practice of fasting is rejected. What matters is abstention from the world. In this context, we would not expect that an admonition toward literal Sabbath observance should appear in *Thomas*. Yet the solution may not be to see a metaphor in the noun "Sabbath." After all, *world* is used in a literal, if abstract sense. It is the verb *fast* that is used in a non-standard way; perhaps this is the case with the verb *to sabbatize* as well. The verb σαββατίζω is not to be understood here in its full sense of *celebrate the Sabbath* but in a more limited sense of *rest* as a synonym for *fast*. It appears as if a traditional saying that urged sincere, literal Sabbath observance has been turned on its head. Perhaps the Thomasine believer is urged to rest, to desist *from* Sabbath observance, especially in its signification as memorial of the creation of the cosmos that the believer is called upon to transcend.[169] This suggestion coincides with that of Baarda, but without drawing on later gnostic

---

[169] The same can be said for the Coptic ⲦⲘⲈⲒⲢⲈ ⲘⲠⲤⲀⲘⲂⲀⲦⲞⲚ ⲚⲤⲀⲂⲂⲀⲦⲞⲚ. To "make the Sabbath a Sabbath" by itself can be heard as an appeal to true, heart-felt Sabbath observance. But the Thomasine Christian was urged to see deeper meanings hidden in the evident. To "make Sabbath" of something would be to rest with regard to it; therefore, to make Sabbath of the Sabbath could mean to rest from it.

writings to read *world* and *Sabbath* as alternative designations of the same object. Consideration of the documented practice of later Christians to hold worship services both on Sabbath and the Lord's Day (Sunday) is appropriate here.[170] When this was done, the Sabbath was a festival day to memorialize creation, whereas the Lord's Day was celebrated as a memorial of the resurrection.[171] This connection of Sabbath and creation may have been what made it objectionable to circles who no longer distinguished between the cosmos as ordered creation, and therefore good, and cosmos as the structure of society opposed to the Christian faith, and therefore bad.

6.3.7 Summary

The combination of fasting and Sabbath observance may have suggested itself from the OT and points to an origin of the saying the Jewish-Christian circles. The phrasing in common with canonical sayings may be the result of literary influence, but it more likely points to an independent witness of tradition, whether oral or from early written sayings collections. Yet the point of the saying is to reinterpret the terminology associated with these common practices of Jewish piety. Fasting is used figuratively as abstention from the world. The reference to the Sabbath is in parallel to this, meaning that here too something other than literal observance of the seventh day of the week is meant. What that is exactly is difficult to ascertain and may have been determined by a culture of oral interpretation in the Thomasine community, now lost to us. If we limit our consideration to the text itself, it appears that while the parallelism of the saying is synonymous, this is only so to the extent that the elements of the two phrases are equivalent, not that they are synonyms. A reading of the saying that takes seriously both the parallel to fasting, in context of the entire *Gospel of Thomas*, and the literal meaning of the terms employed, suggests that the LXX phrase σαββατίζω [τὸ] σάββατον is turned on its head and has come to mean a cessation of Sabbath-observance as a condition of salvation. As such, it can be related both to Paul's teaching in his letter to the Galatians (see above, ch. 3) and the polemic of

---

[170] *Apos. Con.* 2.59.3.
[171] *Apos. Con.* 7.23.3; cf. 2.36.2; 7.36.1.

Barnabas in its present form (see above, 6.2). Yet in contrast to Paul, this abjuration of Sabbath observance did not have its origin in the Gentile mission. It reflects a development within an offshoot of Jerusalem-based Jewish-Christianity on the way to a gnostic form of Christianity.[172] We know too little of the history of the Thomasine community, as well as the date of the composition to know whether external events such as the Bar-Kokhba revolt and the Hadrianic repressions may have influenced such a radical shift, but even without this, the *Gospel of Thomas* bears witness to a variant strand within the first century of the Christian movement.

The Sabbath was not a concern of Thomasine Christians, except insofar as it, along with other practices and concepts inherited from Judaism via Jerusalem-based Christianity could be reinterpreted in light of the specific soteriological concerns of the community.

---

[172] E.g. H. Koester, who sees in its development "a witness for the trajectory that leads from the earliest spiritualizing interpretation of the sayings of Jesus to the full recognition of the gnostic potential of such understanding of Jesus as teacher of divine wisdom" (*History and Literature of Early Christianity* (2d ed.; Berlin, 2000], 158). Among features that could be considered gnostic are the idea of rest as the highest level of human existence, the androgynous Adam, and the encouragement to find the hidden meaning in the sayings as a way of attaining life. On the other hand, there is no fully developed cogmological system with terms such as Hebdomas, Ogdoas or Pleroma.

7
Conclusion

This investigation sought to assess the validity of the Sabbatarian claim that the abandonment of the Sabbath is a post-apostolic phenomenon, and that the NT writings, viewed for themselves rather than in light of subsequent developments, reflect continued observance of the seventh-day Sabbath. The result of my examination of the relevant texts is mixed. On the one hand, the Gospel of Matthew seems to have arisen in an observant community. Even the Lukan writings can sustain a reading that allows for the Sabbath. The Sabbatarian claim founders, however, on the writings of Paul. The view that the Christian movement in the apostolic era was uniformly Sabbath-observant cannot be sustained. Meanwhile, the opposite assertion that either Jesus or his first followers transferred Sabbath observance to the following day also misses the mark. While there is clear evidence in the apostolic era for meetings on the first day of the week, especially evening gatherings for a shared meal (John 20:19, 26; Acts 20:7), there is no warrant for viewing it as a substitute for Sabbath observance. Indeed, the timing could have originally been meant to permit continued participation in Sabbath observances. Before attempting a historical reconstruction that more accurately reflects developments, I will present a detailed summary of the results of my exegetical investigation of the pertinent texts.

7.1 SUMMARY OF RESULTS

In the canonical sequence of the Hebrew scriptures, the Sabbath plays a prominent role from the beginning. Divine rest on the seventh day culminates creation. Nothing is said about a command to humans, although the thought that those who live in knowledge of and close relation to this God would emulate his example is not distant. Nevertheless, nothing is reported about a Sabbath observance by righteous Enoch and Noah, nor by patriarchs Abraham, Isaac and Jacob (Israel). It is said however that Abraham had been tested and was known by God as one who would observe all statutes, allowing subsequent Jewish exegesis to debate whether this implied that he observed the Sabbath.

Both on the narrative level and in historical reconstruction it is the Israelites who first observe the Sabbath. The Sabbath was a feature of life in preexilic Israel. Second Kings 4:23 may be the oldest reference to the Sabbath, an appropriate time for visiting a man of God. This indicates, positively, that a pause from normal labor was connected with the day as well as, negatively, that later restrictions on travel on the day were not yet known. Nothing is said about its origin, nor is there any definition of what is meant by Sabbath, or in what frequency it occurs. Speculations that it may have originated outside of Israel, or that it may once have been a monthly observance connected with the full moon, as an antipode to the beginning of each month, the new moon, find neither confirmation nor refutation.

The time of the Second Temple reflects an increased emphasis on the Sabbath, now clearly equated with the seventh day. The Sabbath features prominently in the Decalogue, in two forms, one connected to the exodus (Deut 5:15), the other to the creation (Exod 20:11). It is given the character of a sign and called a perpetual covenant (Exod 31:12–17). Israel's pollution of the Sabbath is cited as a principle reason for punishment and captivity (Ezek 20:18–24; Lev 26:1–2; Neh 13:15–18). Speculation on the reason for this increased emphasis centers on the need for a cultic observance that could be separated from a temple, one that gave captives in Babylon a sense of identity.

This tradition continues in the intertestamental period. There was no absolute uniformity in practice—strictures may have varied—but the day was held in honor. It was not only a venerated and ancient institution, it was also a key component of Jewish self-identity in the society in which Jesus and his first followers lived. The Jews were widely represented in the Roman world and beyond; they were objects of both attraction and scorn. The Sabbath was the most-often remarked aspect of their faith and practice, showing that viewed from without the Sabbath was an identity marker as well.

The earliest Christian writings known to us are the authentic letters of Paul. They document the existence of a competing mission to the nations that taught Torah-loyalty, culminating in circumcision. Paul perceived this as a threat to his own mission, evoking from him a deeply-reasoned theological response. In his highly-charged letter to his converts in Galatia, he refers to his competitors as *the circumcision*, but the issue at stake between them is not limited to this. In the course of the letter, Paul cites the observance of units of time—days, months, seasons, and years—as evidence of the reenslavement of his readers to the elements of the world (4:10). Paul uses general terms to describe these time units. This is intentional; Sabbath observance is but an illustration of a broader phenomenon. Paul describes the pre-Christian life of his readers (and that to which they are in danger of returning) as a relationship to impersonal forces, the στοιχεῖα and time markers. The new scrupulous observance of Torah-mandated time markers, as a phenomenon, is no different from their earlier involvement with polytheistic worship, in which careful observance of planetary motion, and the time markers that resulted from that, played an important role. This corresponds to Paul's conviction that the God who has called them, the father of Christ and, through adoption, of all believers, is the only personal being properly denoted as *god*. Any competing objects of thought in the spiritual realm are *not-gods* (v. 8), an element of Paul's thought that was in continuity with his Jewish background, in contrast to his stress of the discontinuity of the Christian faith with regard to the Torah. In addition, the religious experience of time—a division of time into sacred and profane—is aligned with an inferior level of experience when compared with the experience of being known by God.

There is no insurmountable difficulty in Paul's use of the term στοιχεῖα τοῦ κόσμου to express the commonality of the new Torah enthusiasm of his audience with their pre-Christian past, nor in his use of the scrupulous observance of time to exemplify this. At any rate, the missionaries would have seen in it a legitimate expression of their Torah-piety. That the reality of the world conforms to the Torah, that cultic observance and times must be in accord with this, and that all of reality breathes of the same divine will as the Torah—that is, that a life in harmony to creation and cult is simply the other side of conformity to the Torah, is all in accord with early Jewish theology. The law possesses therefore soteriological quality, which Paul contests on the basis of his Christology.

Paul's teaching on the law is complex, yet for the purpose of this investigation, it is possible to make certain observations. One is that the law cannot at the same time be the exclusive possession of Israel and have a role in the gathering of the nations. A second is that while the law is at an end as a way of salvation (Rom 10:4), it remains as an expression of the will of God. Nevertheless, there are aspects of the law that are not only not a way of salvation; they also do not express the will of God for Gentile believers. Explicitly, they are the so-called identity markers (circumcision, ritual purity, and the Hebrew calendar). Paul does not systematize this. He does not differentiate between moral and ceremonial law, nor between the Ten Commandments and the rest. Still, his message is clear: faith in Jesus Christ is the way of salvation for all, Jew and Gentile. Jews do not need to stop being Jews to be saved, but believe in Jesus as their promised Messiah. Belief in Jesus as the seed of Abraham in whom all nations would be blessed meant at the same time that Gentiles did not need to become Jews, specifically as expressed by adoption of markers of Jewish identity such as circumcision, nor the observance of days such as the Sabbath. There is no indication that Paul substituted Sunday for the Sabbath. Days were a matter of indifference since time itself had taken on a new quality with the coming of Christ. A later author, writing in Paul's name, has correctly retained the memory that it was Sabbath observance that was at issue (ἑορτῆς ἢ νεομηνίας ἢ σαββάτων; Col 2:16), but has missed the point of why Paul used general terminology.

The synoptic Gospels preserve the memory that Jesus came into conflict with his contemporaries over the Sabbath. This is most widely represented by healing accounts, which were not closely examined in this study. More remarkable is the incident of gleaning grain on the Sabbath (Mark 2:23–28 par.), the only narrated Sabbath dispute in the life of Jesus that does not involve a healing. The disciples have performed an action, but it is Jesus who is held responsible, raising the possibility that the incident is the creation of the post-resurrection community. The investigation showed that the Synoptics understood this pericope in connection with a decision to kill Jesus. The motif of anger provoked by Jesus' words and deeds on the Sabbath, leading to a plot to kill him, seems to have been added at some time after the pericope had been gathered into a collection; it is most likely part of Mark's redactional activity and is a reflection on the role of Jewish leadership in the execution of Jesus by the Romans. It is likely that it also reflects conflict the Christian community experienced with those who retained a strong loyalty to the practices of Judaism. The interest in a postulated pre-Markan collection lay in questions of practice, whereas for Mark, the behavior of the disciples on the Sabbath was the occasion of conflict between Jesus and his environment. The pericope was taken over by both Matthew and Luke. The character of conflict remains, but each author sets his own accents. This is especially the case with Matthew, through a recontexualisation, as well as the insertion of additional material. For instance, Matthew has an additional argument, in keeping with his redactional practice. This concludes in a quotation from Hos 6:6, which is used here for the second time in Matthew's gospel (cf. 9:13), reflecting its importance for this author as an expression of the relation of law and conduct in light of the coming of Christ.

The saying with which Jesus defends the community (Mark 2:27–28), with its categorical subordination of the Sabbath to the lordship of man, stood out enough that it was remembered by his disciples, but was not unthinkable in the discussions of the time. This finding means however that it does not fulfill the criterion of double dissimilarity, and so cannot be accepted with certainty as a word of Jesus. The point on which it fails to fulfill this criterion, however, is not, as often supposed, the teaching of the early church, but with contemporary Judaism. Originally, this two-part logion was about man (collective/individual) in relation to the Sabbath, seen in the perspective of the will of God expressed in creation. In time, Son of Man came to be a christological title, and the statement was understood as applying to the lordship of Jesus over the day. Matthew and Luke independently struck the first half of the saying to emphasize the christological point. The Jesus portrayed here fits neither the revisionist view of Jesus as such a good Jew that conflict was unthinkable, nor the traditional Christian view that Jesus demonstratively violated the Sabbath to prove it no longer was to be kept. Yet it does document the conviction that with the coming of Christ a radical concentration on the law of love, finding concrete expression in concern for human needs, took precedence over all other Torah considerations. It became, in effect, the hermeneutical principle through which the Torah was understood. This incident does not document a break with the Sabbath, but it does reflect a situation in which such a break was possible. There is no express abrogation of the Sabbath in the Synoptics. Given the non-Palestinian location of their redaction, and the changed historical circumstance (e.g., the Pharisees are no longer a competing movement, but have become the elite of post-temple Israel), this is a significant negative finding. Nevertheless, there are clear indications of later developments. On the one hand, the community that transmitted this tradition saw in the Sabbath conflicts a part of the explanation for the hostility of the Jewish elite toward Jesus (Mark, followed by Luke). On the other, there was a reinterpretation of rest as a theological category that found its fulfillment in Jesus, rather than in a period of time (Matthew).

The communities in which the canonical gospels were formulated may well have differed in their own Sabbath practice. There is no reason to believe that Mark's community observed the Sabbath. The Matthean community may have had a different practice. The general tenor of the Gospel, the concern for the law, and specific indications such as Matthew's reworking of the pericope on ritual purity, give us reason to believe that the community was observant—perhaps even to the point of expecting Gentile converts to live according to a Christ-interpreted Torah. Matthew resists the notion that a law-free, pneumatological Christianity should be normative.

Whether or not Jesus thought of himself as the Messiah, the conviction that the imminent Kingdom of God was breaking into the present in his ministry seems central to his self-understanding (Luke 11:20). Those of his words and deeds on the Sabbath that led to conflict (and the tradition retained no other kind) seem to be rooted in this. This provides at one and the same time both the evidence that Jesus is well placed within a first-century Jewish context as well as the seeds of the impetus that led to Christianity becoming a movement that had a separate existence outside of the Judaism that did not share this understanding of Jesus and his mission.

The Sabbath healings recorded in John reflect a heightened level of conflict. Jesus is directly accused of violating the Sabbath (9:16), and even of abolishing it (5:18). Both Jesus the healer and at least one of those healed are portrayed as taking actions that violate Sabbath halakah; this is no coincidence. Yet the stance of the Gospel is that they have not sinned. It is a matter of judgment, however, whether this was a conflict of interpretations between two Sabbath-observant communities that differed in matters of practice, or whether the evangelist is mutely endorsing the charge of the opponents that Jesus has indeed unbound the Sabbath. Crucial in deciding this question is the observation that Jesus responds to this charge by stressing his identity with the Father, who by common—albeit not universal—agreement among Jews was not bound by the Sabbath. The interest of the evangelist is clearly the revelation of the true character of Jesus as the one sent, the Son. John 7:14–24 yields indications that at an earlier stage in the tradition upon which the Gospel draws the teaching of Jesus—and by implication his actions—correspond to the will of God as expressed in the Torah; in its present context, however, the material is used to demonstrate the teaching of the one sent. The coexistence in the incidents of statements that could reflect Torah-loyalty alongside sharp polemic portrayal of mutual rejection, including the charge—not refuted as much as it is transcended—that Jesus has unbound the Sabbath, open the possibility of a diachronic reading of the text. The possibility of a movement from text to history that accompanies every step of this inquiry becomes most apparent here. One way not to do this, however, is to assume, with Rordorf, that the appearances of Jesus to the disciples in Jerusalem following his resurrection are a historical record of the institution of weekly Sunday evening Eucharist. If anything, they reflect the practice of the Johannine community several decades later, after painful expulsion from the synagogue.

To widen the repertoire of texts, and thereby possibly reflect a broader range of early Christian opinions toward the Sabbath, three additional texts were examined. One is in a canonical writing that receives less attention than the Gospels or the Pauline epistles, Hebrews.

Another is from the writings generally referred to as the Apostolic Fathers, and the third is from a gospel that had only come to light in the last century, and whose provenance and age are still matters of debate. Once popular, it was not accepted in the canon.

An investigation of the Book of Hebrews, rich in cultic imagery, contains the statement in Heb 4:9 that a σαββατισμός, a celebration of the Sabbath, remains for the people of God. This is the only NT passage to even remotely express this view, and it is sometimes marshaled in defense of a Sabbatarian position (i.e., the position either that the seventh-day Sabbath should be observed by Christians or that its strictures have been transferred to the first day of the week). An examination of the context of this passage, including the repeated use of κατάπαυσις as the goal of an exhortation of faithfulness, led to the conclusion that the celebration of the Sabbath to which the readers of Hebrews are pointed is both a circumlocution for the rest of God and a redefinition of it. The topos is familiar from Jewish apocalyptic literature from the time preceding and contemporary to Hebrews, but unlike its use there, there is no connection made between celebration of an eternal Sabbath and the faithful observance of a weekly Sabbath in this life. This led to the second main point of investigation, a comparison with two other metaphors for salvation in Hebrews, the altar and the heavenly Jerusalem. This reveals that Hebrews reflects a Christian appropriation of cultic Jewish symbols of salvation. They are transformed in that the symbol is retained without a continuation of the practices that gave rise to the symbolism. This in turn is paradigmatic for the identity-formation of the emergent Christian movement, which through a combination of retention and rejection of its roots sought to situate itself in a tradition while asserting its independence and superiority. Although historically successful, this resulted both in a problematic relationship with its Jewish twin as well as inner-Christian tensions, such as those occasioned by recurrent Sabbatarian movements.

Among all the writings examined, *Barn.* 15 takes the most negative view of Israel and its practices. The Sabbath is included in its radical project of reinterpretation and appropriation. This strategy avoids the difficulties inherent in attempts to distinguish between moral and ritual law in the Torah, attempts that face their greatest difficulty by the presence of the Sabbath command in the Decalogue. In applying this overall strategy to the Sabbath, *Barnabas* proceeds in two steps. First, the Sabbath is reinterpreted as the messianic age at the close of human history. Until that time, neither God nor humankind can truly rest. Secondly, *Barnabas* presents the eighth day as a conscious counterpart to the Sabbath. There is no discussion, however, of how this practice solves the problem diagnosed in Sabbath observance. Further, the Sabbath remains unique. It is the only practice analyzed for which no moral interpretation in the present-day life of believers is offered. Still it does offer evidence of the practice—presented by the author as self-evident—of Christian worship on the eighth day.

The *Gospel of Thomas* mentions Sabbath observance in tandem with fasting, in the process reinterpreting these common practices of Jewish piety (log. 27). The parallel to fasting makes clear that literal observance of the Sabbath is not enjoined on readers; instead, it appears that the expression σαββατίζω [τὸ] σάββατον is a paradox that means that a cessation of Sabbath observance is necessary for salvation.

The most important general result of this investigation has been the discovery that while on the one hand there was diversity of practice with regard to a seventh-day Sabbath in the early Christian community, the subject had, for most strands of Christianity, lost importance when compared to the role that the Sabbath played in Second Temple Judaism (exception: the law observant Christian mission to the Gentiles evident in Galatians). This relative devaluation of the practice took place not in favor of another, analogous worship practice, but as a result of the intensive Christological focus of the community. This was seen in various ways in the present investigation, from the argumentation of Paul in opposing a Torah-observant mission to Galatia, in the use of Sabbath conflicts in the Synoptics, in the answers given by Jesus in the Fourth Gospel, and in the hermeneutical strategy adopted in the writings known as Hebrews and *Barnabas*. This did not immediately answer the question of what rhythm the new community would adopt in the time of its worship practice. It is time now to supplement the exegetical analysis conducted so far in this project with a sketch of how it may have come about that the first day of the week became the Lord's Day, the occasion of weekly gathering for worship.

7.2 HISTORICAL RECONSTRUCTION

One of the most fascinating aspects of early Christianity is the rapid and widespread abandonment of the cultic practice of rest on the seventh day Sabbath, as practiced in the Jewish matrix of the Christian movement. The Jerusalem congregation shared Sabbath practice with their fellows Jews. A century later we find the widespread custom, even among Christians of Jewish descent, of worship on the first day of the week. Combined with this new practice was the conviction that a Christian did not have to observe the Sabbath. Based on the results of the exegesis of pertinent passages, I will now attempt a historical reconstruction.

Although the early followers of Jesus were acculturated in a society that honored the Sabbath, they retained the memory that Jesus had a relatively liberal Sabbath practice, not hesitating to heal on that day, for instance. Sharpened by the impression made by Jesus' violent death, this memory became one of conflict between Jesus and his contemporaries, with the Sabbath being one of the occasions of conflict. This appears to have led to a radical criticism of temple, cult, and Torah by some, characterized as *Hellenists* (Acts 6–7).[1] It is not expressly mentioned that this criticism extended to the Sabbath, but this is assumed. The Hellenists were driven from Jerusalem, but only these (Acts 8:4). The believers who remained—*Hebrews*—combined their faith in Jesus with loyalty to the Torah and its institutions. Yet even they, recalling the practice of Jesus, were less strict in their observance than some of their contemporaries. This more liberal Sabbath practice led to criticism from fellow Jews. This led in turn to a further estrangement from the Sabbath on the part of some, whereas others reacted to this criticism by becoming more conservative in their practice.

The expulsed, meanwhile, settled in Antioch, one of the three largest urban centers in the Empire, and began a Torah-free mission among non-Jews (Acts 11:19–21). Paul was violently opposed to this (Gal 1:13; cf. Acts 8:1–3; 9:1–2), but after an epiphany on the road to Damascus

---

[1]   Brown, *Introduction*, 293–6; more detailed: Martin Hengel, "Zwischen Jesus und Paulus: Die 'Hellenisten,' die 'Sieben'' und Stephanus (Apg 6,1-15; 7,54-8,3)," *ZTK* 72 (1975): 151-206. Overview of the history of discussion since F. C. Baur in Kümmel, *Einleitung*, 127–9.

(Gal 1:15–16; cf. Acts 9:3–8) became an avid adherent of this program, in time becoming its leader. A parallel, Torah-observant mission to the nations developed, leading to frictions that were resolved in a meeting in Jerusalem (Gal 2:1–10; cf. Acts 15:1–29), only to break out anew in Antioch (Gal 2:11–14), after which Paul—apparently on the losing side of the conflict there—withdrew (Acts 15:36–41). Given this inauspicious beginning, the later success of Paul's mission is surprising. The struggles of this controversial missionary leader endowed the movement with a forcefully expressed theology.

In Jerusalem, leaders of the priestly circles took advantage of the interval between the recall of one Roman governor and the arrival of his successor to incite the murder of James, the brother of Jesus, leader of the Jerusalem community (Eusebius, *Hist. eccl.* 2.23.4–18). This is emblematic of the growing tensions within the Jewish community between followers of Jesus and others. These could have been the result of a difference in emphasis: You could be a member of the synagogue and confess Jesus as Messiah, but, for Jews, the Sabbath was central; questions of the Messiah were adiaphora. For the followers of Jesus, it was the other way around.[2] At any rate, it became the opinion of both Christians and Jews that the Jesus movement had failed in their mission to the Jews.[3] And, in their enthusiasm, the early believers met more than once a week. Luke's portrayal of the early, ideal community meeting daily may be an exaggeration, but not far off the mark (Acts 2:46); it corresponds to what has been observed in other charismatic groups. To come together just once a week would have been an impoverishment.

A weakening of the first enthusiasm, reflected in Heb 10:25, encouraged orientation toward a weekly meeting. The Sabbath was no longer a serious possibility; the Pauline heritage ruled it out for those

---

[2]   Adele Reinhartz, *Befriending the Beloved Disciple: A Jewish Reading of the Gospel of John* (New York, 2001), esp. 152–7.

[3]   This at any rate was the perception. Rodney Stark has argued, however, "that Jews continued as a significant source of Christian converts until at least as late as the fourth century and that Jewish Christianity was still significant in the fifth century" (*The Rise of Christianity: How the Obscure, Marginal Jesus Movement Became the Dominant Religious Force in the Western World in a Few Centuries* [Princeton, 1996], 49–71, quotation from 49).

who were converted in a Torah-free mission. The categorical rejection of Sabbaths in Col 2:16 shows this.[4] By this time, there was a widespread pattern of evening meetings after the Sabbath, with a communal meal of sacramental character. This is documented in Acts 20:7, where it is difficult to tell whether these meetings were on Saturday evening or on Sunday evening, but reflected as well in John 20:19–29, where clearly Sunday evening is meant. Pliny reports, in addition to evening meals, meetings that take place before dawn on a certain day, unfortunately, he doesn't say which day this was (*Ep.* X 96). In light of what has been said so far, however, it is unlikely that this was Saturday morning. More likely, it was Sunday morning, before dawn, before going to work.[5] Sunday remained a normal work day throughout the period under investigation. This letter also sheds light on the reason why the evening meetings were assimilated to those in the early morning: to avoid suspicion of subversion. The first literary citation of the phrase by which the first day came to be known, "the Lord's Day," is Rev 1:10. Unfortunately, John the Seer does not tell us what he means by this, so we cannot be sure that he refers to Sunday.[6] The lack of explication indicates, however, that he expects his readers to understand the term, indicating that it was already in use.[7]

[4] The force of this prohibition is against the introduction of the Sabbath in Christian communities in which it is not yet established, as shown by the parallel mention of feasts, which did nothing to inhibit the continued Christian observance of two of the three principle feasts of the Jewish sacred year, Passover and Pentecost, since these simply continued to be observed from the beginning of the Christian movement (Eduard Schwartz, "Osterbetrachtungen" [1906], repr. *Gesammelte Schriften* [Berlin, 1963], 5:1–41, here 6).

[5] If the meetings were on Saturday, and if the Christians were observant, as Sabbatarians allege , there is no need for the meetings to have taken place before dawn.

[6] C. W. Dugmore contends that this and other early uses of the phrase refer to Easter, rather than Sunday ("Lord's Day and Easter," in *Neotestamentica et patristica* [FS O. Cullmann; ed. W. C. van Unnick; Leiden, 1962], 272-81). This view has not won a wide following. Also unlikely, despite the eschatological focus of Rev, is that this phrase (κυριακῇ ἡμέρᾳ) is used in correspondence to the Day of the Lord in the Prophets (ἡμέρα τοῦ κυρίου). The difference in Greek is great enough that it is unlikely to be simply a variation that has the same meaning. On a possible parallel to the earlier attested phrase Lord' Supper, κυριακὸν δεῖπνον, see Rordorf, *Sonntag*, 270.

[7] For more on the early nature of Lord's Day worship, see Rordorf's synthesis of

Jewish Christians lost a unifying figure with the death of James, and a unifying center with the destruction of the temple a few years later. In addition, there are the traditions of their flight. This weakened, but did not destroy, their bond to fellow Jews.[8] The Gospels reflect conflicts with local synagogues (John 9:22; 12:42; 16:2). In the case of Matthew, this may even reflect bitter rivalry for leadership.[9] The Torah-observant part of the Christian movement, weakened by the two Judean revolts and the consolidation of Jewish faith, became marginalized both among its fellow Jews and its fellow Christians, although as we have seen (see above 3.4.1 and 4.3.3), this process extended over a longer period of time than has been assumed.[10]

Nevertheless, Christians continued to gather on the Sabbath in addition to the Lord's Day, especially in the East and in Africa, though we find no teaching that it was wrong to meet on the first day or that one

texts from the first and second centuries in "Ursprung und Bedeutung der Sonntagfeier im frühen Christentum" (1981), repr. in *Lex orandi, lex credendi* (Paradosis 36; Freiburg, Switzerland, 1993), 1–14, here 11–12.

[8]   Michael Avi-Jonah, *The Jews Under Roman and Byzantine Rule: A Political History of Palestine from the Bar Kokhba War to the Arab Conquest* (New York, 1976), 141.

[9]   Anthony J. Saldarini, *Matthew's Christian-Jewish Community* (Chicago Studies in the History of Judaism; Chicago, 1994), esp. 194–206.

[10]   Instead of focusing on the time immediately after the destruction of the temple, 70 C.E., or the suppression of the second Judean revolt (135), it would be advisable to look at the period between 150 and 180, with the difference in viewing Jewish Christianity documented respectively by Justin and Irenaeus. Justin is aware of variety in Jewish Christianity. His comments show that Christology is not a useful tool for distinguishing between Jewish and Gentile Christianity, *pace* the later heresiologists and much modern scholarship, since both adoptionist and pre-existence teaching could be found among both Jewish and Gentile Christians. The key difference was loyalty to the Torah. Justin does not reckon Jewish Christians among heretics; to be a Jewish Christian is not the same as being a heretic. Yet in the source used by Irenaeus for his information on *Ebionites* (first documented use of the term), this is the case. It appears that, under pressure from Marcion and various gnostic groups, the proto-Orthodox party perceived an increased need for self-definition and exclusion in the second half of the second century, and that this led to increased pressure (already evident in Ignatius) for believers to choose between Judaism and Christianity, as if these were mutually exclusive. Yet the Chrysostom sermons show that this was a choice some believers continued to resist into the fourth century.

should only meet on the Sabbath.[11] Worship on the first day of the week seems to be widespread at the close of the era under investigation, but not universal. There are indications that some Christians, even from among the nations, combined a faith in Christ with Sabbath observance of some form. At the same time, the evidence of the gospels of John and Thomas indicate that at least some followers of Jesus from among the Jews no longer observed the Sabbath. It is impossible to stress too greatly, in light of common assumptions to the contrary, that the texts investigated show no indication that Sunday was a substitute for the Sabbath. Instead, the function that the Sabbath had performed seems to have been fulfilled in the minds of Christians by Jesus (this is especially seen in symbolism of true rest in Matt 11:28–30).

Those who explain this development by the status of the Sabbath as an identity marker of the Jewish matrix in which the Christian faith formed and over against which it defined itself are correct, but this explanation falls short if understood only as a sociological process, or as a mechanical exchange. Tensions with regard to the Sabbath preceded expulsion from the synagogue for many communities of Christian Jews (Matthew, John), and the categorical refusal of Paul to permit imposition of "days" on the communities he had gathered from among the nations is earlier yet. If the effect was to resist the assimilation of these converts into Judaism, it is the reason for this refusal that is important, for it reflects a deeply-held theological conviction that coincides with the source of the tension between Christian Jews and their compatriots: the confession of Jesus as the Christ, the Messiah, the fulfilment of all the promises made to Israel. The Sabbath was not rejected in order to form a new identity. The new identity had already been formed by faith in Christ. This led both to a loss of importance of the Sabbath, as well as to its reinterpretation, even among Christian communities that may have continued some form of its observance (Matthew).

This confluence of the Pauline mission and the Matthean and Johannine traditions should not mislead us into thinking that faith in

---

[11] Details of practice for both the East and Ethiopia in Emile Maher Ishaq, "Saturday," *Coptic Encyclopedia* 7:2098–2100. Eusebius even attributes such a practice to the Ebionites (*Hist. eccl.* 3.27.5).

Christ was *ipso facto* irreconcilable with continued literal observance of the Sabbath. The rhetoric of Christ as fulfilment of the hope of Israel does not automatically mean abolition of the practices of Israel, as can be seen in the unbroken continuation of the observance of the Passover (Easter) and Pentecost, albeit with transformed meaning. Nor should we imagine rejection of the Sabbath as the universal step of a unified, pristine original Christianity. As Schwartz observed nearly a century ago, "langsam und schrittweise, in organischem Prozess, löste sich das Christliche vom Jüdischen ab; das Alte und das Neue liegen jahrhundertelang nebeneinander." This organic process "hat sich naturgemäss mit verschiedener Intensität und nicht in gleicher Schnelligkeit überall vollzogen."[12] The intervening years have unearthed additional indications that Schwartz had correctly assessed the development. Given this, it is not the persistent observance of the seven-day Sabbath by *some* Christians that is surprising, but the rapid and widespread abandonment by *most* of the practice, with simultaneous retention of the Jewish seven-day week. Nevertheless, there were from the start groups of Christian Jews who combined faith in Christ with obedience to the Torah, and Paul's letter to the Galatians not only records his theological position but also bears witness to a Torah-observant Christian mission to the nations. The evidence of Ignatius indicates that such a mission outlived Paul or that it arose anew. The contrary position is not the simple product of reaction, but a theological position that situated Jesus where he claimed to be—in the history of Israel. That the OT, even with the NT, can be read in this way is seen in the periodic appearances of such groups. It is here that the disjunction of text and history makes itself felt. For this reason, I will now leave the level of exegetical analysis and historical reconstruction to examine what the persistence into the present of Sabbatarian Christians tells us about the activity of reading and understanding scripture.

---

[12] "Osterbetrachtungen," 2, 36.

7.3 HERMENEUTICAL REFLECTION

The Sabbatarian position is a construction based on a careful and serious reading of scripture. Sabbatarians subscribe to hermeneutical principles that are widely held among Christians, especially those broadly termed fundamentalist or evangelical. Yet most evangelical Christians reject the claim that the seventh-day Sabbath should be observed by all Christians. We are confronted with the paradox that people share the same texts and manner of reading, yet arrive at dramatically opposite conclusions. Part of the problem can be ascribed to historical and exegetical errors in the Sabbatarian position, as the results of this investigation demonstrate, but there is more involved. This manner of reading scripture, for which I will use the term _biblicist_, has three components: (1) a confidence that a text has an objective, verifiable meaning; (2) the assumption that the reader can empty himself or herself of prior notions and arrive at an objective understanding of what scripture says on a given subject; and (3) the belief that the set of writings accepted as holy scripture, as canon, have a singular meaning, despite the long period of time during which they came to be and the wide variety of narrators, transmitters, and editors, most of whom are unknown to us. I would like to focus on the third of these.[13]

The biblicist manner of reading begins with the assumption of the harmony of scripture. In practice, discordances must be resolved by privileging some texts over others, and using these as hermeneutical

[13] The first of these components, confidence in reading a text, has been widely challenged in literary theory in the twentieth century. A useful overview is provided by Terry Eagleton, _Literary Theory: An Introduction_ (2d ed. Minneapolis, 1996). A detailed engagement from an evangelical perspective with these trends, especially the work of Derrida, can be found in Kevin J. Vanhoozer, _Is There a Meaning in this Text? The Bible, the Reader, and the Morality of Literary Knowledge_ (Grand Rapids, Mich., 1998). Not all will find his proposed solution, "interpretive Trinitarianism," convincing. The second component was successfully challenged by the "new hermeneutics" of Hans-Georg Gadamer, particularly in his _Wahrheit und Methode_ (Tübingen, 1960). Gadamer's insistence that the inquiring subject brings prior knowledge, assumptions, and understanding that affect his approach to any text. Indeed, the very questions in which he frames his inquiry, and which condition his results, are a result of these prior conditions. Understanding occurs through a melting of the respective horizons of text and reader.

standards when reading the rest. Those who hold that the scriptures, especially the NT, are literally prescriptive for faith and practice are divided as to whether the Sabbath is to be observed, whether its strictures have been transferred to the Lord's Day, or whether Christians observe Sunday by convention and tradition, but that it is not the Christian Sabbath.[14] Based on their common understanding of the nature and purpose of revelation, however, they would all agree on one thing; only one of these views can be right, and the other two are based on incorrect readings of authoritative scripture.

The Sabbatarian reading strategy is a logical conclusion of the assumed harmony of scripture. The Bible is read as a single book that begins with Genesis, where God himself rests on the seventh-day; the rest of the Bible is then read in light of this. The NT is read beginning with Matthew, in which the law-based conflicts between Jesus and his contemporaries, recorded by all canonical Gospels, as well as many of the non-canonical ones, are qualified by statements such as the one that denies that it was Jesus' intent to abolish the law (5:17–19). By beginning to read the Bible with Genesis, and the NT with Matthew, the Sabbatarians are not unique—except perhaps in their acceptance of the consequences that this has for reading the rest of the scriptures. A third element is not as common. It is to take the designation *general epistles* seriously and to read them before the Pauline epistles (when I say read *before*, I mean assigning privilege to these writings, and using them in order to interpret Paul, although there are some calls within Sabbatarian circles to rearrange the canon to reflect this).[15] Thus, Paul is read not only through the filter of Acts, in which he is presented as faithful to the Torah, but also that of James, which challenges the Pauline slogan, faith without works.

The Sabbatarian position is then a logical consequence of decisions that were made in the selection and organization of the canon, and offers evidence of how the canon can be read in other combinations and

---

[14] The third position is that of the continental Reformers, notably Luther and Calvin. Summary and critique by Paul K. Jewett, *The Lord's Day: A Theological Guide to the Christian Day of Worship* (Grand Rapids, Mich., 1971), 102–6.

[15] E.g. Ernest L. Martin, *Restoring the Original Bible* (Portland, Ore. 1994).

constructions than have been usual. Rather than revealing how the Bible must be understood, it demonstrates a *Sinnpotential* of the canonical scriptures, a way in which they can be understood. Like a kaleidoscope, a shift in perspective yields a drastically altered picture. Not only Sabbatarians, but mainstream Christian leaders of the second to fourth centuries evidently felt the need to domesticate Paul. His letters literally form the middle of the NT—preceded by the Gospels and Acts, followed by other letters and an apocalypse. Structurally, this position is analogous to that of the Sabbath in the decalogue. But Paul is reinterpreted by Luke as a faithful Jew to the end of his days, and the pastorals written in his name to provide order for growing ecclesiastical communities do so without application of the word of the cross, in which Paul found the hermeneutical key that unlocks the meaning of existence. At the same time, the variety of the early Christian movement was not totally excluded from the canon. The "letter" of James and two of the Gospels are products of Jewish communities of believers in Jesus, at least one of which may have still been practicing the Sabbath. Thus, the Sabbatarian reading results in part from a dynamic potential within the NT itself. In the end, however, this variety in the NT witness speaks against their position. Even Matthew's Gospel records conflict over and reinterpretation of the Sabbath, and so could be included in a collection centered around the writings of a missionary who refused its imposition on his converts.

It should come as no great surprise to discover that the canon of the NT is a consensus document. The voices of the unknown authors we call James, Matthew and John are retained, though more irreconcilable forms of Christian Judaism are excluded, and largely lost to us. At the other extreme, the rabid anti-Judaism of Barnabas finds no place in the canon in its final form. The consensus expressed in the NT canon was not only a differentiation from the kind of Christianity expressed by the Ebionites and the Nazarenes, it also rejected the view that saw only a negative value in Israel's experience of God. The proto-Gnosticism of John is retained, albeit with the cosmetic surgery of a final redaction that made it palatable to the mainstream, while the somewhat more Gnostic *Thomas*, from which the Fourth Gospel seems eager to distance itself, is excluded. Meanwhile, at the center, the distinctiveness of Paul is muted, domesti-

cated, by Acts and the Pastorals. It is this that allows Sabbatarian groups
to appeal not only to the OT, but to the NT as well, even to Paul—but
Paul seen through the eyes of Luke.

In the end, this Sabbatarian reading of the scriptures, while possible,
is flawed. It can deal acceptably, if not adequately, with Matthew, but it
founders on Paul, because it is not enough to read Paul as domesticated
by Luke. It is the undomesticated Paul whose voice is decisive in
determining whether the Sabbatarian position is a valid, if non-conform-
ist, reading of the canon. The Sabbatarian position can only be maintained by a reading of Galatians that can not be sustained. To read
Galatians in any other way than as a firm rejection of a Torah-observant
Christian mission to the Gentiles—including a rejection of the imposition
of Sabbath observance—is to misread the text. The concomitant
assertion that the Christian communities in the first one hundred years
after the crucifixion were primarily Sabbath-keeping is a historical error.
Some were—this should not be forgotten—but this was not the norm.

The results of this investigation have demonstrated that the Sabbatarian position can only be maintained by faulty exegesis and historical
ignorance. At the same time, the Sabbatarian position serves as a healthy
reminder that the early Christian movement was not uniformly "orthodox" by later standards. It shares many of the premises of the Torah-
observant mission to the Gentiles in the first century, such as Israel's
experience of God's salvation and the insistence of the church's
continuity with Israel. This can help us avoid a monolithic understanding
of the church today.

Given the number of topics in which the NT reflects variety, it is
telling that in this collection there is no document that explicitly pleads
for Sabbath observance. At the same time, there is no clear statement
mandating Sunday observance. This suggests that matters such as the
timing of worship services were not important, compared to the central
issue of faith in Jesus Christ.

We return to the question with which the investigation began: how
could such a basic practice as the regular observance of holy time be
changed without leaving a literary record of polemical controversy or
reasoned arguments to document the change? The results of this
investigation force a modification of this question. There is some

evidence. Nevertheless, it remains true that it is a small amount compared to the treatment of other topics in the NT. It is possible that this reflects a deep wisdom on the part of Paul, James and the others: a recognition that the time for meeting to worship is much less important than the reason we worship.

This is why Christians can tolerate Sabbatarians in their midst—provided that life in Jesus is celebrated. Their existence is a constant reminder that the content of worship is far more important than its timing. At the same time, the Sabbatarian claim must be firmly and decidedly rejected and resisted. The claim that only those who worship on the seventh-day Sabbath are faithful to the biblical pattern is both mistaken and sectarian—a lamentable mixture.

Articulation of a Lord's Day theology is a later, post-biblical development.[16] This is no reason to dismiss it, but the fact must be kept in mind to avoid the mistake of defending Sunday observance through prooftexting. More importantly, it means that any Lord's Day theology is subsidiary to the Biblical message and must be judged by it.

7.4 RELEVANCE FOR CONTEMPORARY WORSHIP PRACTICE

The present state of the Christian faith, and of the institutions that bear it, raises the question about the Church "as it was supposed to be." For some, the solution would be a return to an earlier, pristine state, while for others, it would be an adaptation of worship patterns to better reflect our digital, global age. For both, the history of the question is vital. To combat the impact of a globalized, digital world in which we are wired 24/7, it is often held that Sunday must remain legally protected. Yet this study has shown that the Sabbath was not abandoned in order to recreate the same institution on another day. The function performed by the Sabbath in the faith of the Jewish people at the time of Jesus became, for Christians, fulfilled in Jesus. This is seen in the Synoptics, John, Paul and Hebrews, but what does this mean for practice today? Is the question of appropriate days for worship even relevant at a time of steadily dwindling attendance at worship services of mainstream denominations

---

[16] A handy summary of developments can be found in Jewett, *Lord's Day*, 87–122.

on both sides of the Atlantic? After all, just because the church once viewed Sunday as a divine command, sometimes in blithe ignorance that the command literally mandates a different day, does not mean that the church has to hold to it today.

The finding that the reason for worship was more important for the first Christians than the day suggests that the reversal of present trends would begin in focusing on why Christians came together in the first place: worshipful celebration of the common faith in Jesus Christ. Where this has gone missing, it accomplishes little to protect Sunday with legal sanctions.

John Riches notes that the emphasis Jesus places on doing good on the Sabbath day is consistent with his view of God, whose holiness does not have to be protected by boundaries.[17] Rather, it is an active force seeking to reconcile the lost by forgiveness and mercy, thus actively overcoming evil and oppression. It is not that the distinction between sacred and profane ceases to exist, but that the sacred no longer is contained in tightly regulated boundaries. To take this a step further than Riches, the implication of this is that "holy time" would no longer be connected with God's rest, but with his activity—with the accomplishment of his work of salvation. The Johannine "my father works until now, as do I" would appear to be, if not an authentic saying of Jesus, nevertheless an appropriate expression of what the Sabbath meant for him. Just as the temple was not rejected but cleansed to be restored to its intended function—a center of prayer—so the Sabbath is a temporal center from which the believer, focusing on the godly will, becomes active in the service of the Kingdom. The consecration of all of life means that not only the Sabbath, but any time is a time for God, and the believer, to be active in overcoming the forces of darkness.

This view has not been sustained by and large in Christianity. The result in fact is too often the opposite. To be fair, it probably could not have been otherwise. Just as notions of purity and holiness continued to find expression in carefully regulated boundaries, so the notion of a regularly recurring, fixed and agreed upon time for rest and worship has been perpetuated. For long periods of its history, the Christian main-

---

[17] John Riches, *Jesus and the Transformation of Judaism* (London, 1980), 112–44.

stream viewed Sunday as a Christian Sabbath, having the status of divine command similar to that of the seventh-day Sabbath in the OT. This view was sustained by the persistent view of the Ten Commandments, the Decalogue, in which the Sabbath command is enshrined, as an epitome of Christian morality. More recently, the abandonment of Sunday blue laws has led to a secularization of all time.

The early Christian movement was characterized by the bursting of boundaries. The posture toward the Sabbath was an expression of this. The boundary between sacred and profane time was transcended. The holiness of God was not characterized as a besieged fortress but as a conquering power, moving out from its center. Holiness, conceived of in terms of time, could become a quality of any moment. It can be asked whether efforts to salvage Sunday are not reflections of a defensive, fortress mentality. If the church retains Sunday as the Lord's Day, it should do so in consciousness that the origin of the practice is not command, but in the common experience of the risen Lord. With this in mind, worship practice must continually be evaluated to ascertain that it continues to be shared celebration of this.[18] From this center, the church could consider other times and forms of worship more fitted to the rhythms of society today.[19]

At the same time, it is important to remember that the Sabbath created a protected "space" for contact with God not only in the form of corporate worship but also for the exercise of personal spirituality. There is potential gain for our society in the recovery of the ideas incorporated in "Sabbath rest." Those who react to this need and practice the discipline of sanctifying time experience a sanctification of life.[20] But care

[18]   Out of the ample recent literature on worship, see A. Daniel Frankforter, *Stones for Bread: A Critique of Contemporary Worship* (Louisville, Ky., 2001) and Michael Horton, *A Better Way: Rediscovering the Drama of God-Centered Worship* (Grand Rapids, Mich., 2002).
[19]   A successful example of this is the series of Friday evening vespers in Zürich's Predigerkirche (http://zh.ref.ch/content/e4/e376/index_ger.html).
[20]   E.g., Lis Harris, *Holy Days: The World of a Hasidic Family* (New York, 1985). An example of the genre of literature that seeks to renew Lord's Day observance by drawing on the example of Jewish Sabbath observance is Marva J. Dawn, *Keeping the Sabbath Wholly: Ceasing, Resting, Embracing, Feasting* (Grand Rapids, Mich., 1989).

must be exercised in the way this is formulated. This investigation has shown that it cannot be justified and propagated through an unhistorical reading of the biblical texts.

Even if the scriptures are not seen as literally prescriptive, there is value in remembering that the Sabbath in the OT was a matter of divine law, taken up into the Decalogue, the quintessence of the requirements made by God on his chosen people. The general tenor of the commands contained in it is reflected by their negative formulation—you shall not—intended to prohibit actions that most of human society understands to be harmful, acts such as murder, adultery, and theft. The Sabbath command stands out by its positive formulation: you shall sanctify the seventh day. The concomitant action proscribed, work, is not normally considered a sin, but is accepted as necessary. Indeed, industriousness is a virtue in other contexts. The Decalogue commands both diligent, industrious activity (six days you shall work), as well as its periodic interruption. This confronts us with the recognition that even such a virtue as diligent labor, the basis of material prosperity as well as the source of satisfaction in a job well done, has its limits. In a time when the best-rewarded jobs go to those willing to ignore the clock, to sacrifice family and health for material gain, this command should be heard.

It should be heard for what it is—a divine command. The God who speaks here makes a claim on the time of his people, in effect, a claim on their lives. Like any divine command, it reveals the nature of life, as well as the nature of the relationship between God and his people. It is a command to rest, to be refreshed. It is evidence that the people addressed are no longer slaves. It is therefore paradigmatic for every divine command, in that it is an invitation, intended to be heard in freedom. The God who lays claim to their time wants to be served in celebration, in songs of praise, not abject fear. Christians confess that the father of whom Jesus spoke is the God who set Israel apart in this way. This divine claim tells us something important about the nature of our existence before that God.

Bibliography

A. SOURCES

Aland, Kurt, and Barbara Aland, eds. *Synopsis of the Four Gospels: Greek-English Edition of the Synopsis Quattuor Evangelorium.* 6th ed. Stuttgart: Deutsche Bibelgesellschaft, 1983 (1972).

Anderson, Gary A., and Michael E. Stone. *A Synopsis of the Books of Adam and Eve.* SBL Early Judaism and Its Literature. Atlanta: Scholars Press, 1994.

The Ante-Nicene Fathers. Edited by Alexander Roberts and James Donaldson. 10 vols. Edinburgh: T. & T. Clark, 1885–1887.

The Apostolic Fathers: An American Translation. Translated by Edgar J. Goodspeed. New York: Harper, 1950.

Augustine. *The Confessions.* Translated by Edward Bouverie Pusey. Pages 1–125 in *Augustine.* Great Books of the Western World 18. Chicago: Encyclopedia Britannica, 1952.

Baillet, M., J. T. Milik, and R. de Vaux, eds. *Les 'Petites Grottes' de Qumran: Exploration de la Falaise, les grottes 2Q, 3Q, 5Q, 6Q, 7Q À 10Q; le rouleau de cuivre.* 2 vols. Discoveries in the Judean Desert of Jordan 3. Oxford: Oxford Univ. Press, 1962.

Barrett, C. K., ed. *The New Testament Background: Selected Documents.* 2d ed. San Francisco: Harper, 1987 (1957).

Barthélemy, D., and J. T. Milik, eds. *Qumran Cave 1.* Discoveries in the Judaean Desert 1. Oxford: Oxford Univ. Press, 1955.

Die Benediktusregel. Lateinisch-Deutsch. Edited by Basilius Steidle. Beuron: Beuroner Kunstverlag, 1978.

Bovon, François, Pierre Geoltrain, and Sever J. Voicu, eds. *Ecrits apocryphes chrétiens.* Bibliothèque de la Pléiade 442. Paris: Gallimard, 1997.

Charlesworth, James H., ed. *The Old Testament Pseudepigrapha.* 2 vols. New York: Doubleday, 1983 (vol. 1), 1985 (vol. 2).

Charlesworth, James H., and Carol A. Newsom, eds. *Angelic Liturgy: Songs of the Sabbath Sacrifice.* The Princeton Theological Seminary Dead Sea Scrolls Project: The Dead Sea Scrolls. Hebrew, Aramaic, and Greek Texts with English Translations 4B. Tübingen: Mohr Siebeck, 1999.

Cross, Frank Moore, and Donald W. Parry, "A Preliminary Edition of a Fragment of 4QSam[b] (4Q52)." *Bulletin of the American Society of Oriental Research* 306 (May 1997): 63–74.

Danby, Herbert. *The Mishnah: Translated from the Hebrew with Introduction and Brief Explanatory Notes.* Oxford: Oxford Univ. Press, 1933.

Denzinger, Heinrich. *Enchiridion symbolorum definitionum et declarationum de rebus fidei et morum*. Edited by Peter Hünermann. 37th ed. Freiburg im Breisgau: Herder, 1991 (1854).

Diels, Hermann, ed. *Die Fragmente der Vorsokratiker*. 11th ed. 3 vols. Edited by Walther Kranz. Zürich: Weidmann, 1964 (1903).

Dio Cassius. *Dio's Roman History*. Translated by Earnest Cary on the basis of the version of Herbert Baldwin Foster. 9 vols. Loeb Classical Library. Cambridge: Harvard Univ. Press, 1914-1927.

Elliger, K., and W. Rudolph. *Biblia Hebraica Stuttgartensia*. 4th ed. Stuttgart: Deutsche Bibelgesellschaft, 1990 (1977).

Eusebius. *The Ecclesiastical History*. Translated by Kirsopp Lake, J. E. L. Oulton and Hugh Jackson Lawlor, Loeb Classical Library. 2 vols. Cambridge: Harvard Univ. Press, 1926, 1932.

Fischer, Joseph A., ed. *Die Apostolischen Väter*. 10th ed. Schriften des Urchristentums 1. Darmstadt: Wissenschaftliche Buchgesellschaft, 1993 (1956).

García Martínez, Florentino, and Eibert J. C. Tigchelaar, eds. *The Dead Sea Scrolls: Study Edition*. 2 vols. Leiden: Brill, 1997–1998.

Grenfell, Bernard P., and Arthur S. Hunt, eds. *The Oxyrhynchus Papyri, Part 1*. Egypt Exploration Fund 1. London: Frowde, 1898.

Guillaumont, A., H.-Ch. Puech, G. Quispel, W. Till, and Yassah 'Abd al Masih, eds. *The Gospel According to Thomas: Coptic Text Established and Translated*. Leiden: Brill, 1959.

Die Heilige Schrift aus dem Grundtext übersetzt: Revidierte Elberfelder Bibel. Wuppertal: Brockhaus, 1985.

Die Heilige Schrift des alten und des neuen Testaments. Zürich: Verlag der Zürcher Bibel, 1931. Repr. 1955.

Hilgenfeld, Adolf. "Barnabae Epistula. Integram graece primum edidit, veterem interpretationem latinam, commentarium criticum et adnotationes." In *Novum Testamentum extra canonem receptum*. Leipzig: Weigel, 1866

Hippolytus. *Refutatio omnium haeresium*. Edited by Miroslav Marcovich. Patristische Texte und Studien 25. Berlin: de Gruyter, 1986.

Horace. *Satires, Epistles, and Ars Poetica*. Translated by H. Rushton Fairclough. Loeb Classical Library. Cambridge: Harvard Univ. Press, 1978.

Horowitz, Charles. *Der Jerusalemer Talmud in deutscher Übersetzung. 1: Berakhoth*. Institut Judaicum der Universität Tübingen. Tübingen: Mohr Siebeck, 1975.

Irenaeus. *Contre les hérésies*. Edited by Adelin Rousseau, Louis Doutreleau, Bertrand Hemmerdinger and Charles Mercier. 9 vols. Sources Chrétiennes. Paris: 1962-1982.

Jerome. *Sancti Eusebii Hieronymi epistulae*. Edited by Isidorus Hilberg. 2 ed. 3 vols. in 4. Corpus scriptorum ecclesiasticorum latinorum 54–56. Vienna: Österreichische Akademie der Wissenschaften, 1996 (1910).

Johannes Chrysostomus, *Acht Reden gegen die Juden*. Edited by R. Brändle. Translated by V. Jegher-Bucher. Bibliothek der griechischen Literatur 41. Stuttgart: Heiersemann, 1995.

Josephus. Translated by H. St. J. Thackeray, Ralph Marcus, Allen Wikgren, and Louis H. Feldman. 13 vols. Loeb Classical Library. Cambridge: Harvard Univ. Press. 1926–1965.

Justin Martyr. *Dialogus cum Tryphone*. Edited by Miroslav Marcovich. Patristische Texte und Studien 47. Berlin: de Gruyter, 1997.

Juvenal. In *Juvenal and Persius*. Translated by G. G. Ramsay. Loeb Classical Library. London: Heinemann, 1965.

Lamsa, George M. *The New Testament According to the Eastern Text: Translated from Original Aramaic Sources*. Philadelphia: Holman, 1933.

Layton, Bentley. *The Gnostic Scriptures: A New Translation with Annotations and Introductions*. New York: Doubleday, 1987.

———, ed. *Nag Hammadi Codex II, 2–7, together with XIII, 2*, Brit. Lib. Or. 4926 (1) and P. Oxy. 1, 654, 655*. Nag Hammadi Studies 20. Leiden: Brill, 1989.

Leipoldt, Johannes. *Das Evangelium nach Thomas: Koptisch und Deutsch*. Texte und Untersuchungen 101. Berlin: Akademie, 1967.

Lightfoot, J. B., ed. *The Apostolic Fathers: 1. S. Clement of Rome. A Revised Text with Introduction, Notes, Dissertation and Translations*. 2 vols. London: Macmillan, 1890.

Lipsius, Ricardus Adelbertus, ed. *Acta Petri, Acta Pauli, Acta Petri et Pauli, Acta Pauli et Theclae, Acta Thaddaei. Acta Apostolorum Apocrypha* 1. Leipzig: Mendelssohn, 1891.

Macarius of Egypt. *Die 50 geistlichen Homilien des Makarios*. Edited by H. Dörries, E. Klostermann, and M. Kroeger. Patristische Texte und Studien 4. Berlin: de Gruyter, 1964.

Ménard, Jacques-É. *L'Évangile selon Thomas*. Nag Hammadi Studies 5. Leiden: Brill, 1975.

Metzger, Marcel, ed. *Les Constitutions Apostoliques*. 3 vols. Sources chrétiennes 320, 329, 336. Paris: Cerf, 1985–1987.

Miller, Robert J., ed. *The Complete Gospels: Annotated Scholars Version*. 3d ed. San Francisco: HarperCollins, 1994 (1992).

Nestle, Eberhard, and Kurt Aland, eds. *Novum Testamentum Graece*. 27th ed. Stuttgart: Deutsche Bibelgesellschaft, 1993 (1898).

Neusner, Jacob. *The Mishnah: A New Translation*. New Haven: Yale Univ. Press, 1988.

Patrologia graeca. Edited by J.-P. Migne. 162 vols. Paris: Vives, 1857–1866. Repr. Tournout: Brepols, n.d.

Patrologia latina. Edited by J.-P. Migne. 217 vols. Paris: Vives, 1844–1864. Repr. Tournout: Brepols, n.d.

Philo. 10 vols., plus 2 suppl. Translated by F. H. Colson and G. H. Whitaker. Loeb Classical Library. Cambridge: Harvard Univ. Press, 1929–1962.

Plutarch. *Moralia*. 2d ed. 11 vols. Edited by W. R. Paton, I. Wegehaupt, M. Pohlenz, and H. Gärtner. Bibliotheca scriptorum Graecorum et Romanorum Teubneriana. Leipzig, Teubner, 1974 (1925).

Pöhlmann, Horst Georg, ed. *Unser Glaube: Die Bekenntnisschriften der evangelisch-lutherischen Kirche. Ausgabe für die Gemeinde.* Gütersloher Taschenbücher/Siebenstern 1289. Gütersloh: Mohn, 1986.

Prigent, Pierre, and Robert A. Kraft, eds. *Épître de Barnabé.* Sources chrétiennes 172. Paris: Cerf, 1971.

Qimron, Elisha, and John Strugnell, eds. *Qumran Cave 4: 5. Miqsat Ma'ase ha-Torah.* Discoveries in the Judean Desert 10. Oxford: Oxford Univ. Press, 1994.

Rahlfs, Alfred, ed. *Septuaginta: Id est Vetus Testamentum graece iuxta LXX interpretes.* Stuttgart: Deutsche Bibelgesellschaft, 1979 (1935).

Resch, Alfred, ed. *Agrapha: Aussercanonische Schriftfragmente.* 2d ed. Texte und Untersuchungen Neue Folge 15.3/4. Leipzig: Hinrichs, 1889.

Robinson, James M., ed. *The Coptic Gnostic Library: A Complete Edition of the Nag Hammadi Codices.* 5 vols. Leiden: Brill, 2000.

Rordorf, Willy, ed. *Sabbat und Sonntag in der Alten Kirche.* Traditio Christiana 2. Zürich: Theologischer Verlag, 1972.

Schneemelcher, Wilhelm, ed. *Neutestamentliche Apokryphen in deutscher Übersetzung.* 6th ed. 2 vols. Tübingen: Mohr Siebeck, 1990.

Segond, Louis, ed. *La Sainte Bible. Qui comprend l'ancien et le nouveau testament traduits sur les texts originaux hébreu et grec.* Geneva: Société Biblique de Genève, 1942.

Sifre zu Numeri. Translated and explained by Dagmar Börner-Klein. Rabbinische Texte, 2. Reihe, Tannaitische Midraschim 3. Stuttgart: Kohlhammer. 1997.

Stern, Menahem. *Greek and Latin Authors on the Jews and Judaism.* 3 vols. Jerusalem: Israel Academy of Sciences and Humanities, 1974–1984.

Strack, Hermann L., and Paul Billerbeck. *Kommentar zum Neuen Testament aus Talmud und Midrasch.* 6 vols. 4th ed. (vols. 1–3); 3d ed. (vol. 4); 2d ed. (vols. 5–6); München: Beck, 1961–1965 (1922–1928).

Tertullian. *Opera.* 2 vols. Corpus Christianorum series latina 1–2. Turnhout: Brepols, 1954.

——, *Adversus Marcionem.* Edited and translated by Ernest Evans. 2 vols. Oxford Early Christian Texts. Oxford: Oxford Univ. Press, 1972.

Vermès, Geza. *The Complete Dead Sea Scrolls in English.* London: Penguin, 1997.

Vööbus, Arthur, ed. *Didascalia Apostolorum in Syriac.* 4 vols. Corpus scriptorum Christianorum orientalium 401-402, 407-408. Paris, 1979.

Wengst, Klaus, ed. *Didache (Apostellehre), Barnabasbrief, Zweiter Klemensbrief, Schrift an Diognet.* Schriften des Urchristentums 2. Darmstadt: Wissenschaftliche Buchgesellschaft, 1984.

Wilckens, Ulrich. *Das Neue Testament übersetzt und kommentiert.* Hamburg: Furche, 1970.

B. LEXICA AND TOOLS

Alsop, John R., ed. *An Index to the Revised Bauer-Arndt-Gingrich Greek Lexicon.* 2d ed. Grand Rapids, Mich.: Zondervan, 1981.

Atiya, Aziz S., ed. *The Coptic Encyclopedia*. 8 vols. New York: Macmillan, 1991.

Balz, Horst, and Gerhard Schneider, eds. *Exegetisches Wörterbuch zum Neuen Testament*. 2d ed. 3 vols. Stuttgart: Kohlhammer, 1992 (1980–1983).

Bauer, Walter. *Griechisch-deutsches Wörterbuch zu den Schriften des Neuen Testaments und der frühchristlichen Literatur*. 6th ed. Edited by Kurt and Barbara Aland. Berlin: de Gruyter, 1988.

Betz, Hans Dieter, Don S. Browning, Bernd Janowski, and Eberhard Jüngel, eds. *Religion in Geschichte und Gegenwart*. 4th ed. 7 vols. to date. Tübingen: Mohr Siebeck, 1998–.

Blass, Friedrich, and Alfred Debrunner. *Grammatik des Neutestamentlichen Griechisch*. Göttinger Theologische Lehrbücher. Edited by Friedrich Rehkopf. 17th ed; Göttingen: Vandenhoeck & Ruprecht, 1990 (1896).

Botterweck, G. Johannes, Helmer Ringgren, and Heinz-Josef Fabry, eds. *Theologisches Wörterbuch zum Alten Testament*. 10 vols. Stuttgart: Kohlhammer, 1970–2000.

Bradley, James E., and Richard A. Muller. *Church History: An Introduction to Research, Reference Works and Methods*. Grand Rapids, Mich.: Eerdmans, 1995.

Buttrick, George Arthur, ed. *The Interpreter's Dictionary of the Bible*. 4 vols. Nashville: Abingdon, 1962. Supplementary volume edited by Keith Crim, n.d.

Cancik, Hubert, and Helmuth Schneider, eds. *Der neue Pauly: Enzyklopädie der Antike*. 16 vols. to date. Stuttgart: Metzlar, 1996–2003.

Coggins, R.J., and J.L. Houlden, eds. *A Dictionary of Biblical Interpretation*. London: SCM, 1990.

Cross, F. L., and E. A. Livingstone, eds. *The Oxford Dictionary of the Christian Church*. 3d ed. Oxford: Oxford Univ. Press, 1997 (1957).

Danker, Frederick William, ed. *A Greek-English Lexicon of the New Testament and Other Early Christian Literature*. 3d ed. Based on Walter Bauer's *Griechisch-deutsches Wörterbuch zu den Schriften des Neuen Testaments und der frühchristlichen Literatur*, sixth edition, ed. Kurt Aland and Barbara Aland, and on previous English editions by W. F. Arndt, F. W. Gingrich, and F. W. Danker. Chicago: Univ. of Chicago Press, 2000 (1957).

Eccles, Lance. *Introductory Coptic Reader: Selections from the Gospel of Thomas with Full Grammatical Explanations*. Kensington: Dunwoody, 1991.

Eliade, Mircea, ed. *The Encyclopedia of Religion*. 16 vols. New York: Macmillan, 1987.

Ferguson, Everett, ed. *Encyclopedia of Early Christianity*. 2d ed. Garland Reference Library of the Humanities 1839. New York: Garland, 1997 (1990).

Freedman, David Noel, ed. *The Anchor Bible Dictionary*. 6 vols. New York: Doubleday, 1992.

Galling, Kurt, ed. *Religion in Geschichte und Gegenwart*. 3d ed. 6 vols. Tübingen: Mohr Siebeck, 1957–1965.

Gelb, Ignace J., Benno Landsberger, A. Leo Oppenheim, and Erica Reiner, eds. *The Assyrian Dictionary of the Oriental Institute of the University of Chicago*. 17 vols. to date. Chicago: Univ. of Chicago, 1956–.

Gesenius, Wilhelm. *Hebräisches und Aramäisches Handwörterbuch über das Alte Testament*. Edited by Frants Buhl. 17th ed., 1915. Repr., Berlin: Springer 1962

Goodspeed, Edgar J. *Index Patristicus sive clavis patrum apostoloricorum operum*. Leipzig: Hinrichs, 1907. Repr. ed. Peabody, Mass: Hendrickson, 1993.

Hatch, Edwin, and Henry A. Redpath, eds. *Concordance to the Septuagint and Other Greek Versions of the Old Testament (Including the Apocryphal Books)*. 2 vols. Oxford, 1897. Suppl. 1906. Repr. 3 vols. in 2, Grand Rapids, Mich.: Baker, 1983.

Hornblower, Simon, and Antony Spawforth, eds. *The Oxford Classical Dictionary*. 3d ed. Oxford: Oxford Univ. Press, 1996.

Jenni, Ernst, and Claus Westermann, eds. *Theologisches Handwörterbuch zum Alten Testament*. 5th ed. 2 vols. München: Kaiser, 1971.

Joüon, Paul. *Grammaire de L'hébreu Biblique*. 4h ed. Rome: Pontifical Biblical Institute, 1982 (1923).

Kittel, Gerhard, and Gerhard Friedrich, eds. *Theologisches Wörterbuch zum Neuen Testament*. 10 vols. Stuttgart: Kohlhammer, 1933–1979. Repr., 1990.

Kraft, Henricus. *Clavis Patrum Apostolicorum*. Darmstadt: Wissenschaftliche Buchgesellschaft, 1964.

Krause, Gerhard, and Gerhard Müller, eds. *Theologische Realenzyklopädie*. 36 vols. Berlin: de Gruyter, 1976–2004.

Lambdin, Thomas O. *Introduction to Sahidic Coptic*. Macon, Geo.: Mercer Univ. Press, 1983.

Liddell, Henry George, Robert Scott, and Henry Stuart Jones. *A Greek-English Lexicon*. 9th ed. Oxford: Oxford Univ. Press, 1940 (1843).

Louw, J. P., and E. A. Nida, eds. *Greek-English Lexicon of the New Testament: Based on Semantic Domains*. 2 ed. 2 vols. New York: United Bible Societies, 1989 (1988).

Metzger, Bruce M. *A Textual Commentary on the Greek New Testament*. 3d ed. London: United Bible Societies, 1975 (1971).

Meyer, Rudolf. *Hebräische Grammatik*. 3rd ed. Sammlung Göschen, 1966–1982. Repr., de Gruyter Studienbuch. Berlin: de Gruyter 1992.

Mills, Watson. *A Computer-Generated Concordance of the Coptic Text of the Gospel According to Thomas*. The Computer Bible 43. Wooster, Ohio: Biblical Research Associates, 1995.

Pauly, A. F. *Paulys Realenzyklopädie der classischen Altertumswissenschaft*. New edition G. Wissowa. 49 vols. Stuttgart: Druckenmüller, 1958–1978.

Pirot, L., and A. Robert, *Dictionnaire de la Bible: Supplement*. 12 vols. to date. Paris: Letouzey, 1928–.

Schiffman, Lawrence H., and James C. VanderKam, eds. *Encyclopedia of the Dead Sea Scrolls*. 2 vols. New York: Oxford Univ. Press, 2000.

Soulen, Richard N. *Handbook of Biblical Criticism*. 2d ed.; Atlanta: John Knox, 1981 (1976).

Temporini, Hildegard, and Wolfgang Haase, eds. *Aufstieg und Niedergang der römischen Welt: Geschichte und Kultur Roms im Spiegel der neueren Forschung*. Part 2, *Principat*. 37 vols. to date. Berlin: de Gruyter, 1974–.

Weingreen, J. *A Practical Grammar for Classical Hebrew.* 2d ed. London: Oxford Univ. Press, 1959 (1939).

Wigram, George. *The Englishman's Greek Concordance of the New Testament.* 9th ed.; London: Bagster 1903 (1840). Repr., Grand Rapids, Mich.: Zondervan, 1970.

———. *The Englishman's Hebrew and Chaldee Concordance of the Old Testament.* London: Samuel Bagster, 1843. Repr., 1971.

Würthwein, Ernst. *Der Text des Alten Testaments: Eine Einführung in die Biblia Hebraica.* 5th ed. Stuttgart: Deutsche Bibelgesellschaft, 1988 (1952).

Ziefle, Helmut W. *Modern Theological German: A Reader and Dictionary.* Grand Rapids, Mich.: Baker, 1997 (previously published separately, 1986, 1992).

C. SECONDARY LITERATURE

Abegg, Martin. "Paul, 'Works of the Law' and MMT." *Biblical Archaeology Review* 20, no. 6 (November/December 1994), 52–55.

Abrahams, I. *Studies in Pharisaism and the Gospels. Second Series.* Cambridge: Cambridge Univ. Press, 1924.

Aichinger, Hermann. "Quellenkritische Untersuchung der Perikope vom Ährenraufen am Sabbat. Mk 2,23–28 par Mt 12,1–8 par Lk 6,1–5." Pages 110–53 in *Jesus in der Verkündigung der Kirche.* Edited by A. Fuchs. Studien zum Neuen Testament und seiner Umwelt 1. Freistadt: Plöchl, 1976.

Albertz, Martin. *Die synoptischen Streitgespräche: Ein Beitrag zur Formgeschichte des Urchristentums.* Berlin: Trowitzsch, 1921.

Albright, W. F., and C. S. Mann. *Matthew: A New Translation with Introduction and Commentary.* Anchor Bible 26. Garden City, N.Y.: Doubleday, 1971.

Allen, E. L. "The Jewish Christian Church in the Fourth Gospel." *Journal of Biblical Literature* 74 (1955): 85–92.

Allison, Dale C. *Jesus of Nazareth: Millenarian Prophet.* Minneapolis: Fortress, 1998.

Alt, Albrecht. *Die Ursprünge des israelitischen Rechts.* Berichte über die Verhandlungen der sächsischen Akademie der Wissenschaften zu Leipzig. Philologisch-historische Klasse 86/1. Leipzig: Hirzel, 1934. Repr. pages 278–332 in *Kleine Schriften zur Geschichte des Volkes Israel 1.* München: Beck, 1953.

Alter, Robert. *The Art of Biblical Narrative.* New York: Basic, 1981.

Anderson, R. Dean, Jr. *Ancient Rhetorical Theory and Paul.* Contributions to Biblical Exegesis & Theology 18. Kampen: Kok Pharos, 1996.

Andreasen, Niels-Erik. *The Old Testament Sabbath: A Tradition-Historical Investigation.* Society of Biblical Literature Dissertation Series 7. Missoula, Mont.: Society of Biblical Literature for the Form Criticism Seminar, 1972.

———. "Recent Studies of the Old Testament Sabbath." *Zeitschrift für die alttestamentliche Wissenschaft* 86 (1974): 453–69.

Andrews, J. N. *History of the Sabbath.* Battle Creek, Mich., 1873. http://www.nisbett.com/sabbath/history/hos-contents.htm, accessed Jan 16, 2003.

Armstrong, Herbert W. *Has Time Been Lost?* 5th ed. Pasadena, Cal.: Ambassador College Press, 1984 (1952)

————. *What Will You Be Doing in the Next Life?* Pasadena, Cal.: Ambassador College Press, 1967.

————. *Which Day is the Christian Sabbath?* Pasadena, Cal.: Ambassador College Press, 1962.

Arnold, Clinton E. "Returning to the Domain of the Powers: *Stoicheia* as Evil Spirits in Galatians 4:3,9." *Novum Testamentum* 38 (1996): 55–76.

Asiedu-Peprah, Martin. *Johannine Sabbath Conflicts as Juridical Controversy*. Wissenschaftliche Untersuchungen zum Neuen Testament. Second Series 132. Tübingen: Mohr Siebeck, 2001.

Attridge, Harold W. *The Epistle to the Hebrews: A Commentary on the Epistle to the Hebrews*. Hermeneia. Philadelphia: Fortress, 1989.

————. "Thematic Development and Source Elaboration in John 7:1–36." *Catholic Biblical Quarterly* 42 (1980): 160–70.

Avemarie, Friedrich. Review of Lutz Doering, *Schabbat: Sabbathalacha und -praxis im antiken Judentum und Urchristentum*. *Theologische Literaturzeitung* 126 (2001): 622–5.

Avi-Yonah, Michael. *The Jews Under Roman and Byzantine Rule: A Political History of Palestine from the Bar Kokhba War to the Arab Conquest*. New York: Schocken, 1976. Repr., Jerusalem: Magnes, 1984.

Baarda, Tjitze. "'If You Do Not Sabbatize the Sabbath . . .': The Sabbath as God or World in Gnostic Understanding (*Ev. Thom.*, Log. 27)." Pages 147–71 in *Essays on the Diatessaron*. Contributions to Biblical Exegesis & Theology 11. Kampen: Kok Pharos, 1994.

————. "The Sabbath in the Parable of the Shepherd, *Evangelium Veritatis 32:18–34*." Pages 133–45 in *Essays on the Diatessaron*. Contributions to Biblical Exegesis & Theology 11. Kampen: Kok Pharos, 1994.

Bacchiocchi, Samuele. *Anti-Judaism and the Origin of Sunday*. Rome: Pontifical Gregorian Univ. Press, 1975.

————. "Un Esame dei testi biblici e patristiici dei primi quattro secoli allo scopo d'accertare il tempe e le cause del sorgere della domenica come giorno del Signore." Ph. D. dissertation, Pontificia Universitate Gregoriana, 1974.

————. *From Sabbath to Sunday: A Historical Investigation of the Rise of Sunday Observance in Early Christianity*. Rome: Pontifical Gregorian Univ. Press, 1977.

————. "John 5:17: Negation or Clarification of the Sabbath?" *Andrews University Seminary Studies* 19 (1981): 3-19.

Back, Sven Olav. *Jesus of Nazareth and the Sabbath Commandment*. Abo: Abo Akademi Univ. Press, 1995.

Baker, Aelred. "Pseudo-Macarius and the Gospel of Thomas." *Vigiliae Christianae* 18 (1964): 215-25.

Bammel, Ernst. "The Cambridge Pericope: The Addition to Luke 6,4 in Codex Bezae." *New Testament Studies* 32 (1986): 404-26.

Banks, Robert. *Jesus and the Law in the Synoptic Tradition*. Society for New Testament Studies Monographs Series 28. Cambridge: Cambridge Univ. Press, 1975.

Barclay, John M. G. *Jews in the Mediterranean Diaspora: From Alexander to Trajan (323 BCE to 117 CE)*. Edinburgh: T. & T. Clark, 1996.

———. "Mirror-Reading a Polemical Letter: Galatians as a Test Case." *Journal for the Study of the New Testament* 31 (1987): 73–93.

Barnard, Leslie William. "The 'Epistle of Barnabas' and its Contemporary Setting." *ANRW* 27.1:159–207. Part 2, *Principat*, 27.1. Edited by H. Temporini and W. Haase. Berlin: de Gruyter, 1993.

Barrett, C. K. "The Eschatology of the Epistle to the Hebrews." Pages 363–93 in *The Background of the New Testament and its Eschatology (FS C. H. Dodd)*. Edited by W. D. Davies and D. Daube. Cambridge: Cambridge Univ. Press, 1956.

———. *Freedom & Obligation: A Study of the Epistle to the Galatians*. London: SPCK, 1985.

———. *The Gospel According to St John. An Introduction with Commentary and Notes on the Greek Text*. 2d ed. London: SPCK, 1978 (1955).

———. *The Gospel of John and Judaism*. Translated by D. M. Smith. London: SPCK, 1975.

Bartelmus, Rüdiger. "Mk 2,27 und die ältesten Fassungen des Arbeitsruhegebots im AT: Biblisch-theologische Beobachtungen zur Sabbatfrage." *Biblische Notizen* 41 (1988): 41–64.

Barth, Gerhard. "Das Gesetzesverständnis des Evangelisten Matthäus." Pages 54–154 in *Überlieferung und Auslegung im Matthäus-Evangelium*. Edited by G. Bornkamm, G. Barth and H. J. Held. 7th ed. Wissenschaftliche Monographien zum Alten und Neuen Testament 1. Neukirchen-Vluyn: Neukirchener Verlag, 1960.

Bauckham, Richard. "For Whom Were the Gospels Written?" Pages 9–48 in *The Gospels for All Christians: Rethinking the Gospel Audiences*. Grand Rapids, Mich.: Eerdmans, 1998.

Baumgarten, Joseph M. "The Counting of the Sabbath in Ancient Sources." *Vetus Testamentum* 16 (1966): 277–86.

Baur, Ferdinand Christian. "Die Christuspartei in der korinthischen Gemeinde, der Gegensatz des petrinischen und paulinischen Christenthums in der ältesten Kirche, der Apostel Petrus in Rom." *Tübinger Zeitschrift für Theologie* 5, no. 4 (1831): 61–206. Repr. pages 1–146 of volume 1 of *Ausgewählte Werke in Einzelausgaben*. Edited by Klaus Scholder. 5 vols. Stuttgart-Bad Cannstatt: Frommann, 1963–1975.

Beare, Francis Wright. "The Sabbath Was Made for Man?" *Journal of Biblical Literature* 79 (1960): 130–36.

Becker, Jürgen. *Das Evangelium nach Johannes*. 3d ed. 2 vols. Ökumensicher Taschenbuch-Kommentar 4. Gütersloh: Mohn, 1991 (1979).

———. *Jesus von Nazaret*. de Gruyter Lehrbücher. Berlin: de Gruyter, 1996.

———. *Paulus der Apostel der Völker*. 3d ed. Uni-Taschenbücher 2014. Tübingen: Mohr Siebeck, 1998 (1989).

Becker, Jürgen, and Ulrich Luz. *Die Briefe an die Galater, Epheser und Kolosser*. Das Neue Testament Deutsch 8/1. Göttingen: Vandenhoeck & Ruprecht, 1998.

Beckwith, Roger T., and Wilfred Stott. *This is the Day: The Biblical Doctrine of the Christian Sunday in its Jewish and Early Church Setting.* Marshall's Theological Library. London: Marshall, Morgan and Scott, 1978.

Beker, J. Christiaan. *Paul the Apostle: The Triumph of God in Life and Thought.* Philadelphia: Fortress, 1980.

Belleville, Linda L. "'Under Law': Structural Analysis and the Pauline Concept of Law in Galatians 3.21–4.11." *Journal for the Study of the New Testament* 26 (1986): 53–78.

Bernard, J. H. *A Critical and Exegetical Commentary on the Gospel According to St. John.* International Critical Commentary. Edinburgh: T. & T. Clark, 1928.

Bernard, Jacques. "La guérison de Bethesda: Harmoniques judéo-hellénistiques d'un récit de miracle un jour de sabbat." *Mélanges de science religieuse* 33 (1976): 3–34.

———. "La guérison de Bethesda un jour de sabbat: Harmoniques judéo-hellénistiques d'un récit de miracle un jour de sabbat (suite)." *Mélanges de science religieuse* 34 (1977): 13–44.

Betz, Hans Dieter. "2 Cor 6:14–7:1: An Anti-Pauline Fragment?" *Journal of Biblical Literature* 92 (1973): 88–108.

———. *Galatians: A Commentary on Paul's Letter to the Churches in Galatia.* Hermeneia. Philadelphia: Fortress, 1979.

Bietenhard, Hans. "'Der Menschensohn'—ὁ υἱὸς τοῦ ἀνθρώπου. Sprachliche und religionsgeshichtliche Untersuchungen zu einem Begriff der synoptischen Evangelien. 1. Sprachlicher und religionsgeschichtlicher Teil." *ANRW* 25,1:265-350. Part 2, *Principat*, 25.1. Edited by H. Temporini and W. Haase. Berlin: de Gruyter, 1982.

Blank, Josef. *Das Evangelium nach Johannes.* 3 vols. in 4. Geistliche Schriftlesung. Neues Testament 4/1–3. Düsseldorf: Patmos, 1977–1981.

Blaschke, Andreas. *Beschneidung: Zeugnisse der Bibel und verwandter Texte.* Texte und Arbeiten zum neutestamentlichen Zeitalter 28. Tübingen: Francke, 1998.

Blinzler, Josef. "Lexikalisches zu dem Terminus τὰ στοιχεῖα τοῦ κόσμου bei Paulus." Pages 429–43 in *Studiorum Paulinorum Congressus Internationalis Catholicus.* Rome: Pontificio Instituto Biblico, 1963.

Bolyki, János. *Jesu Tischgemeinschaften.* Wissenschaftliche Untersuchungen zum Neuen Testament. Second Series 96. Tübingen: Mohr Siebeck, 1998.

Borgen, Peder. "John and the Synoptics." Pages 408–37 in *The Interrelations of the Gospels.* Edited by D. L. Dungan. Bibliotheca ephemeridum theologicarum Lovaniensium 95. Leuven: Leuven Univ. Press, 1990.

Bornkamm, Günther. "Der Auferstandene und der Irdische: Mt 28, 16–20." Pages 171–91 in *Zeit und Geschichte (FS R. Bultmann).* Edited by E. Dinkler. Tübingen: Mohr Siebeck, 1964.

———. "Enderwartung und Kirche im Matthäusevangelium." Pages 13–47 in *Überlieferung und Auslegung im Matthäus-Evangelium.* Edited by G. Bornkamm, G. Barth and H. J. Held. 7th ed. Wissenschaftliche Monographien zum Alten und Neuen Testament 1. Neukirchen-Vluyn: Neukirchener Verlag, 1975 (1960).

———. *Jesus von Nazareth*. 15th ed. Urban-Taschenbücher 19. Stuttgart: Kohlhammer, 1995 (1956).

Bousset, Wilhelm. *Die Religion des Judentums im späthellenisten Zeitalter*. 4th ed. Handbuch zum Neuen Testament 21. Tübingen: Mohr Siebeck, 1966 (1903).

———. *Kyrios Christus: Geschichte des Christusglaubens von den Anfängen des Christentums bis Irenaeus*. 2d ed. Forschungen zur Religion und Literatur des Alten und Neuen Testaments 21. Göttingen: Vandenhoeck & Ruprecht, 1921 (1913).

Bovon, François. *Das Evangelium nach Lukas. 1. Teilband Lk 1,1–9,50*. Evangelisch-Katholischer Kommentar zum Neuen Testament 3/1. Zürich: Benzinger, 1989.

Böcher, Otto, and Klaus Haacker, eds. *Verborum veritas (FS G. Stählin)*. Wuppertal: Brockhaus, 1970.

Braulik, Georg. *Die deuteronomischen Gesetze und der Dekalog: Studien zum Aufbau von Deuteronomium 12–26*. Stuttgarter Bibelstudien 145. Stuttgart: Katholisches Bibelwerk, 1991.

Braun, Herbert. *Spätjüdisch-häretischer und frühchristlicher Radikalismus: Jesus von Nazareth und die essenische Qumransekte*. 2 vols. Tübingen: Mohr Siebeck, 1957.

Brendecke, Arndt. *Die Jahrhundertwenden: Eine Geschichte ihrer Wahrnehmung und Wirkung*. München: Campus, 2000.

Brown, Charles Thomas. *The Gospel and Ignatius of Antioch*. Studies in Biblical Literature 12. New York: Lang, 2000.

Brown, Paterson. "The Sabbath and the Week in Thomas 27." *Novum Testamentum* 34 (1992): 193.

Brown, Raymond E. *The Gospel According to John: A New Translation with Introduction and Commentary*. 2 vols. Anchor Bible 29. Garden City, N.Y.: Doubleday, 1966, 1970.

———. *An Introduction to the New Testament*. Anchor Bible Reference Library. New York: Doubleday, 1997.

Brown, Raymond E., and John P. Meier. *Antioch and Rome: New Testament Cradles of Catholic Christianity*. New York: Paulist, 1983.

Brueggemann, Walter B. *Theology of the Old Testament: Testimony, Dispute, Advocacy*. Minneapolis: Fortress, 1997.

Buchanan, George Wesley. *To the Hebrews: Translation, Comment and Conclusions*. Anchor Bible 36. Garden City, N.Y.: Doubleday, 1972.

Bultmann, Rudolf. *Das Evangelium nach Johannes*. 21st ed. Kritisch-exegetischer Kommentar über das Neue Testament 2. Göttingen: Vandenhoeck & Ruprecht, 1986 (1941).

———. *Die Geschichte der synoptischen Tradition*. 10th ed. Forschungen zur Religion und Literatur des Alten und Neuen Testaments 29. Göttingen: Vandenhoeck & Ruprecht, 1995 (1921).

———. *Der Stil der paulinischen Predigt und die kynisch-stoische Diatribe*. Forschungen zur Religion und Literatur des Alten und Neuen Testaments 13. Göttingen: Vandenhoeck & Ruprecht, 1910. Repr., 1984.

————. *Theologie des Neuen Testaments.* Edited by Otto Merk. 9th ed. Uni-Taschenbücher 630. Tübingen: Mohr Siebeck, 1984 (1953).

————. *Das Urchristentum.* 5th ed. München: Artemis, 1983 (1949). Repr., München: DTV, 1993.

————. "Das Verhältnis der urchristlichen Christusbotschaft zum historischen Jesus." Heidelberg: Carl Winter Universitätsverlag, 1960. Repr. pages 445-69 in *Exegetica: Aufsätze zur Erforschung des Neuen Testaments.* Tübingen: Mohr Siebeck, 1967.

Burkett, Delbert. "The Nontitular Son of Man: A History and Critique." *New Testament Studies* 40 (1994): 504–21.

————. *The Son of Man Debate: A History and Evaluation.* Society for New Testament Studies Monographs Series 107. Cambridge: Cambridge Univ. Press, 1999.

Burton, Ernest De Witt. *A Critical and Exegetical Commentary on the Epistle to the Galatians.* International Critical Commentary 8. Edinburgh: T. & T. Clark, 1921.

Carleton Paget, James. *The Epistle of Barnabas: Outlook and Background.* Wissenschaftliche Untersuchungen zum Neuen Testament. Second Series 64. Tübingen: Mohr Siebeck, 1994.

————. "Jewish Proselytism at the Time of Christian Origins: Chimera or Reality?" *Journal for the Study of the New Testament* 62 (1996): 65–103.

Carson, Donald Arthur. "Jesus and the Sabbath in the Four Gospels." Pages 57–97 in *From Sabbath to Lord's Day: A Biblical, Historical and Theological Investigation.* Edited by Donald Arthur Carson. Grand Rapids, Mich.: Zondervan, 1982.

————, ed. *From Sabbath to Lord's Day: A Biblical Historical and Theological Investigation.* Grand Rapids, Mich.: Zondervan, 1982.

Casey, Maurice. "Culture and Historicity: The Plucking of the Grain (Mark 2.23–28)." *New Testament Studies* 34 (1988): 1–23.

Cassuto, Umberto. *A Commentary on the Book of Genesis.* Translated by Israel Abrahams. 2 vols. Jerusalem: Magnes, 1961.

Cazelles, Henri. "Ex. XXXIV, 21: Traite-t-il du sabbat?" *Catholic Biblical Quarterly* 23 (1961): 223–6. Repr. pages 295-8 in *Autour de l'Exode. (Études).* Sources Bibliques. Paris: Gabalda, 1987.

Chadwick, Henry. *The Early Church.* Pelican History of the Church 1. Harmondsworth: Penguin, 1967.

Charette, B. "'To Proclaim Liberty to the Captives:' Matthew 11.28–30 in the Light of OT Prophetic Expectation." *New Testament Studies* 38 (1992): 290–7.

Charlesworth, James H. *Jesus within Judaism: New Light from Exciting Archaeological Discoveries.* Anchor Bible Reference Library. New York: Doubleday, 1988.

Cohen, Matty. "La controverse de Jésus et des Pharisiens a propos de la cueillette des épis, selon l'Évangile de Saint Matthieu." *Mélanges de Science Religieuse* 34 (1977): 3–12.

Cohen, Shaye J. D. *The Beginnings of Jewishness: Boundaries, Varieties, Uncertainties.* Hellenistic Culture and Society 31. Berkeley and Los Angeles: Univ. of California Press, 1999.

360   Encountering the Rest of God

4
——. "The Political and Social History of the Jews in Greco-Roman Antiquity: The State of the Question." Pages 33–57 in *Early Judaism and Its Modern Interpreters*. Edited by R. A. Kraft and G. W. E. Nickelsburg. Atlanta: Scholars Press, 1986.

Cohn-Sherbok, D. M. "An Analysis of Jesus' Arguments Concerning the Plucking of Grain on the Sabbath." *Journal for the Study of the New Testament* 2 (1979): 31–41.

Conzelmann, Hans. *Grundriss der Theologie des Neuen Testaments*. München: Kaiser 1967. 5th ed. Edited by Andreas Lindemann. Uni-Taschenbücher 1446. Tübingen: Mohr Siebeck, 1992.

Crossan, John Dominic. *The Birth of Christianity: Discovering What Happened in the Years Immediately after the Execution of Jesus*. New York: HarperCollins, 1998.

——. *The Historical Jesus: The Life of a Mediterranean Jewish Peasant*. New York: HarperCollins, 1991.

Crüsemann, Frank. *Bewahrung der Freiheit: Das Thema des Dekalogs in sozialgeschichtlicher Perspektive*. München, 1983.

——. *Die Tora: Theologie und Sozialgeschichte des alttestamentlichen Gesetzes*. München: Kaiser, 1992.

Cullmann, Oscar. "Sabbat und Sonntag nach dem Johannesevangelium. ʼΕΟΣ ʼΑΡΤΙ (Joh. 5,17)." Pages 127–31 in *In Memoriam Ernst Lohmeyer*. Edited by W. Smauch. Stuttgart: Evangelisches Verlagswerk, 1951. Repr. pages 187–91 in *Vorträge und Aufsätze, 1925–1962*. Zürich: Zwingli, 1966.

Culpepper, R. Alan. *Anatomy of the Fourth Gospel: A Study in Literary Design*. Foundations and Facets: New Testament. Philadelphia: Fortress, 1983.

——. "Un exemple de commentaire fondé sur la critique narrative: Jean 5,1–18." Pages 135–51 in *La communauté johannique et son histoire: La trajectoire de l'evangile de Jean aux deux premiers siècles*. Edited by J-D. Kaestli, J.-M. Poffet and J. Zumstein. Le Monde de la Bible 20. Geneva: Labor et Fides, 1990.

Das, A. Andrew. "Another Look at ἐὰν μή in Galatians 2:16." *Journal of Biblical Literature* 119 (2000): 529–39.

Daube, David. "Responsibilities of Master and Disciples in the Gospels." *New Testament Studies* 19 (1972/73): 1–15.

Davies, William D. *The Gospel and the Land: Early Christianity and Jewish Territorial Doctrine*. Berkeley and Los Angeles: Univ. of California Press, 1974.

——. *The Setting of the Sermon on the Mount*. Cambridge: Cambridge Univ. Press, 1964.

Davies, William D., and Dale C. Allison. *A Critical and Exegetical Commentary on the Gospel According to Saint Matthew*. 3 vols. International Critical Commentary. Edinburgh: T. & T. Clark, 1988.

Davis, Philip G. "Christology, Discipleship, and Self-Understanding in the Gospel of Mark." Pages 101–19 in *Self-Definition and Self-Discovery in Early Christianity: A Study in Changing Horizons (FS B. F. Meyer)*. Edited by D. J. Hawkin and T. A. Robinson. Studies in the Bible and Early Christianity 26. Lewiston, Maine: Mellen, 1990.

Dawn, Marva J. *Keeping the Sabbath Wholly: Ceasing, Resting, Embracing, Feasting.* Grand Rapids, Mich.: Eerdmans, 1989.

Dawson, Anne and Michael Lattke, "Nachtrag: Bemerkungen zum Stand der Jesusforschung." Pages 129–58 in Hubert Leroy, *Jesus: Überlieferung und Deutung.* 3d ed. Erträge der Forschung 95. Darmstadt: Wissenschaftliche Buchgesellschaft, 1999 (1978).

De Conick, April D. *Seek to See Him: Ascent and Vision Mysticism in the Gospel of Thomas.* Supplements to Vigiliae Christianae 33. Leiden: Brill, 1996.

Delobel, Joel. "Luke 6,5 in Codex Bezae: The Man Who Worked on the Sabbath." Pages 453–77 in *A cause de l'Évangile. Études sur les Synoptiques et les Actes (FS J. Dupont).* Paris: Cerf, 1985.

Derrett, J. Duncan M. "Judaica in St Mark." Pages 85–100 in *Studies in the New Testament 1: Glimpses of the Legal and Social Presuppositions of the Authors.* Leiden: Brill, 1977.

———. "Luke 6:5D Reexamined." *Novum Testamentum* 37 (1995): 232–48.

Dibelius, Martin. *Die Formgeschichte des Evangeliums.* 5th ed. Tübingen: Mohr Siebeck, 1966 (1919).

———. *Die Geisterwelt im Glauben des Paulus.* Göttingen: Vandenhoeck & Ruprecht, 1909.

———. *Jesus.* 3d ed. Berlin: de Gruyter, 1960 (1939).

Dietzfelbinger, Christian. "Vom Sinn der Sabbatheilungen Jesu." *Evangelische Theologie* 38 (1978): 281–98.

Dodd, C. H. *Historical Tradition in the Fourth Gospel.* Cambridge: Cambridge Univ. Press, 1963.

———. *The Interpretation of the Fourth Gospel.* Cambridge: Cambridge Univ. Press, 1953.

Doering, Lutz. *Schabbat: Sabbathalacha und -praxis im antiken Judentum und Urchristentum.* Texts and Studies in Ancient Judaism 78. Tübingen: Mohr Siebeck, 1999.

Donner, Herbert. "Jesaja 56: 1–7: Ein Abrogationsfall innerhalb des Kanons—Implikationen und Konsequenzen." Pages 165–78 in *Aufsätze zum Alten Testament aus vier Jahrzehnten.* Beihefte zur Zeitschrift für die alttestamentliche Wissenschaft 224. Berlin: de Gruyter, 1994.

Dugmore, C. W. "Lord's Day and Easter." Pages 272–81 in *Neotestamentica et patristica (FS O. Cullmann).* Edited by W. C. van Unnik. Leiden: Brill, 1962, 272–81.

Dunn, James D. G. "4QMMT and Galatians." *New Testament Studies* 43 (1997): 147–53.

———. *The Epistle to the Galatians.* Black's New Testament Commentaries 9. Peabody, Mass.: Hendrickson, 1993.

———. "The Incident at Antioch (Gal. 2.11–18)." *Journal for the Study of the New Testament* 18 (1983): 3–57. Repr. with additional note pages 129–82 in *Jesus, Paul and the Law: Studies in Mark and Galatians.* Louisville, Ky.: Westminster John Knox, 1990.

————. "Mark 2.1–3.6: A Bridge between Jesus and Paul on the Question of the Law." *New Testament Studies* 30 (1984):395–415. Repr. with additional note pages 10–36 in *Jesus, Paul and the Law: Studies in Mark and Galatians*. Louisville, Ky.: Westminster John Knox, 1990.

————. *The Theology of Paul the Apostle*. Grand Rapids, Mich.: Eerdmans, 1998.

Eagleton, Terry. *Literary Theory: An Introduction*. 2d ed. Minneapolis: Univ. of Minnesota, 1996 (1983).

Ebeling, Gerhard. *Die Wahrheit des Evangeliums: Eine Lesehilfe zum Galaterbrief*. Tübingen: Mohr Siebeck, 1981.

Eckstein, Hans-Joachim. *Verheissung und Gesetz: Eine exegetische Untersuchung zu Galater 2,15; 4,7*. Wissenschaftliche Untersuchungen zum Neuen Testament 86. Tübingen: Mohr Siebeck, 1996.

Edelman, Diana Vikander, ed. *The Triumph of Elohim: From Yahwisms to Judaisms*. 2d ed. Contributions to Biblical Exegesis & Theology 13. Grand Rapids, Mich.: Eerdmans, 1995.

Eggenberger, Oswald. *Die Kirchen, Sondergruppen und religiösen Vereinigungen: Ein Handbuch*. 6th ed. Zürich: Theologischer Verlag, 1994 (1969).

Eichrodt, Walther. "Der Sabbat bei Hesekiel: Ein Beitrag zur Nachgeschichte des Prophetentextes." Pages 65–74 in *Lex tua veritas (FS H. Junker)*. Edited by H. Gross and F. Mussner. Trier: Paulinus, 1961.

Eliade, Mircea. *The Myth of the Eternal Return, or, Cosmos and History*. Translated by Willard R. Trask. Bollingen 46. Princeton: Princeton Univ. Press, 1954.

Ellis, E. Earle. "Paul and his Opponents: Trends in Research." Pages 264–98 in vol. 1 of *Christianity, Judaism and other Greco-Roman Cults (FS M. Smith)*. Edited by J. Neusner. Studies in Judaism in Late Antiquity 12. Leiden: Brill, 1975.

Esler, Philip Francis, *Community and Gospel in Luke-Acts: The Social and Political Motivations of Lucan Theology*. Society for New Testament Studies Monograph Series 57. Cambridge: Cambridge Univ. Press, 1987.

Fallon, Francis T. "The Law in Philo and Ptolemy: A Note on the Letter to Flora." *Vigiliae christianae* 30 (1976): 45–51.

Fallon, Francis T., and Ron Cameron. "The Gospel of Thomas: A Forschungsbericht and Analysis." *ANRW* 25.6:4195–251. Part 2, *Principat*, 25.6. Edited by H. Temporini and W. Haase. Berlin: de Gruyter, 1988.

Feazell, J. Michael. *The Liberation of the Worldwide Church of God*. Grand Rapids, Mich.: Zondervan, 2001.

Feld, Helmut. *Der Hebräerbrief*. Erträge der Forschung 228. Darmstadt: Wissenschaftliche Buchgesellschaft, 1985.

Feldman, Louis H. *Jew and Gentile in the Ancient World: Attitudes and Interactions from Alexander to Justinian*. Princeton: Princeton Univ. Press, 1993.

Fieger, Michael. *Das Thomasevangelium: Einleitung, Kommentar und Systematik*. Neutestamentliche Abhandlungen. Neue Folge 22. Münster: Aschendorff, 1991.

Fincke, Andreas. "Lehrkorrekturen." *Materialdienst des Konfessionskundlichen Instituts Bensheim* 59 (1996): 370-1.

Fitzmyer, Joseph A. *The Gospel According to Luke I–IX: A New Translation with Introduction Commentary.* Anchor Bible 28. New York: Doubleday, 1981.

Fortna, Robert T. *The Fourth Gospel and its Predecessor: From Narrative Source to Present Gospel.* Philadelphia: Fortress Press, 1988.

———. *The Gospel of Signs: A Reconstruction of the Narrative Source Underlying the Fourth Gospel.* Society for New Testament Studies Monographs Series 11. Cambridge: Cambridge Univ. Press, 1970.

Frankforter, A. Daniel. *Stones for Bread: A Critique of Contemporary Worship.* Louisville, Ky.: John Knox, 2001.

Fredriksen, Paula. *Jesus of Nazareth, King of the Jews: A Jewish Life and the Emergence of Christianity.* New York: Alfred A. Knopf, 1999.

———. "Judaism, the Circumcision of Gentiles, and Apocalyptic Hope: Another Look at Galatians 1 and 2." *Journal of Theological Studies, New Series* 42 (1991): 532–64.

Frühwald-König, Johannes. *Tempel und Kult: Ein Beitrag zur Christologie des Johannesevangeliums.* Biblische Untersuchungen 27. Regensburg: Pustert, 1998.

Fung, Ronald Y. K. *The Epistle to the Galatians.* New International Commentary on the New Testament. Grand Rapids, Mich.: Eerdmans, 1988.

Funk, Robert Walter. *The Acts of Jesus: The Search for the Authentic Deeds of Jesus.* Polebridge Press. San Francisco: Harper, 1998.

Gadamer, Hans-Georg. *Wahrheit und Methode.* Tübingen: Mohr Siebeck, 1960.

Gager, John G. *The Origins of Anti-Semitism: Attitudes Toward Judaism in Pagan and Christian Antiquity.* New York: Oxford Univ. Press, 1983.

Gärtner, Bertil. *The Theology of the Gospel According to Thomas.* Translated by Eric J. Sharpe. New York: Harper, 1961.

Gnilka, Joachim. *Das Matthäusevangelium.* 2 vols. Herders theologischer Kommentar zum Neuen Testament 1. Freiburg im Breisgau, 1986, 1988.

Goldenberg, Robert. "The Jewish Sabbath in the Roman World up to the Time of Constantine the Great." *ANRW* 19.1:414–47. Part 2, *Principat*, 19.1. Edited by H. Temporini and W. Haase. Berlin, 1979.

Goodman, Martin. *Mission and Conversion: Proselytizing in the Religious History of the Roman Empire.* Oxford: Oxford Univ. Press, 1994.

Grässer, Erich. *An die Hebräer. 1: Hebr 1–6.* Evangelisch-Katholischer Kommentar zum Neuen Testament 17/1. Zürich: Benzinger, 1990.

Gross, Walter. "Erneuerter oder Neuer Bund? Wortlaut und Aussageintention in Jer 31, 31–34." Pages 41–66 in *Bund und Tora: Zur theologischen Begriffsgeschichte in alttestamentlicher, frühjüdischer und urchristlicher Tradition.* Edited by F. Avemarie and H. Lichtenberger. Wissenschaftliche Untersuchungen zum Neuen Testament 92. Tübingen: Mohr Siebeck, 1996.

———. "'Rezeption' in Ex 31, 12–17 und Lev 26, 39–45—Sprachliche Form und theologisch-konzeptuelle Leistung." Pages 45–64 in *Rezeption und Auslegung im Alten Testament und seinen Umfeld (FS O. H. Steck).* Edited by R. G. Kratz and T. Krüger. Freiburg, Switzerland: Editions Universitaires, 1997.

Grünwaldt, Klaus. *Exil und Identität: Beschneidung, Passa und Sabbat in der Priester-schrift.* Bonner biblische Beiträge 85. Frankfurt am Main: Hain, 1992.

Guelich, Robert A. *Mark 1–8:26.* Word Bible Commentary 34. Dallas: Word, 1989.

Guillaumont, Antoine. "ΝΗΣΤΕΥΕΙΝ ΤΟΝ ΚΟΣΜΟΝ (*P. Oxy. 1*, verso, 1,5–6)." *Bulletin de l'Institut français d'archéologie orientale* 61 (1962):15–23.

Gundry, Robert H. *Matthew: A Commentary on his Literary and Theological Art.* Grand Rapids, Mich.: Eerdmans, 1982.

Gunkel, Hermann. *Genesis übersetzt und erklärt.* 3d ed. Göttinger Handkommentar zum Alten Testament 1/1. Göttingen: Vandenhoeck & Ruprecht, 1910 (1901).

———. *Zum religionsgeschichtlichen Verständnis des Neuen Testaments.* 2d ed. Forschungen zur Religion und Literatur des Alten und Neuen Testaments 1. Göttingen: Vandenhoeck & Ruprecht, 1910 (1903).

Haag, Ernst. *Vom Sabbat zum Sonntag: Eine bibeltheologische Studie.* Trierer theologische Studien 52. Trier: Paulinus, 1991.

Haenchen, Ernst. *Die Apostelgeschichte.* 16th ed. Kritisch-exegetischer Kommentar über das Neue Testament 3. Göttingen: Vandenhoeck & Ruprecht, 1977 (1956).

———. *Die Botschaft des Thomas-Evangeliums.* Theologische Bibliothek Töpelmann 6. Berlin: Töpelmann, 1961.

———. "Johanneische Probleme." Pages 78–113 in *Gott und Mensch: Gesammelte Aufsätze.* Tübingen: Mohr Siebeck, 1965.

———. *Das Johannesevangelium: Ein Kommentar.* Tübingen: Mohr Siebeck, 1980.

———. *Der Weg Jesu: Eine Erklärung des Markus-Evangeliums und der kanonischen Parallelen.* 2d ed. Sammlung Töpelmann, 2. Reihe 6. Berlin: Töpelmann, 1968 (1966).

Halbe, Jörn. *Das Privilegrecht Jahwes Ex 34,10–26: Gestalt und Wesen, Herkunft und Wirken in vordeuteronomistischer Zeit.* Forschungen zur Religion und Literatur des Alten und Neuen Testaments 114. Göttingen: Vandenhoeck & Ruprecht, 1975.

Hansen, G. Walter. *Abraham in Galatians: Epistolary and Rhetorical Contexts.* Journal for the Study of the New Testament, Supplements 29. Sheffield: JSOT, 1989.

Hanson, Paul D. *The Dawn of the Apocalyptic.* Philadelphia: Fortress, 1975.

Harnack, Adolf von. *Die Geschichte der altchristlichen Litteratur bis Eusebius. 2/1: Die Chronologie der Litteratur bis Irenäus nebst einleitender Untersuchungen.* Leipzig: Hinrichs, 1897.

———. "Probabilia über die Adresse und den Verfasser des Hebräerbriefes." *Zeitschrift für die neutestamentliche Wissenschaft und die Kunde der Älteren Kirche* 1 (1900): 16–41.

———. *Über die jüngst entdeckten Sprüche Jesu [B. P. Grenfell and A. S. Hunt, ΛΟΓΙΑ IECOY, Sayings of Our Lord from an Early Greek Papyrus, London 1897].* Freiburg: Mohr Siebeck, 1897.

———. *Über einige Worte Jesu die nicht in den kanonischen Evangelien stehen, nebst einem Anhang über die ursprüngliche Gestalt des Vater-Unsers.* Sitzungsberichte der königlich preussischen Akademie der Wissenschaften. Berlin: Reichdruckerei, 1904.

Harris, Lis. *Holy Days: The World of a Hasidic Family.* New York: Summit, 1985.

Helderman, Jan. *Die Anapausis im Evangelium Veritatis: Eine vergleichende Untersuchung des valentinianisch-gnostischen Heilsgutes der Ruhe im Evangelium Veritatis und in anderen Schriften der Nag-Hammadi-Bibliothek.* Nag Hammadi Studies 18. Leiden: Brill, 1984.

Hengel, Martin. *Judentum und Hellenismus: Studien zu ihrer Begegnung unter besonderer Berücksichtigung Palästinas bis zur Mitte des 2. Jhs. v. Chr.* 3d ed. Wissenschaftliche Untersuchungen zum Neuen Testament 10. Tübingen: Mohr Siebeck, 1988 (1969).

———. "Zwischen Jesus und Paulus: Die 'Hellenisten,' die 'Sieben' und Stephanus (Apg 6,1-15; 7,54-8,3)." *Zeitschrift für Theologie und Kirche* 72 (1975): 151-206.

Hill, D. "On the Use and Meaning of Hosea vi.6 in Matthew's Gospel." *New Testament Studies* 24 (1978): 113–6.

Hirsch, Emanuel. *Das vierte Evangelium in seiner ursprünglichen Gestalt verdeutscht und erklärt.* Tübingen: Mohr, 1936.

Hofius, Otfried. *Katapausis: Die Vorstellung vom endzeitlichen Ruheort im Hebräerbrief.* Wissenschaftliche Untersuchungen zum Neuen Testament 11. Tübingen: Mohr Siebeck, 1970.

Holmberg, Bengt. *Sociology and the New Testament: An Appraisal.* Minneapolis: Fortress, 1990.

Honecker, Martin. *Einführung in die Theologische Ethik: Grundlagen und Grundbegriffe.* De Gruyter Lehrbuch. Berlin: de Gruyter, 1990.

Hooker, Morna D. *The Gospel According to Saint Mark.* Black's New Testament Commentaries 2. London: Black's, 1991. Repr., Peabody, Mass.: Hendrickson, 1997.

———. *The Son of Man in Mark: A Study of the Background of the Term "Son of Man" and its Use in St Mark's Gospel.* London: SPCK, 1967.

Horbury, William. "Jewish-Christian Relations in Barnabas and Justin Martyr." Pages 315–45 in *Jews and Christians: The Parting of the Ways, A.D. 70 to 135.* Edited by J. D. G. Dunn. Wissenschaftliche Untersuchungen zum Neuen Testament 66. Tübingen: Mohr Siebeck, 1992.

Horton, Michael. *A Better Way: Rediscovering the Drama of God-Centered Worship.* Grand Rapids, Mich.: Baker, 2002.

Hossfeld, Frank-Lothar. *Der Dekalog: Seine späte Fassungen, die originale Komposition und seine Vorstufen.* Orbis biblicus et orientalis 45. Freiburg, Switzerland: Universitätsverlag, 1982.

Howard, George. *Paul: Crisis in Galatia. A Study in Early Christian Theology.* 2d ed. Society for New Testament Studies, Monograph Series 35. Cambridge: Cambridge Univ. Press, 1991 (1979).

Hübner, Hans. "Der Galaterbrief und das Verhältnis von antiker Rhetorik." *Theologische Literaturzeitung* 109 (1984): 241–50.

———. *Das Gesetz bei Paulus: Ein Beitrag zum Werden der paulinischen Theologie.* 3d ed. Forschungen zur Religion und Literatur des Alten und Neuen Testaments 119. Göttingen: Vandenhoeck & Ruprecht, 1982 (1978).

————. *Das Gesetz in der synoptischen Tradition: Studien zur These einer progressiven Qumranisierung und Judaisierung innerhalb der synoptischen Tradition.* Witten: Luther, 1973.

Hummel, Reinhart. *Die Auseinandersetzung zwischen Kirche und Judentum im Matthäusevangelium.* 2d ed. Beiträge zur evangelischen Theologie 33. München: Kaiser, 1966 (1963).

Hvalvik, Reidar. *The Struggle for Scripture and Covenant: The Purpose of the Epistle of Barnabas and Jewish-Christian Competition in the Second Century.* Wissenschaftliche Untersuchungen zum Neuen Testament. Second Series 82. Tübingen: Mohr Siebeck, 1996.

Jenni, Ernst. *Die theologische Begründung des Sabbatgebotes im Alten Testament.* Theologische Studien 46. Zollikon: Evangelischer Verlag, 1956.

Jeremias, Joachim. *Die Abendmahlsworte Jesu.* 4th ed. Göttingen: Vandenhoeck & Ruprecht, 1967 (1935).

————. *Jesu Verheissung für die Völker.* Franz Delitzsch-Vorlesungen 1953. Stuttgart: Kohlhammer, 1956.

————. *Neutestamentliche Theologie. 1: Die Verkündigung Jesu.* Gütersloh: Mohn, 1971.

————. *Unbekannte Jesusworte.* 3d ed. Abhandlungen zur Theologie des Alten und Neuen Testaments 16. Zürich: Zwingli, 1961 (1948).

————. *Die Wiederentdeckung von Bethesda: Johannes 5,2.* Forschungen zur Religion und Literatur des Alten und Neuen Testaments, Neue Folge 41. Göttingen: Vandenhoeck & Ruprecht, 1949.

Jervell, Jacob. *Die Apostelgeschichte.* Kritisch-exegetischer Kommentar über das Neue Testament 3. Göttingen: Vandenhoeck & Ruprecht, 1998.

Jewett, Paul K. *The Lord's Day: A Theological Guide to the Christian Day of Worship.* Grand Rapids, Mich.: Eerdmans, 1971.

Jones, F. Stanley. *An Ancient Jewish Christian Source on the History of Christianity: Pseudo-Clementine Recognitions 1.27–71.* Texts and Translations 37/Christian Apocrypha Series 2. Atlanta: Scholars Press, 1995.

Kaestli, Jean-Daniel. "Où en est le débat sur le judéo-christianisme?" Pages 243-72 in *Le déchirement juifs et chrétiens au premier siècle.* Edited by D. Marguerat. Le Monde de la Bible 32. Geneva: Éditions Labor et Fides, 1996.

Kahl, Werner. "Ist es erlaubt, am Sabbat Leben zu retten oder zu töten? (Marc. 3:4): Lebensbewahrung am Sabbat im Kontext der Schriften vom Toten Meer und der Mischna." *Novum Testamentum* 40 (1998): 313–35.

Kampen, John. "4QMMT and New Testament Studies." Pages 129–44 in *Reading 4QMMT: New Perspectives on Qumran Law and History.* Edited by J. Kampen and M. J. Bernstein. SBL Symposium Series 2. Atlanta: Scholars Press, 1996.

Käsemann, Ernst. "Das Problem des historischen Jesus." *Zeitschrift für Theologie und Kirche* 51 (1954): 125-53. Repr. pages 187–214 in *Exegetische Versuche und Besinnungen.* 6th ed. 2 vols 1. Göttingen: Vandenhoeck & Ruprecht, 1970 (1960, 1964).

————. "Rechtfertigung und Heilsgeschichte im Römerbrief." Pages 108–39 in *Paulinische Perspektiven.* 2d ed. Tübingen: Mohr Siebeck, 1972 (1969).

————. *Das wandernde Gottesvolk: Eine Untersuchung zum Hebräerbrief.* 2d ed. Forschungen zur Religion und Literatur des Alten und Neuen Testaments 55. Göttingen: Vandenhoeck & Ruprecht, 1957 (1939).

Käser, Walter. "Exegetische Erwägungen zur Seligpreisung des Sabbatarbeiters Lk 6,5D." *Zeitschrift für Theologie und Kirche* 65 (1968): 414–30.

Kieffer, René. "Different Levels in Johannine Imagery." Pages 74–84 in *Aspects on the Johannine Literature.* Edited by L. Hartman and B. Olsson. Coniectanea Biblica, New Testament Series 18. Uppsala: Almqvist & Wiksell, 1987.

Kiilunen, Jarmo. *Die Vollmacht in Widerstreit: Untersuchungen zum Werdegang von Mk 2,1–3,6.* Annales Academiae Scientiarum Fennicae/Dissertationes Humanarum Litterarum 40. Helsinki: Suomalainen Tiedeakatemia, 1985.

Kilpatrick, G. D. "Some Problems in New Testament Text and Language." Pages 198–208 in *Neotestamentica et semitica (FS M. Black),* edited by E. E. Ellis and M. Wilcox. Edinburgh: T. & T. Clark, 1969.

Koch, Klaus. "Monotheismus und Angelologie." Pages 565–81 in *Ein Gott allein? JHWH Verehrung und biblischer Monotheismus im Kontext der israelitischen und altorientalischen Religionsgeschichte.* Edited by Walter Dietrich and Martin A. Klopfenstein. Orbis biblicus et orientalis 139. Freiburg, Switzerland: Editions Universitaires, 1994.

Koester, Craig R. *Hebrews: A New Translation with Introduction and Commentary.* Anchor Bible 36. New York: Doubleday, 2001.

Koester, Helmut. *Ancient Christian Gospels: Their History and Development.* Harrisburg, Penn.: Trinity Press International, 1990.

————. "GNOMAI DIAFOROI: The Origin and Nature of Diversification in the History of Early Christianity." *Harvard Theological Review* 58 (1965): 279–318. Repr. pages 114–57 in *Trajectories through Early Christianity.* Edited by J. M. Robinson and H. Koester. Philadelphia: Fortress, 1971.

————. *History and Literature of Early Christianity.* Vol. 2 of *Introduction to the New Testament.* 2d ed. Berlin: de Gruyter, 2000 (1982).

————. *Synoptische Überlieferung bei den apostolischen Vätern.* Texte und Untersuchungen zur Geschichte der altchristlichen Literatur 65. Berlin: Akademie, 1957.

Kotila, Markku. *Umstrittener Zeuge: Studien zur Stellung des Gesetzes in der johanneischen Theologiegeschichte.* Annales Academiae Scientiarum Fennicae. Dissertationes humanarum litterarum 48. Helsinki: Suomalainen Tiedeakatemia, 1988.

Kraft, Robert A. "Philo and the Sabbath Crisis: Alexandrian Jewish Politics and the Dating of Philo's Works." Pages 131–41 in *The Future of Early Christianity (FS H. Koester).* Edited by B. A. Pearson. Minneapolis: Fortress, 1991.

Kratz, Reinhold Gregor. "Reich Gottes und Gesetz im Danielbuch und im werdenden Judentum." Pages 435–79 in *The Book of Daniel in the Light of New Findings.* Edited by A. S. van der Woude. Leuven: Leuven Univ. Press, 1993.

Kraus, Hans-Joachim. *Gottesdienst in Israel: Studien zur Geschichte des Laubhütten-festes*. 2d ed. Beiträge zur evangelischen Theologie 19. München: Kaiser, 1962 (1954).

Kuhn, Heinz-Wolfgang. *Ältere Sammlungen im Markusevangelium*. Studien zur Umwelt des Neuen Testaments 8. Göttingen: Vandenhoeck & Ruprecht, 1971.

Kümmel, Werner Georg. *Einleitung in das Neue Testament*. 21st ed. Heidelberg: Quelle & Meyer, 1983 (1963).

Kutsch, Ernst. "Der Sabbat—ursprünglich Vollmondtag?" Pages 71–77 in *Kleine Schriften zum Alten Testament*. Berlin: de Gruyter, 1986.

Kysar, Robert. "Expulsion from the Synagogue: A Tale of a Theory." Paper presented at the annual meeting of the SBL, Toronto, 25 November 2002.

La Potterie, Ignace de. *La vérité dans Saint Jean*. 1. *Le Christ et la vérité, L'Esprit et la vérité*. 2 vols. Analecta Biblica 73. Rome: Biblical Institute, 1977.

Laansma, Jon. *"I Will Give You Rest:" The Rest Motif in the New Testament with Special Reference to Mt 11 and Heb 3–4*. Wissenschaftliche Untersuchungen zum Neuen Testament. Second Series 98. Tübingen: Mohr Siebeck, 1997.

Labahn, Michael. *Jesus als Lebensspender: Untersuchungen zu einer Geschichte der johanneischen Tradition anhand ihrer Wundergeschichten*. Beihefte zur Zeitschrift für die neutestamentliche Wissenschaft und die Kunde der älteren Kirche 98. Berlin: de Gruyter, 1999.

———. "Eine Spurensuche anhand von Joh 5.1–18: Bemerkungen zu Wachstum und Wandel der Heilung eines Lahmen." *New Testament Studies* 44 (1998): 159–79.

Lambert, W. G. "A New Look at the Babylonian Background of Genesis." *Journal of Theological Studies* NS 16 (1965): 287–300.

Lapide, Pinchas. *Er predigte in ihren Synagogen: Jüdische Evangelienauslegung*. 4th ed. Gütersloher Taschenbücher Siebenstern 1400. Gütersloh: Mohn, 1985 (1980).

Lee, Dorothy A. *The Symbolic Narratives of the Fourth Gospel: The Interplay of Form and Meaning*. Journal for the Study of the New Testament, Supplements 95. Sheffield: JSOT, 1994.

Lee, Francis Nigel. *The Covenantal Sabbath*. London: Lord's Day Observance Society, 1966.

Leroy, Herbert. *Rätsel und Missverständnis: Ein Beitrag zur Formgeschichte des Johannesevangeliums*. Bonner biblische Beiträge 30. Bonn: Hanstein, 1968.

Levin, Christoph. "Der Dekalog am Sinai." *Vetus Testamentus* 35 (1985): 165–91.

———. *Der Sturz der Königin Atalja: Ein Kapitel zur Geschichte Judas im 9. Jahrhundert v.Chr.* Stuttgarter Bibelstudien 105. Stuttgart: Katholisches Bibelwerk, 1982.

Levine, Etain. "The Sabbath Controversy According to Matthew." *New Testament Studies* 22 (1976): 480–83.

Lewis, Richard B. "Ignatius and the Lord's Day." *Andrews University Seminary Studies* 6 (1968): 46-59.

Liebenberg, Jacobus. *The Language of the Kingdom and Jesus: Parable, Aphorism, and Metaphor in the Sayings Material Common to the Synoptic Tradition and the*

Gospel of Thomas. Beihefte zur Zeitschrift für die neutestamentliche Wissenschaft und die Kunde der älteren Kirche 102. Berlin: de Gruyter, 2001.

Lieu, Judith. "'The Parting of the Ways': Theological Construct or Historical Reality?" *Journal for the Study of the New Testament* 56 (1994): 101–19. Repr. pages 11–29 in *Neither Jew nor Greek? Constructing Early Christianity*. Studies in the New Testament and Its World. London: T. & T. Clark, 2002.

Lincoln, Andrew T. "From Sabbath to Lord's Day: A Biblical and Theological Perspective." Pages 344–412 in *From Sabbath to Lord's Day: A Biblical Historical and Theological Investigation*, edited by D. A. Carson. Grand Rapids, Mich.: Zondervan, 1982.

Lincoln, Bruce. "Thomas-Gospel and Thomas-Community: A New Approach to a Familiar Text." *Novum Testamentum* 19 (1977): 65–76.

Lindars, Barnabas. *The Gospel of John*. New Century Bible. London: Oliphants, 1972.

Lindemann, Andreas. "Jesus und der Sabbat: Zum literarischen Charakter der Erzahlung Mk 3,1–6." Pages 122–35 in *Text und Geschichte: Facetten theologischen Arbeitens aus dem Freundes- und Schülerkreis (FS D. Lührmann)*. Edited by S. Maser and E. Schlarb. Marburg: Elwert, 1999.

Loader, William R. G. *Jesus' Attitude towards the Law*. Wissenschaftliche Untersuchungen zum Neuen Testament. Second Series 97. Tübingen: Mohr Siebeck, 1997.

Lohfink, Norbert. "Zur Dekalogfassung von Dt 5." *Biblische Zeitschrift* NF 9 (1965): 17–32. Repr. pages 193–201 in *Studien zum Deuteronomium und zur deuteronomistischen Literatur*. Vol 1. Stuttgarter biblische Aufsatzbänder: Altes Testament 8. Stuttgart: Katholisches Bibelwerk, 1990.

Lohse, Eduard. "Jesu Worte über den Sabbat." Pages 79–89 in *Judentum, Urchristentum, Kirche (FS Jeremias)*. Edited by W. Eltester. Beiheft zur Zeitschrift für die Neutestamentliche Wissenschaft und die Kunde der älteren Kirche 26. Berlin: Alfred Töpelmann, 1960.

Lüdemann, Gerd. *Antipaulinismus im frühen Christentum*. Vol. 2 of *Paulus der Heidenapostel*. Göttingen: Vandenhoeck & Ruprecht, 1983.

Lührmann, Dieter. "Das neue Fragment des P Egerton 2 (P Köln 255)." Pages 2239–55 in *The Four Gospels 1992 (FS F. Neirynck)*. Edited by F. van Segbroeck, C. M. Tuckett, G. van Belle and J. Verheyden. Bibliotheca Ephemeridum Theologicarum Lovaniensium 100. Leuven: Leuven Univ. Press, 1992.

———. "'Tage, Monate, Jahreszeiten, Jahre' (Gal 4,10)." Pages 428–45 in *Werden und Wirken des Alten Testaments (FS C. Westermann)*. Edited by R. Albertz, H.-P. Müller, H. W. Wolff and W. Zimmerli. Göttingen: Vandenhoeck & Ruprecht, 1980.

Lundbom, Jack R. *Jeremiah 1–20: A New Translation with Introduction and Commentary*. Anchor Bible 21A. New York: Doubleday, 1999.

Luz, Ulrich. *Das Evangelium nach Matthäus. 2: Mt 8–17*. 2d ed. Evangelisch-Katholischer Kommentar zum Neuen Testament 1/2. Zürich: Benzinger, 1996 (1990).

Lybaek, Lena. "Matthew's Use of Hosea 6,6 in the Context of the Sabbath Controversies." Pages 491–9 in *The Scriptures in the Gospels*, edited by C. M. Tuckett.

Bibliotheca Ephemeridum Theologicarum Lovaniensium 131. Leuven: Leuven Univ. Press, 1997.

Malina, Bruce J., and Richard L. Rohrbaugh. *Social-Science Commentary on the Synoptic Gospels*. Minneapolis: Fortress, 1992.

Marcus, Joel. *Mark 1–8: A New Translation with Introduction and Commentary*. Anchor Bible 27A. New York: Doubleday, 1999.

Marguerat, Daniel, and Yvan Bourquin. *La Bible se raconte: Initiation à l'analyse narrative*. Paris: Cerf, 1998.

Marjanen, Antti. "Is *Thomas* a Gnostic Gospel?" Pages 107–39 in *Thomas at the Crossroads: Essays on the Gospel of Thomas*, edited by R. Uro. Studies of the New Testament and its World. Edinburgh: T. & T. Clark, 1998.

———. "Thomas and Jewish Religious Practices." Pages 163–82 in *Thomas at the Crossroads: Essays on the Gospel of Thomas*. Edited by R. Uro. Studies of the New Testament and its World. Edinburgh: T. & T. Clark, 1998.

Martin, Ernest L. *Restoring the Original Bible*. Portland, Ore.: Associates for Scriptural Knowledge, 1994.

Martin, Troy. "Pagan and Judeo-Christian Time-Keeping Schemes in Gal 4.10 and Col 2.16." *New Testament Studies* 42 (1996): 105–19.

Martyn, J. Louis. *Galatians: A New Translation with Introduction and Commentary*. Anchor Bible 33A. New York: Doubleday, 1997.

———. *History and Theology in the Fourth Gospel*. New York: Harper, 1968; 2d ed. Nashville: Abingdon, 1979.

———. *Theological Issues in the Letters of Paul*. Studies of the New Testament and its World. Edinburgh: T. & T. Clark, 1997.

Maurer, Christian. "Steckt hinter Joh 5,17 ein Übersetzungsfehler?" *Wort und Dienst* NF 5 (1957): 130–40.

Mayer-Haas, Andrea J. *«Geschenk aus Gottes Schatzkammer» (bSchab 10b): Jesus und der Sabbat im Spiegel der neutestamentlichen Schriften*. Neutestamentliche Abhandlungen, Neue Folge, 43. Münster: Aschendorff, 2003

McGrath, James F. "A Rebellious Son? Hugo Odeberg and the Interpretation of John 5.18." *New Testament Studies* 44 (1998): 470–73.

McKane, William. *A Critical and Exegetical Commentary on Jeremiah. 1: Introduction and Commentary on Jeremiah 1–25*. International Critical Commentary. Edinburgh: T. & T. Clark, 1986.

Meagher, John C. "As the Twig Was Bent: Antisemitism in Greco-Roman and Earliest Christian Times." Pages 1–26 in *Antisemitism and the Foundations of Christianity*. Edited by Alan T. Davies. New York: Paulist, 1979.

Mealand, D. L. "John 5 and the Limits of Rhetorical Criticism." Pages 258–72 in *Understanding Poets and Prophets (FS G. W. Anderson)*. Edited by A. G. Auld. Journal for the Study of the Old Testament. Supplement series 152. Sheffield: JSOT Press, 1993.

Meeks, Wayne A. "'Am I a Jew?'—Johannine Christianity and Judaism." Pages 163–86 in vol. 1 of *Christianity, Judaism and other Greco-Roman Cults*. Edited by J. Neusner. Studies in Judaism in Late Antiquity 12. Leiden: Brill, 1975.

————. "Equal to God." Pages 309–21 in *The Conversation Continues: Studies in Paul & John (FS J. Louis Martyn)*. Edited by Robert T. Fortna and Beverly Roberts Gaventa. Nashville, Tenn.: Abingdon Press, 1990.

Meier, John P. *A Marginal Jew: Rethinking the Historical Jesus*. 3 vols. to date. Anchor Bible Reference Library. New York: Doubleday, 1991–2001.

Meinhold, Johannes. "Zur Sabbatfrage." *Zeitschrift für die alttestamentliche Wissenschaft* 48 (1930): 121–38.

Merklein, Helmut. *Jesu Botschaft von der Gottesherrschaft: Eine Skizze*. 3d ed. Stuttgarter Bibelstudien 111. Stuttgart: Katholisches Bibelwerk, 1989 (1983).

Metzner, Rainer. "Der Geheilte von Johannes 5—Repräsentant des Unglaubens." *Zeitschrift für die neutestamentliche Wissenschaft und die Kunde der älteren Kirche* 90 (1999): 177–93.

————. *Das Verständnis der Sünde im Johannesevangelium*. Wissenschaftliche Untersuchungen zum Neuen Testament 122. Tübingen: Mohr Siebeck, 2000.

Meyer, Marvin Wayne, and Harold Bloom. *The Gospel of Thomas: The Hidden Sayings of Jesus*. San Francisco: HarperSanFrancisco, 1992.

Michel, Otto. *Der Brief an die Hebräer*. 12th ed. Kritisch-exegetischer Kommentar über das Neue Testament 13. Göttingen: Vandenhoeck & Ruprecht, 1966 (1936).

Moloney, Francis J. *The Gospel of John*. Sacra Pagina 4. Collegeville, Minn.: Liturgical Press, 1998.

Moore, George Foot. *Judaism in the First Centuries of the Christian Era*. 2 vols. Cambridge: Harvard Univ. Press, 1927. Repr., New York: Schocken, 1971.

Moore-Crispin, Derek R. "Gal 4,1–9: The Use and Abuse of Parallels." *Evangelical Quarterly* 60 (1989): 203–23.

Mussner, Franz. *Der Galaterbrief*. Herders theologischer Kommentar zum Neuen Testament 9. Freiburg im Breisgau: Herder, 1974.

Neill, Stephen, and N. T. Wright. *The Interpretation of the New Testament 1861–1986*. Oxford: Oxford Univ. Press, 1988.

Neirynck, Frans. "Jesus and the Sabbath: Some Observations on Mark II.27." Pages 141–68 in *Jésus aux origines de la christologie*. Edited by F. Neirynck. Leuven: Leuven Univ. Press, 1974.

————. "John 5,1–18 and the Gospel of Mark." Pages 703–8 in *Evangelica 2*. Edited by F. Neirynck. Bibliotheca Ephemeridum Theologicarum Lovaniensium 99. Leuven: Leuven Univ. Press, 1991.

————. "John and the Synoptics." Pages 73–106 in *L'Evangile de Jean: Sources, rédaction, théologie*, edited by M. de Jonge. Bibliotheca Ephemeridum Theologicarum Lovaniensium 44. Leuven: Leuven Univ. Press, 1977.

Neirynck, Frans, Theo Hansen and Frans van Segbroek, eds. *The Minor Agreements of Matthew and Luke against Mark with a Cumulative List*. Bibliotheca Ephemeridum Theologicarum Lovaniensium 37. Leuven: Leuven Univ. Press, 1974.

Noth, Martin. *Das dritte Buch Mose: Leviticus*. Altes Testament Deutsch 6. Göttingen: Vandenhoeck & Ruprecht, 1962.

————. *Das zweite Buch Mose: Exodus*. Altes Testament Deutsch 5. Göttingen: Vandenhoeck & Ruprecht, 1958.

Odom, Robert Leo. *Sunday in Roman Paganism*. Tacoma Park, Washington, D.C.: Review & Herald, 1944.

Pagels, Elaine. *The Gnostic Gospels*. New York: Random House, 1979. Repr., Harmondsworth: Penguin, 1990.

Painter, John. *Just James: The Brother of Jesus in History and Tradition*. Studies on Personalities of the New Testament. Columbia: Univ. of South Carolina Press, 1997.

———. *The Quest for the Messiah: The History, Literature and Theology of the Johannine Community*. Edinburgh: T. & T. Clark, 1991.

Pancaro, Severino. *The Law in the Fourth Gospel: The Torah and the Gospel, Moses and Jesus, Judaism and Christianity According to John*. Supplements to Novum Testamentum 42. Leiden: Brill, 1975.

Pesch, Rudolf. *Das Markusevangelium, 1: Einleitung und Kommentar zu Kap. 1,1–8,26*. 4th ed. 2 vols. Herders Theologischer Kommentar zum Neuen Testament 1. Freiburg im Breisgau: Herder, 1984 (1976).

Peterson, Dwight N. *The Origins of Mark: The Markan Community in Current Debate*. Biblical Interpretation Series 48. Leiden: Brill, 2000.

Pettazzoni, Raffaele. "Myths of Beginnings and Creation-Myths." Pages 24–36 in *Essays on the History of Religions*. Studies in the History of Religion 1. Leiden: Brill, 1954.

Porter, Stanley E. *The Paul of Acts: Essays in Literary Criticism, Rhetoric, and Theology*. Wissenschaftliche Untersuchungen zum Neuen Testament 115. Tübingen: Mohr Siebeck, 1999.

Powell, Mark A. *What is Narrative Criticism?* Guides to Biblical Scholarship. New Testament Series. Minneapolis: Fortress, 1990.

Prigent, Pierre. *Les Testimonia dans le Christianisme primitif: L'Épître de Barnabé 1–16 et ses sources*. Études bibliques. Paris: Gabalda, 1961.

Prostmeier, Ferdinand Rupert. *Der Barnabasbrief*. Kommentar zu den Apostolischen Vätern 8. Göttingen: Vandenhoeck & Ruprecht, 1999.

Quispel, Gilles. "The *Gospel of Thomas* Revisited." Pages 218–66 in *Colloque international sur les textes de Nag Hammadi, Québec, 22–25 août 1978*. Edited by B. Barc. Bibliothèque copte de Nag Hammadi 1. Québec: Presse de l'Université de Laval, 1981.

Rabello, Alfredo Mordechai. *The Jews in the Roman Empire: Legal Problems from Herod to Justinian*. Varorium Collected Studies 645. Aldershot: Ashgate, 2000.

Rad, Gerhard von. "Es ist noch eine Ruhe vorhanden dem Volke Gottes: Eine biblische Begriffsuntersuchung." *Zwischen den Zeiten* (1933). Repr. pages 101–8 in *Gesammelte Studien zum Alten Testament*. 3d ed. Theologische Bücherei 8. München: Kaiser, 1965 (1958).

———. *Theologie des Alten Testaments*. 2d ed. 2 vols. München: Kaiser, 1992 (1960).

Räisänen, Heikki. *Paul and the Law*. Tübingen: Mohr Siebeck, 1983. Repr., Philadelphia: Fortress, 1986.

Rein, Matthias. *Die Heilung des Blindgeborenen (Joh 9): Tradition und Redaktion.* Wissenschaftliche Untersuchungen zum Neuen Testament. Second Series 73. Tübingen: Mohr Siebeck, 1995.

Reinhartz, Adele. *Befriending the Beloved Disciple: A Jewish Reading of the Gospel of John.* New York: Continuum, 2001.

Rhoads, David, and Donald Michie. *Mark as Story: An Introduction to the Narrative of a Gospel.* Philadelphia: Fortress, 1982.

Riches, John. *Jesus and the Transformation of Judaism.* London: Darton, 1980.

Riesenfeld, Harald. "Sabbat et jour du seigneur." Pages 210–8 in *New Testament Essays: Studies in Memory of T. W. Manson.* Edited by A. J. B. Higgins. Manchester: Manchester Univ. Press, 1959. Repr., (with minor changes) as "The Sabbath and the Lord's Day." Pages 111–137 in *The Gospel Tradition.* Philadelphia: Fortress, 1970.

Riley, Gregory J. "The Gospel of Thomas in Recent Scholarship." *Currents in Research: Biblical Studies* 2 (1994): 227–52.

Robinson, Gnana. *The Origin and Development of the Old Testament Sabbath: A Comprehensive Exegetical Approach.* Beiträge zur biblischen Exegese und Theologie 21. Frankfurt am Main: Peter Lang, 1988.

Robinson, James M. "The Discovery of the Nag Hammadi Codices." *Biblical Archaeologist* 42 (1979): 206–24.

———. "LOGOI SOPHON: On the Gattung of Q." Pages 71–113 in *Trajectories through Early Christianity.* Edited by J. M. Robinson and H. Koester. Philadelphia: Fortress, 1971.

Roetzel, Calvin J. "Paul and the Law: Whence and Whither?" *Currents in Research: Biblical Studies* 3 (1995): 249–75.

Roloff, Jürgen. *Das Kerygma und der irdische Jesus: Historische Motive in den Jesus-Erzählungen der Evangelien.* Göttingen: Vandenhoeck & Ruprecht, 1970.

Rordorf, Willy. *Der Sonntag: Geschichte des Ruhe- und Gottesdiensttages im ältesten Christentum.* Abhandlungen zur Theologie des Alten und Neuen Testaments 43. Zürich, 1962.

———. "Der Ursprung und Bedeutung der Sonntagsfeier im frühen Christentum." *Liturgisches Jahrbuch* 31 (1981):145–58. Repr. pages 1–14 in *Lex orandi, lex credendi: Gesammelte Aufsätze zum 60. Geburtstag.* Paradosis 36. Freiburg, Switzerland: Universtitätsverlag, 1993.

Rüegger, Hans-Ulrich. *Verstehen, was Markus erzählt: Philologisch-hermeneutische Reflexionen zum Übersetzen von Markus 3,1–6.* Wissenschaftliche Untersuchungen zum Neuen Testament. Second Series 155. Tübingen: Mohr Siebeck, 2002.

Rusam, Dietrich. "Neue Belege zu den στοιχεῖα τοῦ κόσμου (Gal 4,3–9; Kol 2,8.20)." *Zeitschrift für die neutestamentliche Wissenschaft und die Kunde der Älteren Kirche* 83 (1992): 119–25.

Ruszkowski, Leszek. *Volk und Gemeinde im Wandel: Eine Untersuchung zu Jesaja 56–66.* Forschungen zur Religion und Literatur des Alten und Neuen Testaments 191. Göttingen: Vandenhoeck & Ruprecht, 2000.

Saldarini, Anthony J. *Matthew's Christian-Jewish Community.* Chicago Studies in the History of Judaism. Chicago: Univ. of Chicago Press, 1994.

Sanders, E. P. *The Historical Figure of Jesus.* London: Penguin, 1993.

———. *Jesus and Judaism.* Philadelphia: Fortress, 1985.

———. "Jesus and the Constraint of Law." *Journal for the Study of the New Testament* 17 (1983): 19–24.

———. *Judaism: Practice and Belief, 63 BCE–66CE.* London: SCM Press, 1992.

———. *Paul and Palestinian Judaism: A Comparison of Patterns of Religion.* Minneapolis: Fortress, 1977.

———. *Paul, the Law, and the Jewish People.* Philadelphia: Fortress, 1983.

Schäfer, Peter. *Judeophobia: Attitudes toward the Jews in the Ancient World.* Cambridge: Harvard Univ. Press, 1997.

Schaller, Berndt. *Jesus und der Sabbat.* Franz-Delitzsch-Vorlesung 3. Münster: Institut Judaicum Delitzschianum, 1994.

Schenke, Ludger. "Joh 7–10: Eine dramatische Szene." *Zeitschrift für die neutestamentliche Wissenschaft und die Kunde der älteren Kirche* 80 (1989): 172–92.

Schlier, Heinrich. *Der Brief an die Galater.* 13th ed. Kritisch-exegetischer Kommentar über das Neue Testament 7. Göttingen: Vandenhoeck & Ruprecht, 1965 (1949).

Schmidt, Karl Ludwig. *Der Rahmen der Geschichte Jesu: Literarkritische Untersuchungen zur ältesten Jesusüberlieferung.* Berlin: Trowitzsch, 1919. Repr., Darmstadt: Wissenschaftliche Buchgesellschaft, 1964.

Schmidt, Markus. *Weltweite Kirche Gottes: Von Sonderlehren zur Bibel. Sekten, religiöse Sondergemeinschaften, Weltanschauungen* 78. Vienna: Referat für Weltanschauungsfragen, 1998.

Schmidt, Werner H. *Alttestamentlicher Glaube in seiner Geschichte.* 7th ed. Neukirchener Studienbücher 6. Neukirchen-Vluyn: Neukirchener Verlag, 1990 (1968).

———. *Die Schöpfungsgeschichte der Priesterschrift: Zur Überlieferungsgeschichte von Genesis 1,1–2,4a und 2,4b–3,24.* 2d ed. Wissenschaftliche Monographien zum Alten und Neuen Testament 17. Neukirchen-Vluyn: Neukirchener Verlag, 1967 (1964).

Schmidt, Werner H., Holger Delkurt, and Axel Graupner. *Die Zehn Gebote im Rahmen alttestamentlicher Ethik.* Erträge der Forschung 281. Darmstadt: Wissenschaftliche Buchgesellschaft, 1993.

Schmithals, Walter. "Die Häretiker in Galatien." Pages 9–46 in *Paulus und die Gnostiker: Untersuchungen zu den kleinen Paulusbriefen.* Theologische Forschung 35. Hamburg-Bergstedt: Reich, 1965.

Schnackenburg, Rudolf. *Das Johannesevangelium, 2: Kommentar zu Kap. 5–12.* 5th ed. Herders theologischer Kommentar zum Neuen Testament 4/2. Freiburg im Breisgau: Herder, 1971.

Schnelle, Udo. *Antidoketische Christologie im Johannesevangelium: Eine Untersuchung zur Stelle des vierten Evangeliums in der johanneischen Schule.* Forschungen zur Religion und Literatur des Alten und Neuen Testaments 144. Göttingen: Vandenhoeck & Ruprecht, 1987.

————. *Einleitung in das Neue Testament*. 3d ed. Uni-Taschenbücher 1830. Göttingen: Vandenhoeck & Ruprecht, 1999 (1994).

Schoedel, William R. *Ignatius of Antioch: A Commentary on the Letters of Ignatius of Antioch*. Hermeneia. Philadelphia: Fortress, 1985.

Scholtissek, Klaus. *Die Vollmacht Jesu: Traditions- und Redaktionsgeschichtliche Analysen zu einem Leitmotiv markinischer Christologie*. Neutestementliche Abhandlungen, Neue Folge 25. Münster: Aschendorff, 1992.

Schrage, Wolfgang. *Das Verhältnis des Thomas-Evangeliums zur synoptischen Tradition und zu den koptischen Evangelienübersetzungen: Zugleich ein Beitrag zur gnostischen Synoptikerdeutung*. Beihefte zur Zeitschrift für die neutestamentliche Wissenschaft 29. Berlin: Töpelmann, 1964.

Schröter, Jens. *Erinnerung an Jesu Worte: Studien zur Rezeption der Logienüberlieferung in Markus, Q und Thomas*. Wissenschaftliche Monographien zum Alten und Neuen Testament 76. Neukirchen-Vluyn: Neukirchener Verlag, 1997.

Schubert, Kurt. *Jesus im Lichte der Religionsgeschichte des Judentums*. Vienna: Herold, 1973.

Schürer, Emil. *History of the Jewish People in the Age of Jesus Christ (175 B.C.–A.D. 135)*. 2 ed. Edited by G. Vermès, F. Millar, and M. Black. 3 vols. Edinburgh: T. & T. Clark, 1973 (1885).

Schürmann, Heinz. *Das Lukasevangelium. 1: Kommentar zu Kap. 1,1–9,50*. 3d ed. Herders theologischer Kommentar zum Neuen Testament 3,1. Freiburg: Herder, 1984 (1969).

Schwartz, Eduard. "Osterbetrachtungen." *Zeitschrift für die neutestamentliche Wissenschaft und die Kunde der Älteren Kirche* 7 (1906): 1-33. Repr. pages 1–41 of vol. 5 of *Gesammelte Schriften*. Edited by Walther Eltester and Hans-Dietrich Altendorf. Berlin: de Gruyter, 1963.

Schweizer, Eduard. "Altes und neues zu den 'Elementen der Welt' in Kol 2,20; Gal 4,3.9." Pages 111-8 in *Wissenschaft und Kirche (FS E. Lohse)*. Edited by K. Aland and S. Meurer. Texte und Arbeiten zur Bibel 4. Bielefeld: Luther Verlag, 1989.

————. *Das Evangelium nach Markus*. Das Neue Testament Deutsch 1. Göttingen: Vandenhoeck & Ruprecht, 1967.

————. "Die 'Elemente der Welt': Gal 4,3.9; Kol 2,8.20." Pages 245–59 in *Verborum veritas (FS G. Stählin)*. Edited by Otto Böcher and Klaus Haacker. Wuppertal: Brockhaus, 1970. Repr. pages 147–63 in *Beiträge zur Theologie des Neuen Testaments: Neutestamentliche Aufsätze (1955–1970)*. Zürich: Zwingli, 1970.

————. "Mattäus 12,1-8: Der Sabbat—Gebot und Geschenk." Pages 169-79 in *Glaube und Gerechtigkeit (FS R. Gyllenberg)*. Edited by J. Kiilunen, V. Riekkinen and H. Räisänen. Suomen Eksegeettisen Seuran Julkaisuja 38. Helsinki: n. p., 1983.

————. "Der Menschensohn (zur eschatologischen Erwartung Jesu)." *ZNW* 50 (1959): 185–209. Repr. pages 56–84 in *Neotestamentica: Deutsche und Englische Aufsätze 1951–1963*. Zürich: Zwingli, 1963.

————. "Slaves of the Elements and Worshipers of Angels: Gal 4:3, 9 and Col 2:8, 18, 20." *Journal of Biblical Literature* 107 (1988): 455–68.

Scott, Bernard Brandon. "From Reimarus to Crossan: Stages in a Quest." *Currents in Research: Biblical Studies* 2 (1994): 253–80.

Scroggs, Robin. "The Earliest Christian Communities as Sectarian Movement." Pages 1–23 in vol. 2 of *Christianity, Judaism and other Greco-Roman Cults*. Edited by J. Neusner. Studies in Judaism in Late Antiquity 12. Leiden: Brill, 1975.

Sekine, Seizo. *Die Tritojesajanische Sammlung (Jes 56–66) redaktionsgeschichtlich untersucht*. Beihefte zur Zeitschrift für die alttestamentliche Wissenschaft 175. Berlin: de Gruyter, 1989.

Sevenster, J. N. *The Roots of Anti-Semitism in the Ancient World*. Leiden: Brill, 1975.

Shea, William H. "The Sabbath in the Epistle of Barnabas." *Andrews University Seminary Studies* 4 (1966): 149–75.

———. "Sennacherib's Description of Lachish and of Its Conquest." *Andrews University Seminary Studies* 26 (1988): 171–80.

Sigal, Phillip. *The Halakah of Jesus of Nazareth According to the Gospel of Matthew*. Lanham, Md.: Univ. Press of America, 1986.

Sim, David C. *The Gospel of Matthew and Christian Judaism: The History and Social Setting of the Matthean Community*. Studies of the New Testament and its World. Edinburgh: T. & T. Clark, 1998.

Simon, Marcel. *Verus Israel: A Study of the Relations between Christians and Jews in the Roman Empire (AD 135–425)*. Translated by H. McKeating. Oxford: Oxford Univ. Press, 1986. Repr., London: Vallentine, 1996. Translation of *Verus Israel: Étude sur les relations entre chrétiens et juifs dans l'empire romain (135–425)*. 2d ed. Paris: Boccard, 1964 (1948).

Smallwood, E. Mary. *The Jews under Roman Rule from Pompey to Diocletian*. 2d ed. Studies in Judaism in Late Antiquity 20. Leiden: Brill, 1981 (1976).

Smith, D. Moody. "Johannine Studies." Pages 271–96 in *The New Testament and its Modern Interpreters*. Edited by Eldon Jay Epp and George W. MacRae. Atlanta: Scholars, 1989.

———. *John among the Gospels: The Relationship in Twentieth-Century Research*. Minneapolis: Fortress, 1992.

———. "When Did the Gospels Become Scripture?" *Journal of Biblical Literature* 119 (2000): 3–20.

Söding, Thomas. "Die Gegner des Apostels Paulus in Galatien: Beobachtungen zu ihrer Evangeliumsverkündigung und ihrem Konflikt mit Paulus." Pages 132–52 in *Das Wort vom Kreuz: Studien zur paulinischen Theologie*. Wissenschaftliche Untersuchungen zum Neuen Testament 93. Tübingen: Mohr Siebeck, 1997.

Speiser, E. A. *Genesis: A New Translation with Introduction and Commentary*. Anchor Bible 1. Garden City, N.Y.: Doubleday, 1964.

Spicq, Ceslas. *L'Épître aux Hébreux*. 2 vols. Etudes bibliques. Paris: Gabalda, 1952-19-53.

Stähli, Hans-Peter. "Creatio als creatio perpetua?" *Wort und Dienst* NF 10 (1969): 121–9.

Staley, Jeffrey L. "Stumbling in the Dark, Reaching for the Light: Reading Character in John 5 and 9." *Semeia* 53 (1991): 55–80.

Stanton, Graham M. *A Gospel for a New People*. Edinburgh: T & T Clark, 1992.

Stark, Rodney. *The Rise of Christianity: How the Obscure, Marginal Jesus Movement Became the Dominant Religious Force in the Western World in a Few Centuries*. Princeton: Princeton Univ. Press, 1996. Repr., San Francisco: HarperCollins, 1997.

Steck, Odil Hannes. *Der Abschluss der Prophetie im Alten Testament: Ein Versuch zur Frage der Vorgeschichte des Kanons*. Biblisch-theologische Studien 117. Neukirchen-Vluyn: Neukirchner, 1991.

———. "Die Aufnahme von Gen 1 in Jubiläen 2 und 4. Esra 6." *Journal for the Study of Judaism* 8 (1977): 154–82.

———. *Der Schöpfungsbericht der Priesterschrift: Studien zur literarkritischen und überlieferungsgeschichtlichen Problematik von Genesis 1,1–2,4a*. 2d ed. Forschungen zur Religion und Literatur des Alten und Neuen Testaments 115. Göttingen: Vandenhoeck & Ruprecht, 1981 (1975).

———. *Studien zu Tritojesaja*. Beihefte zur Zeitschrift für die alttestamentliche Wissenschaft 203. Berlin: de Gruyter, 1991.

Stemberger, Günter. *Einleitung in Talmud und Midrasch*. 8th ed. overall of the work, first written by Hermann Strack in 1887. München: Beck, 1992.

———. *Juden und Christen im Heiligen Land: Palästina unter Konstantin und Theodosius*. München: Beck, 1987.

Stendahl, Krister. *Paul among Jews and Gentiles*. Philadelphia: Fortress, 1976.

Stern, Menachem. "The Jews in Greek and Latin Literature." Pages 1101–59 in *The Jewish People in the First Century: Historical Geography, Political History, Social, Cultural and Religious Life and Institutions*. Edited by S. Safrai and M. Stern. Assen: Van Gorcum, 1974.

Stolz, Fritz. *Einführung in den biblischen Monotheismus*. Darmstadt: Wissenschaftliche Buchgesellschaft, 1996.

———. "Sabbat, Schöpfungswoche und Herbstfest." *Wort und Dienst* NF 11 (1971): 159–75.

Strecker, Georg. *Der Weg der Gerechtigkeit: Untersuchungen zur Theologie des Matthäus*. 3d ed. Forschungen zur Religion und Literatur des Alten und Neuen Testaments 82. Göttingen: Vandenhoeck & Ruprecht, 1971 (1962).

———. "Zum Problem des Judenchristentums." Appendix to Walter Bauer, *Rechtgläubigkeit und Ketzerei im ältesten Christentum*. 2d ed. Beiträge zur historischen Theologie 10. Tübingen: Mohr Siebeck, 1964, 243-314.

Sumney, Jerry L. *"Servants of Satan," "False Brothers" and Other Opponents of Paul*. Journal for the Study of the New Testament, Supplements 188. Sheffield: Sheffield Academic Press, 1999.

Taylor, Vincent. *The Gospel According to St. Mark: The Greek Text, with Introduction, Notes, and Indexes*. London: Macmillan, 1952.

Theissen, Gerd. *Urchristliche Wundergeschichten: Ein Beitrag zur formgeschichtlichen Erforschung der Synoptischen Evangelien*. 6th ed. Studien zum Neuen Testament 8. Gütersloh: Mohn, 1990 (1974).

Theissen, Gerd, and Annette Merz. *Der historische Jesus: Ein Lehrbuch.* Göttingen: Vandenhoeck & Ruprecht, 1996.

Theissen, Gerd, and Dagmar Winter. *Die Kriterienfrage in der Jesusforschung: Vom Differenzkriterium zum Plausibilitätskriterium.* Novum Testamentum et Orbis Antiquus 34. Freiburg, Switzerland: Universitätsverlag, 1997.

Thomas, Kenneth J. "The Old Testament Citations in Hebrews." *New Testament Studies* 11 (1964/65): 303–25.

Thompson, J. A. *The Book of Jeremiah.* New International Commentary on the Old Testament. Grand Rapids, Mich.: Eerdmans, 1980.

Tilborg, Sjen van. *Imaginative Love in John.* Biblical Interpretation Series 2. Leiden: Brill, 1993.

Tkach, Joseph. *Transformed by Truth.* Sisters, Ore.: Multnomah, 1997.

Tuckett, Christopher M. "Q and Thomas: Evidence of a Primitive 'Wisdom Gospel'?" *Ephemerides theologicae lovanienses* 67 (1991): 346–60.

———. "Thomas and the Synoptics." *Novum Testamentum* 30 (1988): 132–57.

Tugwell, Simon. *The Apostolic Fathers.* Outstanding Christian Thinkers. London: Chapman, 1989.

Turner, M. M. B. "The Sabbath, Sunday, and the Law in Luke/Acts." Pages 99–157 in *From Sabbath to Lord's Day: A Biblical, Historical and Theological Investigation.* Edited by D. A. Carson. Grand Rapids, Mich.: Zondervan, 1982.

Uro, Risto. *Thomas at the Crossroads: Essays on the Gospel of Thomas.* Studies of the New Testament and its World. Edinburgh: Clark, 1998.

Valantasis, Richard. *The Gospel of Thomas.* New Testament Readings. London: Routledge, 1997.

Van Seters, John. *The Life of Moses: The Yahwist as Historian in Exodus-Numbers.* Louisville, Ky.: Westminster John Knox, 1994.

Vanhoozer, Kevin J. *Is There a Meaning in this Text? The Bible, the Reader, and the Morality of Literary Knowledge.* Grand Rapids, Mich.: Zondervan, 1998.

Vanhoye, Albert. *La structure littéraire de l'Épître aux Hébreux.* 2d ed. Studia neotestamentica 1. Paris: Desclée de Brouwer, 1976 (1963).

Vermès, Geza. *Jesus the Jew.* London: Collins, 1973; 2d ed. London: SCM 1983.

Vielhauer, Philipp. "Ἀνάπαυσις: zum gnostischen Hintergrund des Thomasevangeliums." Pages 281–99 in *Apophoreta (FS E. Haenchen).* Edited by W. Eltester and F. H. Kettler. Berlin: Töpelmann, 1964.

———. "Gesetzesdienst und Stoicheiadienst im Galaterbrief." Pages 543–55 in *Rechtfertigung (FS E. Käsemann).* Edited by J. Friedrich, W. Pöhlmann and P. Stuhlmacher. Tübingen: Mohr Siebeck, 1976.

———. "Zum 'Paulinismus' der Apostelgeschichte." *Evangelische Theologie* 10 (1950–51): 1–15.

Vouga, François. *Le cadre historique et l'intention théologique de Jean.* 2d ed. Beauchesne religions 3. Paris, 1981 (1977).

———. *An die Galater.* Handbuch zum Neuen Testament 10. Tübingen: Mohr Siebeck, 1998.

Wahlde, Urban C. von. "The Johannine 'Jews': A Critical Survey." *New Testament Studies* 28 (1982): 33–60.

Wander, Bernd. *Gottesfürchtige und Sympathisanten: Studien zum heidnischen Umfeld von Diasporasynagogen.* Wissenschaftliche Untersuchungen zum Neuen Testament 104. Tübingen: Mohr Siebeck, 1998.

Waxman, Chaim I. "The Sabbath as Dialectic: The Meaning and Role." *Judaism* 31 (1982): 37–44.

Weder, Hans. "Die Menschwerdung Gottes: Überlegungen zur Auslegungsproblematik des Johannesevangeliums am Beispiel von Joh 6." Pages 363–400 in *Einblicke ins Evangelium: Exegetische Beiträge zur neutestamentlichen Hermeneutik. Gesammelte Aufsätze aus den Jahren 1980–1991.* Göttingen: Vandenhoeck & Ruprecht, 1992.

Weinel, Heinrich. *Biblische Theologie des Neuen Testaments: Die Religion Jesu und des Urchristentums.* 3d ed. Grundriss der theologischen Wissenschaften. Tübingen: Mohr Siebeck, 1920.

Weiss, Herold. *A Day of Gladness: The Sabbath Among Jews and Christians in Antiquity.* Columbia: Univ. of South Carolina Press, 2003.

———. "Paul and the Judging of Days." *Zeitschrift für die neutestamentliche Wissenschaft und die Kunde der Älteren Kirche* 86 (1995): 137–53.

———. "The Sabbath Among the Samaritans." *Journal for the Study of Judaism in the Persian, Hellenistic and Roman Period* 25 (1994): 252–73.

———. "The Sabbath in the Fourth Gospel." *Journal of Biblical Literature* 110 (1991): 311–21.

———. "The Sabbath in the Pauline Corpus." Pages 287–315 in *Wisdom and Logos (FS D. Winston).* Edited by David T. Runia and Gregory E. Sterling. Studia Philonica Annual 9. Atlanta: Scholars Press, 1997.

———. "The Sabbath in the Synoptic Gospels." *Journal for the Study of the New Testament* 38 (1990): 13–27.

———. "The Sabbath in the Writings of Josephus." *Journal for the Study of Judaism in the Persian, Hellenistic and Roman Period* 29 (1998): 363–90.

———. "*Sabbatismos* in the Epistle to the Hebrews." *Catholic Biblical Quarterly* 58 (1996): 674–89.

Weiss, Wolfgang. *"Eine neue Lehre in Vollmacht": Die Streit- und Schulgespräche des Markus-Evangeliums.* Beihefte zur Zeitschrift für die neutestamentliche Wissenschaft 52. Berlin: de Gruyter, 1989.

Wellhausen, Julius. *Prolegomena zur Geschichte Israels.* 4th ed. Berlin: Reimer, 1895 (1878).

Wengst, Klaus. *Das Johannesevangelium, 1.* Theologischer Kommentar zum Neuen Testament 4/1. Stuttgart: Kohlhammer, 2000.

———. *Tradition und Theologie des Barnbasbriefes.* Arbeiten zur Kirchengeschichte 42. Berlin: de Gruyter, 1971.

Westermann, Claus. *Genesis 1–11.* 3d ed. Biblischer Kommentar, Altes Testament 1/1. Neukirchen-Vluyn: Neukirchner, 1983 (1974).

Wick, Peter. *Die urchristliche Gottesdienste: Entstehung und Entwicklung im Rahmen der frühjüdischen Tempel-, Synagogen- und Hausfrömmigkeit.* Beiträge zur Wissenschaft vom Alten und Neuen Testament 150. Stuttgart: Kohlhammer, 2002.

Williams, Margaret. "Being a Jew in Rome: Sabbath fasting as an expression of Romano-Jewish identity." Paper presented at the international meeting of the SBL, Rome, July 2001.

Wills, Lawrence. "The Form of the Sermon in Hellenistic Judaism and Early Christianity." *Harvard Theological Review* 77 (1984): 277–99.

Windisch, Hans. *Die Apostolischen Väter 3: Der Barnabasbrief.* Handbuch zum Neuen Testament. Tübingen: Mohr Siebeck, 1920.

Witherington III, Ben. *Grace in Galatia: A Commentary on St. Paul's Letter to the Galatians.* Edinburgh: T. & T. Clark, 1998.

———. *Jesus the Sage : The Pilgrimage of Wisdom.* Minneapolis: Augsburg Fortress, 1994.

Witkamp, L. T. "The Use of Traditions in John 5.1–18." *Journal for the Study of the New Testament* 25 (1985): 19–47.

Wolff, Hans Walter. *Anthropologie des Alten Testaments.* 5th ed. München: Kaiser, 1990 (1973).

Wray, Judith Hoch. *Rest as a Theological Metaphor in the Epistle to the Hebrews and the Gospel of Truth: Early Christian Homiletics of Rest.* Society of Biblical Literature Dissertation Series 166. Atlanta: Scholars Press, 1998.

Yang, Yong-Eui. *Jesus and the Sabbath in Matthew's Gospel.* Journal for the Study of the New Testament. Supplement Series 139. Sheffield: Sheffield Academic Press, 1997.

Zimmerli, Walther. *Ezechiel.* 2 vols. Biblischer Kommentar, Altes Testament 13. Neukirchen-Vluyn: Neukirchner, 1969.

———. *Grundriss der alttestamentlichen Theologie.* 6th ed. Theologische Wissenschaft 3. Stuttgart: Kohlhammer, 1989 (1972).

Zöckler, Thomas. *Jesu Lehren im Thomasevangelium.* Nag Hammadi and Manichaean Studies 47. Leiden: Brill, 1999.

Zumstein, Jean. "Die Endredaktion des Johannesevangeliums." Pages 192–216 in *Kreative Erinnerung: Relecture und Auslegung im Johannesevangelium.* Zürich: Pano, 1999. Translation of "La rédaction finale de l'évangile de Jean (à l'exemple du chap. 21)." In *La communauté johannique et son histoire: La trajectoire de l'évangile de Jean aux dux premiers siècles*, edited by J.-D. Kaestli, J.-M. Poffet and J. Zumstein. Geneva: Labor et Fides, 1990, 207–30.

———. "The Farewell Discourses (John 13:31–16:33) and the Problems of Anti-Judaism." Pages 461–78 in *Anti-Judaism and the Fourth Gospel: Papers of the Leuven Colloquium, 2000.* Edited by R. Bieringer, D. Pollefeyt and F. Vandecasteele-Vanneuville. Assen: Van Gorcum, 2001.

———. "Die johanneische Interpretation des Todes Jesu." Pages 125–44 in *Kreative Erinnerung: Relecture und Auslegung im Johannesevangelium.* Zürich: Pano, 1999. Translation of "L'interprétation johannique de la mort du Christ." Pages

2119–38 in *The Four Gospels 1992*, edited by F. van Segbroeck, C. M. Tuckett, G. Van Belle and J. Verheyden. Leuven: Leuven Univ. Press, 1992.

————. "Das Johannesevangelium: Eine Strategie des Glaubens." Pages 31–45 in *Kreative Erinnerung: Relecture und Auslegung im Johannesevangelium*. Zürich: Pano, 1999. Translation of "L'évangile johannique: Une stratégie de croire." *Recherches de science religieuse* 77 (1989): 217–32.

————. "Der Prozess Jesu vor Pilatus (ein Beispiel johanneischer Eschatologie)." Pages 145–55 in *Kreative Erinnerung: Relecture und Auslegung im Johannesevangelium*. Zürich: Pano, 1999. Translation of "Le procès de Jésus devant Pilate." *Cahiers bibliques de Foi et vie* 31 (1992): 89–101.

————. "Zur Geschichte des johanneischen Christentums." *Theologische Literaturzeitung* 122 (1997): 417–28. Repr. pages 1–14 in *Kreative Erinnerung: Relecture und Auslegung im Johannesevangelium*. Zürich: Pano, 1999.

Index of Ancient Literature

Encountering the Rest of God